The Rambler's
Yearbook & Accommo... ...e

1 9 ...

EDITOR
Charlotte Prager

COVER DESIGN & TYPOGRAPHY
Susan Lishman, Graphique, London

COVER PHOTOGRAPH
Graham Parish—Looking over the
Somerset Levels from Glastonbury Tor

PRINTING
Benham & Co Ltd, Colchester, Essex

TRADE DISTRIBUTION
W. Foulsham & Co Ltd
The Publishing House
Bennets Close
Cippenham, Berks SL1 5AP
☎ (01753) 526769

ADVERTISING
Terry Lock Media Sales
5 & 7 The Crescent Business Centre
30/32 The Crescent
Leatherhead, Surrey KT22 8BL
☎ (01372) 361225/6
Fax (01372) 361228

ACCOMMODATION ADVERTISING
The Ramblers' Association

PUBLISHED BY
The Ramblers' Association
1/5 Wandsworth Road
London SW8 2XX
☎ 0171-582 6878
Fax 0171-587 3799

ISBN 0-900613-89-0
Published November 1996

Stewardship

a decent investment

Your chance to invest for a better world

- The UK's first and largest range of ethical investment funds

- Invests in companies which make a positive contribution to society

- Seeks to avoid companies which harm the world, its people or its wildlife

- A choice of two PEPs and three unit trusts

'I want my investment to benefit companies which are helping rather than harming the world.' (95% of the British adult population agree*)

'I would like to make a profit without anyone getting hurt in the process.' (91% agree)

'I would rather invest in an ethical investment fund than any other sort of investment fund.' (62% agree)

* Source: Friends Provident / NOP Ethical Investment Survey 1996

FRIENDS PROVIDENT

ISSUED BY THE FRIENDS PROVIDENT MARKETING GROUP WHICH IS REGULATED BY THE PERSONAL INVESTMENT AUTHORITY.

Telephone: Unit Trust Dealing Desk 01722 715835   Administration 01722 715834   PEP Enquiries 01722 715836
World Wide Web address: http://www.FriendsProvident.co.uk/Stewardship   email: stewardship@friendsprovident.co.uk

*Please note that the value of an investment and any income from it can go down as well as up and is not guaranteed.
Where a trust or fund invests overseas its value can fluctuate as a result of currency exchange rates.
Full details are available on request from any Friends Provident office. Tax legislation may change.*

CONTENTS

Starting the second half century ... Fifty years of Ramblers Holidays

Unbelievable it may seem, but yes, we've been sending parties of ramblers on holidays overseas for fifty years! Even from the earliest days the company has offered interesting, exciting and challenging holidays, often to remote and not-too accessible areas where the mountains, the hills, or the wilderness offer beautiful, unspoiled, even pristine, scenery.

Over the years, the company has built up an enormous wealth of operating experience, world-wide contacts and hosts of routes and tracks to wonderful places. As the years have passed so the programmes have developed. **There's an enormous variety of pure walking holidays, tough, moderate and easy, then there's cross-country skiing which is somewhat like walking and gliding on snow, and amongst the easiest holidays a wide range of sightseeing programmes often involving a good deal of walking.**

Back in the forties we were in what were then far flung places, like Greece, Algeria and Portugal ~ then three days each way by train. Now, we're in the four corners of the world: **North & South America, New Zealand, South Africa, China, Nepal,** but the greatest part of our programme is amongst the hills and mountains of Europe, now little more than 90 minutes' flight away.

Ramblers' small parties, its leaders and of course the like-minded clients 'make' the holidays; literally hundreds of people come back year after year. Many write in afterwards describing their holiday of a lifetime. Our holidays are meant to be interesting , enjoyable, unregimented and overall with a good essence of fun. On the tougher ones you could well come home with a sense of achievement.

The 1997 brochure with **more than 140 holidays** and over two thousand departures is easily obtained. Please phone, write, e-mail or fax us and one will be sent immediately. Your biggest problem will be in choosing which one, two, or even three to take!

We look forward to welcoming you in 1997, whether married, single, a mountain person happy in a hut in the heavens or a hotel on a hill, or a coastal person enjoying a pleasant hotel with a private bathroom and an easy program

WALLET WARNING:
Becoming addicted to Ramblers Holidays can damage your wealth.

Ramblers Holidays, Box 43, Welwyn Garden, AL8 6PQ
Tel: 01707 331133 Fax: 01707 333276
E-mail: Ramhols@dial.pipex.com

4

Editor's Foreword

Welcome to the Rambler's Yearbook 1997! We hope you will find it a friendly and useful companion in your discovery or rediscovery of our beautiful countryside.

This edition is slimmer than recent ones but don't be fooled — it has more pages than ever before. But it *will* fit more easily into your rucksack. The paper it is printed on is designed to be thin and the Italian company that has manufactured it has strict standards concerning care for the environment.

Seasoned readers will notice several new arrivals to this edition — a full index of all four parts of the Accommodation Guide; six more long distance paths; a list of local authorities responsible for public rights of way; some thoughts and tips on safety in the hills; a section on accommodation suitable for groups; and a vastly expanded listing of equipment shops. Users of the Accommodation Guide can now see at a glance where they can take their dog; whether or not their hosts are members of the Ramblers' Association; and any tourist board classification awarded to the establishment.

Local authority restructuring has provided us with an obstacle course throughout the production of the listings this year. Explanations of the method used are given where necessary. The continuing reorganisation of counties during 1997 invites even more havoc next year and the Editor will be pleased to consider any suggestions of alternative ways of presenting the material.

To inspire you on those wintry mornings, we reproduce below some verses from a kindred spirit of the 19th Century — part of Gerard Manley Hopkins' *Inversnaid*.

> Degged with dew, dappled with dew
> Are the groins of the braes that the brook treads through,
> Wiry heathpacks, flitches of fern,
> And the beadbonny ash that sits over the burn.
>
> What would the world be, once bereft
> Of wet and of wildness? Let them be left,
> O let them be left, wildness and wet;
> Long live the weeds and the wilderness yet.

Even the faint-hearted should take courage from that!

The Ramblers' Association exists to facilitate, for the benefit of everyone, the enjoyment and discovery on foot of Britain's countryside; and to promote respect for the life of the countryside.

The association protects rights of way; campaigns for freedom to roam over uncultivated open country; and defends the beauty of the countryside.

The association is a democratic, voluntary organisation, registered as a charity (no.306089).

A view of the year ahead from Ramblers' Director Alan Mattingly

EARLY ON NEW YEAR'S DAY 1997, hundreds of revellers will be pulling on their boots and stepping out into the bracing air for the final day of the Ramblers' Festival of Winter Walks.

A full week's programme of 290 walks aimed particularly at new recruits will have ensured **January and February** see a significant increase in membership of the Association from its September 96 level of 117,000. Thousands of people, from all parts of Britain, will pursue their new year's resolutions to get fit and discover their countryside, by taking up walking with the Ramblers.

March will see the publication of the first of four 1997 editions of the colour magazine, *Rambling Today,* free to members and packed with news of Ramblers' campaigns and information about walking opportunities at home and abroad.

April will be conference month, when delegates from all over Britain will meet at Loughborough University in Leicestershire for the 1997 Ramblers' General Council meeting. At this truly democratic gathering, members' representatives gather to affirm - or to change Ramblers' policy.

Delegates may be fortunate enough to visit nearby Bradgate Park, one of the few patches of woodlands and heath which are all that is left of ancient Charnwood Forest. There, they will be able to wander at will, and to reflect on the pressing need to protect and extend these wildlife-rich open spaces, of which so few remain in lowland Britain.

The weekend of **May 17th and 18th** will mark a high point in the "Free Your Paths" campaign. At scores of walks, rallies and other events around the country, RA members and supporters will be asked to give their backing to the Ramblers' campaign to have all 140,000 miles of rights of way in England and Wales put in good order by the end of this century. In Scotland, the RA will be campaigning for the removal of barriers to long-used public paths, and for the creation of a much more extensive network of footpaths for local communities throughout the country.

The ever-popular Family Rambling Day will once again take place on the last Sunday of **June**, sponsored this year by Country Holidays and Countrywide. Children taking part are asked to ensure that their parents are well-behaved.

By the time the holiday months of **July and August** arrive, the 1997 general election will have come and gone and we shall know who will form the next government. RA campaigners will be working hard to prepare for the parliamentary session that will follow, urging ministers to act on RA's "election manifesto" - a list of ten or more key action points aimed at protecting our beautiful countryside and ensuring that everyone can explore it peacefully, on foot. High on the list will be a plea for effective measures to save our rapidly-dwindling heritage of hedgerows and dry stone walls - features of the landscape which make such a sublime contribution to the attractiveness of our countryside.

On Sunday **September 28th**, the RA will hold its national Access Day. This event will press for the implementation of another central aspect of the RA's plans for new countryside legislation - namely, a government Bill to allow the public to wander freely on foot over mountain, moorland and other uncultivated open country, subject to sensible restrictions.

During the autumn months of **October and November** hundreds of local RA volunteers will be preparing for another season of practical footpath work - clearing paths of overgrown vegetation, repairing stiles and footbridges, and waymarking miles of paths across the countryside. Their work will benefit local communities everywhere.

December, and the year will have turned full circle to another Festival of Winter Walks, from Christmas to New Year's Day. Boots will crunch over frost-hardened ground, and views over distant, snow-covered hills will be razor-sharp. It will be a great way to end the year.

The Ramblers' Association

WALKING IS FOR EVERYONE

In 1935, rambling groups across Britain united to form a new national association to speak with one voice on behalf of 1,200 individual members and 300 affiliated clubs. In the years since then, walking has become recognised as one of the healthiest and certainly the most accessible forms of exercise for people of all ages. Figures from the government's latest General Household Survey show that 4 in 10 adults regularly go for a walk of two miles or more for pleasure.

The RA aims to bring a love and understanding of the countryside to the minority of the population who never walk there, either because they do not have the means, because their mobility is impaired by disablement, or simply because they have not yet had the opportunity to discover the sense of liberation and enjoyment that walking for pleasure in the outdoors can bring.

FOOTPATHS

Throughout the year, our members go quietly about their work surveying, clearing, waymarking and building footbridges and stiles on England and Wales' unique network of 140,000 miles of paths designated as rights of way. Parts of this network have been neglected and abused by landowners over the years and the RA is actively supporting the Countryside Commission's declared intention of getting the entire network fully open and useable by the year 2000.

The RA played a key role in securing the Rights of Way Act 1990, which at last provides legislation to deal effectively with illegal ploughing and cropping of footpaths. This was an important step towards achieving the CC's goal, which is fully supported by the government.

The RA is recognised as a much-respected source of expertise. It seeks to have illegal obstructions on rights of way removed and, where necessary, prosecutes offenders. It urges farmers to obey the law on ploughing and rights of way and calls upon local authorities and the government to ensure that these and other laws are respected. The RA seeks restrictions on the grazing of dangerous animals such as bulls in fields containing pubic rights of way. It presses for new rights of way to be created where necessary.

At local level voluntary footpath secretaries oppose public path closures and diversions that are not in the public interest. In Scotland, local groups also carry out valuable footpath work and press for new rights of way to be created.

OPEN LAND

Ramblers work towards defending and extending public access on foot to open country. The RA's primary aim is to win a legal freedom to roam on all common land in England and Wales and on moorland and mountain areas throughout Britain.

The RA also seeks wider rights of access to private forests and woodlands. In 1994, RA campaigning contributed to the government deciding not to privatise the Forestry Commission. But this is only a partial victory as woodlands previously open to the public are still being sold into private hands. Since 1981, almost half of all Forestry Commission woodlands have been sold, usually without public access agreements in place. The RA is calling for legislation to ensure that the public's right of access to these woodlands is protected once they pass into private hands.

We stress the need for wider access to riverside and coastal land.

COUNTRYSIDE

The RA campaigns to protect and enhance the natural beauty of rural Britain. This can mean anything from opposing damaging new quarry developments in the Mendip Hills and the Isle of Harris to taking part in annual Tidy Britain campaigns. Recently, the RA has opposed plans to extend Spaunton Quarry in the Yorkshire Dales and the construction of a huge polo arena on an Area of Outstanding Natural Beauty in West Sussex.

The Association is in the forefront of campaigns to minimise the damage caused by military training in national parks and other beautiful countryside. In particular, the RA has renewed its call for an end to live firing in national parks. In Otterburn, where the MOD is planning to rebuild roads so that they can carry heavy firing equipment, the RA has called for a public inquiry. This inquiry is due to begin in 1997. (See Useful Addresses section of this Yearbook for telephone lines giving details of firing times on military training areas.)

We fight to protect green belts and believe that all major agricultural and forestry operations should be subject to planning control.

The RA has also been prominent in campaigns to protect and improve public transport in rural areas. Bus and rail services are of vital importance to families without private transport who wish to explore the countryside on foot. You will find details of public transport enquiry lines on page 73.

PARLIAMENTARY WORK

In Parliament the RA lodges petitions against certain bills and offers advice to MPs and members of the House of Lords on legislation of concern to the walking public. Through the good offices of sympathetic MPs of all parties the RA is able to promote questions and debates in the House of Commons. It also sends regular deputations to ministers.

Each year we submit evidence and papers to a host of public inquiries, committees of inquiry, parliamentary committees, government departments and other public bodies.

The RA commissions research and publishes reports on matters of particular concern. It organises conferences, seminars, public meetings, rallies, etc. to publicise and gain support for its objectives.

We have been particularly successful over

the years in promoting our campaigns through the media. This is achieved by issuing a steady stream of well-researched news releases.

The RA works closely with allied environmental and recreational organisations, particularly through the Council for National Parks, the Central Council of Physical Recreation, and "Link" groups in England, Scotland and Wales.

Overall, the association aims to present a well-argued and well-publicised case which is demonstrably supported by a substantial body of public opinion. Over the years, the application of these techniques has achieved a great deal.

Information about current campaigns is conveyed to members in the RA's journal and in campaign broadsheets. A summary of each year's activity is contained in the annual report, which is available to all members on request.

RAMBLERS IN ACTION IN THE EARLY DAYS

The RA's work in the 1990s is the continuation of a tradition which has its roots in the industrial revolution of the early 19th century. England's first footpath protection society was formed in York in 1824. Two years later the Manchester Association for the Preservation of Ancient Footpaths was founded and in Scotland, a federation of walking clubs, centred on Glasgow, was set up in 1892.

Later, in the face of strong threats to open spaces in London, the Commons Preservation Society (now called the Open Spaces Society) was formed in 1865. It was instrumental in forming the first English Federation of Rambling Clubs in 1905. It was not until 1919 that this London-based federation was joined by a similar organisation in

Manchester, quickly followed by new federations in Liverpool, Sheffield, the Midlands and other mostly urban centres.

At an historic meeting in the Peak District in 1931 a resolution was passed that a National Council of Ramblers' Federations be formed. In 1935 it was agreed that the title should be changed to the Ramblers' Association. A national organisation for ramblers had finally been established.

NATIONAL PARKS CAMPAIGN

Although the RA had no paid staff until 1952, it was remarkably effective in its early years. In particular, it spearheaded a campaign which led to the passing of the National Parks and Access to the Countryside Act 1949.

The RA's first full-time Secretary, Tom Stephenson, played a key role in that campaign — not least by organising well-publicised treks in the Pennines for influential MPs. Tom Stephenson's book, *Forbidden Land* (Manchester University Press 1989), describes in detail many early RA campaigns, including that for the 1949 Act.

In the years which followed, the RA worked tremendously hard to put the Act's provisions into effect.

Definitive maps of rights of way were drawn up by county councils throughout England and Wales. RA volunteers collected every available scrap of evidence and submitted thousands of claims for rights of way to include on the maps. Many are the paths we walk today that would probably have disappeared years ago had it not been for the RA's vigilance in those years.

The 1949 Act provided for the creation of national parks in England and Wales. With the RA campaigning for their early designation, ten parks were established within a few years. The RA in Scotland is still actively pursuing a campaign to get precious natural areas like the Cairngorms designated as national parks.

The Act also offered a mechanism for securing a right to roam over mountain and moorland through access agreements and orders. The RA won several such agreements in the Peak District, and later some in the Yorkshire Dales and the Forest of Bowland.

The creation of long distance paths was also an aim of the 1949 Act; and Tom Stephenson's Pennine Way was the first such route to be established.

It took much longer to complete the route than the RA had hoped (it was opened in 1965), but it was soon followed by several others. Most of these long distance paths were based on routes proposed, and surveyed in detail, by the RA.

Further parliamentary lobbying by the RA in the 1960s led to the Countryside Act 1968, which, among other things, gave county councils in England and Wales a duty to signpost rights of way.

An RA-led campaign in the 1970s helped greatly to strengthen national park authorities in England and Wales; and to secure for them more resources to protect their parks.

SAVING FOOTPATHS

Throughout most of its history, the RA has fought not only to open up neglected footpaths, but also to save them from closure in programmes of path "rationalisation". In this, the RA has been largely successful. In particular, RA lobbying led to a defeat of the government in the House of Lords in 1981. Ministers had intended to abolish what is in effect a right of appeal by objectors against proposals by local authorities to close rights of way. Had this proposal been enacted, many rights of way now enjoyed by the public would surely have been wiped off the map.

In the 1970s, the RA had been the first to criticise tax concessions which fuelled much of the conifer afforestation causing so much damage to scenery and wildlife in the uplands — especially in Scotland. After years of RA campaigning, these concessions were abolished by the Chancellor in 1988. Since then, the Forestry Commission has made major changes to its policy, by placing much more emphasis on the planting of broadleaved woodlands.

ORDNANCE SURVEY

In the 1960s, the RA persuaded the Ordnance Survey to show on its popular maps rights of way as depicted on definitive maps. Thus, for the first time, walkers had ready access to maps showing precisely where they had a right to walk in the countryside.

But then the maps themselves came under threat. On more than one occasion, the RA fought off attempts by some sections of the government to withdraw what we now know as the Pathfinder (1:25,000) Series. These maps, which show field boundaries and paths (including, in England and Wales, public rights of way) and which are therefore vital for cross-country navigation, were finally completed as a national series in 1989. The Ordnance Survey at that time acknowledged that the series had been saved by the RA. Although the Pathfinder series is now to be replaced by the more "tourist-friendly" Explorers, the principle – to provide maps for walkers at the 1:25,000 scale – remains intact

In 1995, the RA won a further victory when the Ordnance Survey issued for the first time a map showing previously unpublished public rights of way (white roads) as well as National Trust and Forest Enterprise Access land. In 1996 the popular support for this move led to a pledge by the OS to show white roads on all 1:50,000 (Landranger) maps, the whole series to be completed in 6 years.

STRUCTURE

Much of the RA's work is done at area and group level with guidance and back-up from its offices in London, Wales and Scotland. The governing body is the 200-strong General Council which meets once a year. Here, delegates from the areas and from affiliated organisations debate and establish RA policy. General Council also elects the Executive Committee, which is responsible for implementing the policies and making sure the association's funds are used appropriately. The Executive Committee also employs staff, most of which are based at the London office. Staff are also employed to run Wales and Scotland offices and Wales and Scotland also have their own Councils.

VOLUNTEERS

The RA relies on its hundreds of volunteers working in their neighbourhoods to reinforce and carry out its aims and policies. In many cases it is their diligence that sparks off major changes in legislation affecting walkers' rights. It is they who are walking, clearing and keeping open our wonderful network of footpaths, spreading a love of the countryside with walks programmes and newsletters and firing enthusiasm in local campaigns. There are 53 RA areas in England, Wales and Scotland (the RA is not at present active in Northern Ireland) running 400 local groups.

THE RA NATIONAL EXECUTIVE COMMITTEE, OCTOBER 1996

President	Janet Street-Porter
Chairman	Kate Ashbrook
Vice-Chairman	David Grosz
Treasurer	Jack Ibbott
Chairman, Scottish Council	Kate Walsham
Chairman, Welsh Council	Geoffrey Williams

Other members: Jo Bird, Tony Drake, Geoff Eastwood, Peter Gould, Peter Harwood, Geoffrey Kirby, Cath MacKay, Pam Roberts and Des Whicher.

MEMBERS OF STAFF OCTOBER 1996

DIRECTOR'S SECTION

Responsible for overall management of RA staff; access and countryside issues; Ordnance Survey matters; "Let's Get Going" project; information on walking in the countryside; production of *Rambling Today*.

Director	Alan Mattingly
Director's Personal Assistant	Janice Samuel
Assistant Director (Access)	David Beskine
Personal Assistant (Access)	Sandra Law
RA Secretary	Andrew Dalby
Information Officer	Andrew McCloy
Policy Officer (Countryside)	Penelope Kemp
Rambling Today Editor	Annabelle Birchall
Editor's Assistant	Denise Noble

DEPUTY DIRECTOR'S SECTION

Responsible for rights of way matters (England).

Deputy Director	John Trevelyan
Senior Policy Officer	Janet Davis
Policy Officer	Eugene Suggett
Administration Assistant	Olive Lacey
Administration Assistant	Donna O'Brien

FINANCE & ADMINISTRATION SECTION

Responsible for financial services and financial management; office administration, central office reception.

Head of Finance	Frank Syratt
Accountant	David Carter
Finance Assistant	Anthony Wyght
Administration Secretary	Gwen Campbell
Administration Assistant	Martin Ogilvie
Receptionist	Teham Riley

MEMBERSHIP SECTION

Responsible for administration of the RA membership system; production of *The Rambler's Yearbook*

Assistant Director	Adrian Ritchie
Section Supervisor	Carol Harding
Administration Assistant	Vanessa Crawford
Administration Assistant	Pam Gheerow
Administration Assistant	Wendy Farr
Yearbook Editor	Charlotte Prager

PUBLICITY AND DEVELOPMENT SECTION

Responsible for recruitment of members; marketing, including media coverage; fundraising; Family Rambling Day and the Festival of Winter Walks; projects to help Areas and Groups find more volunteers.

Assistant Director	Catharine Gunningham
Press & Publicity Officer	Sue Bond
Press Officer	George Hill
Fundraising & Marketing Officer	
	VickyFurnival
Local Groups Officer	Jacquetta Fewster
Publicity Assistant/PA	Katey Avis

WELSH OFFICE

Promotion of many of the RA's objectives in Wales. Based at Ty'r Cerddwyr, High Street, Gresford, Wrexham, Clwyd LL12 8PT. Tel. (01978) 855148, Fax (01978) 854445.

Welsh Officer	Beverley Penney
Personal Assistant	Bronwen Williams
Deputy Welsh Officer	Sue Gittins

SCOTTISH OFFICE

Promotion of many of the RA's objectives in Scotland. Based at Crusader House, Haig Business Park, Markinch, Fife KY7 6AQ. Tel. (01592) 611177, Fax (01592) 611188.

Scottish Officer	Dave Morris
Depute Scottish Officer	Ian McCall
Administration Officer	Linda Johnson

FINANCE

The association's main source of income – over £1¼ million in 1996 – is the subscriptions of its members and affiliated bodies and the repayments of tax which the Association can recover on those subscriptions paid under deed of covenant. Currently, 25 per cent of this income is paid to areas for area and group finance. The rest is used at national level, although a good deal of this is used to support local campaigns and local RA work.

The second most important source of income – £240,000 in 1996 – is regular grants from the Ramblers' Association Trust. The Trust is financed by Ramblers' Association Services Ltd (RAS). This is a commercial company which (through its subsidiary, Ramblers Holidays) organises walking, mountaineering, trekking, skiing and sightseeing holidays at home and abroad. The main purpose of the Trust is to support the work of the Ramblers' Association. Much of the RA's campaigning and other work at national level could not be carried out without this support.

Members will appreciate from this that it is of vital importance to the RA that Ramblers Holidays continues to be a flourishing and profitable organisation. Members are therefore urged to take their holidays with Ramblers Holidays whenever they can (see their listing in the Useful Addresses section of this book).

Other important sources of funding are: donations from members (£125,000 in 1996) and the Christmas Raffle (£67,000 in 1995).

Income from legacies is another very important source of funds (£200,000 in 1996). All members are urged to mention the RA in their wills (see later).

Valuable financial support also comes from business sponsorship. The RA has a close relationship with Countrywide Holidays, who were the sponsors of Family Rambling Day in 1994, 1995 and 1996. In 1997 this event will be sponsored by Country Holidays and Countrywide. Regatta Great Outdoors have sponsored our Membership Card and Fibre One the 1997 Festival of Winter Walks.

Expenditure on the RA's work was £2.1 million in 1996. Regular reports of this work are published in *Rambling Today*, free to members.

A full copy of the Ramblers' Association's current annual report and accounts can be supplied without charge to any RA member or affiliated organisation, on request to the association's office in London.

PUBLICATIONS, SALES AND INFORMATION SERVICE

RA central office offers a modest information service to anyone who wants to go walking in the countryside. A range of publications and information sheets on various aspects of country walking in Britain is available. For a list of these please send a stamped addressed envelope to the London office. We are unable to offer detailed advice on individual walking holidays and tours.

For publications on guides to some long distance paths, see the chapter on those routes in this Yearbook.

Members can also obtain advice on walking gear – for further details see regular articles on equipment in the RA's journal. For addresses of retail outlets see the Equipment section of this Yearbook.

For details of some RA publications on footpaths see the Access Section in this Yearbook.

MEMBERSHIP SUBSCRIPTION RATES 1996/7

Ordinary Membership £17.

Joint Membership (for two people living at the same address) £21

Reduced Ordinary Membership* £8.50

Reduced Joint Membership* £10.50

Life Membership £600 (£300**)

Affiliated local organisations £17

* For members under 18; students; and disabled, retired and other unwaged persons.

**For persons over 60 years of age.

See page 323 for special membership offer.

Over 40% of members pay their subscriptions by direct debit, which saves them trouble and greatly reduces our administration costs and bank charges. Members are informed of the date and amount of each payment well in advance and can, of course, cancel the arrangement at any time.

As a charity, the RA recovers tax on payments made under deeds of covenant. These currently benefit us by over £80,000 a year, at no extra cost to members. For more information on covenants please contact the membership department in London.

BENEFITS AND RESPONSIBILITIES OF RA MEMBERSHIP

On joining the RA, members are sent: a membership card; our Yearbook; the 60 page colour magazine *Rambling Today* every quarter; and the appropriate area newsletter when available. Most groups will also automatically supply their members with their programme of walks; some groups only supply them on request. All members then receive as benefits of membership free copies of each issue of:

- *Rambling Today*, the RA's quarterly colour magazine;

- the appropriate area newsletter, published up to four times a year.

In addition, members of the RA may:

- join a local group of their choice without further charge and take part in rambles and social programmes organised by that or any other group;

- borrow maps (Ordnance Survey Landranger, Outdoor Leisure and Explorer series,) from the RA map lending library at a nominal charge. (See Maps section).

On joining the Ramblers' Association each member agrees "to respect the countryside, its beauty and wildlife and to promote access to it on foot." The association insists that those taking part in walks and other events organised by the RA respect the life of the countryside by leaving no litter, doing no unnecessary damage, keeping dogs under control, etc.

The RA, many of whose members live in or close to the countryside, is mindful of the needs and concerns of rural communities. It is keen to work with members of these communities - and in particular with farmers, farmworkers and landowners - to ensure that the social, economic and environmental well-being of rural areas is maintained and improved.

INFLUENCING POLICIES, AND PLAYING A PART IN RAMBLERS' ASSOCIATION WORK

All RA members are entitled to attend and vote at the annual general meetings of their area and group. They can propose motions for debate at their annual meetings and they can stand for election to their area and group committees.

Through their areas, members may also seek election as delegates to General Council, where national policy is determined and to which areas may submit motions. Members of General Council may in turn stand for election to the Executive Committee.

In Wales and Scotland, members can, through their areas and groups, seek election to the Welsh and Scottish Councils and their committees.

The RA is always in need of help from willing volunteers. In particular, we need more members to lead walks, to help working parties clear and waymark footpaths; to help members with special needs to go on walks; to do a variety of administration tasks; to serve on local committees; and to take on key posts such as footpath secretary, publicity officer or community link officer according to whichever skills, interests or ideas they may have.

If you can help, contact your local area or group secretary or attend your local RA annual meeting and offer to stand for the group's committee. All offers will be most gratefully received!

LEAVING A LEGACY TO THE RA

As someone who derives great pleasure and satisfaction from walking in our beautiful countryside, you will no doubt share the RA's wish that future generations may also enjoy that pleasure.

But our footpaths and countryside face

THE RAMBLERS

many threats. More than ever, the vigilance of the Ramblers' Association is needed to save our heritage for ramblers of the future.

The RA is constantly campaigning to keep footpaths open and to safeguard our traditional right to roam across the hills, mountains and common land of Britain. And we are fighting to protect the natural beuaty of the countryside—its hedgerows and woodlands, its heathlands and downs.

What we bequeath to our successors may depend on a bequest from you to the RA. Income from legacies is of enormous importance to the RA in helping us to achieve the association's objectives. May we therefore appeal to you to leave a legacy to the Ramblers' Association?

Anyone can leave a legacy to the RA. You don't have to be a member. The simplest form of bequest is one which gives the RA a specific sum of money. The words to use in your will for this are:

"I give the sum of .... pounds to the Ramblers' Association of 1/5 Wandsworth Road, London SW8 2XX for its general purposes. I further direct that the receipt of the treasurer, director or other proper officer of the Ramblers' Association for the time being shall be a full and sufficient discharge for my Executors or Trustees."

Alternatively, you can leave to the RA a share of your Estate; or the residue of your Estate after making other bequests. If you have already made a will, you can easily amend it or add to it by signing a codicil.

Further details of all these options are set out in a free RA leaflet on legacies obtainable from the RA's office in London.

RAMBLERS' WILL-MAKING SERVICE

The RA's solicitors provide a special will-making service for RA members and supporters. Further details of this service are given in the RA's legacy leaflet. Alternatively, you can write to them direct – without obligation. Write to: Jerry Pearlman, Brooke, North & Goodwin, Crown House, Great George Street, Leeds LS1 3BR Tel. 0113-283 2100.

You will then receive a questionnaire which, when completed, will give Brooke, North & Goodwin the information they need to draw up your will. All the information you provide will of course be treated in strict confidence and will not be revealed to any third party, including the RA.

At the time of publication, the basic charge for this service will be only £35 + VAT for one person and £60 + VAT for a couple with similar wishes for what to include in their wills. These charges may change to keep abreast of rising costs and may not apply in cases of special complexity.

So please think of those who will follow in your footsteps: ramblers of the future will be glad of your legacy.

THE RAMBLERS

Ramblers' Area and Group Contacts

Four hundred groups all over England, Wales and Scotland form the body of the Ramblers' Association. The groups carry out vital work in their localities — clearing and maintaining footpaths, organising walks programmes, giving publicity to rights of way and access issues and, of course, walking together.

We list here the area and group secretaries. They are all volunteers and many work from home. Some are happy to have their telephone numbers published; others are not. If you telephone, please do so at reasonable times.

The details are correct at October 1996 but changes do take place during the year in both officers and the groups themselves (i.e. some are disbanded and some are formed). At the present time, for example, three new groups are being formed in the South Oxfordshire area but at the time of going to press, elections for officers have not yet been held.

England

AVON

AREA SECRETARY
Ms S C Popham, 56 Falcon Drive, Stoke Dean, Patchway, Bristol, BS12 5RB

GROUP SECRETARIES
Bath Mrs M Starbuck, 33 South View Road, Bath, Avon, BA2 3RW
Bristol Mr J A Grant, 103 Queensholm Crescent, Downend, Bristol BS16 6LJ. ☎ 0117-957 3450
Kingswood Monica Davis, 11 Deerhurst, Kingwood, Bristol, BS15 1XH. ☎ 0117-909 0535
Norton Radstock Mrs S Haddon, 4 Dymboro Close, Midsomer Norton, Bath, Avon, BA3 2QS
Southwold (Yate) Miss S S Naqui, 3 Brake Close, Sherbourne Park, Bradley Stoke, Bristol, BS12 8BA. . ☎ 0117-969 7246

BEDFORDSHIRE

AREA SECRETARY
Mr Ian Lindsay, 9 Harrow Road, Leighton Buzzard, Beds, LU7 8UF. ☎ (01525) 370907

GROUP SECRETARIES
Flit Vale Ms G M Brown, 21 Castle Road, Bedford, MK40 3PL
Ivel Valley Mrs J C Idle, 74 Denmark Street, Bedford, MK40 3TH. ☎ (01234) 353708
Lea & Icknield Mr K Warlow, 110 Talbot Road, Luton, Beds, LU2 7RW. ☎ (01582) 612105
Leighton Buzzard Mr Tony Harding, 32 Garden Leys, Leighton Buzzard, Beds, LU7 8PQ
North Bedfordshire Mrs J Edwards, Newfield, 16 Rushden Road, Milton Ernest, Beds, MK44 1RU. ☎ (01234) 822244
Ouse Valley Mr Malcolm Lewis, 7 High Street, Oakley, Bedfordshire, MK43 7RG. ☎ (01234) 822294
South Bedfordshire Miss R M Seymour, 110 Luton Road, Toddington, Dunstable, Beds, LU5 6DG

> **Do you know your rights when you're out walking in the countryside? See pages 32-39**

BERKSHIRE

AREA SECRETARY
Mr Cliff Lambert, 'Marandella', 73 Fifth Road, Newbury, Berkshire, RG14 6DT. ☎ (01635) 32842

GROUP SECRETARIES
East Berkshire Mr Gerald Barnett, 9 Fremantle Road, High Wycombe, Bucks, HP13 7PQ. ☎ (01494) 522404

Great Park Mrs Joan Bird, 9 Martin Close, Windsor, Berkshire, SL4 5SP. ☎ (01753) 866583

Loddon Valley Mr Nick Price, 5 Dunbar Drive, Woodley, Berkshire, RG5 4HA. ☎ (01734 697153

Mid Berkshire Ms E Cuff, Donkey Pound Cottage, Beech Hill, Reading, Berkshire, RG7 2AX. ☎ (01734) 882674

Pang Valley Mr Peter Harris, 106 St Peters Avenue, Caversham, Reading, RG4 7DR. ☎ (01734) 479187

South East Berks Mr J Moules, 50 Qualitas, Roman Hill, Bracknell, Berks, RG12 7QG. ☎ (01344) 421002

West Berkshire Mrs J M Young, 10 Porchester Road, Newbury, Berks, RG14 7QJ. ☎ (01635) 42006

BUCKINGHAMSHIRE & W MIDDLESEX

AREA SECRETARY
Mr D Bradnack, 47 Thame Road, Haddenham, Bucks, HP17 8EP. ☎ (01844) 291069

GROUP SECRETARIES
Amersham & District Mr K Evans, 4 Ruckles Way, Amersham, Buckinghamshire, HP7 0BZ. ☎ (01494) 725838

Aylesbury & District Mr C A R Bostle, 11 Field Close, The Coppice, Aylesbury, Bucks, HP20 1XR. ☎ (01296) 27717

Hillingdon Mrs P A Morris, 3 The Uplands, Ruislip, Middx, HA4 8QN. ☎ (01895) 633162 (membership enquiries Mr Massey ☎ (01895) 230199)

Milton Keynes & District Mrs J M Hussey, 33 Lavender Grove, Walnut Tree, Milton Keynes, Bucks, MK7 7DB. ☎ (01908) 691089

North West London Miss H O Lee, 12b Wellesley Road, Harrow, Middlesex, HA1 1QN. ☎ 0181-863 7628

West London Miss J Jefcoate, 25 Willow Grove, Ruislip, Middx, HA4 6DG. ☎ (01895) 63345

Wycombe District Mr J L Esslemont, 4 Park Farm Way, Lane End, High Wycombe, Buckinghamshire, HP14 3EG. ☎ (01494) 881597

CAMBRIDGESHIRE

AREA SECRETARY
Mr G Smith, 74 Maitland Avenue, Cambridge, CB4 1TB. ☎ (01223) 510665

GROUP SECRETARIES
Cambridge Mrs Alison Harrison, 61 Harlestones Road, Cottenham, Cambridge, CB4 4TR

Huntingdonshire Mrs Betty Aveling, 164 Hartford Road, Huntingdon, Cambs, PE18 7XQ. ☎ (01480) 454866

Peterborough Mr P Bennett, 24 Albany Walk, Woodston, Peterborough, PE2 9JN

CORNWALL

AREA SECRETARY
Mrs S Oliver, "Trenoweth", Viaduct Hill, Hayle, Cornwall, TR27 5HT. ☎ (01736) 752121

GROUP SECRETARIES
Bude/Stratton Mr J H Fitch, Sunbeams, Widemouth Bay, Bude, Cornwall, EX23 0AW. ☎ (01288) 361301

Camel District (Wadebridge) Mr George Burke, 5 Sherwood Drive, Bodmin, Cornwall, PL31 2PR. ☎ (01208) 73489

Caradon Mrs Barbara Roberts, Trees, Lanreath, Loow, Cornwall, PL13 2NU

Carrick Mrs J M Ingleby-oddy, Stratton House, Stratton Terrace, Falmouth, Cornwall, TR11 2SY

Newquay Margaret Baker, 86 Bonython Road, Newquay, Cornwall, TR7 3AL. ☎ (01637) 878208

Restormel Mr Roger Smith, Fieldhaven, 18 St Sulien, Luxulyan, Bodmin, Cornwall, PL30 5EB. ☎ (01726) 75721

West Cornwall (Penwith & Kerrier) Mrs S Oliver, "Trenoweth", Viaduct Hill, Hayle, Cornwall, TR27 5HT. ☎ (01736) 752121

DERBYSHIRE
WEST DERBYSHIRE, AMBER VALLEY, DERBY, SOUTH DERBYSHIRE AND EREWASH DISTRICTS OF DERBYSHIRE.
SEE ALSO SOUTH YORKSHIRE & NORTH EAST DERBYSHIRE AREA; MANCHESTER AREA

AREA SECRETARY
Mr J G Riddall, Hills View, Far Hill, Bradwell, Sheffield, S30 2HR. ☎ (01433) 620467

GROUP SECRETARIES
Amber Valley Vacant
Derby Mr D H G Varley, 27 Amber Road, Allestree, Derby, DE22 2QB. ☎ (01332) 551552

Derbyshire Dales Mr C Gale, 1 Masson Terrace, Church Street, Tansley, Matlock, Derbyshire, DE4 5FD. ☎ (01629) 580554

Erewash District Mr A Beardsley, 14 York Avenue, Sandiacre, Nottingham, NG10 5HB. ☎ 0115-939 2554

DEVON

AREA SECRETARY

Mrs E Linfoot, 14 Blaydon Cottages, Blackborough, Cullompton, Devon, EX15 2HJ. ☎ (01884) 266435

GROUP SECRETARIES

Bovey Tracey Mrs Margaret Dart, 47 Kiln Close, Bovey Tracey, Newton Abbot TQ13 9YL.

East Devon Mrs J English, 10 St Johns Close, Colyton, Devon, EX13 6TG

Exeter & District Mrs J W Mills, 1a Hampton Buildings, Blackboy Road, Exeter, Devon, EX4 6SR. ☎ (01392) 413073

Moorland Dr B Le G Waldron, 'Peebles', Bendarroch Road, West Hill, Ottery St Mary, Devon, EX11 1UR

North Devon Mrs Joan Long, 12 Bradiford, Barnstaple, Devon, EX31 4AD. ☎ (01271) 76274

Plymouth Mrs J W M Perkins, 59 Godding Gardens, Southway, Plymouth, Devon, PL6 6NF. ☎ (01752) 776517

South Devon Mr R A Woolcott, The Lodge, Manor Park, Seymour Drive, Watcombe Torquay, TQ2 8PY. ☎ (01803) 313430

South Hams Mr Bruce Hall, Whiteacres, West Charleton, Kingsbridge, Devon, TQ7 2AB. ☎ (01548) 531605

Tavistock Mr H Hodge, Binnicknowle, 138 Old Exeter Rd, Tavistock, Devon, PL19 0JB. ☎ (01822) 613970

Teignmouth & Dawlish Miss J Dawkins, 6 The Close, Windward Lane, Holcombe, Devon, EX7 0JH. ☎ (01626) 863724

Tiverton Miss C P L Cooke, 9 St Lawrence Close, Tidcombe, Tiverton, Devon, EX16 4ED. ☎ (01884) 256254

Totnes Mrs N M Adams, 7 Courtfield, Totnes, Devon, TQ9 5RQ. ☎ (01803) 862829

DORSET

AREA SECRETARY

Mr Brian Panton [acting Sec], 5 Nicholas Gardens, Ensbury Park, Bournemouth, Dorset, BH10 4BA. ☎ (01202) 526954

GROUP SECRETARIES

East Dorset Mr Andy Hopkinson, 32 Nugent Road, Hengistbury Head, Bournemouth, Dorset, BH6 4ET. ☎ (01202) 418955

North Dorset Mr A T Combridge, Green Bushes, North Rd, Sherborne, Dorset, DT9 3JN

South Dorset Mrs Val Barnes, Broadstone Barn, Walditch, Bridport, Dorset, DT6 4LA. ☎ (01308) 427430

West Dorset Mr Peter Mccarthy, 3 Home Farm Close, Uploders, Bridport, Dorset, DT6 4RS. ☎ (01308 485418

COUNTY DURHAM

SEE NORTHERN AREA AND NORTH YORKSHIRE & SOUTH DURHAM AREA

EAST YORKSHIRE & DERWENT

EAST RIDING OF YORKSHIRE, YORK AND THE OLD RURAL DISTRICTS AND TOWNS OF DERWENT, EASINGWOLD, FLAXTON, MALTON, NORTON, AND FILEY; PART OF SCARBOROUGH, RYEDALE AND HAMBLETON

AREA SECRETARY

Mrs M A Cumberland, 33 Mill Lane, Acaster Malbis, York, YO2 1UJ. ☎ (01904) 708479

GROUP SECRETARIES

Beverley Mr J Roach, Hollins, The Park, Swanland, North Humberside, HU14 3LU. ☎ (01482) 632117

Driffield Mr J R Jefferson, Delamere, 2 Spellowgate, Driffield, North Humberside, YO25 7BB. ☎ (01377) 252412

Hull & Holderness Mr G Armstrong, 9 Moseley Hill, Bilton, Kingston Upon Hull, HU11 4ES

Ryedale Mr J Atkinson, Quarry Garth, Broughton, Malton, North Yorkshire, YO17 0QG. ☎ (01653) 692478

Scarborough & District Ms A K Thornton, 62 Hillcrest Avenue, Scarborough, North Yorkshire, YO12 6RQ. ☎ (01723) 376490

York Miss V Silberberg, 41 North Parade, Bootham, York, YO3 7AB. ☎ (01904) 628134

ESSEX

ESSEX PLUS LONDON BOROUGHS OF WALTHAM FOREST, RED-BRIDGE, HAVERING, BARKING AND NEWHAM

AREA SECRETARY
A Vincent-Jones, 2 Porchester Close, Emerson Park, Hornchurch, Essex, RM11 2HH. ☎ (01708) 473253

GROUP SECRETARIES
Brentwood Mrs B Stoten, 10 Toppesfield Avenue, Wickford, Essex, SS12 0PB. ☎ (01268) 735447

Chelmer & Blackwater Ms Elaine Bane, Hide-away, Hackmans Lane, Cock Clarks, Chelmsford, CM3 6RE

Colchester Mrs M E Hobby, Weathercock Cottage, East Mersea Road, West Mersea, Essex, CO5 8SL

Friends Group Audrey Wiseman, Royston, Main Road, Bicknacre, Chelmsford, Essex, CM3 4HA. ☎ (01245) 224749

Greenways Mr P H E Griffiths, 27 Daltons Fen, Pitsea, Basildon, Essex SS13 1JE.

Havering & East London Mrs S Green, 5 Salcombe Drive, Chadwell Heath, Romford, Essex, RM6 6DU. ☎ 0181 599 4719

North West Essex Mr G Pattenden, 234 Cressing Road, Braintree, Essex, CM7 3PQ. ☎ (01376) 327535

Redbridge Mr L I Goldsmith, 11 Holland Park Avenue, Newbury Park, Essex, IG3 8JR

Rochford & Castle Point Ms L R Fletcher, 40 Hambro Ave, Rayleigh, Essex, SS6 9NJ. ☎ (01268) 780716

South East Essex Mrs Joyce Law, 4 Nobles Green Close, Leigh-on-Sea, Essex, SS9 5QH

Stort Valley Mr C Taylor, 6 Acorn Mews, Bush Fair, Harlow, CM18 6NA

Tendring District Miss B A Wackett, 103 Butchers Lane, Walton-on-Naze, Essex, CO14 8UD. ☎ (01255) 671205

Thurrock Mr S G Dyball, 29 Bishops Road, Corringham, Stanford Le Hope, Essex, SS17 7HB. ☎ (01375) 676442

Uttlesford Vacant

West Essex Mr H F Matthews, Glen View, London Road, Abridge, Essex, RM4 1UX. ☎ (Membership Enquiries only 0181-989 6851)

GLOUCESTERSHIRE

AREA SECRETARY
Mrs M Rear, 106 Malleson Road, Gotherington, Cheltenham, Glos, GL52 4EY. ☎ (01242) 674470

GROUP SECRETARIES
Cirencester Mrs L Cook, 9 Partridge Way, Cirencester, Glos, GL7 1BH. ☎ (01285) 658477

Cleeve Mrs M Davies, 6 Manor Lane, Gotherington, Cheltenham, GL52 4QX. ☎ (01242) 673928

Forest of Dean Mr F F Gray, 2 Church Gardens, Lydney, Glos, GL15 5EF. ☎ (01594) 842513

Gloucester David Butler, 1 Sovereign Chase, Staunton, Glos, GL19 3NW. ☎ (01452) 840172

Mid-Gloucestershire Mrs J C Smieja, 18 Sandy Lane, Charlton Kings, Cheltenham, Glos, GL53 9BZ. ☎ (01242) 511809

North Cotswold Miss J A Smith, 2 Hammond Drive, Northleach, Cheltenham Glos, GL54 3JF. ☎ (01451) 860817

South Gloucestershire Mr M Garner, Southcot, The Headlands, North Woodchester, Stroud, Glos, GL5 5PS. ☎ (01453) 873625

HAMPSHIRE

AREA SECRETARY
Mr M L Malpass, The Coach House, Rareridge Lane, Bishops Waltham, Hants, SO32 1DX. ☎ (01489) 893777

GROUP SECRETARIES
Alton Mrs S Fleck, 10 Bow Street, Alton, Hants, GU34 1NY. ☎ (01420) 541230

Andover Mrs M A Inness, 6 Bremen Gardens, Archers Grange, Andover, Hants, SP10 4QL. ☎ (01264) 362387

Basing & Hook Mrs J E Davies, 23 Church View, Hartley Wintney, Hants, RG27 8LN. ☎ (01252) 844969

Eastleigh Mr John Cawley, Melin Jy, Uppermoors Road, Brambridge, Eastleigh, Hants, SO50 6HW. ☎ (01962) 715201

Meon Mrs J Giles, The Laurels, Brookside Drive, Sarisbury Green, Southampton, SO31 6ER. ☎ (01489) 583430

New Forest Trevor Davies, 7 Boundstone, Hythe, Southampton, SO45 5AZ. ☎ (01703) 848700

North East Hants Mr Brian Austen, Kappa Crucis, Hillside Road, Farnham, Surrey, GU9 9DW. ☎ (01252) 314826

Portsmouth & Southsea Mrs F M Jones, 38 Grant Road, Farlington, Portsmouth, Hants, PO6 1DX. ☎ (01705) 381878

Romsey Mrs E Drinkwater, 19 Bassett Green Village, Southampton, SO16 3ND. ☎ (01703) 767308

South East Hants Ms J Rowe, 19 Crystal Way, Waterlooville, Hants, PO7 8NB. ☎ (01705) 266039

Southampton Mrs Valerie Harvey, 21 Kingsfold Avenue, Townhill Park, Southampton, Hants, SO18 2PY. ☎ (01703) 582445.

Waltham Mr Pat Sayers, 8 Stirling Court, Frosthole Crescent, Fareham, Hants, PO15 6DH

Winchester Alan Charles, Melbury House, Stoke Charity Road, Kingsworthy, Winchester SO23 7LS. ☎ (01962) 886897.

Watford & Three Rivers Ms C J Gransby, 24 Richards Close, Bushey, Watford, WD2 3JB. ☎ [contact G Seaman ☎ (01923) 673214

HEREFORD & WORCESTER

AREA SECRETARY
Mr Derek Starkey, 39 Sandpiper Crescent, Malvern, Worcs, WR14 1UY. ☎ (01886) 832064

GROUP SECRETARIES
Bromsgrove Mrs S A Woodbury, 13 Victoria Road, Bromsgrove, Worcs, B61 0DW. ☎ (01527) 873441
Evesham Ms Y D H Williams, 51 Bridge Street, Pershore, Worcs, WR10 1AL
Hereford Mr A G Rowe, 67 Quarry Road, Tupsley, Hereford, HR1 1ST. ☎ (01432) 269182
North Herefordshire Mrs G A Pennington, 3 Glebbe Cottages, Eardisland, Leominster, Herefordshire, HR6 9BD. ☎ (01544) 388110
Redditch Mrs P Hammond, 11 Clifton Crescent, Solihull, W Midlands, B91 3LG. ☎ 0121-704 9399
Worcester Miss J Hollis, 57 Sandys Road, Barbourne, Worcester, WR1 3HE. ☎ (01905) 20868
Wyre Forest Mr C E Baston, 14 Cardinal Drive, Kidderminster, Worcs, DY10 4RY. ☎ (01562) 68442

HERTFORDSHIRE & NORTH MIDDLESEX

HERTFORDSHIRE PLUS LONDON BOROUGHS OF BARNET, ENFIELD AND HARINGEY

AREA SECRETARY
Mr D S Allard, 8 Chilcourt, Royston, Herts, SG8 9DD ☎ (01763) 242677.

GROUP SECRETARIES
Dacorum Mr D Saxby, 62 High Firs Crescent, Harpenden, Herts, AL5 1NA. ☎ (01582) 715633 (Membership enquiries Mr Spicer (01582) 760323)
East Hertfordshire Miss P A Hemmings, 20 East Road, Bishops Stortford, Herts, CM23 5JG. ☎ (01279) 506248
Finchley & Hornsey Ms C Cahn, 153 North View Road, London, N8 7ND. ☎ 0181-347 9561
North Hertfordshire Mr R T Jarvis, 17 Moormead Close, Hitchin, Herts, SG5 2BA. ☎ (01462) 422837
North London & South Herts Mrs M Pearce, 2 The Glade, Winchmore Hill, London, N21 1QE. ☎ 0181 882 7668
Royston Mr M J Lee, 6 The Shires, Royston, Herts, SG8 9HX. ☎ (01763) 247579

HUMBERSIDE

SEE EAST YORKSHIRE & DERWENT AREA AND LINCOLNSHIRE & SOUTH HUMBERSIDE AREA

INNER LONDON

AREA SECRETARY
Mr D Purcell., 8 Dryburgh Mansions, London, SW15 1AJ. ☎ 0181-788 1373

GROUP SECRETARIES
Blackheath Mr D Bollen, 119a Culverley Rd, Catford, London, SE6 2JZ. ☎ 0181-244 0557.
Hammersmith & Wandsworth Mr J E G Stebbings, 45 Abdale Road, London, W12 7ER. ☎ 0181-743 0250
Hampstead Mr K D Jones, Flat 4, 144 Agar Grove, Camden, London, NW1 9TY. ☎ 0171-485 2348
Kensington & Westminster Ms J M Mack, 8n Grove End House, Grove End Road, London, NW8 9HN. (Membership enquiries: s.a.e to Joceline Morrison, 87 Campden Hill Court, London W8 7HW)
North East London Mr P Weaire, 25 Cromer Road, Leyton, London, E10 6JA. ☎ 0181-556 3884
South Bank Mr M R Jackson, Flat 7, 57 Crystal Palace Road, East Dulwich, London, SE22 9EX

ISLE OF WIGHT

AREA SECRETARY
Mrs Phyllis Griffiths, 21 Milne Way, Shide, Newport, Isle Of Wight, PO30 1YF. ☎ (01983) 527715

GROUP SECRETARIES
Isle of Wight Mrs G D Wardle, 32 Marina Avenue, Appley, Ryde, Isle Of Wight, PO33 1NJ. ☎ (01983) 566726

KENT

KENT PLUS LONDON BOROUGHS OF BEXLEY AND BROMLEY

AREA SECRETARY
Mr Peter Skipp, 81 New Street Hill, Bromley, Kent, BR1 5BA. ☎ 0181-857 8571

GROUP SECRETARIES
Ashford (Kent) Mrs L V Percival, 2 Cloth Hall Gardens, Biddenden, Ashford, Kent, TN27 8AT

AREA AND GROUP CONTACTS

Bromley Mr Peter Skipp, 81 New Street Hill, Bromley, Kent, BR1 5BA

Canterbury Mrs E Holt, 36 Dundonald Rd, Ramsgate, Kent, CT11 9PU. ☎ (01843) 581051

Dartford Bill Ripper, 45 Bradbourne Rd, Bexley, Kent, DA5 1NS. ☎ (01322) 554259

Maidstone Mr M P Finnimore, 12 Laurel Grove, Kingswood, Maidstone, Kent, ME17 3PS.
☎ (01622) 843208

Medway Mrs D M Ashdown, 94a Hollywood Lane, Wainscott, Rochester, Kent, ME3 8AR

North West Kent Sylvia Hogg, 111 Dorchester Avenue, Bexley, Kent, DA5 3AN. ☎ 0181-301 5428

Romney Marsh Ms A M Graham, 47 Taylors Lane, St Marys Bay, Romney Marsh, Kent, TN29 0HB

Sevenoaks Mr Paul Dunn, 110 Brittains Lane, Sevenoaks, Kent, TN13 2NE

Tonbridge & Malling Mrs J A Jones, 85 Norman Road, West Malling, Maidstone, Kent, ME19 6RN.
☎ (01732) 842212

Tunbridge Wells Mrs M Booker, 1 Elphicks Place, Tunbridge Wells, Kent, TN2 5NB. ☎ (01892) 530284

White Cliffs Mrs E A Govier, 20 Castle Rd, Sandgate, Folkestone, Kent, CT20 3AG. ☎ (01303) 240570

LAKE DISTRICT

CUMBRIA PLUS LANCASTER DISTRICT OF LANCASHIRE

AREA SECRETARY
Mr Peter Jones, 44 High Fellside, Kendal, Cumbria, LA9 4JG. ☎ (01539) 723705

GROUP SECRETARIES
Carlisle Miss A M Cole, 101 Etterby Lea Crescent, Stanwix, Carlisle, CA3 9JR. ☎ (01228) 46544

Furness Mr W Scott, 55 Ainslie Street, Barrow In Furness, Cumbria, LA14 5AY. ☎ (01229) 831871

Grange over Sands Mr R B Stubbs, 2 Netherwood Gardens, Off Lindale Road, Grange Over Sands, Cumbria, LA11 6EL. ☎)015395) 35794

Kendal Mr Gerald Cole, The Barn, Holme Lyon, Burneside, Nr Kendal, Cumbria, LA9 6QX.
☎ (01539) 727837

Lancaster Mrs P Gilligan, 22 Endsleigh Grove, Lancaster, LA1 2TX. ☎ (01524) 68853

Penrith Mrs Christine Roberts, 11 Friars Rise, Penrith, Cumbria, CA11 8DF. ☎ (01768) 63771

West Cumbria Mr David Woodhead, Cropple How, Birkby, Ravenglass, Cumbria, CA18 1RT.
☎ (01229) 717270

LANCASHIRE

SEE LAKE DISTRICT AREA; MID LANCASHIRE AREA; NORTH EAST LANCASHIRE AREA

LEICESTERSHIRE & RUTLAND

AREA SECRETARY
Mr M Statham, 201 Maplewell Road, Woodhouse Eaves, Leicester, LE12 8QY. ☎ (01509) 890779

GROUP SECRETARIES
Coalville Miss Fiona Andrews, 78 Blackwood, Coalville, Leicester, LE67 4RF. ☎ (01530) 812242

Hinckley Mr Sid Hindmarsh, 9 Croft Close, Wolvey, Hinckley, Leicestershire, LE10 3LE.
☎ (01455) 220418

Leicester Mr H E Lomas, 44 Stretton Road, Leicester, LE3 6BJ

Loughborough & District Mrs J Noon, 8 Ribble Drive, Barrow-upon-Soar, Loughborough, Leics, LE12 8LJ

Lutterworth Mrs B T Wilkinson, 6 Marylebone Drive, Lutterworth, Leicestershire, LE17 4DL.
☎ (01455) 553254

Melton Mowbray Mrs P A Posey, 8 Owen Drive, Melton Mowbray, Leics, LE13 1TS

Rutland Mr Gerry Neild, 49 Stamford Road, Oakham, Leics, LE15 6HZ. ☎ (01572) 722514

LINCOLNSHIRE

LINCOLNSHIRE INCLUDING THE UNITARY AUTHORITIES OF NORTH AND NORTH EAST LINCOLNSHIRE, FORMERLY HUMBERSIDE

AREA SECRETARY
Mr S W Parker, 129 Broughton Gardens, Brant Road, Lincoln, LN5 8SR. ☎ (01522) 534655

GROUP SECRETARIES
Boston Mr R L Ruskin, 4 Garfits Lane, Boston, Lincs, PE21 7ES. ☎ (01205) 353540

Gainsborough Mrs P Mcclure, The Cottage, 52 Aisby, Gainsborough, Lincs, DN21 5RF. ☎ (01427) 838789

Grantham Mrs D Bean, 185 Harlaxton Road, Grantham, Lincs, NG31 7AG. ☎ (01476) 565090

Grimsby & Louth Mrs Julia Light, 223 Station Road, New Waltham, Grimsby, Lincs, DN36 4PF.
☎ (01472)821941

Horncastle Mr P Johnson, 'Justwe', Highgate Lane, Sutton On Sea, Lincs, LN12 2LJ. ☎ (01507) 442400

Lincoln Mrs Miriam Smith, 2 Belgravia Close, Forest Park, Lincoln, LN6 0QJ. ☎ (01522) 682479

Scunthorpe Mr N J Good, 21 Rivermeadow, Brigg, DN20 9JW. ☎ (01652) 653072

Skegness Mrs G Malcolm, 10 Saxby Avenue, Skegness, Lincs, PE25 3JZ. ☎ (01754) 764687

Sleaford Mr G Rodgers, 10 Spring Gardens, Newfield Road, Sleaford, Lincs, NG34 7AU.
☎ (01529) 303979

Spalding Mrs M Widdows, 8 St Annes Way, Spalding, Lincs, PE11 3PA. ☎ (01775) 766372

Stamford Mr Bob Hadfield, 95 Northorpe, Thurlby, Bourne, Lincs, PE10 0HZ. ☎ (01778) 426417

LONDON

FOR INNER LONDON BOROUGHS SEE INNER LONDON AREA.
FOR OUTER LONDON BOROUGHS SEE BUCKINGHAMSHIRE & WEST MIDDLESEX AREA; HERTFORDSHIRE & NORTH MIDDLESEX AREA; KENT AREA; SURREY AREA

MANCHESTER

FORMER GREATER MANCHESTER PLUS HIGH PEAK DISTRICT OF DERBYSHIRE

AREA SECRETARY

Mr T Perkins, 34 Grangethorpe Drive, Burnage, Manchester, M19 2LG. ☎ 0161-225 2650

GROUP SECRETARIES

Bolton Mr D Smethurst, 108 Green Lane, Bolton, Lancs, BL3 2HX. ☎ (01204) 532011

Bury Dr M B Carter, 6 Abbeystead Drive, Lancaster, Lancs, LA1 4QU

New Mills Mrs M Nother, The Firs, Buxton Road, Whaley Bridge, Via Stockport, Cheshire, SK12 7JY. ☎ (01663) 732123

Oldham Janet Hewitt, 2 Hillside Avenue, Carrbrook, Stalybridge, Cheshire, SK15 3NE. ☎ (01457) 834769

Rochdale Mrs N E Tupling, 4 Four Lanes Way, Norden, Rochdale, Lancs, OL11 5TL. ☎ (01706) 42376

Stockport Ms C Wickens, 5 Essex Avenue, Cheadle Heath, Stockport, SK3 0JA. ☎ 0161-477 5803

Wigan & District Mr P Taylor, 11 Corfe Close, Aspull, Wigan, Lancs, WN2 1UW

MERSEYSIDE AND WEST CHESHIRE

MERSEYSIDE PLUS CHESTER AND ELLESMERE PORT DISTRICTS OF CHESHIRE

AREA SECRETARY

Miss G F Thayer, 53 Bramwell Avenue, Prenton, Birkenhead, Merseyside, L43 0RQ. ☎ 0151-608 9472

GROUP SECRETARIES

Cestrian (Chester) Mrs F Edwards, 32 Wetherby Way, Little Sutton, South Wirral, L66 4NY. ☎ 0151-339 1178

Liverpool Miss G F Thayer, 53 Bramwell Avenue, Prenton, Birkenhead, Merseyside, L43 0RQ

Southport Mr D Wall, 22 Dunbar Crescent, Southport, Lancs, PR8 3AB

St Helens Mr P J McGurk, 156 Brynn Street, St Helens, Lancs WA10 1HX.

Wirral Mrs E B Rendle, 5 Axholme Close, Thingwall, Wirral, Merseyside, L61 1BH. ☎ 0151-648 1535

MID LANCASHIRE

LANCASHIRE: BLACKPOOL, FYLDE, PRESTON, SOUTH RIBBLE, CHORLEY, WEST LANCASHIRE AND WYRE BOROUGHS

AREA SECRETARY

Mr D Kelly, 4 Buttermere Close, Bamber Bridge, Preston, Lancs, PR5 4RT. ☎ (01772) 312027

GROUP SECRETARIES

Chorley Mrs M Schmuhl, 106 Spring Meadow, Clayton-le-woods, Leyland, Lancs, PR5 2LY

Fylde Mr M J Bloomfield, 4 Rockingham Road, Bispham, Blackpool, Lancs, FY2 0LP

Garstang & District Mrs C Stenning, 20 Meadowcroft Avenue, Catterall, Garstang, Lancs, PR3 1ZH. ☎ (01995) 601478

Preston Mr A Manzie, 3 Ruthin Court, Dunbar Road, Ingol, Preston, Lancs, PR2 3YE. ☎ (01772) 736467

South Ribble Mr D Kelly, 4 Buttermere Close, Bamber Bridge, Preston, Lancs, PR5 4RT. ☎ (01772) 312027

West Lancashire Mr W G Wright, 49 Riverview, Tarleton, Preston, Lancs, PR4 6ED. ☎ (01772) 812034

NORFOLK

AREA SECRETARY

Mr John Harris, 7 Lowther Road, Eaton Rise, Norwich, NR4 6QN. ☎ (01603) 623070

GROUP SECRETARIES

Dereham Mr G J D Price, 48 Bittering Street, Gressenhall, Dereham, Norfolk, NR20 4EB

Fakenham Sandra Harrod, 45 Creake Gate Road, Wighton, Wells-next-the-Sea, Norfolk, NR23 1PP

Great Yarmouth Miss J Roberts, 1 Mission Place, Estcourt Road, Great Yarmouth, Norfolk, NR30 4JF. ☎ (01493) 852818

King's Lynn Mr J Tomkin, 24 Langland, Gayton Road, Kings Lynn, Norfolk, PE30 4TH

Norwich Mrs J Worsfold, 5 Lucerne Close, Old Catton, Norwich, NR6 7DG

Sheringham & District Mrs B Page, 41 Cromer Road, Holt, Norfolk, NR25 6EV

Southern Norfolk Mr G H Head, 9 Henley Road, Norwich, NR2 3NL

Swaffham Mrs C Wright, 12 Southlands, Swaffham, Norfolk, PE37 7PE

Wensum Mr A J Beckingham, Kilwhang, Beechwood Avenue, Aylmerton, Norwich, Norfolk, NR11 8QQ.

NORTH AND MID CHESHIRE

AREA SECRETARY
Mr R E Jones, 56 Greystone Road, Penketh, Warrington, WA5 2ER

GROUP SECRETARIES
Halton Mrs P Jones, 3 William Street, Widnes, Cheshire, WA8 6RN

Vale Royal and Knutsford Mrs A Slade, 13 Norbury Close, Knutsford, Cheshire, WA16 8JP.
☎ (01565) 633997

Warrington Mr J R Reese, 2 Freshfields Drive, Padgate, Warrington, Cheshire, WA2 0QY.
☎ (01925) 821166

NORTH EAST LANCASHIRE

LANCASHIRE: RIBBLE VALLEY, PENDLE, BURNLEY, ROSSENDALE, BLACKBURN AND HYNDBURN DISTRICTS

AREA SECRETARY
Mrs S Baxendale, 101 Blackburn Road, Clayton-le-Moors, Accrington, Lancs, BB5 5JT.
☎ (01254) 235049

GROUP SECRETARIES
Blackburn & Darwen Miss M G Brindle, 103 School Lane, Guide, Blackburn, BB1 2LW.
☎(01254) 671269

Burnley & Pendle Mrs J Kay, 19 Barrowford Road, Colne, Lancs, BB8 9QP. ☎ (01282) 866890

Clitheroe Mr B Brown, 2 Chorlton Terrace, Barrow, Whalley, Clitheroe, Lancs, BB7 9AR.
☎ (01254) 822851

Hyndburn Miss J H Addison, 77 Catlow Hall Street, Oswaltwistle, Accrington, Lancs, BB5 3EZ.
☎ (01254) 235844

Rossendale Mr Alan Johnson, 10 Pendle Close, Bacup, Lancashire, OL13 9JY. ☎ (01706) 877521

> **Do you know your rights when you're out walking in the countryside?**
> **See pages 32-39**

NORTH YORKS & SOUTH DURHAM

CLEVELAND; CO. DURHAM EXCEPT DERWENTSIDE, DURHAM AND CHESTER-LE-STREET DISTRICTS; NORTH YORKSHIRE; PRESENT RICHMONDSHIRE DISTRICT AND THE FORMER URBAN AND RURAL DISTRICTS OF BEDALE, HELMSLEY, KIRKBYMOORSIDE, NORTHALLERTON, PICKERING, STOKESLEY, THIRSK AND WHITBY NOW FORMING PART OF THE HAMBLETON AND RYDALE DISTRICT. SEE ALSO WEST RIDING AREA; EAST YORKSHIRE AREA

AREA SECRETARY
Mr A Patterson, 141 Castle Road, Redcar, Cleveland, TS10 2NF. ☎ (01642) 474864

GROUP SECRETARIES
Barnard Castle Mrs J M Martin, 8 Kirk View, Barnard Castle, Co Durham, DL12 8HE

Cleveland Mr A Patterson, 141 Castle Road, Redcar, Cleveland, TS10 2NF. ☎ (01642) 474864

Crook & Weardale Mrs V W Bartlett, Coronation Cottage, Hamsterley, Bishop Auckland, Co Durham, DL13 3PT

Darlington Mr A Hutchinson, 1 Caithness Way, Darlington, Co Durham, DL1 3QS.
☎ (01325) 482164

North Yorks Moors Vacant

Northallerton Mr M F Kent, 131 Valley Road, Northallerton, North Yorkshire, DL6 1SN.
☎ (01609) 777618

Richmondshire Mrs B Forde, Hargill House, Gilling West, Richmond, North Yorkshire, DL10 5LJ.
☎ (01748) 824156

NORTHAMPTONSHIRE

AREA SECRETARY
Mr M J Tebbutt, 4 Manfield Way, Kettering Road, Northampton, NN3 6NA. ☎ (01604) 643352

GROUP SECRETARIES
Corby Angela Matthews, 11 Stavanger Close, Corby, Northants, NN18 9HT. ☎ (01536) 746280

Daventry Jenny Warner, 41 Harmans Way, Weedon, Northampton, NN7 4PB

Kettering Miss E M Wildman, 36 Skeffington Close, Geddington, Northants, NN14 1BA

Northampton Mr A K Grainger, 26 Lumbertubs Lane, Northampton, NN3 6AH. ☎ (01604) 492265

Towcester & District Mr J Mckeon, 1 Maidenhead Avenue, Bradwell Common, Milton Keynes, Bucks, MK13 8NA. ☎ (01908) 674867

Wellingborough & District Mr B Gotch, 30 Church Street, Finedon, Wellingborough, Northants, NN9 5NA. ☎ (01933) 680032

NORTHERN

AREA SECRETARY
Mr T M Pollard, 1 Derwentwater Gardens, Whickham, Newcastle On Tyne, NE16 4EY. ☎ 0191-488 7693

GROUP SECRETARIES
Alnwick Mr J Sim, 18 Chapel Lands, Alnwick, Northumberland, NE66 1EL. ☎ (01665) 605212

Berwick Mr W D Gill, 3 Knowes Close, Hutton, Berwick Upon Tweed, TD15 1TS. ☎ (01289) 386791

Chester le Street Mrs D Seeney, 3 Pennycross Road, Pennywell, Sunderland, SR4 0NW.
☎ 0191-534 5323

Derwentside Mr Neville Hartley, 51 Foxhills Crescent, Lanchester, Co. Durham, DH7 0PW.
☎ (01207) 520204

Durham City Mr C Ludman, 5 Church Street, Durham, DH1 3DG. ☎ 0191-386 6886

Hexham Mrs S Harding, 28 Hackwood Park, Hexham, Northumberland, NE46 1AX.
☎ (01434) 607210

Morpeth Miss M Siggens, 17 Kingswell, Carlisle Lea, Morpeth, Northumberland, NE61 2TY.
☎ (01670) 518031

Ponteland Mr K Shuttleworth, Medburn Cottage, Medburn, Ponteland, Newcastle Upon Tyne, NE20 0JE. ☎ (01661) 824741

Sunderland Mr B W Bell, 104 Tunstall Road, Sunderland, SR2 9BD. ☎ 0191-520 1028

Tyneside Miss M E Ramsdale, 36 Frankland Drive, Whitley Bay, Tyne & Wear, NE25 9DS.
☎ 0191-252 1949

NORTHUMBERLAND

SEE NORTHERN AREA

NOTTINGHAMSHIRE

AREA SECRETARY
Mr A J Staniforth, 2 Park View, Mapperley, Nottingham, NG3 5FD. ☎ 0115-952 2840

GROUP SECRETARIES
Broxtowe Mrs Kathleen Caster, 40 Cromwell Road, Beeston, Nottingham, NG9 1DG. ☎ 0115-925 6287

Collingham Mr V Pennell, 2 Oaklands Close, Collingham, Newark, Nottingham, NG23 7RQ.
☎ (01636) 893152

Dukeries Mrs S R Moore, 9 Rufford Rd, Edwinstowe, Notts, NG21 9HX. ☎ (01623) 822264

Gedling Sue Hallam, 10 Lime Tree Gardens, Lowdhan, Nottingham, NG14 7DJ. ☎ 0115-9617755

Harworth & Bircotes Mrs G D Houghton, The Cottage, Main Street, Harworth, Doncaster, DN11 8LB. ☎ (01302 742021

Hucknall Mrs Joan Niblett, 180 Papplewick Lane, Hucknall, Nottingham, NG15 8EH. ☎ 0115-952 1240

Newark Mr K E Martin, 32 Fosse Road, Farndon, Newark, Notts, NG24 4ST. ☎ (01636) 73563

Nottingham Mrs M F Staniforth, 2 Park View, Mapperley, Nottingham, NG3 5FD.
☎ 0115-952 2840

Ravenshead Jenny Abrahams, 14 Longdale Avenue, Ravenshead, Nottingham, NG15 9EA.
☎ (01623) 792352

Retford Mrs Irene Gore, The Old Rectory, Fledborough, Newark, Notts, NG22 0UU

Rushcliffe Mr R Parrey, 61 West Leake Road, Kingston On Soar, Notts, NG11 0DN.
☎ 0115-983 0730

Southwell Mrs K P Shale, 32 Riverside, Southwell, Nottinghamshire, NG25 0HA

Vale of Belvoir Carol Crook, 6 Nottingham Road, Bottesford, Nottingham, NG13 0AP.
☎ (01949) 842662

Worksop Mrs F M Lennox, 50 Shepherds Ave, Worksop, Notts, S81 0JB. ☎ (01909) 486473

OXFORDSHIRE

AREA SECRETARY
Mr P Barbour, 31 West Street, Chipping Norton, Oxon, OX7 5EU. ☎ (01608) 641081

GROUP SECRETARIES
Bicester & Kidlington Mrs Rose Stratford, 8 Queens Court, Bicester, Oxon, OX6 8JX

Cherwell Mrs Dianna Lathbury, 74 Valley Road, Brackley, Northants, NN13 7DQ. ☎ (01280) 704320

Didcot & Wallingford Vacant.

Henley & Goring Vacant.

Oxford Mrs E M Steane, 36 Harpes Road, Summertown, Oxford, OX2 7QL. ☎ (01865) 52531

South Oxfordshire Mrs M Broster, Munts Mill, Castle Lane, Wallingford, Oxon, OX10 0BN.
☎ (01491) 836654

Thame & Wheatley Vacant.

Vale of White Horse Mr P Lonergan, 35 Cherwell Close, Abingdon, OX14 3TD. ☎ (01235) 530174

West Oxfordshire Dr A E Cobb, Hillside Cottage, 3 Dyers Hill, Charlbury, Oxford, OX7 3QD.
☎ (01608) 810283

SHROPSHIRE

If you need to telephone anyone listed here please do so at a reasonable time

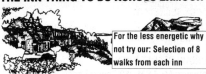

SOUTH & EAST CHESHIRE

CHESHIRE; CREWE & NANTWICH AND CONGLETON DISTRICTS PLUS EASTERN SECTION OF MACCLESFIELD DISTRICT

AREA SECRETARY

Mrs B Gray, 56 Lear Drive, Wistaston, Cheshire, CW2 8DS. ☎ (01270) 67517

GROUP SECRETARIES

Congleton Mr R W Foden, 50 Portree Drive, Holmes Chapel, Cheshire, CW4 7JB. ☎ (01477) 535924

East Cheshire Mrs B Salter, 10 Highfield Road, Bramhall, Stockport, Cheshire, SK7 3BE. ☎ 0161-439 1418

South Cheshire Mrs D Mccarthy, 6 Carisbrooke Close, Wistaston, Crewe, Cheshire, CW2 8JD. ☎ (01270) 68486

SOUTH YORKS & N.E.DERBYSHIRE

FORMER SOUTH YORKSHIRE PLUS NORTH EAST DERBYSHIRE; CHESTERFIELD, AND BOLSOVER DISTRICTS OF DERBYSHIRE

AREA SECRETARY

Mr T M Howard, 334 Manchester Road, Crosspool, Sheffield, S10 5DQ

GROUP SECRETARIES

Barnsley & Penistone Mr A Ridge, 53 Stead Lane, Hoyland, Barnsley, South Yorkshire, S74 0AD

Bolsover District Miss S Lee, 72 Langworth Road, Bolsover, Nr Chesterfield, Derbyshire, S44 6HW. ☎ (01246) 825189

Chesterfield & North East Derbyshire Mr A Hunt, 108 Peveril Road, Newbold, Chesterfield, Derbyshire, S41 8SG

Dearne Valley Mr D A Phillips, 4 Lower Malton Road, Scawsby, Doncaster, South Yorkshire, DN5 8SF

Doncaster Mrs M Thompson, 31 Broom Hill Drive, Cantley 6, Doncaster, DN4 6QZ. ☎ (01302) 371093

Rotherham Metro District Mrs J I Williams, 10 Spinney Field, Rotherham, S60 3HW. ☎ (01709) 531289

Sheffield Mrs Pat Peters, 751 Gleadless Road, Sheffield, S12 2QD. ☎ 0114-239 8505

STAFFORDSHIRE

STAFFORDSHIRE PLUS DUDLEY, SANDWELL, WALSALL AND WOLVERHAMPTON DISTRICTS OF FORMER WEST MIDLANDS

AREA SECRETARY

Mr C J Brookes, 34 Nethersole Street, Polesworth, Tamworth, Staffs, B78 1EE. ☎ (01827) 894023

GROUP SECRETARIES

Chase & District Mr P Baker (acting secretary), 2 Anker Close, Burntwood, Staffordshire, WS7 9JW. ☎ (01543) 672983

East Staffordshire Cherie Churchill, The Oaklands, Brakenhurst Lane, Newchurch, Burton-on-Trent, DE13 8QR

Lichfield Mrs Margaret Haywood, 64 Whitehouse Road, Dordon, Nr Tamworth, Staffs, B78 1QS. ☎ (01827) 893060

Sandwell Mr A Phillips, 39 Farm Road, Langley, Oldbury, Warley

South Staffordshire Mrs V Wilkinson, 20 Princefield Avenue, Penkridge, Stafford, ST19 5HG

Stoke/Newcastle Mr R H Clamp, 61 Downing Avenue, Basford, Newcastle, Staffs, ST5 0LB

Stone Mr A J Trimmings, 1 Beechwood Drive, Stone, Staffordshire, ST15 0EH

Stourbridge Mrs Joan Crowe, 29 Stennels Avenue, Halesowen, West Midlands, B62 8QJ. ☎ 0121-422 1698

Walsall Mr P Holder, 13 Wolverhampton Road, Wedges Mills, Cannock, Staffordshire, WS11 1ST. ☎ (01922) 410167

Wolverhampton Mrs Janet Heaton, 3 Greenacres, Tettenhall, Wolverhampton, West Midlands, WV6 8SR. ☎ (01902) 753623

SUFFOLK

AREA SECRETARY

Mr G Pratt, 3 Sidegate Avenue, Ipswich, Suffolk, IP4 4JJ. ☎ (01473) 724656

GROUP SECRETARIES

Alde Valley Mrs M K Hall, Deben Lodge, Wickham Market, Woodbridge, Suffolk, IP13 0RF. ☎ (01728) 746837

Bury St Edmunds Mrs J V Bowerman, 16 Sutton Close, Bury St Edmunds, Suffolk, IP32 7EP

Ipswich & District Mr K Chittleborough, 63 Bell Lane, Kesgrave, Ipswich, Suffolk, IP5 7JL. ☎ (01473) 623431

Newmarket & District Ms L C Macer, 48 Queensway, Soham, Ely, Cambridgeshire, CB7 5BX

Stowmarket Mr Tony Buck, 23 Alexander Drive, Needham Market, Ipswich, Suffolk IP6 8XQ. ☎ (01449) 721121

Sudbury Mr J E D'eye, 14 Croft Lea, Little Waldingfield, Sudbury, Suffolk, CO10 0SL

Waveney Mr R Whitmore, 15 Oaklands, Blackwater Covert, Southwold, Suffolk, IP18 6RD

SURREY

SURREY PLUS LONDON BOROUGHS OF RICHMOND, KINGSTON, MERTON, SUTTON AND CROYDON

AREA SECRETARY
Mr G Butler, 109 Selsdon Park Road, South Croydon, CR2 8JJ

GROUP SECRETARIES
Croydon Mrs J Wood, 37 Eskdale Gardens, Purley, Surrey, CR8 1ET
East Surrey Ms B S Witherington, 14 Treetops, Hillside Road, Whyteleafe, Surrey, CR3 0BY.
☎ (01883) 626793
Epsom Mrs J Thomson, 24 Manor House Court, West Street, Epsom, KT18 7RN. ☎ (01372) 727351
Farnham & District Mrs M Rice, Heathercroft, 6 Vicarage Gate, Onslow Village, Guildford, GU2 5QJ
Godalming & Haslemere Mrs R J Bryant, Kinfauns Cottage, Petworth Road, Witley, Godalming, GU8 5QW. ☎ (01483) 421612
Guildford Mr J G Quinton, 176 Guildford Park Avenue, Guildford, GU2 5NH
Kingston Mr M Lake, 87 Porchester Road, Kingston-upon-Thames, Surrey, KT1 3PW.
(☎ membership enquiries only 0181-977 0817)
Mole Valley Miss C Simpson, 14 Embleton Walk, Hampton, Middlesex, TW12 3YU
Reigate Mrs E A Booth, 1 Brokes Crescent, Reigate, Surrey, RH2 9PS
Richmond Mr E J Masters, 21 Alder Road, Mortlake, London, SW14 8ER
Staines Mrs J Currie, 24 Ecton Road, Addlestone, Surrey, KT15 1UE. ☎ (01932) 848276
Surrey Heath Mrs C Norris, 11 Warwick Close, Camberley, Surrey, GU15 1ES. ☎ (01276) 26821
Sutton/Wandle Valley Mr J C Parkin, 59 Beechwood Court, West Street Lane, Carshalton, Surrey, SM5 2QA. ☎ 0181-773 0048
Woking & District Mrs A Brown, Beckdale House, White Hart Lane, Wood Street Village, Guildford, Surrey, GU3 3EA

SUSSEX

EAST AND WEST SUSSEX

AREA SECRETARY
Mrs N Etherton, Hazards, Blackness Rd, Crowborough, East Sussex, TN6 2NA.
☎ (01892) 654850

GROUP SECRETARIES
Arun-Adur Miss E J Clunes, 14 Oxen Court, Oxen Avenue, Shoreham By Sea, Sussex, BN43 5AS.
☎ (01273) 452360

Beachy Head Mr A S Bancroft, 21 Terminus Avenue, Bexhill-on-Sea, East Sussex, TN39 3LS.
☎ (01424) 221133
Brighton & Hove Miss A Palmer, 12 Warmdene Road, Patcham, Brighton, East Sussex, BN1 8NL
Crawley & North Sussex Miss S M Darby, 14 Chevening Close, Broadfield, Crawley, RH11 9QU.
☎ (01293) 533242
Heathfield & District Mrs R Brown, Chant House, Hornshurst Road, Rotherfield, Nr Crowborough, Sussex, TN6 3ND. ☎ (01892) 852153
High Weald Walkers Mrs N Etherton, Hazards, Blackness Rd, Crowborough, East Sussex, TN6 2NA.
☎ (01892) 654850
Horsham & Billingshurst Mrs Janet M Barber, 7 Stirling Way, Horsham, West Sussex, RH13 5RX
Mid Sussex Mr M Monk, 5 Sharrow Close, Haywards Heath, West Sussex, RH16 3AY
Rother Mrs S M Ward, 33 Alma Villas, St Leonards-on-sea, East Sussex, TN37 6QU. ☎ (01424) 441018
South West Sussex Mrs P Brannigan, 19 Somerton Green, Felpham, Bognor Regis, W. Sussex, PO22 8EZ

TYNE & WEAR

SEE NORTHERN AREA

WARWICKSHIRE

WARWICKSHIRE PLUS BIRMINGHAM, COVENTRY AND SOLIHULL DISTRICTS OF FORMER WEST MIDLANDS

AREA SECRETARY
Mr M Bird, 16 Melford Hall Road, Solihull, West Midlands, B91 2ES. ☎ 0121-705 1118

GROUP SECRETARIES
Castle Bromwich Mrs J Mackey, 9 Tackford Close, Castle Bromwich, Birmingham, B36 9TA.
☎ 0121-749 4760
City of Birmingham Ms C D Dittrich, Po Box 4364, West Bromwich, West Midlands, B70 7AA
Coventry Mr A J Meek, 4 Square Lane, Corley Ash, Coventry, CV7 8AX. ☎ (01676) 541836
Mid Warwickshire Mrs S M Coates, 40 Windy Arbour, Kenilworth, CV8 2AS. ☎ (01926) 55123
Rugby Mrs F Debonnaire, 3 Montgomery Drive, Bilton, Rugby, Warks, CV22 7LA. ☎ (01788) 812213
Solihull Mrs S M Woolley, 43 Ferndown Road, Solihull, W Midlands, B91 2AU. ☎ 0121-705 5753
South Birmingham Mrs J Whitehead, 88 Marsham Road, Kings Heath, Birmingham, B14 5HE.
☎ 0121-474 3181
Southam Linda Dodd, 6 Mayfield Road, Southam, Leamington Spa, Warks, CV33 0JX.
☎ (01926) 812381

Stratford upon Avon Ms J A Smith, 3 Preston-on-Stour, Stratford-on-Avon, Warwickshire, CV37 8NG. ☎ (01789) 450360

Sutton Coldfield Mr G C Baker, 29 Shelley Drive, Sutton Coldfield, West Midlands, B74 4YD. ☎ 0121-323 2223

WEST MIDLANDS

SEE WARWICKSHIRE AREA AND STAFFORDSHIRE AREA

WEST RIDING

THE METROPOLITAN AREA OF WEST YORKSHIRE PLUS CRAVEN, HARROGATE, AND SELBY (WEST OF RIVER OUSE) DISTRICTS OF NORTH YORKSHIRE

AREA SECRETARY

Mr Keith Wadd, 25 Rossett Beck, Harrogate, North Yorkshire, HG2 9NT. ☎ (01423) 872268

GROUP SECRETARIES

Bradford Ms E E Donovan, 4 Draughton Street, Bradford, BD5 9QQ. ☎ (01274) 724214

Calderdale Mrs D F Hall, 11 School Close, Ripponden, Halifax, Yorks, HX6 4HP. ☎(01422) 823440

Castleford & Pontefract Vacant

Craven Mr M G Leigh, 8 Castle View, Barnoldswick, Lancs, BB8 5PN. ☎ (01282) 816795

Dewsbury Emley Footpaths Association, Mr E Shaw, 15 Rectory Lane, Emley, Nr Huddersfield, HD8 9RR. ☎ (01924) 848364

Harrogate Mrs M J Clack, 40 Woodlands Grove, Harrogate, North Yorkshire, HG2 7BG. ☎ (01423) 884481

Huddersfield Mr J M Lieberg, 11 Woodroyd Avenue, Honley, Huddersfield, West Yorks, HD7 2LG. ☎ (01484) 662866. Publications: 0113-267 4797

Keighley Mr J Maude, 50 Cliffe Lane South, Baildon, Bradford, West Yorkshire, BD17 5LB

Leeds Mrs M Webb, 21 Chandos Avenue, Roundhay, Leeds, LS8 1QU. ☎ 0113-293 1358

Lower Wharfedale Mr F L Straw, 2 Victoria Cres, Horsforth, Leeds, LS18 4PR. ☎ 0113-258 7861

Ripon Mr P Harrison, Mill Corner, 26 Moorside Avenue, Ripon, North Yorkshire, HG4 1TA

Wakefield Mr P E J Baldwin, 57 Sycamore Copse, Wakefield, West Yorkshire, WF2 8DQ. ☎ (01924) 362218

Wetherby Mrs Yvonne Sumner, 37 Hudson Way, Wighill Lane, Tadcaster, North Yorkshire, LS24 8JF. ☎ (01937) 834172

WEST YORKSHIRE

SEE WEST RIDING AREA

WILTSHIRE

AREA SECRETARY

Mr R L Cornish, `ashcott', Bowdens, Urchfont, Devizes, Wilts, SN10 4SQ

GROUP SECRETARIES

Chippenham Mr B Howlett, 66 Hardens Mead, Chippenham, Wilts, SN15 3AE

Mid Wiltshire Mrs M White, 367 Quemerford, Calne, Wilts, SN11 8LF. ☎ (01249) 816009

North East Wilts Mr J T Hartley, 100 Upham Road, Swindon, Wilts, SN3 1DW. ☎ (01793) 525912

South Wiltshire Mr Graham Carter, 33 Hilltop Way, Salisbury, Wilts, SP1 3QY. ☎ (01722) 328298

West Wiltshire Ms M Hollingworth, Foxglove Cottage, 5 The Bank, North Bradley, Trowbridge, Wilts, BA14 9RP. ☎ (01225) 753897

Scotland

Not all RA areas correspond to administrative areas since the creation of unitary authorities throughout Scotland in 1996. Descriptions of the areas below are therefore sometimes approximate.

CALEDONIAN (HIGHLAND AND ISLANDS)

THE UNITARY AUTHORITIES OF HIGHLAND; THE WESTERN ISLES; ORKNEY AND SHETLAND

AREA SECRETARY

Mr J Holms, 'Fernbank', Killin, Perthshire, FK21 8UW. ☎ (01567) 820511

GROUP SECRETARIES

Inverness Vacant

ARGYLL & BUTE

SEE STRATHCLYDE, DUMFRIES & GALLOWAY AREA

CENTRAL, FIFE AND TAYSIDE

THE UNITARY AUTHORITIES OF ANGUS; CITY OF DUNDEE; CLACK-MANANSHIRE; FLAKIRK; FIFE; PERTH & KINROSS; AND STIRLING

AREA SECRETARY

Mr A Costello, 9 Adam Crescent, Stenhousemuir, Larbert, Stirlingshire, FK5 4DG. ☎ (01324) 553393

GROUP SECRETARIES

Alyth & District Mrs A E May, Elmgrove, High Street, Alyth, Perthshire, PH11 8DW. ☎ (01828) 632263

Brechin & District Mr G Mitchell, 4 Gellatly Place, High Meadow, Brechin, DD9 6BS ☎ (01356) 624562.

Broughty Ferry Ms E Paterson, 9 Cardean Street, Dundee, DD4 6PS

Dundee & District Ms S G Knight, 1e St Peter Street, Dundee, DD1 4JJ. ☎ (01382) 641733

Glenrothes Ms E Yardley, 55 Skibo Avenue, Glenrothes, Fife, KY7 4PX. ☎ (01592) 772387

Kirkcaldy District Mrs M A Harvey, 2 Nicol Drive, Burntisland, Fife, KY3 9JB

Perth & District Mrs M K Mackay, 28 Langside Road, Perth, PH1 2LB. ☎ (01738) 629915

St Andrews Ms K Douglas, Thornton Farmhouse, Birkhill, Nr Cupar, KY15 4QN

Stirling District Dr E Smeaton, 4 Hill Street, St Ninians, Stirling, FK7 0DH. ☎ (01786) 473987

West Fife Mrs U Mansnerus-Watson, 48 Lilac Grove, Dunfermline, Fife, KY11 5AP. ☎ (01383) 720096

DUMFRIES & GALLOWAY

SEE STRATHCLYDE, DUMFRIES & GALLOWAY

GRAMPIAN

THE UNITARY AUTHORITIES OF ABERDEENSHIRE; CITY OF ABERDEEN; MORAY; NAIRN PART OF HIGHLAND

AREA SECRETARY

Mrs M J Catto, 9 Aboyne Gardens, Garthdee, Aberdeen, AB1 7BW. ☎ (01224) 583998 (fax)

GROUP SECRETARIES

Aberdeen Miss A M Mitchell, 32 Gordon Road, Mannofield, Aberdeen, AB15 7RL. ☎ (01224) 322580

Inverurie Ms M T Corley, 41 Elmbank Terrace, Aberdeen, AB2 3NN. ☎ (01224) 488197

Moray Mrs M Mackenzie, 102 Milnefield Avenue, New Elgin, Elgin, IV30 3EL. ☎ (01343) 544134

Stonehaven Mrs E A Simpson, 4 Craigpark, Nigg, Aberdeen, AB1 4BD. ☎ (01224) 878286

LOTHIAN & BORDERS

THE UNITARY AUTHORITIES OF CITY OF EDINBURGH; EAST LOTHIAN; MIDLOTHIAN; SCOTTISH BORDERS; WEST LOTHIAN

AREA SECRETARY

A Homan-Elsy, 55 Deanburn Road, Linlithgow, West Lothian, EH49 6EY. ☎ (01506) 842897

GROUP SECRETARIES

Balerno Mr J B Murray, 62 Thomson Road, Currie, Edinburgh, EH14 5HW. ☎ 0131-449 2046

Bathgate Mr R N Nicol, 7 Meadowpark Road, Brookfield, Bathgate, West Lothian, EH48 2SJ. ☎ (01506) 656515

Coldstream A Pritchard, Lees Lodge, Coldstream, Berwickshire, TD12 4LG. ☎ (01890) 2107

Dalkeith & District Mrs D Mckeane, 4 Carlowrie Place, Gorebridge, Midlothian, EH23 4XL. ☎ (01875) 820924

East Berwickshire Mrs M Reid, Millbank Lodge, Eyemouth, Berwickshire, TD14 5RE

Edinburgh Ms E A Tett, 3RD Floor, 38 Warrender Park Terr, Edinburgh, EH9 1EB

Jedburgh Vacant

Linlithgow Mr J B Davidson, 16 Friars Way, Linlithgow, EH49 6AX. ☎ (01506) 842504

Livingston Mrs V Mcgowan, 4 Larbert Avenue, Deans, Livingston, EH54 8QJ. ☎ (01506) 438706

Musselburgh Mr G C Edmond, 54 Northfield Gardens, Prestonpans, Scotland, EH32 9LG. ☎ (01875) 810729

North Berwick Mrs M Allan, 10 Amisfield Pk, Haddington, East Lothian, EH41 4QE. ☎ (01620) 824938

Tweeddale Mrs P E Armstrong, Velvet Hall Cottage, Innerleithen, Peeblesshire, EH44 6RD. ☎ (01896) 830342

PERTH & KINROSS

SEE CENTRAL, FIFE AND TAYSIDE AREA

SCOTTISH BORDERS

SEE LOTHIAN AND SCOTTISH BORDERS

STIRLING

SEE CENTRAL, FIFE AND TAYSIDE AREA

STRATHCLYDE, DUMFRIES & GALLOWAY

THE UNITARY AUTHORITIES OF ARGYLL & BUTE; CITY OF GLASGOW; DUMFRIES & GALLOWAY; EAST, NORTH & SOUTH AYRSHIRE; EAST & WEST DUNBARTONSHIRE; EAST RENFREW; MORVERN PART OF HIGHLAND AUTHORITY; INVERCLYDE; NORTH & SOUTH LANARKSHIRE; RENFREWSHIRE; BIGGAR PART OF SCOTTISH BORDERS AUTHORITY

AREA SECRETARY

Mrs E Lawie, Burnside Cottage, 64 Main Street, Glenboig, Lanarkshire, ML5 2RD. ☎ (01236) 872959

GROUP SECRETARIES

Bearsden & Milngavie Mrs J Hird, 54 Borland Road, Bearsden, Glasgow, G61 2ND

Biggar Mrs P M Mccrone, 1 Viewpark Road, Biggar, ML12 6BG

Clyde Valley Miss A Gray, 51 Burnblea Street, Hamilton, ML3 6RF

Cumbernauld & Kilsyth Mr A Brierley, 31 Lairds Hill Place, Kilsyth, Glasgow, G65 9EX

Cunninghame Mrs M D Windsor, Fernbank, 20 Dalry Road, Beith, Ayrshire, KA15 1AU

Dumfries & Galloway Mr T Key, The Bungalow, High Kelton Farm, Glencaple Road, Dumfries & Galloway, DG1 4UA. ☎ (01387) 770464

Eastwood Mr G Howat, 20 Inverewe Way, Newton Mearns, Glasgow, G77 6XH

Glasgow Mr J Riddell, 61 Balcarres Avenue, Glasgow, G12 0QE. ☎ 0141-334 5586

Kilmarnock & Loudoun Ms E A Garrod, 16 West Grove, Troon, Ayrshire, KA10 7BG

Monklands Mrs E J Evans, 3 Fifth Avenue, Airdrie, ML6 7EH. ☎ (01236) 763255

Paisley Miss E S Brownlie, 17 Clarence Street, Paisley, PA1 1PS

South Ayrshire Mr S Wyllie, 6 Corrie Place, Troon, Ayrshire, KA10 6TZ. ☎ (01292) 311924

Strathkelvin Mrs S Gray, 35 Woodside Avenue, Lenzie, Glasgow, G66 4NG

Wales

DYFED

THE UNITARY AUTHORITIES OF CARMARTHENSHIRE, CEREDIGION AND PEMBROKESHIRE

AREA SECRETARY

Mr G D Williams, Maesquarre, Bethlehem Road, Llandeilo, Dyfed, SA19 6YA. ☎ (01558) 822960

GROUP SECRETARIES

Aberystwyth Mrs S A Kinghorn, 16 Bryn Glas, Llanbadarn, Aberystwyth, Dyfed, SY23 3QR. ☎ (01970) 624965

Cardigan & District Ms S J Brown, Parc Manordeifi, Cilgerran, Cardigan, Dyfed, SA43 2PG. ☎ (01239) 682776

Carmarthenshire Mr E M Davies, Bryneusydd, Llangunnor, Carmarthen, Dyfed, SA31 2PH. ☎ (01267) 238524

Dinefwr Mr David Foot, Ty Isaf, Taliaris, Llandeilo, Dyfed, SA19 7DE. ☎ (01550) 777623

Lampeter Mrs E K Davies, Ardwyn, Llanybydder, Carmarthenshire SA40 9UB. ☎ (01570) 480041

Llanelli Mrs P Davies, 56 Coleshill Terrace, Llanelli, Dyfed, SA15 3DA. ☎ (01554) 770077

Pembrokeshire Mr P C A Kimberley, 4 Scotchwell View, Prendergast, Haverfordwest, Pembrokeshire, SA61 2RE. ☎ (01437) 768341

GLAMORGAN

THE UNITARY AUTHORITIES OF SWANSEA,; WEST GLAMORGAN; BRIDGEND; RHONDDA,CYNON TAFF; VALE OF GLAMORGAN; CARDIFF; AND CAERPHILLY

AREA SECRETARY

Mr Terry Squires, 7 Glan-yr-Afon, Pontyclun, Mid Glamorgan, CF72 9BJ. ☎ (01443) 223526

GROUP SECRETARIES

Bridgend & District Mr J R Sanders, 3 Bryn Rhedyn, Pencoed Bridgend, Mid Glam, CF35 6TL. ☎ (01656) 861835

Cardiff Mr Robin Hamilton, Acting Secretary, 10 Lon Ty'n y Cae, Cardiff, CF4 6DD. ☎ (01222) 624652

Cynon Valley Mr David James, Cwmtydu, 2 Plasdraw Rd, Aberdare, CF44 0NR. ☎ (01685) 874600

Merthyr Valley Mr Gerry Horsey, 1 Raglan Grove, Castle Park, Merthyr Tydfil, Mid Glamorgan, CF48 1JE

Penarth & District Ms M Cooper, 13 Gainsborough Court, Bridge St, Penarth, S. Glam, CF64 2LJ. ☎ (01222) 703585

Taff Ely Ms Noelle Clay, 31 Wyndham Street, Ton Pentre, Pentre, Mid Glamorgan, CF4 7BA. ☎ (01443) 437697

Vale of Glamorgan Mr David Cobourne, 9 The Verlands, Cowbridge, South Glamorgan, CF71 7BY. ☎ 01446 773301

West Glamorgan Miss P Gresty, 48 Phillip Street, Manselton, Swansea, SA5 9NL. ☎ (01792) 298202

GREATER GWENT

THE UNITARY AUTHORITIES OF MONMOUTHSHIRE; TORFAEN; NEWPORT; AND BLAENAU GWENT

AREA SECRETARY

Mr Allan Jones, Coed-y-cefn, 5 Craig Road, Hengoed Mid Glamorgan, CF82 7JJ. ☎ (01433) 813285

GROUP SECRETARIES

Gelligaer Miss A Price, 27 Tredomen Terrace, Ystarad Mynach, Mid Glamorgan, CF82 7BW. ☎ (01443) 862541

Lower Wye Mrs Jan Lavis, 25 Anwyll Close, Caerleon, Newport, Gwent, NP6 1TJ. ☎ (01633) 423484

North Gwent Mr A Nicholas, 31 Windsor Road, Brynmawr, Gwent, NP3 4HE. ☎ (01495) 311088

Pontypool Mrs S Woods, 17 Ludlow Close, Llanyravon, Cwmbran, Gwent, NP44 8JQ

South Gwent Mr R J Davies, Flat 29, Uplands Court, Rogerstone, Newport, Gwent, NP1 9FW. ☎ (01633) 895067

Walking Group 18-40 Miss L Mead, 9 Kerry Place, Wrexham, Clwyd, LL12 7DA. ☎ (01978) 263256

Wrexham Mr Paul Davies, 32 Peel Street, Wrexham, Clwyd, LL13 7TR. ☎ (01978) 362253

Ynys Mon Miss J Tyldesley, 32 High Street, Menai Bridge, Isle Of Anglesey, Gwynedd, LL59 5EF. ☎ (01248) 716939

NORTH WALES

THE UNITARY AUTHORITIES OF ISLE OF ANGLESEY; CONWY; DENBIGHSHIRE; FLINTSHIRE; GWYNEDD; AND WREXHAM

AREA SECRETARY
Mr J Robinson, 2 Graig Cottages, Pontfadog, Llangollen, Clwyd, LL20 7AU. ☎ (01691) 718771

GROUP SECRETARIES
Bangor-Bethesda Mr Eifion Williams, 44 Gorwel, Llanfairfechan, Gwynedd, LL33 0DU. ☎ (01248) 680042

Caernarfon Ms E Watkin, Ty N Lon, Bethel, Caernarfon, LL55 1UW. ☎ (01248) 671243

Clwydian Miss T K Wilsher, 3 Bellevue Court, Tenters Square, Wrexham, Clwyd, LL13 7LY. ☎ (01978) 353885

Conwy Valley Mrs S Owens, 3 Abbey Drive, Rhos-on-sea, Colwyn Bay, Clwyd, LL28 4PD. ☎ (01492) 546847

Deeside Mr Jim Irvine, 30 St Davids Drive, Connahsquay, Deeside, Clwyd, CH5 4SR. ☎ (01244) 818577

Dwyfor Mr S Caplan, 19 Stanley Road, Criccieth, Gywnedd, LL52 0EH. ☎ (01766) 522238

Merionnydd Miss P J Hadley, Harddwch Y Gader, Pencefn, Dolgellau, Gwynedd, LL40 2ER. ☎ (01341) 422367

South Clwyd Mr Goff Oldaker, 'Gwynfa', Llanarmen D.c., Llangollen, Clwyd, LL20 7LF. ☎ (01691) 600287

Vale of Clwyd Mrs A Devenport, Woodlands, Bishopswood Road, Prestatyn, LL19 9PL. ☎ (01745) 888814

POWYS

AREA SECRETARY
Mr P Jennings, Garnfawr, Hundred House, Llandrindod Wells, Powys, LD1 5RP. ☎ (01982) 570334

GROUP SECRETARIES
Brecon Mrs M Probert, Pyrgad, Duffryn Crawnon, Llangynidr, NP8 1NU. ☎ (01874) 730558

Dyfi Valley Mr David Bunyan, Brynhyfryd, Eglwysfach, Machynlleth, Powys, SY20 8SX. ☎ (01654) 781337

East Radnor Mr P Jennings, Garnfawr, Hundred House, Llandrindod Wells, Powys, LD1 5RP. ☎ (01982) 570334

Welshpool Mrs Gwen Evans, Moorwood, Leighton, Welshpool, Powys, SY21 8LW. ☎ (01938) 580352

AREA AND GROUP CONTACTS

Access to the Countryside

· ·

A brief guide to the law relating to access on foot to the British countryside

England and Wales— rights of way

Below are answers to the questions people most often ask about rights of way.

WHAT IS A RIGHT OF WAY?

A right of way in the countryside is either a footpath, a bridleway or a byway. On footpaths the public has a right of way on foot only. On bridleways it also has a right of way on horseback and on a pedal cycle. Byways are open to all classes of traffic, including motor vehicles. Legally, a public path is part of the Queen's highway and subject to the same protection in law as all other highways, including trunk roads.

WHAT ARE MY RIGHTS ON A PUBLIC RIGHT OF WAY?

The public's right is to pass and repass along the way. You can also take with you a "natural accompaniment", which includes a dog. However, you should ensure that dogs are under close control. On suitable paths, a "natural accompaniment" could also include a pram or a pushchair.

HOW DO I KNOW WHETHER A PATH IS A PUBLIC RIGHT OF WAY OR NOT?

The safest evidence is the definitive map of public rights of way. These maps are available for public inspection at county, district and outer London borough council offices. Some are also available for inspection in libraries and some are sold by the councils concerned. In addition, public rights of way information derived from them, as amended by subsequent orders, is shown by the Ordnance Survey on its 1:25,000 scale

(Explorer, Outdoor Leisure and Pathfinder) and 1:50,000 scale (Landranger) maps. But note that a path not shown on the definitive map may still be a public right of way, and application may be made to the surveying authorities (see below) for ways to be added to the definitive map.

HOW DOES A PATH BECOME PUBLIC?

Some paths are created formally, by agreement between the landowner and local authority, by legal order made by the authority or by the landowner simply dedicating the path for public use. But others become public through "presumed dedication". This applies where the public use the path as a right of way for 20 years and there is no evidence that the landowner intended that it should not be dedicated as a right of way.

DOES A PATH CEASE TO BE A RIGHT OF WAY IF IT IS NOT USED?

No. The legal principle is "Once a highway, always a highway". But a local authority can make an order to close a path: the public have a right to object (see question below).

WHO OWNS THE PATHS?

The surface of the path is for most purposes considered to belong to the highway authority, but the soil under the path remains the property of the owner of the surrounding land.

HOW WIDE SHOULD A PATH BE?

The theory is that the path should be whatever width was dedicated to the public. This width may be recorded in the statement accompanying the definitive map. But in many cases the proper width will be a matter of what has been past practice on that particular path.

ARE HORSES AND PEDAL CYCLES (INCLUDING MOUNTAIN BIKES) ALLOWED ON PUBLIC PATHS?

Horse-riders have a right to use bridleways, as the name implies, and the 1968 Countryside Act gave cyclists the same right, provided they give way to walkers and horse-riders. Neither group has the right to use footpaths, but if they do they are not committing a criminal offence unless a byelaw or traffic regulation order forbids their use on that path, although they may be a nuisance.

IS IT ILLEGAL TO DRIVE CARS OR MOTOR CYCLES ON PUBLIC PATHS?

Anyone who drives a vehicle on a footpath or bridleway without permission is committing an offence. This does not apply if the driver stays within 15 yards of the road and only goes on the path to park. The owner of the land, however, can still order vehicles off even within 15 yards from the road. Races or speed trials on paths are forbidden. Permission for other types of trials on paths may be sought from the local authority, if the landowner consents.

WHAT IS A ROAD USED AS A PUBLIC PATH?

RUPPS, as they are commonly known, are a type of way shown on the definitive map which is usually unsurfaced and may or may not carry vehicular rights. This classification is now in process of abolition and all RUPPS will eventually be reclassified as either footpaths, bridleways or byways open to all traffic.

WHICH COUNCILS DEAL WITH PATHS?

The councils to which duties have been given as highway and definitive map surveying authorities are the unitary authorities where they exist and county councils where there are still counties and districts. A full list of these authorities is given on page 40. The list is as of October 1996. More unitary authorities will be created in April 1997 and April 1998. Highway authorities have a general duty "to assert and protect the rights of the public to the use and enjoyment" of paths in their area and "to prevent as far as possible the stopping up or obstruction" of such paths. They should therefore deal with any deliberate obstruction such as a barbed wire fence or crops across a path. They are also legally responsible for maintaining the surface of the path (including bridges) and keeping it free of overgrowth. Shire district councils are entitled to take over the maintenance of public paths from the county councils if they wish and may by agreement take over other responsibilities from the county council. Parish councils (in England) and community councils (in Wales) also have the power to maintain paths (see the RA leaflet *Paths for People* — details below). Highway authorities have the power to require owners to cut back overhanging growth from the side of a path.

WHO IS SUPPOSED TO LOOK AFTER STILES AND GATES ON A PATH?

Maintaining these is primarily the owner's responsibility, but the highway authority (or the district council if it is maintaining the path) must contribute a quarter of the cost if asked and may contribute more if it wishes. If the landowner fails to keep his stiles and gates in proper repair the authority can, after 14 days' notice, do the job itself and send the bill to the owner.

ARE ALL THE PATHS SUPPOSED TO BE SIGNPOSTED?

Highway authorities have a duty to put up signposts at all junctions of footpaths, bridleways and byways with metalled roads. But there is no time limit within which this job must be completed. Also parish and community councils can relieve authorities of the obligation for particular paths. Highway authorities also have a duty to waymark paths so far as they consider it appropriate.

WHAT IS WAYMARKING?

Waymarking is a means of indicating the line or direction of a path at points where it may be difficult to follow. The Countryside Commission has recommended a standard system of painted arrows for waymarking - yellow for footpaths, blue for bridleways and red for byways.

IS IT ILLEGAL TO PLOUGH UP OR OTHERWISE DISTURB THE SURFACE OF A PATH SO AS TO MAKE IT INCONVENIENT TO USE?

No, if the path is a footpath or bridleway running across a field and the farmer could not conveniently avoid disturbing the surface; yes, if the path is a byway, or any other footpath or bridleway. However, in the former case, the farmer must make good the surface within 24 hours of the disturbance (two weeks if the disturbance is the first one for a particular crop). A path so restored must be reasonably convenient to use, must have a minimum width of one metre for a footpath and two metres for a bridleway, and its line must be clearly apparent on the ground.

WHAT HAPPENS IF A PATH SURFACE HAS BEEN DISTURBED BUT NOT RESTORED?

A highway authority may serve notice on the occupier and, if necessary, then restore the path itself and send the bill to the occupier. The authority may also prosecute the person responsible for the disturbance.

WHAT ABOUT CROPS GROWING ON OR OVER A PATH?

The farmer has a duty to prevent a crop (other than grass) from making the path difficult to find or follow. The minimum widths given previously (question before last) apply here also, but if the path is a field-edge path they are increased to 1.5 metres for a footpath, three metres for a bridleway. You have every right to walk through crops growing on or over a path, but stick as close as you can to its correct line. Report the problem to the highway authority: it has power to prosecute the farmer or cut the crop and send him the bill.

WHAT IS AN OBSTRUCTION ON A PATH?

Anything which interferes with your right to proceed along it, e.g. a barbed wire fence across the path or a heap of manure dumped on it. Dense undergrowth is not normally treated as an obstruction but is dealt with under path maintenance.

CAN I REMOVE AN OBSTRUCTION TO GET BY?

Yes, provided that (a) you are a bona fide traveller on the path and have not gone out for the specific purpose of moving the obstruction and (b) you remove only as much as is necessary to get through. If you can easily go round the obstruction without causing any damage, then you should do so. But report the obstruction to the highway authority and/or the RA: see details of our Reporting Path Problems leaflet below.

HOW CAN I HELP THE RA DEAL WITH PATH PROBLEMS?

To help the RA tackle path problems, you can:

(a) Send full details to the highway authority and to the RA. Use the Path Problem Report form at the end of this book.

(b) Ask the farmer or landowner concerned to clear the obstruction.

(c) Take part in RA footpath clearance working parties.

(d) If the problems persist, write to your local councillors about them.

(e) Send letters to local newspapers seeking support for any representations you may be making.

(f) If the authority fails to take action, consider complaining to the local ombudsman.

CAN A FARMER KEEP A BULL IN A FIELD CROSSED BY A PUBLIC PATH?

Bulls of a recognised dairy breed (Ayrshire, British Friesian, British Holstein, Dairy Shorthorn, Guernsey, Jersey and Kerry) are banned from fields crossed by public paths under all circumstances. All other bulls are banned unless accompanied by cows or heifers. If a bull or any other animal acts in a way which endangers the public, an offence may be committed under health and safety legislation.

CAN A LANDOWNER CLOSE OR DIVERT A PATH?

No. Closure and diversion (i.e. change of a path's route) can only be carried out by local authorities or central government. Under the commonest procedure for closure, a local authority is empowered to make an order to close a path if it considers it is no longer needed for public use. A notice that the council has made an order must be published in a local paper and also placed at both ends of the path. It must allow at least 28 days for objections. These must be heard at a public inquiry taken by an inspector from the Department of the Environment (or Welsh Office), or by private hearing if the

Department so decides, or they may be considered in writing if the objectors agree.

Path diversions may not take place if the new path will be substantially less convenient to the public than the existing one, and account must also be taken of the effect the diversion will have on public enjoyment of the way as a whole. Paths may also be closed or diverted under The Town and Country Planning Act 1990 "in order to enable development to be carried out in accordance with planning permission". The procedure for these orders, and for diversion orders under the Highways Act, is the same as for closure orders. There are also provisions for highway authorities to apply to magistrates courts for closure or diversion of paths, and for closure and diversion orders to be made in other circumstances, e.g. construction of new roads, railways and reservoirs, both on a permanent and temporary basis.

WHAT IS A MISLEADING NOTICE?

A misleading notice is one calculated to deter you from using a public right of way - for example, a notice saying PRIVATE at the point where a public footpath enters a park. Such notices should be reported immediately to the highway authority. They are illegal on paths shown on the definitive map.

WHAT IS A PERMISSIVE PATH?

A path which is not a right of way but which is made available to the public on a concessionary basis. This may be informally, or via a formal agreement with the local authority. The less formal the arrangement, the greater the chance that permission will be withdrawn without warning.

ACCESS TO THE COUNTRYSIDE

England and Wales: Access

The text below is an edited extract from _Out in the Country_, an excellent booklet available from the Countryside Commission (details below). The extracts are published with the commission's kind permission.

There is no general right of access to the countryside, but walkers do have freedom to wander in many areas.

First, there are places intended for _public use_. Town parks and recreation grounds are obvious examples, but there are equivalent areas in the countryside, such as picnic sites and country parks. These are maintained primarily for the enjoyment of visitors.

Second, there is access to some areas defined as _"open country"_. This is any area consisting wholly or mainly of mountain, moor, heath, down, cliff, sea foreshore, beach, or sand dunes. The term also includes woodland, as well as rivers and canals and their banks if in the countryside. Although this is usually private land, local authorities are able to make access agreements or orders with the owner or occupier to give the public a legal right of access to the land. Access will be subject to certain restrictions. You may not be able to camp, for example, and you may have to keep a dog on a lead. Access may also be suspended temporarily, for example to reduce the risk of fire during very dry weather, or to prevent the spread of a livestock disease, or to allow shooting to take place.

However, relatively few _access agreements_ have been made; many are in the Peak District National Park. Where an access agreement has been made you are likely to see signs permitting entry at places where roads and paths cross the boundary. They are sometimes marked on Ordnance Survey maps. In these areas, so long as you remain in the open countryside and do not enter enclosed land where crops are growing, or walk on to other land that is obviously private, legally you are not a trespasser.

Access to some pockets of countryside is now being provided under the Countryside Stewardship and similar schemes.

In other places there is no formal agreement with the local authority but you can still enter the land at the invitation of the landowner so long as you observe the conditions laid down.

For example, the National Trust owns common land and other open country, especially on the coast and in the Lake District, and it is Trust policy to allow the public onto their open land. Most _Forestry Commission_ woodlands and plantations are also open to the public, often with car parking and other facilities provided. Some private woodlands are also open to the public, including most of those owned by the Woodland Trust. (The Forestry Trust for Conservation and Education publishes a useful guide to private woodland—see below)

There is also limited access to some _nature reserves_ - e.g. some reserves owned by English Nature and the Countryside Council for Wales. English Nature reserves are now being shown on Ordnance Survey maps.

Elsewhere, there are areas where, although the landowner has never given formal permission for the public to enter his land, people have nevertheless been doing so for a long time. This de facto access, established by tradition, is extensive but is unprotected by law.

There are 1.37 million acres of _common land_ in England and Wales, most of which is in private ownership. There is a legal right of access for the public to only about one-fifth of it.

It is only "common" in the sense that certain people, other than the owner, have

ACCESS TO THE COUNTRYSIDE

rights over the land - e.g. to graze sheep or cattle. There is, however, de facto access to much common land.

All commons are registered. You can see the register of commons in a particular area, and a map showing them, at the county or London borough council office.

In London and some other areas around our older towns and cities the common land now belongs to the local authority and has been dedicated, or set aside, for public enjoyment. Epping Forest is an example. Legally, such common land has become a public open space, with the special provision that it must not be enclosed. There is also legal access to common land in the Lake District fells, because this country was formerly part of an Urban District; and to common land in Dartmoor where special legislation applies.

Some *moorland* water-gathering grounds are open to people on foot by virtue of special nineteenth-century legislation. Land in the Elan Valley, central Wales and land around Thirlmere and Haweswater in the Lake District are examples.

Village greens were originally reserved for the recreation of the inhabitants of the parish, but most are open to the public as well.

Beaches are owned, like any other areas of land. The public usually has access to them, although there is no right to cross private land in order to reach a beach. Many beaches are owned by local authorities and dedicated for public use, while still more have been used by the public for many years and are presumed to have been dedicated. Much coastline is also owned by the National Trust and is open to the public.

The *foreshore* is slightly different. This is defined as the region lying between the high and low tide line, limited on the landward side to the medium line between neap and spring high tides. It is marked on Ordnance Survey maps. This strip usually belongs to the Crown. There is no public right of access on foot to it, but when it is covered by water there is a public right of navigation over it. As any barrier designed to exclude people at low tide would interfere with boaters' rights at high tide, in practice there is usually freedom of access to the foreshore.

Access to Scotland's countryside

There is a long-standing tradition of freedom of access to land in Scotland, although of late that tradition, which is not protected in law, has been challenged in many areas. An important part of the same tradition is that walkers show respect for the land and in particular take care not to disrupt deer stalking and grouse shooting (the same respect should also be shown in England and Wales, of course).

As in England and Wales, there is often freedom of access to nature reserves and to land owned by the Forestry Commission and the National Trust for Scotland - although all this access is technically a concession offered by the owner and is not enjoyed by right.

There are hardly any access agreements in Scotland and there is no common land. Rights of way exist in Scotland as well as England and Wales, although the acts of Parliament dealing with rights of way in Scotland are separate from those applying in England and Wales. The law in Scotland is set out clearly in the Scottish Rights of Way Society's booklet "Rights of Way, A Guide to the Law in Scotland" (see the Address Directory elsewhere in the Yearbook).

Most rights of way in Scotland came into existence under common law. According to the Society, "the essential requirements for the creation of a right of way under the common law are these:

(1) The track must run from one public place to another public place;

(2) The track must follow a more or less defined route;

(3) The track must have been used openly and peaceably by members of the public without the permission, express or implied, of the landowners;

(4) It must have been so used without substantial and effective interruption for a period of 20 years or more."

The key differences between rights of way law in Scotland and in England and Wales include the following:

(1) There are no definitive maps of rights of way in Scotland. But local authorities may maintain registers of paths which they believe to be public rights of way.

(2) The "once a highway, always a highway" maxim which applies in England and Wales does not apply to rights of way in Scotland. A right of way in Scotland may be lost if the landowner can show that it has not been used by the public for a continuous period of twenty years.

(3) In England and Wales, the duty to protect rights of way falls on the highway authorities. In Scotland, planning authorities have this duty which is "to keep open and free from obstruction or encroachment any public right of way which is wholly or partly within their area. The planning authorities in Scotland are the unitary authorites (see list beginning on page 40).

Trespass (England, Wales and Scotland)

Trespass is not normally a criminal offence, so a notice saying "Trespassers Will Be Prosecuted" was, prior to the Criminal Justice and Public Order Act 1994 (see below), virtually meaningless. That apart, legal action normally arises only if damage to property occurs. However, in England and Wales it is theoretically possible to be sued for simple trespass, although a landowner, in addition to asking for legal costs, could only recover nominal damages in such a case. In Scotland, you cannot be sued for damages merely because you are trespassing.

If you trespass and are requested to leave, you have no right to stay. The landowner may take steps to eject trespassers who refuse to leave, but they must use no greater force than is reasonable in the circumstances. There is no clear definition of what is "reasonable" in this context. Where, as in Scotland, there has been a long tradition of free access to the countryside, it could be argued that the use of any physical force to remove a trespasser is not reasonable. Trespass with an intention to reside may be a criminal offence under some circumstances, as may trespass on military land.

Trespass is now also a criminal offence under the Criminal Justice and Public Order Act 1994. This provides for the arrest, fining or imprisonment of anyone who commits aggravated trespass, i.e. trespass with "intention" to disrupt a lawful activity, such as grouse shooting. The effect of the Act is yet to be tested but the RA fears that it could criminalise walkers who may cause inadvertent disruption while not on a right of way.

REPORTING PATH PROBLEMS

To report a problem on a public right of way send us as much information as possible, including the date when you found the problem and a grid reference. The details will then be passed to the appropriate local footpath secretary for investigation. You can use the path problem report form at the end of this book or in the Reporting Path Problems leaflet (see below).

The more path users show their concern for the state of the rights of way network, by complaining about trouble spots, the better. You should consider reporting bad cases to the local highway authority as well as to the RA. A list of highway authorities is given on page 40.

RA PUBLICATIONS ON RIGHTS OF WAY (ENGLAND AND WALES)

The second edition of the RA's book, *Rights of Way: a guide to law and practice*, which is recognised as the definitive work on the subject, was published in 1992, and is available for £12.00 plus £2.00 p&p from RA Sales.

Footpath Worker, a bulletin containing reports of decision letters on public path orders, court cases and other matters of interest to those concerned with public paths is available from the RA, price £6.50 for a volume of 4 issues.

FREE RA LEAFLETS

Available from RA central office. Please enclose an s.a.e.

Defending Public Paths – a leaflet on the RA's work protecting paths and the campaign to open all 140,000 miles of rights of way before the year 2000.

Paths for People – a leaflet explaining the powers and opportunities for parish and community councils to care for and improve their local footpaths. A version in Welsh is also available from RA Welsh office.

Planning for Public Paths – a leaflet for developers and planning authorities aimed at preventing the obstruction of rights of way by new buildings.

Ploughed and Cropped Paths – a leaflet explaining the law on ploughing and cropping of public paths.

Reporting Path Problems – a leaflet incorporating a path problem report form.

Please note that these publications are relevant to England and Wales only.

OTHER USEFUL PUBLICATIONS

There are some useful Countryside Commission publications on rights of way and access to the countryside in England:

Out in the Country - where you can go and what you can do;

A Guide to Definitive Map Procedures;

Waymarking Public Paths;

A Guide to Procedures for Public Path Orders;

Managing Public Access.

These booklets are available from Countryside Commission Postal Sales, PO Box 124, Walgrave, Northampton NN6 9TL. (Tel 01604) 781848. No charge is made for single orders but for orders of more than ten copies please inquire.

The Countryside Council for Wales has produced Welsh versions of *Out in the Country* and *Managing Public Access*. Available free of charge from CCW, Plas Penrhos, Ffordd Penrhos, Bangor, Gwynedd LL57 2LQ. Tel. (01284) 370444

Woodlands to Visit in England & Wales £4.99 including post and packing from the Forestry Trust for Conservation and Education, The Old Estate Office, Englefield Road, Theale, Reading, Berks RG7 5DZ.

Highway Authorities

The Ramblers' Association is constantly working towards keeping our many miles of footpaths open and free from obstruction. You can help by reporting any problems you encounter. You can send your report either to the Ramblers' Association in the area concerned (in which case the local footpath officer will take the matter up with the local authority) or direct to the local authority. **If you choose the latter, please send a copy to the local RA local contact as well.** (See list starting on page 16).

The following listing is of the authorities in England, Wales and Scotland as at October 1996. Changes in local authority structure will continue to take place throughout the life of this book. Each county or unitary authority has its own department for dealing with rights of way. The inner London boroughs, rightful members of this listing, have not been included for reasons of space.

In England and Wales your report should be addressed to the Public Rights of Way Officer of the appropriate authority, in Scotland to the Director of Planning. If the problem is within a National Park, the report should be made to the National Park Authority. (See list in the Useful Addresses section of this Yearbook).

If you find it helpful, use the Path Problem Report form at the back of this book to describe the nature of the obstruction. Make sure you report **what** the problem is, **where** it is and **when** it was you noticed it. Further forms are available from RA offices.

England

Barnsley Town Hall, Barnsley S70 2TA. ☎ (01226) 770770.

Bath & North East Somerset The Guildhall, Bath BA1 5AW. ☎ (01225) 477000.

Bedfordshire County Hall, Bedford MK42 9AP. ☎ (01234) 363222

Berkshire Shire Hall, Shinfield Park, Reading RG2 9XD. ☎ (01734) 875444.

Birmingham The Council House, Victoria Square, Birmingham B1 1BB. ☎ 0121-235 9944.

Bolton Town Hall, Bolton BL1 1RU. ☎ (01204) 522311.

Bradford City Hall, Bradford BD1 1HY. ☎ (01274) 752111.

Bristol The Council House, College Green, Bristol BS1 5TR. ☎ 0117-922 3959.

Buckinghamshire County Hall, Aylesbury HP20 1UA. ☎ (01296) 395000.

Bury Town Hall, Knowsley Street, Bury BL9 0SW. ☎ 0161-705 5000.

Calderdale Northgate House, Northgate, Halifax HX1 1UN. ☎ (01422) 357257.

Cambridgeshire Shire Hall, Castle Hill, Cambridge. ☎ (01223) 317111.

Cheshire County Hall, Chester CH1 1SF. ☎ (01244) 602424.

Cornwall County Hall, Truro TR1 3AY. (01872) 322000.

Coventry Council House, Coventry CV1 5RR. (01203) 833333.

Cumbria The Courts, Carlisle CA3 8LZ. ☎ (01228) 23456.

Derbyshire County Offices, Matlock DE4 3AG. ☎ (01629) 580000.

Devon County Hall, Topsham Road, Exeter EX2 4QD. ☎ (01392) 382000.

Doncaster 1 Priory Place, Doncaster DN1 1BN. ☎ (01302) 734000.

Dorset County Hall, Colliton Park, Dorchester DT1 1XJ. ☎ (01305) 251000.

Dudley The Council House, Dudley DY1 1HF. ☎ (01384) 456000.

Durham County Hall, Durham DH1 5UL. ☎ 0191-386 4411.

Essex County Hall, Chelmsford CM1 1LX. ☎ (01245) 492211.

Gateshead Civic Centre, Gateshead NE8 1HH. ☎ 0191-477 1011.

Gloucestershire Shire Hall, Gloucester GL1 2TG. ☎ (01452) 425000.

Gloucestershire (South) The Council Offices, Castle Street, Thornbury, Bristol BS12 1HF. ☎ (01454) 416262.

Hampshire The Castle, Winchester SO23 8UJ. ☎ (01962) 841841.

Hatlepool Civic Centre, Hartlepool TS24 8AY. ☎ ☎ (01429) 266522.

Hereford & Worcester County Hall, Spetchley Road, Worcester WR5 2NP. ☎ (01905) 763763.

Hertfordshire County Hall, Hertford SG13 8DE. ☎ (01992) 555644.

Isle of Wight County Hall, High Street, Newport PO31 1UD. ☎ (01983) 821000.

Kent Director of Highways and Transportation, Springfield, Maidstone ME14 2LQ. ☎ (01622) 671411.

Kingston upon Hull Guildhall, Alfred Gelder Street, Hull HU1 2AA. ☎ (01482) 223111.

Kirklees Oldgate House, 2 Oldgate, Huddersfield HD1 6QQ. ☎ (01484) 422133.

Knowsley Municipal Buildings, Archway Road, Huyton, Knowsley, Merseyside L36 9UX. ☎ 0151-443 2242.

Lancashire County Hall, Preston PR1 8XJ. ☎ (01772) 254868.

Leeds 19 Wellington Street, Leeds LS1 4RR. ☎ 0113-234 8080.

Leicestershire County Hall, Glenfield, Leicester LE3 8RA. ☎ 0116-232 3232.

Lincolnshire Director of Highways and Planning, Fourth Floor, City Hall, Beaumont Fee, Lincoln LN1 1DN. ☎ (01522) 553055.

Lincolnshire (North) 18 Bigby Street, BriggDN20 8ED. ☎ (01652) 655972.

Lincolnshire (North East) Municipal Offices, Town Hall Square, Grimsby DN31 1HU.

Liverpool Municipal Buildings, Dale Street, Liverpool L69 2DH. ☎ 0151-236 2047.

LONDON BOROUGHS (outer boroughs only)

Barking & Dagenham Civic Centre, Dagenham RM10 7BN. ☎ 0181-592 4500.

Barnet The Town Hall, The Burroughs, NW4 4BG. ☎ 0181-359 2000.

Bexley Civic Offices, Broadway, Bexleyheath DA6 7LB. ☎ 0181-303 7777.

Brent Town Hall, Forty Lane, Wembley HA9 9EZ. ☎ 0181-937 1007.

Bromley Civic Centre, Stockwell Close, Bromley BR1 3UH. ☎ 0181-464 3333.

Croydon Taberner House, Park Lane, Croydon CR9 3JS. ☎ 0181-686 4433.

Ealing Town Hall, New Broadway, Ealing W5 2BY. ☎ 0181-579 2424.

Enfield Civic Centre, Silver Street, Enfield EN1 3XA. ☎ 0181-366 6565.

Haringey Civic Centre, PO Box 264, High Road N22 4LE. ☎ 0181-975 9700.

Harrow Civic Centre, Harrow, Middx HA1 2UW. ☎ 0181-863 5611.

Havering Mercury House, Mercury Gardens, Romford RM1 3DS. ☎ (01708) 772222.

Hillingdon Civic Centre, Uxbridge UB8 1UW. ☎ (01895) 250111.

Hounslow Civic Centre, Lampton road, Hounslow TW3 4DN. ☎ 0181-570 7728.

Kingston upon Thames Guildhall, Kingston upon Thames KT1 1EU. ☎ 0181-546 2121.

Merton Civic Centre, London Road, Morden SM4 5DX. ☎ 0181-543 2222.

Newham Town Hall, East Ham E6 2RP. ☎ 0181-472 1430.

Redbridge Town Hall, High Road, Ilford IG1 1DD. ☎ 0181-478 3020.

Richmond upon Thames Civic Centre, 44 York Street, Twickenham TW1 3BZ. ☎ 0181-891 1411.

Sutton Civic Offices, St Nicholas Way, Sutton SM1 1EA. 0181-770 5000.

Waltham Forest Town Hall, Forest Road, Walthamstow E17 4JF. ☎ 0181-527 5544.

Manchester Town Hall, Manchester M60 2LA. ☎ 0161-234 5000.

Middlesbrough PO Box 99a, Municipal Buildings, Middlesbrough TS1 2QQ. ☎ (01642) 245432.

Newcastle upon Tyne Civic Centre, Newcastle-upon-Tyne NE99 2BN. 0191-232 8520.

Norfolk County Hall, Martineau Lane, Norwich NR1 2DH. ☎ (01603) 222222.

Northamptonshire County Hall, Northampton NN1 1DN. ☎ (01604) 236236.

Northumberland County Hall, Morpeth NE61 2EF. ☎ (01670) 533000.

Nottinghamshire County Hall, West Bridgford, Nottingham NG2 7QP. ☎ 0115-982 3823.

Oldham PO Box 160, Civic Centre, West Street, Oldham OL1 1UG. ☎ 0161-911 3000.

Oxfordshire County Hall, Oxford OX1 1ND. ☎ (01865) 792422.

Redcar & Cleveland Langbaurgh Town Hall, Fabian Road, PO Box 8, South Bank TS6 9AR. ☎ (01642) 456564.

Rochdale PO Box 15, Town Hall, Rochdale OL16 1AB. ☎ (01706) 47474.

Rotherham Civic Building, Walker Place, Rotherham S65 1UF. ☎ (01709) 382121.

Salford Salford Civic Centre, Chorley Road, Swinton M27 5DA. ☎ 0161-794 4711.

Sandwell The Sandwell Council House, Oldbury, Warley B69 3DE. ☎ 0121-569 2200.

Sefton Town Hall, Southport, Merseyside PR8 1DA. (01704) 533133.

Sheffield Town Hall, Sheffield S1 2HH. ☎ 0114-273 5003.

Shropshire The Shire Hall, Abbey Foregate, Shrewsbury SY2 6ND. ☎ (01743) 251000.

Solihull PO Box 18, Council House, Solihull B91 3QS. ☎ 0121-704 6000.

Somerset County Hall, Taunton TA1 4DY. ☎ (01823) 255258.

Somerset (North) Town Hall, Weston-super-Mare BS23 1UJ. ☎ (01934) 631701.

St Helens Town Hall, St Helens WA10 1HP. ☎ (01744) 456000.

Stockport Town Hall, Stockport SK1 3XE. ☎ 0161-480 4949.

Stockton-on-Tees PO Box 11, Municipal Buildings, Church Road, Stockton-on-Tees TS18 1LD. ☎ (01642) 670067.

Suffolk St Helens Court, County Hall, Ipswich IP4 2JS. ☎ (01473) 230000.

Sunderland Civic Centre, Sunderland SR2 7DN. ☎ 0191-553 1000.

Surrey County Hall, Penrhyn Road, Kingston upon Thames KT1 2DN. ☎ 0181-541 8800.

Sussex (East) Pelham House, St Andrew's Lane, Lewes BN7 1UN. ☎ (01273) 481000.

Sussex (West) County Hall, Chichester PO19 1RQ. ☎ (01243) 777100.

Tameside Council Offices, Wellington Road, Ashton-under-Lyne, Tameside OL6 6DL. ☎ 0161-342 8355.

Trafford Trafford Town Hall, Stretford M32 0YT. ☎ 0161-912 1212.

Tyneside (North) 14 Northumberland Square, North Shields NE30 1PZ. ☎ 0191-257 5544.

Tyneside (South) Town Hall & Civic Offices, South Shields NE33 2RL. ☎ 0191-427 1717.

Wakefield Town Hall, Wakefield WF1 2HQ. ☎ (01924) 306090.

Walsall Civic Centre, Walsall WS1 1TP. ☎ (01922) 650000.

Warwickshire Shire Hall, Warwick CV34 4RR. ☎ (01926) 410410.

Wigan New Town Hall, Library Street, Wigan WN1 1YN. ☎ (01942) 244991.

Wiltshire County Hall, Trowbridge BA14 8JG. ☎ (01225) 713000.

Wirral Town Hall, Brighton Street, Wallasey L44 8ED. ☎ 0151-638 7070.

Wolverhampton Civic Centre, St Peter's Square, Wolverhampton WV1 1RG. ☎ (01902) 27811.

York The Guildhall, York YO1 1QN. ☎ (01904) 551000.

Yorkshire (East Riding of) 74 Lairgate, Beverley HU17 8EU. ☎ (01482) 887700.

Yorkshire (North) County Hall, Northallerton DL7 8AD. ☎ (01609) 780780.

Scotland

Aberdeen Town House, Broad Street, Aberdeen AB9 1AQ. ☎ (01224) 522000.

Aberdeenshire Woodhill House, Westburn Road, Aberdeen AB16 5GB. ☎ (01224) 682222.

Angus County Buildings, Market Street, Forfar DD8 1BX. ☎ (01307) 461460.

Argyll & Bute Kilmory Castle, Lochgilphead, Argyll PA31 8RT. ☎ (01546) 602127.

Ayrshire (East) Council Offices, London Road Centre, London Road, Kilmarnock KA3 7DG. ☎ (01563) 576000.

Ayrshire (North) Cunninghame House, Firar's Croft, Irvine KA12 8EE. ☎ (01294) 324100.

Ayrshire (South) Council Offices, Wellington Square, Ayr KA7 1DR. ☎ (01292) 612000.

Clackmannanshire Council Offices, Greenfield, Alloa FK10 2AD. ☎ (01259) 450000.

Dumfries & Galloway Council Offices, English Street, Dumfries DG1 2DD. ☎ (01387) 261234.

Dunbartonshire (East) Council Offices, Tom Johnston House, Civic Way, Kirkintilloch G66 4TJ. ☎ 0141-776 9000.

Dunbartonshire (West) Council Offices, Garshake Road, Dunbarton G82 3PU. ☎ (01389) 737000.

Dundee Council Offices, 21 City Square, Dundee DD1 3BY. ☎ (01382) 434000.

Edinburgh City of Edinborough Council, George IV Bridge, Edinburgh EH1 1UQ. ☎ 0131-200 2000.

Falkirk Municipal Buildings, Falkirk FK1 5RS. ☎ (01324) 506070.

Fife Fife House, North Street, Glenrothes, Fife KY7 5LT. ☎ (01592) 414141.

Glasgow City Chambers, George Square, Glasgow G2 1DU. ☎ 0141-287 2000.

Highland Highland Council, Glenurquhart Road, Inverness IV3 5NX. ☎ (01463) 702000.

Inverclyde Municipal Buildings, Clyde Square, Greenock PA15 1LX. ☎ (01475) 724400.

Lanarkshire (North) Civic Centre, Motherwell ML1 1TW. (01698) 266166.

Lanarkshire (South) Council Offices, Almada Street, Hamilton ML3 0AA. ☎ (01698) 454444.

Lothian (East) Council Buildings, Haddington, East Lothian EH41 3HA. ☎ (01620) 827827.

Lothian (West) West Lothian House, Almondvale North, Livingstone EH54 6QG. ☎ (01506) 777000.

Midlothian Midlothian House, 40 Buccleuch Street, Dalkeith EH22 1DJ. ☎ 0131-663 2881.

Moray Council Offices, High Street, Elgin IV30 1BX. ☎ (01343) 543451.

Orkney Islands Council Offices, School Place, Kirkwall, Orkney KW15 1NY. ☎ (01856) 873535.

Perth & Kinross Council Offices, 2 High Street, Perth PH1 5PH. ☎ (01738) 475000.

Renfrewshire Municipal Buildings, Cotton Street, Paisley PA1 1BU. ☎ 0141-842 5000.

Renfrewshire (East) Council Offices, Eastwood Park, Rouken Glen Road, Giffnock G46 6UG. ☎ 0141-621 3000.

Shetland Islands Town Hall, Lerwick ZE1 0HB. ☎ (01595) 693535.

Scottish Borders Council Headquarters, Newtown St Boswells, Melrose TD6 0SA. ☎ (01835) 824000.

Stirling Council Offices, Viewforth, Stirling FK8 2ET. ☎ (01786) 443322.

Western Isles Council Offices, Sandwick Road, Stornoway, Isle of Lewis PA87 2BW. ☎ (01851) 703773.

Wales

Anglesey Council Offices, Llangefni, Anglesey LL77 7TW. ☎ (01248) 750057.

Blaenau Gwent Municipal Offices, Civic Centre, Ebbw Vale NP3 6XB. ☎ (01495) 350555.

Bridgend PO Box 4, Civic Offices, Angel Street, Bridgend CF31 1LX. ☎ (01656) 643643.

Caerphilly Civic Centre, Pontllanfraith, Blackwood NP2 2YW. ☎ (01495) 226622.

Cardiff County Hall, Atlantic Wharf, Cardiff CF1 5UW. ☎ (01222) 872020.

Carmarthenshire County Hall, Carmarthen SA31 1JP. ☎ (01267) 233333.

Ceredigion Penmorfa, Aberaeron SA46 0PA. ☎ (01545) 570881.

Conwy Civic Centre, Abergele Road, Colwyn Bay LL29 8AR. ☎ (01492) 515271.

Denbighshire Council Offices, Ruthin LL15 1YN. ☎ (01824) 702201.

Flintshire Shire Hall, Mold CH7 6NB. ☎ (01352) 704476.

Gwynedd Caernarfon LL55 1SH. ☎ (01286) 672255.

Merthyr Tydfil Civic Centre, Castle Street, Merthyr Tydfil CF47 8AN. ☎ (01685) 723201.

Monmouthshire County Hall, Cwmbran NP44 2XH. ☎ (01633) 832114.

Neath Port Talbot Civic Centre, Port Talbot SA13 1PJ. ☎ (01639) 875200.

Newport Civic Centre, Newport NP9 4UR. ☎ (01633) 244491.

Pembrokeshire Haverfordia House, Winch Lane, Haverfordwest SA61 2DN. ☎ (01437) 763313.

Powys County Hall, Llandrindod Wells LD1 5LG. ☎ (01597) 826000.

Rhondda, Cynon, Taff Borough Council, The Pavillions, Clydach Vale, Rhondda. ☎ (01222) 780456

Swansea The Guildhall, Swansea SA1 3SN. ☎ (01792) 471111.

Torfaen Civic Centre, Pontypool NP4 6YB. ☎ (01495) 762200.

Vale of Glamorgan Civic Offices, Holton Road, Barry CF63 4RU. ☎ (01446) 700111.

Wrexham Guildhall, Wrexham LL11 1AY. ☎ (01978) 292108.

Maps

MAPS FOR WALKERS

The Ordnance Survey are the main (but not only) producers of maps in Britain and some series are particularly useful for walkers because of their large scale and the range of features shown. Those described below all show public rights of way.

Landranger series: 1:50,000 or 2cm to 1km or 1¼" to the mile. There are 204 maps covering the whole of England, Wales and Scotland. They show many landmarks and buildings, telephones, churches and pubs and topographical information such as grid squares, contour lines and heights of hills.

Outdoor Leisure series: 1:25,000 or 4cm to 1km or 2½" to the mile. They cover popular tourist and walking areas. They show field boundaries, stone walls and fences and more buildings and points of interest.

Pathfinder series: also at the 1:25,000 scale but covering the whole country. The maps cover smaller areas than the Outdoor Leisure series and show field boundaries. However, see below.

NEWS FROM ORDNANCE SURVEY

The OS will be phasing out the Pathfinder series and extending the Explorer maps to cover the whole country at the 1:25,000 scale (except for those areas covered by the Outdoor Leisure series). There are currently 15 maps in the Explorer series and 37 in the Outdoor Leisure. There will eventually be 350 maps at the 1:25,000 scale. The Explorer maps cover a larger area than the Pathfinders and are deemed a better buy by virtue of their more colourful design and inclusion of tourist information.

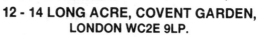

THE RA AND ORDNANCE SURVEY

The Ramblers' Association works very closely with Ordnance Survey to ensure that walkers' needs are taken care of in the maps produced. Last year we announced that the OS had published one map (Landranger sheet 124) showing whether or not the public has access to a range of paths known as "white roads". Previously, it had not been possible to tell from the maps which of these were private and which public. The move was so popular that the OS have now decided to include this information on all Landranger maps.

A Ramblers' Association publication

NAVIGATION AND LEADERSHIP
– a manual for walkers

Available from Ramblers' London office price £8.95 plus £1 p&p. Reduction for RA areas & groups.

An indispensable guide to map reading, using a compass and leading a group. The book is packed with illustrations, exercises and ideas for dealing with all manner of troublesome situations!

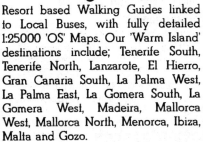

'Warm Island' Walking Guides

Resort based Walking Guides linked to Local Buses, with fully detailed 1:25000 'OS' Maps. Our 'Warm Island' destinations include; Tenerife South, Tenerife North, Lanzarote, El Hierro, Gran Canaria South, La Palma West, La Palma East, La Gomera South, La Gomera West, Madeira, Mallorca West, Mallorca North, Menorca, Ibiza, Malta and Gozo.

".. a real sense of intimacy with the writers, Ros and David .. keen on local -style bars .. excellent on public transport .. a sense of mild adventure shared. Many will value this aspect."
Daily Telegraph - Travel Bookshelf.
£4.50 each from bookshops or from
    Discovery Walking Guides Ltd
    10 Tennyson Close. Dallington.
    Northampton NN5 7HJ.

THE RA MAP LIBRARY

The library at RA national office stocks the Landranger 1:50,000 maps, the Outdoor Leisure 1:25,000 maps and limited numbers of Harvey's "Superwalker" waterproof 1:25,000 maps and OS Explorer maps. A recent addition to the library is a complete set of the 1:50,000 Discovery series of maps for Northern Ireland. All these are available on loan to RA members only (Pathfinder 1:25,000 maps are NOT stocked.) No more than 10 maps may be borrowed at any one time.

There is a charge of 30p per map for a period of six weeks from the date of issue, plus postage and packing. Borrowers are responsible for returning maps in good condition, and will be charged for loss or damage.

To order maps, telephone or write at least ten days in advance (if possible) to the Map Library Service stating the number(s) of the map(s) required, the date you want them and your membership number. Please do not send any money with your order, as an invoice will be sent with the maps. This should be paid when the maps are returned.

Write to Martin Ogilvie at the RA Central office in London. Tel. 0171-582 6878.

All Hostels, bunkhouses and B&Bs listed in this book have 6-figure grid references

MAPS

Useful Addresses

ACTION WITH COMMUNITIES IN RURAL ENGLAND (ACRE)
Somerford Court, Somerford Road, Cirencester, Glos GL7 1TW. ☎ (01285) 653477
IDENTIFIES RURAL PROBLEMS, ENCOURAGES SELF-HELP AND ADVISES ON RURAL POLICIES; NATIONAL ASSOCIATION OF RURAL COMMUNITY COUNCILS.

ASSOCIATION FOR THE PROTECTION OF RURAL SCOTLAND
Gladstone's Land, 483 Lawnmarket, Edinburgh EH1 2NT. ☎ 0131-225 7012
GIVES ADVICE AND INFORMATION ON MATTERS AFFECTING RURAL AREAS IN SCOTLAND. ENCOURAGES APPROPRIATE DEVELOPMENT.

BACKPACKERS CLUB
Jim & Maggie Beed, 49 Lyndhurst Road, Exmouth, EX8 3DS. ☎ (01395) 26515.
A CLUB FOR LIGHT WEIGHT CAMPERS INCLUDING AN ADVISORY AND INFORMATION SERVICE ON LIGHT WEIGHT EQUIPMENT.

BRITISH HORSE SOCIETY
British Equestrian Centre, Stoneleigh, Nr Kenilworth, Warks CV8 2LR. ☎ (01203) 696697
PROMOTES THE UPKEEP OF BRIDLEWAYS AND ENCOURAGES SAFETY AND TRAINING OF HORSES AND RIDERS.

BRITISH MOUNTAINEERING COUNCIL
177-179 Burton Road, Manchester M20 2BB. ☎ 0161-445 4747.
PROMOTES THE INTERESTS OF BRITISH MOUNTAINEERS IN THE UK AND OVERSEAS.

BRITISH ORIENTEERING FEDERATION
Riversdale, Dale Road North, Darley Dale, Matlock, Derbys DE4 2HX. ☎ (01629) 734042

BRITISH TRUST FOR CONSERVATION VOLUNTEERS (BTCV)
36 St Mary's Street, Wallingford, Oxon OX10 0EU. ☎ (01491) 839766
INVOLVES VOLUNTEERS IN PRACTICAL CONSERVATION WORK TO PROTECT AND IMPROVE THE ENVIRONMENT. AFFILIATED GROUPS NATIONWIDE. RUNS NATURAL BREAK WORKING HOLIDAYS.

BRITISH UPLAND FOOTPATH TRUST
PO Box 96, Manchester M20 2FU. ☎ 01204 529905.
AIMS TO IMPROVE THE QUALITY AND STANDARD OF FOOTPATH WORKS AND DEAL WITH EROSION PROBLEMS.

BRITISH WATERWAYS
Willow Grange, Church Road, Watford WD1 3QA. ☎ (01923) 226422.
RESPONSIBLE FOR THE MAINTENANCE & SAFETY OF 2,000 MILES OF CANALS AND RIVERS.

BYWAYS & BRIDLEWAYS TRUST
St Mary's Business Centre, Oystershell Lane, Newcastle-upon-Tyne NE4 5QS. ☎ 0191-233 0770
AIMS TO PROTECT AND DEVELOP BYWAYS, BRIDLEWAYS AND PUBLIC RIGHTS OF WAY IN GENERAL BY PUBLISHING INFORMATION AND HOLDING TRAINING COURSES.

CAMPAIGN FOR THE PROTECTION OF RURAL WALES (Ymgyrch Diogelu Cymru Wledig)
Ty Gwyn, 31 High Street, Welshpool, Powys SY21 7JP. ☎ (01938) 552525/556212
13 BRANCHES IN WALES. SIMILAR AIMS TO THOSE OF CPRE.

CAMPING & CARAVANNING CLUB LTD
Greenfields House, Westwood Way, Coventry CV4 8JH. ☎ (01203) 694995

CAMPING & OUTDOOR LEISURE ASSOCIATION (COLA)
Morrit House, Station Approach, South Ruislip HA4 6SA. ☎ 0181-842 1111.
ORGANISE TRADE EXHIBITITIONS FOR THE OUTDOOR LEISURE INDUSTRY

CIVIC TRUST
17 Carlton House Terrace, London, SW1Y 5AW. ☎ 0171-930 0914
AIMS TO STIMULATE INTEREST IN, AND ACTION FOR, THE IMPROVEMENT OF THE ENVIRONMENT THROUGHOUT THE UK.

CIVIC TRUST FOR WALES (Treftadaeth Cymru)
4th Floor, Empire House, Mount Stuart Square, Cardiff CF1 6DH. ☎ (01222) 484606

COMMON GROUND
Seven Dials Warehouse, 44 Earlham Street, London WC2H 9LA. ☎ 0171-379 3109
PROMOTES CONSERVATION BY ENCOURAGING LOCAL ACTION. MAKES PRACTICAL LINKS WITH ALL BRANCHES OF THE ARTS.

COUNCIL FOR NATIONAL PARKS (CNP)
246 Lavender Hill, London SW11 1LJ. ☎ 0171-924 4077
WORKS TO PROTECT BRITAIN'S NATIONAL PARKS AND PROVIDES A FORUM FOR DISCUSSION AMONG INTERESTED ORGANISATIONS.

COUNCIL FOR THE PROTECTION OF RURAL ENGLAND (CPRE)
Warwick House, 25 Buckingham Palace Road, London SW1W 0PP. ☎ 0171-976 6433
CONCERNED WITH THE PROTECTION OF THE COUNTRYSIDE. CAMPAIGNS FOR THE CAUSE OF CONSERVATION.

COUNTRYGOER PROJECT
15 Station Road, Knowle, Solihull, West Midlands B93 0HL. ☎ (01564) 778323.
PROMOTES THE USE OF PUBLIC TRANSPORT TO GAIN ACCESS TO THE COUNTRYSIDE AND PUBLISHES INFORMATION ABOUT SERVICES AND ROUTES.

COUNTRY LANDOWNERS' ASSOCIATION (CLA)
16 Belgrave Square, London SW1X 8PQ.
☎ 0171-235 0511
PROMOTES AND PROTECTS THE INTERESTS OF RURAL AND AGRI-
CULTURAL LANDOWNERS.

COUNTRYSIDE COMMISSION
John Dower House, Crescent Place, Cheltenham,
Glos GL50 3RA. ☎ (01242) 521381
OFFICIAL GOVERNMENT BODY. ADVISES AND SUPPORTS CONSER-
VATION AND COUNTRYSIDE RECREATION POLICY AND PRACTICE.

COUNTRYSIDE COMMISSION PUBLICATIONS
PO Box 124, Walgrave, Northampton NN6 9TL.
☎ (01604) 781848

COUNTRYSIDE COUNCIL FOR WALES
(Cyngor Cefn Gwlad Cymru)
Plas Penrhos, Penrhos Road, Bangor, Gwynedd LL57
2LQ. ☎ (01248) 370444
STATUTORY BODY RESPONSIBLE FOR THE PROTECTION OF NATURE
AND THE COUNTRYSIDE IN WALES.

COUNTRYWIDE HOLIDAYS
Grove House, Wilmslow Road, Didsbury, Manchester
M20 2HU.☎ 0161-446 2226.
ORGANISES WALKING HOLIDAYS FROM 8 CENTRES IN BRITAIN. CO-
SPONSORS (WITH COUNTRY HOLIDAYS) OF FAMILY RAMBLING DAY.

CYCLISTS' TOURING CLUB
Cotterell House, 69 Meadrow, Godalming, Surrey
GU7 3HS. ☎ (01483) 417217
REPRESENTS CYCLISTS IN MATTERS AFFECTING USE OF ROADS,
ACCESS TO THE COUNTRYSIDE. CLUB ACTIVITIES.

DEPARTMENT OF THE ENVIRONMENT
2 Marsham Street, London SW1P 3EB.
☎ 0171-212 3434

ECOLOGY BUILDING SOCIETY
18 Station Road, Cross Hills, near Keighley, W Yorks
BD20 7EH ☎ (01535) 635933
SPECIALISES IN MAKING ADVANCES FOR PROPERTIES USING MOST
ECOLOGICALLY EFFICIENT USE OF LAND.

ENGLISH HERITAGE
Fortress House, 23 Savile Row, London W1X 1AB.
☎ 0171-973 3000
CARES FOR OVER 350 PROPERTIES OPEN TO THE PUBLIC;
PROMOTES THE CONSERVATION OF ENGLAND'S HISTORIC BUILT
HERITAGE.

ENGLISH NATURE
Northminster House, Northminster Road,
Peterborough PE1 1UA. ☎ (01733) 340345
STATUTORY BODY RESPONSIBLE FOR ADVISING GOVERNMENT AND
OTHERS ON NATURE CONSERVATION IN ENGLAND.

ENGLISH TOURIST BOARD
Thames Tower, Blacks Road, Hammersmith, London
W6 9EL. ☎ 0181-846 9000.

ENVIRONMENT AGENCY
Rio House, Waterside Drive, Aztec West,
Almondsbury, Bristol BS12 4UD. ☎ (01454) 624400.

General enquiries ☎ (0645) 333111
GOVERNMENT AGENCY SET UP TO PROTECT AND ENHANCE THE
ENVIRONMENT.

ENVIRONMENTAL NEWS & INFORMATION SERVICE
1 Kensington Gore, London SW7 2AR.
☎ 0171-823 8842.
ORGANISATION DISSEMINATING NEWS ABOUT ENVIRONMENTAL
AND CONSERVATION MATTERS.

EUROPEAN RAMBLING ASSOCIATION
Europaische Wandervereinigung e.V., Reichstrasse 4,
D6600 Saarbrucken, Germany
AIMS TO FURTHER WALKING AND CLIMBING, CARE FOR AND
PROTECT THE COUNTRYSIDE, AND CREATE EUROPEAN LONG
DISTANCE PATHS. SEE ALSO EUROPE SECTION OF THIS YEARBOOK.

FARM HOLIDAY BUREAU
National Agricultural Centre, Stoneleigh Park,
Kenilworth, Warks CV8 2LZ. ☎ (01203) 696909
NETWORK OF FARMING FAMILIES OFFERING COUNTRY HOLIDAYS.

FARMING & WILDLIFE ADVISORY GROUP
National Agricultural Centre, Stoneleigh, Kenilworth,
Warks CV8 2RX. ☎ (01203) 696699
CONCERNED WITH COUNTRYSIDE AND CONSERVATION OF
WILDLIFE IN THE CONTEXT OF PRACTICAL FARMING.

FIELDFARE TRUST
67a The Wicker, Sheffield S3 8HT.
☎ 0114-270 1668
SUPPORTS INITIATIVES WHICH ENABLE PEOPLE WITH SPECIAL
NEEDS TO ENJOY THE COUNTRYSIDE

FIELD STUDIES COUNCIL
Central Services, Preston Montford, Montford Bridge,
Shrewsbury, Shrops SY4 1HW. ☎ (01743) 850674
ENCOURAGES FIELD WORK AND RESEARCH THROUGH ITS FIELD
CENTRES. RUNS COURSES.

FORESTRY COMMISSION
231 Corstorphine Road, Edinburgh EH12 7AT.
☎ 0131-334 0303
GOVERNMENT DEPARTMENT. RESPONSIBLE FOR ESTABLISHING
AND MANAGING FORESTS IN GB FOR A VARIETY OF USES.

FREEWHEELERS
225 Low Friar Street, Newcastle-upon-Tyne NE1 5UE.
☎ 0191-222 0090.
NATIONAL LIFT-SHARING AGENCY.

FRIENDS OF THE EARTH (FOE)
26/28 Underwood Street, London N1 7JQ.
☎ 0171-490 1555
and:
FRIENDS OF THE EARTH (SCOTLAND)
Bonnington Mill, 70-72 Newhaven Road, Edinburgh
EH6. ☎ 0131-554 9977
ENVIRONMENTAL CAMPAIGNING ORGANISATIONS.

FRIENDS OF THE LAKE DISTRICT
The Secretary, No 3, Yard 77, Highgate, Kendal,
Cumbria LA9 4ED. ☎ (01539) 720788
WORKS TO PROTECT AND ENHANCE THE COUNTRYSIDE OF THE
LAKE DISTRICT. REPRESENTS THE CPRE WITHIN CUMBRIA.

FRIENDS OF THE RIDGEWAY
c/o Nigel Forward, 90 South Hill Park, London NW3 2SN. ☎ 0171-794 2105
AIMS TO PRESERVE THE RIDGEWAY NATIONAL TRAIL FOR QUIET RECREATION USE.

GAY OUTDOOR CLUB (G.O.C.)
PO Box 24, Minehead, Somerset TA24 8YZ.
MIXED CLUB ORGANISES WALKS, CYCLING, SWIMMING, MOUNTAINEERING, OVERSEAS HOLIDAYS ON A REGIONAL GROUP BASIS.

GLENMORE LODGE
Aviemore, Inverness-shire PH22 1QU.
☎ (01479) 861276
SCOTTISH NATIONAL SPORTS CENTRE. ORGANISES COURSES ON MOUNTAIN ACTIVITIES, CLIMBING, AND WINTER SKILLS.

GREENPEACE LIMITED
Greenpeace House, Canonbury Villas, London N1 2PN. ☎ 0171-865 8100
PROMOTES PEACEFUL BUT UNCOMPROMISING ACTION IN DEFENCE OF THE ENVIRONMENT.

HF HOLIDAYS
Imperial House, Edgware Road, London NW9 5AL.
☎ 0181-905 9556
ORGANISES WALKING HOLIDAYS IN BRITAIN FROM 19 CENTRES

INLAND WATERWAYS ASSOCIATION
114 Regent's Park Road, London NW1 8UQ.
☎ 0171-586 2510/2556
PROMOTES RESTORATION AND DEVELOPMENT OF INLAND WATERWAYS FOR TRADE AND RECREATION.

JOHN MUIR TRUST
13 Wellington Place, Leith, Edinburgh EH6 7JD.
PROMOTES THE CARE OF WILD PLACES THROUGH RAISING FUNDS TO PURCHASE THREATENED AREAS.

LONDON GREEN BELT COUNCIL
13 Oakleigh Park Avenue, Chislehurst, Kent BR7 5PB
☎ 0181-467 5346
VOLUNTARY BODY MADE UP OF NATIONAL, REGIONAL AND LOCAL ORGANISATIONS CONCERNED WITH THE PROTECTION OF LONDON'S GREEN BELT.

LONDON WALKING FORUM
Lee Balley Riogional Park Authority, Myddelton House, Bulls Cross, Enfield EN2 9HG.
☎ (01992) 713838.
AIMING TO LINK UP LONDON'S OPEN SPACES TO CREATE A NETWORK OF WALKS.

LONG DISTANCE WALKERS ASSOCIATION
c/o Les Maple, 21 Upcroft, Windsor, Berks SL4 3NH.
☎ (01753) 866685
AIMS TO FURTHER THE INTERESTS OF THOSE WHO ENJOY LONG DISTANCE WALKING.

MARINE CONSERVATION SOCIETY
9 Gloucester Road, Ross-on-Wye, Hereford & Worcester HR9 5BU. ☎ (01989) 566017.
AIMS TO PROTECT THE BEACHES AND SEAS AROUND OUR COASTS.

MILITARY RANGES
THESE NUMBERS CAN BE USED FOR OBTAINING INFORMATION ON TIMES AND DATES WHEN FIRING WILL BE TAKING PLACE.
Castle Martin, Dyfed ☎ (01646) 661321 x4280
Dartmoor ☎ (01837) 52939
Lulworth, Dorset ☎ (01929) 462721 x4819/4859
Otterburn, Northumberland ☎ 0191-239 4201
Salisbury Plain, Wiltshire ☎ (01980) 620819
Thetford, Norfolk ☎ (01842) 855235

MOUNTAINEERING COUNCIL OF SCOTLAND
National Officer, Kevin Howett, Flat 1R, 71 King Street, Crieff PH7 3HB. ☎ (01764) 654962
AIMS TO PROMOTE MOUNTAINEERING IN SCOTLAND. GOVERNING BODY FOR THE SPORT IN SCOTLAND.

NATIONAL FARMERS' UNION
164 Shaftesbury Avenue, London WC2H 8HL.
☎ 0171-331 7200
REPRESENTS THE INTERESTS OF FARMERS AND GROWERS.

and

NATIONAL FARMERS' UNION SCOTLAND
The Rural Centre, West Mains, Inglestone, Newbridge, Mid-Lothian EH28 8LT.☎ 0131-335 3111

and

NATIONAL FARMERS' UNION WALES
Llys Amaeth, Queen's Square, Aberystwyth, Dyfed SY23 2EA. ☎ (01970) 612755

NATIONAL PARKS
THE MAIN OFFICES OF THE NATIONAL PARKS ARE LISTED BELOW. IN MOST JNSTANCES THERE WILL BE AN INFORMATION OFFICER WHO CAN ANSWER QUESTIONS OR SEND LEAFLETS. ALL THE NATIONAL PARKS RUN INFORMATION CENTRES WHERE YOU CAN OBTAIN BOOKS, MAPS, WALKS INFORMATION ETC. SOME OF THESE ARE ONLY OPEN IN SUMMER.

Brecon Beacons
National Park Office, 7 Glamorgan Street, Brecon, Powys LD3 7DP. ☎ (01874) 624437

The Broads Authority
Thomas Harvey House, 18 Colegate, Norwich NR3 1BQ. ☎ (01603) 610734

Dartmoor
National Park Authority, Parke, Haytor Road, Bovey Tracey, Newton Abbot, Devon TQ13 9JQ.
☎ (01626) 832093

Exmoor Exmoor House, Dulverton, Somerset TA22 9HL. ☎ (01398) 323665

Lake District National Park Office, Brockhole, Windermere, Cumbria LA23 1LJ. ☎ (015394) 46601

Northumberland National Park Dept, Eastburn, South Park, Hexham, Northumberland NE46 1BS.
☎ (01434) 605555

North York Moors National Park Office, The Old Vicarage, Bondgate, Helmsley, N Yorks YO6 5BP. ☎ (01439) 770657

Peak District National Park Office, Baslow Road, Bakewell, Derbyshire DE45 1AE. ☎ (01629) 814321

Pembrokeshire Coast National Park Dept, County Offices, St Thomas' Green, Haverfordwest, Pembrokeshire, Dyfed SA61 1QZ. ☎ (01437) 764636

Snowdonia National Park Office, Penrhyndeudraeth, Gwynedd LL48 6LS. ☎ (01766) 770274/770701

Yorkshire Dales National Park Authority, Hebden Road, Grassington, Skipton, N Yorks BD23 5LB. ☎ (01756) 752748

NATIONAL TRUST
36 Queen Anne's Gate, London SW1H 9AS. ☎ 0171-222 9251
PROTECTS, THROUGH OWNERSHIP, COUNTRYSIDE, COASTLAND AND MANY HISTORIC BUILDINGS IN ENGLAND.

NATIONAL TRUST (NORTHERN IRELAND)
Rowallane House, Saintfield, Ballynahinch, Co Down BT24 7LH. ☎ Saintfield (01238) 510721

NATIONAL TRUST FOR SCOTLAND
5 Charlotte Square, Edinburgh EH2 4DU. ☎ 0131-226 5922

NORTHERN IRELAND TOURIST BOARD
St Anne's Court, 59 North Street, Belfast BT1 1NB. ☎ (01232) 246609

OPEN SPACES SOCIETY
5a Bell Street, Henley-on-Thames, Oxon RG9 2BA. ☎ (01491) 573535
AIMS TO PROTECT COMMON LAND, OPEN SPACES AND FOOTPATHS.

ORDNANCE SURVEY
Romsey Road, Maybush, Southampton, Hants SO16 4GU. ☎ (01703) 792000
NATIONAL MAPPING AGENCY OF GREAT BRITAIN.

ORDNANCE SURVEY OF NORTHERN IRELAND
Colby House, Stranmillis Court, Belfast BT9 5BJ. ☎ Belfast. (01232) 661244

OUTDOOR WRITERS GUILD
7 Camwood, Clayton Green, Bamber Bridge, Preston PR5 8LA.
ASSOCIATION OF PROFESSIONALS INVOLVED IN OUTDOOR WRITING AND PHOTOGRAPHY.

PEAK & NORTHERN FOOTPATHS SOCIETY
r D Taylor, 15 Parkfield Drive, Tyldesley, Manchester M29 8NR. ☎ 0161-790 4383
AIMS TO PRESERVE THE RIGHTS OF THE PUBLIC TO USE THE PUBLIC HIGHWAYS IN THE EIGHT NORTHERN COUNTIES.

PEDESTRIANS ASSOCIATION
126 Aldersgate St, London EC1A 4QJ. ☎ 0171-490 0750

PLAS-Y-BRENIN
Capel Curig, Gwynedd LL24 0ET. ☎ (01690) 720214
NATIONAL MOUNTAIN CENTRE. ORGANISES COURSES ON MOUNTAIN WALKING AND LEADERSHIP, NAVIGATION & CLIMBING

RAILWAY DEVELOPMENT SOCIETY
2 Clematis Cottages, Hopton Bank, Cleobury Mortimer, Kidderminster DY14 0HF. ☎ (01584) 890807
VOLUNTARY NATIONAL PRESSURE GROUP FOR THE RETENTION AND MODERNISATION OF RAILWAY SERVICES.

RAILWAY RAMBLERS
12 Harefield Gardens, Middleton-on-Sea, Bognor Regis PO22 6EQ. ☎ (01243) 582242
PROMOTES THE PRESERVATION OF DISUSED RAILWAY LINES FOR WALKING AND CYCLING.

RAMBLERS' ASSOCIATION SCOTLAND
Crusader House, Haig Business Park, Markinch, Fife KY7 7AQ. ☎ (01592) 611177

RAMBLERS' ASSOCIATION WALES
Ty'r Cerddwyr, High Street, Gresford, Wrexham, Clwyd LL12 8PT. ☎ (01978) 855148

RAMBLERS HOLIDAYS LTD
Box 43, Welwyn Garden City, Herts AL8 6PQ. ☎ (01707) 331133
GUIDED WALKING, SKIING AND SIGHTSEEING HOLIDAYS ABROAD. GUIDED WALKING HOLIDAYS IN THE LAKE DISTRICT.

RED ROPE
18 Ormskirk Road, Upholland, Lancs WN8 0AG. ☎ (01695) 625336.

ROYAL SOCIETY FOR THE PROTECTION OF BIRDS (RSPB)
The Lodge, Sandy, Beds SG19 2DL. ☎ (01767) 680551

SCOTTISH COUNTRYSIDE ACTIVITIES COUNCIL
7 Lawson Ave, Banchory, Kincardineshire AB31 3TW.
AN UMBRELLA GROUP OF ORGANISATIONS WITH INTERESTS IN COUNTRYSIDE RECREATION IN SCOTLAND.

SCOTTISH FIELD STUDIES ASSOCIATION
Kindrogan Field Centre, Enochdhu, Blairgowrie, Perthshire PH10 7PG. ☎ (01250) 881286
RUNS RESIDENTIAL COURSES ON ALL ASPECTS OF NATURAL HISTORY AND THE COUNTRYSIDE, INCLUDING WALKING.

SCOTTISH NATURAL HERITAGE
12 Hope Terrace Edinburgh EH9 2AS. ☎ 0131-447 4784.
BODY FORMED BY THE MERGER OF THE COUNTRYSIDE COMMISSION FOR SCOTLAND AND THE NATURE CONSERVANCY COUNCIL FOR SCOTLAND.

SCOTTISH OFFICE
New St Andrew's House, Edinburgh EH1 3TG. ☎ 0131-556 8400
THE PRINCIPAL GOVERNMENT DEPARTMENTS THAT DEAL WITH COUNTRYSIDE AND ACCESS MATTERS.

SCOTTISH RIGHTS OF WAY SOCIETY
Unit 2, John Cotton Business Centre, 10/2 Sunnyside, Edinburgh EH7 5RA. ☎ 0131-652 2937
PRESERVES, DEFENDS AND SEEKS TO ESTABLISH PUBLIC RIGHTS OF WAY IN SCOTLAND.

SCOTTISH SPORTS COUNCIL
Caledonia House, South Gyle Edinburgh EH12 9DQ. ☎ 0131-317 7200

SCOTTISH TOURIST BOARD
23 Ravelston Terrace, Edinburgh EH4 3EU. ☎ 0131-332 2433

SCOTTISH WILDLIFE TRUST
Cramond House, Kirk Cramond, Cramond Glebe Road, Edinburgh EH4 6NS
VOLUNTARY ORGANISATION FOR THE CONSERVATION OF ALL FORMS OF WILDLIFE AND THEIR HABITATS IN SCOTLAND.

SCOTTISH YOUTH HOSTELS ASSOCIATION
7 Glebe Crescent, Stirling FK8 2JA. ☎ (01786) 451181

SHELL BETTER BRITAIN CAMPAIGN
c/o Peter Woodward, Red House, Hill Lane, Great Barr, Birmingham B43 6LZ
HELPS VOLUNTARY GROUPS UNDERTAKING COMMUNITY ENVIRONMENTAL PROJECTS.

SOCIETY OF SUSSEX DOWNSMEN
93 Church Road, Hove, East Sussex BN3 2BA. ☎ (01273) 771906
AIMS TO PRESERVE AND PROTECT THE SOUTH DOWNS.

SPORTS COUNCIL
16 Upper Woburn Place, London WC1H 0QP. ☎ 0171-388 1277
AIMS TO FOSTER THE PRACTICE OF SPORT AND RECREATION AMONG THE PUBLIC AT LARGE.

SPORTS COUNCIL FOR WALES
National Sports Centre for Wales, Sophia Gardens, Cardiff CF1 9SW. ☎ (01222) 397571

TOWN & COUNTRY PLANNING ASSOCIATION
17 Carlton House Terrace, London SW1Y 5AS. ☎ 0171-930 8903
AIMS TO IMPROVE THE ENVIRONMENT THROUGH EFFECTIVE PLANNING, PUBLIC PARTICIPATION AND SUSTAINABLE DEVELOPMENT.

TRANSPORT 2000
Walkden House, 10 Melton Street, London NW1 2EJ. ☎ 0171-388 8386
CAMPAIGNS FOR TRANSPORT POLICIES THAT WILL NOT HARM THE ENVIRONMENT AND WILL MOST BENEFIT THE PUBLIC.

TRANSPORT USERS CONSULTATIVE COMMITTEE
Golden Cross House, 8 Duncannon St, London WC2N 4JF. ☎ 0171-839 7338
STATUTORY CONSUMER COMMITTEES COVERING THE VARIOUS REGIONS OF BRITAIN. THEY MONITOR THE QUALITY OF RAIL SERVICES AND PURSUE RAIL USERS' UNRESOLVED COMPLAINTS.

ULSTER FEDERATION OF RAMBLING CLUBS
Mary Doyle, 27 Slievegallion Drive, Belfast BT11 8JN. ☎ (01232) 624289
AIMS TO PROTECT AND PROMOTE THE COUNTRYSIDE AND WALKING.

WALES TOURIST BOARD (Bwrdd Croeso Cymru)
Brunel House, 2 Fitzalan Road, Cardiff CF2 1UY. ☎ (01222) 499909

WELSH OFFICE
Cathays Park, Cardiff CF1 3NQ. ☎ (01222) 825111.

THE WILDLIFE TRUSTS
The Green, Witham Park, Waterside South, Lincoln LN5 7JR. ☎ (01522) 544400
DEALS WITH ALL ASPECTS OF WILDLIFE PROTECTION. NATIONAL ORGANISATION OF THE 47 WILDLIFE TRUSTS AND WATCH, THE JUNIOR CLUB FOR YOUNG ENVIRONMENTALISTS.

THE WOODCRAFT FOLK
13 Ritherdon Road, London SW17 8QE. ☎ 0181-672 6031

WOODLAND TRUST
Autumn Park, Dysart Road, Grantham, Lincs NG31 6LL. ☎ (01476) 581111.
AQUIRES WOODS THROUGHOUT BRITAIN TO SAFEGUARD THEIR AMENITY, WILDLIFE AND LANDSCAPE VALUE.

WWF - WORLD WIDE FUND FOR NATURE (UK)
Panda House, Weyside Park, Godalming, Surrey GU7 1XR. ☎ (01483) 426444
MAJOR ENVIRONMENTAL CAMPAIGNING AND FUND-RAISING BODY: PART OF A WORLD-WIDE NETWORK.

YORKSHIRE DALES SOCIETY
Otley Civic Centre, Cross Green, Otley, W Yorks LS21 1HD. ☎ (01943) 607868/461938)
AIMS TO ADVANCE PUBLIC KNOWLEDGE AND TO PRESERVE THE LANDSCAPE AND NATURAL BEAUTY OF THE DALES.

YOUTH HOSTELS ASSOCIATION
Trevelyan House, 8 St Stephen's Hill, St Albans, Herts AL1 2DY. ☎ (01727) 855215
AIMS TO HELP ALL PEOPLE OF LIMITED MEANS TO A GREATER KNOWLEDGE, LOVE AND CARE OF THE COUNTRYSIDE, BY PROVIDING YOUTH HOSTEL AND CAMPING BARN ACCOMMODATION, AND A WIDE RANGE OF OUTDOOR RECREATION, LEISURE AND ENVIRONMENTAL EDUCATION PROGRAMMES.

YOUTH HOSTELS ASSOCIATION OF NORTHERN IRELAND
22 Donegall Road, Belfast BT12 5JN. ☎ (01232) 324733.

The Ramblers in Europe

ANDORRA
Andorran Mountain Federation, Carrer Bra. Riberaygua 39, 5e, Andorra la Vella, Principat D'Andorrà.

AUSTRIA
ÖAV-Sektion Weitwanderer, p/a Thaliastrasse 159/3/16, A-1160, Vienna.

BELGIUM
Grote Routepaden, Van Stralenstraat 40, B-2060, Antwerp. ☎ Antwerp (03) 232 72 18. Fax 231 81 26.
Les Sentiers de Grande Randonée (SGR), Boîte Postale 10, B-4000, Liège 1.

BULGARIA
Bulgarian Tourist Union, Zentralrat, 75 Vassil Levski Blvd, BG-1000 Sofia.

CZECH REPUBLIC
Czeck Touring Club, Mezi Stadiony, 16017 Prague 6.

DENMARK
Landsforeningen Dansk Vandrelaug (Danish Ramblers Association), Kulturvet 7, 1, DK-1175 Copenhagen K.

ESTONIA
Estonian Sport-Tourism Union, Raekoja Plats 18, EE-0001 Tallinn.

FINLAND
Finnish Travel Association, PO Box 776, SF-00101 Helsinki.

FRANCE
Centre d'Information de la FFRP, 64 rue de Gergovie, -75014 Paris.
☎ Paris 45 45 31 02. Fax 43 95 68 07.
Club Bosgien/Vogesenklub-Comité Central, 16 rue Sainte Hélène, F-67000 Strasbourg.

GERMANY
Verband Deutscher Gebirgs und Wandervereine, Postfach 103213, D-66032 Saarbrucken.

GREECE
Hellenic Federation of Mountaineering Clubs, Milioni, GR-10673 Athens.

HOLLAND
Foundation for Long-Distance Footpaths, (SLAW) Postbus 846, NL-3800 AV Amersfoort. ☎ (033) 65 5 60.

HUNGARY
Magyar Termeszetbarat Szovetseg (Hungarian Nature-Friends Association), Postafiok 483, H-1396 Budapest 5.

ICELAND
Ütivist, Hallveigarstig 1, PO Box 236 IS-121 Reykjavik.

IRELAND
Irish Youth Hostel Association, 61 Mountjoy Square Sth., IRL-Dublin 7.

ITALY
Federazione Italiana Escursionismo, Via La Spezia 58r, 1-16149 Genova.
Associazione Sentiero Italia, via San Gervasio 12, 1-50131 Firenze Fl.

LUXEMBOURG
Ministère du Tourisme, 6 Avenue Emile Reuter, Boite Postale 86, L-2010 Luxembourg.

NORWAY
Norwegian Mountain Touring Association, Postboks 7 Sentrum, N-0101 Oslo.
☎ (+47) 22 82 28 00. Fax 22 82 28 01.

POLAND
Polish Tourist Association, ul. Senatorska 11, PL-00-075 Warsaw. ☎ +48 22 26 22 51. Fax /25 05.

PORTUGAL
Clube de Actividades de Ar Livre, Rua Maria Pia 479-A, P-1350 Lisbon.

ROMANIA
Romanian Ramblers Association, Valea Calugareasca 15, Bl. Z 1 ap. 58, Sector 6, R-77472 Bucharest.

SLOVAKIA
Klub Slovenskych Turistov (Slovak Tourist Club), Junacka 6, SK-83280, Bratislava

SLOVENIA
Komisija za evropske pespoti, Erjavceva 15, SLO-61000 Ljubljana.

SPAIN
Federación Española de Montana y Escalada, Alberto Aguilera 3-4, E-28015 Madrid.
Federacio d'Entitats Excursionistes de Catalunya, Rambla 61, 1r, E-08002 Barcelona.

SWEDEN
Swedish Touring Club (STF), Box 25, S-10120 Stockholm. ☎ 08 790 32 00. Fax 08 20 80 16.

SWITZERLAND
Schweizer Wanderwege (Swiss Hiking Federation), Im Hirshalm 49, CH-4125 Riehen.

Safety in the Hills

Following the bad winter of 1993/4, when an unusually high number of mountain accidents had been reported, the House of Commons Scottish Affairs Committee decided to conduct an inquiry into the mountain rescue services and their ability to cope with the pressure.

A lot of sensational news reporting had fuelled ideas that the tax payers' money was being wasted by ill-prepared people taking to the hills, that those using the hills for sport ought to be insured and that the rescue services ought to be manned by, or at least consist largely of, paid 'professionals' rather than volunteers. The Committee was met with a fierce and proud response from those in charge of mountain rescue operations in Scotland: keep off our fantastic service; no other system would work as well as the one we have whose great strength is the good will and mutual respect and co-operation between the police, volunteer rescuers and the RAF. But please do give us money to expand our training and public information initiatives. People using the hills need to be more aware of the amount of risk they can take relative to their experience, skill and state of physical fitness. These sentiments are strongly echoed by the Scottish Mountain Rescue Teams' counterparts in England and Wales.

Mountain rescuers, it seems, are a valiant breed, mostly active and experienced mountaineers themselves, who are motivated not least by the realistic fear that they or their nearest and dearest may need rescuing one day. When asked how they would respond to the introduction to a 'professional' (i.e. paid) rescue service, they answered to a man – or woman (not many!) – that they wished to remain a volunteer force. They explained that a salaried team would bring about the decline of the volunteer force which is made up of most of those best equipped to do the job. Mountaineers would be unlikely to volunteer their services if others were being paid to do the job and there simply would not be enough experienced 'professionals' to provide the service. Errors would inevitably be made. For example, the point at which a search is initiated for a missing person is a subtle judgement. It is important to avoid the expense and unnecessary effort and danger of launching a search only to find the person walking down the mountain fit and well an hour or so later. A paid team would be bound to instigate searches too early for fear of being sued for negligence. This would certainly be a waste of public funds.

According to statistics reported in *The Handbook of the Mountain Rescue Council*, the main causes of accidents among hillwalkers are slippages, exhaustion and what they call 'incompetence'. Those who wish to avoid this demeaning epithet had better make sure their boots are in good order, their map and compass skills impeccable and that their determination to keep within their own limits of stamina and skill knows no bounds. It is heartening to note, however, that the numbers of accidents caused by the said incompetence has dropped dramatically in recent years from 186 in 1990 to 34 in 1995. Surely we can take this to mean that efforts to educate the public in mountain awareness are proving successful.

Many accidents in the hills are preceded by impulsive decision-making. Sometimes, it is absolutely necessary to change one's plans – if you see bad weather coming or a member of the group is slower than expected, for example. But there is a difference between doing this in an informed and considered way, where you know alternative routes, to acting on a whim. As the *Handbook of the Mountain Rescue Council* points out, often more that half the enjoyment from a venture is in the planning phase and forethought has added to, not detracted from, an experience. The Ramblers' Association publication *Navigation and Leadership* gives detailed advice on planning, leadership, compass and map reading and much more.

What comes across very strongly in the Scottish report, published in 1996, is that hill walkers, climbers and others using the mountains for recreation are bringing in a huge amount of money into an economically vulnerable area. Half a million of us visit the Highlands each year and the industry resulting from this accounts for 3% of all employment in the area. To put it in perspective, we are bringing in more money than the next biggest industry, forestry, which totals £72 million a year.

There was one good laugh to be had from the Scottish Affairs Committee inquiry. Asked if rescue teams were ever called out on false alarms, Mr Dunlop, a member of Lochaber team, told the story of a woman who came down a mountain saying her husband had dislocated his knee. A helicopter had been sent to find him but a while later the husband came striding down the mountain. "Well, what do you call that? Is that a false alarm? " asked Mr Dunlop.

"Grounds for divorce" came the reply!

SAFETY IN THE HILLS

Some dos and don'ts for being safe in the hills

- Go with a group if you have any doubts about your experience and competence. The figures show many more injuries to people walking alone than members of groups.

- Leave information with someone you know or in your car which will help rescuers find you should this become necessary.

Take courses to learn hill craft. There are lots of them advertised in the walking press including Rambling Today.

Don't keep quiet till you're exhausted. Swallow your pride and let the leader know in good time that you are running out of steam. Then a new plan can be thought out.

Don't overestimate your own stamina. Don't underestimate the effect of cold weather and carrying a heavier weight than usual. They will deplete your energy and reduce your speed.

Concentrate on what you're doing and place each step carefully, especially on your way down when most accidents occur.

- Keep the group close together especially in a mist. It is easy to lose a person.

- Carry more food and warm clothing than for lowland walking.

- Don't rely on mobile phones to get you out of trouble, nor global positioning systems. They may not work and could give you a false sense of confidence.

- In the winter carry ice axe and crampons and know how to use them.

- Carry a survival bag.

- Call on emergency services only if you cannot deal with the situation yourselves.

- Carry a whistle and torch. If the worst happens, blow or flash six times then stop for a minute, then repeat until help comes. Send one person for help, keep at least one with the patient.

- Know basic first aid and keep the injured person warm. They will lose body heat more quickly than you.

Long Distance Paths

This section gives details of over 60 long distance paths. New to the listing this year are the Cumbria Coastal Way, Grand Union Canal Walk, Severn Way, Solent Way, Stour Valley Path and White Peak Way. Publishers of any books or pamphlets mentioned are given at the end of the section. **These publications are not available from the RA unless stated.** Postage & packing might be charged for mail order purchases. The B&B guide in this Yearbook gives a cross-reference to any address which is within 2 miles of any of these routes. There are of course plenty of other paths not on this list and these do not have a cross-reference in the B&B Guide.

In many cases the degree of difficulty of a path is given in the description. First timers are advised to try such paths as the West Mendip Way, South Downs Way or canal or riverside routes, for example, and to avoid the harder paths like the Cambrian Way, Coast to Coast Walk and Pennine Way. It is important to know your own daily limit with whatever weight you will be carrying. It should be possible to plan accommodation along the way by using the B&B and/or Hostels & Bunkhouses parts of the Accommodation Guide in this book, combined with any accommodation guides specific to the path in question.

The Long Distance Walkers' Handbook describes 350 paths and this year for the first time we give a brief mention to 35 lesser known paths near the end of the section in four regional summaries.

Map numbers referred to are 1:50,000 in the Ordnance Survey Landranger series. Some areas are also covered by larger scale (1:25,000) maps in the Explorer, Outdoor Leisure or Pathfinder series. See Maps section (page 44).

Symbols used in this section:

🌢 Path designated a National Trail.

❁ Official long distance path in Scotland.

∗ Path added to this list for the first time in this edition.

(M) Publication includes detailed maps.
(A) Publication includes places to stay.

ANGLES WAY

Great Yarmouth to Knettishall Heath
77 miles (123km)
The 'Broads to Brecks Path' along the Suffolk/Norfolk border, from the meandering Waveney via Diss and the Little Ouse to the sandy heaths of Breckland. Links: Icknield Way; Peddars Way; Weavers Way.
Maps 134 • 144 • 156
Youth hostels Great Yarmouth
Publications
THE ANGLES WAY (MA)
BY NORFOLK AND SUFFOLK RA AREAS. £1.80. AVAILABLE PLUS POSTAGE FROM RA CENTRAL OFFICE.
LANGTON'S GUIDE TO THE WEAVERS WAY AND ANGLES WAY (MA)
LANGTON'S GUIDE. £6.95.

CALDERDALE WAY

Circular from Clay House, Greetland
50 miles (80 km)
Mostly along the course of the River Calder this route explores the industrial archaeology of West Yorkshire and encircles old mill towns such as Hebden Bridge and Todmorden. Links: Pennine Way.
Maps 103 • 104 • 110
Youth hostels Mankinholes
Publications
THE CALDERDALE WAY (M)
BY CALDERDALE WAY ASSOCIATION. TO BE PUBLISHED SHORTLY.
THE CALDERDALE WAY; WALK THE CALDERDALE WAY BY BUS.
BOTH BY AND FROM METROPOLITAN BOROUGH OF CALDERDALE.
FREE LEAFLETS (SAE).

CAMBRIAN WAY

Cardiff to Conwy
274 miles (440 km)
Pioneered by the RA's Tony Drake, this high-level traverse of Wales is as exhilarating as it is challeng-

ing, and is definitely for experienced mountain walkers only. Via the Brecon Beacons, Cader Idris and Snowdonia. Links: Dyfi Valley Way; Taff Trail; Glyndwr's Way. For more information contact the Cambrian Way Walkers Association, Llanerchindda Farm, Cynghordy, Llandovery, SA20 0NB.

Maps 115 • 124 • 135 • 146/147 • 160 • 161 • 171

Youth hostels Cardiff, Capel-y-ffin, Llwyn-y-celyn, Ystradfellte, Llanddeusant, Bryn Poeth Uchaf, Tyncornel, Dolgoch, Blaencaron,Ystumtuen, Kings, Bryn Gwynant, Pen-y-pass, Idwal Cottage, Rowen.

Publications
CAMBRIAN WAY: THE MOUNTAIN CONNOISSEUR'S WALK (MA)
BY A. J. DRAKE - AUTHOR, PUBLISHER AND ENQUIRIES (SEE PUB-
LISHERS' ADDRESSES). £4.50. ALSO AVAILABLE PLUS POSTAGE
FROM RA CENTRAL OFFICE.
CAMBRIAN WAY LOGBOOK AND INFORMATION PACK BY AND FROM
CAMBRIAN WAY WALKERS' ASSOCIATION (SEE ABOVE). FREE.

CHESHIRE RING CANAL WALK

Circular from Macclesfield

97 miles (155km)

A towpath walk along six separate canals, including the Macclesfield, Peak Forest, Bridgewater and Trent & Mersey. Both rural and urban, it visits Congleton, Kidsgrove, Middlewich and passes through central Manchester.

Maps 108 • 109 • 118

Youth hostels Manchester

Publications
THE CHESHIRE RING CANAL WALK (M)
SET OF 11 BOOKLETS BY CHESHIRE COUNTY COUNCIL. £1.00 PER
BOOKLET OR £8.00 FOR FULL SET
THE CHESHIRE RING BY JOHN MERRILL. FOOTPRINT PRESS. £4.95.

CLEVELAND WAY

Helmsley to Filey Brigg

110 miles (177 km)

Sometimes strenuous, but always varied and scenic, this enticing trail takes you from the high heather moors to the plunging North Sea cliffs and bays, via Osmotherley, Whitby and Scarborough. Links: Wolds Way; Coast to Coast Walk.

Maps 93 • 94 • 99 • 100 • 101

Youth hostels Boggle Hole, Helmsley, Osmotherley, Scarborough, Whitby. YHA camping barns Kildale Barn, Farndale Barn.

Publications
NATIONAL TRAIL GUIDE: CLEVELAND WAY (M)
BY IAN SAMPSON. AURUM PRESS. £9.99.
WALKING THE CLEVELAND WAY AND THE MISSING LINK (M)
BY MALCOLM BOYES. CICERONE PRESS. £5.99.
THE CLEVELAND WAY COMPANION (M)
BY PAUL HANNON. HILLSIDE PUBLICATIONS. £5.99.
CLEVELAND WAY ACCOMMODATION GUIDE (A)
AVAILABLE FROM THE CLEVELAND WAY PROJECT OFFICER. SAE.

COAST TO COAST WALK

St. Bees to Robin Hood's Bay

190 miles (304 km)

Wainwright's well-walked route across the Lake District, Yorkshire Dales and North York Moors can be taxing for inexperienced walkers. Links: Cumbria Coastal Way; Cumbria Way; Pennine Way; Cleveland Way.

Maps 89 • 90 • 91 • 92 • 93 • 94 • 98 • 99 (and see Outdoor Leisure 33, 34)

Youth hostels Ennerdale, Black Sail, Honister Hause, Borrowdale, Grasmere, Helvellyn, Patterdale, Kirkby Stephen, Tebay, Keld, Grinton Lodge, Osmotherley, Boggle Hole. YHA camping barns Farndale Barn, Brompton-on-Swale Barn, Richmond Barn, Low Row Barn, Westerdale Barn, Lovesome Hill Barn. YHA Coast to Coast Booking Bureau: YHA Northern Region, PO Box 11, Matlock, Derbys DE4 2XA (enclose large SAE).

Publications
A COAST TO COAST WALK (M)
BY A. WAINWRIGHT. MICHAEL JOSEPH. £9.99.
THE COAST TO COAST WALK (M)
BY PAUL HANNON. HILLSIDE PUBLICATIONS. £7.99.
COAST TO COAST WALK ACCOMMODATION GUIDE (A)
BY AND FROM NORTH YORK MOORS ADVENTURE CENTRE. £3.00.
ALSO AVAILABLE PLUS POSTAGE FROM RA CENTRAL OFFICE. £2.30.
THE NORTHERN COAST TO COAST WALK (MA)
BY TERRY MARSH. CICERONE. £7.99.
AN INTRODUCTION TO THE COAST TO COAST WALK
FREE FACT SHEET AVAILABLE FROM RA CENTRAL OFFICE (SAF).

ALSO SEE: ALTERNATIVE COAST TO COAST WALK (M)
BY DENNIS BROOK AND PHIL HINCHLIFFE. CICERONE PRESS. £9.99.
(NEW AND IMAGINATIVE WALNEY ISLAND TO HOLY ISLAND ROUTE.)

COTSWOLD WAY

Chipping Campden to Bath

100 miles (161 km)

An attractive, well-waymarked route along the escarpment of the Cotswolds. Devised by Glos Area RA and now designated a future National Trail. Links: Heart of England Way.

Maps 150 • 151 • 162 • 163 • 172

Youth hostels Bath

Publications
COTSWOLD WAY HANDBOOK (A)
BY GLOS AREA RA. £1.50. AVAILABLE PLUS POSTAGE FROM RA
CENTRAL OFFICE.
THE COTSWOLD WAY (M)
BY MARK RICHARDS. REARDON PUBLISHING. £3.95. ALSO AVAIL-
ABLE PLUS POSTAGE FROM RA CENTRAL OFFICE.
THE COTSWOLD WAY (M)
BY ANTHONY BURTON. AURUM PRESS. £9.99.
AN INTRODUCTION TO THE COTSWOLD WAY
FREE FACT SHEET AVAILABLE FROM RA CENTRAL OFFICE (SAE).

CUMBRIA WAY

Ulverston to Carlisle

70 miles (112 km)

A great week's walk through the heart of the Lake District, via Coniston, Langdale, Borrowdale and Keswick. Links: Coast to Coast Walk; Cumbria Coastal Way.

Maps 85 • 90 • 97

Youth hostels Coniston, Elterwater, Borrowdale, Derwentwater, Keswick, Carrock Fell, Skiddaw House, Carlisle. YHA Cumbria Way Booking Bureau: YHA Northern Region, PO Box 11, Matlock, Derbys DE4 2XA (enclose large SAE).

Publications
THE CUMBRIA WAY
BY JOHN TREVELYAN. DALESMAN PUBLISHING. £4.95. ALSO AVAILABLE PLUS POSTAGE FROM RA CENTRAL OFFICE.
GUIDE TO THE CUMBRIA WAY (MA)
BY PHILLIP DUBOCK. MIWAY PUBLISHING. £3.75.

* CUMBRIA COASTAL WAY

Milnthorpe to Carlisle

150 miles (240 km)

From Morecambe Bay to the Solway Firth, this new and as yet little-explored trail is a great way of discovering the quieter side of Cumbria; via Ulverston, Barrow and St Bees Head. Links: Cumbria Way; Coast to Coast Walk.

Maps 85 • 89 • 96 • 97

Youth hostels Arnside, Carlisle.

Publications
THE CUMBRIA COASTAL WAY (M)
BY IAN AND KRYSIA BRODIE. ELLENBANK PRESS. £7.99.
CUMBRIA COASTAL WAY
BY AND FROM CUMBRIA COUNTY COUNCIL. FREE LEAFLET (SAE).

DALES WAY

Ilkley to Bowness-on-Windermere

81 miles (130 km)

From the Yorkshire Dales to the Lake District, most of this attractive trail sticks to riverside and valley. Links: Pennine Way. For more information contact the Dales Way Association, Dalegarth, Moorfield Road, Ilkley, West Yorks LS29 8BL

Maps 97 98 104

Youth hostels Linton, Kettlewell, Dentdale, Kendal, Windermere.

Publications
THE DALES WAY HANDBOOK (A)
BY WEST RIDING AREA RA. £1.20. AVAILABLE PLUS POSTAGE FROM RA CENTRAL OFFICE.
THE DALES WAY
BY COLIN SPEAKMAN. DALESMAN PUBLISHING. £5.95. AVAILABLE PLUS POSTAGE FROM RA CENTRAL OFFICE.

DALES WAY COMPANION (M)
BY PAUL HANNON. HILLSIDE PUBLICATIONS. £5.99.
THE DALES WAY BY ANTHONY BURTON. AURUM PRESS. £10.99.

DYFI VALLEY WAY

Aberdyfi to Borth

108 miles (172 km)

From the mouth to the source of the beautiful Afon Dyfi, traditionally the frontier between north and south Wales, then back down the other side. Via Machynlleth and the Centre for Alternative Technology. Links: Cambrian Way; Glyndwr's Way.

Maps 124 • 125 • 135 • 136

Youth hostels Corris, Borth

Publications
THE DYFI VALLEY WAY (M)
BY LAURENCE MAIN. WESTERN MAIL. £7.95.

ESSEX WAY

Epping Station to Harwich Quay

81 miles (130 km)

From Epping Forest, on the edge of north east London, to the coast at Harwich, via Dedham Vale and Constable country.

Maps 167 • 168 • 169

Youth hostels Epping

Publications
THE ESSEX WAY (MA)
BY AND FROM ESSEX COUNTY COUNCIL. £3.00.

GLYNDWR'S WAY

Knighton to Welshpool

120 miles (193 km)

Linking with the Offa's Dyke Path at each end, this mid Wales route goes as far west as Machynlleth (Dyfi Valley Way), and in between enjoys a range of scenery including rough moorland and hillside. Via Llanidloes and Lake Vyrnwy.

Maps 125 • 126 • 135 • 136 • 148

Youth hostels None

Publications
16 ROUTE DESCRIPTION LEAFLETS (M) AND ACCOMMODATION LEAFLET (A) BY AND FROM POWYS COUNTY COUNCIL. NEW EDITION EXPECTED SOON.
OWAIN GLYNDWR'S WAY (M)
BY RICHARD SALE. CONSTABLE. £9.95.

* GRAND UNION CANAL WALK

Paddington, London to Gas Street Basin, Birmingham

145 miles (234 km)

Britain's first National Waterway Walk, linking London and Birmingham city centres. Scenic and undemanding towpath walking, via Tring, Braunston and Warwick. Links: Heart of England Way; London Countryway; Ridgeway.

Maps 139 • 151 • 152 • 165 • 176

Youth hostels Ivinghoe

Publications
THE GRAND UNION CANAL WALK (M)
BY ANTHONY BURTON AND NEIL CURTIS. AURUM PRESS. £9.99.
THE GRAND UNION CANAL WALK (M)
BY CLIVE HOLMES. CICERONE PRESS. £6.99.
GRAND UNION CANAL WALK ACCOMMODATION LIST (A)
BY AND FROM BRITISH WATERWAYS. £1.50.

GREENSAND WAY

Haslemere to Ham Street

105 miles (169 km)

South of London and the North Downs, this gentle walk along the greensand hills of Surrey and Kent visits Haslemere, Dorking and Sevenoaks. Links: North Downs Way; Vanguard Way; London Countryway; Wealdway; Saxon Shore Way.

Maps 186 • 187 • 188 • 189

Youth hostels Hindhead, Holmbury St Mary.

Publications
GREENSAND WAY (SURREY SECTION) (M)
BY AND FROM SURREY COUNTY COUNCIL. £2.50.
THE GREENSAND WAY IN KENT (M)
BY AND FROM KENT COUNTY COUNCIL. £2.95. ALSO AVAILABLE PLUS POSTAGE FROM RA CENTRAL OFFICE.
GREENSAND WAY USER'S GUIDE (A)
AVAILABLE FROM SURREY COUNTY COUNCIL. £1.00.

HEART OF ENGLAND WAY

Cannock Chase to Bourton-on-the-Water

100 miles (161 km)

Gentle, rural route through the Midlands, via Lichfield, Henley- in-Arden and Alcester. Links Oxfordshire Way; Cotswold Way; Staffordshire Way. For more information contact the Heart of England Way Association, 7 Park Lane, Lower Quinton, Stratford on Avon CV37 8SP.

Maps 127 • 128 • 139 • 140 • 150 • 151 • 163

Youth hostels None

Publications
THE HEART OF ENGLAND WAY WALKERS GUIDE (M)
BY JOHN ROBERTS. WALKWAYS. £5.50.

ICKNIELD WAY

Ivinghoe Beacon to Knettishall Heath

105 miles (169 km)

This part of the so-called Great Ridgeway, a route used since prehistoric times, takes travellers from the Chilterns into East Anglia. Links Angles Way; Ridgeway; Peddars Way. For more information

contact the Icknield Way Association, 19 Boundary Road, Bishops Stortford, Herts CM23 5LE.

Maps 144 • 154 • 155 • 165 • 166

Youth hostels Ivinghoe, Brandon.

Publications
THE ICKNIELD WAY - A WALKER'S GUIDE (M)
BY AND FROM ICKNIELD WAY ASSOCIATION (SEE ABOVE). £4.50.
ALSO AVAILABLE PLUS POSTAGE FROM RA CENTRAL OFFICE.

ISLE OF MAN COASTAL PATH

Circular from Douglas

75 miles (121 km)

A fine coastal walk, but the rugged cliffs and moorland can make it a strenuous undertaking. Also known as The Gull's Road, or 'Raad Ny Foillan'.

Maps 95

Youth hostels None

Publications
ISLE OF MAN COASTAL PATH
BY AILEEN EVANS. CICERONE PRESS. £5.99. (INCLUDES DESCRIPTIONS OF THE HERRING WAY AND MILLENNIUM WAY.)
WALKING THE ISLE OF MAN COASTAL PATH
BY JOHN MERRILL. FOOTPRINT PRESS. £3.95.

ISLE OF WIGHT COASTAL PATH

Circular from Ryde

65 miles (105 km)

Island-walking at its best, via clifftops and bays, salt-marshes and chines; and makes for a terrific 4/5 day outing. Good public transport and cross-island linking paths.

Maps 196

Youth hostels Sandown, Totland Bay.

Publications
ISLE OF WIGHT COASTAL PATH (M)
SERIES OF 4 LEAFLETS BY AND FROM ISLE OF WIGHT COUNTY COUNCIL. 35P EACH OR £1.40 FOR THE SET.
THE ISLE OF WIGHT COASTAL PATH (MA)
BY JOHN MERRILL. FOOTPRINT PRESS. £3.25.

KERRY WAY

Circular from Killarney

135 miles (215km)

The Republic of Ireland's longest trail, through Killarney National Park and from Glenbeigh around the Iveragh Peninsula. On footpaths, green roads and a few surfaced lanes. Mainly low-level.

Maps OS (Eire) Discovery Series (1:50 000) 78 • 83 • 84 • 85

Publications
THE KERRY WAY MAP GUIDE (M)
CORDEE. PRICE TO BE ANNOUNCED.
ALSO SEE: WAYMARKED TRAILS OF IRELAND
BY MICHAEL FEWER. MOORLAND PUBLISHING. £9.99.

LANDSKER BORDERLANDS TRAIL

Circular from Canaston Bridge, Dyfed

60 miles (96km)

Attractive tour of the 'frontier' land between Pembrokeshire and Carmarthenshire, east of the Cleddau estuary (and centred on Narberth). Connects with the 60-mile semi-coastal 'South of the Landsker Trail' (details from SPARC).

Maps 158

Youth hostels Lawrenny (opening April 1997)

Publications
THE LANDSKER BORDERLANDS TRAIL (M)
LAMINATED ROUTE CARDS BY SPARC. £2.50.

LONDON COUNTRYWAY

Circular from Box Hill

205 miles (330 km)

Not to be confused with the LOOP (London Outer Orbital Path) which is still under construction, this mammoth circular walking route keeps between 12 and 30 miles from the city centre. Links: Wealdway; Saxon Shore Way; Essex Way; Vanguard Way; North Downs Way; Thames Path.

Maps 165 • 166 • 167 • 175 • 177 • 186 • 187 • 188

Youth hostels Tanners Hatch, Windsor, Bradenham, Epping, Kemsing.

Publications
A GUIDE TO THE LONDON COUNTRYWAY (M)
BY KEITH CHESTERTON. CONSTABLE. £5.95.

NORTH DOWNS WAY

Farnham to Dover

141 miles (227 km)

Via Box Hill, Otford and Wye, with an optional loop to Canterbury, this pleasant National Trail can be walked in day stretches from London. Links: Wealdway; Greensand Way; London Countryway; Vanguard Way; Saxon Shore Way.

Maps 178 • 179 • 186 • 187 • 188 • 189

Youth hostels Tanners Hatch, Holmbury St Mary, Kemsing, Rochester, Canterbury, Dover.

Publications
NATIONAL TRAIL GUIDE: NORTH DOWNS WAY (M)
BY NEIL CURTIS. AURUM PRESS. £9.99.
THE NORTH DOWNS WAY - A USER'S GUIDE (MA)
BY AND FROM KENT COUNTY COUNCIL. £1.00.
NORTH DOWNS WAY (SURREY SECTION) (M)
LEAFLET BY AND FROM SURREY COUNTY COUNCIL. 60P.
A GUIDE TO THE PILGRIM'S WAY AND NORTH DOWNS WAY
BY C. J. WRIGHT. CONSTABLE. £10.95.
NORTH DOWNS WAY BY TRAIN; WILDLIFE ON THE NDW; HISTORIC
BUILDINGS AND ARCHAEOLOGY (NDW); HISTORICAL CHURCHES
(NDW). KENT COUNTY COUNCIL. FREE LEAFLETS.

OFFA'S DYKE PATH

Chepstow to Prestatyn

168 miles (270 km)

A handsome, sometimes exacting south-north National Trail through the unspoilt Welsh borders, via Hay-on-Wye, Knighton, Welshpool and Llangollen. Links: Glyndwr's Way; Wye Valley Walk. For more information contact the Offa's Dyke Association, Offa's Dyke Centre, West Street, Knighton, Powys LD7 1EW.

Maps 116 • 117 • 126 • 137 • 148 • 161 • 162

Youth hostels St Briavel's Castle, Monmouth, Capel-y-ffin, Clun Mill.

Publications
NATIONAL TRAIL GUIDE (2 VOLS) - OFFA'S DYKE PATH SOUTH:
CHEPSTOW TO KNIGHTON (M) AND OFFA'S DYKE PATH NORTH:
KNIGHTON TO PRESTATYN (M)
BOTH BY ERNIE & KATHY KAY AND MARK RICHARDS. AURUM
PRESS. £9.99 EACH.
OFFA'S DYKE PATH: ACCOMMODATION AND TRANSPORT (A)
BY AND FROM OFFA'S DYKE ASSOCIATION (SEE ABOVE). £1.50.
ALSO AVAILABLE PLUS POSTAGE FROM RA CENTRAL OFFICE.
LANGTON'S GUIDE TO THE OFFA'S DYKE PATH (MA)
LANGTON'S GUIDES. £12.99.

OXFORDSHIRE WAY

Bourton-on-the-Water to Henley-on-Thames

65 miles (105 km)

An easy, lowland path that keeps to the north of Oxford, connecting the Cotswolds to the Chilterns. Links: Thames Path; Ridgeway.

Maps 163 • 164 • 165 • 175

Youth hostels Stow-on-the-Wold

Publications
THE OXFORDSHIRE WAY (M)
BY AND FROM OXFORDSHIRE COUNTY COUNCIL. £5.99.

PEDDARS WAY AND NORFOLK COAST PATH

Knettishall Heath, near Thetford, to Cromer

94 miles (138 km)

A trail of two halves: first a Roman road across the low Norfolk countryside via Castle Acre to Holme-next-the-Sea; then a scenic coastal walk past Wells-next-the-Sea and Sheringham. Links: Angles Way; Weavers' Way; Icknield Way.

Maps 132 • 133 • 144

Youth hostels Brandon, Hunstanton, Sheringham.

Publications
NATIONAL TRAIL GUIDE: PEDDARS WAY AND NORFOLK COAST
PATH (M) BY BRUCE ROBINSON. AURUM PRESS. £10.99.
LANGTON'S GUIDE TO THE PEDDAR'S WAY AND NORFOLK COAST
PATH (MA). BY ANDREW DURHAM. LANGTON'S GUIDES. £6.95.

LONG DISTANCE PATHS

WALKING THE PEDDAR'S WAY & NORFOLK COAST PATH WITH THE
WEAVERS WAY (MA) FROM NORFOLK AREA RA, 7 LOWTHER ROAD,
NORWICH NR4 6QN. £2.40.

PEMBROKESHIRE COAST PATH

Amroth to Cardigan

186 miles (299 km)

Via Tenby, Pembroke and Fishguard, the trail takes in high clifftop, wide bays and hidden harbours. Stunning scenery, but some demanding walking from St David's Head to Cardigan.

Maps 145 • 157 • 158

Youth hostels Poppit Sands, Pwll Deri, Trevine, St. David's, Broad Haven, Marloes Sands, Manorbier, Newport, Pentlepoir, Penycwm (Solva).

Publications
NATIONAL TRAIL GUIDE: PEMBROKESHIRE COAST PATH (M)
BY BRIAN JOHN. AURUM PRESS. £9.99.
THE PEMBROKESHIRE COASTAL PATH (MA)
BY DENNIS KELSALL. CICERONE PRESS. £9.99.
ACCOMMODATION GUIDE (A) (£1.50) AND MILEAGE CHART (10P)
FROM PEMBROKESHIRE COAST NATIONAL PARK. (SEE USEFUL
ADDRESSES SECTION, NATIONAL PARKS)

PENNINE WAY

Edale to Kirk Yetholm

256 miles (412 km)

Opened in 1965 it was Britain's first official long distance path, and it remains one of the toughest, if grandest, with long upland stretches of exposed moorland and minimal facilities. Don't make this your first trail. Links: Calderdale Way; Dales Way; Ribble Way; Coast to Coast Walk. For more information contact the Pennine Way Association, 29 Springfield Park Avenue, Chelmsford, Essex CM2 6EL.

Maps 74 • 80 • 86 • 87 • 91 • 92 • 98 • 103 • 109 • 110

Youth hostels Edale, Crowden, Mankinholes, Haworth, Earby, Malham, Stainforth, Hawes, Keld, Baldersdale, Langdon Beck, Dufton, Alston, Green-

head, Once Brewed, Bellingham, Byrness, Kirk Yetholm. YHA camping barns Holwick Barn. YHA Pennine Way Booking Bureau: YHA Northern Region, PO Box 11, Matlock, Derbys DE4 2XA (large SAE).

Publications
NATIONAL TRAIL GUIDE (2 VOLS) - PENNINE WAY SOUTH: EDALE TO
BOWES (M) AND PENNINE WAY NORTH: BOWES TO KIRK YETHOLM
(M) BOTH BY TONY HOPKINS. AURUM PRESS. £9.99 EACH.
PENNINE WAY COMPANION (M)
BY A. WAINWRIGHT. MICHAEL JOSEPH. £9.99.
PENNINE WAY ACCOMMODATION AND CAMPING GUIDE (A)
90P. AVAILABLE PLUS POSTAGE FROM RA CENTRAL OFFICE.
AN INTRODUCTION TO THE PENNINE WAY
FREE FACT SHEET AVAILABLE FROM RA CENTRAL OFFICE (SAE).
ALSO SEE: ALTERNATIVE PENNINE WAY (M)
BY DENIS BROOK AND PHIL HINCHLIFFE. CICERONE PRESS. £8.99.
(ASHBOURNE TO JEDBURGH ROUTE.)

RIBBLE WAY

Dolphin Inn, Longton to Gayle Moor, south of Hawes

72 miles (118 km)

An interesting mouth to source route, from near Preston to high on the Pennine moors; via Ribchester, Clitheroe, Gisburn and Settle. Links: Pennine Way; Dales Way.

Maps 98 • 102 • 103

Youth hostels Stainforth ('Taitlands'). YHA camping barns: Giggleswick, Downham and Hurst Green.

Publications
THE RIBBLE WAY (M)
BY GLADYS SELLERS. CICERONE PRESS. £5.99.
THE RIBBLE WAY BY AND FROM LANCS COUNTY COUNCIL. 90P.

THE RIDGEWAY ✿

Overton Hill, near Avebury to Ivinghoe Beacon

85 miles (137 km)

From Avebury to the Thames at Goring it is a high, open downland track, then it enters the wooded Chilterns and a more pastoral landscape. Links: Wessex Ridgeway; Icknield Way; Thames Path; Oxfordshire Way. For further details contact Friends of the Ridgeway, 90 South Hill Park, London NW3 2SN.

Maps 165 • 173 • 174 • 175

Youth hostels Ivinghoe, Bradenham, The Ridgeway, Streatley.

Publications
NATIONAL TRAIL GUIDE: THE RIDGEWAY (M)
BY NEIL CURTIS. AURUM PRESS. £9.99.
EXPLORING THE RIDGEWAY (A)
BY ALAN CHARLES. COUNTRYSIDE BOOKS. £4.95. ALSO AVAILABLE
FROM RA CENTRAL OFFICE.
1. RIDGEWAY INFORMATION & ACCOMMODATION GUIDE. £1.50.
2. RIDGEWAY INFORMATION LEAFLET PACK. £2.00.
3. RIDGEWAY ROUTE PACKS (WALKS AND EVENTS). £2.00.
4. FAMILY WALKS ACTIVITY BOOK. £2.75.
ALL AVAILABLE FROM THE RIDGEWAY OFFICE AT OXFORDSHIRE
COUNTY COUNCIL.

LONG DISTANCE PATHS

ROBIN HOOD WAY

Starts at Nottingham Castle, ends at various places

105 miles (165 km)

A long distance path with a series of circular off-shoots, usually beginning at Nottingham Castle, that explores Sherwood Forest and the Nottinghamshire countryside north of the Trent.

Maps 120 • 129

Youth hostels None

Publications
THE ROBIN HOOD WALKS (M)
(INCLUDES 14 CIRCULAR WALKS BASED ON THE TRAIL) BY NOTTINGHAM WAYFARERS' RAMBLING CLUB. CORDEE. £4.95.

SAINTS WAY

Padstow to Fowey

37 miles (59km)

A short and easy route of footpaths and lanes across the peninsula vaguely tracing the steps of Celtic saints.

Maps 200 • 204

Youth hostels Golant

Publications
THE SAINTS WAY (MA) BY CORNWALL COUNTY COUNCIL. £2.50.

SAXON SHORE WAY

Gravesend to Rye

135 miles (217 km)

From marsh and pebbly bays to chalk cliffs, this diverse route around Kent's coast is full of surprises and historical connections. Links: Greensand Way; North Downs Way; London Countryway.

Maps 177 • 178 • 179 • 189

Youth hostels Broadstairs, Dover.

Publications
SAXON SHORE WAY (M) BY BEA COWAN. AURUM PRESS. £9.99.
SAXON SHORE WAY WALKS: SHORNE AND HIGHAM MARSHES;
BROCKHILL COUNTRY PARK (£1.45 EACH); SWALE HERITAGE TRAIL
(£1.95). BY AND FROM KENT COUNTY COUNCIL.

✳ SEVERN WAY

66 miles (105 km)

Tewkesbury to Pill, near Avonmouth

East bank route via Gloucester and Slimbridge. There are plans to extend the route upstream via Shrewsbury and Welshpool all the way to the Severn's source near Plynlimon, potentially making it a river walk to match the Thames.

Maps 150 • 162 • 172

Youth hostels Slimbridge

Publications
GUIDE TO THE SEVERN WAY: EAST BANK (M)

BY STANLEY GIDMAN. GLOS COUNTY COUNCIL. £3.50. (COVERS GLOS SECTION ONLY: TEWKESBURY TO SHEPPERDINE)

SHROPSHIRE WAY

Circular from Wem

125 miles (201 km)

This trail is a great way to get to know the Shropshire countryside, visiting Shrewsbury, Ludlow, the Stiperstones, Clun, the Clee Hills, Wenlock Edge and the Wrekin, with extensions north towards Chester and west to link with the Offa's Dyke Path.

Maps 117 • 126 • 127 • 137 • 138

Youth hostels Bridges, Clun Mill, Ironbridge, Ludlow, Shrewsbury, Wheathill, Wilderhope Manor.

Publications
RAMBLER'S GUIDE TO THE SHROPSHIRE WAY
BY SHROPSHIRE AREA RA. AVAILABLE FROM POWNEY'S BOOKSHOP
(SEE PUBLISHERS' ADDRESSES). £5.99 (ADD £1.00 POSTAGE).

✳ SOLENT WAY

Milford-on-Sea to Emsworth

60 miles (96 km)

With yachts, ferries and supertankers your constant companions, Hampshire's seaboard walk via Portsmouth and Southampton will never be dull. Includes a stretch through the New Forest.

Maps 195 • 196 • 197

Youth hostels Portsmouth

Publications
EXPLORING THE SOLENT WAY (M)
BY ANNE-MARIE EDWARDS. COUNTRYSIDE BOOKS. £5.95. (ALSO
INCLUDES AN EXTENSION TO CHRISTCHURCH, DORSET.)
THE SOLENT WAY
HAMPSHIRE COUNTY COUNCIL. FREE LEAFLET.

SOUTH DOWNS WAY

Eastbourne to Winchester

106 miles (171 km)

The South East's premier trail, across the billowing, green downs of Sussex and through the woods and farmland of Hampshire. Splendid walking. Links: Vanguard Way; Wealdway; Three Castles Path.

Maps 185 • 197 • 198 • 199

Youth hostels Eastbourne, Alfriston, Telscombe, Truleigh Hill, Arundel, Winchester.

Publications
NATIONAL TRAIL GUIDE: SOUTH DOWNS WAY (M)
BY PAUL MILLMORE. AURUM PRESS. £10.99.
ALONG THE SOUTH DOWNS WAY TO WINCHESTER (MA)
BY THE SOCIETY OF SUSSEX DOWNSMEN. £5.00. AVAILABLE PLUS
POSTAGE FROM RA CENTRAL OFFICE.
THE SOUTH DOWNS WAY & THE DOWNS LINK
BY KEV REYNOLDS. CICERONE PRESS. £5.99.

LONG DISTANCE PATHS

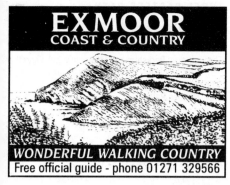

EXMOOR
COAST & COUNTRY

WONDERFUL WALKING COUNTRY
Free official guide - phone 01271 329566

SOUTH WEST COAST PATH

Minehead to Poole

approximately 600 miles (965 km)

Britain's longest and perhaps most exhilarating National Trail, incorporating most of the coastline of Somerset, Dorset, Devon and Cornwall. Sometimes tough, always rewarding, enjoy it for a day or a fortnight at a time. Links: Tarka Trail; Two Moors Way; Wessex Ridgeway. For more information contact the South West Way Association, Windlestraw, Penquit, Ermington, Ivybridge, Devon PL21 0LU.

Maps Somerset and North Devon: 180 • 181 • 190
Cornwall 190 • 200 • 201 • 203 • 204
South Devon 192 • 193 • 201 • 202
Dorset 193 • 194 • 195

Youth hostels Minehead, Lynton, Instow, Elmscott, Boscastle, Tintagel, Treyarnon Bay, Newquay, Perranporth, Land's End, Penzance, Coverack, Pendennis Castle, Boswinger, Golant, Plymouth, Salcombe, Maypool, Beer, Bridport, Litton Cheney, Lulworth Cove, Swanage.

Publications
NATIONAL TRAIL GUIDE (4 VOLS) - SOUTH WEST COAST PATH: MINEHEAD TO PADSTOW (M) BY ROLAND TARR; PADSTOW TO FALMOUTH (M) BY JOHN MACADAM; FALMOUTH TO EXMOUTH (M) BY BRIAN LE MESSURIER; EXMOUTH TO POOLE (M) BY ROLAND TARR. AURUM PRESS. £10.99 EACH.
SOUTH WEST WAY ASSOCIATION GUIDE (A)
£3.99. AVAILABLE PLUS POSTAGE FROM RA CENTRAL OFFICE.
SOUTH WEST WAY VOL 1: MINEHEAD TO PENZANCE (M) AND VOL 2: PENZANCE TO POOLE (M)
BOTH BY MARTIN COLLINS. CICERONE PRESS. £8.99 EACH.

SOUTHERN UPLAND WAY

Portpatrick to Cockburnspath

212 miles (341 km)

A long and solitary coast to coast route across southern Scotland, via Sanquhar, Moffatt, St Mary's Loch and Melrose. Its remoteness deters the crowds, which is recommendation enough. Links to the Pennine Way via the newly-opened St Cuthbert Way.

Maps 67 • 73 • 74 • 77 • 78 • 79 • 82

Youth hostels Minnigaff, Kendoon, Wanlockhead, Broadmeadows, Melrose, Abbey St. Bathans, Coldingham.

Publications
THE SOUTHERN UPLAND WAY (M)
BY ROGER SMITH. INCLUDES TWO 1:50,000 ROUTE MAPS. HMSO. £17.50.
SOUTHERN UPLAND WAY INFORMATION & ACCOMMODATION LEAFLET (A).AVAILABLE FROM DUMFRIES & GALLOWAY REGIONAL COUNCIL. FREE.
A GUIDE TO THE SOUTHERN UPLAND WAY
BY DAVID WILLIAMS. CONSTABLE. £9.95.

SPEYSIDE WAY

Tugnet, on the coast at Spey Bay, to Tomintoul, in the Cairngorm foothills

45 miles (81 km)

Spey Bay to Ballindalloch provides fairly easy walking, but then it climbs steeply. The last section is remote and exposed.

Maps 28 • 36

Youth hostels Tomintoul.

Publications
THE SPEYSIDE WAY (MA)
INFORMATION PACK BY AND FROM MORAY COUNCIL. FREE (SAE).

STAFFORDSHIRE WAY

Mow Cop Castle to Kinver Edge

93 miles (148 km)

A trail that offers a splendid combination of rocky outcrops, canal towpaths, woodland and sandy heathland. Via Leek, Uttoxter, Abbots Bromley and Penkridge. Links: Heart of England Way.

Maps 118 • 127 • 128 • 138

Youth hostels Dimmingsdale, Meerbrook.

Publications
STAFFORDSHIRE WAY (M)
BY AND FROM STAFFORDSHIRE COUNTY COUNCIL. £5.00. PLUS ACCOMMODATION LEAFLET (A) (FREE).
THE STAFFORDSHIRE WAY
BY LES LUMSDON AND CHRIS RUSHTON. SIGMA LEISURE. £6.95.
WHERE TO STAY ALONG THE STAFFORDSHIRE WAY (A)
BY STAFFS AREA RA. ALSO AVAILABLE FROM RA CENTRAL OFFICE. FREE (SAE).

✳ STOUR VALLEY PATH

60 miles (96 km)

Newmarket to Cattawade, Suffolk

Attractive, gentle trail following the course of the meandering River Stour via Sudbury, most of which forms the Suffolk/Essex border. Classic English lowland countryside. Links: Icknield Way; Essex Way.

Maps 154 • 155 • 168 • 169

Youth hostels None

Publications
STOUR VALLEY PATH (MA)
BY AND FROM SUFFOLK COUNTY COUNCIL. £1.80.

TAFF TRAIL

Cardiff to Brecon

55 miles (88km)

Walking and cycling route via towpaths and former railways lines along the Taff valley, from Cardiff Bay to the Brecon Beacons via Llandaff, Pontypridd and Merthyr Tydfil. Links: Cambrian Way.

Maps 160 • 161 • 170 • 171

Youth hostels Cardiff, Llwyn-y-Celyn.

Publications
THE TAFF TRAIL (M)
BY JEFF VINTER. ALAN SUTTON PUBLISHING. £6.99.

TARKA TRAIL

Usually started at Barnstaple

180 miles (290 km)

Forms a huge figure of eight around the Devon countryside, centred on Barnstaple, and includes sections of coast and moorland. Links: South West Coast Path; Two Moors Way.

Maps 180 • 191

Youth hostels Ilfracombe, Instow, Lynton. YHA camping barns Great Potheridge, Higher Cadham, Chenson, Sticklepath.

Publications
THE TARKA TRAIL: A WALKER'S GUIDE
BY THE TARKA PROJECT. DEVON BOOKS. £3.95.

THAMES PATH

Thames Head, Gloucestershire to Thames Barrier, London

180 miles (288 km)

The newest National Trail is a majestic riverside walk from a Cotswold meadow to a capital city. Via Lechlade, Oxford, Henley and Windsor. Links: Oxfordshire Way; Ridgeway; London Countryway.

Maps 163 • 164 • 174 • 175 • 176

Youth hostels Oxford, Streatley, Windsor, London.

Publications
NATIONAL TRAIL GUIDE: THE THAMES PATH (M)
BY DAVID SHARP. AURUM PRESS. £12.99. (INCLUDES ROUTE DESCRIPTION FOR BOTH BANKS FROM TEDDINGTON TO THE BARRIER.) ALSO AVAILABLE PLUS POSTAGE FROM RA CENTRAL OFFICE.

Do you know your rights when you're out walking in the countryside?
See pages 32-39

LONG DISTANCE PATHS

THREE CASTLES PATH

Windsor to Winchester

60 miles (96 km)

Through rural Berkshire and Hampshire following the 13th century journeys of King John via his castle at Odiham. Links: London Countryway; South Downs Way; Thames Path.

Maps 175 • 186 • 185

Youth hostels Windsor, Winchester

Publications
THREE CASTLES PATH (M)
BY EAST BERKS RA. (ACCOMMODATION LEAFLET (A) ALSO AVAILABLE.) £2.50. GUIDEBOOK AVAILABLE PLUS POSTAGE FROM RA CENTRAL OFFICE.

TWO MOORS WAY

Ivybridge to Lynmouth

103 miles (166 km)

Linking Dartmoor to Exmoor and the north Devon coast, this hilly and attractive route via Drewsteignton is not waymarked on the open moor, and use of a compass may be necessary. Links: South West Coast Path; Tarka Trail. For more information contact the Two Moors Way Association, 'Coppins', The Poplars, Pinhoe, Exeter, Devon EX4 9HH.

Maps 180 • 181 • 191 • 202

Youth hostels Lynton, Exford, Bellever. YHA camping barns Holne, Runnage, Watercombe.

Publications
TWO MOORS WAY (M)
BY AND FROM TWO MOORS WAY ASSOCIATION. £3.00. ALSO AVAILABLE PLUS POSTAGE FROM RA CENTRAL OFFICE.
TWO MOORS WAY ACCOMMODATION LEAFLET (A)
FROM TWO MOORS WAY ASSOCIATION (SEE ABOVE). 25P (SAE).
THE TWO MOORS WAY (M)
BY JAMES ROBERTS. CICERONE PRESS. £5.99.

ULSTER WAY

Circular from Belfast

570 miles (920 km)

A massive route encircling nearly the whole of Northern Ireland, via the Mournes and the Sperrins, the lakes of Fermanagh, and the Antrim and Causeway coasts. Many sections remain little-walked, and waymarking is not continuous.

Maps 18 Discovery maps (1:50 000) cover the route. Details from Ordnance Survey of Northern Ireland (see Useful Addresses)

Publications
WALKING THE ULSTER WAY
BY ALAN WARNER. APPLETREE PRESS. £5.95
AN INFORMATION GUIDE TO WALKING (14 CIRCULAR WALKS ON THE ULSTER WAY) (M) AND ACCOMMODATION LEAFLET (A). FROM NORTHERN IRELAND TOURIST BOARD. BOTH FREE.

VANGUARD WAY

Croydon to Seaford

63 miles (101 km)

East Croydon Station is the unlikely start for this pleasant walk via Crockham Hill and Forest Row to the south coast at Seaford, East Sussex. Links: North Downs Way; London Countryway; Wealdway; South Downs Way.

Maps 187 • 188 • 199 • 198

Youth hostels Blackboys, Alfriston.

Publications
THE VANGUARD WAY (MA)
BY VANGUARDS RAMBLING CLUB. £1.35
AVAILABLE PLUS POSTAGE FROM RA CENTRAL OFFICE.
THE WEALDWAY AND THE VANGUARD WAY (M)
BY KEV REYNOLDS. CICERONE PRESS. £4.99.

VIKING WAY

Barton-upon-Humber to Oakham

140 miles (225 km)

From underneath the Humber Bridge along the Lincs Wolds to Horncastle, then via Lincoln and gentle lowland scenery to end near Rutland Water. Recently improved route. Links: Wolds Way via the Humber Bridge.

Maps 112 • 113 • 121 • 122 • 130 • 141

Youth hostels Lincoln, Woody's Top, Thurlby.

Publications
NEW, OFFICIAL GUIDE DUE OUT EARLY 1997. CONTACT LIN-
COLNSHIRE COUNTY COUNCIL FOR DETAILS.
VIKING WAY FACT SHEET (A)
BY AND FROM LINCS COUNTY COUNCIL (A4 SAE/35P POSTAGE).
BARDNEY TO LINCOLN (RECOMMENDED ALTERNATIVE ROUTE) AND
VIKING WAY ACCOMMODATION LEAFLET (A). 30P EACH (SAE). BOTH
AVAILABLE FROM LINCOLNSHIRE AREA RA, CHLORIS HOUSE, 208
NETTLEHAM ROAD, LINCOLN LN2 4DH.
THE VIKING WAY (M) BY JOHN STEAD. CICERONE PRESS. £5.99.

WEALDWAY

Gravesend to Eastbourne

80 miles (129 km)

Another north-south route to the sea, via Ashdown Forest and the ancient Weald of Kent and Sussex. Links: North and South Downs Ways; Greensand Way; London Countryway; Saxon Shore Way; Vanguard Way.

Maps 117 • 188 • 198 • 199

Youth hostels Blackboys, Alfriston, Eastbourne.

Publications
THE WEALDWAY (M)
BY GEOFFREY KING. £3.50. ALSO AVAILABLE PLUS POSTAGE FROM
RA CENTRAL OFFICE OR FOLLOWING ADDRESS.
WEALDWAY ACCOMMODATION LEAFLET (A). £1.00. AVAILABLE
FROM RAMBLERS' ASSOCIATION, 11 OLD LONDON ROAD,
BRIGHTON, SUSSEX BN1 8XR.

THE WEALDWAY AND THE VANGUARD WAY (M)
BY KEV REYNOLDS. CICERONE PRESS. £4.99.

WEAVERS WAY

Cromer to Great Yarmouth

56 miles (90 km)

An inland route through rural Norfolk and the unspoilt Norfolk Broads, via Aylsham and North Walsham. Links with the Peddars Way and Norfolk Coast Path at one end and the Angles Way at the other.

Maps 133 • 134

Youth hostels Great Yarmouth

Publications
LANGTON'S GUIDE TO THE WEAVERS WAY AND ANGLES WAY (MA)
LANGTON'S GUIDES. £6.95.
WALKING THE PEDDAR'S WAY & NORFOLK COAST PATH WITH THE
WEAVERS WAY (MA) FROM NORFOLK AREA RA, 7 LOWTHER ROAD,
NORWICH NR4 6QN. £2.40.

WESSEX RIDGEWAY

Marlborough to Lyme Regis

136 miles (219 km)

From the Wessex Downs via the edge of Salisbury Plain and Cranborne Chase to the Dorset coast. Waymarked in places. Links: South West Coast Path; Ridgeway National Trail.

Maps 173 • 183 • 184 • 193 • 194 • 195

Youth hostels None

Publications
WALK THE WESSEX RIDGEWAY IN DORSET (MA)
BY PRISCILLA HOUSTOUN. DORSET PUBLISHING COMPANY. £5.95.
(DORSET SECTION ONLY.)

WEST HIGHLAND WAY

Milngavie, Glasgow, to Fort William

95 miles (153 km)

Via the shores of Loch Lomond, the vastness of Rannoch Moor, and the grandeur of Glencoe, this relatively short trail is deservedly popular. But beware the summer midges, and don't underestimate the mountain weather and conditions.

Maps 41 • 50 • 56 • 57 • 64

Youth hostels Rowardennan, Crianlarich, Glen Nevis.

Publications
WEST HIGHLAND WAY (M)
BY ROGER SMITH. INCLUDES 1:50,000 ROUTE MAP. HMSO. £14.95.
WEST HIGHLAND WAY INFORMATION & ACCOMMODATION LEAFLET
(A). AVAILABLE FROM WEST HIGHLAND WAY PATH MANAGER
(SOUTH). FREE.
THE WEST HIGHLAND WAY (M)
BY ANTHONY BURTON. AURUM PRESS. £9.99.

WEST MENDIP WAY

Wells to Uphill, Weston-super-Mare

30 miles (48 km)

A short, scenic and undulating route across the Mendip Hills to the sea, visiting Wookey Hole and Cheddar Gorge. Can be continued eastwards along the newly-formed East Mendip Way, from Wells to Frome via Shepton Mallet.

Maps 182

Youth hostels Cheddar

Publications
THE WEST MENDIP WAY (M)
BY ANDREW EDDY. £1.75. WESTON-SUPER-MARE HERITAGE CENTRE.

* WHITE PEAK WAY

Circular from Bakewell

90 miles (144 km)

A circular route through the glorious limestone country of Derbyshire's White Peak, broken down into seven stages that all finish at youth hostels.

Maps 110 • 119

Youth hostels Bakewell, Youlgreave, Ilam, Hartington, Ravenstor, Castleton, Hathersage. YHA White Peak Way Booking Bureau: YHA Northern Region, PO Box 11, Matlock, Derbys DE4 2XA (large SAE).

Publication
THE WHITE PEAK WAY (M)
BY ROBERT HASLAM. CICERONE PRESS. £4.99.

THE WICKLOW WAY

Marlay Park, south of Dublin, to Clonegal

82 miles (132 km)

A varied route that begins on the southern edge of Dublin, then climbs through the Dublin and Wicklow Mountains, and ends in the gentle farmland of County Carlow.

Maps Sheet 50 • 56 • 62 - Wicklow (1:50 000) from OS (Eire). £3.90.

Publications
THE COMPLETE WICKLOW WAY (M)
BY J. B. MALONE. O'BRIEN PRESS. £5.95.
THE WICKLOW WAY MAP GUIDE (INCLUDES 1:50,000 ROUTE MAP) FROM EASTWEST MAPPING. £5 (INCL. POSTAGE).
ALSO SEE: WAYMARKED TRAILS OF IRELAND
BY MICHAEL FEWER. MOORLAND PUBLISHING. £9.99.

WOLDS WAY

Filey to Hessle, Kingston upon Hull

79 miles (127 km)

Linking the North Sea to the River Humber, this unfashionable National Trail explores the gentle chalk hills of the Yorkshire Wolds, via Market Weighton.

Links: Cleveland Way; Viking Way.

Maps 100 • 101 • 106 • 107

Youth hostels Thixendale.

Publications
NATIONAL TRAIL GUIDE: WOLDS WAY (M)
BY ROGER RATCLIFFE. AURUM PRESS. £9.99.

WYE VALLEY WALK

Chepstow to Rhayader

107 miles (172 km)

Follows the course of the lovely River Wye via Monmouth, Ross-on- Wye, Hereford and Builth Wells, usually along the riverbank and sometimes high up the valley sides. Links: Offa's Dyke Path.

Maps 147 • 148 • 149 • 161 • 162

Youth hostels St Briavel's Castle, Monmouth, Welsh Bicknor.

Publications
WYE VALLEY WALK (HAY-ON-WYE TO RHAYADER) (M)
SET OF 8 CARDS BY AND FROM POWYS COUNTY COUNCIL. £2.50. NEW, OFFICIAL GUIDE TO WHOLE ROUTE DUE OUT SOON.
ACCOMMODATION GUIDE (A)
BY AND FROM POWYS COUNTY COUNCIL. FREE.
WALKING DOWN THE WYE (M)
BY DAVID HUNTER. CICERONE PRESS. £6.99.

OTHER TRAILS

For full details of what maps and guidebooks you will need and where to get hold of them consult the *Long Distance Walkers' Handbook* by the LDWA (A & C Black, £9.99); or the RA's series of 22 *Regional Walking Guides* (short booklets that cost 25p each + 25p postage, from RA central office).

SOUTHERN & SW ENGLAND

Connecting the North and South Downs Way is the 30-mile **Downs Link**, while the **Sussex Border Path** extends for over 150 miles from Emsworth to Rye along rights of way as close to the county border as possible, and joining it at Emsworth is Hampshire County Council's 71-mile **Wayfarer's Walk**. The **Leland Trail** follows a quiet 38-mile route through south Somerset, from Alfred's Tower to Ham Street; while the **King's Way**, developed by Hampshire RA, links Portchester to Winchester. In South East London the 39-mile **Green Chain Walk** joins dozens of green spaces, commons and parks; and heading west the **Kennet & Avon Canal Path** runs for 86 miles from Reading to Bristol. Also worth exploring is the newly-created **North Cotswold Diamond Way**, a 60-mile circular walk from Moreton in Marsh.

CENTRAL & EASTERN ENGLAND

The 102-mile **Hereward Way** crosses the Fens from Oakham to Thetford; while further south the **North Bucks Way** connects Chequers Knap and Milton Keynes, and is one of a network of trails throughout the county. The **Suffolk Coast and Heaths Path** runs for 50 miles south from Lowestoft, and the **Jurassic Way** from Banbury to Stamford. Two other new but much longer trails are the **Midshires Way**, 225 miles from Bledlow to Stockport, and the **Macmillan Way**. This stretches 235 miles from Oakham to Abbotsbury in Dorset, and all profits are donated to the Cancer Relief Macmillan Fund. Currently under development is the **Lee Valley Walk**, which will run the length of the valley from Bow in East London to Luton when complete.

NORTHERN ENGLAND

Cheshire County Council manage the short but scenic **Sandstone** and **Gritstone Trails**; while the **Cestrian Link Path** usefully connects the Offa's Dyke and Pennine Way National Trails (Prestatyn to Edale). The **Nidderdale Way** is a circular, 53-mile route around the moors of North Yorkshire; while in the North East the **Weardale Way** (Monkwearmouth to Cowshill, 78 miles) and the **Teesdale Way** (Middleton-in-Teesdale to Middlesbrough, 140 miles) explore the lengths of two enticing Pennine rivers. On the West Coast avoid the Lake District crowds by exploring the **Westmorland Way** (Appleby to Arnside) or **Eden Way**, 91 miles along the Eden valley from near Carlisle to

Mallerstang. And in Lancashire the 45-mile **Pendle Way** and newly-created **Lancashire Coastal Way** are both full of interest. Finally, 1996 saw the opening of the **Trans Pennine Trail**, the new coast to coast route from Southport (Liverpool) to Hornsea (Hull).

SCOTLAND, WALES & IRELAND

In Scotland the **Fife Coast Path** is under development, and will eventually link the Firths of Forth and Tay. Meanwhile in the Borders the newly-opened **St Cuthbert Way** connects the Southern Upland Way (at Melrose) with the Pennine Way (at Kirk Yetholm), and stretches 62 miles to the North Sea at Lindisfarne. Three short but attractive trails in South Wales to explore are the **Sirhowy Valley Walk** from Tredegar to Newport, **Usk Valley Walk** from Caerleon to Brecon via Abergavenny, and the **Coed Morgannwg Way** via the wooded hills east of Neath. The **Mortimer Trail**, through the Marches between Ludlow and Kington, is also recommended. For long distance walkers planning to cross the Irish Sea contact the Irish Tourist Board for a copy of *Walking Ireland: The Waymarked Ways*, an excellent booklet guide to the top 20 trails in Ireland (it includes the **Dingle Way, Beara Way, Leitrim Way** and **Slieve Bloom Way**). Contact ITB, 150 New Bond Street, London W1Y 0AQ or Bord Failte, Baggot Street Bridge, Dublin 2, Ireland.

PUBLISHERS' ADDRESSES

APPLETREE PRESS TITLES DISTRIBUTED BY BOOKPOINT LTD, 39 MILTON PARK, ABINGDON, OXFORD OX14 4TD
AURUM PRESS 25 BEDFORD AVENUE, LONDON WC1B 3AT
BRITISH WATERWAYS MARSWORTH JUNCTION, WATERY LANE, MARSWORTH, TRING, HERTS HP23 4LZ
METROPOLITAN BOROUGH OF CALDERDALE TOURIST INFORMATION CENTRE, PIECE HALL, HALIFAX HX1 1RE
CHESHIRE COUNTY COUNCIL HERITAGE AND RECREATION, GOLDSMITH HOUSE, HAMILTON PLACE, CHESTER CH1 1FE
CICERONE PRESS 2 POLICE SQ, MILNTHORPE, CUMBRIA LA7 7PY
CLEVELAND WAY PROJECT OFFICER NORTH YORK MOORS NATIONAL PARK OFFICE, THE OLD VICARAGE, BONDGATE, HELMSLEY, NORTH YORKS YO6 5BP
CONSTABLE 3 THE LANCHESTERS, 162 FULHAM PALACE ROAD, LONDON W6 9ER

CORDEE 3A DE MONTFORT STREET, LEICESTER LE1 7HD
CORNWALL COUNTY COUNCIL TRANSPORTATION AND ESTATES, CASTLE CANYKE ROAD, BODMIN PL31 1DZ
COUNTRYSIDE BOOKS HIGHFIELD HOUSE, 2 HIGHFIELD AVENUE, NEWBURY, BERKS RG14 5DS
CUMBRIA COUNTY COUNCIL RIGHTS OF WAY SECTION, CONSULTANCY AND DESIGN DIVISION, VIADUCT ESTATE ROAD, CARLISLE, CUMBRIA CA2 5BN
DALESMAN PUBLISHING CLAPHAM, VIA LANCASTER LA2 8EB
DEVON BOOKS (SEE HALSGROVE)
DORSET PUBLISHING COMPANY (SEE HALSGROVE)
A. J. DRAKE 2 BEECH LODGE, WOODLEIGH, 67 THE PARK, CHELTENHAM, GLOS GL50 2RX
DUMFRIES & GALLOWAY REGIONAL COUNCIL DEPT OF ENVIRONMENT & INFRASTRUCTURE, PLANNING & BUILDING CONTROL SERVICES, KIRKBANK, ENGLISH ST, DUMFRIES DG1 2DD
EASTWEST MAPPING BALLYREDMOND, CLONEGAL, ENNISCORTHY, CO WEXFORD, IRELAND
ELLENBANK PRESS PARK HILL SOUTH, CAMP ROAD, MARYPORT, CUMBRIA CA15 6JN
ESSEX COUNTY COUNCIL WAYS THROUGH ESSEX, PLANNING DEPT, COUNTY HALL, CHELMSFORD CM1 1LF
FOOTPRINT PRESS 19 MOSELEY STREET, RIPLEY, DERBYS DE5 3DA
GLOUCESTERSHIRE COUNTY COUNCIL RIGHTS OF WAY SECTION, ENVIRONMENT DEPT, GLOS COUNTY COUNCIL, BEARLAND, GLOUCESTER GL1 2TH
HALSGROVE HALSGROVE HOUSE, LOWER MOOR WAY, TIVERTON BUSINESS PARK, TIVERTON, DEVON EX16 6SS
HAMPSHIRE COUNTY COUNCIL COUNTRYSIDE AND COMMUNITY DEPT, MOTTISFONT COURT, HIGH STREET, WINCHESTER, HANTS SO23 8ZF
HILLSIDE PUBLICATIONS 11 NESSFIELD GROVE, KEIGHLEY, WEST YORKS BD22 6NU
HMSO PUBLICATIONS PO BOX 276, LONDON SW8 5DR
ISLE OF WIGHT COUNTY COUNCIL WALKING LEAFLETS AVAILABLE FROM SHANKLIN TOURIST INFORMATION CENTRE, HIGH STREET, SHANKLIN, ISLE OF WIGHT PO37 6JJ
KENT COUNTY COUNCIL ACCESS & RECREATION OFFICER, PLANNING DEPT, SPRINGFIELD, MAIDSTONE, KENT ME14 2LX
LANCASHIRE COUNTY COUNCIL PLANNING DEPT, PO BOX 160, EAST CLIFF COUNTY OFFICES, PRESTON PR1 3EX
LANGTON'S GUIDES ASHLEIGH, RADLEY ROAD, HALAM, NEWARK, NOTTS NG22 8AQ
LINCOLNSHIRE COUNTY COUNCIL ENVIRONMENTAL SERVICES DEPT, COUNTY OFFICES, LINCOLN LN1 1YL
MICHAEL JOSEPH (PENGUIN) 27 WRIGHTS LANE, LONDON W8 5TZ
MIWAY PUBLISHING PO BOX 2, KESWICK, CUMBRIA CA12 4GA

MOORLAND PUBLISHING MOOR FRAM ROAD, AIRFIELD INDUSTRIAL ESTATE, ASHBOURNE, DERBYS DE6 1HD
MORAY DISTRICT COUNCIL DEPT OF LEISURE AND LIBRARIES, DISTRICT HEADQUARTERS, HIGH STREET, ELGIN, MORAYSHIRE IV30 1BX
NORTHERN IRELAND TOURIST BOARD 11 BERKELEY STREET, LONDON W1X 6BU
NORTH YORK MOORS ADVENTURE CENTRE PARK HOUSE, INGLEBY CROSS, NORTHALLERTON, NORTH YORKS DL6 3PE
O'BRIEN PRESS 20 VICTORIA ROAD, DUBLIN 6, IRELAND
ORDNANCE SURVEY (EIRE) PHOENIX PARK, DUBLIN 8, IRELAND (MAPS ALSO AVAILABLE FROM STANFORDS, CORDEE AND OTHER UK OUTLETS)
OXFORDSHIRE COUNTY COUNCIL DEPARTMENT OF LEISURE AND ARTS, COUNTRYSIDE SERVICES, LIBRARY HEADQUARTERS, HOLTON, OXFORD OX33 1QQ
POWNEY'S BOOKSHOP 4-5 ST ALKMUND'S PLACE, SHREWSBURY SY1 1UJ
POWYS COUNTY COUNCIL RIGHTS OF WAY SECTION, PLANNING DEPT, COUNTY HALL, LLANDRINDOD WELLS, POWYS LD1 5LE
RA CENTRAL OFFICE 1/5 WANDSWORTH ROAD, LONDON SW8 2XX FOR LOCAL RA PUBLICATIONS SEE RA AREA CONTACTS SECTION
REARDON PUBLISHING 56 UPPER NORWOOD STREET, LECKHAMPTON, CHELTENHAM, GLOS GL53 0DU
SIGMA LEISURE 1 SOUTH OAK LANE, WILMSLOW, CHESHIRE SK9 6AR
SPARC (SOUTH PEMBROKESHIRE PARTNERSHIP FOR ACTION WITH RURAL COMMUNITIES) THE OLD SCHOOL, STATION ROAD, NARBERTH, PEMBROKESHIRE SA67 2LE
STAFFORDSHIRE COUNTY COUNCIL CULTURAL & RECREATIONAL SERVICES DEPT, SHIRE HALL, MARKET ST, STAFFORD ST16 2LQ
SUFFOLK COUNTY COUNCIL DEDHAM VALE AND STOUR VALLEY PROJECT, ENVIRONMENT AND TRANSPORT DEPT, ST EDMUND'S HOUSE, ROPE WALK, IPSWICH, SUFFOLK IP4 1LZ
SURREY COUNTY COUNCIL INFORMATION CENTRE, PLANNING DEPT, COUNTY HALL, KINGSTON-UPON-THAMES, SURREY KT1 2DT
ALAN SUTTON PUBLISHING TITLES DISTRIBUTED BY LITTLEHAMPTON BOOK SERVICES, 10-14 ELDON WAY, LINESIDE ESTATE, LITTLEHAMPTON, WEST SUSSEX BN17 7HE
VANGUARDS RAMBLING CLUB 109 SELSDON PARK ROAD, SOUTH CROYDON, SURREY CR2 8JJ
WALKWAYS 8 HILLSIDE CLOSE, BARTLEY GREEN, BIRMINGHAM B32 4LT
WEST HIGHLAND WAY PATH MANAGER (SOUTH) BALLOCH CASTLE, BALLOCH, DUMBARTONSHIRE G53 8LX
WESTERN MAIL & ECHO LTD HAVELOCK STREET, CARDIFF CF1 1XR
WESTON-SUPER-MARE HERITAGE CENTRE 3-6 WADHAM STREET, WESTON-SUPER-MARE, AVON BS23 1JY

STILWELL'S NATIONAL TRAIL COMPANION 1997

AT LAST! Where to stay and where to eat along 39 paths - the basic logistics for walkers. B&Bs, hostels and pubs are listed in the exact order they appear Along each route. Everything the walker wants - maps, grid references, distance from path, vehicle pick-up, tourist board grades, packed lunches and drying facilities. The perfect companion to the usual 'route only' guides. Now you can walk a path in stages or at the weekends - devise your own holiday! The perfect companion to the usual 'route only' guides.

Price £9.95 from WH Smith & all good bookshops (ISBN 1-900861-00-3) or for £10.95 (inc p&p) from Stilwell Publishing Ltd, 59 Charlotte Rd, London, EC2A 3QT, (0171 739 7179)

Paths Featured in Stilwell's

Pennine Way • South Downs Way • North Downs Way
Viking Way • Offa's Dyke • Thames Path • Ridgeway
Peddars Way & Norfolk Coast Path • Coast to Coast
Pembrokeshire Coast Path • South West Coastal Path
Dales Way • Ulster Way • Cotswold Way • Wealdway
Cleveland Way • Ribble Way • Southern Upland Way
Speyside Way • Fife Coastal Path • Glyndwr's Way
Kerry Way • Cambrian Way • Heart of England Way
Essex Way • Greensand Way • Hadrian's Wall
Hereward Way Wye Valley Walk • Oxfordshire Way
Wolds Way • Cumbria Way • West Highland Way
Shropshire Way • Staffordshire Way • Wicklow Way
Two Moors Way • Beara Way • Vanguard Way
Dingle Way • Wayfarers Walk • Wessex Ridgeway

Walking Holidays in Britain

The organisations listed here vary wildly in the scale of their operations. Some are large enough to train their own leaders and cover long-distance paths and walking areas all over the country (these are listed under the Great Britain heading). Others are smaller outfits focusing on a particular range of hills or stretch of coastline that they know intimately (these are listed under the country they operate in). You can choose guided or unescorted tours or to go with your group or sign up as an individual. Most offer baggage transfer. Some will tailor the walk to your own individual needs.

We only give the briefest of details so it's worth asking a lot of questions to make sure you book the holiday that suits you.

Apart from Ramblers Holidays who operate all over the world, the holidays listed deal only with Britain and Ireland and we welcome the particularly strong presence of holidays in Ireland in this edition. It is not a definitive list of all walking holidays available and the RA has not tried them out! All the companies or organisations have been contacted personally and have paid to be included.

Great Britain

BLACK DRAGON OUTDOOR EXPERIENCES

7 Ethelbert Drive, Charlton, Nr. Andover, Hants SP10 4EP. ☎ (01264) 357313.
Wales & Scotland • Classic mountaineering, mountain walking, rock climbing, scrambling, navigation, alpine walking.

COUNTRYWIDE HOLIDAYS

Grove House, Wilmslow Road, Didsbury, Manchester M20 2HU. ☎ 0161-446 2226.
Comprehensive selection of escorted and independent walking holidays in Britain.

INSTEP LINEAR WALKING HOLIDAYS

35 Cokeham Road, Lancing, W Sussex BN15 0AE. ☎/Fax (01903) 766457.
EMail: walking@instep.demon.co.uk
Unescorted walking holidays, national trails • Coast to Coast a speciality • Luggage service.

SUMMITS AFOOT

Freepost (MID 00177), Birmingham B28 0BR.
☎ 0121-693 5787.
England & Wales • Tailormade hillwalking trips •
National Parks • Short breaks or longer • Everything
organised.

WALKING WITH WATER

HEHNB, Basingstoke Canal Centre, Mytchett Place
Road, Mytchett, Surrey GU16 6DD.
☎ (0831) 566373. Fax (01252) 371758.
Walking/cruising along Britain's canals • Based on
our travelling hotelboats.

England

ADVENTURELINE

North Trefula Farm, Redruth, Cornwall TR16 5ET.
☎/Fax (01209) 820847.
Walking holidays through Cornwall's best scenery •
Coast, moors, estuaries, farmland.

ALBION LEISURE SERVICES

PO Box 348, Cheltenham GL52 6ZH.
☎ (01242) 254771. Fax (01242) 234056.
Cotswolds • Walking & cycling holiday packages •
Accommodation booking and luggage transfer.

APPLEBYS WALKING HOLIDAYS

8 Whitehead Hill, Scarborough, North Yorks
YO11 1PF. ☎ (01723) 500647.
North Yorkshire (East) • Guided walks Monday-Friday
• Excellent food/accommodation • Small & friendly.

COLD KELD GUIDED WALKING HOLIDAYS

Fell End, Ravenstonedale, Cumbria CA17 4LN.
☎/Fax (015396) 23273.
Cumbria • En suite accommodation • Delectable din-
ing • Singles welcome • All abilities • £235 per week.

COTSWOLD WALKING HOLIDAYS

10 Royal Parade, Bayshill Road, Cheltenham GL50
3AY. ☎/Fax (01242) 254353.
Cotswolds, Oxfordshire, Gloucestershire • Guided
and self-guided walks for individuals, groups and
companies.

THE COUNTRYMAN HOTEL

Victoria Road, Camelford, Cornwall PL32 9XA.
☎ (01840) 212250.
North Cornwall • Guided and self-guided walks •
Small groups and individuals welcome • B&B also.

DISCOVERY TRAVEL

12 Towthorpe Road, Haxby, York YO3 3ND.
☎ (01904) 766564.
Coast to Coast, Yorkshire Dales, North York Moors •
Self-guided walking and cycling holidays • Luggage
transfer • Accommodation booked.

THE EARNLEY CONCOURSE

Earnley, Chichester, West Sussex PO20 7JL.
☎ (01243) 670392. Fax (01243) 670832.
West Sussex/Eastern Hampshire • Weekend walking
breaks and summer walking weeks, including South
Downs Way.

FOOTPRINTS OF SUSSEX

47 Hills Road, Steyning, West Sussex BN44 3QG.
☎ (01903) 814506.
Walking holidays on the South Downs — as featured
on BBC2.

LIGHTFOOT WALKING HOLIDAYS

Nanquitho, Calloose Lane, Leedstown, Hayle,
Cornwall TR27 5ET. ☎ (01736) 850715.
Cornish Coastal Path • Unescorted • Carefully
selected accommodation • Luggage transported •

WALKING HOLIDAYS

MAJOR TAKEAHIKE

The Exmoor White Horse Inn, Exford, West Somerset TA24 7PY. ☎ (01643) 831229. Fax (01643) 831246.
Exmoor/North Devon • Walking holidays on Exmoor from inn to inn • B&B also.

MOUNTAIN GOAT HOLIDAYS AND TOURS

Victoria Street, Windermere, Cumbria LA23 1AD. ☎ (015394) 45161.
Minicoach daily tours throughout Lakeland • Holidays in most National Parks.

THE OLD FURNACE WALKING HOLIDAYS

Greendale, Oakamoor, Staffs ST10 3AP. ☎ (01538) 703331. Fax (01538) 703337.
Peak District • Specifically for single people • Guided weekends and breaks.

ORCHARD TRAILS

5 Orchard Way, Horsmonden, Tonbridge, Kent TN12 8JX. ☎/Fax (01892) 722680.
Unescorted walking and cycling holidays in Kent and East Sussex • Luggage transported daily.

SWALEDALE WALKING GUIDES

Tarn at Leaves, 9 Wathcote Close, Richmond, North Yorkshire DL10 7DX. ☎ (01748) 825487.
Yorkshire Dales • Guided walking breaks for groups • Fully inclusive • From ancient Dales inn.

WALKER'S GUIDED LAKELAND HOLIDAYS

66 Warbreck Hill Road, Blackpool FY2 9UH. ☎ (01253) 592332.
Long-distance/historic walking tours in Cumbria and Yorkshire Dales • Different accommodation each night.

YOUTH HOSTELS ASSOCIATION— NORTHERN ENGLAND

PO Box 11, Matlock, Derbyshire DE4 2XA. ☎ (01629) 825850.
Guided walking holidays • Luggage transport and full board • Booking service for independent walkers.

Scotland

ABOUT ARGYLL WALKING HOLIDAYS

John Fisher, The Old Inn, Strachur, Argyll PA27 8DG. ☎/Fax (01369) 860274.
Argyll & the Isles • Guided walks • Luggage transported • Hills, history, wildlife • Accommodation carefully selected.

ALBA WALKING HOLIDAYS

24 Lundavra Road, Fort William, Inverness-shire PH33 6LA. ☎ (01397) 704964.
Western Highlands and Islands • Walking and scrambling holidays all year • Professional mountain walking guides.

Please mention the Rambler's Yearbook when booking your holiday

WALKING HOLIDAYS

AVALON TREKKING SCOTLAND

Bowerswell Lane, Kinnoull, Perth PH2 7DL.
☎/Fax (01738) 624194.
Scotland and Northern England • Fully supported guided walking along long distance footpaths • Comfortable accommodation.

C-N-DO SCOTLAND WALKING HOLIDAYS & CLIMBING COURSES

77 John Player Building, Stirling FK7 7RP.
☎/Fax (01786) 445703.
Established 1984 • Year round walking • Meanders • Munros • LDPs • Scrambling • Climbing.

ISLE OF SKYE

Mrs C Rayner, Givendale, Heron Place, Portree, Isle of Skye IV51 9EU. ☎ (01478) 612183.
Isle of Skye • Quality B&B • Guided and self-guided walks.

MOUNTAIN CRAFT

Glenfinnan, Fort William PH37 4LT.
☎ (01397) 722213. Fax (01397) 722300.
Highlands and Islands • Instructional mountaineering courses and holidays plus private guiding • Established 1986.

NORTH-WEST FRONTIERS

18a Braes, Ullapool, Ross-shire IV26 2SZ.
☎/Fax (01854) 612628.
e-mail: 101717.451 @ compuserve.com
North-West Highlands & Islands • Seven day holidays at three grades • Centres include Ullapool, Skye, Torridon, Harris, Gairloch • Coastal walks to mountain ridges • Established 1986.

RUA REIDH LIGHTHOUSE (R)

Rua Reidh Lighthouse, Melvaig, Gairloch, Ross-shire IV21 2EA. ☎ (01445) 771263.
N W Highlands of Scotland • Seven days walking in Highlands • All grades • Magnificent location.

Wales

DINEFWR TREKS

Caban Cwmffynnon, Cefn Gorwydd, Llangammarch Wells, Powys LD4 4DW. ☎ (01591) 610638.
Personally guided and self-guided walks in heart of Wales • Accommodation in guest houses. See also Hostels section.

HIGH TREK SNOWDONIA

Tal-y-Waen, Deiniolen, Gwynedd LL55 3NA.
☎/Fax (01286) 871232.
Guided or self-guided trekking, navigation • Climbing, Winter Walking and other weekend courses.

HILLSCAPE

Blaen-y-Ddôl, Pontrhydygroes, Ystrad Meurig, Cardiganshire SY25 6DS.
☎ (01974) 282640.
40 varied walks of 5-20 miles • Idyllic setting • En-suite rooms • Imaginative home cooking.

LLANELLI FESTIVAL OF WALKS 1997

56 Coleshill Terrace, Llanelli, Dyfed SA15 3DA.
☎ (01554) 770077.
Llanelli Ramblers' popular Spring Bank Holiday walking and social event, 23-26 May 1997.

PEMBROKESHIRE – WALK ON THE WILD SIDE

Unit 5, Merlin Court, Winch Lane, Haverfordwest SA61 1SB.
☎ (01437) 767655. Fax (01437) 769196.
Walking holidays in the Pembrokeshire Coast National Park • Luggage transfer.

WANDERING IN WALES

2 Castle Terrace, Montgomery, Powys SY15 6PB.
☎ (01686) 668737.
Remote Mid Wales • Inclusive weekly package for groups • Border to coast.

WYSK WALKS

Church Farm, Mitchell Troy, Monmouth, Gwent NP5 4HZ. ☎ (01600) 712176.
Guided and self-guided walkers • Wye Valley, Black Mountains, Offa's Dyke Path and Wye Valley Walk • Character accommodation. See also B&B section.

WALKING HOLIDAYS

Ireland

CASTLEBAR'S INTERNATIONAL FOUR DAYS' WALKS

Newantrim Street, Castlebar, County Mayo.
☎ 00353 94 24102.
Ireland's most prestigious rambles • From July 3rd-6th 1997.

CLIMBERS INN, KERRY HIGHLANDS

Glencar, Killarney, County Kerry.
☎ 00353 66 60101 Fax 66 60104.
Highlands of Kerry • Excellent food and accommodation • Pub, shop, post office, walking books, maps.

COUNTRYSIDE TOURS

10 Prince of Wales Tce, Bray, County Wicklow.
☎ 00353 1 276 0733. Fax 00353 1 276 0734.
Guided and self-guided walking holidays throughout Ireland including Northern Ireland.

DONEGAL WALKING HOLIDAYS

Sessiagh Cottage, Woodhill, Dunfanaghy, County Donegal.
☎ 00353 74 36376.
North West Donegal • One-centre and three-centre walking hlidays to explore spectacular area • Small groups.

ENJOY IRELAND HOLIDAYS

Ainsworth Street, Blackburn, Lancs BB1 6AZ.
☎ (01254) 692899. Fax (01254) 693075.
Specialists in walking holidays and other activities in Ireland, North and South.

HERITAGE RAMBLES

Woodhouse, Cheekpoint, County Waterford.
☎ 00353 51 382629. Fax 00353 51 382689.
Ireland • Archaeology, history, literature, comfort included in 3-14 day guided encounters.

IRISH WAYS WALKING HOLIDAYS

The Old Rectory, Ballycanew, Gorey, County Wexford. ☎/Fax 00353 55 27479.
Guided and independent holidays in Ireland • Donegal, Connemara, Kerry, Wicklow.

WALKING HOLIDAYS

Public Transport

The Ramblers' Association enthusiastically supports initiatives which facilitate the use of public transport in the countryside and which help people from towns and cities to reach the countryside.

The **Countrygoer** project publishes an annual travel guide and newsletters for its subscribers. Both give essential information on bus and rail services to beautiful countryside. For three issues of *Countrygoer News* and an annual *Countrygoer Travel Guide* send a cheque for just £3 (made payable to Countrygoer) to Transport Marketing, 15 Station Road, Knowle, Solihull, West Midlands B93 0HL. Tel: (01564) 771901.

See the ad on page 75 for details of *Doe's Directory of Bus Timetables* and *The Great Britain Bus Timetable*.

TBC Hotline gives timetable information on all trains and express coaches and is available from 6am-9pm on (0891) 910910.

There is plenty of public transport information now on the Internet and this can be obtained on the Web site entitled **UK Public Transport Information** at: http://www.compulink.co.uk/~aus-an/ptinfo/

Two publications available from May 1997 will interest travellers to Wales and Scotland. *Getting Around Wales* and *Getting Around the Highlands and Islands* give timetables for trains, ferries, coaches and buses, for both full and part time services, for the summer season. They cost £2.50 each and are available from Tourist Information Centres in Scotland and Wales or from the publishers, Southern Vectis, Nelson Road, Newport, Isle of Wight PO30 1RD.

We list here public transport enquiry lines for each county or unitary authority. These should give you detailed timetable information. Where there is no enquiry line, a number for general queries is given. Where several unitary authorities share a line, these have been banded together.

England

The old county of **AVON** Enquiry Line: 0117-955 5111 (0800-2000 daily).

BEDFORDSHIRE Enquiry Line: (01234) 228337 (0830-1600 M-F).

BERKSHIRE 0118-923 4524.

BUCKINGHAMSHIRE Enquiry Line: (0345) 382000 (0700-2000 M-F, 0800-2000 Sat & Sun).

CAMBRIDGESHIRE (01223) 317740.

CHESHIRE Enquiry Line: (01244) 602666 (0800-1800 M-F, 0900-1300 Sat).

CORNWALL (01872) 322142.

CUMBRIA Enquiry Line: (01228) 606000 (0900-1700 M-F; 0900-1200 Sat).

DERBYSHIRE Enquiry Line: (01332) 292200 (0700-2000 daily).

DEVON Enquiry Line: (01392) 382800 (0830-1700 M-F).

DORSET (01305) 224535.

DURHAM Enquiry Line: 0191-383 3337 (0800-1700 Mon-Thurs; 0800-1630 Fri).

ESSEX Enquiry Line: (0345) 000333 (0700-2000 daily).

GLOUCESTERSHIRE Enquiry Line: (01452) 425543 (0745-1700 M-F).

HAMPSHIRE Enquiry Line: (0345) 023067 (0900-1700 M-F).

HARTLEPOOL BOROUGH COUNCIL Enquiry Line (01429) 523555 (0830-1700 M-F)

HEREFORD & WORCESTER Enquiry Line: 0345 125436 (0800-1900 M-F; 0900-1700 weekends).

HERTFORDSHIRE Enquiry Line: 0345 244344 (0830-1730 M-F).

ISLE OF WIGHT Enquiry Line: (01983) 823710 (0830-1700 Mon-Thurs; 0830-1630 Fri).

ISLES OF SCILLY (01720) 422537.

KENT Enquiry Line: (0800) 696996 (0800-2030 M-F; 0900-1700 weekends).

KINGSTON UPON HULL (01482) 612026.

LANCASHIRE Enquiry Line: (01257) 241693 (0900-1730 M-F; 0900-1700 Sat).

LEICESTERSHIRE Enquiry Line: 0116-251 1411 (0800-2000 Mon-Sat).

LINCOLNSHIRE Enquiry Line: 01522 553135 (0815-1645 M-F).

LINCOLNSHIRE (North East) (01472) 324490.

MIDDLESBROUGH, REDCAR & CLEVELAND, STOCKTON ON TEES Enquiry Line (01642) 444777 (0830-1700 M-F)

NORFOLK Enquiry Line: (0500) 626116 (0830-1700 M-Sat).

NORTH LINCOLNSHIRE (01724) 297444.

NORTHAMPTONSHIRE (01604) 236712.

NORTHUMBERLAND Enquiry Line: (01670) 533128 (0900-1700 M-F).

NOTTINGHAMSHIRE Enquiry Line: 0115-924 0000 (0700-2000 daily).

OXFORDSHIRE (01865) 810405.

SHROPSHIRE Enquiry Line: (0345) 056785 (0830-1745 M-F; 0830-1700 Sat).

SOMERSET (01823) 255695.

STAFFORDSHIRE Enquiry Line: (01785) 223344 (0815-1730 M-F; 0830-1330 Sat).

SUFFOLK Enquiry Line: (01473) 583358 (0845-1800 M-F; 0900-1230 Sat).

SURREY Enquiry Line: (01737) 223000 (0700-1900 M-F; 0900-1700 weekends).

SUSSEX (East) Enquiry Line: (01273) 474747 (0900-1700 Mon-Thurs; 0900-1630 Fri).

SUSSEX (West) (01243) 777556.

WARWICKSHIRE Enquiry Line: (01926) 414140 (0830-1730 M-Thurs; 0830-1700 Fri).

WILTSHIRE Enquiry Line: (0345) 090899 (0800-1800 M-F).

YORK (CITY) (01904) 551402.

YORKSHIRE (East Riding) (01482) 884163.

YORKSHIRE (North) (01609) 780780.

Scotland

ABERDEENSHIRE & MORAY (01224) 664580.

ANGUS Enquiry Line: (01307) 461775 (0800-1700 M-F).

ARGYLL & BUTE (01546) 604657.

CLACKMANNANSHIRE Enquiry Line: (01786) 442707 (0900-1700 M-F).

DUMFRIES & GALLOWAY Enquiry Line: (0345) 090510 (0900-1700 M-F).

DUNDEE Enquiry Line: (01382) 303125 (0900-1600 M-F).

LOTHIAN (East), MIDLOTHIAN & EDINBURGH Enquiry Line: (0800) 232323 (0830-1630 M-F).

LOTHIAN (West) Enquiry Line: (01506) 775288 (0830-1700 M-Thurs; 0830-1600 Fri).

FALKIRK Enquiry Line: (01324) 504724 (0900-1630 M-F).

FIFE Enquiry Line: (01592) 414141 (0900-1600 M-F).

HIGHLAND (01463) 702613.

ORKNEY (01856) 873535.

PERTH & KINROSS Enquiry Line: (0345) 413883 (0800-1730 M-F).

SCOTTISH BORDERS (01835) 824000.

SHETLAND (01595) 744850.

STIRLING Enquiry Line: (01786) 442707 (0900-1700 M-F).

WESTERN ISLES (01851) 703773.

Wales

ANGLESEY (01248) 752459.

BLAENAU GWENT,MONMOUTHSHIRE, NEWPORT AND TORFAEN Enquiry Line: (01495) 355444 (0900-1700 M-F).

BRIDGEND (01656) 643420.

CAERPHILLY (01495) 235223.

CARDIFF (01222) 873252.

CARMARTHENSHIRE Enquiry Line: (01267) 231817 (0900-1700 M-F).

CEREDIGION (01545) 572504.

CONWY Enquiry Line: (01492) 575412 (0900-1700 M-F).

DENBIGHSHIRE Enquiry Line: (01824) 706858 (0830-1645 M-Thurs; 0830-1615 Fri).

FLINTSHIRE Enquiry Line: (01352) 704035 (0830-1645 M-Thurs; 0830-1615 Fri).

GWYNEDD (01286) 679535.

MERTHYR TYDFIL (01685) 388993 ext. 240.

NEATH PORT TALBOT (01792) 222722.

PEMBROKESHIRE Enquiry Line: (01437) 764551 (0900-1700 M-F).

POWYS (01597) 826643.

RHONDDA CYNON TAFF (01222) 820627.

SWANSEA (01792) 636233.

VALE OF GLAMORGAN (01446) 704687.

WREXHAM Enquiry Line: (01978) 363760 (0900-1700 Mon, Tue, Thurs, Fri) 0900-1300 (Wed) 0900-1200 Sat)

Metropolitan Areas

LONDON TRANSPORT Enquiry Line: 0171-222 1234 (24 hour).

GREATER MANCHESTER Enquiry Line: 0161-228 7811 (0800-2000 daily).

MERSEYSIDE (MERSEYTRAVEL) Enquiry Line: 0151-236 7676 (0800-2000 daily).

SOUTH YORKSHIRE Enquiry Line: (01709) 515151 (0800-1800 Mon-Sat; 0900-1700 Sun).

STRATHCLYDE Enquiry Line: 0141-226 4826 (0700-2100 Mon-Sat; 0900-1930 Sun).

TYNE & WEAR Enquiry Line: 0191-232 5325 (0800-2000 Mon-Sat; 0900-1700 Sun).

WEST MIDLANDS PTE (CENTRO) Enquiry Line: 0121-200 2700 (0730-2230 daily).

WEST YORKSHIRE Enquiry Line: 0113-245 7676 (0800-1900 Mon-Sat; 0900-1730 Sun).

BUS AND RAIL INFORMATION

For a source of accurate, up-to-date information about public transport use one of the following.

Doe's Directory of Bus Timetables

This lists addresses, Head Office and Enquiry Office, telephone and fax numbers of all major operators, counties and regions, with details of their latest timetables, inclusive cost £5 post-free within Europe; £6 (Sterling) to any other address in the world. Cheques payable to B S Doe, 25 Newmorton Road, Bournemouth BH9 3NU. Tel: 01202 528707. Published twice yearly.

The Great Britain Bus Timetable

(incorporating Doe's Bus/Rail Guide)

Approx. 1,000 pages and published January, June & September, this has full timetables for virtually all inter-urban and rural bus services in Britain, plus details of rail interchange, and comes with an all-Britain bus and rail map. £11, post-free within Europe. Annual subscription (commencing any date): £30. Rates for outside Europe on request. Cheques payable to Southern Vectis, Nelson Road, Newport, Isle of Wight PO30 1RD. Tel: 01983 522456.

PUBLIC TRANSPORT

Equipment Directory

An alphabetical listing by town of as many shops as we could find

Marshall Ltd, 186 George Street, **Aberdeen**
☎ 01224 636952

Graham Tiso, 26 Netherkirkgate, **Aberdeen**
☎ 01224 634934

Outdoor Mountain Ski & Gear, 88 Fonthill Road,
Aberdeen ☎ 01224 573952

Badlands, 10 Bridge St, **Aberystwyth**
☎ 01970 625453

Walkabout, 3 East St. Helens Street, **Abingdon**, Oxon
☎ 01235 527704

H M Supplies, 27 Grosvenor Road, **Aldershot**
☎ 01252 342788

Wild Spirit, 9 Narrowgate, **Alnwick**, Northumberland
☎ 01665 604961

Cunningham Stewart, 1-2 Rydal Road, **Ambleside**
☎ 015394 32636

The Climbers Shop, Compston Corner, **Ambleside**
☎ 015394 32297

Gaynor Sports, Market Cross, **Ambleside**
☎ 015394 33305

Fox's, 1 London Road, **Amersham**, Bucks
☎ 01494 431431

Amersham Outdoor Sports, 11 Hill Avenue,
Amersham, Bucks ☎ 01494 722574

Eden Rambler, Low Wend, **Appleby**, Cumbria
☎ 017683 52601

Peglers, 69 Tarrant Street, Arundel, W Sussex
☎ 01903 883375

Riley's Outdoor Centre, 10 Shawcroft Centre, Dig St,
Ashbourne, Derbys ☎ 01335 346364

Track & Trail, 30-32 St John St, **Ashbourne**
☎ 01335 346403

Riley's Outdoor Centre, 10 Shawcroft Centre, Dig St,
Ashbourne, Derbys ☎ 01335 346364

Outdoor Action, 214 Stamford St, **Ashton under Lyne**
☎ 0161-343 2151

Ramblers, 20 Buckingham Street, **Aylesbury**, Bucks
☎ 01296 20163

Frasers of Ayr,47 Burns Statue Square, **Ayr**,
Strathclyde ☎ 01292 266029

Track Trail, Gramby Road, **Bakewell**, Derbys
☎ 01629 815483

Mid Antrim Camping, 20 Broughshane Sreet,
Ballymena, Co Antrim ☎ 01266 47187

Hitch 'n' Hike, High Peak Garden Centre, **Bamford**,
Hope Valley, Derbys ☎ 01433 651013

THE GREAT OUTDOOR EQUIPMENT SPECIALIST

For everything in outdoor wear, climbing and lightweight camping equipment it's worth taking a trip to **Graham Tiso**.

You'll find everything you'll ever need for outdoors ... indoors at **Graham Tiso**.

And because our staff share your interest you can be sure they're looking after your interests.

ABERDEEN	BELFAST	EAST KILBRIDE	GLASGOW	LEITH
26 Netherkirkgate	12-14 Cornmarket	53 The Plaza	129 Buchanan Street	13 Wellington Place
01224 634934	01232 231 230	0135 523 8383	0141 248 4877	0131 554 0804
AYR	DUNDEE	EDINBURGH	INVERNESS	STIRLING
228 High Street	22-24 Whitehall Street	Rose Street Precinct	41 High Street	Thistle Centre
0129 228 8885	01382 221153	0131 225 9486	01463 716617	01786 464737

Sports Outdoor & Ski, Cornhill House, Market
Square, **Banbury**, Oxon ☎ 01925 273700

Four Seasons, 44 The Bank, **Barnard Castle**, Co
Durham ☎ 01833 637829

John Pollock, 67 High Street, **Barnet**, Herts
☎ 0181-440 3994

Barnsley Outdoor Centre, 35 Peel Parade, **Barnsley**,
W Yorks ☎ 01226 200120

Moor Walking, 12 Silver Street, **Barnstaple**, Devon
☎ 01271 23585

The Outdoor Centre, Gisburn Road, **Barrowford**,
Lancs ☎ 01282 611129

B C H Camping & Leisure, 30 Southgate, **Bath**
☎ 01225 460200

Rickards of Bath, 11 Northumberland Place, **Bath**
☎ 01225 464107

Oswald Bailey, 8 The Mall, Southgate, **Bath**
☎ 01225 463202

Beaten Track, Unit 2-13, Ross's Court, **Belfast**
☎ 01232 236016

77

Home Stores, 433 Lisburn Road, **Belfast**
☎ 01232 381284

CBSI Scout Store, 253 Antrim Road, **Belfast**
☎ 01232 352549

Beverley Walking Centre, 2 Butcher Row, **Beverley**, Humberside ☎ 01482 861908

BJ Camping & Clothing, High Sreet, **Billericay**, Essex ☎ 01277 624372

Taunton Leisure, 1045 Stratford Road, Hall Green, **Birmingham** ☎ 0121-777 3337

Camping & Outdoor Centre, 62 New Street, **Birmingham** ☎ 0121-643 2474

Oswald Bailey, 111 Bull Ring Centre, **Birmingham** ☎ 0121-643 2474

Snow & Rock, 14 Priory Queensway, **Birmingham** ☎ 0121-236 8280

YHA Adventure Shops, 90-98 Corporation Street, **Birmingham** ☎ 0121-236 7799

Windrow Sports, 5-7 Fore Bondgate, **Bishop Aukland**, Durham ☎ 01388 603759

Outdoor Action, 26 King Sreet, **Blackburn**, Lancs ☎ 01254 671945

Rivington Camping Ltd, 59a Chorley New Road, Horwich, Nr **Bolton**, Lancs ☎ 01204 699550

Outdoor World, 79-83 Rimrose Road, **Bootle** ☎ 0151-944 2202

Oswald Bailey, 106 Commercial Road, **Bournemouth** ☎ 01202 558797

Camping & Outdoor Centre, 7 Gervis Place, **Bournemouth** ☎ 01202 558797

Allan Austin, Jacob Street Mills, Manchester Road, **Bradford** ☎ 01274 728674

Hill & Dale, 38 Manningham Lane, **Bradford** ☎ 01274 730257

Out and About, 2 Elcho Sreet, **Brae**, Peebles ☎ 01721 723590

Jons Work & Leisure Store, 11 Sandpit Lane, **Braintree**, Essex ☎ 01376 320436

Field & Trek, 23-25 & 41 Kings Road, **Brentwood** ☎ 01277 222230 and mail order ☎ 01277 233122

Camping & Outdoor Centre, 24 St James's Street, **Brighton** ☎ 01273 684281

YHA Adventure Shops, 126-127 Queen's Road, **Brighton** 01273 821554

YHA Adventure Shops, 10-12 Fairfax Street, **Bristol** ☎ 0117-929 7141

Oswald Bailey, 61 Horsefair, **Bristol** ☎ 0117-929 3523

Taunton Leisure, 72 Bedminster Parade, **Bristol** ☎ 0117-963 7640

Camping & Outdoor Centre, 9-10 Transom House, Victoria Street, **Bristol** ☎ 0117-926 4892

Kingswood Caravan & Camping Centre, 137-145 High Street, Kingswood, **Bristol** ☎ 0117-960 0205

Marcruss Stores, 181 Hotwells Road, **Bristol** ☎ 0117-929 7427

Survival Shop (West) Ltd, 48 Bond Street, **Bristol** ☎ 0117-922 6663

Oswald Bailey, High Street, **Bromsgrove**, Hereford & Worcester ☎ 01527 871562

Hill & Dale, 46 Church Sreet, **Burnley**, Lancs ☎ 01282 31241

Stepping Out, 55 St John's Sreet, **Bury St Edmunds**, Suffolk ☎ 01284 763150

H M Supplies, 157-159 London Road, **Camberley**, Surrey ☎ 01276 20550

Hughes, 92 Mill Road, **Cambridge** ☎ 01223 576611

Open Air Cambridge Ltd, 11 Green Street, **Cambridge** ☎ 01223 324666

YHA Adventure Shops, 6-7 Bridge Street, **Cambridge** ☎ 01223 353956

Field & Trek, 3 Palace Street, **Canterbury**, Kent ☎ 01227 470023

Camping & General, Charlfleets, **Canvey Island**, Essex ☎ 01268 692141

Up & Under, 490 Cowbridge Road East, Victoria Park, **Cardiff** CF5 1BL ☎ 01222 578579

YHA Adventure Shops, 13 Castle Street, **Cardiff** ☎ 01222 399178

Cardiff Sportsgear, 81 Whitchurch Road, **Cardiff** ☎ 01222 621757

Camping & Outdoor Centre, 10 Duke Street, **Cardiff** ☎ 01222 390887

Freetime, 3 West Tower Street, **Carlisle**, Cumbria ☎ 01229 47349

Denis English Mountain Sports, 139/141 Lowther Sreet, **Carlisle**, Cumbria ☎ 01228 30239

Outdoor Style, Jacksons Lane, **Carmarthen**, Dyfed ☎ 01267 221422

The Old Barn, Market place, **Castleton**, Sheffield ☎ 01433 620528

Bowden James & Sons, 50-54 The Square, **Chagford**, Devon ☎ 01647 433271

Kent Camping, 39 High Street, **Chatham**, Kent ☎ 01634 402255

Outdoor Pursuits Centre, 38-40 High Street, **Chatham**, Kent ☎ 01634 826582

Ski Plus, Navigation Road, **Chelmsford**, Essex ☎ 01245 264143

The Outdoor Centre, 44 Winchcombe St, **Cheltenham** ☎ 01242 242200

EQUIPMENT SHOPS

Snow & Rock, 99 Fordwater Road, **Chertsey,** Surrey ☎ 01932 566886

Camp & Climb, 95-97 Brook Street, **Chester** ☎ 01244 311174

Yeomans Army Stores Head Office, The Warehouse, Markham Road, **Chesterfield** ☎ 01246 232419

Wilderness Ways, 26-28 Park Road, **Chesterfield,** ☎ 01246 201437

Great Outdoors, 195 Chatsworth Road, **Chesterfield,** ☎ 01246 220287

Cairnsmore, 51 West Street, **Chichester,** W Sussex ☎ 01243 721321

Rohan, 1 Priory Lane Shopping Centre, Northgate, **Chichester,** W Sussex ☎ 01243 787214

Oswald Bailey, 2 Saxon Square, **Christchurch,** Dorset ☎ 01202 483043

Camp-Trek UK, 23a Castle St, **Cirencester,** Glos ☎ ☎ 01285 641401

Hikers Way, Kingsway Sports, 139 Grimsby Road, **Cleethorpes,** Humberside ☎ 01472 601616

Ken Varey, 4 Newmarket Street, **Clitheroe,** Lancs ☎ 01200 23267

Leisure & Camping, 61 North Station Road, **Colchester** ☎ 01206 766056

Camping & Outdoor Centre, 16 Short Wyre Street, **Colchester,** Essex ☎ 01206 577040

Conwy Outdoor Shop, 9 Castle Street, **Conwy,** Gwynedd ☎ 01492 593390

Lynes, Well Street, Off Corporation Street, **Coventry** 01203 223512

Kit Bag, 121 Far Gosford Sreet, **Coventry,** Warks ☎ 01203 222624

Jacksons of Old Arley, Unit 8 Springhill Industrial Estate, Arley, **Coventry,** Warks ☎ 01676 540878

Outdoor Bound, 9 Hay Lane, **Coventry,** Warks ☎ 01203 630330

OBI Camping Centre, 5 Westgate Street, **Cowbridge,** S Glamorgan ☎ 01446 772498

Camping & Outdoor Centre, 37-39 George's Walk, **Croydon** ☎ 0181-688 1730

Field & Trek, 32 Church Street, **Croydon,** Surrey ☎ 0181-680 8798

Sgt. Pepper, 27 Bonnygate, **Cupar,** Fife ☎ 01334 654862

Power Sports Depot, 63-65 Green Lane, **Derby** ☎ 01332 348311

Prestidge Ski & Climb, 47 Queen Street, **Derby** ☎ 01332 342245

Birds of Dereham, 6 Norwich Street, **Dereham,** Norfolk ☎ 01362 692941

The Outdoor Store, 2 High Sreet, **Dingwall,** Highland ☎ 01349 861418

DMC Mountain Sports, Unit 2, Fraser House, Netherall Road, **Doncaster** ☎ 01302 341756

Don Valley, Littleworth Lane, Old Rossington, Nr **Doncaster,** S Yorks ☎ 01302 868408

Great Western Camping, 35 Great Western Road, **Dorchester** ☎ 01305 266800

Dorchester Rambler, 40 Trinity Street, **Dorchester** ☎ 01305 251411

Pattie's of Dumfries, 109 Queensberry Sreet, **Dumfries** ☎ 01387 252891

EQUIPMENT SHOPS

Frasers, 80/90 Friars Vennel, **Dumfries**
☎ 01387 267327

Graham Tiso, 22 Whitehall Street, **Dundee**
☎ 01382 21153

Munros Specialist Outdoor Shop, 14 Bank Sreet, Aberfeldy, **Dundee** ☎ 01887 820008

Summits Ltd, 5 Bridge Sreet, **Dunfermline**, Fife
☎ 01383 730181

Wild Rover, 53 The Plaza, **East Kilbride**
☎ 013552 38383

Outdoor Life, 3 High Street, Old Town, **Eastbourne**, E Sussex ☎ 01323 25372

Oswald Bailey, 15 Market Street, **Eastleigh**, Hants
☎ 01703 613238

Nevisport Ltd, 81 Shandwick Place, **Edinburgh**
☎ 0131-229 1197

Camping & Outdoor Centre, 77 Southbridge, **Edinburgh** ☎ 0131-225 3339

One Step Ahead, 177 Morningside Road, **Edinburgh**
☎ 0131-447 0999

The Outdoor Trading Co, 130 Rose Sreet, **Edinburgh**
☎ 0131-225 4609

Leith Army Stores, 7-10 Brunswick Place, **Edinburgh**
☎ 0131-556 2337

Graham Tiso, Rose Street Precinct, **Edinburgh**
☎ 0131-225 9486

High Land Outdoor, 41 South Sreet, **Elgin**, Grampian
☎ 01343 540774

BAC Outdoor Leisure, Central Hall, Coronation St, **Elland**, W Yorks ☎ 01422 371146

Taunton Leisure, 110 Fore Street, **Exeter**
☎ 01392 410534

WALKING BOOT REPAIRS

Speedy Service

Avg. 2 days in workshop

Traditional Craftsman Quality Repairs on trainers to hob nail boots, Timberland moccasins to riding boots.
For Construction, Soling & Price guide
**Please phone: 01392 59423
or fax: 01392 410610**

Parkhouse & SON Est. 1948

129 Sidwell Street, Exeter EX4 6RY

Thomas Moore of Exeter, 102 Fore Street, **Exeter**,
☎ 01392 55711

Challenge Sports, 25 Bank Street, **Falkirk**
☎ 01324 612328

Cornish Rambler, 11 Arwenack Street, **Falmouth**, Cornwall ☎ 01326 314760

Boots & Saddle Wear, 175 Fleet Road, **Fleet**, Hants
☎ 01252 616889

S B & S Camping, The Square, **Forest Row**, E Sussex
☎ 01342 822740

The Outdoor Store, 97 High Sreet, **Forfar**, Tayside
☎ 01307 465471

Leisure Time, 10 The Esplanade, **Fowey**, Cornwall
☎ 01726 832207

Outside Now, 173 Byres Road, **Glasgow**
☎ 0141-339 2202

The Survival Shop, 158 Buchanan Street, **Glasgow** G1 ☎ 0141-332 9750

Graham Tiso, 129 Buchanan Street, **Glasgow**
☎ 0141-248 4877

Adventure 1, 38 Dundas Street, **Glasgow** G1
☎ 0141-353 3788

Highrange Sports, 200 Great Western Road, **Glasgow** G4 ☎ 0141-332 5533

Catstycam, The Outdoor Shop, **Glenridding**, Cumbria
☎ 017684 82351

Field & Trek, 74 Westgate Street, **Gloucester**
☎ 01452 416549

Oswald Bailey, 24 The Oxebode, **Gloucester**
☎ 01452 305555

Anglefield Corner, Eastbourne Road, South **Godstone**, Surrey RH9 8JG ☎ 01342 893881

Outdoor World, G.O. Red Lion Square, **Grasmere**, Cumbria ☎ 015394 35614

Vango, 70 East Hamilton Street, **Greenock**, Strathclyde ☎ 01475 744122

The Outdoor Scene, 4-6 Regent Arcade, Old Market Place, **Grimsby**, Lincs ☎ 01472 240763 Mail order also

J A Norris, 62 Pasture St, **Grimsby**, Lincs
☎ 01472 350408

West Riding Camping, The Tannery, Halifax Road, Hipperholme, **Halifax**, W Yorks ☎ 01422 844500

Springhill Camping, Denholme Road, Burnley Rd, Luddenden Foot, **Halifax**, W Yorks
☎ 01422 883164

Summits Outdoor Gear, 30 Gateside Street, **Hamilton**
☎ 01698 427783

Out and About, 18 Bower Road, **Harrogate**
☎ 01423 561592

Wilderness Ways, 71 Station Parade, **Harrogate**
☎ 01423 562874

Camping & Outdoor Centre, 104 Hinders Road, **Harrow**, Middx ☎ 0181-427 3809

Base Camp, 16 The Galleria, **Hatfield**, Herts
☎ 01707 267815

Outdoor Trading Post, Unit 51, The Galleria, Comet Way, **Hatfield**, Herts ☎ 01707 256606

Outside Ltd, Main Road, **Hathersage**, Derbys
☎ 01433 651936 and

Filarinskis of Havant, 26-28 East Street, **Havant**,
Hants ☎ 01705 499599

Footloose, Borogate, **Helmsley**, N Yorks
☎ 01439 770886

Ramblers, 1 Marlowes, **Hemel Hempstead**, Herts
☎ 01442 214631

The Complete Outdoors, London Road, Bourne End,
Hemel Hempstead, Herts ☎ 01442 873133

Campestral, Wargrave Road, **Henley on Thames**,
Oxon ☎ 01491 575829

Out & About, 11 King St, **Hereford**
☎ 01432 274084

Fewsters Camping Equipment, 48 Priestpopple,
Hexham, Northumberland ☎ 01434 607040

Bartletts of Hillingdon, 1-2 Rosslyn Parade, Uxbridge
Road, **Hillingdon,** Middx ☎ 0181-573 2076

J & R Camping & Leisure, Eggington Road, **Hilton**,
Derbys ☎ 01283 733525

Dodwell's Leisure, **Hinckley**, Leics ☎ 01455 632625

Eskdale Outdoor Shop, Eskdale Green, **Holmrook**,
Cumbria ☎ 019467 23223

Mountain Trail, 49 High Sreet, **Holywood**, N Ireland
☎ 01232 428529

Annapurna, 1 Market Square, **Horsham**, W Sussex
☎ 01403 850895

Hill & Dale, 17 Southgate, **Huddersfield**
☎ 01484 425103

Blackburns Outdoor Pursuits, 171 Bradford Rd,
Huddersfield, W Yorks ☎ 01484 531561

Wet & Wild Adventure Sports, 619 Anlaby Road, **Hull**
☎ 01482 354076

Broadman Ltd, Wiltshire Road, **Hull**
☎ 01482 561181

Sports & Fashions, 51 High Sreet, **Huntingdon,**
Cambs ☎ 01480 454541

Ilkeston Camping & Leisure, 138 Nottingham Road,
Ilkeston, Derbys ☎ 0115-930 9457

Graham Tiso, 41 High Street, **Inverness**
☎ 01463 716617

W D Macpherson & Sons, 34 Church Sreet,
Inverness ☎ 01463 711427

High Land Outdoor, 73 Castle Sreet, **Inverness**
☎ 01463 236406

Craigdon Sports, Craigdon House, High Street,
Inverurie, Grampian ☎ 01467 625855

Stepping Out, 10 Gt Colman Sreet, **Ipswich**, Suffolk
☎ 01473 211647

Camping & Outdoor Centre, 7-9 Tacket Street,
Ipswich ☎ 01473 254704

Speaks Field & Fell, 3-11 Lawkholme Cres, **Keighley**,
W Yorks ☎ 01535 603979

Wild Places, 93 Highgate, **Kendal**, Cumbria
☎ 01539 724419

Kendal Survival Shop, 1 Kent View, **Kendal**, Cumbria
☎ 01539 729699

Outsider, 2a Charlton Road, **Keynsham**, Avon
☎ 0117-986 0030

Lang & Hunter, 12 Thames Street, **Kingston,** Surrey
☎ 0181-546 5427

Outdoor Pursuits, 81 Penny Sreet, **Lancaster**
☎ 01524 843663

Harry Robinson, 4-5 New Road, **Lancaster**
☎ 01524 66610

Lockwoods, 125 Rugby Road, **Leamington Spa,**
Warks ☎ 01926 339388

Maughans, 20 The Parade, **Leamington Spa**, Warks
☎ 01926 428685

Kathmandu Trekking, 5 Crabtree Lane, Great
Bookham, **Leatherhead**, Surrey ☎ 01372 454773

Wilderness Ways, 100a Gelderd Road, **Leeds**
☎ 0113-245 8002

Wilderness Ways, 30 Woodhouse Lane, **Leeds**
☎ 0113-244 4715

Camping & Outdoor Centre, 62 The Headrow, **Leeds**
☎ 0113-245 7273

EQUIPMENT SHOPS

YHA Adventure Shops, 119-121 Vicar Lane, **Leeds** 0113-246 5339

Centresport, 57-59 New Briggate, **Leeds**, W Yorks ☎ 0113-245 2917

The Great Outdoors, 1 Ivegate, Yeadon, **Leeds** ☎ 0113-250 4686

Yak & Yeti, 3 Smithfield Centre, **Leek**, Staffs ☎ 01538 371038

J & R Camping & Leisure, Byron St, Off Lee Circle, **Leicester** ☎ 0116-255 1595

Roger Turner, 52a London Road, **Leicester** ☎ 0116-255 1952

City Surplus, 79 Granby St, **Leicester** ☎ 0116-255 0208

Canyon Mountain Sports, 92 Granby St, **Leicester** ☎ 0116-255 7957

Graham Tiso, 13 Wellington Place, **Leith** ☎ 0131-554 0804

Mailorder ☎ 01202 747096

Linsports Outdoor Centre, 21 Silver St, **Lincoln** ☎ 01522 524674

Camping & Ski Shack, 113-5 Portland Sreet, **Lincoln** ☎ 01522 560961

The Base Camp, 54 High Street, **Littlehampton**, W Sussex ☎ 01903 723853

Camp 'A' Tent, 92 St John's Road, Crosby, **Liverpool** L22 9QQ ☎ 0151-920 9535

YHA Adventure Shops, 25 Bold Street, **Liverpool** ☎ 0151-709 8063

Outside, Old Baptist Chapel, High Street, **Llanberis**, Gwynedd ☎ 01286 871534

Wayfarers Outdoor Leisure, Park Crescent, **Llandrindod Wells**, Powys ☎ 01597 825100e

Hard Ruck, 127a Oxford Street, **London** W1 ☎ 0171-437 3386

Ben Nevis Clothing,237 Royal College Street, **London** NW1 ☎ 0171-485 9989

Paul's Camping & Clothing Store, 170 Muswell Hill Broadway, **London** N10 ☎ 0181-444 6511

Backpacking Centre, 44 Birchington Road, **London** ☎ 0171-328 2166

Camping & Outdoor Centre, 41 Ludgate Hill, **London** EC4 ☎ 0171-329 8757

Joe's Outdoor Centre, 26 Station Road, **London** NW10 ☎ 0181-961 8300

Snow & Rock, 150 Holborn, **London** EC1 ☎ 0171-831 6900

Camping & Outdoor Centre, 27 Buckingham Palace Road, **London** SW1 ☎ 0171-834 6007

Field & Trek, 105 Baker Street, **London** W1 ☎ 0171-224 0049

Snow & Rock, 188 Kensington High Street, **London** W8 ☎ 0171-937 0872

B T Cullum, 199 Wandsworth High Street, **London** SW18 ☎ 0181-874 2346

Tarpaulin & Tent Co, 101-103 Brixton Hill, **London** SW2 ☎ 0181-674 ☎ 0121

Taunton Leisure, 557-561 Battersea Park Road, **London** SW11 ☎ 0171-924 3838

YHA Adventure Shops, 14 Southampton Street, Covent Garden, **London** WC2 ☎ 0171-836 8541

YHA Advenutre Shops, Campus Travel Shops, 52 Grosvenor Gardens, Victoria, **London** SW1 ☎ 0171-823 4739

Bob's Surplus Stores, 2 Rupert Road, Chiswick, **London** W4 1LX ☎ 0181-994 8665

YHA Adventure Shops, 174 Kensington High Street, **London** W8 ☎ 0171-938 2948

Crystal Palace Camping, 15-17 Central Hill, **London** ☎ 0181-766 6060

Arnolds Leisure, 154-156 Broadway, West Ealing, **London** ☎ 0181-840 7383

Backpacker, 136 Charing Cross Road, **London**, WC2 ☎ 0171-836 1160

CSD Chelsea, E Block, Duke of Yorks HQ, Kings Road, Chelsea, **London** SW3 ☎ 0171-730 3386

Mclains Outdoor Wear, 144 Holloway Road, **London** N7 ☎ 0171-607 8413

John Pollock, 157 High Raod, **Loughton**, Essex ☎ 0181-508 6626

Mullen Marine, Kinnego Marina, **Lurgan** ☎ 01762 343911

Leisure Fayre, 60 High Street, **Lyndhurst**, Devon ☎ 01703 283445

Compass Point, 2 Church Road, **Lytham**, Lancs ☎ 01253 795597

Pennine Leisure, Brookside Mill, Crossall St, **Macclesfield**, Cheshire ☎ 01625 420167

Greenstiles, Heol Penrallt, **Machynlleth** ☎ 01654 703543

Camping & Outdoor Centre, 2-4 Granada House, Gabriels Hill, **Maidstone**, Kent ☎ 01622 763008

Cave & Crag, Cove Centre, **Malham**, N Yorks ☎ 01729 830432

YHA Adventure Shops, 166 Deansgate, **Manchester** ☎ 0161-834 7119

Camping & Outdoor Centre, 7 Oldham Street, **Manchester** ☎ 0161-835 1016

Walkwise, 14 Harehill Road, Littleborough, Greater **Manchester** ☎ 01706 371911

Ellis Brigham Mountain Sports, Wellington Mills, Duke Street, **Manchester** 3 ☎ 0161-834 6366

EQUIPMENT SHOPS

82

Regatta Great Outdoors, Risol House, Mercury Way, Urmston, **Manchester** 41 ☎ 0161-747 2971

W Slack & Sons, 38 Rosemary St, **Mansfield**, Notts ☎ 01623 24449

Mansfield Outdoor Leisure, 21 Chesterfield Rd South, **Mansfield**, Notts ☎ 01623 25236

Wilderness Ways, 100 Newport Road, **Middlesbrough**, Cleveland ☎ 01642 248916

Keyne Camping & Leisure, 15 Stacey Bushes Trading Centre, **Milton Keynes**, Bucks ☎ 01908 227090

Walkmoors, 18b Park St, **Minehead**, Somerset ☎ 01643 707192

Northumbria Mountain Sports, 59 Bridge Sreet, **Morpeth**, Northumberland ☎ 01670 513276

Clobber, 33 Windsor Rd, **Neath**, W Glam ☎ 01639 639316

TAM Leisure, 180-186 Kingston Road, **New Malden**, Surrey ☎ 0181-949 5435

Worsleys Army & Navy Stores, 62 Lymington Road, **New Milton**, Hants ☎ 01425 638220

Angling & Outdoors, 14 Garden Walk, Metro Centre, **Newcastle-upon-Tyne** ☎ 0191-460 8733

Wilderness Ways, 100-104 Grainger Street, **Newcastle-upon-Tyne** ☎ 0191-232 4941

M L Great Outdoors, 89/98 Grainger Market, **Newcastle-upon-Tyne** ☎ 0191-261 8371

Freemans Outdoor Centre, 1 Bigg Market, **Newcastle-upon-Tyne** ☎ 0191-232 1646

Newport Scout & Guide Shop, 10 Commercial Road, **Newport**, Gwent ☎ 01633 214082

Kitstop, 17 Carlsbrook Road, **Newport**, Isle of Wight ☎ 01983 528593

Carey Wear, 16 Union Street, **Newton Abbot**, Devon ☎ 01626 334430

Percy Hodge (Sports) Ltd, 104-106 Queen Street, **Newton Abbot,** Devon ☎ 01626 54923

Gilroy Wilson Shoes, 7 Market Street, **Northwich**, Cheshire ☎ 01606 42577

Outdoor Life, 14 High St, **Norton**, Cleveland ☎ 01642 553034

Outdoor Centre, Elm Hill, **Norwich** ☎ 01603 625645

Norwich Camping Company, 56 Magdalen Street, **Norwich** ☎ 01603 615525

Venturesport, 17 Westlegate, **Norwich** ☎ 01603 613378

Roger Turner, 120 Derby Road, **Nottingham**

Camping & Outdoor Centre, 3-7 St Jeames's Street, **Nottingham** ☎ 0115-948 4571

Wilderenss Ways, 21 St Peters Gate, **Nottingham** ☎ 0116 950 3455

Castle Mountain & Moor, 40-44 Maid Marian St, **Nottingham** ☎ 0115-941 4059

Kit Bag, 22 Pool Bank Sreet, **Nuneaton**, Warks ☎ 01203 641033

Nancy Black, 18-19, Argyll Sqare, **Oban**, Strathclyde ☎ 01631 562550

Dartmoor Equipment, The Manse New Road, **Okehampton**, Devon ☎ 01837 52967

Caseys, Stephen Smith's Garden Centre, Pool Rd, **Otley**, W Yorks ☎ 01943 465462

Camping & Outdoor Centre, 17 Turl Street, **Oxford** ☎ 01865 247110

YHA Adventure Shops, 9-10 St Clements (The Plain), **Oxford** ☎ 01865 247948

Touchwood Sports, 107 St Aldates, **Oxford** ☎ 01865 725220

Touchwood Sports, 426 Abingdon Road, **Oxford** ☎ 01865 246551

Summits Outdoor Gear, 96 Causeyside Street, **Paisley**, Strathclyde ☎ 0141-887 5536

Penrith Survival Equipment, The Square, **Penrith**, Cumbria ☎ 01931 714444

General Clothing Stores, 1-3 Adelaide Street, **Penzance**, Cornwall ☎ 01736 64369

Camping & Outdoor Centre, 97 Bridge Street, **Peterborough** ☎ 01733 61000

Outdoor Adventure, 6 Hereward Cross, Broadway, **Peterborough**, Cambs ☎ 01733 341381

Wright Outdoors, 5-7 Lincoln Road, **Peterborough**, Cambs ☎ 01733 312184

Hereward Ski & Walking, 14 Fenlake Business Centre, **Peterborough**, Cambs ☎ 01733 893647

Rock & Rapids, 2-4 Mutley Plain, **Plymouth**, Devon ☎ 01752 227264

Mountain Action, 50 Faraday Mill, Prince Rock, **Plymouth**, Devon ☎ 01752 226923

Camping & Outdoor Centre, 4-6 Royal Parade, **Plymouth** ☎ 01752 662614

M & T Crossley, Tordoff, Newgate, **Pontefract**, W Yorks ☎ 01977 702002

Outdoor Adventure, 34 Station Road, Lower Parkstone, **Poole**, Dorset ☎ 01202 735639

Oswald Bailey, 31Kingland Crescent, **Poole**, Dorset ☎ 01202 675495

Gullivers Travels, 52 Commercial Road, Parkstone, **Poole**, Dorset ☎ 01202 747096

Wolfpack Trading Post, 52 Commercial Road, **Poole**, Dorset

Mountain Top Products, 48 St Mary's Road, **Portsmouth**, Hants ☎ 01705 730667

Safari, Unit 44 Kingwell Path, Cascade Shopping Centre, **Portsmouth** ☎ 01705 829410

Out 'n' About, 25 Breck Road, **Poulton-le-Fylde**, Lancs ☎ 01253 892445

Leisure Croft, 279 Victoria Road, **Prestatyn** ☎ 01745 853646

Camping & Outdoor Centre, 23 Miller Arcade, **Preston**, Lancs ☎ 01772 250242

Outdoor Action, 132 Church St, **Preston**, Lancs ☎ 01772 561970

Glacier Sport Ltd, 40/41 Lune Sreet, **Preston**, Lancs ☎ 01772 821903

Grips, 58 Eastwood Road, **Rayleigh**, Essex ☎ 01268 776661

BJ Camping & Clothing, 156/8 High Sreet, **Rayleigh**, Essex ☎ 01268 7422347

YHA Adventure Shops, 3 Market Place, **Reading** ☎ 01734 587722

Carter's, 99 Caversham Road, **Reading** ☎ 01734 599022

Hills Clothiers, 25 Queen St, **Redcar**, Cleveland ☎ 01642 484854

Ray Ward Gunsmith, 4 Holland Close, **Redhill**, Surrey ☎ 01737 766715

Lang & Hunter, 16 Hill Rise, **Richmond**, Surrey ☎ 0181-940 9283

Milletts Camping & Countrywear, Unit 7 The Furlong Centre, **Ringwood**, Hants ☎ 01425 480047

Royston Outdoor, 13 Kneesworth Sreet, **Royston**, Herts ☎ 01763 243195

White & Bishop, 29-31 Clifton Road, **Rugby**, Warks ☎ 01604 230901

Backpack Caravan, 13 Hill St, **Saffron Walden**, Essex ☎ 01799 525639

Outdoor Gear Camping Goods, 17 Cross Keys, Chequer, **Salisbury** ☎ 01722 331290

Edlas, 16 Winchester Street, **Salisbury**, Wilts ☎ 01722 327316

Oswald Bailey, Old George Mall, **Salisbury**, Wilts ☎ 01722 328689

YHA Adventure Shops, 9 Priory Square, The Maltings, **Salisbury** ☎ 01722 422122

Bosses & Slaves, 34 Victoria Road, **Scarborough**, North Yorks ☎ 01723 500051

Leisureways, 38 Victoria Rd, **Scarborough**, N Yorks ☎ 01723 368777

Lyon Equipment, Dent, **Sedbergh**, Cumbria ☎ 015396 25493

Castleberg Sports, Cheapside, **Settle**, N Yorks ☎ 01729 823751

Cave & Crag, Market Place, **Settle**, N Yorks ☎ 01729 823877

Foothills, 11 Edgedale Rd, **Sheffield** ☎ 0114-258 6228

Outside, Mowbray Sreet, **Sheffield** ☎ 0114-279 7427

Camping & Outdoors, 13 Castle Foregate, **Shrewsbury** ☎ 01743 355168

Craven Rambler, 15/17 Coach St, **Skipton**, N Yorks ☎ 01756 796166

Sleat Trading, Armadale Pier, **Sleat**, Isle of Skye ☎ 01471 844265

Field & Trek, 313 High Street, **Slough**, Bucks ☎ 01753 554252

Four Points, 12-13 The Village Shopping Centre, High Street, **Slough**, Bucks ☎ 01753 691027

Cape Hill Camping, 118 Windmill Lane, **Smethwick**, Warley, W Mids ☎ 0121-555 5866

Oswald Bailey, 48 Station Road, **Solihull** ☎ 0121-705 3226

S K Camping & Leisurewear, Walkers Garden Centre, 17 Frederick St, **South Shields** ☎ 0191-455 3978

McRed's Ramble In, 74 Dean Road, **South Shields** ☎ 0191-456 6402

Camping & Outdoor Centre, 9 East Street, **Southampton** ☎ 01703 334462

Oswald Bailey, 109 Above Bar Street, **Southampton** ☎ 01703 333687

YHA Adventure Shops, 14 High Street, **Southampton** ☎ 01703 235847

Hill & Dale, 39 Burnley Rd, **Sowerby Bridge** ☎ 01422 833360

The Outdoor Shop Alternative, 36 London Road, **St Albans**, Herts ☎ 01727 833586

Short & Curlys, 140-142 St Albans Road, **St Annes**, Blackpool ☎ 01253 726800

County Wise, 6 Victoria Place, **St Austell**, Cornwall ☎ 01726 70780

Weathergear, 42 Polkyth Road, **St Austell**, Cornwall ☎ 01726 66183

Sgt. Pepper, 5 Mercat Wynd, Market Sreet, **St Andrews**, Fife ☎ 01334 478097

Stafford Outdoor Leisure, 38 Mill Street, **Stafford** ☎ 01785 40594

Rugged Outdoors, Northumberland House, Drake Avenue, **Staines**, Middx ☎ 01784 466616

YHA Adventure Shops, 133 High Street, **Staines**, Middx ☎ 01784 452987

County Hardware Ltd, Unit 6, Ind Estate, **St Columb Major**, Cornwall ☎ 01637 881275

Countryside Ski & Climb, 118 High St, **Stevenage**, Herts ☎ 01438 740214

New Heights, 26 Barnton Street, **Stirling** ☎ 01786 449236

Alpenstock, 35 St Petersgate, **Stockport** ☎ 0161-480 3660

Blake Maurice Ltd, 12 Mill Road, **Stokenchurch**, Bucks ☎ 01494 483971

Hi-Peak Leisure Ltd, Stafford House, Clouth St, Hanley, **Stoke-on-Trent**, Staffs ☎ 01782 268102

Outdoor Professional, 24 Radford Sreet, **Stone**, Staffs ☎ 01785 817658

The Outdoor Shop, 27-31 High St, **Stony Stratford**, Bucks ☎ 01908 568913

Stowmarket Caravan & Leisure Centre, Bury Road, **Stowmarket**, Suffolk ☎ 01449 612677

Geoff Turner, Outdoor People, Unit 11, Charles Ind. Estate, Stowupland Road, **Stowmarket**, Suffolk ☎ 01449 675511

Rohan Designs, 23-24 Wood St, **Stratford-upon-Avon**, Warks ☎ 01789 414498

M L Great Outdoors,9 The Bridges, **Sunderland**, Tyne & Wear ☎ 0191-567 2727

Reynolds Outdoor Centre, 6 Derwent Sreet, **Sunderland**, Tyne & Wear ☎ 0191-565 7945

SSS Camping Centre, 9 Market St, Huthwaite, **Sutton in Ashfield**, Notts ☎ 01623 511181

Midwest Camping, Wyndley Garden Centre, Lichfield Road, **Sutton Coldfield** ☎ 0121-308 7279

EQUIPMENT SHOPS

85

Taunton Leisure, 206 High St, **Swansea**
☎ 01792 476515

Leisure Quest, Parc Tawe, North Dock, **Swansea**
☎ 01792 646647

High Adventure, 6 Wind St, **Swansea**
☎ 01792 648712

Taunton Leisure, 40 East Reach, **Taunton**
☎ 01823 332987

The Wearhouse, 32 North Street, **Taunton**
☎ 01823 333291

Kounty Kit, 22-23 West Street, **Tavistock,** Devon
☎ 01822 613089

Supersales of Totnes, 90 High Street, **Totnes,** Devon
☎ 01803 862737

Elements Outdoor Leisure, 71 High Street, **Totnes**,
Devon ☎ 01803 862255

BCH Camping & Leisure, 8-12 Islington, **Trowbridge**,
Wilts ☎ 01225 764977

Rohan Travel & Leisure, Town Quay, **Truro**, Cornwall
☎ 01872 260042

Penrose Outdoors, Town Quay, **Truro**, Cornwall
☎ 01872 70213

Country Trails, 39 Mount Pleasant, **Tunbridge Wells**,
Kent ☎ 01892 539002

Adventure Shop, 83 Clayton St, **Tyneside**
☎ 0191-233 1572

Silver Trek, 198 High Street, **Uxbridge**, Middx
☎ 01895 850895

Countrywise, 27 Molesworth Street, **Wadebridge**,
Cornwall ☎ 01208 812423

Outdoor Focus at Rentatent, Twitch Hill, Horbury,
Wakefield ☎ 01924 275131

Mountain High, 9 The Bull Ring, **Wakefield**
☎ 01924 296219

Mitchells, Hostingley Lane, Middlestown, **Wakefield**
☎ 01924 272877

Kenmar Camping & Leisure, Spring Green Nurseries,
Pontefract Road, Sharleston, **Wakefield**
☎ 01924 864494

Somerset Camping & Leisure, A38 Bridgwater Road,
Walford Cross, W Monkton, Somerset
☎ 01823 413333

White Mountain, 31a Stafford Street, **Walsall**, W
Mids ☎ 01922 722422

Whites, 147 Warrington Market, **Warrington**
☎ 01925 631531

Outdoor World, Mersey Building, Winwick Road,
Warrington, Cheshire ☎ 01925 634794

Adventure Centre, Evans House, Orford Lane,
Warrington, Cheshire ☎ 01925 411385

Cheshire Leisure, 30-42 Knutsford Road,
Warrington, Cheshire ☎ 01925 630554

Waterlooville Camping & Angling, 157a London
Road, **Waterlooville**, Hants ☎ 01705 252610

Tradewinds, 4 Park Road, **Wellingborough**,
Northants ☎ 01933 276632

Alexander W, 29 Broad St, **Welshpool**
☎ 01938 552329

Marcruss Stores, 52a Meadow Street, **Weston-super-
Mare**, Avon ☎ 01934 415041

The Wearhouse, 62 St Mary Street, **Weymouth**,
Dorset ☎ 01305 761791

Outdoor World, 49 Ilfracombe Gardens, **Whitley Bay**,
Tyne & Wear ☎ 0191-251 4388

Hugh Lewis & Sons, 29-31 Moor Lane, **Widnes**,
Cheshire ☎ 0151-424 7316

Active Leisure (Standish), Cannells Garden Centre,
Back Lane, Appley Bridge, **Wigan**, Lancs
☎ 01257 422945

Oswald Bailey, 5 Crown Mead Centre, **Wimborne**,
Dorset ☎ 01202 880366

Up & Away of **Winchester**

CTC Leisure, 89-91 Corn St, **Witney**
☎ 01993 771080

Midwest Camping, Codsall Garden Centre, Codsall,
Wolverhampton ☎ 01902 845404

White Mountain, 22 Worcester Street,
Wolverhampton, W Mids ☎ 01902 773395

Hillfolk, 28-32 High Sreet, **Wooler**, Northumberland
☎ 01668 281735

The Wearhouse, 21 The Cross, **Worcester**
☎ 01905 617727

Camping & Outdoor Centre, 20 Brighton Road,
Worthing, Sussex ☎ 01903 232028

The Wearhouse, 84 Middle Street, **Yeovil**, Somerset
☎ 01935 71260

Wilderness Ways, 9 Colliergate, **York**
☎ 01904 639567

Camping & Outdoor Centre, 3 Queen's House, Mickle
Gate, **York** ☎ 01904 653567

EQUIPMENT SHOPS

The Accommodation Guide

This year there are four parts to the Accommodation Guide.

Part I **Hostels and Bunkhouses**;

Part II **Accommodation Suitable for Groups**;

Part III **Self-catering Accommodation**;

Part IV **Bed & Breakfast**.

If you are looking for accommodation in a particular place rather than of a certain sort, go to the Index at the back of the book. This will refer you to the place of your choice in any of the four sections.

We have done our best to jump through the various hoops put up by the recent and ongoing re-organisation of counties. The listings in the Guide are organised by country, then county order or unitary authority where these exist. Sometimes we have banded together authorities which are small in size or where there are fewer listings — in particular, central Scotland, north east Scotland, north east Wales and south Wales. We have tried to create a system which has accuracy and logic and also takes account of the ways people think about the British Isles. However, we are unlikely to have pleased all of the people. We hope you can find your way around.

We have introduced some new symbols:

This appealing character 🐾 means you may be able to take your dog after consultation with the proprietor. The symbol is not used where only a Guide Dog would be accepted, nor when the dog is not allowed in the building but only in outside kennel or car.

Ⓜ means the advertiser is a member of the Ramblers' Association.

Ⓟ means a packed lunch is available.

Not all symbols are used in every section.

For instance, we did not ask the proprietors of group centres if they would take dogs. On the other hand Ⓟ for packed lunch is only given in the Groups section. A full key to the symbols used in the Guide is given on the last page of the book.

Tourist Board classifications These are given for the first time in this edition. However, we have not given any other classifications such as the AA or RAC. In England, a system of Crowns is used to explain the extent of facilities at a catered establishment (1-5 Crowns) and Keys (1-5 again) for self-catering. After the number of Crowns or Keys is sometimes given a mark of quality. These are: Listed, Approved, Commended, Highly Commended and De Luxe. In Scotland, Crowns are awarded for both catered and self-catering establishments. In Wales, either Grades (1, 2, 3 etc.) or Dragons are used for self-catering. In Ireland establishments are graded by Stars. Other Tourist Board awards are for holiday parks and these are Rose (England), Thistle (Scotland) and Ticks (Wales). For a fuller explanation of the classifications, consult your local Tourist Information Centre.

We have abbreviated in the following rather obvious way:

Cr for Crown; k for Key; App for Approved; List for Listed; C for Commended; and HC for Highly Commended.

If you don't know what type of accommodation you want but you do know where you want to stay, use the **index** which will guide you to the place of your choice in any of the four sections. The index begins on page 309.

Please keep sending recommendations to the Editor. It is the best way we have of keeping high standards in the Yearbook.

Hostels, Bunkhouses and Camping Barns

This section lists stopovers of all kinds. There are stone tents, "luxury" hostels with en suite rooms and hot showers, and a wide variety in between. There are many YHA hostels but not a full list (and, sadly, hardly any YHA Camping Barns). Some centres listed here are primarily for groups, but they should all be open to individuals as well. If you have to book, this is stated. Any centres catering solely for groups are now in a new section entitled Accommodation Suitable for Groups.

We give in each case the price per night, whether or not meals and/or self-catering facilities are available, long-distance paths nearby, times of year the hostel or barn is closed and items of special interest such as wheelchair access. If no months of closure are given, the establishment is open all year.

A 6-figure map reference has been given in most cases together with the sheet number of the appropriate Ordnance Survey 1:50,000 Landranger map.

Only prices for adults have been included. Most of the establishments listed here accept children at a reduced rate.

Any walking routes mentioned in the entries are as supplied by the organisers and are not checked.

The type of establishment is indicated in each case next to its name:

CB = Camping Barn A redundant farm building converted to provide basic shelter. Little or no privacy. Limited facilities. Toilets may be chemical. Sleeping areas are usually not divided between the sexes and there are wooden sleeping platforms. Camping barns are often described as stone tents.

BB = Bunkhouse Barn A converted farm building, better equipped than the camping barn. Stoves and cooking facilities provided. Toilets may be chemical. Separate sleeping areas for each sex but little privacy. Bunk beds are provided.

B = Bunkhouse Other kinds of converted buildings, simply but comfortably furnished. They can be run by hotels, sporting estates or individuals. Cooking facilities and utensils provided. Separate sleeping areas for each sex with beds or bunks. Showers and drying facilities provided.

IH = Independent Hostel A privately run hostel. Similar to YHA hostels but the standards and conditions will vary from hostel to hostel. Some provide meals but majority are self-catering. Sheet sleeping bag liners usually required.

OC = Outdoor Centre Often available to groups only. See also special section on accommodation suitable for groups in this Yearbook.

YHA = Youth Hostels Association hostel YHA hostels conform to standards of welcome, comfort, cleanliness, security, privacy and care for the environment, as established by Hostelling International. Open to all ages, you have to be a member of the YHA—you can join on arrival for only £9.50 (this includes a discount booklet). Price per night is £3.85-£7.65 for under 18s and £5.65-£11.20 for adults (except at some city hostels). Self-catering kitchens are provided, plus most hostels offer good value meals (see individual entries). Other facilities include drying rooms, cycle sheds and communal areas. Accommodation is in comfortable bunk-bedded rooms, with all bedding provided. There are often rooms for couples and families, as well as the single sex dormitories.

SYHA = Scottish Youth Hostels Association.

England

BEDFORDSHIRE

IVINGHOE YOUTH HOSTEL (YHA)
The Old Brewery House, Ivinghoe, Nr Leighton Buzzard LU7 9EP.
☎ (01296) 668251. Map 165/945161.
Meals available • Icknield Way, North Bucks Way and The Ridgeway.

BERKSHIRE

STREATLEY-ON-THAMES YOUTH HOSTEL (YHA)
Hill House, Reading Road, Streatley, Reading RG8 9JJ.
☎ (01491) 872278. Map 174/591806.
Meals available • The Ridgeway and Thames Path.

BUCKINGHAMSHIRE

BRADENHAM YOUTH HOSTEL (YHA)
The Village Hall, Bradenham, High Wycombe HP14 4HF.
☎ (01494) 562929. Map 165/828972.
SC only • London Countryway and The Ridgeway.

BRADWELL VILLAGE YOUTH HOSTEL (YHA)
Manor Farm, Vicarage Road, Bradwell Village, Milton Keynes MK13 9AG.
☎ (01908) 310944. Map 152/831395.
SC only • Meals for groups if pre-booked.

JORDANS YOUTH HOSTEL (YHA)
Welders Lane, Jordans, Beaconsfield HP9 2SN.
☎ (01494) 873135. Map 175, 176/975910.
SC only.

CORNWALL

BOSCASTLE HARBOUR YOUTH HOSTEL (YHA)
Palace Stables, Boscastle PL35 0HD.
☎ (01840) 250287. Map 190/096915.
Meals available • South West Coast Path.

BOSWINGER YOUTH HOSTEL (YHA)
Gorran, St Austell PL26 6LL.
☎ (01726) 843234. Map 204/991411.
Meals available • South West Coast Path.

COVERACK YOUTH HOSTEL (YHA)
Park Behan, School Hill, Coverack, Helston TR12 6SA.
☎ (01326) 280687. Map 204/782184.
Meals available • South West Coast Path.

LAND'S END (ST JUST) YOUTH HOSTEL (YHA)
Letcha Vean, St Just-in-Penwith, Penzance TR19 7NT.
☎ (01736) 788437. Map 203/364305.
Meals available • South West Coast Path.

PERRANPORTH YOUTH HOSTEL (YHA)
Droskyn Point, Perranporth TR6 0DS.
☎ (01872) 573812. Map 204/752544.
SC only • South West Coast Path.

TINTAGEL YOUTH HOSTEL (YHA)
Dunderhole Point, Tintagel PL34 0DW.
☎ (01840) 770334. Map 200/047881.
SC only • South West Coast Path.

TREYARNON BAY YOUTH HOSTEL (YHA)
Tregonnan, Treyarnon, Padstow PL28 8JR.
☎ (01841) 520322. Map 200/859741.
Meals available • South West Coast Path.

CUMBRIA

ALSTON YOUTH HOSTEL (YHA)
The Firs, Alston CA9 3RW.
☎ (01434) 381509. Map 86/717461.
Meals available • Pennine Way.

BENTS BARN (CB)
Bents Farm, Newbiggin-on-Lune, Kirkby Stephen
Book through Keswick Information Centre, 31 Lake Road, Keswick CA12 5DQ.
☎ (017687) 72803/(015396) 23681.
Map 91/708065.
Bednight £3 • Meals and SC • Coast to Coast Walk • Sleeps 12.

BLACK SAIL YOUTH HOSTEL (YHA)
Black Sail Hut, Ennerdale, Cleator CA23 3AY.
Map 89/194124. No phone
Meals available • Coast to Coast walk.

BORROWDALE YOUTH HOSTEL (YHA)
Longthwaite, Keswick CA12 5XE.
☎ (017687) 77257. Map 89/254142.
Meals available • Coast to Coast walk, Cumbria Way.

BUTTERMERE YOUTH HOSTEL (YHA)
King George VI Memorial Hostel, Buttermere, Cockermouth CA13 9XA.
☎ (017687) 70245. Map 89/178168.
Meals available.

CARLISLE YOUTH HOSTEL (YHA)
Etterby House, Etterby, Carlisle CA3 9QS.
☎ (01228) 23934. Map 85/386569.
Meals available • Cumbria Way.

CARROCK FELL YOUTH HOSTEL (YHA)
High Row Cottage, Haltcliffe, Hesket Newmarket, Wigton CA7 8JT.
☎ (016974) 78325. Map 90/358355.
Meals available • Cumbria Way.

COCKERMOUTH YOUTH HOSTEL (YHA)
Double Mills, Cockermouth CA13 0DS.
☎ (01900) 822561. Map 89/118298.
Meals available.

CONISTON COPPERMINES YOUTH HOSTEL (YHA)
Coppermines House, Coniston LA21 8HP.
☎ (015394) 41261. Map 96/289986.
Meals available • Cumbria Way.

DENTDALE YOUTH HOSTEL (YHA)
Cowgill, Dent, Sedbergh LA10 5RN.
☎ (015396) 25251. Map 98/773850.
Meals available • Dales Way.

DUFTON YOUTH HOSTEL (YHA)
Redstones, Dufton, Appleby CA16 6DB.
☎ (017683) 51236. Map 91/688251.
Meals available • Pennine Way.

ELTERWATER YOUTH HOSTEL (YHA)
Elterwater, Ambleside LA22 9HX.
☎ (015394) 37245. Map 90/327046.
Meals available • Cumbria Way.

ENNERDALE YOUTH HOSTEL (YHA)
Cat Crag, Ennerdale, Cleator CA23 3AX.
☎ (01946) 861237. Map 89/142141.
Meals available • Coast to Coast walk.

ESKDALE YOUTH HOSTEL (YHA)
Boot, Holmrook CA19 1TH.
☎ (019467) 23219. Map 89/195010.
Meals available.

GRASMERE THORNEY HOW YOUTH HOSTEL (YHA)
Thorney How, Grasmere, Ambleside LA22 9QW.
☎ (015394) 35591. Map 90/332084.
Meals available • Coast to Coast walk.

GREENHEAD YOUTH HOSTEL (YHA)
Greenhead, Carlisle CA6 7HG.
☎ (016977) 47401. Map 86/659655.
Meals available • Pennine Way.

HELVELLYN YOUTH HOSTEL (YHA)
Greenside, Glenridding, Penrith CA11 0QR.
☎ (017684) 82269. Map 90/366173.
Meals available • Coast to Coast walk.

HONISTER HAUSE YOUTH HOSTEL (YHA)
Honister Hause, Seatoller, Keswick CA12 5XN.
☎ (017687) 77267. Map 89/224135.
Meals available• Coast to Coast Walk
Cumbria Way.

KIRKBY STEPHEN YOUTH HOSTEL (YHA)
Fletcher Hill, Market Street, Kirkby Stephen CA17 4QQ.
☎ (017683) 71793. Map 91/774085.
Meals available • Coast to Coast walk.

ROWRAH HALL (OC)
Frizington CA26 3XH.
☎ (01946) 861029. Map 89/056184.
Bednight £5 • Meals available • No SC • Near Coast to Coast Walk • Family rooms • Large groups OK • Closed Jan/Feb.

SKIDDAW HOUSE YOUTH HOSTEL (YHA)
Bassenthwaite, Keswick CA12 4QX.
☎ (016974) 78325. Map 89/288291.
SC only • Cumbria Way.

STICKLEBARN BUNKHOUSE (B)
Great Langdale, Nr Ambleside LA22 9JU.
☎ (015394) 37356. Map 90/294064.
Bednight £10 • Meals • No SC • Cumbria Way.

STRIDING EDGE HOSTEL (IH)
Greenside, Glenridding, Nr Penrith. Map 90/364174.
Book through Nat. Park Information Centre, 31 Lake Road, Keswick CA12 5DQ.
☎ (017687) 73700.
Bednight around £6 • SC only • Coast to Coast Walk.

SWIRRAL BARN (CB)
Greenside, Glenridding, Nr Penrith. Map 90/364174.
Book through Nat. Park Information Centre as for Striding Edge above.
Bednight around £3 • No SC, no meals • Coast to Coast Walk.

TEBAY YOUTH HOSTEL (YHA)
The Old School, Tebay, Penrith CA10 3TP.
☎ (015396) 24286. Map 91/618045.
Meals available • Coast to Coast Walk.

THIRLMERE YOUTH HOSTEL (YHA)
The Old School, Stanah Cross, Keswick CA12 4TQ.
☎ (017687) 73224. Map 90/318190.
Meals available.

WASTWATER YOUTH HOSTEL (YHA)
Wasdale Hall, Wasdale, Seascale CA20 1ET.
☎ (019467) 26222. Map 89/145045.
Meals available.

WINDERMERE YOUTH HOSTEL (YHA)
High Cross, Bridge Lane, Troutbeck, Windermere LA23 1LA.
☎ (015394) 43543. Map 90/405013.
Meals available • Dales Way.

DERBYSHIRE

BAKEWELL YOUTH HOSTEL (YHA)
Fly Hill, Bakewell DE45 1DN.
☎ (01629) 812313. Map 119/215685.
Meals available • White Peak Way.

BRETTON YOUTH HOSTEL (YHA)
Nr Eyam. Book through J & E Whittington, 7 New Bailey, Crane Moor, Sheffield S30 7AT.
☎ 0114-288 4541. Map 119/200870.
SC only.

BUXTON YOUTH HOSTEL (YHA)
Sherbrook Lodge, Harpur Hill Road, Buxton SK17 9NB.
☎ (01298) 22287. Map 119/062772.
Meals available.

CASTLE FARM (CB)
Middleton by Youlgrave, Bakewell DE45 1LS.
☎ (01629) 636746. Map 119/198633.
Bednight £3 • No SC nor meals • Alternative Penine Way, White Peak, Limey Way.

CROWDEN YOUTH HOSTEL (YHA)
Peak National Park Hostel, Crowden, Hadfield, Hyde SK14 7HZ.
☎ (01457) 852135. Map 110/073993.
Meals available • Pennine Way.

ELTON YOUTH HOSTEL (YHA)
Elton Old Hall, Main Street, Elton, Matlock DE4 2BW.
☎ (01629) 650394. Map 119/224608.
SC only and snack meals • Limestone Way.

HATHERSAGE YOUTH HOSTEL (YHA)
Castleton Road, Hathersage S30 1AH.
☎ (01433) 650493. Map 110/226814.
Meals available • White Peak Way.

LANGSETT YOUTH HOSTEL (YHA)
Nr Penistone.
Book through J & E Whittington, 7 New Bailey, Crane Moor, Sheffield S30 7AT.
☎ 0114-288 4541. Map 110/211005.
SC only.

MEERBROOK YOUTH HOSTEL (YHA)
c/o Elton Old Hall, Main Street, Elton, Matlock DE4 2BW.
☎ (01629) 650394. Map 119/989608.
SC only • Staffordshire Way.

NEW BUILDINGS FARM BUNK BARN (B)
New Buildings Farm, Ashleyhay, Wirksworth, Matlock DE4 4AH.
☎ (01629) 823191. Map 119/296518.
Bednight £6 • Sole use £60 • SC only • Sleeps 12/14 • Showers, heating • Mid-Shires Way, High Peak Trail.

PEAK NATIONAL PARK CENTRE CAMPING BARNS
13 Camping Barns throughout the Peak District.
☎ (01433) 620373.

SHINING CLIFF YOUTH HOSTEL (YHA)
c/o Elton Old Hall, Main Street, Elton, Matlock DE4 2BW.
☎ (01629) 650394. Map 119/335522.
SC only.

STANLEY FARM BUNKERBARN CENTRE (BB, IH)
Stanley Farm, Chunal, Glossop.
☎ (01457) 863727. Map 110/033905.
Bednight £8 • SC only • Pennine Way.

THORPE FARM BUNKHOUSE (B)
Thorpe Farm, Hathersage, Sheffield S30 1BQ.
☎ (01433) 650659. Map 110/223824.
Bednight midweek £6 or £80 sole use • SC only • Heating, showers, drying facilities • Food nearby..

YOULGRAVE YOUTH HOSTEL (YHA)
Fountain Square, Youlgreave, Nr Bakewell DE4 1UR.
☎ (01629) 636518. Map 119/210641.
Meals available • Limestone Way & White Peak Way.

DEVON

BEER YOUTH HOSTEL (YHA)
Bovey Combe, Townsend, Beer, Seaton EX12 3LL.
☎ (01297) 20296. Map 192/223896.
Meals available • South West Coast Path.

BELLEVER YOUTH HOSTEL (YHA)
Postbridge, Yelverton PL20 6TU.
☎ (01822) 880227. Map 191/654773.
Meals available • Two Moors Way.

DARTINGTON YOUTH HOSTEL (YHA)
Lownard, Dartington, Totnes TQ9 6JJ.
☎ (01803) 862303. Map 202/782622.
SC only.

DARTMOOR EXPEDITION CENTRE (B, BB, OC)
Rowden, Widecombe-in-the-Moor, Newton Abbot TQ13 7TX.
☎ (01364) 621249. Map 191/699764.
Bednight £5.50 • SC or meals by arrangement • Two Moors Way • Groups also.

ELMSCOTT (HARTLAND) YOUTH HOSTEL (YHA)
Elmscott, Hartland, Bideford EX39 6ES.
☎ (01237) 441367. Map 190/231217.
SC only • South West Coast Path.

ILFRACOMBE YOUTH HOSTEL (YHA)
Ashmour House, 1 Hillsborough Terrace, Ilfracombe EX34 9NR.
☎ (01271) 865337. Map 180/524476.
Meals available • South West Coast Path Tarka Trail.

INSTOW YOUTH HOSTEL (YHA)
Worlington House, New Road, Instow, Bideford EX39 4LW.
☎ (01271) 860394. Map 180/842303.
Meals available • South West Coast Path.

LOPWELL CAMPING BARN (CB)
Lopwell Dam, Lopwell, Nr Yelverton.
☎ (01752) 696408. Map 201/475650.
Book through West Devon Borough Council, Kilworthy Park, Tavistock PL19 0BZ.
☎ (01822) 615911.
Bednight £3.50 • SC only • West Devon Way.

LYNTON YOUTH HOSTEL (YHA)
Lynbridge, Lynton EX35 6AZ.
☎ (01598) 753237. Map 180/720487.
Meals available • South West Coast Path, Two Moors Way, Tarka Trail.

MAYPOOL YOUTH HOSTEL (YHA)
Maypool House, Galmpton, Brixham TQ5 0ET.
☎ (01803) 842444. Map 202/877546.
Meals available • South West Coast Path.

PLUME OF FEATHERS INN BUNKHOUSE (B/CB/IH)
Plume of Feathers Inn, The Square, Princetown, Tavistock PL20 6QG.
☎ Princetown (01822) 890240. Map 191/591735.
Bednight from £3-£5.50 • SC and meals • B&B and campsite also.

SALCOMBE YOUTH HOSTEL (YHA)
'Overbecks', Sharpitor, Salcombe TQ8 8LW.
☎ (0154884) 2856. Map 202/728374.
Meals available • South West Coast Path.

STEPS BRIDGE YOUTH HOSTEL (YHA)
Dunsford, Exeter EX6 7EQ.
☎ (01647) 252435. Map 191/802882.
SC only.

WATERCOMBE BUNK BARN (YHA BARN)
Watercombe Farm, Cornwood, Ivybridge.
Book through 60 Compton Ave, Mannamead, Plymouth PL3 5DA.
☎ (01752) 668846/(01271) 24420.
Map 202/625613.
Bednight £3.50 or £38 group • SC only • Closed Oct-Feb • Two Moors Way • Family room • Unisex or separate sleeping • Shower • Disabled facilities.

DORSET

LITTON CHENEY YOUTH HOSTEL (YHA)
Litton Cheney, Dorchester DT2 9AT.
☎ (01308) 482340. Map 194/548900.
SC only • South West Coast Path.

LULWORTH COVE YOUTH HOSTEL (YHA)
School Lane, West Lulworth, Wareham BH20 5SA.
☎ (01929) 400564. Map 194/832806.
Meals available • South West Coast Path.

COUNTY DURHAM

BALDERSDALE YOUTH HOSTEL (YHA)
Blackton, Baldersdale, Barnard Castle DL12 9UP.
☎ (01833) 650629. Map 91/931179.
Meals available • Pennine Way.

EDMUNDBYERS YOUTH HOSTEL (YHA)
Low House, Edmundbyers, Consett DH8 9NL.
☎ (01207) 55651. Map 87/017500.
SC only.

HUDEWAY CENTRE (IH, OC)
Stacks Lane, Middleton-in-Teesdale, Barnard Castle DL12 0QR.
☎ (01833) 640012. Map 92/943257.
Bednight £7 • £10 B&B • £15 full board or SC • Pennine Way • Ground floor available.

LANGDON BECK YOUTH HOSTEL (YHA)
Langdon Beck, Forest-in-Teesdale, Barnard Castle DL12 0XN.
☎ (01833) 622228. Map 91/860304.
Meals available • Pennine Way.

ESSEX

CASTLE HEDINGHAM YOUTH HOSTEL (YHA)
7 Falcon Sq, Castle Hedingham, Halstead CO9 3BU.
☎ (01787) 460799. Map 155/786355.
Meals available • Wheelchair access.

EPPING FOREST YOUTH HOSTEL (YHA)
Wellington Hall, High Beach, Loughton IG10 4AG.
☎ 0181-508 5161. Map 167/408983.
SC only • Essex Way, London Countryway.

SAFFRON WALDEN YOUTH HOSTEL (YHA)
1 Myddylton Place, Saffron Walden CB10 1BB.
☎ (01799) 523117. Map 154/535386.
Meals available.

GLOUCESTERSHIRE

DUNTISBOURNE ABBOTS YOUTH HOSTEL (YHA)
Duntisbourne Abbots, Cirencester GL7 7JN.
☎ (01285) 821682. Map 163/970080.
Meals available.

THE FOUNTAIN LODGE (B, IH)
Opposite. old railway station, Parkend,
Lydney GL15 4JD.
☎ (01594) 562189.
Bednight £7.50 • SC and meals.

STOW-ON-THE-WOLD YOUTH HOSTEL (YHA)
Stow-on-the-Wold, Cheltenham GL54 1AF.
☎ (01451) 830497. Map 163/191258.
Meals available • Oxfordshire Way.

HAMPSHIRE

BURLEY YOUTH HOSTEL (YHA)
Cottesmore House, Cott Lane, Burley, Ringwood
BH24 4BB.
☎ (01425) 403233. Map 195/220028.
Meals available.

WINCHESTER YOUTH HOSTEL (YHA)
The City Mill, 1 Water Lane, Winchester SO23 0ER.
☎ (01962) 853723. Map 185/486293.
Meals available • South Downs Way, Three Castles
Path.

HEREFORD & WORCESTER

MALVERN HILLS YOUTH HOSTEL (YHA)
18 Peachfield Rd, Malvern Wells, Malvern WR14 4AP.
☎ (01684) 569131. Map 150/774440.
Meals available.

WELSH BICKNOR YOUTH HOSTEL (YHA)
Welsh Bicknor Rectory, Nr. Goodrich, Ross-on-Wye
HR9 6JJ.
☎ (01594) 860300. Map 162/591177.
Meals provided • Family rooms • Wye Valley Walk.

ISLE OF WIGHT

SANDOWN YOUTH HOSTEL (YHA)
The Firs, Fitzroy Street, Sandown PO36 8JH.
☎ (01983) 402651. Map 196/597843.
Meals available • Isle of Wight Coastal Path.

**TOTLAND BAY (WEST WIGHT) YOUTH HOSTEL
(YHA)**
Hurst Hill, Totland Bay PO39 0HD.
☎ (01983) 752165. Map 196/324865.
Meals available • Isle of Wight Coastal Path.

KENT

BROADSTAIRS YOUTH HOSTEL (YHA)
Thistle Lodge, 3 Osborne Road, Broadstairs, Isle of
Thanet CT10 2AE.
☎ (01843) 604121. Map 179/390679.
SC only • Saxon Shore Way.

**CAPSTONE FARM (ROCHESTER) YOUTH HOSTEL
(YHA)**
377 Capstone Road, Gillingham ME7 3JE.
☎ (01634) 400788. Map 178/781654.

KEMSING YOUTH HOSTEL (YHA)
Church Lane, Kemsing, Sevenoaks TN15 6LU.
☎ (01732) 761341. Map 188/555588.
Meals available • London Countryway, North Downs
Way.

KIPPS (IH)
40 Nunnery Fields, Canterbury CT1 3JT.
☎ (01227) 786121. Map 179/151570.
Bednight £9.95 (dorm), £12.95 (single) • SC only •
North Downs Way, Pilgrims Way • Sleeps 36.

LANCASHIRE

EARBY YOUTH HOSTEL (YHA)
Glen Cottage, Birch Hall Lane, Colne BB8 6JX.
☎ (01282) 842349. Map 103/915468.
SC only • Pennine Way.

ENTWISTLE CAMPING BARN (CB)
Hall Shore Croft, Overshores Road, Entwistle, Near
Bolton. Book through Jumbles Information Centre,
Waterfold car park, Bradshaw Road, Bolton.
☎ (01204) 853360. Map 109/725175.
Bednight £2 • Deposit £10 • No SC or meals —
camping gear required.

MANKINHOLES YOUTH HOSTEL (YHA)
Mankinholes, Todmorden OL14 6HR.
☎ (01706) 812340. Map 103/960235.
Meals available • Calderdale Way & Pennine Way.

MORRIS HOUSE CAMPING BARN (CB)
Dean Head Lane, Rivington. Book through Great
House Barn Information Centre, Rivington Lane,
Horwich, Bolton BL6 7SB.
☎ (01204) 691549. Map 109/629159.
Bednight £2 • Deposit £10 • No SC or meals—
camping gear required.

SLAIDBURN YOUTH HOSTEL (YHA)
King's House, Slaidburn, Clitheroe BB7 3ER.
☎ (01200) 446656. Map 103/711523.
SC only.

SUNNYHURST CAMPING BARN (CB)
Adjacent to Sunnyhurst Hey Reservoir, access via Earnsdale Road, Darwen. Book through Great House Barn Information Centre, Rivington Lane, Horwich, Bolton BL6 7SB.
☎ (01204) 691549. Map 103/678221.
Bednight £2 • Deposit £10 • No SC or meals—camping gear required.

LEICESTERSHIRE

COPT OAK YOUTH HOSTEL (YHA)
Whitwick Road, Copt Oak, Markfield LE67 9QB.
☎ (01530) 242661. Map 129/482129. SC only.

SWAN LODGE (BB)
Station Road, Upper Broughton, Melton Mowbray LE14 3BH.
☎ (01664) 823686. Map 129/677260.
Bednight £5 or £30 groups • SC only • Mixed sleeping area • Heating and TV • Mid-Shires Way.

LINCOLNSHIRE

THURLBY YOUTH HOSTEL (YHA)
16 High Street, Thurlby, Bourne PE10 0EE.
☎ (01778) 425588. Map 130/097168.
SC only • Wheelchair access • Viking Way.

WOODY'S TOP YOUTH HOSTEL (YHA)
Ruckland, Nr Louth LN11 8RQ.
☎ (01507) 533323. Map 122/332786.
SC only • Viking Way.

GREATER MANCHESTER

GLOBE FARM BUNKHOUSE (IH)
Globe Farm, Huddersfield Road, Standedge, Delph, Oldham OL3 5LU.
☎ Saddleworth (01457) 873040. Map 109/012097.
Bednight £6.50 • Meals and SC • Camping and ensuite B&B also • On Pennine Way.

Do you know your rights when you're out walking in the countryside?

Do you know what to do if you find your way blocked?

Do you know what's happening to our woodlands and forests?

Read what the Ramblers are doing about these matters on pages 6-39.

NORFOLK

COURTYARD FARM (BB)
Ringstead, Hunstanton PE36 5LQ.
☎ (01485) 525369. Map 132/729400.
Bednight £4 • SC only • Peddars Way.

DEEPDALE GRANARY BUNKHOUSE (B)
Deepdale Farm, Burnham Deepdale, Kings Lynn PE31 8DD. ☎ (01485) 210256. Map 132/803443.
Bednight £7.50 • SC only • Norfolk Coast Path.

GREAT YARMOUTH YOUTH HOSTEL (YHA)
2 Sandown Road, Great Yarmouth NR30 1EY.
☎ (01493) 843991. Map 134/529083.
Meals available • Weavers Way.

HUNSTANTON YOUTH HOSTEL (YHA)
15 Avenue Road, Hunstanton PE36 5BW.
☎ (01485) 532061. Map 132/674406.
Meals available • Peddars Way.

KING'S LYNN YOUTH HOSTEL (YHA)
Thoresby College, College Lane, King's Lynn PE30 1JB.
☎ (01553) 772461. Map 132/616199.
SC only • Meals for groups if pre-booked.

NORTHAMPTONSHIRE

BADBY YOUTH HOSTEL (YHA)
Church Green, Badby, Daventry NN11 3AS.
☎ (01327) 703883. Map 152/561588.
SC only.

NORTHUMBERLAND

ACOMB YOUTH HOSTEL (YHA)
Acomb, Hexham NE46 4PL.
☎ (01434) 602864. Map 87/934666.
SC only.

BELLINGHAM YOUTH HOSTEL (YHA)
Woodburn Road, Bellingham, Hexham NE48 2ED.
☎ (01434) 220313. Map 80/843834.
SC only • Pennine Way.

BORDER FOREST CARAVAN PARK BUNKHOUSE (B)
(FORMERLY BYRNESS CARAVAN PARK)
Cottonshopeburnfoot, Nr Otterburn.
☎ (01830) 520259. Map 80/780014.
Bednight £7 • SC only • Pennine Way.

HADRIAN'S WALL BACKPACKERS (B, IH)
Hadrians Lodge, Hindshield Moss, North Road,
Haydon Bridge.
☎ (01434) 688688. Map 86/
Bednight £8 • SC or meals • Closed Jan-Feb •
Hadrians Wall Path • Disabled toilets and ground
floor accommodation • Licensed bar.

HOLMEHEAD FARM (CB)
Hadrians Wall, Greenhead, Via Carlise CA6 7HY.
☎ (016977) 47402. Map 86/661659.
Bednight from £3 • SC only • Pennine Way, Hadrians
Wall Path • Pub nearby.

JOINERS SHOP BUNKHOUSE (B)
Preston, Chathill NE67 5ES.
☎ (01665) 589245. Map 75/183254.
Bednight £5.50 • SC only.

NINEBANKS YOUTH HOSTEL (YHA)
Orchard Hse, Mohope, Ninebanks, Hexham NE47 8DO.
☎ (01434) 345288. Map 86/771514.
SC only.

ROCK HALL SCHOOL (IH)
Rock, Alnwick NE66 3SB.
☎ (01665)˙579224. Map 81/235196.
Half board £17 • No SC • Closed Nov-Feb.

WOOLER YOUTH HOSTEL (YHA)
30 Cheviot Street, Wooler NE71 6LW.
☎ (01668) 281365. Map 75/991278.
Meals available • St Cuthberts Way.

NOTTINGHAMSHIRE

IGLOO TOURIST HOSTEL (IH)
110 Mansfield Road, Nottingham NG1 3HL.
☎ 0115-947 5250.Map 129/569417.
Bednight £8.50 • SC only • Robin Hood Way, Trent
Valley Way.

OXFORDSHIRE

CHARLBURY YOUTH HOSTEL (YHA)
The Laurels, The Slade, Charlbury OX7 3SJ.
☎ (01608) 810202. Map 164/361198.
Meals available • Wheelchair access

OXFORD BACKPACKERS HOSTEL (IH)
9 Hythe Bridge Street, Oxford OX1 2EW.
☎ (01865) 721761. Map 164/508063..
Bednight £9 • SC only • Oxford Canal Walk and
Oxford Circular Path.

THE RIDGEWAY YOUTH HOSTEL (YHA)
The Court Hill Ridgeway Centre, Court Hill, Wantage
OX12 9NE.
☎ (012357) 60253. Map 174/393851.
Meals available • Wheelchair access • The Ridgeway.

SHROPSHIRE

BRIDGES LONG MYND YOUTH HOSTEL (YHA)
Ratlinghope, Shrewsbury SY5 0SP.
☎ (01588) 650656. Map 137/395965.
Meals available • Shropshire Way.

CLUN MILL YOUTH HOSTEL (YHA)
The Mill, Clun, Nr Craven Arms SY7 8NY.
☎ (01588) 640582. Map 137/303812.
SC only • Shropshire Way, Offa's Dyke Path.

LUDLOW YOUTH HOSTEL (YHA)
Ludford Lodge, Ludford, Ludlow SY8 1PJ.
☎ (01584) 872472. Map 137, 138/513741.
Meals available • Shropshire Way.

STOKES BARN (BB)
Newtown House Farm, Much Wenlock TF13 6DB.
☎ (01952) 727293. Map 69/609999.
Bednight £6 • Meals available • Shropshire Way •
Family rooms • Campsite also • .

WHEATHILL YOUTH HOSTEL (YHA)
Malthouse Farm, Wheathill, Bridgnorth WV16 6QT.
☎ (01746) 787236. Map 138/613818.
SC only • Shropshire Way.

WILDERHOPE MANOR YOUTH HOSTEL (YHA)
The John Cadbury Mem. Hostel, Easthope, Much
Wenlock TF13 6EG.
☎ (01694) 771363. Map 137, 138/544928.
Meals available • Shropshire Way.

SOMERSET

CHEDDAR YOUTH HOSTEL (YHA)
Hillfield, Cheddar BS27 3HN.
☎ (01934) 742494. Map 182/455534.
Meals available • West Mendip Way.

CROWCOMBE HEATHFIELD YOUTH HOSTEL (YHA)
Denzel House, Crowcombe Heathfield, Taunton
TA4 4BT.
☎ (01984) 667249. Map 181/138339.
SC only

EXFORD (EXMOOR) YOUTH HOSTEL (YHA)
Exe Mead, Exford, Minehead TA24 7PU.
☎ (0164383) 1288. Map 181/853383.
Meals available • Two Moors Way.

MINEHEAD YOUTH HOSTEL (YHA)
Alcombe Combe, Minehead TA24 6EW.
☎ (01643) 702595. Map 181/973442.
Meals available • South West Coast Path.

QUANTOCK HILLS (HOLFORD) YOUTH HOSTEL (YHA)
Sevenacres, Holford, Bridgwater TA5 1SQ.
☎ (01278) 741224. Map 181/145416.
SC only • Meals for groups if pre-booked.

STREET YOUTH HOSTEL (YHA)
The Chalet, Ivythorne Hill, Street BA16 0TZ.
☎ (01458) 442961. Map 182/480345.
SC only.

STAFFORDSHIRE

DIMMINGSDALE YOUTH HOSTEL (YHA)
Little Ranger, Dimmingsdale, Oakamoor, S-O-T, ST10 3AS.
☎ (01538) 702304. Map 119/052436.
SC only • Staffordshire Way.

SUFFOLK

BLAXHALL YOUTH HOSTEL (YHA)
Heath Walk, Blaxhall, Woodbridge IP12 2EA.
☎ (01728) 688206. Map 156/369570.
Meals available.

BRANDON YOUTH HOSTEL (YHA)
Heath House, off Warren Close, Bury Road, Brandon IP27 0BU.
☎ (01842) 812075. Map 144/786864.
Meals available • Hereward Way, Icknield Way.

SURREY

HINDHEAD YOUTH HOSTEL (YHA)
Devils Punch Bowl, Thursley, Nr Godalming GU8 6NS.
☎ (0142 860) 4285. Map 186/892368
SC only • Greensand Way.

TANNERS HATCH YOUTH HOSTEL (YHA)
Polesden Lacey, Dorking RH5 6BE.
☎ (01372) 452528. Map 187/140515.
SC only • London Countryway, North Downs Way.

EAST SUSSEX

ALFRISTON YOUTH HOSTEL (YHA)
Frog Firle, Alfriston, Polegate BN26 5TT.
☎ (01323) 870423. Map 199/518019.
Meals available • South Downs Way, Vanguard Way, Wealdway.

BLACKBOYS YOUTH HOSTEL (YHA)
Blackboys, Uckfield TN22 5HU.
☎ (01825) 890607. Map 199/521215.
SC only • South Downs Way, Vanguard Way, Wealdway.

EASTBOURNE YOUTH HOSTEL (YHA)
East Dean Road, Eastbourne BN20 8ES.
☎ (01323) 721081. Map 199/588990.
SC only • South Downs Way, Wealdway.

FOXHOLE CAMPING BARN & CAMPSITE (CB)
Seven Sisters Country Park, Exceat, Nr Seaford BN25 4AD. Book through the Rangers Office (as above).
☎ (01323) 870280. Map 199/523583.
Bednight £3 • No meals or SC • Closed Xmas • South Downs Way.

HASTINGS YOUTH HOSTEL (YHA)
Guestling Hall, Rye Road, Guestling, Hastings TN35 4LP.
☎ (01424) 812373. Map 199/848133.
Meals available.

TELSCOMBE YOUTH HOSTEL (YHA)
Bank Cottages, Telscombe, Lewes BN7 3HZ.
☎ (01273) 301357. Map 198/405033.
SC only • South Downs Way.

WEST SUSSEX

ARUNDEL YOUTH HOSTEL (YHA)
Warningcamp, Arundel BN18 9QY.
☎ (01903) 882204. Map 197/032076.
Meals available • South Downs Way.

GUMBER BOTHY CAMPING BARN (CB)
Gumber Farm, Slindon, Nr Arundel.
☎ (01243) 814554 (day) 814484 (eve). Map 197/961119.
Bednight £5 • SC only Breakfast food available • Closed Nov-Dec • Disabled facilities • South Downs Way.

TRULEIGH HILL YOUTH HOSTEL (YHA)
Tottington Barn, Truleigh Hill, Shoreham-by-Sea BN43 5FB.
☎ (01903) 813419. Map 198/220105.
Meals available • South Downs Way.

TYNE & WEAR

BYRNESS YOUTH HOSTEL (YHA)
7-8 Otterburn Green, Byrness, Newcastle-upon-Tyne NE19 1TS.
☎ (01830) 520424. Map 80/764027.
SC only • Pennine Way.

EAST RIDING OF YORKSHIRE

BEVERLEY FRIARY YOUTH HOSTEL (YHA)
The Friary, Friar's Lane, Beverley HU17 0DF.
☎ (01482) 881751. Map 107/038393.
Meals available.

NORTH YORKSHIRE

AIRTON QUAKER HOSTEL (IH)
Airton, nr Skipton BD23 4AE. Book through Mr & Mrs G Parker, The Nook, Airton, Nr Skipton BD23 4AE.
☎ (01729) 830263. Map 103/904592.
Bednight £4 • SC only • Pennine Way.

AYSGARTH YOUTH HOSTEL (YHA)
Aysgarth, Leyburn DL8 3SR.
☎ (01969) 663260. Map 98/012844.
Meals available • Herriot Way.

BARDEN BUNK BARN (BB)
Barden Tower, Barden, Nr Skipton BD23 6AS.
☎ (01756) 720330. Map 104/050571.
Bednight approx. £6 • SC • Sleeps 24 • Dales Way • Closed Jan/Feb.

THE BARNSTEAD (BB)
Stacksteads Farm, Ingleton, Carnforth LA6 3HS.
☎ Ingleton (015242) 41386. Map 98/686724.
Bednight £7 • SC only • Wheelchair access.

BENT RIGG FARM (BB, IH)
Ravenscar, Scarborough.
☎ (01723) 870475. Map 94/984008.
Bednight £4 • SC only • Lyke Wake Walk and Cleveland Way.

DUB COTE BUNKHOUSE (B/BB)
Dub Cote Farm, Horton-in-Ribblesdale, Nr Settle BD24 0ET.
☎ (01729) 860238. Map 98/819715.
Bednight £6.30 • SC only • Family rooms available • Closed Jan-March • Pennine Way, Ribbleway.

ELLINGSTRING YOUTH HOSTEL (YHA)
Lilac Cottage, Ellingstring, Ripon HG4 4PW.
☎ (01677) 60216. Map 99/176835.
SC only.

GRANGE FARM BARN (BB)
Grange Farm, Hubberholme, Skipton BD23 5JE.
☎ (01756) 760259. Map 98/935773.
Bednight £5 mid-week • Weekends groups only £210 for 2 nts, sleep 18 • SC only • Dales Way.

HALTON GILL BUNK BARN (BB)
Halton Gill, Skipton BD23 5QN.
Book through Mrs A Cowan, Ellershaw Farm, Halton Gill, Skipton BD23 5QN.
☎ (01756) 770241. Map 98/879765.
Bednight £6-£6.50 • SC only • Sleeps 40 • Heated • Pennine Way.

HARBOUR GRANGE (B)
Spital Bridge, Whitby YO22 4EG.
☎ (01947) 600817. Map 94/901104.
Bednight £8 • Groups £145 • Jan-Mar groups only • Cleveland Way, Coast to Coast Walk.

HAWES YOUTH HOSTEL (YHA)
Lancaster Terrace, Hawes DL8 3LQ.
☎ (01969) 667368. Map 98/867897.
Meals available • Herriot Way & Pennine Way.

HELMSLEY YOUTH HOSTEL (YHA)
Carlton Lane, Helmsley YO6 5HB.
☎ (01439) 770433. Map 100/616840.
Meals available • Cleveland Way & Ebor Way.

HILL TOP FARM (B)
Walden, West Burton, Leyburn DL8 4LE.
☎ (01969) 663341. Map 98/010860.
Bednight £4.50 • SC only • Groups (10-14) £60 • Buckden Pike, Coverdale.

INGLETON YOUTH HOSTEL (YHA)
Greta Tower, Ingleton, Carnforth LA6 3EG.
☎ (015242) 41444. Map 98/695733.
Meals available.

KELD YOUTH HOSTEL (YHA)
Keld Lodge, Upper Swaledale, Richmond DL11 6LL. ☎ (01748) 886259. Map 91/891009.
Meals available • Herriot Way, Coast to Coast walk & Pennine Way.

KETTLEWELL YOUTH HOSTEL (YHA)
Whernside House, Kettlewell, Skipton BD23 5QU.
☎ (01756) 760232. Map 98/970724.
Meals available • Dales Way.

LINTON YOUTH HOSTEL (YHA)
The Old Rectory, Linton-in-Craven, Skipton BD23 5HH.
☎ (01756) 752400. Map 98/998627.
Meals available • Dales Way.

LOCKTON YOUTH HOSTEL (YHA)
The Old School, Lockton, Pickering YO18 7PY.
☎ (01751) 60376. Map 94/844900.
SC only • Link through the Tabular Hill.

MALTON YOUTH HOSTEL (YHA)
47 York Road, Derwent Bank, Malton YO17 0AX.
☎ (01653) 692077. Map 100/779711.
Meals available.

OSMOTHERLEY YOUTH HOSTEL (YHA)
Cote Ghyll, Osmotherley, Northallerton DL6 3AH.
☎ (01609) 883575. Map 100/461981.
Meals available • Cleveland Way, Coast to Coast walk & Lyke Wake Walk.

PUNCH BOWL INN AND BUNKHOUSE (B)
Low Row, Swaledale, Richmond DL11 6PF.
☎ Richmond (01748) 886233. Map 99/987484.
Bednight from £6.50 • Meals or SC • Coast to Coast Walk.

SCARBOROUGH YOUTH HOSTEL (YHA)
The White House, Burniston Road, Scarborough YO13 0DA.
☎ (01273) 361176. Map 101/026907.
Meals available • Cleveland Way & Link through the Tabular Hills.

SKIRFARE BRIDGE DALES BARN (BB)
Northcote, Kilnsey, Skipton BD23 5PT.
☎ Grassington (01756) 752465. Map 98/973688.
Bednight £7 • SC or meals by arrangement • Sleeps 25 • Heated • Groups only weekends • Dalesway.

THIXENDALE YOUTH HOSTEL (YHA)
The Village Hall, Thixendale, Malton YO17 9TG.
☎ (01377) 288238. Map 100/843610.
SC only • Wolds Way.

TIMBERLODGE (B)
Pinecroft, Ingleton, Carnforth LA6 3DP
☎ (015242) 41462. Map Map 98/699719.
Bednight £7 • SC only • Facilities for wheelchair users • Drying room.

WEST END OUTDOOR CENTRE (B)
Whitmoor Farm, West End, Summerbridge, Harrogate HG3 4BA.
☎ (01943) 880207. Map 104/146575.
Bednight £5-£7 • 30 people in 9 bedrooms • SC only • Family room available.

WHEELDALE YOUTH HOSTEL (YHA)
Wheeldale Lodge, Goathland, Whitby YO22 5AP.
☎ (01347) 86350. Map 94/813984.
Meals available.

WHITBY YOUTH HOSTEL (YHA)
East Cliff, Whitby YO22 4JT.
☎ (01947) 602878. Map 94/902111.
Meals available • Esk Valley Walk & Cleveland Way.

YORK YOUTH HOTEL (IH)
11/13 Bishophill Senior, York YO1 1EF.
☎ (01904) 625904. Map 105/600515.
Bednight £9 • SC Meals for groups.

WEST YORKSHIRE

FOREST FARM BUNKHOUSE (B)
Forest Farm, Mount Road, Marsden, Huddersfield HD1 6NN.
☎ Huddersfield (01484) 842687. Map 110/041104.
Bednight £6.50 • SC and breakfast • Pennine Way and Alternative Pennine Walk.

Scotland

ARGYLL & BUTE

JEREMY INGLIS HOSTEL (IH)
21 Airds Crescent, Oban.
☎ (01631) 565065. Map 49/860295.
Bednight £6.50-£7 (includes continental breakfast) • SC only • Private rooms available.

OBAN YOUTH HOSTEL (SYHA)
Esplanade, Oban, Argyll PA34 5AF.
☎ (01631) 562025. Map 49/854307.
Bednight £8.15 • SC only.

CENTRAL BELT

THE AUTHORITIES OF AYRSHIRE (EAST, NORTH & SOUTH), CLACK-MANNANSHIRE, DUNBARTONSHIRE (WEST & EAST), DUNDEE CITY, EDINBURGH CITY, FALKIRK, FIFE, GLASGOW CITY, INVERCLYDE, LANARKSHIRE (NORTH & SOUTH), LOTHIAN (EAST & WEST), MID-LOTHIAN, RENFREWSHIRE & EAST RENFREWSHIRE,

ARDGARTAN YOUTH HOSTEL (SYHA)
Arrochar, Dunbartonshire G83 7AR.
☎ (013012) 362. Map 56/272028.
Bednight £7.35 • Meals available • Arrochar Alps, Argyll Forest Park.

EDINBURGH EGLINTON YOUTH HOSTEL (SYHA)
18 Eglinton Crescent, Edinburgh EH10 4EZ.
☎ 0131-337 1120. Map 66/238735.
Bednight £10.95 (inc. breakfast) • Meals available.

GLASGOW YOUTH HOSTEL (SYHA)
7/8 Park Terrace, Glasgow G3 6BY.
☎ 0141-332 3004. Map 64/575662.
Bednight £10.95 (inc. breakfast) • Meals available • West Highland Way.

HOSTELS, BUNKHOUSES AND CAMPING BARNS   ENGLAND   SCOTLAND

NEW LANARK YOUTH HOSTEL (SYHA)
Wee Row, Rosedale Street, New Lanark ML11 9DJ.
☎ (01555) 666710. Map 71/878429.
Bednight £9.25 (Inc. breakfast) • Meals available •
Clydeside Walkway.

PRINCES STREET WEST (IH)
3 Queensferry Street, Edinburgh. Book through
H/Office Festival City Properties, 48 Lochrin
Buildings, Edinburgh.
☎ 0131-228 8575.
SC only • Closed July/Aug • Linen provided • Heated •
Bar.

HIGHLAND

ACHMELVICH YOUTH HOSTEL (SYHA)
Recharn, Lairg, Sutherland IV27 4JB.
☎ (01571) 844480. Map 15/059248.
Bednight £4.40 • SC only.

AITE CRUINNICHIDH (IH)
1 Achluachrach, By Roy Bridge, Inverness-shire
PH31 4AW. ☎ (01397) 712315. Map 41/301810.
Bednight £7 • SC only • Near Ben Nevis.

ASSYNT FIELD CENTRE (IH)
Inchnadamph Lodge, Inchnadamph, Assynt, Lairg,
Sutherland IV27 4HL.
☎ (01571) 822218. Map 15/253218.
B&B £11.50 (bed), £8.75 (bunk) • SC only for
evenings • Closed Jan/Feb • Inchnadamph to East
Coast Path • Drying room • Group discounts.

THE AULTGUISH INN (B)
By Garve, Ross-shire IV23 2PQ.
☎ (01997) 455254. Map 20/351705.
Bednight £6 inc. bath • Em available • No SC •
Blackbridge to Styrathcarron path.

AVIEMORE YOUTH HOSTEL (SYHA)
25 Grampian Road, Aviemore PH22 1PR.
☎ (01479) 810345. Map 36/893119.
Bednight £7.15 • SC only • Wheelchair access •
Speyside Way, Cairngorms.

BADACHRO BUNKHOUSE (B)
Badachro, Gairloch, Ross-shire IV21 2AA.
☎ (01445) 741291. Map 19/778737.
Bednight £7 or £9 with duvet • SC only • South
Erradale to Badachro path.

BOTHAN AIRIGH BUNKHOUSE (B)
Insh, Kingussie, Inverness-shire PH21 1NT.
☎ (01540) 661051. Map 35/815017.
Bednight £6 plus electricity • SC only • Scotland
Cross Country Walk.

CANNICH YOUTH HOSTEL (SYHA)
Beauly, Inverness-shire IV4 7LT.
☎ (01456) 415244. Map 26/339315.
Bednight £5.75 • SC only • Wheelchair access.

CARBISDALE CASTLE YOUTH HOSTEL (SYHA)
Culrain, Sutherland IV24 3DP.
☎ (01549)421232. Map 21/574954.
Bednight £10.05 (inc. breakfast) • Meals available.

NEWTONMORE INDEPENDENT HOSTEL (IH)
Craigellachie House, Main Street, Newtonmore,
Inverness-shire PH20 1DA.
☎ (01540) 673360. Map 35/713989.
Bednight £8 • SC • Meals nearby • Breakfast by
arrangement • No smoking • B&B also • Speyside
Way Extension.

GERRY'S ACHNASHELLACH HOSTEL (IH)
Craig, Achnashellach, Strathcarron, Wester-Ross
IV54 8YU. ☎ (01520) 766232. Map 25/037493.
Bednight £7 • SC only• No smoking • Family rooms •
Coulin Pass, Corrie Lair, Glen Uig routes.

GLEN AFFRIC BACKPACKERS HOSTEL (IH)
Cannich By Beauly, Inverness IV4 7LT.
☎ (01456) 415263. Map .26/341316.
Bednight £4.80 • SC only.

GLENCOE YOUTH HOSTEL (SYHA)
Glencoe, Ballachulish, Argyll PA39 4HX.
☎ (01855) 811219. Map 41/118577.
Bednight £7.35 • SC only • Wheelchair access • West
Highland Way.

GLENFESHIE HOSTEL (IH)
Balachcroick House, Glenfeshie, Kincraig, Inverness-
shire. ☎ (01540) 651323. Map 33, 36/850009.
Bednight £8 inc. porridge • SC and evening meals •
Mountaineering centre also.

GLEN NEVIS YOUTH HOSTEL (SYHA)
Glen Nevis, Fort William, Inverness-shire PH33 6ST.
☎ (01397) 702336. Map 41/127716.
Bednight £7.35 • SC only • Wheelchair access • West
Highland Way, Ben Nevis footpath.

GREY CORRIE LODGE (B/IH)
Roybridge, Inverness-shire PH31 4AN.
☎ (01397) 712236. Map 41,34/277814.
Bednight £7.50-£8.50 • SC and meals.

INCHREE BUNKHOUSE HOSTEL (IH)

Onich, Fort William, Inverness-shire PH33 6SD.
☎ (01855) 821287. Map 41/025632.
Bednight £6 • SC and pub/restaurant • West Highland
Way and Ultimate Challenge walks • SC chalets also.

JOHN O'GROATS YOUTH HOSTEL (SYHA)

Canisbay, Nr Wick, Caithness KW1 4YH.
☎ (01955) 611424. Map 12/348721.
Bednight £5.75 • SC only.

KIRKBEAG HOSTEL (IH)

Kirkbeag, Kincraig, Kingussie, Inverness-shire
PH21 1ND.
☎ (01540) 651298. Map 35/840068.
Bednight £8.50 • SC only • Breakfast by arrangement
• B&B also.

LOCHBUIE CROFT (IH)

Strone Road, Newtonmore, Inverness-shire
PH20 1BA.
☎ (01540) 673504. Map 35/720001.
Bednight £9 • SC only • Laggan to Kingussie path.

LOCH MORLICH YOUTH HOSTEL (SYHA)

Glenmore, , Inverness-shire PH22 1QY.
☎ (01479) 861238. Map 36/976099.
Bednight £7.35 • Meals available • Foot of
Cairngorms.

LOCH NESS BACKPACKERS LODGE (IH)

Coiltie Farmhouse, East Lewiston, Drumnadrochit.
(01456) 450807. Map 26/2951.
Bednight £8.50-£9 • SC only • Well-equipped
kitchens • Heated • Proposed Great Glen Way.

THE OLD SMIDDY (B/OC)

The Smiddy Bunkhouse, Snowgoose Mountain
Centre, Station Road, Corpach, Fort William
PH33 7LS.
(01397) 772467. Map 41/100767.
Bednight £7.50 • SC only • West Highland Way,
proposed Great Glen Way.

PITLOCHRY YOUTH HOSTEL (SYHA)

Knockard Road, Pitlochry PH16 5HJ.
☎ (01796) 472308. Map 52/943584.
Bednight £7.35 • Meals available.

RATAGAN YOUTH HOSTEL (SYHA)

Glenshiel, Kyle, Ross-shire IV40 8HP.
☎ (01599) 511243. Map 33/918199.
Bednight £7.35 • SC only.

SAIL MHOR CROFT HOSTEL (IH)

Camusnagaul, Dundonnell, Ross-shire IV23 2QT.
☎ (01854) 633224. Map 19/064893.
Bednight £7.25-£7.50 • SC and meals • Closed
Xmas/New Year • An Teallach Ridge route.

THE STOP-OVER (IH)

The Square, Grantown on Spey, Moray PH26 3HQ.
Book through The Strathspey Estate Office,
Heathfield, Grantown-on-Spey, Moray PH26 3LG.
☎ (01479) 872529. Map 36/039284.
Bednight £8-£12 • SC for groups, meals on request •
One room equipped for disabled • See Groups
section also.

TORRIDON YOUTH HOSTEL (SYHA)

Torridon, Ross-shire IV22 2EZ.
☎ (01445) 791284. Map 25/904559.
Bednight £7.35 • SC only.

TORRIE SHIELING (IH)

Inverie, Knoydart, Inverness-shire PH41 4PL.
☎ (01687) 462669. Map 33/775998.
Bednight £13 • SC only • 3 bunkrooms, 1 ensuite •
Sleeps 12 • Kinlochleven-Inverie route.

ULLAPOOL YOUTH HOSTEL (SYHA)

Shore Street, Ullapool, Ross-shire IV26 2UJ.
☎ (01854) 612254. Map 19/129940.
Bednight £7.35 • SC only • Inverpolly Nature Reserve.

WEST HIGHLAND LODGE (B/OC/IH)

Kinlochleven, Argyll PA40 4RT.
☎ (01855) 831471. Map 41/186617.
Bednight £6 • SC only • West Highland Way.

ISLE OF ARRAN

CORRIE CROFT (B)

Corrie, Isle of Arran. Book through Douglas Park,
Brodick, Isle of Arran.
☎ (01770) 302203/810253. Map 69/024430.
Bednight £5.20 • SC only.

LOCHRANZA YOUTH HOSTEL (SYHA)

Lochranza, Isle of Arran KA27 8HL.
☎ (01770) 830631. Map 62, 69/935504.
Bednight £5.75 • SC only.

ISLE OF ISLAY

ISLAY YOUTH HOSTEL (SYHA)

Port Charlotte, Isle of Islay, Argyll PA48 7TX.
☎ (01496) 850385. Map 60/259584.
Bednight £5.75 • SC only.

ISLE OF LEWIS

GALSON FARM BUNKHOUSE (B)

South Galson HS2 0SH.
☎ (01851) 850492. Map 8/437592.
Bednight £8 • SC and meals.

ISLE OF MULL

SHIELING HOLIDAYS (CB, B, OC)
Craignure, Isle of Mull.
☎ (01680) 812496. Map 49/724369.
Bednight £5-£8.50 • SC on site, pub food nearby •
Closed Nov-Mar.

ISLE OF RAASAY

RAASAY YOUTH HOSTEL (SYHA)
Creachan Cottage, Isle of Raasay, Kyle IV40 8NT.
☎ (01478) 660240. Map 32/553378.
Bednight £4.40 • SC only.

ISLE OF SKYE

BROADFORD YOUTH HOSTEL (SYHA)
Broadford IV49 9AA.
☎ (014718) 22442. Map 32/641237.
Bednight £7.35 • SC only.

GLENBRITTLE YOUTH HOSTEL (SYHA)
Glenbrittle, Carbost IV47 8TA.
☎ (01478) 640278. Map 32/408224.
Bednight £5.75 • SC only • Cuillin hills.

RUBHA PHOIL FOREST GARDEN (B)
Rubha Phoil, Armadale Pier, Armadale, Sleat
IV45 8RS.
No phone. Map 32/640046.
Bednight £5 • SC only • Meals nearby • Sleeps 5 in
Eco-bothy.

SKYEWALKER INDEPENDENT HOSTEL (IH)
Fiscavaig Road, Portnalong IV47 8SL.
☎ (01478) 640250. Map 32/348348.
Bednight £6 • Meals and SC • Wheelchair access •
Base for groups • Shop, café on site.

SLEAT INDEPENDENT HOSTEL (IH)
Kilmore, Sleat IV44 8RG.
☎ (01471) 844440. Map 32/657070..
Bednight £6 • SC only.

SLIGACHAN BUNKHOUSE & COTTAGES (B)
Sligachan, Isle of Skye IV47 8SW.
☎ (01478) 650303. Map 32/484298.
Bednight £6 • SC on site, meals nearby • Closed
Nov/Dec • Cuillin mountains.

> **Please mention the Rambler's Yearbook
> when booking your accommodation**

NORTH EAST SCOTLAND
THE UNITARY AUTHORITIES OF CITY OF ABERDEEN, ABERDEEN-
SHIRE, ANGUS AND MORAY

BRAEMAR YOUTH HOSTEL (SYHA)
Corrie Feragie, 21 Glenshee Road, Braemar,
Aberdeenshire AB35 5YQ.
☎ (013397) 41659. Map 43/155909.
Bednight £7.35 • SC only • Jock's Road.

GLENDOLL YOUTH HOSTEL (SYHA)
Clova, Kirriemuir, Angus DD8 4RD.
☎ (01575) 550236. Map 44/278763.
Bednight £5.75 • SC only • Jock's Road.

JENNY'S BOTHY (IH)
Dellachuper, Corgarff, by Strathdon, Aberdeenshire
AB36 8YP.
☎ Strathdon (019756) 51449/6. Map 37/269079.
Bednight £7 • SC only • Ring before arrival • Families,
groups, individuals.

ORKNEY ISLANDS

BROWNS HOSTEL (IH)
45-47 Victoria Street, Stromness, Orkney KW16 3BS.
☎ (01856) 850661. Map 6, 7/254090.
Bednight £7.50-£8 • SC only • Near clifftop paths.

PERTH & KINROSS

BRAINCROFT BUNKHOUSE (B, IH)
Braincroft, Crieff, Perthshire PH7 4JZ.
☎ (01764) 670140. Map 52/803231.
Bednight £8 or £9 ensuite • SC only • Access and
facilities for wheelchair users.

SCOTTISH BORDERS

KIRK YETHOLM YOUTH HOSTEL (SYHA)
Kelso, Roxburghshire TD5 8PG.
☎ (01573) 420631. Map 74/820280.
Bednight £5.75 • SC only • Pennine Way.

MELROSE YOUTH HOSTEL (SYHA)
Priorwood, Melrose TD6 9EF.
☎ (01896) 822521. Map 73/549339.
Bednight £7.35 • Meals available • Close to Eildon hills.

WANLOCKHEAD YOUTH HOSTEL (SYHA)
Lotus Lodge, Wanlockhead, by Biggar, Lanarkshire
ML12 6UT.
☎ (01659) 74252. Map 71/874131.
Bednight £5.75 • SC only • Southern Upland Way.

STIRLING

EASTER DRUMQUHASSLE FARM (B)
Gartness Road, Drymen, Stirlingshire.
☎ (01360) 660893. Map 57/486872.
Bednight £6 • Meals or SC • West Highland Way •
Camping also.

KILLIN YOUTH HOSTEL (SYHA)
Killin, Perthshire FK21 8TN.
☎ (01567) 820546. Map 51/569338.
Bednight £5.75 • SC only.

ROWARDENNAN YOUTH HOSTEL (SYHA)
Rowardennan, by Drymen G63 0AR.
☎ (01360) 870259. Map 56/359992.
Bednight £7.35 • Meals available • Wheelchair access
• West Highland Way.

STIRLING YOUTH HOSTEL (SYHA)
St John Street, Stirling FK8 1DU.
☎ (01786) 473442. Map 57/7993.
Bednight £10.95 (includes breakfast) • Meals available • Wheelchair access.

Wales

ANGLESEY

OUTDOOR ALTERNATIVE (IH/OC)
Cerrig-yr-Adar, Rhoscolyn, Holyhead, Anglesey LL65
2NQ.
☎ (01407) 860469. Map 114/278752.
Bednight £9 • Meals (book) or SC • Wheelchair
access and toilet • Anglesey Coast Path.

CARMARTHENSHIRE

BRYN POETH UCHAF YOUTH HOSTEL (YHA)
Hafod-y-Pant, Cynghordy, Llandovery SA20 ONB.
☎ (01550) 750235. Map 146, 147/796439.
Cambrian Way • No smoking.

LLANDDEUSANT YOUTH HOSTEL (YHA)
The Old Red Lion, Llanddeusant, Llangadog,
SA19 6UL.
☎ (01550) 740634/740619. Map 160/776245.
Family rooms available • Cambrian Way • No
smoking.

CEREDIGION

BLAENCARON YOUTH HOSTEL (YHA)
Blaencaron, Tregaron SY25 6HL.
☎ (01974) 298441. Map 146, 147/713608.
No smoking.

DOLGOCH YOUTH HOSTEL (YHA)
Dolgoch, Tregaron SY25 6NR.
☎ (01222) 222122. Map 147/806561.
Cambrian Way • No smoking.

POPPIT SANDS YOUTH HOSTEL (YHA)
Sea View, Poppit, Cardigan, SA43 3LP.
☎ (01239) 612936. Map 145/144487.
Pembrokeshire Coast Path • No smoking.

TYNCORNEL YOUTH HOSTEL (YHA)
Llanddewi-Brefi, Tregaron SY25 6PH.
☎ (01222) 222122. Map 146, 147/751534.
Cambrian Way • No smoking.

YSTUMTUEN YOUTH HOSTEL (YHA)
Glantuen, Ystumtuen, Aberystwyth SY23 3AE.
☎ (01970) 890693. Map 135, 147/735786.
Cambrian Way • No smoking.

CONWY

CAPEL CURIG YOUTH HOSTEL (YHA)
Plas Curig, Capel Curig, Betws-y-Coed LL24 OEL.
☎ (01690) 750225. Map 115/726579.
Meals provided • Family rooms.

CONWY YOUTH HOSTEL (YHA)
Larkhill, Sychnant Pass Road, Conwy LL32 8AJ.
☎ (01492) 593571. Map 115/775773.
Meals provided • Family rooms • Wheelchair access
and facilities.

LLEDR VALLEY YOUTH HOSTEL (YHA)
Lledr House, Pont-y-Pant, Dolwyddelan, LL25 ODQ.
☎ (01690) 750202. Map 115/749534.
Meals provided.

ROWEN YOUTH HOSTEL (YHA)
Rhiw Farm, Rowen, Conwy LL32 8YW.
☎ (01492) 530627. Map 115/747721.
Cambrian Way.

WILLIAMS BARN CAMPSITE (CB and B)
Gwern-y-Gof Isaf Farm, Capel Curig, Betws-y-Coed
LL24 OEU. ☎ (01690) 720276. Map 115/686602.
Bednight £3-£4 • SC only • CB sleeps 18, Barn 6 •
Camping also • Cambrian Way.

Do you know your rights when you're out walking in the countryside?
See pages 32-39

GWYNEDD

BRYN DINAS BUNKHOUSE/HOSTEL (BH/IH)
Nant Gwynant, Beddgelert, Caernarfon LL55 4NH.
☎ (01766) 890234. Map 115/625503.
Bednight £6 • SC • Foot of Snowdon south side.

BRYN GWYNANT YOUTH HOSTEL (YHA)
Bryn Gwynant, Nant Gwynant, Caernarfon LL55 4NP.
☎ (01766) 890251. Map 115/641513.
Meals provided • Family rooms available • Cambrian Way.

CABAN CADER IDRIS (B, IH)
Islawrdref, Dolgellau LL40 1TS.
Book through Mrs Dafydd Rhys, Caban Cader Idris, Talsarn, Llanllechid, Bangor LL57 3AJ. ☎ (01248) 600478/(01766) 762588.
Map 124/682169.
SC only • Groups also (19) • Cambrian Way, Mawddach Estuary • Hot showers • Drying room.

CHAMOIS MOUNTAINEERING CENTRE (B, OC, IH)
Ceunant, Waunfawr, Caernarfon.
Book through Les Pinnington, 1 Mauretania Riad, Liverpool L4 6SR.
☎ 0151-525 3425. Map 115/532608.
Bednight £4.80 • SC • .Closed Bank Holidays • Unwardened.

HEIGHTS HOTEL (IH)
High Street, Llanberis LL55 4NB.
☎ (01268) 871179. Map 115/579602.
Bednight £7 • B&B £10.50 • No SC • EM available • Groups also (45) • Club dinners • Some ensuite rooms.

IDWAL COTTAGE YOUTH HOSTEL (YHA)
Nant Ffrancon, Bethesda, Bangor LL57 3LZ.
☎ (01248) 600225. Map 115/648603.
Meals provided.

JESSE JAMES' BUNKHOUSE (IH)
Buarth y Clytiau, Penisarwaen, LL55 3DA.
☎ Llanberis (01286) 870521. Map 115/566638.
Bednight from £6.75 • SC or meals • No smoking • Family bunk rooms available • Groups also (36).

KINGS (DOLGELLAU) YOUTH HOSTEL (YHA)
Kings, Penmaenpool, Dolgellau LL40 1TB.
☎ (01341) 422392. Map 124/683161.
Meals provided, family rooms available • Cambrian Way.

LLANBEDR (NR HARLECH) YOUTH HOSTEL (YHA)
Plas Newydd, Llanbedr, Barmouth, LL45 2LE.
☎ (01341) 241287. Map 124/585267.
Meals provided • Family rooms available.

LLANBERIS YOUTH HOSTEL (YHA)
Llwyn Celyn, Llanberis, Caernarfon LL55 4SR.
☎ (01286) 870280. Map 115/574596.
Meals provided.

THE OLD SCHOOL BUNKHOUSE (B)
Hen Ysgol, Pant Glas, N W Snowdonia LL51 9EQ.
☎ (01286) 660701. Map 123/456474.
Bednight £4.50 • Discount for groups • SC • B&B also • Lon Eifion path • Snowdon Peninsular.

PLAS TAN-Y-GRAIG (IH)
Beddgelert LL55 4LT.
☎ (01766) 890329. Map 115/591482.
Bednight £7.50 • Meals available, no SC • Bike hire.

SNOWDON RANGER YOUTH HOSTEL (YHA)
Rhyd Ddu, Caernarfon LL54 7YS.
☎ (01286) 650391. Map 115/565550.
Meals provided.

MONMOUTHSHIRE

CAPEL-Y-FFIN YOUTH HOSTEL (YHA)
Capel-y-Ffin, Abergavenny, Gwent. NP7 7NP.
☎ (01873) 890650. Map 161/250328.
Meals provided • Offa's Dyke Path, Cambrian Way • No smoking.

MONMOUTH YOUTH HOSTEL (YHA)
Priory Street School, Priory St, Monmouth NP5 3NX.
☎ (01600) 715116. Map 162/508130.
Offa's Dyke Path, Cambrian Way.

OLD RECTORY (B)
Llangattock-Lingoed, Nr Abergavenny.
☎ (01873) 821326.
Bednight £4 • SC only • Camping also • Offa's Dyke.

SMITHY'S BUNKHOUSE (B)
Lower House Farm, Pantygelli, Abergavenny.
☎ (01873) 853432/(0585) 257788.
Map 161/305178.
Bednight £6-£7 • SC • Offa's Dyke, Cambrian Way.

NORTH EAST WALES

THE AUTHORITIES OF DENBIGHSHIRE, FLINTSHIRE & WREXHAM

CYNWYD YOUTH HOSTEL (YHA)
The Old Mill, Cynwyd, Corwen LL21 OLW.
☎ (01490) 412814. Map 125/057409.
No smoking.

MAESHAFN YOUTH HOSTEL (YHA)
Holt Hostel, Maeshafn, Mold CH7 5LR.
☎ (01222) 222122. Map 117/208606.
No smoking.

PEMBROKESHIRE

HAMILTON GUEST HOUSE & BACKPACKER LODGE (IH)
21/23 Hamilton Street, Fishguard SA65 9HL.
☎ (01348) 874797. Map 157/958370.
Bednight £8-£10 inc. continental breakfast • SC also • Camping also • Pembrokeshire National Park.

MANORBIER YOUTH HOSTEL (YHA)
Manorbier, Nr. Tenby SA70 7TT.
☎ (01834) 871803. Map 158/081975.
Meals provided • Family rooms • Wheelchair access and facilities • Pembrokeshire Coast Path.

MARLOES SANDS YOUTH HOSTEL (YHA)
Runwayskiln, Marloes, Haverfordwest SA62 3BH.
☎ (01646) 636667. Map 157/778080.
Pembrokeshire Coast Path • No smoking.

NEWPORT (PEMBS) YOUTH HOSTEL (YHA)
Lower St Mary's Street, Newport SA42 0TS.
☎ (01239) 820080. Map 145/058393.
Pembrokeshire Coast Path • No smoking • Family rooms.

PENTLEPOIR YOUTH HOSTEL (YHA)
The Old School, Pentlepoir, Saundersfoot SA9 9BJ.
☎ (01834) 812333. Map 158/116060.
Meals provided • Pembrokeshire Coast Path • No smoking.

PENYCWM (SOLVA) YOUTH HOSTEL (IH, YHA)
Hafod Lodge, Whitehouse, Penycwm, Nr. Solva, Haverfordwest SA62 6LA.
☎ (01437) 720959. Map 157/857250.
Bednight £7.45-£8.25 • Meals provided or SC • Family rooms available • Pembrokeshire Coast Path • No smoking.

PWLL DERI YOUTH HOSTEL (YHA)
Castell Mawr, Tref Asser, Goodwick SA64 0LR
☎ (01348) 891233. Map 157/891387.
No smoking

ST. DAVID'S YOUTH HOSTEL (YHA)
Llaethdy, St. David's, Haverfordwest SA62 6PR.
☎ (01437) 720345. Map 157/739276.
Pembrokeshire Coast Path.

TREVINE YOUTH HOSTEL (YHA)
11 Ffordd-yr-Afon, Trefin, Haverfordwest SA62 5AU.
☎ (01348) 831414. Map 157/840324.
Family rooms available • Pembrokeshire Coast Path • No smoking.

TYCANOL FARM CAMP SITE (B)
Newport SA42 0ST.
☎ (01239) 820264. Map 157, 145/043396.
Bednight £6 • SC only • Pembrokeshire Coast Path.

POWYS

CABAN CWMFFYNNON (BB)
Cefn Gorwydd, Llangammarch Wells LD4 4DW.
☎ (01591) 610638. Map 147/907439.
Bednight £7.50 • SC only • No smoking • See also Walking Holidays section (Dinefwr Treks).

CORRIS YOUTH HOSTEL (IH, YHA)
Canolfan Corris, Old Road, Corris, Machynlleth SY20 9QT.
☎ (01654) 761686. Map 124/754080.
Bednight £7.25 • Meals or SC • Family rooms • Closed Dec-Feb • No smoking • Dyfi Valley Way, Cambrian Way • 'Green' educational hostel.

GLASCWM YOUTH HOSTEL (YHA)
The School, Glascwm, Llandrindod Wells LD1 5SE.
☎ (01982) 570415. Map 148/158532.

THE HELD BUNKHOUSE (BB)
Cantref, Brecon LD3 8LT.
☎ (01874) 624646. Map 160/036266.
Bednight £7.50 • SC • Taff Trail.

LLWYN-Y-CELYN YOUTH HOSTEL (YHA)
Libanus, Brecon LD3 8NH.
☎ (01874) 624261. Map 160/973225.
Meals provided • Cambrian Way.

LLYSDINAM FIELD CENTRE (OC)
Newbridge on Wye, Llandrindod Wells LD1 6NB.
☎ (01597) 860308. Map 147/009586.
Bednight £5.95 + VAT • Groups only • SC • On Wye Valley Walk.

STONECROFT HOSTEL (IH)
Dolecoed Road, Llanwrtyd Wells.
☎ (01591) 610332. Map 147/878467.
Bednight £8-£10 • SC • Breakfast available • Some private rooms • EM nearby • Well heated • Riverside garden • Ground floor.

TREKKERS BARN (CB, BB)
Castle Inn, Pengenffordd, Nr Talgarth LD3 0EP.
☎ (01874) 711353. Map 161/174296.
Bednight £4-£5 • SC or meals • Toilets, heating, bunks, no kitchen • Cambrian Way.

TRERICKET MILL BUNKHOUSE (B/IH)
Erwood, Builth Wells LD2 3TQ.
☎ (01982) 560312. Map 148, 161/112415.
Bednight £7.50 • SC • Meals available • Pub nearby • Camping & B&B also • On Wye Valley Walk.

TYDDU BUNKHOUSE (B)
Heart of Wales Riding School, Tyddu, Dolau, Llandrindod Wells.
☎ (01597) 851884. Map 07,17/128665.
Bednight £5 • SC and meals • Closed July, August.

WALES   HOSTELS, BUNKHOUSES AND CAMPING BARNS

TYDDU FARM BUNKHOUSE

LUXURIOUS MODERN BUNKHOUSE

C/H • Full Kitchen Facilities
Sleeps 36 in five rooms • 5 toilets • Showers
• TV lounge • Dining room
Self-catering £5 per person
Full Board £15   B&B £7.50

Close to Offa's Dyke, Elan Valley (The
Lakeland of Wales), Glyndwrs Way and the
Wye Valley Walk, adjoining Radnor Forest.
10 miles from RSPB Red Kite feeding
centre at Rhayader.

Minibus available for transport to walks or
the nearest pub. Closed July and August.

Details from
David Vipont, Tyddu, Penybont, Dolau,
Llandrindod Wells, Powys LD1 5TB
Tel/Fax 01597 851884

TY'N-Y-CAEAU YOUTH HOSTEL (YHA)

Groesffordd, Brecon LD3 7SW.
☎ (01874) 665270. Map 160/074288.
Meals provided.

UPPER CANTREF FARM BUNKHOUSE (B/BB)

Cantref, Brecon LD3 8LR.
☎ (01874) 665223. Map 160/057258.
Bednight £8.50 • SC only • Wheelchair facilities.

SOUTH WALES

THE AUTHORITIES OF BLAENAU GWENT, BRIDGEND, CARDIFF, CAER-
PHILY, MERTHYR TYDFIL, NEWPORT, NEATH PORT TALBOT,
RHONDDA CYNON TAFF, SWANSEA & TORFAEN.

PORT EYNON YOUTH HOSTEL (YHA)

The Old Lifeboat House, Port Eynon, Swansea, West
Glamorgan. SA3 1NN.
☎ (01792) 390706. Map 159/468848.

YNYS HYWEL (CB, OC)

Cwmfelinfach, Crosskeys, Gwent NP1 7JX.
☎ (01495) 200113. Map 157/187911.
Bednight £3 in barn SC, £18 B&B groups in centre •
Sirhowy Valley Walk.

YSTRADFELLTE YOUTH HOSTEL (YHA)

Tai'r Heol, Ystradfellte, Aberdare, Mid Glamorgan
CF44 9JF.
☎ (01639) 720301. Map 160/925127.
Cambrian Way • No smoking.

Ireland

CORNAGHER CENTRE (IH)

Ballinamore, County Leitrim.
☎ 078-36453.
Bednight £6 • SC or restaurant • Luxury hostel in
Lakelands of Ireland • 24 beds • Showers • Bike hire.

HOMEFIELD WALKING & CYCLING CENTRE (IH)

Homefield House, Bayview Avenue, Bundoran,
County Donegal.
☎ 072-41288. Map 16/823589 Discovery Series.
Bednight £10-£12 • SC and meals • Wheelchair
accessible • Guides available • Ulster Way.

INDEPENDENT HOLIDAY HOSTELS OF IRELAND

Independent Holiday Hostels of Ireland, 57 Lower
Gardiner Street, Dublin 1.
☎ Int. 353-1-836 4700. Fax 353-1-836 4710.
Free, comprehensive list of 140 hostels in Ireland.
Dorm beds from £5 per night. Meals, private/family
rooms and camping available at many hostels.

PADDY MOLONEY'S DOOLIN HOSTEL (IH)

Fisher Street, Doolin, County Clare.
☎ 065-74006.
Bednight from £6 • Group rates also • SC and meals •
Closed Dec • On Burren Way • Conference room •
Wheelchair facilities • B&B also • Groups welcome.

THE RING LYNE (IH)

Chapeltown, Valentia Island, County Kerry.
☎ 066-76103.
Bednight £7 • SC and meals • Disabled toilet •
Camping also.

SHEPHERD'S LODGE (B)

Near Newcastle, Morne Mountains, County Down.
Book through Pinkertons, 8 Church Lane, Quorn,
Loughborough, Leics LE12 8DP.
☎ (01509) 413866.
Bednight £6.50 • SC only • Close to Ulster Way • SC
SC apartments also.

WATERVILLE LEISURE HOSTEL (IH)

Waterville, County Kerry.
☎ 066-74644.
Bednight £6 • SC only • Closed Oct-March.

Accommodation Suitable for Groups

The centres listed here include many which are tried and tested by RA groups and recommended to us. They vary as widely in type, standards, price, facilities and size as you would expect the diverse groups using them to vary in their requirements. There are hotels, hostels, university halls of residence, cabins in the woods, farmhouses. Perhaps there is something for everyone.

Twenty of the entries are National Trust **Basecamps**. The Basecamps are all self-catering, with cooking facilities, a lounge area and dormitories with bunk beds. They are heated (unless stated); towels and sheets are not provided. They are all situated in National Trust land and are frequently used by groups taking part in conservation work. Prices given are approximate and there is normally a minimum stay of two nights.

Pre-booking for any group is essential. We give an address which is sometimes approximate (exact address can be obtained on booking), a contact name and phone number. Any grid reference is as supplied by the establishment. We say if the accommodation is self-catering (**SC**) or catered (**B&B** or **DB&B**); how many rooms of different types (S single, D double, T twin, F family or dorms); what, if any, tourist board classification has been awarded (see page 87 for a fuller explanation of these); months open (eg 9-6 means open from September to June) — some establishments are only open to outside groups for a few months of the year. Other details given:

P packed lunches available

B at least one room has private bathroom and/or toilet

D there are clothes drying facilities

S there is some restriction on smoking (this could be anything from no smoking in dining room to no smoking at all)

R accommodation is less than 2 miles from a railway station

Discount neg. A discount may be negotiated for such factors as size of group, time of year, mid-week or number of nights.

Not all accommodation for groups is listed here — there are plenty of places able to take large numbers in the other three accommodation sections. See also the index.

England

CAMBRIDGESHIRE

Wicken Fen (The Ganges) Basecamp (NT), nr Ely (9 miles) • ☎ (01353) 723095/720274 • Wicken Fen Nature Reserve • 1-12 • £3.50-£5.50 p/night • Max 30 people • Cold in winter, parking 300m from building • See intro for Basecamp details.

CHESHIRE

Dunham Massey (The Barn) Basecamp (NT), Little Bollington, nr Altrincham • ☎ 0161-928 1760 • Mrs Mary Owen • 1-12 • £352 p/week • Max 20 people • D • See intro for Basecamp details.

CORNWALL

Beach Head Basecamp (NT), Bedruthan Steps, near Newquay • ☎ (01872) 552412 • Ralph Calvert • Max 14 • £50 per nt for group • 9-6 • D. See intro for details of Basecamps.

Chyvarloe Basecamp (NT), nr Helston • ☎ (01326) 561407 • Robin Howard • 1-12 • £50 p/nt for group • Max 14 people • D • See intro for Basecamp details.

Treglyn Farm, St Minver, Wadebridge PL27 6RG • Near Rock • ☎ (01208) 862359 • Map 200/974765 • 1-12 • SC • 11 cottages sleeping total of 44 or 60 inc. bed-settees • Min. £95 for 2-4 Winter, max. £695 for 6-8 Summer • Discount neg • P D S

☆ **Bude Haven Hotel**, Flexbury Avenue, Bude EX23 8NS • Mrs M Bird • ☎ (01288) 352305 • 9-6 • B&B from £18.50, DB&B from £28.50 • Discount neg • Max 24 • S2 D4 T4 F2 • P B D S • 3Cr/C • Licensed; full CH • B&B also.

Bude Haven Hotel – Bude

Lovely Edwardian house. Quietly situated close to the magnificent coast path and town. All rooms en-suite (most with baths). Excellent home cooking, comfort and great hospitality guarantee you an enjoyable stay.

Telephone 01288 352305

☆ **Housel Bay Hotel**, The Lizard TR12 7PG • ☎ (01326) 290417 • Mr & Mrs Mespopiams • 1-12 • B&B from £28 • Discount neg • Max 40 • S4 D9 T7 F1 • P B D S • 3Cr/HC • .

CUMBRIA

"Birslack Grange", Levens, Nr Kendal LA8 8PA. • ☎ (015395) 60989 • John & Jean Carrington-Birch • Map 97/866486 • B&B £16 • Max 16 • T8 F2 • 1-11 • P B D S • Westmorland Way & Cumbria Cycle Way.

Bongate House, Appleby in Westmorland • Anne & Malcome Dayson • ☎ (017683) 51245/51423 • Map 91/689200 • 1-12 NX • B&B £17-£19.50 • Discount neg • Max 18-20 • S1 D3 T2 F2 • P B D R • 3Cr/C Large garden

Howtown Outdoor Centre, Ullswater, Penrith CA10 2ND • ☎ (017684) 86508 • Steve Mitchell • Bednight £7, meals available, no SC • 1 free place out of 12 • Min 12, max 30 males, 30 female • Dorms for 4 • P B D S • Outdoor courses available.

The Old School, Tebay CA10 3TP • ☎ (015396) 24286 • Dave & Pat Weatherley • Map 91/618044 • 2-11 • SC and B&B • SC £7.50 • Volume discount • Max 46 • T3 F1, plus 2 dorms • P B D S • Hillcraft courses available.

Richmond House, Eskin Street, Keswick CA12 4DG • ☎ (017687) 73965 • Nigel Stephenson • 1-12 NX • B&B and SC • B&B £15 • Max 20 • S3 D4 T3 F1 • P B S • 3 Cr/C.

☆ **Smallwood Hotel**, Compston Road, Ambleside • ☎ (015394) 32330 • Colin Harrison • 1-12 NX • B&B £21.50 • D7 T3 F3 • P B D • 3Cr/C • Additional accommodation in neighbouring properties.

Striding Edge Hostel, Greenside, Glenridding, Nr Penrith • Book through National Park Information Centre • (017687) 72803 • Map 90/364174 • SC only • £112 Mon-Thurs, £132 Fri-Sun • Max 18 • 1-12 • Dorms for 2 & 4 • D S.

Kirkbeck House, Lake Road, Coniston LA21 8EW • ☎ (015394) 41358 • Map 96,97/301973 • 1-12 NX • B&B £14 • Discount neg • Max 9 • S1 D2 T1 F1 • P D • Meals nearby.

☆ **The Lupton Centre**, Back Lane, Sedbergh • ☎ (015396) 20303 • Mr D M Parratt • 1-12 • B&B and SC • B&B £14, half board £20, full board £25 • SC £9 • Min 12, Max 44 • S20 D6 F1 Dorm for 14 • P B D S.

ACCOMMODATION SUITABLE FOR GROUPS IN ENGLAND

DERBYSHIRE

Champion House, Edale, Sheffield S30 2ZA • ☎ (01433) 670254 • Adrian Murray-Leslie • Map 123855 • SC £8.50- caterers by arrangement • 1-12 • Min 14, max 34 • T4 F9 • Ⓑ Ⓓ Ⓢ Ⓡ • Youth centre but adult groups also, usually midweek.

Hardwick Hall (The Croft) Basecamp (NT), Doe Lea, nr Chesterfield • ☎ (01246) 851787 • The Warden • 1-12 • £2.50 p/nt, min £50 • Max 20 people • Ⓓ • See intro for Basecamp details.

The Wharf Shed, Near Cromford, Matlock • ☎ (01629) 534561 • Mr P Smith • 1-12 • Map 315561 • SC • Max 28 • £140 per nt • Dorms for 12 and 2 with bunks • Ⓓ Ⓡ • Parking nearby, 2 washrooms.

Hopton Cottage, Hopton, Nr Wirksworth • ☎ (01629) 534561 • Mr P Smith • 1-12 • Map 254547 • SC • Max 12 • £57.50 per nt. • Dorms for 8 and 4 with bunks • Ⓓ • No bed linen, parking for 5 cars, 2 washrooms.

☆ **The Bulls Head Hotel**, Youlgrave, Nr Bakewell • ☎ (01629) 636307 • 1-12 NX • B&B £14-£20 • Max 16 • Discount neg • D4 F2 • Ⓟ Ⓑ Ⓓ Ⓢ.

THE BULLS HEAD HOTEL
Youlgrave, Nr Bakewell,
Derbyshire
01629 636307

A homely family run pub in the heart of the Peak District. Situated in between the Lathkill Dale and the Bradford Dale. Ideal location for walking and touring.

☆ **Westminster Hotel**, 21 Broad Walk, Buxton SK17 6JR • ☎ (01298) 23929 • Derek Stephens • 2-11 • B&B £21, DB&B £29 • Max 24 • D6 T6 • Ⓟ Ⓑ Ⓓ Ⓡ • 3Cr.

WESTMINSTER HOTEL
21 Broad Walk, Buxton, Derbys SK17 6JR
Tel. 01298 23929
Fax. 01298 71121

AA QQQQ Selected

RAC Highly Acclaimed

A small family hotel offering the personal services of the proprietors and enjoying the best location in Buxton, overlooking the pavilion gardens and near amenities. All rooms en suite with colour TVs and drinks facilities. Varied but traditional menus. Ample car parking. DB&B from £29 pp per night min. 2 nights (3 nights May to September).

Want to know more about the tourist board classifications? See page 87

DEVON

Sheldon Centre, Dunsford, Exeter EX6 7LE • (01647) 252203 • Hillary Hanson • 2-12 • Map 191/ 840871 • SC • From £5 • Min 4, max 52 • S8 D/T9 dorms for 12 and 16 • Ⓑ Ⓢ • Converted farm buildings.

☆ **Dartmoor Expedition Centre**, Rowden, Widecombe-in-the-Moor, Newton Abbot TQ13 7TX • (01364) 621249 • John Earle • 1-12 • Map 699764 • B&B and SC • SC £5.50 • Min 6, max 32 • Dorms • Ⓟ Ⓓ Ⓢ • Bunkhouses 300m high on Two Moors Way.

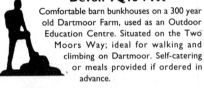

DARTMOOR EXPEDITION CENTRE
Rowden, Widecombe,
Devon TQ13 7TX

Comfortable barn bunkhouses on a 300 year old Dartmoor Farm, used as an Outdoor Education Centre. Situated on the Two Moors Way; ideal for walking and climbing on Dartmoor. Self-catering or meals provided if ordered in advance.

Details Tel. 01364 621249

☆ **Torquay Leisure Hotels**, Belgrave Road, Torquay TQ2 5HL • (01803) 291333 • Kerstin Dannan • 1-12 • B&B and SC • B&B £37, DB&B £51 • Discount neg • Max 220 • S12 D23 T36 F27 • Ⓟ Ⓑ Ⓓ Ⓡ • 3-4Cr/C.

TORQUAY LEISURE HOTELS
ideal for
DARTMOOR & SOUTH WEST COAST PATH

4 CONTRASTING HOTELS PLUS SELF CATERING APARTMENTS ON A SINGLE SEVEN ACRE SITE 450 YARDS FROM THE SEA FRONT OFFERING AN UNRIVALLED CHOICE OF ACCOMMODATION.

GROUPS OF ALL SIZES WELCOME

SUPERB LEISURE FACILITIES • EXCELLENT SERVICE • NIGHTLY ENTERTAINMENT • LAUNDERETTE & DRYING ROOM • INDOOR & OUTDOOR SWIMMING POOLS

DERWENT • VICTORIA • TOORAK • CARLTON
BELGRAVE ROAD, TORQUAY, TQ2 5HL
01803 291333

☆ **Rosemont Guest House**, Greenbank Terrace, Yelverton PL20 6DR • (01822) 852175 • Paul Lepper • 1-12 • B&B £18 • Discounts neg. • Max 18 • S2 D3 T2 F2 • Ⓑ Ⓓ • List/C • Dartmoor National Park.

The Rosemont
Guest House

Greenbank Terrace, Yelverton, Devon
Between Plymouth & Tavistock
Ideal rambling base, situated on the Western edge of Dartmoor National Park. Spacious Edwardian house overlooking the Green. Close to all amenities. Hearty moorish breakfast. ETB Commended. Drying facilities. Warm welcome.
Paul & Jane Lepper
Tel Yelverton (01822) 852175

☆ **Royal York & Faulkner Hotel**, Esplanade, Sidmouth EX10 8AZ • ☎ 0800 220714 • 2-12 • Peter Hook • Max 110 • DB&B avail. • Group rates neg.• S22 D9 T29 F8 • P B D S • 4 Cr/C.

The Royal York & Faulkner Hotel

English Tourist Board
👑👑👑👑 COMMENDED

Esplanade, Sidmouth, South Devon
Charming Regency hotel on the centre of Sidmouth's delightful Esplanade.
Long established family run hotel with emphasis on personal and efficient service coupled with all amenities, excellent standard of furnishings and a good range in indoor leisure facilities.

Ideally situated for walking the superb coastal paths and inland walks offering stunning flora, fauna and views.

Regular Host to Rambling Associations.
Special Groups Rates Available.
For a full information pack containing a series of guided walks and maps
Freephone 0800 220714

Please mention the Rambler's Yearbook when booking your accommodation

---

Bicton College of Agriculture, East Budleigh, Budleigh Salterton EX9 7BY • ☎ (01395) 568353 • Student Services Manager • No groups Xmas and term time • Map 071866 • B&B £18, DB&B £27 • Discounts neg. • S184 T12 F3 Dorms for 14 • P B D S • Sports facilities, arboretum.

DORSET

☆ **Churchview Guesthouse**, Winterbourne Abbas • ☎ (01305) 889296 • Michael & Jane Deller • 1-12 • B&B £18.50-£25, DB&B £29.50-£37 • Discount neg • Min 6, max 18 • D6 T3 • P B D S • 3Cr/C.

Churchview Guest House
Winterbourne Abbas, Dorchester DT2 9LS

Our beautiful 17C Guest House is ideal for groups wishing to explore West Dorset. We cater for up to 18 (more by arrangement with local B&Bs). Delicious meals. Two lounges and bar.
Call Michael and Jane Deller ☎ 01305 889296

Fernhill Hotel & Self Catering Chalets, Charmouth • ☎ (01297) 560492 • Terry or Debbie Bridges • 2-11 • B&B and SC • £5-£30 • Max 150 • S2 D6 T2 F4 • P B D • 3Cr • Set in 14 acres of country hillside.

☆ **White Lodge Hotel**, Grosvenor Road, Swanage BH19 2DD • ☎ (01929) 422696 • John Hutchins • 1-12 • B&B £20 • Max 30 • S1 D4 T5 F4 • P B D S • 3Cr/C.

The White Lodge Hotel
Grosvenor Road, Swanage
Dorset BH19 2DD
Situated 3 mins from Durlston Country Park and 5 mins from Swanage Bay, in quiet road. A homely and friendly hotel with excellent meals, fully licensed, large rooms with en suite and tea & coffee-making facilities. Mini-breaks between Dec & Jan.
Colour TV. Discount for groups.
Tel. John & Chris Hutchins
Swanage (01929) 422696

HAMPSHIRE

☆ **The Wessex Centre**, Sparsholt College, Sparsholt, Winchester SO21 2NF • ☎ (01962) 797259/776647 • Map 185/424320 • 1-12 NX • B&B £20 • Discounts neg • Max 200 • S275 D1 T40 • P B D S • Some rooms 3 Cr.

☆ See Display Advertisement

HERTFORDSHIRE

Chilterns Basecamp (NT), near Berkhamstead • ☎ (01442) 842488 • Jeremy Sutton, Warden • 1-12 • £250 p/week • Max 20 people • Ⓓ • See intro for Basecamp details.

ISLE OF WIGHT

☆ **Hambledon Hotel**, 11 Queens Road, Shanklin PO37 6AW • ☎ (01983) 862403 • Norman Birch • 1-12 • B&B £18 • Discount neg • Max 30 • S2 D5 T1 F4 • Ⓟ Ⓑ Ⓓ Ⓡ • 3Cr/C • Free use of indoor leisure facilities nearby; special ferry rates.

☆ **Appley, Bondi, Roseglen, Rowborough & White House Hotels**, Shanklin • ☎ (01983) 862666 • Denis Squires • 9-5 • B&B £18 • Discount neg • Min 10, max 80 • S10 D15 T20 F5 • Ⓟ Ⓑ Ⓓ Ⓡ • 3Cr • All hotel proprietors are walking club members.

KENT

Ripple Down House, Dover Road, Ringwould, Deal CT14 8HE • ☎ (01304) 364854 • Chas Matthews • 1-12 • Map 362484 • DB&B and Ⓟ £31 Mar-June, less other times • Discounts for children • Min 20, max 43 • S1 T1 F6 • Ⓓ Ⓢ Ⓡ • An environmental education centre.

Howard Basecamp (NT), Scotney Castle Estate, nr Lamberhurst • ☎ (01892) 890651 • David Soesan (National Trust office) • 1-12 • £470 p/week • Max 19 people • Ⓓ • See intro for Basecamp details.

Abbey House Hotel, 5-6 Westbourne Gardens, Off Sandgate Road, Folkestone CT20 2JA • ☎ (01303) 255514 • 1-12 • B&B £18 • Discounts neg • Max 38 • S3 D3 T5 F4 • Ⓟ Ⓑ Ⓓ Ⓢ Ⓡ • 2Cr • Near sea and coastal park.

NORFOLK

University of East Anglia, Norwich NR4 7TJ • ☎ (01603) 592941 • Closed term time and Xmas • B&B and SC • B&B £21 • Discount neg • Max 1,500 • S1,500 and a few twins • Ⓟ Ⓑ Ⓓ Ⓢ Ⓡ • In parkland with Broad, near city centre.

The Old Red Lion, Bailey Street, Castle Acre PE32 2AG • ☎ (01760) 755557 • Alison Loughlin • Map 818151 • 1-12 • B&B and SC • B&B £10, bed only £8.50 • Max 20-24 • D1 T2 and dorms for 6 and 9 • Ⓟ Ⓢ • Exclusively wholefood catering; modest 'conference' facilities.

SHROPSHIRE

☆ **Belvedere Guest House**, Burway Road, Church Stretton SY6 6DP • ☎ (01694) 722232 • Don & Rita Rogers • 1-12 NX • Map 137/451941 • B&B £22 • Discount neg • Max 22-24 • S3 D4 T3 F2 • Ⓟ Ⓑ Ⓓ Ⓢ Ⓡ • 3Cr/C • Close to National Trust hill country.

☆ See Display Advertisement

The Cecil Guesthouse, Sheet Road, Ludlow SY8 1LR • ☎ (01584) 872442 • Maurice or Gillian Phillips • 1-12 NX • Map 137/525742 • B&B £18.50 • Min 10, max 17 • Discount neg • S2 D1 T5 F1 P B D S R • 2Cr/C.

☆ **Big Mose Basecamp (NT)**, Mose, Quatford, Bridgnorth • (National Trust) • Mrs J Pomery • ☎ (01746) 780008 • 1-12 • Map 138/757901 • SC • £55 for group • Max 22 • Bunk beds • Dorms for 8, 4 and 2 • D S

BIG MOSE BASECAMP
MOSE, SHROPSHIRE

Ideal centre for walking and touring •
Hostel style self-catering accommodation
for up to 22 people • Full central heating •
Fire alarm system throughout •
Fully equipped – just bring a pillow
case/sleeping bag • Situated in farmland
on the National Trust estate at Dudmaston.
Four miles South East of Bridgnorth in
the hamlet of Mose.
Map re. OS Sheet 138/757901.
01746 780008
THE NATIONAL TRUST

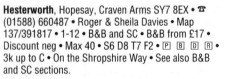

Hesterworth, Hopesay, Craven Arms SY7 8EX • ☎ (01588) 660487 • Roger & Sheila Davies • Map 137/391817 • 1-12 • B&B and SC • B&B from £17 • Discount neg • Max 40 • S6 D8 T7 F2 • P B D R • 3k up to C • On the Shropshire Way • See also B&B and SC sections.

The Bear Hotel, Salop Road, Oswestry • ☎ (01691) 652093 • Mrs L Lucks • B&B £23 • Max 17 • 1-11 • Discount neg • S3 D4 T2 F1 • P B D • 3Cr/C.

SOMERSET

Baymead Hotel, Longton Grove Road, Weston-super-Mare BS23 1LS • ☎ (01934) 622951 • Bob or Cilla Cutler • 1-12 • Map 182/320618 • B&B from £18 • EM £5 • Free organiser place • Max 59 • S10 D8 T12 F3 • P B D S R • 3Cr • Central location, quiet area.

Cross Tree House, Lopen TA13 5JX • Book through Prof G B Milner • ☎ (01460) 240476 • 1-12 • Map 193/426144 • SC • £6-£12 p/person p/nt • Min 8, max 16 • 9-6 midweek • D3 F5 • P D S 17thC Thatched farmhouse, log fires.

STAFFORDSHIRE

The Michael Hutchinson Residential Centre, Hollinsclough, Nr Longnor • Map 065665 • John Carrington • ☎ 0115-955 0010 • SC • £5 per nt • Min 10, max 28 • Closed Mid-week most of May, June, July • D S

SUFFOLK

☆ **Colston Hall**, Badingham, Nr Framlingham, Woodbridge IP13 8LB • ☎ (01728) 638375 • John & Liz Bellefontaine • Map 156/316672 • 1-12 NX • B&B £20 • Discount neg • Max 24 • S1 D3 T4 F3 • P B D S • 2Cr/C.

COLSTON HALL
Badingham, Nr Framlingham,
Woodbridge, Suffolk IP13 8LB

Our spacious Elizabethan farmhouse provides en suite accommodation amidst a wealth of heavy beams and Suffolk bricks. We cater for parties who wish to explore the many good local walks. We look forward to meeting you.

☎ **01728 638375**

 Commended

SURREY

Felbury House, Holmbury St Mary, Dorking RH5 6NL • John Fidgett • ☎ (01306) 730929 • 1-12 NX• Full board £20 • Discount neg • Max 45 • ST15 F5 • P B D S R • Qualified leaders available.

Henman Basecamp (NT), Leith Hill, nr Dorking • ☎ (01306) 711777 • Paul Redsell, Warden • 1-12 • £4 p/nt • Max 16 people • See intro for Basecamp details.

Hunter Basecamp (NT), Haslemere • ☎ (01428) 652359 • Dudley Malone, Warden • 10-6 mainly midweek • £4 • Max 19 people • R • See intro for Basecamp details.

SUSSEX

Barn House, Rodmell, Lewes • ☎ (01273) 477865 • Ian & Bernadette Fraser • 3-1 • B&B £25 • EM by arrangement for large parties • Discount neg • Max 16 • S1 D5 T3 • P B D S R

Slindon Basecamp (NT), Slindon, nr Arundel • ☎ (01243) 814554 • Mark Wardle • 10-6 • £5 p/nt, min £50 • Max 16 people • D • See intro for Basecamp details.

Gumber Bothy (NT), Slindon, nr Arundel • ☎ (01243) 814554 • Mark Wardle • 4-10 • £5 p/nt, min £50 • Max 27 people • Ⓓ • South Downs Way • Very basic accommodation, no access by car, no heating.

Marina House Hotel, 8 Charlotte Street, Brighton • ☎ (01273) 605349/679484 • 1-12 • Map 198/319038 • B&B £15-£22.50 • Max 50 • S4 D11 T4 F7 • Ⓟ Ⓑ Ⓡ • 3Cr.

University of Brighton (Varley Hall, Coldern Lane and Phoenix Brewery, Southover Street) • ☎ (01273) 643167 • Evelyn Mohan • 7-9 • B&B and SC • SC £9.50 per nt • Min 15, max 495 • S 750 • Ⓟ Ⓑ Ⓓ Ⓢ Ⓡ • One centre near South Downs Way, the other in centre of Brighton.

Stafford House, 91 Keymer Road, Hassocks BN6 8QJ • ☎ (01273) 845530 • Barbara Lees • B&B and SC • B&B £11.30, Full board £30.85, SC £8.70 • All plus VAT • Min 15, max full board 45, max SC 25 • S31 T6 • Ⓟ Ⓓ Ⓢ Ⓡ • Cooked breakfast extra.

North Acres, Streat BN6 8RX • ☎ (01273) 890278 • John Eastwood • Map 352154 • 1-12 • B&B £11 • Discount neg. • Min 6, max 20 • S1 T2 F3 (bunks) • Ⓟ Ⓓ Ⓢ Ⓡ • Close to South Downs Way.

Bridge House, 18 Queen Street, Arundel BN18 9JG • ☎ (01903) 882142/0500 323224 • Jack Hutchinson • 1-12 NX • Map 197/020069 • B&B £15-£22 • Discount neg • S2 D9 T2 F6 • Ⓟ Ⓑ Ⓓ Ⓢ Ⓡ • 3Cr/C.

WEST MIDLANDS

HILLSCOURT

Conference Centre

ROSE HILL, REDNAL, BIRMINGHAM
SITUATED IN THE LICKEY HILLS
COUNTRY PARK, WHERE BIRMINGHAM
ENDS AND THE WORCESTERSHIRE
COUNTRYSIDE BEGINS, HILLSCOURT IS
AN IDEAL BASE FROM WHICH TO
EXPLORE THE LOCAL AREA.

*A Warm Welcome Awaits
Plus Excellent Facilities:*

● LICENSED BAR AND EXCELLENT CATERING -
● TV AND TELEPHONE IN ALL ROOMS -
● ALL ROOMS EN SUITE -
● LAUNDRY AND DRYING FACILITIES.

TEL: 0121-457 8370

☆ **Hillscourt Conference Centre**, Rose Hill, Rednal, Birmingham B45 8RS • ☎ 0121-457 8370 • Matthew Baker • 1-12 • B&B £27.50-£37 • Discount neg • Max 65 • S49 D1 T8 • Ⓟ Ⓑ Ⓓ Ⓢ Ⓡ.

Bilberry Hill Centre, Rose Hill, Rednal, Birmingham B31 3RL • ☎ 0121-453 3531• Mike Smith/Shirley Bateman • 1-12 • B&B and SC • SC £5.50, meals negotiable • Min 15, max 67 • S18 T5 and dorms • Ⓟ Ⓡ • Situated in Lickey Hills Country Park.

WILTSHIRE

Farmers Hotel, 1 Silver Street, Warminster BA12 8PS • G Brandani • ☎ (01985) 213815 • 1-12 • B&B £17 • Discount neg • Max 30 • S8 D4 T5 F3 • Ⓟ Ⓑ Ⓓ Ⓡ • 1Cr.

White Hart Hotel, 2 London Road, Calne SN11 0AB • Miss Orlandi • ☎ (01249) 812413 • 1-12 • B&B £18-£20 • Discount neg • Max 25 • S3 D4 T4 F3 • Ⓟ Ⓑ Ⓓ • 1Cr • Old coaching inn, part 16thC.

Stourhead Basecamp (NT), nr Gillingham • ☎ (01747) 840509 • Mrs Hilary Ward, Warden • 1-12 • £70-£80 p/nt for group • Max 18 people • Ⓓ • Lecture room • See intro for Basecamp details.

NORTH YORKSHIRE

Bransdale Mill Basecamp (NT), near Helmsley (but remote - 9 miles) • ☎ (01751) 431693 • Myles Lea • £5.50 per person • Max 12 • Ⓓ • See intro for Basecamp details.

Brimham Rocks Basecamp (NT), Summerbridge, Nidderdale • ☎ (01423) 780688 • Peter Meese, Warden • 2-12 • £546 p/week for group , £42 p/nt • Max 13 people • Ⓓ • No heating in dorms • See intro for Basecamp details.

☆ **Cober Hill**, Cloughton, Scarborough YO13 0AR • ☎ (01723) 870310 • Carol Webster • 1-12 • Map 101/010948 • DB&B and lunch or Ⓟ £28 • Winter discount • Min 20, Max 80 • S21 D11 T28 F10 • Ⓟ Ⓑ Ⓓ Ⓢ

Cober Hill

**Cloughton, nr Scarborough
North Yorkshire YO13 0AR**

On the fringe of N York Moors National Park, 6 miles north of Scarborough. Ideally situated for walking moors and coastal paths. Cleveland Way. We cater for ramblers; good food; good beds; plenty of drying rooms. Special party rates, brochure on request.
Tel. Scarborough (01723) 870310

ENGLAND

ACCOMMODATION SUITABLE FOR GROUPS

113

Miresfield Farm, Malham, Skipton BD23 4DA • ☎ (01729) 830414 • Vera Sharp • B&B £22 • Discounts 3nts • Max 30 • S1 D5 T5 F3 • P B D S • 3Cr • 3 ground floor rooms suitable for people with walking difficulties.

North York Moors Adventure Centre, Park House, Ingleby Cross, Northallerton DL6 3PE • ☎ (01609) 882571 • 1-12 NX • Map 453995 • B&B £14 • Discount neg. • Min 8, max 24 • S2 D2 T2 F3 • P D • Ideal for rambling groups for weekends.

Yorkshire Dales Field Centre, Square House, Church Street, Giggleswick, Settle BD24 0AQ • ☎ (01729) 824180 • Alexandra Barbour • 1-12 • Map 98/812641 • B&B and SC • B&B £13, SC £8.50 • Min 12, max 32 • S2 D1 F5 • P D S R • Group bookings only.

The Carlton Lodge, Bondgate, Helmsley YO6 5EY • ☎ (01439) 770557 • Chris Parkin • 1-12 • Map 100/614839 • B&B from £29.50 • Discount neg • Min 8, max 24 • D8 T3 F1 • P B D S • 3Cr/Comm • Situated in the North York Moors National Park.

WEST YORKSHIRE

☆ **Stones Environmental Training Centre**, Rochdale Rd, Ripponden, Sowerby Bridge • ☎ (01422) 824030 • Book through Mr C Haigh • 1-12 • Map 110/031189 • SC £3.50 • Min 20, max 42 • F4 and dorms for 14 • D S • Centrally heated; large recreational room.

Pennine setting
Ripponden, HALIFAX
Excellent walking •
See South Pennines map 031189 •
Easy access M62 (J22) • Self-catering
hostel • Sleeps 42 • Comfortable •
Central heating • Large kitchen •
Dining room • Recreation/lounge •
Good parking • Sole use •
Inexpensive — £3.50 per person per
night • Minimum charge £70 per
night • Detailed brochure available.

☎ 01422 824030

The Glenmoor Centre, Wells Road, Ilkley LS29 9JF • ☎ (01943) 436270 • Mrs M Cairns or Ms K Crowther • 1-12 • B&B and SC • B&B £12.50-£20 • Min 10, max 32 • S8 T12 • P B S R • Recreation area.

Scotland

CENTRAL BELT

☆ **Oatridge Agricultural College**, Ecclesmachan, Broxburn EH52 6NH • ☎ (01506) 854387 • Ivor Santer • 1-12 • B&B and SC • B&B £15.15 • Min 6, max 100 • S190 D20 F20 • P B D S R • Student accommodation near Edinburgh • Sports facilities.

University of St Andrews, Fife • ☎ (01334) 463000 • Mrs Marjorie Brechin, Conference & Group Services • Map 59/512168 • Closed term times • B&B and SC • B&B £20.25 • Discount neg • Min 10 • S1412 D466 T202 F31 • P B D S • List/App up to 3Cr/Comm.

DUMFRIES & GALLOWAY

Merkland House, Buccleuch Place, Moffat, Dumfriesshire DG10 9AN • ☎ ☎ (01683) 220957 • Andy and Lorna Tavener • 1-12 • B&B £15-£18 • Discount 4 nts • Max 12 • S1 D2 F2 • P B D S • 2Cr/C.

Corsbie Villa, Newton Stewart, Wigtownshire DG8 6JB • ☎ (01671) 402124 • Edward Gladstone • 1-12 • Map 665404 • B&B £16.50 • Max 21 • S1 D3 T4 F2 • P D S • Licensed bar.

HIGHLAND

Cougie Lodge, Tomich, Strathglass, Inverness-shire IV4 7LY • Mrs V A Pocock • Phone messages Tomich PO ☎ (01456) 415212 • 4-10 • Map 240210 • SC £6-£8.50 p/nt • Discount neg • Max 12 • D2 T3 F1 • B D • Accommodation in cabin and caravan.

☆ **The Stop-Over**, The Square, Grantown on Spey, Moray • ☎ (01479) 872529 • Sue Redfearn • 1-12 • B&B and SC • SC £8-£12 • Meals available • Discount neg • Max 27 • D1 and bunk rooms for 4, 6 and 8 • P D S • One room plus shower ground floor equipped for disabled.

THE STOP-OVER
Grantown on Spey, Moray

Opened in April 1995, the Hostel provides excellent accommodation for 27 people in 9 bunkrooms. There are 5 shower rooms/bathrooms and 2 separate WCs, a large TV room and dining room. There are disabled facilities on the ground floor.

Situated in The Square, the Stop-Over gives access to a wide variety of sports and interests in the area and is an ideal base for anyone visiting the Scottish Highlands.

Meals can be provided or self-catering facilties may be available if preferred. Prices from £8 per person per night. Discounts available for sole use.

Please contact The Strathspey Estate Office Heathfield, Grantown on Spey, Moray PH26 3LG Tel. (01479) 872529/873121

Nethy House, Nethy Bridge, Inverness-shire PH25 3DS • ☎ (01479) 821370 • Richard & Patricia Eccles • 1-12 NX • Map 002207 • B&B and SC • Prices neg • Min 15 catered, max 63 • S4 plus bunk rooms • Ⓟ Ⓓ • Flexible to needs of the group; bar and lecture facilities.

☆ **Glenmore Lodge**, Aviemore, Inverness-shire PH22 1QU • ☎ (01479) 861276 • Tony Mitchell • 1-12 NX • Map 36/987095 • B&B and SC • DB&B and Ⓟ £26 • Max 75 • S1 T23 F3 • Ⓟ Ⓑ Ⓓ Ⓢ

PERTH & KINROSS

Dunolly House, Taybridge Drive, Aberfeldy PH15 2BL • ☎ (01887) 820298 • Scot Hermiston • 1-12 • B&B and SC • DB&B and Ⓟ £19.50, SC £7.50 • Discounts neg • Min 8, max 60 • D5 T1 F7 plus 5 bunk rooms • Ⓟ Ⓑ Ⓓ • List/App and 1Cr (SC) • Childrens activities arranged; walking guides available.

SCOTTISH BORDERS

Bailey Mill, Bailey, Newcastleton, Roxburghshire TD9 0TR • ☎ (016977) 48617 • Mrs Pam Copeland • 1-12 • B&B and SC • B&B from £15, SC from £25 per cottage (1-4) • Discount neg • Max 38 • S2 D4 T2 F3 • Ⓟ Ⓑ Ⓓ • 3k/Comm • Leisure and health facilities on site plus trekking.

Netherurd House, Blyth Bridge, West Linton, Peeblesshire EH46 7AQ • ☎ (01968) 682208 • Miss Claire Thomson • 1-12 NX • Map 117446 • Catered accommodation - prices on application • Min 6, max 40 • S6 T8 F5 • Ⓟ Ⓓ Ⓢ • Outdoor activities available • SC also.

STIRLING

Invervey Hotel, Tyndrum, By Crianlarich, Perthshire FK20 8RY • ☎ (01838) 400219 • John Riley • 1-12 NX • Map 50/329302 • B&B £27 • Discount neg • Max 40 • S5 D5 T7 F4 • Ⓟ Ⓑ Ⓓ Ⓢ Ⓡ • 2Cr/App.

☆ **Dounans Centre**, Aberfoyle, Stirling • ☎ (01899) 221115 • Lesley Baird • Mid 2-mid 12 • Map 528013 • Full board £19.50, B&B available • Discount neg • Min 10, max 260 • S20 F20 • Bunk beds in chalets • Ⓟ Ⓑ Ⓢ • Outdoor courses of all kinds available.

Please mention the Rambler's Yearbook when booking your accommodation

☆ See Display Advertisement

SCOTTISH CENTRES

Aberfoyle, Biggar, Meigle,
West Linton

4 outdoor centres in Scotland suitable for groups
of 10 persons or more : fully catered, all bedding
provided.

tel: 01899 221115

Wales

Betws-y-Coed (Dinas) Basecamp (NT), ☎ (01492)
860123 • John Anderson (National Trust North
Wales) • £400 p/week, £60 p/nt • Max 17 • 1-12 • Ⓓ
Ⓡ • See intro for Basecamp details.

ACCOMMODATION SUITABLE FOR GROUPS · WALES

CEREDIGION

☆ **University of Wales, Aberystwyth** • ☎ (01970)
621960 • James Wallace • Closed term time • B&B
and SC • SC £12-£15 • Max 900 • S900 • Ⓟ Ⓑ Ⓢ
Ⓡ

CONWY

☆ **Broadway Hotel**, Mostyn Broadway, Llandudno
LL30 1AA • ☎ (01492) 876398 • Mr & Mrs Tura • 11-
3 • DB&B £21 • Organiser free • S7 D8 T5 F13 • Ⓟ
Ⓑ Ⓓ Ⓢ Ⓡ • 2Cr • Centrally situated.

GWYNEDD

☆ **Dolgoch Falls Hotel**, Abergynolwyn, Tywyn LL36
9UW • ☎ (01654) 782258 • 3-10 • B&B £19.50 •
Discount neg. • Max 20 • S1 D3 T2 plus annex • Ⓟ
Ⓑ Ⓓ Ⓢ Ⓡ

Ffrondderw Private Hotel, Stryd-y-Fron, Bala LL23
7YD • ☎ (01678) 520301 • Mr T G Jones • 3-11 •
Map • 125/916362 • B&B £15-£21 • Discount neg • EM
available • Min 12, max 17 • S2 D2 T2 F3 • Ⓟ Ⓑ Ⓓ
Ⓢ • 3Cr/C • Special diets OK.

Penbryn Croft, Cader Road, Dolgellau LL40 1RW • ☎ (01341) 422815 • Mrs Ann Jones • 1-12 NX • B&B £16 • One in 10 free • Max 14 • D3 T3 • P D S

Plas Menai National Watersports Centre, Llanfairisgaer, Caernarfon • ☎ (01248) 670964 • 1-12 • B&B £15-£22 • Discount neg • T34 • P B D S • 3Cr • Disabled access • Mountaineering courses available • Snowdonia.

☆ **Chamois Mountaineering Centre** • Ceunant Waunfawr, Caernarfon • Les Pinnington, 1 Mauretania Road, Liverpool L4 6SR • ☎ 0151-525 3425 • Closed Bank Holidays • Map 115/532608 • SC £4.80 • Bunk rooms for 4, 6 and 8 • D S • No resident warden.

CHAMOIS MOUNTAINEERING CENTRE
Near Llanberis, Snowdonia

Spacious self-catering group accommodation
8 bedrooms with bunkbeds
Available for groups of 15-40
Showers, drying room, well-equipped kitchen
Separate dining room and lounge
Coach access and parking
£4.80 per person per night
All enquiries/bookings to
Less Pinnington
1 Mauretania Road, Liverpool L4 6SR
0151-525 3425

MONMOUTHSHIRE

Beaufort Hotel, Beaufort Square, Chepstow NP6 5EP • ☎ (01291) 622497 • Michael Collins • 1-12 • B&B £24-£26 • Min 8, max 36 • Discount neg • S6 D7 T4 F2 • P B D R • 3Cr/HC • Restaurant and bar menu.

The Riverside Hotel, Cinderhill Street, Monmouth NP5 3RY • ☎ (01600) 715577 • Rodney Dodd • 1-12 • Map 162/504123 • DB&B £27-£36 • Max 34 • D6 T9 F2 • P B D • 4Cr/HC • On Offa's Dyke walk.

☆ **Ty'r Morwydd House**, Pen-y-Pound, Abergavenny NP7 5UD • ☎ (01873) 855443 • 1-12 NX • B&B £14 EM £6 • Discount neg. • Max 72 • S30 D2 T18 F4 • P D S R • WTB Approved.

Smithy's Bunkhouse, Lower House Farm, Pantygelli, Abergavenny • ☎ (01873) 853432 • Neil or Katy Smith • 1-12 • Map 161/304178 • B&B and SC • SC £6 • Discount neg • Min 6, max 24 • 2 dorms • P D S R • Bunkhouse & SC cottages also.

NORTH EAST WALES

Chirk Castle Basecamp (NT), Chirk, nr Oswestry • ☎ (01691) 777701 • 1-12 • £400-£500 p/week • Max 14 people • R • Offa's Dyke Path • See intro for Basecamp details.

Erddig Basecamp (The Yale Hostel) (NT), nr Wrexham • ☎ (01978) 355314 • The Warden • 1-12 • £105-£280 p/week • Max 18 • D R • See intro for Basecamp details.

PEMBROKESHIRE

Penycwm (Solva) Youth Hostel, Whitehouse, Penycwm, Haverfordwest SA62 6LA • ☎ (01437) 720959 • Kenneth Cross • 1-12 • Map 157/857250 • B&B £11.45, DB&B £13.05, SC £8.55 • T2 plus dorms for 4 and 6 • P B S • Luxury hostel.

High Noon, Lower Lamphey Road, Pembroke SA71 4AB • ☎ (01646) 683736 • Sherilea Barnikel • 1-12 • Map 157/990011 • B&B £17-£19.50 • Discount neg • Max 17 • S3 D3 T2 F2 • P B D S R • 3Cr/C • On Pembrokeshire Coastal Path.

☆ See Display Advertisement

☆ **Lochmeyler**, Llandeloy, Nr Solva, Haverfordwest SA62 6LL • ☎ (01348) 837724 • Mrs M Jones • 1-12 • Map 157/855275 • B&B £15-£20, EM £10 see display • Discount neg • Max 30 • 12 rooms various • P B D S • 4Cr Deluxe.

Walking in Pembrokeshire

Lochmeyler is a 220-acre dairy farm in centre of St. David's Peninsula. Twelve ensuite rooms all have colour TV & videos (free video library), tea-making facilities, hair dryer, heating, electric blankets, telephones. Four-poster beds available. No smoking in bedrooms.

We have two lounges (one for smokers) with log fires for winter breaks. Our traditional farmhouse cooking uses local produce with home-baked rolls & desserts; vegetarians can be catered for. Children welcome. Each bedroom has a National Park pack which includes all the walks in Pembrokeshire, OS maps & booklets on boat trips, birdwatching, flowers. Drying facilities. Plenty of wildlife trails, ponds and streams. Credit cards accepted.

DAILY RATE

B&B from £20, BB & evening meal from £32.50

WEEKLY RATE

B&B from £140, BB & evening meal £210 (p/p)

RAC Guest House of the Year.
WTB 4 Crowns Deluxe
Brochure & literature from
**Mr & Mrs Jones, Lochmeyler
Pen-y-Cwm, Llandeloy, Solva,
Haverfordwest, Pembrokeshire SA62 6LL.
Tel (01348) 837724   Fax (01348) 837622**

POWYS

Forest Lodge Farmhouse, Libanus, Brecon • ☎ (01874) 676446 • Liz Daniel, Brecon Beacons Holiday Cottages • 1-12 • SC • Whole house: £450 per weekend, £800 per week • Max 30 • Varied rooms • B D • Other large farmhouses also.

Eagle Hotel, New Radnor LD8 2SN • ☎ (01544) 350208 • Angela Hoy • 1-12 • Map 148/212609 • B&B £12.50-£19 except Xmas • 1 free place/10 bookings • D2 T2 F2 or dorms for 6 • P B D S • 1Cr • Outdoor activities available; Transport from Offa's Dyke.

☆ **Neuadd Arms Hotel**, Llanwrtyd Wells LD54 4RB • ☎ (01591) 610236 • Gordon Green • 1-12 NX • B&B £20, full board £31 • Discount neg • Max 33 • S7 D5 T8 • P B D R • 2Cr • By Cambrian mountains; walking guide provided free.

Pencerric Gardens Hotel, Llandrindod Road, Builth Wells • ☎ (01982) 553226 • Robert Southcott • 1-12 • DB&B £40 • Discount neg • Max 40 • S2 D3 T12 F3 • P B D R • 4Cr • Guided walks; special breaks.

☆ **The Beacons**, 16 Bridge Street, Brecon LD3 8AH • ☎ (01874) 623339 • Mr & Mrs Jackson • 1-12 NX • Map 042285 • B&B £16.50 • Discount neg. • Max 30 • S1 D4 T3 F2 • P B D S • 3Cr/C.

Liverpool House, East Street, Rhayader LD6 5EA • ☎ (01597) 810706 • Mrs Ann Griffiths • 1-12 • Map 147/972681 • B&B £14 • Winter discount • Max 18 • S1 D3 T1 F3 • P B D S • 3Cr.

☆ **Elan Valley Lodge**, Rhayader LD6 5HN • ☎ (01597) 811143 • 1-12 • Map 147/932648 • £72.50 per weekend, full board and guided walks • T7 F5 • P B D S • WTB accredited activity centre.

Ireland

COUNTY KERRY

The Ring Lyne, Chapeltown, Valentia Island • ☎ (066) 76103 • Mrs Frances or Sean O'Sullivan • 1-12 • B&B and SC • SC £7 • Discount neg • Min 22, max 30 • D5 T2 F3 • P D • Independent hostel with own chef.

Self-catering Accommodation

The 1996 Ramblers' Yearbook was the first to include self-catering accommodation in a separate chapter and judging by your response to it there are just as many walkers who like to find a home of their own for a week as there are those who like to B&B it.

You are urged to make full enquiries before booking any self-catering accommodation. We give only a minimum of information here.

We ask downers to give the following details:

- Number and type of properties they own or deal with;
- Number of people the accommodation is intended to accommodate (you are advised to check the number of bedrooms on booking);
- Price of the smallest property at low season (usually assumed to be outside of school holidays and during the winter months)

and the biggest at high season—you are advised to check prices and extra charges ;

- Any months of closure;
- Any tourist board classification awarded. An explanation of these is given on page 87. A range of awards may be given where there is more than one property;
- A few words of each advertiser's choosing—there is no regularity whatsoever in these delightfully individual contributions!
- Whether or not a dog may be brought (🐕) **upon arrangement**. Where an advertiser owns several properties, dogs may be allowed in some but not others. Always ask.
- If there are any smoking restrictions (Ⓢ) – again, restrictions might apply to some properties and not others;
- If there is a train station within 2 miles (ℝ);
- A contact name and telephone number.

SELF-CATERING ACCOMMODATION   ENGLAND

120

BUCKINGHAMSHIRE

Bledlow Ridge • Cottage • Sleeps 5-6 • £200-£300 • 3k/C • Secluded small farm, large garden; Ridgeway • Mrs N E Gee ☎ (01844) 344416 • Ⓢ 🖾 • B&B also

CHESHIRE

Chisworth • Stable conversion cottage • Sleeps 6 • £150-£300 • 3k/C • Magnificent views, open fires, ground floor • Monica Sidebottom ☎ (01457) 866536 • Ⓡ • B&B also

Langley, Macclesfield • Cottage • Sleeps 2 • £100-£190 • 3k/C • M M Birch ☎ (01260) 252230 • Ⓡ • B&B also

Macclesfield/Buxton • Cottage • Sleeps 7 • £160-£300 • 3k/C + disabled • Peaceful, secluded, breathtaking views; walker's haven • Mrs F Waller ☎ (01260) 227229 • 🖾

CORNWALL

Blisland/St Tudy • 6 cottages • Sleeps 2-5 • £90-£320 • Traditional cottages near Bodmin Moor • Mrs M Pestell ☎ (01208) 850146

Boscastle • Bungalow • Sleeps 10 • £275-£650 • 5k/C • Sea views; all fuels free; log fire • Mrs Cheryl Nicholls ☎ (01840) 250545 • Ⓢ • B&B also

Bude • Caravans • Sleeps 2-6 • £50-£225 • Closed Nov-Easter • List/App • Tourers, campers, walking groups - transport arranged • Mr & Mrs Woods ☎ (01288) 361380 • 🖾

Fowey • 12 cottages & flats • Sleeps 2-6 • £100-£400 • 2-4k/up to C • Out of season short breaks available • Fowey Harbour Cottages ☎ (01726) 832211 • 🖾

Fowey • 6 flats • Sleeps 2-7 • £160-£725 • 1-4k/HC • Boathouse, launderette, balconies/roof terrace, games room • Ms J Grundy ☎ (01527) 575929

Hayle • Bungalow • Sleeps 8-9 • £130-£290 • Closed Nov-Apr • Sea view, beach 100 yards • I R V Langford ☎ (01932) 560503 • Ⓡ 🖾

Hellandbridge • 7 Cottages & riverside cabins • Sleeps 2-6 • £100-£400 • On River Camel/Camel Trail • Mike & Julie Aitken ☎ (01208) 74408 • Transport from station

Kilkhampton, Bude • Cottage • Sleeps 5 • £100-£300 • Quiet, comfortable, close to coast & lakes • Mr & Mrs P Lucock ☎ (01303) 844289 • 🖾

Please mention the Rambler's Yearbook when booking your accommodation

☆ **Lanhydrock, Bodmin** • 8 cottages • Sleeps 2-8 • £110-£575 • 4-5k/HC • Pat Smith ☎ (01208) 74405 • Ⓡ 🖾

Lanreath, nr Looe • 2 cottages • Sleeps 2-6 • £85-£325 • Barn conversion; winter short breaks available • Mr T E Gamble ☎ (01503) 220289 • 🖾 • B&B also

Launceston • 8 cottages • Sleeps 2-8 • £140-£595 • 3-4k/up to HC • Heated indoor swimming pool open all year • J A Chapman ☎ (01566) 772141

Lizard Point • Clifftop Chalet • Sleeps 2-3 • £89-£185 • On coastal path, magnificent sea views • ☎ (01326) 290300 • Ⓢ

☆ See Display Advertisement

ENGLAND

SELF-CATERING ACCOMMODATION

Looe • Cottage • Sleeps 6 • £125-£340 • 2k/C • Shower & basin main bedroom; linen supplied • Mrs J Mickleburgh ☎ (01503) 272349 • Ⓡ

☆ **Lostwithiel** • Cottages • Sleeps 2-6 • £135-£490 • 4k/HC • Excellent walks from your front door • Tim & Nicky Reed ☎ (01208) 873618 • Ⓡ 🐾

TREDETHICK FARM COTTAGES

Exceptional cottages on edge of Fowey valley. Beautiful walks from your front door. Ideal base for coastline, wooded valley and moorland walking. Maps & info. on best walks in the area are provided.

� ♛♛♛ Highly Commended

WINNERS OF 4 AWARDS

Tel. *01208 873618*

☆ **Lostwithiel** • 2 houses, 4 cottages, 3 flats • Sleeps 2-6 • £140-£535 • 4-5k/C • Waterside; peace & quiet; excellent walking • Mr H F Edward-Collins ☎ (01208) 872444 • Ⓡ 🐾

English Tourist Board
COMMENDED
UP TO ♛♛♛♛♛

LANWITHAN FARM, LOSTWITHIEL PL22 0LA
TWO WATERSIDE COTTAGES
Seven other cottages set in 110 acre Georgian Estate with parkland running down to the River Fowey. Private fishing & dinghy. Tennis court, games room, ample heating, log fires. All with gardens. Excellent walks and wildlife.
Brochure 01208 872444

Mabe, Falmouth • Converted barn • Sleeps 6 • £200-£600 • Set on footpath; beautiful countryside • Mark & Keren Barrett ☎ 0181-202 8136 • Ⓡ 🐾

Mevagissey • 4 flats • Sleeps 4-5 • £120-£230 • A H Robins ☎ (01726) 843352 • 🐾

Mullion Cove • 25 timber lodges • Sleeps 2-6 • £130-£425 • 5 ticks • 200 yds coastal footpath, 1 mile village • Pauline Story ☎ (01326) 240496 • Ⓢ 🐾 • B&B also

Newquay • 4 courtyard cottages • Sleeps 2-8 • £150-£650 • Beams, antique furnishings, some four-poster beds • Mrs J Schofield ☎ (01637) 874695

Porthleven • Cottage • Sleeps 2 • £120-£150 • Electricity & bedding included • Mrs C Cookson ☎ (01326) 574493 • 🐾 • B&B also

☆ **Rock (nr)** • 10 cottages, 1 bungalow • Sleeps 2-8 • £99-£695 • Quality cottages, quiet location, beautiful view • James Bloye ☎ (01208) 862359 • Ⓢ 🐾 • Groups also

---

Treglyn Farm, Rock
North Cornwall
Quality Cottages in Quiet Country location • Superb Views • Ideal base for Walking, Golf, Sailing, Surfing • Suit groups or individuals • Cottages from £99 per week.

01208 862359

St Austell • Cottage • Sleeps 2-6 • £85-£450 • 4k/up to HC • Cosy cottages on working farm • Mrs Judith Nancarrow ☎ (01726) 67111 • 🐾

St Austell • 27 chalets & bungalows • Sleeps 2-8 • £85-£420 • Closed Jan-Feb • 5 ticks • Lovely tranquil park, convenient central location • Mrs M King ☎ (01726) 74283 • Ⓡ 🐾

St Erth, Hayle • 2 converted barns • Sleeps 4 • £100-£200 • Log burning fire; long weekends available • Mrs Sue Crutchfield ☎ (01736) 755529 • Ⓡ 🐾

☆ **St Mawgan** • 1 cottage, 6 bungalows • Sleeps 2-5 • £85-£295 • Closed Nov-Mar (bungalows) • 2-3k/App • One mile from large Sandy beech; coastal walks • Mr & Mrs Alexander ☎ (01637) 860460 • 🐾

ST MAWGAN
RETORRICK MILL

Stone cottage and six holiday bungalows set in nine acres in quiet wooded valley. One mile large sandy beach and coastal footpath. Newquay six miles, Padstow nine miles. Tourist board Approved. Short breaks. Cottage open all year.
Tel. (01637) 860460

☆ **Stithians** • 11 cottages • Sleeps 2-8 • £100-£400 • Converted Cornish farmstead; groups, families, couples • Peter Stokes ☎ (01209) 860863 • 🐾

STITHIANS, NR FALMOUTH
COTTAGES AND APARTMENTS

£100 to £400 per week

1-4 double/twin bedrooms. Couples, families and small groups. Courtyard conversion of older Cornish Farmstead, 5 miles equidistant North and South coasts. Bed linen, colour TV, ample parking. 3/4 days breaks—cottages from £70. Brochure from resident proprietors:

Mr & Mrs Peter Stokes, Higher Trewithen, Stithians, Truro, Cornwall TR3 7DR
Tel. 01209 860863

Zennor • Cottage • Sleeps 4 • £150-£295 • Sea and Moorland views, walks leaflets • Dr E Gynn ☎ (01736) 794183 • Ⓢ • B&B also

CUMBRIA

Alston • Bungalow • Sleeps 6 • £160-£325 • 4k/HC • Luxury two-bedroom bungalow • Mrs Pat Dent ☎ (01434) 381383 • Ⓢ 🐾 • B&B also

Ambleside • 7 lodges • Sleeps 4-6 • £135-£325 • Closed Dec-Feb • 2k/up to C • Secluded woodland setting in central Lakeland • Gareth Evans ☎ (015394) 36583

Ambleside • Flat • Sleeps 4 • £90-£120 • Opens onto garden; private parking • P F Quarmby ☎ (015394) 32326 • 🐾

Applethwaite, Kewick • Cottage • Sleeps 5 • £185-£395 • At foot of Skiddaw; panoramic views • Mrs M J Matthews ☎ (017687) 78243 • 🐾

Bassenthwaite Village • 3 cottages, 1 flat • Sleeps 2-20 • £90-£550 • Character cottages for couples/families/groups • Mrs Alison Trafford ☎ (017687) 76393 • 🐾

Bowness-on-Windermere • Flat • Sleeps 4 • £145-£195 • Closed Nov-Mar • Modern flat, lake view, no children under 10 • Mrs J Kay ☎ (01925) 755612

☆ **Bowness-on-Windermere** • 1 cottage, 5 flats • Sleeps 2-6 • £100-£355 • Closed Jan-Feb • 3-4k/C • Edwardian mansion, Sylvan setting, secluded walks • Mrs P Fanstone ☎ (015394) 45557 • Ⓡ

Bowness-on-Windermere • Flat • Sleeps 2-4 • £100-£195 • Lake views, central situation; well-equipped • Mr & Mrs E Jones ☎ 0151-228 5799 • Ⓡ

Braithwaite • Cottage • Sleeps 4 + cot • £190-£260 • Parking; heating included; walking from door • Shirley Thompson ☎ (01768) 864541 • Ⓢ

☆ **Buttermere** • 6 apartments, 1 cottage • Sleeps 4-6 • £295-£495 • 5k/HC • Dishwashers, microwaves, ovens, south facing patios • Bridge Hotel Reception ☎ (017687) 70252 • 🐾 • B&B also

☆ **Caldbeck** • 7 cottages • Sleeps 2-8 • £142-£561 • 4k/up to HC • Leisure club membership; activity/pub guides • Jennifer or Andy Collard ☎ (016974) 76254 • 🐾

Caldbeck (near) • 2 cottages • Sleeps 4-6 • £125-£375 • 4k/C • Remote setting in northern Lake District • Fran and Robin Jacobs ☎ (016974) 78430 • 🐾

Coniston • Flat • Sleeps 2 • £90-£125 • Available for weekend or midweek breaks • M Nicholson ☎ (015394) 41415 • 🐾

Coniston • 2 chalet bungalows • Sleeps 2-6 • £100-£250 • Closed Dec-Jan • Quiet location overlooking lake; owner-maintained • Mrs Anne Hall ☎ (015394) 41558 • 🐾

☆ **Coniston, Lake District** • Flats • Sleeps 2-6 • £65-£225 • 2-3k/App • Private parking • Mr & Mrs A Jefferson ☎ (01204) 419261 • 🐾. For display ad see over.

☆ See Display Advertisement

Dent • Cottage • Sleeps 6-8 • £100-£330 • Mrs Marlene Williamson ☎ (01539) 625353 • 🏠

Elterwater • Flat • Sleeps 2 • £240 • Closed Nov-Mar • Beautifully situated; peaceful; in Elterwater village • Audrey Whittle ☎ (015394) 37278 • Ⓢ • B&B also

Eskdale, Lake District • 1 Cottage, 1 house • Sleeps 8-16 • £230-£1200 • 4-5k/C • Peaceful location amid spectacular scenery • Mrs D M Postlethwaite ☎ (019467) 23235 • Ⓢ Ⓡ

Grange-over-Sands • Cottage • Sleeps 5 • £120-£320 • Quiet secluded garden with patio • Mr W J Lambert ☎ (015395) 32116 • Ⓡ 🏠 • B&B also

☆ **Grasmere** • 4 apartments, 1 cottage • Sleeps 2-6 • £177-£421 • Closed 2/11-10/2 • Richard Fowler ☎ (015394) 35417 • 🏠

Beck Steps

Self Catering Apartments & Cottage
IN THE CENTRE OF GRASMERE

OVERLOOKING THE VILLAGE GREEN
Four self contained apartments with parking, designed, furnished and equipped to a high standard, together with a detached stone cottage on the banks of the River Rothay – providing an excellent centre for walks and drives to all parts of the National Park.
For brochures or enquiries
Tel 015394 35417

☆ **Grasmere** • 5 apartments + extra bedrooms for groups • Sleeps 2-4 or groups • £150-£315 • 3k/C • Free membership of local health club • Hugh McLarity ☎ 0151-727 1144 • Ⓢ

GRASMERE LODGE
FOREST SIDE, GRASMERE

🔑 🔑 🔑 Commended

Converted Coach House providing five one-bedroomed self-contained apartments with boot drying room. Ancillary bedrooms provide additional sleeping accommodation for the larger groups. Sorry no smoking and no pets. Ideal for all graded walks with direct access to Rydal Fell.
FREE membership of local Exclusive Health Club with linen, towels, TV, microwave and parking included in price. Open all year.
Full weeks £189-£325 with half weeks available in winter.
15% discount on published prices to members of the Ramblers' Association.
Tel/Fax 0151-727 1144

Grayrigg • Cottage • Sleeps 6 • £150-£280 • 3k/HC • Spacious non-smoking accommodation; price all-inclusive • Mrs D Johnson ☎ (01539) 824345 • Ⓢ • B&B also

Hawkshead • Cottage • Sleeps 5 • £195-£305 • 3k/C • Central for walking Lakes; garden, parking • Mrs S Dewhurst ☎ (015394) 36340 • Ⓢ 🏠

Hawkshead/Sawrey • Cottages & apartments • Sleeps 2-8 • £150-£400 • 3-5k/HC • Magnificent mountain and lake views • Mrs J Haddow ☎ (015394) 36280

Ireby • 3 cottages • Sleeps 4-6 • £185-£398 • 3-4k/HC • Superb views of Skiddaw and Caldbeck fells • Mrs D Darnton ☎ (016973) 71547 • 🏠

Keswick • 2 flats, 1 house • Sleeps 2-6/7 • £180-£450 • 3-4k/HC • Fitted to high standards, cleanliness guaranteed • J Miller ☎ (017687) 72553 • Ⓢ • B&B also

Keswick • Apartment • Sleeps 8 • £295-£325 • Country setting; built 1843; parking; weekends • Mr & Mrs Oakey ☎ (017687) 72692 • 🏠

SELF-CATERING ACCOMMODATION   ENGLAND

☆ **Keswick (Portinscale)** • 1 cottage, 3 flats • Sleeps 2-6 • £95-£280 • 3k/C • Central heating & parking • Mary & Oliver Bull ☎ (01889) 505678 • Ⓢ 🐾

DERWENTWATER

ETB ♈♈♈
COMMENDED

Traditional stone Lakeland building now four comfortable well-equipped self-catering holiday suites at Portinscale village on Derwentwater, 1 mile from Keswick.
Ideal centre for walking.
Central heating and linen included.
Parking. Open all year. Short breaks.
Prices £95 to £280.
Some reductions for two people only.
Mary and Oliver Bull
Tel 01889 505678

BASSENTHWAITE HALL FARM COTTAGE HOLIDAYS

By a stream with ducks!

Character cottages for couples/families/walking parties.
BASSENTHWAITE VILLAGE, NEAR KESWICK
Telephone 017687 76393 for colour brochure

Loweswater • 2 cottages • Sleeps 4-6 • £150-£180 • Quiet country location, ideal for walking • D Bell ☎ (01900) 85227 • 🐾

Motherby • Cottage • Sleeps 4-6 • £120-£210 • Converted coach house • Mrs Jacquie Freeborn ☎ (017684) 83368 • 🐾 • B&B also

Newlands Valley, Keswick • Cottage • Sleeps 4 • £160-£240 • 3k/C • Extremely pleasantly situated amongst Cumbrian mountains • Mrs Beaty ☎ (017687) 78278 • Ⓢ

Portinscale, Keswick • Bungalow • Sleeps 4 • £145-£255 • Linen supplied, pets welcome, car park • Mr & Mrs Jackson ☎ (017687) 73070 • 🐾 • B&B also

Santon, Holmrook • House • Sleeps 6-8 • £75-£200 • Working farm, near footpath and pub • Mr H W Cook ☎ (019467) 26270

☆ **Sedbergh** • 1 bungalow, 2 caravans • Sleeps 2-6 • £90-£280 • Closed Dec-Feb (caravans) • Quiet, peaceful; lovely views; secluded wooded setting • Mike & Liz Clark ☎ (015396) 20537 • 🐾 • B&B also

Staveley • Cottage • Sleeps 4-6 • £180-£250 • Central village location, short breaks available • Mrs A Bunn ☎ (01376) 513037 • Ⓢ Ⓡ 🐾

☆ **Staveley** • 4 cottages • Sleeps 2-6 • £135-£240 • 3k/App • Spectacular views, great walks from farm • Mrs Jean Dace ☎ (01539) 821030 • Ⓡ 🐾

Ullswater • 16 properties - cottages, lodges, coach house • Sleeps 2-6 • £116-£392 • 1-4k/up to C • Private 300 acre estate below Helvellyn • Stephen Foxall ☎ (017684) 82308 • 🐾

☆ **Wastwater Lake** • 3 apartments • Sleeps 4-5 • £180-£275 • 3k/C • Near Wastwater Lake, 8 miles to coast • Mrs J Burnett ☎ (019467) 26243 • 🐾

☆ See Display Advertisement

SELF-CATERING ACCOMMODATION ENGLAND

DERBYSHIRE

Flash • Flats in converted barn • Sleeps 2-6 • £80-£280 • 3k/App • Superb views, excellent walking & trekking centre • Mrs E Andrews ☎ (01298) 22543 •

Hartington • 2 cottages • Sleeps 2-4 • £150-£320 • 4k/HC • Exposed beams, log fire, glorious location • Mrs F Skemp ☎ (01298) 84447

Hathersage • Cottage • Sleeps 7 • £160-£350 • 4k • Near bunkhouse; by bridle way; working farm • Jane Marsden ☎ (01433) 650659 • ℝ ℅

☆ **Hope** • 4 cottages • Sleeps 2-6 • £140-£330 • 4k/HC • Superb location for walking • Mrs P M Mason ☎ (01433) 620291 • ℝ

Hope • Cottage • Sleeps 2 • £150-£235 • Closed Nov-Apr • 3k/C • Peak District; walkers paradise; peaceful location • Mrs Julie Hadfield ☎ (01433) 621955 • ⒮ ⓘ

☆ **Hope** • 3 cottages • Sleeps 2-6 • £140-£300 • 4k/C • Delightful riverside setting bordering Hope village • Mrs Dorothy Neary ☎ (01433) 620214 • ℝ ℅

Ilam • 1 farmhouse, 1 cottage • Sleeps 7-12 • £150-£475 • 4k/C • Mrs Muriel Richardson ☎ (01538) 308202 • ℅ • B&B also

Mayfield, Ashbourne • Cottage • Sleeps 3 • £150-£275 • 3k/HC • Mrs C & Mr K Mellor ☎ (01335) 344422 • ⒮ • B&B also

☆ **Peak District (nr Buxton)** • 10 apartments • Sleeps 2-8 • £120-£450 • Many free leisure facilities • J A Jackson ☎ (01298) 872591

Wirksworth (near) • Farm cottage • Sleeps 6-8 • £140-£240 • Good walking, wildlife; short breaks available • Mr & Mrs Wiltshire ☎ (01629) 823191 • Bunkhouse also

Wootton, nr Ashbourne • 5 cottage-style apartments & games room • Sleeps 2-6 • £95-£450 • 4k/HC • Old stone barn, ideal walking country • Ann Thompson ☎ (01335) 324433 • ℅

DEVON

☆ **Bickington, Newton Abbot** • 1 farmhouse, 1 flat, 2 converted barns • Sleeps 1 (bedsit) -7 • £83-£494 • Closed Xmas • Clean, warm; off the beaten track • Liz & Gray Ross ☎ (01626) 821496 • ⒮ ℅ • B&B also. For Display ad see over.

Dunsford, Teign Valley • 2 cottages • Sleeps 2-5 • £110-£270 • Peaceful farmland; lovely views; woodland walks • Mrs Jean May ☎ (01647) 252784 • Ⓢ

☆ **East Allington, Kingsbridge** • 1 farmhouse cottage, 1 converted barn • Sleeps 11 each • £200-£650 • Working farm, short breaks, lovely walks and views • Mrs Jean A Turner ☎ (01548) 521327 • 🏠

Hartland • Bungalow • Sleeps 6 • £200-£250 • Aga; CH; rural position; parking; garden • Mrs N Johns ☎ (01237) 441218 • 🏠

High Bickington • Cottage • Sleeps 2 • £145-£125 • Transport for senior citizens and non-drivers • Marion Cooke ☎ (01769) 560158 • Ⓢ

Holne, Ashburton • Cottage • Sleeps 5 • £155-£378 • Closed Nov-Apr • 3k/App • Devon hearth, electric chair lift, parking • Mrs Anne Mortimore ☎ (01364) 631235 • Ⓢ 🏠 • B&B also

☆ **Hope Cove, Kingsbridge** • Bungalow • Sleeps 1-8 • £200-£550 • 4k/HC • Mrs Cuming ☎ (01548) 561873

Ilfracombe • Apartments • Sleeps 2-6 • £120-£450 • 4k/HC • Harbourside manor house on coastal path • Dawn Marshall ☎ (01271) 862446 • 🏠

Ilfracombe • 4 apartments • Sleeps 1-4 • £85-£265 • Closed Nov-Feb • 3k/App • Magnificent sea views; adjacent coastal path • Don & Tricia Lawson ☎ (01271) 863126

Mid-Devon • Cottage • Sleeps 5 + cot • £110-£400 • 4k/C • Idyllic situation by Two Moors Way • Mrs V Blake ☎ (01363) 84288 • 🏠

☆ **Modbury** • Cottages • Sleeps 2-6 • £142-£399 • 3-4k/HC • Working farm; short breaks; beautiful countryside • Cathy Evans ☎ (01548) 830842 • 🏠

Morebath, nr Bampton • 4 cottages • Sleeps 3-8 • £160-£190 • Closed Nov-Apr • 4k/C • Edge Exmoor; 8 miles Wimbleball Lake • Mrs P Krombas ☎ (01398) 331465/(01392) 74039 • 🏠

☆ **Moretonhampstead** • 7 barn conversions - cottages & flats • Sleeps 2-6 • £90-£320 • Closed Jan-Dec • 2-3k/C • Judith Harvey ☎ (01647) 440835 • 🏠

ENGLAND

SELF-CATERING ACCOMMODATION

Moretonhampstead • Flat • Sleeps 4-6 • £80-£250 • Stunningly beautiful views of Dartmoor • Sally Radcliffe ☎ (01647) 440560 • 🏠

☆ **Mortehoe (Woolacombe)** • Flats • Sleeps 4-6 • £155-£410 • Mrs D A Vause ☎ (01483) 222644 • 🏠

☆ **Newton Ferrers, Plymouth** • Cottages • Sleeps 2-12 • £240-£1300 • 2k/C • Fabulous coastal walks • Sandy Cherrington ☎ (01752) 872235 • Ⓢ 🏠 • B&B also

North Bovey, Dartmoor • 6 cottages • Sleeps 2-5 • £100-£480 • 4k/HC • Stunning countryside, superb wildlife, cosy cottages • Susan Horn ☎ (01647) 40455 • 🏠

North Devon • 16 apartments & cottages • Sleeps 2-7 • £195-£674 • 3-4k/C-HC • Family owned, superb settings, short breaks • Nicky Faull ☎ (01271) 50611

Okehampton • 2 cottages • Sleeps 2-6 • £95-£165 • ETB member; heart of Devon; Tarka trail • Mrs M E Stevens ☎ (01837) 52305 • 🏠

Parracombe, Exmoor • 2 cottages - barn conversion • Sleeps 6 • £150-£390 • Closed Feb • 4k/HC • Secluded; on footpath; CH; short breaks • Mandy Chadwick ☎ (01598) 763315

☆ **Parracombe, Exmoor** • Cottage • Sleeps 8 • £90-£140 • Open fire in sitting room • Rosemary Lewis ☎ 0181-688 7078 • 🏠

Peter Tavey (nr), West Dartmoor • 1 barn conversion, 1 wing of farmhouse • Sleeps 2-6 • £120-£320 • 2k/App • Moorland position, idyllic walking base • Mr & Mrs Boswell ☎ (01822) 810687 • 🏠

☆ **Sidford, nr Sidmouth** • 7 cottages • Sleeps 4-6 • £160-£460 • 4-5k/HC • Mrs L Dillon ☎ (01395) 514162 • 🏠

Sidmouth • 1 cottage, 4 bungalows • Sleeps 2-6 • £120-£320 • Up to 4k/HC • Ideally situated for coastal path walking • Margaret Goddard ☎ (01395) 516065 • Ⓢ 🏠

South Zeal • Flats and chalet • Sleeps 2-4 • £90-£205 • 3k • Peter Wilkens ☎ (01837) 840209 • 🏠 • B&B also

☆ **Wembury Bay, Plymouth** • 50 chalets • Sleeps 2-6 • £165-£460 • Closed Dec-Mar • 4 ticks • R E Stansell ☎ (01752) 862382 • 🏠. For display ad see over

☆ See Display Advertisement

DORSET

Beaminster • Flat • Sleeps 2 • £150-£175 • 1k/App • Working farm; Wessex Way; informal, happy atmosphere • Judy Thompson ☎ (01308) 862537 • Ⓢ • B&B also

Bridport • Bungalow • Sleeps 4-6 • £160-£340 • 4k/C • Linen & fuel included; owners always available • Dan & Ann Walker ☎ (01308) 422941 • Ⓢ 🐾 • B&B also

Charmouth • 35 chalets • Sleeps 2-7 • £120-£309 • Closed Dec-Jan • Set in 14 acres of hillside • Terry & Debbie Bridges ☎ (01297) 560492 • 🐾 • B&B and groups also

☆ **Corfe Castle, Purbeck** • 3 apartments, 1 bungalow • Sleeps 2-8 • £150-£400 • Working farm; short breaks; beautiful countryside • Mrs Ann Fry ☎ (01929) 481066 • Ⓢ

Lulworth Cove • Flat • Sleeps 2 • £160-£175 • Closed Nov-Mar • Near Dorset Coastal Path • J M Palmer ☎ (01929) 400235 • Ⓢ 🐾

Lyme Regis • House • Sleeps 6 • £300-£425 • Grade II; belltower with cells; on coast • Mr & Mrs G Broom ☎ (01297) 489343 • Ⓢ

Lyme Regis • Two flats • Sleeps 4-5 • £100-£325 • 3k/App-3k/C • Central location; parking; 2 minutes beach • Mr D W Sweet ☎ 0117-950 4575 • 🐾

☆ **Marnhull** • Cottage • Sleeps 5 • £95-£290 • 2k/C • Superb views, very quiet • Gil Espley ☎ (01258) 820412 • Ⓢ • B&B also

Shaftesbury • 4 cottages, 1 flat • Sleeps 2-5 • £135-450 • 4k/C • Family farm, magnificent views, log res • Mrs Susan Smart ☎ (01747) 811830 • Ⓢ 🐾

Swanage • 5 apartments in house • Sleeps 2-6 • £85-315 • Closed Nov-Feb • 5 minutes town, beach, coastal path • Joe Gadston ☎ (01929) 423503 • 🐾

West Bexington • 3 cottages • £70-£450 • Closed Jan-Feb • 3k/App • On organic farm, sloping to Chesil Beach • Mrs M Josephine Pearse ☎ (01308) 897784

West Lulworth • Cottage • Sleeps 3 + 2 children • £160-£325 • Log fire; converted WI hall in centre of lage • A Cake ☎ (01202) 741938 • 🐾

West Lulworth • House • Sleeps 5-6 • £130-£300 • rge garden; near coastal paths and Cove • Ulla hari ☎ (01929) 400581 • 🐾 • B&B also

Weymouth • Flats • Sleeps 6 • £150-£400 • 2-3k/C • Georgian house with panoramic sea views • Mrs Veronica Brown ☎ (01305) 814152 • Ⓡ 🐾

Yetminster, nr Sherborne • 2 cottages • Sleeps 1-6 • £95-£230 • 3k/App • Comfortable, quiet, ideal for touring • Mrs Jane Warr ☎ (01935) 872305 • Ⓡ

COUNTY DURHAM

Blanchland, Consett • Cottage • Sleeps 6 • £120-£235 • Closed Nov-Mar • 3k/C • Loraine & Irene Bainbridge ☎ (01434) 675247/675296

Cotherstone, Teesdale • Cottage • Sleeps 4 • £150-£250 • 4k/HC • Private fishing available; on Teesdale Walk • Louise Horsley ☎ (01430) 422562 • Ⓢ 🐾

Holwick, Middleton-in-Teesdale • 2 Cottages • Sleeps 6-9 • £150-£550 • 4k/HC • Character cottages, edge of moors, Pennine Way • Peter Raine ☎ (01833) 640261

Middleton-in-Teesdale • Farmhouse • Sleeps 6-8 • £160-£325 • 4k/C • Central heating; quiet & private situation • Mrs June Dent ☎ (01833) 640349 • 🐾 • B&B also

Newbiggin-in-Teesdale, nr Middleton • Cottage • Sleeps 4-6 • £140-£285 • 3k/C • Lovely views; superb walking from doorstep • Mr R Burman ☎ 0161-860 7123

Startforth, nr Barnard Castle • Cottage • Sleeps 4 • £95-£170 • Closed Dec-Feb • 2k/App • Working farm, walking area, quiet location • Mrs G E Hodgson ☎ (01833) 621009 • 🐾

Wolsingham, Weardale • 5 cottages • Sleeps 2-5 • £135-£320 • Up to 4k/HC • Short breaks; working farm • Judith Stephenson ☎ (01388) 527285 • 🐾

Wolsingham-in-Weardale • Terraced cottage • Sleeps 4 • £120-£198 • 2k/C • Open fire; excellent walking area • Mrs M Gardiner ☎ (01388) 527538 • 🐾

GLOUCESTERSHIRE

☆ **Blockley** • 11 cottages • Sleeps 2-6 • £140-£546 • 4-5k/C-HC • Character cottages, winter breaks, idyllic setting • Mrs Katie Batchelor ☎ (01386) 700237

SELF-CATERING ACCOMMODATION IN ENGLAND

131

Chalford, Stroud • 4 cottages, 2 flats • Sleeps 2-6 • £120-£290 • Closed Nov-Mar • 3k/App • Secluded Cotswold hill farm in Golden Valley • Julian Usborne ☎ (01285) 760262 •

Chipping Campden • Coach house flat • Sleeps 2-3 • £100-£250 • Closed Nov-Feb • 4k/C • Magnificently situated on Cotswold Way • Mrs J Whitehouse ☎ (01386) 840835 •

St Briavels • 3 cottages • Sleeps 2-6 • £196-£396 • 4k/HC • Very peaceful location with wonderful views • Gillie Peacock ☎ (01594) 530393 •

Stanton • Cottage • Sleeps 6 • £230-£375 • 3k/C • Quiet, beautiful, unspoilt village near Broadway • Mrs V Ryland ☎ (01386) 584339/584270 •

HAMPSHIRE

Barton-on-Sea • Annexe of house • Sleeps 4 • £200-£310 • Closed Xmas • 3k • Ideal touring area; sea & forest • Mrs E P Carter ☎ (01425) 615211 • S R • B&B also

Fordingbridge (near) • Wing of thatched cottage • Sleeps 4 • £140-£310 • Excellent walking - New Forest, Cranborne Chase • Sue Sollars ☎ (01425) 653032

Lockerley • Thatched cottage • Sleeps 5 • £125-£210 • Mrs R J Crane ☎ (01794) 340460 •

Milford-on-Sea • Wing of Listed building • Sleeps 4-6 • £110-£250 • Period house, lovely garden; Solent Way • Mrs J M Halliday ☎ (01590) 642077 •

New Forest • Modern cottage • Sleeps 6 • £225-£465 • 4k/C • Very comfortable, quiet position, within forest • Mr & Mrs Cintra ☎ (01703) 282200 • R

New Forest • Thatched cottage • Sleeps 6-7 • £195-£395 • Log fires, garden, stream • Alison Du Cane ☎ 0171-727 5463 • S R

Warsash • Flat • Sleeps 4 • £95-£190 • 3k/C • 10 minute walk from Solent Way • Mrs E Paxton ☎ (01489) 572907 • R

HEREFORD & WORCESTER

Bircher Common • Farmhouse • Sleeps 6 • £175-£300 • Magnificent setting; walker's paradise outside door • Wendy Clare ☎ (0973) 463389/(01568) 780812 •

☆ **Broadway, Worcestershire** • Cottage • Sleeps 2 • £130-£180 • 3k/C • 18thC, oak-beamed throughout, listed building • Liz Dungate ☎ (01895) 834357

Bromyard • Flat • Sleeps 5 • £100-£150 • Closed Nov-Apr • 3k • Ideal area for touring • Mrs E M Whiteley ☎ (01885) 482294 • S • B&B also

Malvern (West) • Garden flat • Sleeps 2-4 • £95-£160 • 4k/C • Conservatory, use of garden, drying room • Mrs S Matthews ☎ (01684) 567328 • R

☆ **Malvern (near)** • 7 cottages • Sleeps 2-6 • £164-£461 • 4k/HC • Short breaks in winter months • Mr & Mrs D Berisford ☎ (01886) 880607

Malvern Hills • 1 cottage, 2 apartments • Sleeps 2-6 • £160-£395 • 4k/HC • Beautifully appointed characte cottages; excellent walking • Mrs D J Knight ☎ (01684) 564448 • S R

☆ **Much Cowarne** • 4 cottages • Sleeps 2-8 • £175-£600 • 4k/HC • Malvern Hills/Wye Valley - free maps & guides • Mr R M Bradbury ☎ (01432) 820317 •

Pershore (near) • Flat • Sleeps 3 • £150-£225 • Closed Dec • 3k • Listed Georgian farmhouse; lovely views • Mrs Sally Dodwell ☎ (01386) 553117 • R

Ross-on-Wye • Cottages • Sleeps 4-6 • £170-£418 • 4-5k/C-HC • Situated in beautiful valley for walks • Ian Jenkins ☎ (01432) 840390 • 🐾

Upper Lyde • Cottage • Sleeps 5 • £140-£280 • Closed Nov-Apr • 3k/C • Rural location; three bedrooms;central heating • Mrs A M White ☎ 0114-236 4357 • Ⓢ

ISLE OF WIGHT

Colwell Bay • Bungalow • Sleeps 4 • £100-£300 • Closed Dec-Jan • 3k • Delightful yachting sea views over Solent • Jill Howard ☎ (01590) 683871 • Ⓢ Ⓡ

Freshwater • Bungalow • Sleeps 4-5 • £145-£320 • Closed Nov-Feb • 3k/C • Sea/downs views, quiet, ideal walking • Jo & Dare Barry ☎ (01983) 529901 • Ⓢ Ⓡ

KENT

Goudhurst • 3 cottages • Sleeps 2-6 • £150-£500 • 5k/HC • Short breaks out of season #80 3 nights • Marion Fuller ☎ (01580) 212175 • Ⓢ 🐾

Old Wives Lees, Chilham • Cottage • Sleeps 5 • £185-£440 • 4k/C • Pilgrims Way; quality accommodation adjacent orchards • Mrs Darby ☎ (01372) 720723 • Ⓢ Ⓡ

Ramsgate • 1 house, 2 apartments • Sleeps 3-6 • £115-£320 • 3-4k/C • Comfortable, homely; short breaks; coastal walks • Mrs P J Martin ☎ (01843) 592945 • Ⓢ Ⓡ

Sevenoaks • Cottage • Sleeps 2-5 • £240-£380 • Closed Nov-Apr • Convenient for many National Trust properties • Lynda Gilbert ☎ (01732) 461008 • Ⓢ Ⓡ

Upper Hardres, nr Canterbury • Cottage • Sleeps 4 • £200-£300 • Closed Jan-Feb • 4k • Barn conversion, edge of meadow • Mrs Sheila Wilton ☎ (01227) 709375 • Ⓢ

Wrotham, Sevenoaks • 4 timber lodges • Sleeps 4-6 • £240-£480 • Closed Mid Jan-Mid Feb • 3k/HC • Top of North Downs near Pilgrim's Way • Gerry Morel ☎ (01732) 822415 • Ⓡ

LANCASHIRE

Borwick, Carnforth • 5 cottages (barn conversions) • Sleeps 4-6 • £195-£438 • 4k/C • Covered swimming pool May-Sept; games room • Mrs Morphy ☎ (01524) 732586 • 🐾

Brindle, nr Chorley • Cottage • Sleeps 4 • £180-£230 • 4k/C • Centrally heated, beamed cottage; telephone; parking • Mrs Pat McDade ☎ (01254) 852913 • 🐾

Chipping, Clitheroe • 4 properties • Sleeps 2-8 (total 16) • £75-£360 • Up to 5k/HC • Exposed beams; CH; meals available • Mrs Pat Gifford ☎ (01995) 61332/(0589) 279063 • 🐾 • B&B also

Chipping, Forest of Bowland • Flat • Sleeps 2 • £125-£195 • 4k/HC • AONB, fell country, wonderful views, parking • Mrs J Porter ☎ (01995) 61160 • 🐾

Croston • Converted barn • Sleeps 6 • £260-£395 • 5k/HC • Picturesque setting in rural village • D McMillan ☎ (01772) 600222 • Ⓡ 🐾

Longridge, Preston • Coach house • Sleeps 2 • £115-£185 • 3k/C • Drying room, cycle store, pub nearby • ☎ (01772) 785925 • Ⓢ

Ribble Valley • Cottage • Sleeps 3-4 • £145-£235 • 3k/HC • Margaret Berry ☎ (01200) 424176 • Ⓡ 🐾 • B&B also

Slaidburn • Semi-detached cottage • Sleeps 2-4 • £150 • Farmhouse close by; convenient for shop and inn • Mrs S Parker ☎ (01200) 446288

Yealand Redmayne • 3 cottages • Sleeps 4-6 • £90-£320 • 3-4k/C • Working farm, lovely walking in AONB • Mrs Susan Clarke ☎ (015395) 63276 • 🐾

LEICESTERSHIRE & RUTLAND

Belton-in-Rutland • Cottage • Sleeps 2 • £150-£185 • Closed Jan-Feb • Heavily beamed and quaint; stream outside • Mrs Patricia L Brown ☎ (01572) 717440 • Ⓢ 🐾

Belton-in-Rutland • Flat • Sleeps 4-6 • £150-£225 • 3k/C • On Macmillan Way; pub, shop in village • Richard & Vanessa Peach ☎ (01572) 717279 • Ⓢ 🐾 • B&B also

Edith Weston, Rutland • 4 stone cottages • Sleeps 2-5 • £150-£375 • 4-5k/HC • Privately owned, restful home from home • Mrs Kitty Walmsley ☎ (01780) 64001 • 🐾 • Disabled access

LINCOLNSHIRE

Bloxholm, nr Donnington, Sleaford • Cottage • Sleeps 4 • £130-£170 • 3k • Log fire, quiet village, scenic walks • Mrs H Gillatt ☎ (01526) 860347 • 🐾

Dorrington • 2 Victorian cottages • Sleeps 5 • £150-£275 • 3-4k/C • Local walks, short breaks, central heating • Janet Crafer ☎ (01526) 378222 • Ⓡ 🐾

Ropsley • Cottage • Sleeps 2 • £140-£175 • 4k/HC • Early 18thC, village location, highest standards • Mr & Mrs Hogan ☎ (01476) 585620 • 🐾

NORFOLK

Barton Turf • Cottage • Sleeps 2 • £110-£200 • Closed Jan-Mar • Period cottage; well equipped; dinghy available • Mr G Morgan ☎ (01692) 536057 • 🐾 • B&B also

☆ See Display Advertisement

Foxley, Dereham • 7 converted stables, 2 cottages • Sleeps 3-7 • £135-£350 • 3k/App • 365 acres mature woodland; ideal for ramblers • Mr P Davis ☎ (01362) 688523 • 🐾

Holme-next-the-Sea • Cottage • Sleeps 6+1 • £250-£750 • Closed Nov-Mar • 3k/HC • Traditional flint and brick Norfolk cottage • Mrs R Morison ☎ (01485) 533068 • 🐾

Neatishead, Norfolk Broads • Cottage • Sleeps 6 • £160-£350 • Peaceful Broads village; pub/shop nearby • Sue Wrigley ☎ (01692) 630233 • 🐾 • B&B also

☆ **Norwich** • House • Sleeps 5 • £220-£280 • 3k/C • Near bus station • Sally Clarke ☎ (01603) 615819 • Ⓡ • B&B also

---

NORWICH
SPACIOUS CITY CENTRE HOUSE
KINGSLEY ROAD

Quiet cul-de-sac 5-10 mins walk to bus station, shops, castle. Sleeps 5 in 3 bedrooms. £220-£280 per week. Includes CH, linen, towels.

👑👑👑 Commended

Tel or fax 01603 615819

Ringstead • 17thC cottage • Sleeps 4 • £160-£290 • Short breaks; log fire; CH; garden • Vivienne Scott ☎ (01553) 671694 • 🐾

NORTHAMPTONSHIRE

Sibbertoft, Market Harborough • Chalet • Sleeps 4 • £120-£220 • 3k/C • Peaceful lakeside setting • Mary & Jasper Hart ☎ (01858) 880886 • 🐾 • B&B also

NORTHUMBERLAND

Alwinton • Chalets • Sleeps 7 • £200 • Mrs Christine Pulman ☎ (01669) 650341 • 🐾 • B&B also

Amble • Cottage • Sleeps 4 • £115-£210 • 3k/HC • Cosy centrally heated cottage by beach • Mrs Eileen O'Kane ☎ 0191-273 6044 • 🐾

Bellingham, nr Kielder/Hadrians WI • Cottage • Sleeps 4 • £200-£360 • Closed Nov-Mar • 4k/HC • Near Kielderlake; walking, mountain biking, sailing • Ken & Joy Gaskin ☎ (01434) 220361 • B&B also

Branton • 9 cottages • Sleeps 2-6 • £175-£640 • 4-5k/HC • Indoor pool, gym, sauna, games room • Peter Moralee ☎ (01665) 578263 • 🐾

Chatton • 2 cottages • Sleeps 5-8 • £195-£360 • 4k/C • Coast, moors, unspoilt open countryside • Mrs J E May ☎ (01453) 842175 • 🐾

Crookham • Cottage • Sleeps 4 • £90-£300 • 3k/C • Convenient for Cheviot Hills, coast and Tweed Valley • Heather Pentland ☎ (01890) 820201

Embleton • Cottages • Sleeps 2-10 • £100-£300 • 2-4k/App-HC • Five miles wildlife trail on farm • Douglas Turnbull ☎ (016655) 79235 • 🐾

Glanton, nr Alnwick • Cottage • Sleeps 4 • £130-£300 • 4k/C • Inglenook fireplace, stone cottage, near Cheviots • Mrs P Clough ☎ (01661) 822662

Longbyre, Greenhead • Cottage • Sleeps 2 • £120-£180 • Closed Jan-Feb • 3k/C • Near Hadrian's Wall and Pennine Way • Mrs B Smith ☎ (016977) 47471 • Ⓢ 🐾 • B&B also

Rothbury • Cottage • Sleeps 4 • £135-£300 • Olde world, enclosed garden, centrally heated • Mr & Mrs Hewison ☎ (01669) 620144 • 🐾 • B&B also

Thropton, Morpeth • Cottage • Sleeps 5 • £135-£305 • 3k/C • Mrs H Farr ☎ (01665) 574672 • B&B also

Wark • Cottage • Sleeps 4 • £170-£270 • Closed Nov-Mar • On working farm; ideal walking area • Mrs A Nichol ☎ (01434) 230260 • 🐾 • B&B also

OXFORDSHIRE

Burford, Cotswolds • Cottage • Sleeps 2 • £150-£190 • Open fireplace; ancient honeystone building; electricity included • Mrs N T Pollock ☎ (01305) 784915

Cotswolds • 4 cottages • Sleeps 2 +2 • £200-£389 • 5k/HC • Unusually high quality; 70 acres farm & woods • David & Nena Barbour ☎ (01608) 683270 • Ⓢ

SHROPSHIRE

Bishop's Castle • 3 cottages • Sleeps 2-6 • £100-£275 • 3k/C • Fully inclusive; short breaks available • Mrs Audrey Price ☎ (01588) 638170 • 🐾

☆ **Cardington** • 1 flat, 1 chalet • Sleeps 2-4 • £70-£140 • D V Jones ☎ (01694) 771366 • Ⓢ

CARDINGTON

Nr Church Stretton, Shropshire

Two self-contained units on small touring caravan site. Views south to Caer Caradoc and Wenlock Edge. Sleep 4. £70-£140 per week. Short breaks. Open all year. Brochure or enquiries.

David Jones 01694 771366

ENGLAND

SELF-CATERING ACCOMMODATION

134

Church Stretton • Bungalow • Sleeps 6 • £160-£260 • 5k/C • Well equipped; beautiful views; golf course • Louise or Rosemary Powell ☎ (01694) 723159 • Ⓡ 🐾

Church Stretton • Bungalow • Sleeps 4 • £145-£190 • 3k/C • Immaculately kept; homely accommodation; beautiful countryside • Mrs Wendy Lewis ☎ (01694) 723173 (eve)/751212 (day) • Ⓡ

Clun Valley • 11 cottages & flats • Sleeps 2-8 • £85-£310 • 3k/up to C • Beautiful area, caring owners, short breaks • Roger & Sheila Davies ☎ (01588) 660487 • Ⓡ 🐾 • B&B also

Clunton • Caravan • Sleeps 4 • £125-£180 • Closed Nov-Mar • Amid superb walking country, free brochure • Mr & Mrs R Pledge ☎ (01462) 733182

Hope, Shropshire Marches • Cottage • Sleeps 5 • £135-£275 • 3k/C • Spectacular countryside, wonderful walking; leaflet available • D R Stacey ☎ (01743) 891210 • 🐾

Ironbridge • Flat • Sleeps 2 • £100-£150 • 3k/C • Tollhouse flat by famous Iron Bridge • Mrs P M Gillott ☎ (01952) 433522 • 🐾

☆ **Longden, nr Shrewsbury** • Cottage • Sleeps 3 • £170-£230 • 3k/HC • Mr & Mrs J E Jones ☎ (01743) 718323

Much Wenlock • Cottage • Sleeps 5 • £140-£270 • Closed Oct-Mar • 3k/C • Situated on Wenlock Edge; short breaks • Mrs Suzanne Hill ☎ (01952) 727293 • Ⓢ 🐾 • Bunkbarn also

Much Wenlock, Church Stretton • Barn • Sleeps 6-7 • £140-£300 • 3k/C • Good Pub Guide; garden; children welcome • Patrick Egan ☎ (01694) 771206 • Ⓢ 🐾 • B&B also

Stiperstones • Cottage • Sleeps 4 • £90-£150 • 2k/C • Breathtaking scenery; shop and inn nearby • Roy & Sylvia Anderson ☎ (01743) 791401 • 🐾 • B&B also

Wentnor, Bishops Castle • Converted barn • Sleeps 2-3 • £95-£145 • 3k/C • Large garden; close to Stiperstones & Longmynd • Barry Preston ☎ (01588) 650671

SOMERSET

☆ **Allerford** • Flats • Sleeps 2-3 • £185-£270 • Peacefully situated beside ancient packhorse bridge • Sheila Wright ☎ (01643) 862475 • 🐾 • B&B also

Bath • Cottage • Sleeps 5 • £125-£250 • Closed Oct-June • Mrs M Gould ☎ (01225) 316578 • Ⓡ 🐾 • B&B also

☆ **Dulverton** • 7 cottages • Sleeps 1-6 • £135-£400 • Closed Feb • 4k/HC • Katharine Harris ☎ (01392) 433524 • 🐾

Dunster, Exmoor • Beach chalet • Sleeps 4 • £90-£175 • Closed Nov-Apr • Quiet, private, sandy beach and sanctuary • Terry Simkins ☎ (01380) 828369 • Ⓡ

☆ **Glastonbury** • 8 cottages • Sleeps 2-6 + cot • £168-£490 • 2-4k/C • Indoor heated swimming pool • Mrs Avril Coles ☎ (01458) 83235. For display ad see over.

GLASTONBURY, SOMERSET

Middlewick Farm Holiday Cottages, Wick Lane

Mrs Avril Coles

Tel. 01458 832351

Eight delightful cottages with olde worlde charm and country style decor with indoor heated swimming pool. Also B&B. Can cater for 2-32 people. Short breaks ...vember-Easter, otherwise weekly.

Higher Wambrook, Chard • Converted barn • Sleeps 4 • £165-£245 • Peaceful, rural, lovely views, attractive barn • Mrs Kay Clegg ☎ (01460) 62583 • S

Hinton St George • Cottage • Sleeps 6 • £100-£280 • Thatched, walled garden, Inglenook, lovely walks • Gillian McKinsey ☎ (01689) 810609 • 🐾

Holford, Quantocks • Flatlet • Sleeps 2 • £65-£100 • Garden outlook, excellent walking, short breaks • Mrs C Taylor ☎ (01278) 741292 • S

Ilminster • House • Sleeps 6 • £170-£320 • Former toll house, Grade II Listed • Mr & Mrs Crowhurst ☎ (01275) 847181 • 🐾

Montacute • Cottage • Sleeps 2-6 • £180-£350 • 3k/C • Peaceful, comfortable; short or long walks nearby • George & Pat Baggesen ☎ (01935) 824487 • S 🐾

Norton Sub Hamdon • Converted stable • Sleeps 2-4 • £120-£200 • Closed Nov-Feb • 2k/HC • In peaceful village with inn and store • Mrs Jacqueline Fisher ☎ (01935) 881789

Simonsbath, Exmoor • 4 cottages, 1 flat • Sleeps 1-6 • £110-£440 • 2-4k/HC • Ideal base for walking holiday • Jane Styles ☎ (01643) 831222 • 🐾

Wheddon Cross, Exmoor • 6 cottages • Sleeps 2-6 • £110-£450 • 4k/HC • Quality comfort, cleanliness; outstanding, peaceful location • Tammy Cody-Boutcher ☎ (01643) 841249 • S 🐾 • B&B also

STAFFORDSHIRE

Kingsley • Cottage • Sleeps 2-5 • £165-£195 • 3k/App • Cosy, all-inclusive rambler's rest • Linda Salmon ☎ (01538) 754762 • 🐾

Leek (nr), Staffordshire moorlands • 2 flats on farm • Sleeps 6-7 • £110-£200 • 3k/App • Within walking distance of 2 pubs serving meals • Edith & Alwyn Mycock ☎ (01538) 308213 • 🐾

Winkhill • Cottages • Sleeps 2-7 • £120-£325 • 4k/C • 3 miles Alton Towers • Mrs J Saul ☎ (01538) 308298 • 🐾 • B&B also

> Please mention the Rambler's Yearbook when booking your accommodation

SUFFOLK

Darsham • Converted 17thC granary • Sleeps 4 • £135-£295 • Out of season weekends #35 per night • Mrs Bloomfield ☎ (01728) 668459 • S R • B&B also

Pakenham • Studio cottage • Sleeps 2 • £130-£230 • Closed Oct-Apr • Shared swimming pool, unheated • Mr A Nawrot ☎ (01359) 231149 • S R

SURREY

Holmbury St Mary • 2 units • Sleeps 2-4 • £140-£290 • 3-4k/C • Converted farm buildings on Greensand Way • Gill Hill ☎ (01306) 730210 • 🐾 • Category 3 accessibility. B&B also

EAST SUSSEX

Alfriston • Flat • Sleeps 2 or family of 4 • £180-£200 • Beautiful area, close to South Downs Way • Mrs Fay Smith ☎ (01323) 870407 • S

☆ **Ashdown Forest** • 5 single-storey cottages • Sleeps 4-5 • £199-£367 • 3k/C • John or Linda Francis ☎ (01825) 712377 • 🐾

ASHDOWN FOREST

Five two-bedroom cottages on small farm with extensive views over forest. Excellent walking and riding on and around forest. Includes heating, linen, colour TV, microwave, sleeps 4. Prices £199-£367. One dog welcome. For further details Tel 01825 712377.

ETB 🎋🎋🎋 Commended

Herstmonceux • Cottage • Sleeps 4 • £225-£420 • 4k/HC • Beams, inglenooks; surrounded by farmland walks • Mrs J K Gilday ☎ (01323) 832175/(01732) 770054

Magham Down • House • Sleeps 4-5 • £220-£325 • 4k/C • Well equipped, quiet rural location • Mr Geoffrey Daintree ☎ (01825) 890365

Telscombe Village & Folkington • 1 converted barn, 3 cottages • Sleeps 2-10 • £120-£645 • 3-5k/HC • Delightful rural cottages, South Downs Way • Anne Kennedy ☎ (01273) 858221 • R 🐾 • Groups also

WEST SUSSEX

Compton, nr Chichester • Flat • Sleeps 2 • £105-£160 • Ideal for walking South Downs • Mr J Buchanan ☎ (01705) 324555 day/631248 eve • 🐾

Henfield • 1 cottage, 1 flat • Sleeps 3-5 • £120-£270 • 3k/C • On footpath close to South Downs • Mrs M W Carreck ☎ (01273) 492546 • 🐾

Slindon • Flat • Sleeps 4 • £135-£300 • In NT village; views to coast • Peter & Sarah Fuente ☎ (01243) 814440 • 🐾 • B&B also

WARWICKSHIRE

Ilmington • House • Sleeps 3 + 1 • £155-£210 • 4k/C • Off-season short breaks available • David Price ☎ (01608) 682215 • Ⓢ

Long Marston, nr Stratford-on-Avon • 2 flats, 1 cottage • Sleeps 2-6 • £140-£270 • 3k/App • Historic country house near Heart of England Way • Mrs G H Jenkins ☎ (01789) 720705 • 🐾

Mousley End, Hatton • Cottage • Sleeps 4-6 • £225-£450 • 4k/HC • Set in outstanding countryside • Clive Bevins ☎ (01926) 484577 • Ⓡ 🐾

WILTSHIRE

Devizes • Caravan • Sleeps 4-6 • £150-£200 • Closed Nov-Mar • Alongside Kennet & Avon canal towpath • Colin & Cynthia Fletcher ☎ (01380) 828254 • 🐾

Malmesbury • Converted barn • Sleeps 2-3 • £150-£210 • 3k/C • Working farm; pets; linen, electricity free • Edna Edwards ☎ (01666) 823310 • 🐾

Pewsey • Thatched cottage • Sleeps 3 • £185-£265 • Closed Nov-Feb • 3k/C • Peaceful, in grounds of timber-framed manor • Mr C L G Sangster ☎ (01672) 563479 • Ⓢ Ⓡ 🐾

Steeple Ashton, nr Bath • Cottage • Sleeps 1-6 • £169-£349 • 4k/C • Cottage in picturesque Wiltshire village • Mr N A Sharples ☎ 0121-353 5258 • 🐾

EAST YORKSHIRE

Beverley (nr) • 12 cottages • Sleeps 1-6 • £160-£427 • 4-5k/HC • Yorkshire Wolds views • Mrs Pauline Greenwood ☎ (01430) 422230 • 🐾 • B&B also

NORTH YORKSHIRE

Appleton-le-Moors • Cottage • Sleeps 1-4 • £145-£245 • Closed Dec • 3k/C • Superb walking area, ideal for coast • Mrs B Firth ☎ 0113-258 8940

Askrigg • Cottage • Sleeps 6 + 2 children • £130-£325 • Village location, ideal walking/touring country • Jane Grant ☎ (01332) 550489 • 🐾

Askrigg • Cottage • Sleeps 4 • £150 • Lounge with open fire • Mrs B Bowe ☎ (01969) 650535 • 🐾 • B&B also

☆ **Aysgarth Falls** • Cottage • Sleeps 5 • £128-£240 • 3k/C • Wensleydale; unspoiled village; centre National Park • M C Mason ☎ (01792) 371602 • Ⓢ 🐾

☆ **Barningham, Richmond** • Cottage • Sleeps 2-6 • £130-£270 • 3k/C • Wonderful walks, moors, dales, log fires • S M Catton ☎ (01833) 621374 • Transport from station

Bishop Wilton (near) • 2 cottages • Sleeps 4 • £137-£225 • Closed Feb • 3k • Half a mile from the Minster Way • Mr & Mrs R B Sleightholme ☎ (01759) 368400 • 🐾

Boroughbridge • 2 cottages • Sleeps 2-6 • £200-£350 • 3k/C • 18th century working family farm • Rowena Naish ☎ (01423) 322045 • Ⓢ • B&B also

Borrowby, Staithes • Cottage • Sleeps 5 • £90-£220 • Converted, modernised cottage; fantastic sea views • Mrs A Welford ☎ (01947) 840505

Buckden, nr Skipton • 13 cottages • Sleeps 2-6 • £255-£449 • Indoor pool, private saunas, brochure • Susan & David Lusted ☎ (01756) 760877 • Ⓢ 🐾 • Only one small dog allowed

☆ **Carlton-in-Coverdale** • 2 cottages • Sleeps 1-6 • £120-£279 • 2-3k/C • Ideal Yorkshire Dales walking base • Peter R Wright ☎ (01705) 736651 • Ⓢ. For display ad see over.

☆ See Display Advertisement

SELF-CATERING ACCOMMODATION • ENGLAND

☆ **Chopgate, North York Moors** • 2 cottages • Sleeps 2-5 • £137-£290 • Near Coast to Coast, Cleveland Way and Lykewake walks • Mrs Jean Bowles ☎ (01642) 778254 • B&B also

☆ **Cloughton, Scarborough** • 4 cottages • Sleeps 2-7 • £90-£395 • 3-4k/HC • Quiet, peaceful, beautiful views • Mrs M A Martin ☎ (01723) 870924 • B&B also

Egton Bridge, Whitby • Cottage • Sleeps 4 • £100-£135 • Situated by river Esk; centre point for walks • Mrs M White ☎ (01947) 895279 • Ⓢ Ⓡ 🐾

Fearby, nr Masham • 2 cottages • Sleeps 5 • £200-£250 • Closed Nov-Mar • Double glazed, built in Yorkshire stone • J & V McCourt ☎ (01765) 689477 • Camping also - 4 ticks

☆ **Glaisdale** • 2 cottages • Sleeps 4 • £250-£396 • 5k/HC • Tom Spashett ☎ (01947) 897242 • Ⓢ Ⓡ • B&B also

Grassington • Apartment • Sleeps 2-4 • £110-£220 • 3k/C • Large, comfortable accommodation, overlooking village square • Ann Wadsworth ☎ (01253) 404726 • 🐾

Great Ayton • Cottage • Sleeps 3 • £150-£230 • 3k/C • Charming village beside North York moors • L M Juckes ☎ (01642) 723504 • Ⓢ Ⓡ

Grosmont • House • Sleeps 6 • £150-£325 • 4k/C • Near village and Coast to Coast and Eak Valley walks • Mrs B Howard ☎ (01947) 895314 • Ⓡ

Hawes • Cottage • Sleeps 4 • £140-£250 • 3k/C • Overlooking River Ure and Shunner Fell • Kate Empsall ☎ (01969) 650565 • Ⓢ 🐾 • B&B also

Horton-in-Ribblesdale • Cottage • Sleeps 4/5 • £100-£195 • Centre Three Peaks; well equipped, clean • Mrs S E Lambert ☎ (01729) 860367

Hovingham • Cottage • Sleeps 6 • £280-£330 • 4k/C • On Ebor Way, near Fosseway, Cleveland Way and Lyke-Wake walk • Mrs J James ☎ (01439) 788241 • 🐾

Kirkby Malham • 4 cottages, 4 apartments • Sleeps 2-6 • £180-£435 • 4k/HC • Idyllic private hamlet; superb walking/touring • Pam Hall ☎ (01729) 830293 • 🐾

Low Row, Richmond • Cottage • Sleeps 6 • £110-£240 • Superb walking & touring; secluded; spectacular views • Kathleen Hird ☎ (01748) 886243

Malham • 3 Cottages, 1 flat • Sleeps 2-6 • £140-£285 • Centre of village amidst limestone scenery • Mrs G Boocock ☎ (01729) 830317 • B&B also

Malton • Cottage • Sleeps 5 • £180-£295 • 2k/C • Farmhouse B&B also available; rural situation • Marion Shaw ☎ (01653) 694970 • Ⓢ

Newsham, Richmond • Cottage • Sleeps 6 • £105-£250 • Detached; working farm; quiet; walking area • Mrs S E Bainbridge ☎ (01833) 621252 • 🐾

Pateley Bridge • Cottage • Sleeps 6-8 • £165-£360 • 5k/HC • Ideal for Nidderdale Way • Mrs Anne Rack ☎ (01423) 711001 • 🐾

☆ **Pickering, Ryedale** • 7 cottages (1 & 2 storey) • Sleeps 2-7 • £175-£550 • 4k/HC • Gateway to the North Yorkshire moors • Penny & Julian Fearn ☎ (01751) 473974

Gateway to the North Yorkshire Moors
Keld Head Farm Cottages
Pickering, North Yorkshire

English Tourist Board
HIGHLY COMMENDED

Seven character stone cottages one and two storey, set around a secluded courtyard, each with open beamed ceilings and stone fire places. Superbly equipped, CH, double glazed, private parking, landscaped gardens and children's play area. Sleeps two to seven. All cottages have linen, towels, TV, radio, microwave, toaster, coffee maker etc. provided. Open all year. Off peak senior citizen discount. Short breaks.
Contact Penny & Julian Fearn.
Tel: 01751 473974 post code YO18 8LL

Reeth, Swaledale • 3 cottages • Sleeps 3-7 • £170-£385 • 4k/up to HC • All inclusive tariff; all comforts provided • Mrs P R E Procter ☎ (01748) 884273 • 🐾

☆ **Robin Hood's Bay** • Cottage • Sleeps 6 • £135-£275 • Mrs G R Astley ☎ (01332) 882637 • 🐾

ROBIN HOOD'S BAY

Three-bedroomed centrally heated cottage in the heart of the village • Sleeps up to 6 • 3 minutes walk to the sea • Ideal for holidays or short breaks all year round • For brochure or enquiries

Tel 01332 882637

Ryedale • 2 cottages • Sleeps 2-6 • £125-£285 • Closed Nov-Mar • Pretty village, convenient for York, moors, Dales • ☎ (01653) 628656 • 🐾

Sawley, Ripon • 4 cottages • Sleeps 2-7 • £95-£275 • 2k/C • Peaceful location near Fountains Abbey & Dales • A C Cook & Mrs J R Cook ☎ (01765) 620658 • Ⓢ 🐾

Sedbusk, Hawes, and West Burton • 2 cottages • Sleeps 4-8 • £155-£350 • 4k/HC • Lovely character old Dales stone cottages • Anne Fawcett ☎ (01969) 667481 • 🐾

Stockton on Forest, York • 5 cottages • Sleeps 2-8 • £150-£300 • Closed Oct-Mar • 150 year old renovated farmworkers cottages • Mike Cundall ☎ (01904) 400600 • 🐾

Thormanby • 2 cottages • Sleeps 4-6 • £130-£300 • CH; open fires; quiet lane • Rachel Ritchie ☎ (01845) 501417 • 🐾 • B&B also

☆ **Wensleydale** • 3 cottages • Sleeps 4-7 • £155-£320 • Own grounds, unrestricted views, short breaks • Mrs Pat Cooper ☎ (01677) 460315 • 🐾

Moorcote
Wensleydale, North Yorkshire

Three fully-equipped cottages • Sleep 4-7 • Four acres of private grounds overlooking Jervaulx Abbey • A haven for bird watchers and a walker's paradise • Well-behaved pets welcome • Holidays or short breaks.
Enquiries Tel. 01677 460315

Wensleydale • 9 cottages and bungalow farmhouses • Sleeps 2-10 • £120-£498 • 3-4k/up to HC • Comfort and quality at reasonable prices • Brenda Stott ☎ (01969) 667359 • 🐾 • Groups also

Whitby • Flats • Sleeps 2-4 • £98-£260 • Panoramic harbour views, winter breaks, non-smoking • Pat Beale ☎ (01947) 810534 • Ⓢ Ⓡ • B&B also

Worton, nr Askrigg • 3 cottages • Sleeps 2-8 • £150-£450 • Up to 4k?HC • Open fires; central heating; super views • Mike & Pamela Hague ☎ (01969) 650652 • 🐾

WEST YORKSHIRE

Haworth • Cottage • Sleeps 3-4 • £130-£180 • Closed Oct-Mar • 3k/C • Famous Bronte village; beautiful moorland walks • Pam Pennington ☎ (01535) 642986 • Ⓢ Ⓡ 🐾

Hebden Bridge • Cottage • Sleeps 4 • £130-£225 • 3k/C • Working dairy farm; fresh produce available • Mrs Sue Reynard ☎ (01845) 524529 • Ⓡ 🐾

Todmorden • Stone cottage • Sleeps 2-4 • £118-£160 • 3k/C • Close to Calderdale and Pennine Way • Mrs H Grieve ☎ (01706) 812086 • Ⓡ 🐾

Yeadon • Cottage • Sleeps 4 • £165-£250 • Cosy; easy reach of Emmerdale, Bronte country & Dales • Mrs I Croft ☎ 0113-250 4198 • Ⓡ 🐾

FOR THE KEY TO SYMBOLS USED IN THIS GUIDE, SEE THE LAST PAGE OF THE BOOK

☆ See Display Advertisement

Scotland

ARGYLL & BUTE

Barcaldine, nr Oban • Chalet • Sleeps 2 • £175-£220 • Closed Jan-Feb • Lochside location; wonderful views; interesting walking • Jock & Jonquil Slorance ☎ (01631) 720265 • Ⓢ 🐾

Duror, Argyll • Flat • Sleeps 6 • £90-£220 • Mrs Elspeth Malcolm ☎ (01631) 740259 • 🐾

Kilmartin, Argyll • 2 cottages • Sleeps 2-4 • £150-£320 • Working farm nestling among coastal hills • Barbara Caulton ☎ (01546) 810281 • Ⓢ 🐾

Loch Fyne (shore) • Cottage • Sleeps 6 • £196-£288 • Price includes sea/river fishing and boat • John Rankin ☎ (01738) 632580 • 🐾

Lochavich • 2 cottages • Sleeps 2-4 • £120-£300 • 4Cr/C • Peaceful glen in regional scenic area • Mrs G Dalton ☎ (01866) 844212

CENTRAL BELT

Clyde Valley, South Lanarkshire • Stone cottages • Sleeps 2-7 • £160-£430 • 3Cr/C-5Cr/HC • Unique heritage cottages on private estate • Richard Carmichael ☎ (01899) 308336 • Ⓢ 🐾

Dunure, by Ayr • Bungalow • Sleeps 6 • £140-£275 • 4Cr/C • Convenient for golf, touring, fishing, walking • Mrs Lesley Wilcox ☎ (01292) 500223 • 🐾 • B&B also

Edinburgh • Flat • Sleeps 5 • £300-£475 • 4Cr/C • Unrestricted parking; first floor; residential area • Jim Donaldson ☎ 0131-337 1066 • Ⓢ Ⓡ

Pentland Hills, nr Edinburgh • 1 cottage, 1 farmhouse wing • Sleeps 5-6 • £190-£420 • 4Cr/C & 5Cr/HC • Car essential; Trossachs; Borders close; brochure • Geraldine Hamilton ☎ (01501) 785205 • 🐾

DUMFRIES & GALLOWAY

Castle Douglas • Cottage • Sleeps 6 • £150-£320 • 4Cr/C • Working farm, beautiful countryside, linen supplied • Mrs Elizabeth Millar ☎ (01557) 820283 • 🐾

HIGHLAND

Aviemore • 12 log cabins & chalets • Sleeps 2-6 • £196-£567 • 2Cr/C-5Cr/deluxe • Superb location by Cairngorm Mountains • Pine Bank Chalets ☎ (01479) 810000 • Ⓡ 🐾 • Groups also

Diabaig, Ross & Cromarty • Caravan • Sleeps 4 • £28-£40 • Closed Dec-Feb • Harbour nearby, hill walker's paradise • Mrs I Ross ☎ (01445) 790268 • B&B also

Fort William • Flat • Sleeps 2-4 • £160-£220 • 2Cr/C • Good base for walking West Highlands • Charles Moore ☎ (01397) 702535 • Ⓢ Ⓡ 🐾 • B&B also

Glen Coe • Cottage • Sleeps 6 • £250-£450 • Closed Nov • 4Cr • Spacious stone house, two bathrooms • Ray Darker ☎ (01855) 811553 • Ⓢ

Glen Nevis, Fort William • Cottage, 2 apartments & bunkhouse • Sleeps 2-5 • £220-£280 • 3Cr/C-4Cr/Comm • Situated at Ben Nevis Footpath • Mrs Diane Young ☎ (01397) 702240 • Ⓡ 🐾 • B&B also

Glenelg, nr Shiel Bridge • 1 bungalow, 6 chalets, 1 caravan • Sleeps 2-6 • £100-£310 • Bungalow 4Cr/C • Laundry & indoor games room on site • M & E Lamont ☎ (01599) 522231 • 🐾

Inveralligin, Torridon • Cottage • Sleeps 6 • £200-£280 • Ideally situated for climbing and walking • Mrs Mary Mackay ☎ (01445) 791333 • 🐾 • B&B also

Invergarry • Cottage • Sleeps 6 • £100-£290 • 3k/C • Many interesting forest walks, Munros accessible • Mrs M Waugh ☎ (01809) 501335 • 🐾 • B&B also

Invergarry, Inverness-shire • Cottage, flat, house • Sleeps 2-12 • £430-£700 • Miss J Ellice ☎ (01809) 501287

Kincraig • 2 cottages • Sleeps 4 • £120-£300 • 3Cr/C • Nick Thompson ☎ (01540) 651377 • 🐾 • B&B also

Kintail, Skye & Lochalsh • Caravan • Sleeps 2-4 • £100 • Lochside location, wonderful views, Munro country • Mrs Jean Camilli ☎ (01599) 511266 • Ⓢ

Kishorn • 2 chalets • Sleeps 4 • £100-£200 • Closed Nov-Mar • 2Cr/App • Quiet location, mountain and loch views • Penny Van Hinsbergh ☎ (01520) 733253 • 🐾

Lochcarron • Cottages & caravans • Sleeps 3-6 • £100-£300 • 3Cr/App-4Cr/C • Walking, wildlife, birds, boating, magnificent views • Mrs C Mackay ☎ (01520) 722281 • 🐾

Newtonmore • Cottage • Sleeps 6 • £200 upwards • 3Cr/C • Central heating, open fire, drying room • Mary Mackenzie ☎ (01540) 673504 • Ⓡ 🐾 • Hostel also

☆ **Northern Cairngorms** • Log chalets • Sleeps 6-12 • £315-£630 • Closed Xmas • Tony Mitchell ☎ (01479) 861276 • Ⓢ 🐾

SELF-CATERING ACCOMMODATION SCOTLAND

☆ **Onich, Fort William** • 4 cottages • Sleeps 4-6 • £180-£320 • 2Cr/C • Mr & Mrs W Murray ☎ (01855) 821257 •

Onich, Fort William • Chalets • Sleeps 4-25 • £160-£359 • 2-3Cr/C • Pub/restaurant on site, real ales • Paddy Heron ☎ (01855) 821287 •  • Bunkhouse also

☆ **Onich, Fort William** • 2 cottages, 1 flat, 5 caravans • Sleeps 4-5 • £185-£350 • 4Cr/C-HC • A W MacLean ☎ (01855) 821359 •

Poolewe, Ross-shire • 6 bungalows • Sleeps 6 • £160-£395 • 4Cr/HC • Main bedrooms en-suite • F M Hughes ☎ (01445) 781454 •

☆ **Strontian, Argyll** • Scandinavian log houses • Sleeps 8 • £220-£495 • 4Cr/HC • G Hanna ☎ (01967) 402409 •

ISLE OF ARRAN

Blackwaterfoot • Cottage • Sleeps 2-4 • £175-£280 • Centrally heated, near beach & village, Aga • Mrs M Bannatyne ☎ (01770) 830237 •

ISLE OF EIGG

• Croft house • Sleeps 7 • £120-£200 • Beautiful island with views of Skye and Rum • Peter Wade-Martins ☎ (01362) 668435

ISLE OF SKYE

Dunvegan • 5 cottages & chalets • Sleeps 2-4 • £100-£320 • 2Cr/App-3Cr/C • Outstanding walks on doorstep; short breaks • Mr Jerry Cox ☎ (01470) 521231 •

Glen Eynort, nr Glenbrittle • Cottage • Sleeps 6 • £180-£220 • Walks start from doorstep • R Van Der Vliet ☎ (01478) 640320 •

Kildonan, nr Edinbane • Sleeps 4 • £140-£190 • Closed Nov-Mar • Mrs Barbara Herbert ☎ (01470) 582285 •

NORTH EAST SCOTLAND

Lintrathen, Kirriemuir, Angus • Bunglaow/log house • Sleeps 4-6 • £160-£360 • 4Cr/C-5Cr/HC • Excellent views in lovely countryside • Moira Clark ☎ (01575) 560213 •  • B&B also

Strathdon, Aberdeenshire • 2 cottages, 1 house • Sleeps 7-8 • £180-£260 • 3Cr/C • Mrs Elizabeth Ogg ☎ (019756) 51238 •  • B&B also

☆ See Display Advertisement

SCOTLAND

SELF-CATERING ACCOMMODATION

141

SCOTTISH BORDERS

Newcastleton • 4/5 cottages/flats • Sleeps 2-36 • £78-£448 • 3k/C • Sauna, solarium, jacuzzi, pony trekking • Mrs P Copeland ☎ (016977) 48617 • 🖾 • Groups also

Wales

CARMARTHENSHIRE

Llandeilo (near) • 6 cottages • Sleeps 3-8 • £190-£600 • Closed Jan-Feb • 4 dragons • Exceptionally comfortable; idyllic situation; catering available • Mrs M E Jones ☎ (01550) 777448 • Ⓡ 🖾 • Wheelchair access grade 2

Myddfai, Llandovery • Cottage • Sleeps 4-6 • £120-£220 • Spacious stable conversion in peaceful setting • Gill Swan ☎ (01550) 720494 • Ⓢ 🖾 • B&B also

CEREDIGION

Borth • 5 cottages • Sleeps 2-10 • £145-£569 • 5 dragons, Welcome Host • Nature reserve adjacent; coastal/mountain walks • Bob Trubshaw ☎ (01970) 871233 • Ⓡ 🖾 • Disabled access grade 2 award

Clarach Bay • 60 caravans • Sleeps 4-8 • £105-£385 • Closed Nov-Mar • 5 ticks, Welcome Host • Beach front location; coastal/mountain walks • Gwynn Jenkins ☎ (01970) 828900 • 🖾 • Disabled access grade 2 award

CONWY

Betws-y-Coed • Cottage • Sleeps 5 • £145-£275 • 4 dragons • Panoramic views, central heating, peaceful surroundings • Nerys Evans ☎ (01492) 640438 • 🖾

GWYNEDD

☆ **Barmouth** • Flat • Sleeps 6 • £135-£275 • Sea views • Mrs G R Astley ☎ (01332) 882637 • Ⓡ 🖾

Beddgelert • House • Sleeps 6 • £55-£240 • Snowdon path and inn nearby; views • Sue & Michael Davies ☎ 0181-670 2756

Bontddu, nr Dolgellau • Cottage • Sleeps 6-9 inc. children • £95-£190 • Estuary, waterfall, wildish garden; short breaks • Lindsey March ☎ (01803) 866870 • 🖾

Crogen, Llandderfel • Converted barn • Sleeps 2-4 • £150-£250 • Closed Dec • Incredible views; hill walking; short breaks • Dee & Peter Smith ☎ (01490) 440346 • B&B also

Dolgellau • Flat & caravan • Sleeps 2-4 • £100-£230 • Both equipped to a high standard • Mrs D M Rowlands ☎ (01341) 422638 • Ⓢ • B&B also

Dolgellau • 2 cottages, 2 parts country house • Sleeps 2-9 • £106-£535 • Could accommodate 21. Cadair's foothills • Mr G B Gauntlett ☎ (01341) 423481 • 🖾

Dolgellau • Flat • Sleeps 4 • £160-£250 • Closed Nov-Feb • WTB grade 4 • Lovely grounds, riverside setting, spacious parking • Mrs R Le Tissier ☎ (01341) 423487 • Ⓢ

Harlech • Cottage • Sleeps 4 • £60-£85 • Closed Nov-Easter • Situated village centre, close beach, mountains • Mrs Owen ☎ 0181-894 9204 • Ⓡ 🖾

Llanberis (nr), Snowdonia • Large house • Sleeps up to 40 • £4.80 per night • Closed Bank Hol.w/ends • Unwardened, all bookings through Les Pennington • ☎ 0151-525 3425 • Ⓢ • Groups also

Llanuwchllyn • Cottage • Sleeps 6-8 • £160 • Isolated; mountain views; wood stove; no TV • J H Gervis ☎ (01992) 892331 • Ⓡ 🖾

Lleyn Peninsula • Farmhouse and caravan • Sleeps 6 • £85-£150 • Closed Oct-Easter (house) • Comfortable, clean accommodation; situated on B4417 • Mrs J M Roberts ☎ (01758) 770261 • 🖾

Nant Gwynant • House • Sleeps 12 • £290-£620 • Unique situation, 14 acres, garden, lake • Harvey Lloyd ☎ (01286) 871057 • 🖾

☆ **Pwllheli** • 9 cottages on farm • Sleeps 2-8 • £94-£199 • 4-5 dragons • Mrs S R Ellis ☎ (01758) 612536 • Ⓢ Ⓡ 🖾

☆ **Snowdonia** • Cottage • Sleeps 5 • £175-£250 • Well-equipped; lovely views and garden • A Garnsey ☎ (01323) 891179/(01766) 770770 •

Spacious cottage on edge of National Park, 1½ miles from Port Merion • Beautiful views Peaceful garden above the village • Sleeps 5-6 in three bedrooms • Modern bathroom • Two lounges • Large kitchen • Laundry room • Ring for details.

Mrs A Garnsey   01323 891179 or 01766 770770

Tanygrisiau, Vale of Ffestiniog • Cottage • Sleeps 4-6 • £110-£265 • 3 dragons • Doorstep walking; short breaks; linen; heating • Mrs M deWardt ☎ (01642) 722409 • Ⓢ Ⓡ

MONMOUTHSHIRE

Abergavenny • Cottage • Sleeps 2 • £150-£200 • 3 dragons • Excellent views; peaceful yet accessible; working farm • Sandra Belcham ☎ (01873) 856682 • • B&B also

Abergavenny • 4 cottages • Sleeps 3-6 • £160-£350 • 4Cr • Indoor swimming pool; working farm; brochure • Richard Sage ☎ (01873) 857357 • Ⓡ

Abergavenny • 2 cottages • Sleeps 4-6 • £100-£250 • 4/5 Dragons • Peaceful, near Offa's Dyke & Three Castles • Mrs S C Pritchard ☎ (01873) 821219 •

PEMBROKESHIRE

Broad & Little Haven • 4 cottages • Sleeps 2-9 • £95-£385 • 4 dragons • 200 yards from coastal path • R Llewellin ☎ (01437) 781552 • • B&B also

Glanrhyd • Cottage • Sleeps 4 • £120-£205 • Closed Jan-Feb • 3 dragons • Central heating; 3 miles coastal path • Ralph & Janet Stammers ☎ (01239) 881615 •

Pembrokeshire National Park • Cottage • Sleeps 5 • £150-£300 • 4 dragons • On coastal path, outstanding views • Mrs E A Webber ☎ (01646) 636254 • • B&B also

Porthgain, St Davids • 3 cottages, 9 cedar lodges • Sleeps 2-9 • £115-£495 • 3-4 dragons • Spectacular sea views, peaceful location • Steve Craft ☎ (01348) 831220 • Ⓢ • Groups also

Solva • Cottage • Sleeps 2-4 • £75-£350 • 4 dragons • TV, microwave; linen provided (not towells) • S Murphy ☎ 0181-446 6532 •

☆ **Solva** • 4 cottages • Sleeps 4-6 • £130-£420 • 5 dragons • Old stone cottages in glorious countryside • Sarah Griffiths ☎ (01348) 831224 •

POWYS

Border country • Cottage • Sleeps 7-8 + cot • £140-£250 • Closed Nov-Easter • Near Offa's Dyke; log fire • Mrs J E Pinches ☎ (01544) 370219

Brecon Beacons • 1 bungalow + 1 farmhouse or 2 apartments • Sleeps 2-15 • price not supplied • 4-5 dragons • Walk direct from accommodation onto mountains • Ann Phillips ☎ (01874) 665329 •

Llanfair Caereinion • Cottage • Sleeps 6 • £185-£275 • 4 dragons • 17thC oak-beamed cottage in country town • Peter Brown ☎ 0171-359 1281 • Ⓢ

Llangynidr • Cottage • Sleeps 6 • £150-£250 • 4 dragons • Stone cottage in heart of National Park • Mrs C J King ☎ (01794) 512342 •

Montgomeryshire • 3 cottages • Sleeps 4-6 • £160-£315 • Closed y • Period cottages in beautiful countryside; brochure • Ruth Macklin Smith ☎ (0589) 282004 • Ⓢ

☆ **Pontsticill** • 4 cottages & houses • Sleeps 4-10 • £300-£500 • 5 dragons • Fitted kitchens, Aga cooker, serviced daily • Michael Hurley ☎ (01685) 723627 • Ⓢ • B&B also. For display ad see over.

☆ See Display Advertisement

SELF-CATERING ACCOMMODATION WALES

Ireland

COUNTY DOWN

☆ **Morne Mountains** • 1 farmhouse, 1 cottage • Sleeps 6-10 • £250-£500 • Secluded, traditional; hill walking - near Ulster Way • D Davies ☎ (01509) 413866 • 🏕 • Camping & bunkhouse also

Morne Mountains, Co Down • Apartment • Sleeps 2-4 • £145-£195 • NITB 3 star • Short breaks; on promenade; foot of mountains • Mrs Kathleen Calvert ☎ (013967) 26081

COUNTY KERRY

Annascaul • Bungalow • Sleeps 4 • £80-£180 • Bord Failte App • Lake, sea, mountains; near Annascaul village • Kathleen O'Connor ☎ (066) 57168 • 🏕 • B&B also

Caherciveen • Cottage • Sleeps 4-6 • £200-£240 • ITB 3 star • Lovely location, convenient to all amenities • Mary Landers ☎ 066 72997 • B&B also

Kells, Ring of Kerry • Cottage • Sleeps 4-6 • £170-£300 • Modernised farmhouse, peat fire, idyllic setting • Mr Richard Paddy ☎ (01622) 764007 • Ⓢ

Lauragh (Healy Pass Road) • Cottage • Sleeps 5-6 • £110-£190 • Magnificent view of sea & countryside • Mrs Mary Moriarty ☎ 00353 64 83131 • 🏕

COUNTY WATERFORD

Ballymacarbry • Cottage • Sleeps 6 • price not supplied • ITB 4 star • Heart of Nire Valley; walking maps available • Eileen Ryan ☎ 052 36141 • 🏕

COUNTY WICKLOW

☆ **Glendalough** • Bungalow • Sleeps 1-8 • £200-£250 • 3 star • Ideal hill-walking area; car essential • Susan McDonnell ☎ 003531 285 9218 • 🏕

Glenealy, Ashford • Cottage • Sleeps 7 • £120-£250 • ITB 3 star • Own exclusive local walking guidebook /map • Mary Byrne ☎ 404 44614 • B&B also

The B&B Accommodation Guide

THE KEY TO THE SYMBOLS USED IN THIS GUIDE IS ON THE LAST PAGE

Welcome to the 1997 B&B Accommodation Guide! There are several developments in the Guide this year. One is a special section for centres offering accommodation suitable for groups. This begins on page 106. However, it is important to note that many places big enough to take groups are still listed in the other three sections, including this one.

We have for the first time included any tourist board classification awarded to the establishment (but not any from other bodies such as the AA or Which?). See page 87 for a brief explanation of them and how we have abbreviated them. The classifications give certain assurances of what standards and facilities to expect. Not all proprietors choose to take part in the tourist board scheme. Some feel that in order to do so they are required to take the individuality out of their accommodation and put it in a straight jacket. Or, that in order to obtain a certain grading, they may be expected to provide facilities which seem inconsequential to their particular clientele (such as a trouser press in an outlying farm clearly only visited by hill walkers). So don't pass by somewhere that doesn't have a tourist board grading. A telephone call to make a booking will usually tell you a good deal (but don't forget to cancel if you change your mind).

We have introduced some new symbols this year.

⚲ means you may be able to take your dog after consulting with the proprietor.

🌙 means the proprietor is a member of the Ramblers' Association (a key to all symbols is on the last page of the book).

This edition also sees for the first time an index. This guides you to the place of your choice in any of the four accommodation sections. It also helps you find villages or hamlets which are part of an address but too small to have a heading of their own.

As always, many of the entries in this guide come from readers' recommendations. As we are not able to vet the establishments, this is a most valuable resource. Please keep your recommendations coming in, by letter, telephone or by using the form on page 325.

Many providers of accommodation write to us saying how much they enjoy having walkers to stay. Equally, many readers tell us what wonderful hospitality they have received up and down the country. Clearly, many users of this book are plugging the Yearbook and encouraging proprietors to place a listing.

The entries are listed in order of country—England, Isle of Man, Scotland, Wales and Ireland in that order; then in alphabetical order of county or unitary authority, and then by place. See page 87 for an explanation of how we have dealt with the new unitary authorities in organising these listings. The place might be a village or town or even a hamlet and the choice is determined by a number of elements—proximity to a long distance path; its ease of access to a resort or walking centre; or on occasion, the request of an advertiser. It is not possible to standardise this procedure and it is done by consulting maps and guides. If the place is within 2 miles of one of the long distance paths listed in our selection starting on page 54, the name of that path is given after the place name. As some "places" are sprawling, it is always best to check the location on a map.

Six-figure grid references are given for each entry and the maps referred to, unless otherwise stated, are the Ordnance Survey Landranger series, scale 1:50,000.

Finally—a disclaimer. The information in the guide is based on details received from proprietors during 1996. The RA cannot be held responsible for errors or omissions.

THE ACCOMMODATION GUIDE

145

AVON

COUNTY NO LONGER EXISTS. ENTRIES PREVIOUSLY LISTED HERE
WILL NOW BE FOUND UNDER EITHER GLOUCESTERSHIRE OR
SOMERSET

BEDFORDSHIRE

■ LUTON
ICKNIELD WAY

Mrs L Frances Spinner, "Spinners", 46 Hill Rise, LU3
3EE. ☎ (01582) 508327 • Map 166/055252 • BB **B** •
EM book first £4, 6-8pm • S1 T1 • 1-12 NX • Ⓓ Ⓢ
Ⓡ

■ PULLOXHILL (Bedford)

Judy Tookey, Pond Farm, 7 High Street, MK45 5HA.
☎ (01525) 712316 • Map 153/063340 • BB **B** • D1 T1
F1 • 1-12 • Ⓓ • List • Food nearby

■ SANDY

Mrs J M Strong, Orchard Cottage, 1 High Street,
Wrestlingworth, SG19 2EW. ☎ (01767) 631355 •
Map 153/258471 • BB **B** • S2 D1 T1 • 1-12 NX • Ⓓ
Ⓢ • 1Cr/C

Mrs Margaret Codd, Highfield Farm, Great North
Road, SG19 2AQ. ☎ (01767) 682332 • Map
153/166515 • BB **C/D** • D/S2 T/S2 F/S2 • 1-12 NX • Ⓑ
Ⓓ Ⓢ Ⓡ 🐾 • 2Cr/HC

BERKSHIRE

■ COMPTON (Newbury)
RIDGEWAY

M Jarett, The Forge House, RG20 6QS. ☎ (01635)
578387 • Map 174/521800 • BB **B** • EM book first £8,
7pm • T1 • 4-10 NX • Ⓥ Ⓑ Ⓓ Ⓢ 🐾

Garry & Liz Mitchell, The Compton Swan Hotel, High
Street, RG20 6NL. ☎ (01635) 578269 • Map
174/520799 • BB **D** • EM £6, 9.30pm • D1 T3 F1 • 1-
12 • Ⓥ Ⓑ Ⓓ Ⓢ 🐾 • Caravan also

■ COOKHAM
THAMES PATH

Cynthia Crowe, Wylie Cottage, School Lane, SL6 9QJ.
☎ (01628) 520106 • Map 175/895851 • BB **C** • D1 T1
• 1-12 NX • Ⓓ Ⓢ Ⓡ 🐾 Ⓜ • List

■ HIGHCLERE (Newbury)

Westridge Open Centre, Andover Road, RG20 9PJ. ☎
(01635) 253322 • Map 174/436604 • BB **A** • EM book
first £5, 6.30pm • S3 T2 • 1-12 NX • Ⓥ Ⓓ Ⓢ • Extra
charge for cooked breakfast. Closed public holidays

■ MAIDENHEAD
THAMES PATH & LONDON COUNTRYWAY

Mrs Caroline Street, Sheephouse Manor, Sheephouse
Road, SL6 8HJ. ☎ (01628) 776902 • Map
175/898831 • BB **D** • S2 D2 T1 • 1-12 NX • Ⓑ Ⓓ Ⓡ
🐾 Ⓜ • 2Cr/C • SC also

Mrs B Fox, 48 Birdwood Road, SL6 5AP. ☎ (01628)
70198 • Map 175/865809 • BB **C** • D1 T1 • 1-12 NX •
Ⓑ Ⓢ Ⓡ

■ WARGRAVE
THAMES PATH

Heather Carver, Windy Brow, 204 Victoria Road,
RG10 8AJ. ☎ (01734) 403336 • Map 175/794788 •
BB **C/D** • S1 D2/3 T2/3 F1 • 1-12 NX • Ⓑ Ⓓ Ⓢ Ⓡ 🐾
• List • House is on opposite side from path

■ WINDSOR
THAMES PATH

Mrs Joyce, "The Laurells", 22 Dedworth Road, SL4
5AY. ☎ (01753) 855821 • Map 175,176/952765 • BB
B • T2 • 1-12 NX • Ⓑ Ⓓ Ⓢ Ⓡ 🐾

Mrs Ford, 57 Grove Road, SL4 1JD. ☎ (01753)
853600 • Map 175,176/966762 • BB **C** • T1 F1 • 1-12
NX • Ⓑ Ⓓ Ⓢ Ⓡ • List

BUCKINGHAMSHIRE

■ ASKETT (Princes Risborough, Aylesbury)
RIDGEWAY

Mrs Christine Ramsay, The Bell House Barn,
Crowbrook Road, HP27 9LS. ☎ (01844) 346107 •
Map 165/812050 • BB **B** • S1 T2 • 1-12 NX • Ⓓ Ⓡ 🐾

■ AYLESBURY
GRAND UNION CANAL WALK

Elaine & Gordon Sanders, Baywood Guest House, 98
Weston Road, Aston Clinton, HP22 5EJ. ☎ (01296)
630612 • Map 165/870120 • BB **B/C** • EM book first
£7.50 (for groups) • S2 D4 T4 F1 • 1-12 NX • Ⓥ Ⓑ
Ⓓ 🐾

Mrs V A Taylor, B and B at 103, 103 London Road,
Aston Clinton, HP22 5LD. ☎ (01296) 631313 • Map
165/893114 • BB **C** • S1 T2 • 2-12 • Ⓓ Ⓢ • List/C

■ BLEDLOW RIDGE (High Wycombe)
RIDGEWAY

Mrs N E Gee, Old Callow Down Farm, Wigans Lane,
HP14 4BH. ☎ (01844) 344416 • Map 165/787000 •
BB **B/C** • EM book first £8, 7pm • T2 • 1-12 NX • Ⓥ
Ⓑ Ⓓ Ⓢ 🐾 • 2Cr • SC also

■ EDLESBOROUGH (Dunstable, Beds)
RIDGEWAY & ICKNIELD WAY

Mr & Mrs Lloyd, Ridgeway End, 5 Ivinghoe Lane,
LU6 2EL. ☎ (01525) 220405 • Map 165/974183 • BB
C • S1 D2 T1 • 1-11 NX • Ⓑ Ⓓ Ⓢ

■ **GREAT KINGSHILL (High Wycombe)**

Mrs M A Davies, Hatches Farm, Hatches Lane, HP15 6DS. ☎ (01494) 713125 • Map 165/873980 • BB **B** • D1 T1 • 1-12 NX • Ⓓ • List/C

■ **HANSLOPE (Milton Keynes)**

Mr & Mrs N Stacey, Woad Farm, Tathall End, MK19 7NE. ☎ (01908) 510985 • Map 152/815471 • BB **C** • EM book first £8 • D/S1 T/S1 • 1-12 • Ⓓ Ⓢ 🐾 • List/C

■ **HIGH WYCOMBE**

Belmont Hotel, 9 Priory Avenue, HP13 6SQ. ☎ (01494) 527046 • Map 175/866932 • BB **D** • EM book first £7+ • S8 D1 T9 F2 • 1-12 NX • Ⓥ Ⓑ Ⓓ Ⓢ Ⓡ

■ **MARLOW**
THAMES PATH & LONDON COUNTRYWAY

Mrs S Bendall, 5 Pound Lane, SL7 2AE. ☎ (01628) 482649 • Map 175/848861 • BB **C/D** • D1 T1 • 1-11 NX • Ⓓ Ⓢ Ⓡ • List/C • Food nearby

Mr & Mrs B Wells, Merrie Hollow, Seymour Court Hill, Marlow Road, SL7 3DE. ☎ (01628) 485663 • Map 175/837889 • BB **C** • EM book first £8, 7-8pm • D1 T1 • 1-12 • Ⓥ Ⓢ Ⓡ 🐾 • List/C

Mrs Mary Cowling, Acha Pani, Bovingdon Green, SL7 2JL. ☎ (01628) 483435 • Map 175/834869 • BB **B** • EM book first £5 • S1 D1 T1 • 1-12 • Ⓥ Ⓑ Ⓓ Ⓡ 🐾 • List/C

■ **QUAINTON (Aylesbury)**

M Rolley, The White Hart, HP22 4AS. ☎ (01296) 655234 • Map 165/747200 • BB **D** • EM £6, 7-9pm • D1 F1 • 1-12 NX • Ⓥ Ⓑ Ⓓ

■ **SAUNDERTON (High Wycombe)**
RIDGEWAY

Hunter's Gate, Deanfield, HP14 4JR. ☎ (01494) 481446 • Map 165/809975 • BB **B/C** • S1 D1 T1 • 1-12 • Ⓑ Ⓓ Ⓡ 🐾 • List

■ **STOKENCHURCH (High Wycombe)**

Mrs S E McKelvey, Gibbons Farm, Bigmore Lane, Horsley's Green, HP14 3UR. ☎ (01494) 482385 • Map 175/782946 • BB **C** • EM book first £5, 6-7pm • S4 D1 T1 F2 • 1-12 • Ⓥ Ⓑ Ⓓ Ⓢ

■ **WENDOVER (Aylesbury)**
RIDGEWAY & GRAND UNION CANAL WALK

Mrs Y MacDonald, 46 Lionel Avenue, HP22 6LP. ☎ (01296) 623426 • Map 165/863085 • BB **B** • S3 T1 • 1-12 NX • Ⓓ Ⓢ Ⓡ 🐾

Mrs G Samuels, 17 Icknield Close, HP22 6HG. ☎ (01296) 623859 • Map 165/871081 • BB **B** • S1 D/F1 1 F1 • 1-12 NX • Ⓓ Ⓢ Ⓡ

Mrs E C Condie, 26 Chiltern Road, HP22 6DB. ☎ (01296) 622351 • Map 165/865082 • BB **A** • S2 T/F2 • 1-12 NX • Ⓓ Ⓢ Ⓡ 🐾 Ⓜ • SC also

■ **WEST WYCOMBE (High Wycombe)**

The Swan Inn, HP14 3AE. ☎ (01494) 527031 • Map 175/829945 • BB **C** • S1 D2 T1 F1 • 1-12 NX • Ⓡ

CAMBRIDGESHIRE

■ **CALDECOTE**

☆ Margaret & George Baigent, Avondale, 35 Highfields, CB3 7NX. ☎ (01954) 210746 • Map 154/358590 • BB **C** • D1 T1 F1 • 1-12 NX • Ⓑ Ⓓ 🐾

Avondale
35 Highfields, Caldecote

Small exclusive bungalow, offering friendly accommodation. Situated in peaceful village location surrounded by wooded areas, and interlaced with bridle paths and long country walkways. TV, tea/coffee facilities, weekly rates.

Margaret & George Baigent
Tel. 01954 210746

■ **CAMBRIDGE**

☆ Bon Accord House, 20 St Margaret's Square, off Cherry Hinton Road, CB1 4AP. ☎ (01223) 411188/246568 • Map 154/469565 • BB **C** • S5 D3 T1 • 1-12 NX • Ⓑ Ⓓ Ⓢ Ⓡ • List

BON ACCORD HOUSE
20 St Margaret's Square
(off Cherry Hinton Road)
Cambridge CB1 4AP

Quietly situated family run guest house about 1½ miles south of the centre of this historic city.
AA listed and RAC acclaimed. ETB listed.
Entirely no smoking
B&B from £17.50. Visa & Mastercard welcome
Prop: Mr & Mrs Northrop
Tel. 01223 411188

Mrs R Boorman, Antwerp Guest House, 36 Brookfields, Mill Road, CB1 3NW. ☎ (01223) 247690 • Map 154/473575 • BB **C** • S1 D3 T3 F1 • 1-12 NX • Ⓑ Ⓓ Ⓢ Ⓡ Ⓜ • 2Cr

Mrs M Sanders, 145 Gwydir Street, CB1 2LJ. ☎ (01223) 356615 • Map 154/462579 • BB **B** • T1 • 1-12 NX • Ⓓ Ⓢ Ⓡ

Mrs D J Wyatt, The Willows, 102 High Street, Landbeach, CB4 4DT. ☎ (01223) 860332 • Map 154/477650 • BB **B** • S2 D1 T1 • 1-12 • Ⓓ Ⓢ Ⓡ 🐾

☆ See Display Advertisement

■ FORDHAM

☆ E R Eccles, Inglenook, 42 Carter Street, CB7 5NG. ☎ (01638) 720387 • Map 154/628708 • BB **B/C** • T5 F1 • 1-12 NX • Ⓑ Ⓓ

INGLENOOK GUEST HOUSE
42 Carter St, Fordham, Ely, Cambs

Situated 4 miles North of Newmarket on A142 Ely Rd. En suite accommodation with tea/coffee facilities and colour TV. Within easy travelling distance of Cambridge, the nature reserve of Wicken Fen, Constable country and many National Trust properties.

ETB 2 crowns Approved   Tel 01638 720387

■ HEMINGFORD GREY (Huntingdon)

Willow Guest House, 45 High Street, PE18 9BJ. ☎ (01480) 494748 • Map 153/295706 • BB **C** • S2 D2 T1 F2 • 1-12 • Ⓑ Ⓓ Ⓢ

■ KIRTLING (Newmarket, Suffolk)

☆ Mrs Ann Bailey, Hill Farm, CB8 9HQ. ☎ (01638) 730253 • Map 154/682583 • BB **C** • EM book first £12.50, 7-9.30pm • S1 D1 T1 • 1-12 NX • Ⓑ Ⓓ 🐾 Ⓜ • 3Cr

---

"Hill Farm"
Kirtling, Newmarket

Picturesque 400-year-old farmhouse with superb views of rural Studland. Tea/coffee facilities, CH, en suites available. Log fires, TV lounge, games room. Excellent home-cooking with menu choice. Special diets by arrangement. Licensed. Fire certificate. Access at all times. £22 single room, £40 double. Evening meal £12.50.

🥄🥄🥄   **Tel. 01683 730253**   **AA** QQQ

■ WISBECH

P J Parish, Ravenscourt Guest House, 138 Lynn Road, PE13 3DP. ☎ (01945) 585052 • Map 131,143/466102 • BB **B** • S1 D2 T1 F1 • 1-12 NX • Ⓑ Ⓓ Ⓢ

CHESHIRE

■ CHISWORTH (Broadbottom, Hyde)

M Sidebottom, Shire Cottage Farmhouse, Benches Lane, SK14 6RY. ☎ (01457) 866536 • Map 109/981912 • BB **C** • S1 D/T1 F1 • 1-12 • Ⓑ Ⓓ Ⓡ 🐾 Ⓜ • 2Cr/C • SC also

■ CHURCH MINSHULL (Crewe)

Mrs A M Charlesworth, Higher Elms Farm, Minshull Vernon, CW1 4RG. ☎ (01270) 522252 • Map 118/669607 • BB **B/C** • S1 D1 T2 F1 • 1-12 • Ⓑ Ⓓ Ⓢ

■ CONGLETON
CHESHIRE RING CANAL & STAFFORDSHIRE WAY

Mrs Sheila Kidd, Yew Tree Farm, North Rode, CW12 2PF. ☎ (01260) 223569 • Map 118/895667 • BB **C** • EM book first £10, 6.30pm • D1 T2 • 1-12 • Ⓥ Ⓑ Ⓓ Ⓢ • List/C

■ FRODSHAM

3 Shepherds House, off Manley Road, WA6 6HW. ☎ (01928) 734424 • Map 117/519754 • BB **A/B** • S1 D1 • 1-12 NX • Ⓑ Ⓓ Ⓢ Ⓡ 🐾

■ LANGLEY (Macclesfield)
CHESHIRE RING CANAL

Mrs M Birch, High Low Farm, SK11 0NE. ☎ (01260) 252230 • Map 118/944715 • BB **B** • D1 T1 F1 • 1-12 NX • Ⓢ Ⓡ • 1Cr • SC also

■ MALPAS

Mrs Sally-Ann Chesters, Millmoor Farm, Nomansheath, SY14 8ED. ☎ (01948) 820304 • Map 117/512470 • BB **B/C** • EM book first £10, 6-7.30pm • D2 T1 • 1-12 • Ⓥ Ⓑ Ⓓ 🐾 • List

Mrs Rosemary Bourne, Pool Farm, Bickerton, SY14 8LN. ☎ (01829) 782411 • Map 117/511522 • BB **C** • D2 T1 • 3-10 • Ⓑ Ⓓ Ⓢ • Food nearby

■ NANTWICH

Mrs Georgina West, Stoke Grange Farm, Chester Road, CW5 6BT. ☎ (01270) 625525 • Map 118/615564 • BB **C** • D1 T1 F1 • 1-12 • Ⓑ • 2Cr/C • Food nearby. SC also

■ NORTHWICH
CHESHIRE RING CANAL

Mrs S M Schofield, Ash House Farm, Chapel Lane, Acton Bridge, CW8 3QS. ☎ (01606) 852717 • Map 117/587755 • BB **C** • S1 D1 T1 F1 • 1-12 NX • Ⓓ Ⓢ Ⓡ 🐾

■ SIDDINGTON (Macclesfield)

Hazel Rush, The Golden Cross Farm, SK11 9JP. ☎ (01260) 224358 • Map 118/848707 • BB **B** • S2 D2 • 1-12 NX • Ⓑ Ⓓ Ⓢ • 2Cr

■ TARPORLEY

Mr & Mrs Sutcliffe, Roughlow Farm, Willington, CW6 0PG. ☎ (01829) 751199 • Map 117/537673 • BB **D** • EM book first £15, 7.30pm • D1 T2 F1 • 1-12 • Ⓑ Ⓓ Ⓢ • 2Cr/C

■ TARVIN (Chester)

Mrs R Rutter, Moss Heyes, CH3 8NG. ☎ (01829) 740227 • Map 117/500660 • BB **B** • S1 D1 T1 • 3-10 NX • Ⓓ Ⓢ

Vegetarian food is often available by arrangement — JUST ASK

ENGLAND   CAMBRIDGESHIRE   CHESHIRE
B&B ACCOMMODATION

■ TIMBERSBROOK (Congleton)
CHESHIRE RING CANAL & STAFFORDSHIRE WAY

Pedley House Farm, CW12 3QD. ☎ (01260) 273650 • Map 118/897637 • BB **B** • EM book first £10 • D/T1 F1 • 1-12 NX • Ⓥ Ⓓ

■ WINCLE (Macclesfield)
Mrs Susan Brocklehurst, Hill Top Farm, SK11 0QH. ☎ (01260) 227257 • Map 118/965661 • BB **C** • EM book first £9, 6-6.30pm • T2 • 3-11 • Ⓥ Ⓑ Ⓓ Ⓢ 🐾 • SC also

■ WYBUNBURY (Nantwich)
☆ Mrs Jean Callwood, Lea Farm, CW5 7NS. ☎ (01270) 841429 • Map 118/716489 • BB **B** • EM book first £9, 7pm • D1 T1 F1 • 1-12 NX • Ⓑ Ⓓ 🐾 • 2Cr/C

LEA FARM
Wrinehill Road
Wybunbury
Nantwich
Cheshire
CW5 7NS
♨ ♨ Commended

Charming farmhouse, set in landscaped gardens where peacocks roam, 150 Acre Dairy Farm, Delightful Bedrooms. All amenities some en-suite, Snooker/Pool Table. Fishing available.

Tel: 01270 841 429 *AA* RẶC

CLEVELAND
SEE NORTH YORKSHIRE FOR SALTBURN ENTRIES

CORNWALL

■ BOSCASTLE
SOUTH WEST COAST PATH

☆ Trerosewill Farmhouse, Paradise, PL35 0DL. ☎ (01840) 250545 • Map 190/094906 • BB **C** • EM £16, 6.30pm • S1 D3 T1 F2 • 1-12 NX • Ⓥ Ⓑ Ⓓ Ⓢ • 3Cr/HC • SC also

TREROSEWILL FARMHOUSE
BOSCASTLE

B&B accommodation in the heart of the heritage coast close to the South West Coast Path. En suite, CH. Traditional Cornish cooking. Superb coastal & rural views. One way walks (packed lunches on request).

☎ **(01840) 250545**

W J & E Purslow, Orchard Lodge, Gunpool Lane, PL35 0AT. ☎ (018405) 250418 • Map 190/099907 • BB **B/C** • D4 T2 • 3-11 • Ⓑ Ⓓ Ⓢ

■ BUDE
SOUTH WEST COAST PATH

☆ Mornish Hotel, 20 Summerleaze Crescent, EX23 8HJ. ☎ (01288) 352972 • Map 190/216066 • BB **C** • EM £8.75, 6.30-7pm • D5 T2 F3 • 3-10 • Ⓥ Ⓑ Ⓓ Ⓢ 🐾

MORNISH HOTEL
SUMMERLEAZE CRESCENT
BUDE EX23 8HJ

Situated on Cornwall's N Coastal Path, we offer a warm welcome, full hotel facilities incl. central heating, all rooms en suite, TVs, and a drying room. Price £18.75 B&B. Evening meal £8.75. Children and pets catered for. Secure cycle shed.

Tel. Bude (01288) 352972 for details

M & E Payne, Pencarrol Guest House, 21 Downs View, EX23 8RF. ☎ (01288) 352478 • Map 190/207071 • BB **B** • EM book first £8, 6.30pm • S2 D4 T1 F1 • 1-11 • Ⓥ Ⓑ Ⓓ

☆ Margaret Bird, Bude Haven Hotel, Flexbury Avenue, EX23 8NS. ☎ (01288) 352305 • Map 190/210071 • BB **C/D** • EM £10, 6.30-7.30pm • S2 D5 T3 F3 • 1-12 • Ⓥ Ⓑ Ⓓ • 3Cr/C • Groups also

BUDE HAVEN HOTEL
AA ETB ♨♨♨
★★

Bude *Haven*

Flexbury Avenue, Bude, Cornwall
Tel 01288 352305
A warm and friendly welcome awaits you at our detached 13 beds hotel, where all rooms are fully ensuite with tea & coffee making facilities & colour TVs. Excellent home cooked food. Special diets catered for. We have full central heating and a secure drying/storage room. Ideal centre for fabulous walks right on coast path. Open all year.

The Meva-Gwin Hotel, Upton, EX23 0LY. ☎ (01288) 352347 • Map 190/202049 • BB **C** • EM £8.95, 6.30pm • S2 D4 T1 F5 • 4-10 NX • Ⓥ Ⓑ Ⓓ Ⓢ • 3Cr/C • SC also

☆ See Display Advertisement

Peter & Mary Kimpton, "Kisauni", 4 Downs View, EX23 8RF. ☎ (01288) 352653 • Map 190/217071 • BB **B** • EM £6.50-£7.25, 6-7pm • S1 D3 T1 F3 • 1-12 • Ⓥ Ⓑ Ⓓ 🐾 Ⓜ

Mike & Jan Williams, "Seabreeze", 5 Hartland Terrace, EX23 8JY. ☎ (01288) 355922 • Map 190/207065 • BB **B/C** • D1 T2 F1 • 1-12 NX • Ⓥ Ⓑ Ⓢ • App

■ CALLINGTON

Mrs T C Wills, Dozmary, Tors View Close, Tavistock Road, PL17 7DY. ☎ (01579) 383677 • Map 201/364697 • BB **B** • D1 T1 F1 • 1-11 • Ⓑ Ⓢ • 1Cr/C

■ CALSTOCK

☆ Tamar Valley Riverside Accom, Kelly Cottage, Lower Kelly, PL18 9RX. ☎ (01822) 832380 • Map 201/432687 • BB **C** • EM book first £10 • S1 D1 T2 F1 • 1-12 • Ⓥ Ⓑ Ⓓ Ⓢ Ⓡ

■ CAMELFORD

Mrs Deborah Reeve, The Countryman Hotel, Victoria Road, PL32 9XA. ☎ (01840) 212250 • Map 200/100830 • BB **B** • EM book first £10, 7-8.30pm • S1 D/T8 F2 • 1-12 • Ⓥ Ⓑ Ⓓ 🐾

■ CRACKINGTON HAVEN (Nr Bude)
SOUTH WEST COAST PATH

☆ Coombe Barton Inn, EX23 0JG. ☎ (01840) 230345 • Map 190/143967 • BB **C** • EM £10, 6-10pm • S2 D3 T2 F1 • 3-10 NX • Ⓥ Ⓑ Ⓓ Ⓢ 🐾 • 3Cr

Ann & John Radford, Penkenna House, EX23 0JG. ☎ (01840) 230201 • Map 190/143969 • BB **B** • D1 T1 • 1-12 NX • Ⓓ Ⓢ

■ FALMOUTH
SOUTH WEST COAST PATH

☆ The Grove Hotel, Grove Place, TR11 4AU. ☎ (01326) 319577 • Map 204/794323 • BB **C** • EM £9, 7-9pm • S2 D3 T6 F4 • 1-11 • Ⓥ Ⓑ Ⓓ Ⓢ Ⓡ 🐾 • SC also

Rod & Penny Jones, Esmond House, Emslie Road, TR11 4BG. ☎ (01326) 313214 • Map 204/813319 • BB **B** • S1 D3 T2 F1 • 1-12 NX • Ⓑ Ⓓ Ⓢ Ⓡ 🐾

■ FOWEY
SOUTH WEST COAST PATH & SAINTS WAY

Fowey Hall, PL23 1ET. ☎ (0172683) 3104 • Map 200/121515 • BB **C/D** • EM £9.50, 7pm • S11 T22 F8 • 1-12 • Ⓥ Ⓓ Ⓢ Ⓜ • Groups also

Mr & Mrs Moore, "Church View", Lanteglos Highway, PL23 1ND. ☎ (01726) 870108 • Map 200/147536 • BB **A** • D1 T1 • 1-12 NX • Ⓑ Ⓓ 🐾 • Transport from path

Rick & Wai Chee Nisbet, The Wheelhouse, 60 The Esplanade, PL23 1JA. ☎ (01726) 832452 • Map 200/122514 • BB **C** • S1 D1 T1 F1 • 1-12 • Ⓑ Ⓓ Ⓢ • Food nearby

■ GORRAN HAVEN (St Austell)
SOUTH WEST COAST PATH

Llawnroc Inn, PL26 6NU. ☎ (01726) 843461 • Map 204/010416 • BB **C** • EM £4.50, 7-9pm • S1 D3 T2 F2 • 1-12 • Ⓥ Ⓑ Ⓓ Ⓢ 🐾 • 3Cr/HC

■ GUNNISLAKE

Sandhill Manor Hotel, PL18 9DR. ☎ (01822) 832442 • Map 201/428712 • BB **C** • EM £10, 7pm • S2 D3 T2 F2 • 3-11 NX • Ⓥ Ⓑ Ⓓ Ⓢ Ⓡ

■ HAYLE
SOUTH WEST COAST PATH

Mrs Anne Cooper, 54 Penpol Terrace, TR27 4BQ. ☎ (01736) 752855 • Map 203/558378 • BB **B** • S1 D1 T1 • 1-11 • Ⓓ Ⓢ Ⓡ Ⓜ

Mrs M P Quick, Poplar Villa Guest House, 1 Penmare Terrace, TR27 4PH. ☎ (01736) 752357 • Map 203/571382 • BB **B** • S2 D2 T1 • 1-11 • Ⓓ Ⓡ ⚲

■ LANIVET (Bodmin)
SAINTS WAY

Mrs Joy Rackham, High Cross Farm, PL30 5JR. ☎ (01208) 831341 • Map 200/026634 • BB **A** • EM £8, 6.30pm • D1 T1 F1 • 1-12 NX • Ⓓ Ⓢ

Margaret Oliver, Tremeere Manor, PL30 5BG. ☎ (01208) 831513 • Map 200/046642 • BB **A/B** • EM book first £7 • D2 T1 • 3-11 • Ⓑ Ⓓ Ⓢ • SC also

■ LANLIVERY (Bodmin)
SAINTS WAY

Mrs Amanda Penk, Lynnwood, PL30 5BX. ☎ (01208) 872326 • Map 200/083587 • BB **B** • EM book first £6 • D1 T1 F1 • 1-12 • Ⓥ Ⓓ Ⓢ Ⓡ ⚲

■ LANREATH (Looe)

Mrs B C Gamble, Rowan Lodge, PL13 2NX. ☎ (01503) 220289 • Map 201/181568 • BB **B** • EM book first £10.50, 7.30pm • S1 D3 T1 • 1-12 NX • Ⓥ Ⓑ Ⓓ ⚲ • SC also

■ LANSALLOS
SOUTH WEST COAST PATH & SAINTS WAY

Mrs Sue Shakerley, Carneggan, Lanteglos, Fowey, PL23 1NW. ☎ (01726) 870327 • Map 201/162522 • BB **C/D** • T2 F1 • 1-12 NX • Ⓑ Ⓓ • SC also

■ LISKEARD

Mrs N Strudwick, Elnor Guest House, 1 Russell Street, PL14 4BP. ☎ (01579) 342472 • Map 201/250642 • BB **B/C** • EM book first £12, 6pm • S4 D3 T1 F1 • 1-12 NX • Ⓑ Ⓓ Ⓢ Ⓡ • 2Cr/C

■ LOOE
SOUTH WEST COAST PATH

☆ Marwinthy Guest House, East Cliff, East Looe, PL13 1DE. ☎ (01503) 264382 • Map 201/257532 • BB **B/C** • S1 D2 T1 F1 • 1-10 • Ⓑ Ⓓ Ⓢ Ⓡ ⚲

Mrs Angela Eastley, Little Larnick Farm, Pelynt, PL13 2NB. ☎ (01503) 262837 • Map 201/233542 • BB **B/C** • D1 T1 F1 • 2-11 • Ⓑ Ⓓ Ⓢ Ⓡ • 2Cr

---

Melvyn and Pauline Neaves, Schooner Point Guest House, 1 Trelawney Terrace, Polperro Road, PL13 2AG. ☎ (01503) 262670 • Map 201/252537 • BB **A/B/C** • EM book first £8, 6.30pm • S2 D3 F1 • 1-12 NX • Ⓥ Ⓑ Ⓓ Ⓢ Ⓡ

■ MANACCAN (Helston)
SOUTH WEST COAST PATH

Mr & Mrs J H Whale, Porthvean, Gillan, TR12 6HL. ☎ (01326) 231204 • Map 204/783251 • BB **B** • T1 • 1-12 • Ⓑ Ⓓ Ⓢ ⚲ Ⓜ

■ MARHAMCHURCH (Bude)
SOUTH WEST COAST PATH

☆ Hideaway Farm Holidays, Tackbeare Farm, EX23 0HH. ☎ (01288) 381264 • Map 190/250012 • BB **C** • EM £8, 6.30pm • 1-12 • Ⓥ Ⓑ Ⓓ Ⓢ

■ MORWENSTOW (Bude)
SOUTH WEST COAST PATH

Monica Heywood, Cornakey Farm, EX23 9SS. ☎ (01288) 331260 • Map 190/208157 • BB **B** • EM £7, 6.30pm • D2 F1 • 1-12 NX • Ⓥ Ⓑ Ⓓ Ⓢ • List/C

■ MULLION (Helston)
SOUTH WEST COAST PATH

Mrs J Tyler Street, Trenance Farmhouse, TR12 7HB. ☎ (01326) 240639 • Map 203/673184 • BB **B/C** • D2 T1 • 3-10 • Ⓑ Ⓓ ⚲ • 2Cr/C • SC also

☆ June Lugg, Tregaddra Farm, Cury Cross Lanes, TR12 7BB. ☎ (01326) 240235 • Map 203/701219 • BB **C** • EM book first £9, 6.30pm • S1 D2 T1 F1 • 1-12 • Ⓑ Ⓓ Ⓢ • 3Cr/HC

CORNWALL • ENGLAND • ACCOMMODATION B&B

151

■ MULLION COVE (Helston)
SOUTH WEST COAST PATH

Pauline Story, Criggan Mill, TR12 7EU. ☎ (01326) 240496 • Map 203/667180 • BB **B** • EM book first £7.50 • S4 D4 T4 F4 • 4-10 • Ⓥ Ⓑ Ⓓ Ⓢ 🐾 • SC timber lodges also

■ NEWQUAY
SOUTH WEST COAST PATH

☆ S R Harper, Chichester, 14 Bay View Terrace, TR7 2LR. ☎ (01637) 874216 • Map 200/813614 • BB **B** • EM book first £5, 6.30pm • S2 D2 T2 F1 • 3-11 • Ⓥ Ⓑ Ⓓ Ⓢ Ⓡ Ⓜ • 1Cr/C

INTEREST HOLIDAYS

SPRING AND AUTUMN
GUIDED MINERAL
COLLECTING
HERITAGE AND

WALKING WEEKS

IN LOVELY CORNWALL

14 BAY VIEW TERRACE - NEWQUAY - TR7 2LR Tel: 01637 874216

Doreen & Allan Connor, Belair Guest House, 28 Edgcumbe Avenue, TR7 2NH. ☎ (01637) 876503 • Map 200/817618 • BB **A/B** • EM book first £5, 6pm • S2 D3 T1 F1 • 1-12 • Ⓑ Ⓓ Ⓢ Ⓡ

☆ Tregurrian Hotel, Watergate Bay, TR8 4AB. ☎ (01637) 860280 • Map 200/842649 • BB **C/D** • EM £8.50, 6.45-7.30pm • S4 D10 T5 F8 • 3-10 NX • Ⓥ Ⓑ Ⓓ • 3Cr

TREGURRIAN HOTEL
Watergate Bay, nr Newquay,
AA **   Cornwall   👑👑👑

Overlooking beach, 20 yards from coastal path. Swimming pool. Most rooms with en suite bathrooms. 3 miles from Newquay, 3 miles from Bedruthan Steps. Spectacular coastal scenery and walking. Groups welcome.

Tel 01637 860280

Mrs Jean Wilson, Manuels Farm, Quintrell Downs, TR8 4NY. ☎ (01637) 873577 • Map 200/834600 • BB **C** • EM book first £12, 6.30pm • S1 D2 F1 • 1-12 NX • Ⓑ Ⓓ Ⓢ Ⓡ 🐾 • 2Cr/HC • SC also

Valerie & Frank Tatam, Harrington Guest House, 25 Tolcarne Road, TR7 2NQ. ☎ (01637) 873581 • Map 200/817617 • BB **B** • EM book first £6, 6pm • D3 F4 • 1-12 NX • Ⓥ Ⓑ Ⓓ Ⓡ Ⓜ

■ NORTH HILL (Launceston)

Mrs S Doney, Botternell Farm, PL15 7NS. ☎ (01579) 362386 • Map 201/278745 • BB **B** • D2 T1 • 3-10 • Ⓓ Ⓢ 🐾

■ PADSTOW
SOUTH WEST COAST PATH & SAINTS WAY

Mr & Mrs Champion, 8 Treverbyn Road, PL28 8DW. ☎ (01841) 532551 • Map 200/921749 • BB **C** • S1 D2 T1 • 2-12 NX • Ⓑ Ⓓ Ⓢ

Cross House Hotel, Church Street, PL28 8BG. ☎ (01841) 532391 • Map 200/916755 • BB **D** • EM book first £10.25, 7pm • S1 D4 T1 F1 • 1-12 • Ⓥ Ⓑ Ⓓ 🐾

☆ Michael & Pat Walker, The Old Mill Country House, Little Petherick, PL27 7QT. ☎ (01841) 540388 • Map 200/918721 • BB **D** • D5 T2 • 3-10 • Ⓑ Ⓓ Ⓢ

THE OLD MILL COUNTRY HOUSE
Little Petherick

16th Century corn mill with waterwheel. Streamside gardens. Period furnishings. Two miles from Padstow. Area of Outstanding Natural Beauty. On Saints Way walk, near coastal paths and Camel Trail. Ensuite from £25. Light suppers available. Minimum age 14 years. AA   RAC.

Padstow (01841) 540388

Mrs Sheila Shadbolt, "Trelooan", Treporth, Porthcothan Bay, PL28 8LS. ☎ (01841) 521158 • Map 200/858716 • BB **B** • D1 T1 • 1-12 NX • Ⓓ

Linda Green, 20 Grenville Road, PL28 8EX. ☎ (01841) 532756 • Map 200/915750 • BB **B/C** • D1 T2 • 1-12 NX • Ⓑ Ⓓ Ⓢ

■ PENZANCE
SOUTH WEST COAST PATH

Mrs Champion, 16 Provis Road, Alverton, TR18 4QQ. ☎ (01736) 60171 • Map 203/463296 • EM book first £6, 7pm • S2 T2 • 1-12 • Ⓥ Ⓓ Ⓢ Ⓡ 🐾

☆ Mrs G Ash, Torre Vene, Lescudjack Terrace, TR18 3AE. ☎ (01736) 64103 • Map 203/475308 • BB **A/B** • EM £8.50, 6.30pm • S2 D4 T4 F4 • 1-12 • Ⓥ Ⓓ Ⓡ

TORRE-VENE
Lescudjack Terrace, Penzance
Cornwall TR18 3AE

Well-appointed guesthouse, delightful views of harbour, Mount's Bay. Friendly 'home from home' atmosphere. Ideal overnight stop for Isles of Scilly. Close to railway, coach stations and coastal paths. Good home cooking, EM optional. B&B bands A & B. A warm welcome awaits you.

Mrs G Ash Tel. 01736 64103

"Penalva", Alexandra Road, TR18 4LZ. ☎ (01736) 69060 • Map 203/466301 • BB **A/B** • S2 D3 T1 F1 • 1-12 • B D S R • 3Cr

John & Cherry Hopkins, Woodstock Guest House, 29 Morrab Road, TR18 4EZ. ☎ (01736) 369049 • Map 203/472300 • BB **A/B** • S2 D2 T2 F2 • 1-12 • B R • 2Cr

Sally Adams, Tremearne Farmhouse, Bone Valley, Heamoor, TR20 8UG. ☎ (01736) 64576 • Map 203/443305 • BB **C** • EM book first £12.50, 7pm • D2 T1 F2 • 1-12 NX • V B D S R ❧ ⓜ • SC also

Teresa & Roy Stacey, Lynwood Guest House, 41 Morrab Road, TR18 4EX. ☎ (01736) 65871 • Map 203/472300 • BB **A/B** • S1 D2 T2 F2 • 1-12 • B D R ❧ • 2Cr/App • Food nearby

☆ Shan & Dave Glenn, Trewella Guest House, 18 Mennaye Road, TR18 4NG. ☎ (01736) 63818 • Map 203/469298 • BB **A/B** • EM book first £7, 6.30pm • S2 D4 F2 • 3-10 • V B S R ❧

■ PERRANPORTH
SOUTH WEST COAST PATH

Yvonne Morgan, The Morgans', 3 Granny's Lane, TR6 0HB. ☎ (01872) 573904 • Map 204,200/758538 • BB **C** • S1 D4 T2 F2 • 3-1 NX • B D S ❧ • 3Cr/C • Food nearby

■ PERRANUTHNOE (Penzance)
SOUTH WEST COAST PATH

Geary & Moira Skinner, The Dubban, TR20 9NR. ☎ (01736) 710273 • Map 203/537296 • BB **B** • EM book first £9.95, 6-8pm • D1 T2 • 5-10 • V D S

■ POLRUAN (Fowey)
SOUTH WEST COAST PATH & SAINTS WAY

Mrs B E Blamey, Holly House, 18 Fore Street, PL23 1PQ. ☎ (01726) 870478 • Map 200/126508 • BB **B** • T3 • 1-10 NX • S ❧ ⓜ • Ferry nearby

Mr & Mrs B Wilde, Quayside House, PL23 1PA. ☎ (01726) 870377 • Map 200/126510 • BB **B** • D2 T2 F1 • Closed Dec-Easter • D S ❧

■ PORT ISAAC
SOUTH WEST COAST PATH

R Baker, The Shipwright Inn, The Terrace, PL29 3SG. ☎ (01208) 880305 • Map 200/999807 • BB **C** • EM £5-£10, 7-9.30pm • D1 T3 • 1-12 • V B D • SC also

☆ Gavin & Tammy Benger, Rockmount, 12 The Terrace, PL29 3SG. ☎ (01208) 880629 • Map 200/999807 • BB **B** • EM book first £9 • S2 D2 T1 F2 • 1-12 • V D S

■ PORTH (Newquay)
SOUTH WEST COAST PATH

"Sea Drift", 79 Penhallow Road, TR7 3BZ. ☎ (01637) 872311 • Map 200/831620 • BB **B** • EM book first £6, 6pm • D2 T1 F1 • 1-12 NX • V B S R ❧ • SC also

■ PORTHCURNO (Penzance)
SOUTH WEST COAST PATH

J Ring, "Corniche" Guest House, Trebehor, TR19 6LX. ☎ (01736) 871685 • Map 203/376239 • BB **B** • EM £3.95-£6.50, till 9pm • S1 D3 T1 F1 • 1-12 NX • V D S ⓜ

■ PORTHLEVEN (Helston)
SOUTH WEST COAST PATH

Mr & Mrs R Cookson, Pentre House, Peverell Terrace, TR13 9DZ. ☎ (01326) 574493 • Map 203/629254 • BB **B** • S2 D1 T1 • 3-10 • D S ❧ • SC also

■ PORTLOE (Truro)
SOUTH WEST COAST PATH

Mrs Clare Holdsworth, Tregain Licensed Restaurant & Tea Room, TR2 5QU. ☎ (01872) 501252 • Map 204/935395 • BB **C** • EM £3.50-£20, 7-8.30pm • S1 T1 • 3-10 • V D S ❧

■ PORTREATH (Redruth)
SOUTH WEST COAST PATH

Philip & Elaine Allen, "Sycamore Lodge", Primrose Terrace, TR16 4JS. ☎ (01209) 842784 • Map 203/659452 • BB **C** • EM book first £8, 6-7.30pm • S1 D1 T1 • 1-12 NX • V D S

☆ See Display Advertisement

■ PORTSCATHO (Truro)
SOUTH WEST COAST PATH

Christine Toms, Hillside House, 8 The Square, TR2 5HW. ☎ (01872) 580523 • Map 204/876354 • BB **B** • S1 D3 T1 F1 • 1-12 • B D ♨ • Meals nearby

■ POUGHILL (Bude)
SOUTH WEST COAST PATH

Sally-Ann Trewin, Lower Northcott Farm, EX23 9EQ. ☎ (01288) 352350 • Map 190/223077 • BB **C** • EM from £8, 6.30pm • S1 D1 T1 F2 • 1-12 • V B D S ♨ • 2Cr/C

■ ROCK (Wadebridge)
SOUTH WEST COAST PATH

Roskarnon House Hotel, PL27 6LD. ☎ (01208) 862785 • Map 200/933757 • BB **C/D** • EM from £10, 7-8pm • S2 D3 T3 F4 • 3-10 • V B D ♨ Ⓜ • 3Cr

Mrs Barbara Martin, Silvermead, PL27 6LB. ☎ (01208) 862425 • Map 200/933757 • BB **B** • EM book first £9.50, 6-8pm • S3 D2 T2 F2 • 1-12 • V B D S ♨ • 3Cr/C

■ SENNEN COVE (Penzance)
SOUTH WEST COAST PATH

David & Janet Gallie, "Polwyn Cottage", Old Coastguard Row, TR19 7DA. ☎ (01736) 871349 • Map 203/350264 • BB **B/C** • D1 T1 • 1-12 NX • B D ♨ • Transport also

■ ST AGNES
SOUTH WEST COAST PATH

☆ Mrs Gill-Carey, Penkerris, Penwinnick Road, TR5 0PA. ☎ (01872) 552262 • Map 204/720501 • BB **A/B/C** • EM book first £8.50, 6.30pm • S1 D2 T2 F2 • 1-12 • B D ♨ • 2Cr

Trewarren, Mithian Downs, TR5 0PY. ☎ (01872) 553851 ∘ Map 204/742498 ∘ BB **B/C** ∘ EM book first £5 (mostly veg.), 6-7pm • S1 D2 T1 F1 • 2-12 NX • V B D S ♨ • SC also

■ ST AUSTELL
SOUTH WEST COAST PATH

Shirley Mathieson, 11 Coastguard Terrace, Charlestown, PL25 3NJ. ☎ (01726) 72828 • Map 204, 200/039515 • BB **A** • D1 T1 • 1-12 NX • D S R ♨ Ⓜ

■ ST ISSEY (Wadebridge)
SOUTH WEST COAST PATH & SAINTS WAY

Mr & Mrs B Mealing, Trevorrick Farm, PL27 7QH. ☎ (01841) 540574 • Map 200/921732 • BB **C** • EM book first £8, 6-7.30pm • D1 T1 F1 • 1-12 • V B D ♨ • 2Cr • SC also

■ ST IVES
SOUTH WEST COAST PATH

Mrs M E McPherson, Ren-roy Guest House, 2 Ventnor Terrace, TR26 1DY. ☎ (01736) 796971 • Map 203/515405 • BB **B** • EM book first £6.50 • S1 D2 T1 F1 • 1-12 NX • V D R Ⓜ • List

☆ Sandra & Steve Herbert, Lyonesse Hotel, Talland Road, TR26 2DF. ☎ (01736) 796315 • Map 203/518401 • BB **C** • S1 D9 T1 F4 • 2-11 • B D S R Ⓜ

☆ David Watson, Chy-an-Dour Hotel, Trelyon Avenue, TR26 2AD. ☎ (01736) 796436 • Map 203/524398 • BB **D** • EM £14.75, 7-8pm • D11 T9 F3 • 1-12 NX • V B D S R • 3Cr/C

Left margin: CORNWALL   ENGLAND   B&B ACCOMMODATION

■ **ST JUST (Penzance)**
SOUTH WEST COAST PATH

Mary Stokes, Boswedden House Hotel, Cape Cornwall, TR19 7NJ. ☎ (01736) 788733 • Map 203/359319 • BB **C** • S1 D4 T2 F1 • 2-11 • B D S • 2Cr

☆ Alison & Bob Hartley, Bosavern House, TR19 7RD. ☎ (01736) 788301 • Map 203/370304 • BB **B/C** • S1 D3 T2 F4 • 3-11 • B D S • 2Cr

BOSAVERN HOUSE

ST JUST, PENZANCE

Lovely 17thC family-run, licensed guesthouse, set in beautiful grounds overlooking the Cornish seascape or the nearby moors. A half mile from the coastal path. A warm welcome, superb breakfasts, delicious cream teas and log fires will make your stay a memorable one.

ETB ☎ **01736 788301**

■ **ST KEVERNE (Helston)**
SOUTH WEST COAST PATH

Mrs R Kelly, Trevinock, TR12 6QP. ☎ (01326) 280498 • Map 204/802216 • BB **B** • EM book first £7.50, 6.30pm • S2 D2 • 3-10 • V D S • SC also

■ **ST LEVAN (Penzance)**
SOUTH WEST COAST PATH

Pam Armitage, Higher Bosistow, Nanjizal, TR19 6JJ. ☎ (01736) 871269 • Map 203/366234 • BB **B** • EM £6.50, 6-8pm • S1 D1 T1 • 1-12 NX • V D S • App

■ **ST WENN (Bodmin)**
SAINTS WAY

Mrs Marilyn Hawkey, Tregolls Farm, PL30 5PG. ☎ (01208) 812154 • Map 200/983661 • BB **A/B** • EM book first £7.50, 7pm • S1 D1 T1 F1 • 1-12 NX • V B D S

■ **THE LIZARD (Helston)**
SOUTH WEST COAST PATH

☆ Housel Bay Hotel, Housel Cove, TR12 7PG. ☎ (01326) 290417/290917 • Map 203/703124 • BB **D** • EM £10-£15, 7-9pm • S4 D9 T7 F1 • 1-12 • V B D S Ⓜ • 3Cr/HC • Groups also

Housel Bay Hotel
The Lizard

Elegant Victorian hotel at Britain's most southerly coast. AA/RAC/ETB Highly Commended. 2/3/4 day breaks & weekly terms. Spectacular position overlooking lovely sandy cove. Cornish Coastal Path runs through hotel garden. Fully licensed. Stylish restaurant & bar snacks. All rooms en suite with satellite TV.

☎ **01326 290417**

Jan & Steve Kilmister, Parc Brawse House Hotel, Penmenner Road, TR12 7NR. ☎ (01326) 290466 • Map 203/701120 • BB **B/C** • EM book first £10, 7pm • S1 D3 T2 F1 • 1-12 • V B D S • 2Cr/C

■ **TINTAGEL**
SOUTH WEST COAST PATH

☆ Bossiney House Hotel, PL34 0AX. ☎ (01840) 770240 • Map 200/066887 • BB **D** • EM £13.50, 7-8pm • D11 T7 F1 • 3-10 NX • V B D • 3Cr/App

BOSSINEY HOUSE HOTEL
TINTAGEL

Close to Coastal Path. Ideal for ramblers wishing to explore this scenic part of North Cornwall. The hotel offers excellent facilities, hospitality, home cooking. En-suite rooms, seaviews, heated indoor pool and Sauna. Group discounts.

Tel. 01840 770240 **Fax. 01840 770501**

AA** RAC** ETB Approved

The Old Malt House, Fore Street, PL34 0DA. ☎ (01840) 770461 • Map 200/054890 • BB **B/C** • EM £9.50, 6.30-8.30pm • S1 D5 T2 • 3-10 • V B • 2Cr/C

■ **TREEN, ST LEVAN, PORTHCURNO (Penzance)**
SOUTH WEST COAST PATH

Mrs A Jilbert, Penver House Farm, TR19 6LG. ☎ (01736) 810778 • Map 203/394231 • BB **B** • S/T1 D1 • 1-12 NX • B D S

■ **TREGONY (Truro)**

Sandra Collins, Tregonan, TR2 5SN. ☎ (01872) 530249 • Map 204/955452 • BB **B** • D2 T1 • 3-10 • V D S • 1Cr/C

■ **TRURO**

Bridget Dymond, Trevispian Vean Farm Guest House, St Erme, TR4 9BL. ☎ (01872) 79514 • Map 204/857483 • BB **C** • EM book first £8, 6.30pm • D6 T3 F3 • 3-10 • V B D S • 3Cr/C • Groups also

■ **WHITSAND BAY**
SOUTH WEST COAST PATH

Kathy Ridpath, Fir Cottage, Lower Tregantle, Antony, PL11 3AL. ☎ (01752) 822626 • Map 201/391537 • BB **B** • EM £6, 6-7pm • S1 F2 • 1-12 NX • D

Sylvia White, Higher Tregantle Farm, Antony, PL11 3AY. ☎ (01752) 822245 • Map 201/396529 • BB **A** • EM £5 • S2 D1 T1 F1 • 1-12 NX • D S

■ **WIDEMOUTH BAY (Bude)**
SOUTH WEST COAST PATH

Bay View Inn, Marine Drive, EX23 0AW. ☎ (01288) 361273 • Map 190/201022 • BB **A/B/C** • EM £5.50, 7-9.30pm • S2 D3 T1 F3 • 1-12 • V B D S • List

■ ZENNOR (St Ives)
SOUTH WEST COAST PATH

Mrs N I Mann, Trewey Farm, TR26 3DA. ☎ (01736) 796936 • Map 203/455375 • BB **B** • S1 D2 T1 F2 • 3-10 • Ⓥ Ⓓ Ⓢ ⅏

Sue & John Wilson, Tregeraint House, TR26 3DB. ☎ (01736) 797061 • Map 203/451378 • BB **B** • D2 T1 F1 • 1-12 NX • Ⓓ Ⓢ

Dr E Gynn, Boswednack Manor, TR26 3DD. ☎ (01736) 794183 • Map 203/442378 • BB **B/C** • EM book first £9 veg only, 7pm • S1 D2 T1 F1 • 1-12 NX • Ⓥ Ⓑ Ⓓ Ⓢ • SC also

CUMBRIA

■ ALSTON
PENNINE WAY

Mrs Pat Dent, Middle Bayles Farm, CA9 3BS. ☎ (01434) 381383 • Map 86,87/707450 • BB **B/C** • EM book first £10, 6pm • D1 F1 • 5-3 NX • Ⓑ Ⓓ Ⓢ • 2Cr/C • SC also

High Loaning Head Adventure Centre, Garrigill, CA9 3EY. ☎ (01434) 381929 • Map 86,87/747417 • BB **A** • EM £6 • F6 • 1-12 • Ⓓ Ⓢ ⅏ • SC and bunkhouse also

Mrs V Thompson, "Nentholme" B&B, The Butts, CA9 3JQ. ☎ (01434) 381523 • Map 86,87/719467 • BB **B** • EM book first £9, 7-8pm • S1 D4 T3 F2 • 1-12 • Ⓥ Ⓑ Ⓓ Ⓢ • 2Cr • SC also

Mrs Jean Best, Chapel House, CA9 3SH. ☎ (01434) 381112 • Map 86,87/721464 • BB **B** • EM book first £6, 7pm • S1 D1 F1 • 1-12 NX • Ⓥ Ⓑ Ⓓ Ⓢ • List/App

■ AMBLESIDE

Fisherbeck Farmhouse, Old Lake Road, LA22 0DH. ☎ (015394) 32523 • Map 90/377039 • BB **B** • S1 D2 T2 F1 • 3-11 • Ⓓ Ⓢ ⅏ • 2Cr

Mrs A Ryder & Mrs J Hitchen, Invergowrie Guest House, Lake Road, LA22 0DB. ☎ (015394) 33479 • Map 90/376041 • BB **B/C** • S1 D5 • 2-10 • Ⓑ Ⓓ • 2Cr/C

The Rysdale Hotel, Rothay Road, LA22 0EE. ☎ (015394) 32140 • Map 90/374043 • BB **B/C/D** • S3 D5 T1 • 1-12 NX • Ⓑ Ⓓ Ⓢ ⅏ Ⓜ • 2Cr/C

Broadview Guest House, Low Fold, Lake Road, LA22 0DN. ☎ (015394) 32431 • Map 90/377036 • BB **B/C** • D3 T1 F2 • 2-11 • Ⓑ Ⓓ Ⓢ • List/C

Mr & Mrs Doano, Thorneyfield Guest House, Compston Road, LA22 9DJ. ☎ (015394) 32464 • Map 90/375044 • BB **B/C** • S1 D2 T1 F3 • 1-12 NX • Ⓑ Ⓓ Ⓢ • 2Cr/C • Groups also

☆ John Horne, The Horseshoe Hotel, Rothay Road, LA22 0EE. ☎ (015394) 32000 • Map 90/374043 • BB **D** • EM £10.50, 7-8.30pm • S1 D13 T4 F2 • 1-12 • Ⓥ Ⓑ Ⓓ Ⓢ ⅏ • 3Cr

☆ Mrs J Boulton, Windlehurst, Millans Park, LA22 9AG. ☎ (015394) 33137 • Map 90/375046 • BB **B/C** • S1 D2 F3 • 1-12 NX • Ⓑ Ⓓ Ⓢ ⅏ • 2Cr

☆ Chris & Jane, Brantfell, Rothay Road, LA22 0EE. ☎ (015394) 32239 • Map 90/374043 • BB **B/C** • EM £12, 7pm • S2 D4 T1 • 1-12 • Ⓥ Ⓑ Ⓓ Ⓢ ⅏ • 2Cr/App

Mrs K Siddall, Cross Parrock, 5 Waterhead Terrace, LA22 0HA. ☎ (015394) 32372 • Map 90/377030 • BB **B** • EM book first £9, 6.30pm • D2 T1 • 1-12 NX • Ⓥ Ⓓ Ⓢ

Loughrigg Brow, LA22 9SA. ☎ (015394) 32229 • Map 90/450068 • BB **C/D** • EM £9.50, 7pm • S4 D2 T12 F6 • 1-12 • Ⓥ Ⓓ Ⓢ Ⓜ • Groups also

Barnes Fell Guest House, Low Gale, LA22 0BB. ☎ (015394) 33311 • Map 90/377042 • BB **B/C/D** • EM book first £12.50, 7.30pm • D3 • 1-12 • Ⓥ Ⓑ Ⓓ Ⓢ ⅏ • List/C

CUMBRIA　CORNWALL　ENGLAND　B&B ACCOMMODATION

☆ The Old Vicarage, Vicarage Road, LA22 9DH. ☎ (015394) 33364 • Map 90/373044 • BB **C/D** • S2 D8 T2 F2 • 1-12 • Ⓑ Ⓓ Ⓢ 🍴 • 2Cr/C

The Old Vicarage

Vicarage Road, Ambleside, Cumbria

Tranquil setting in heart of village. Own car park. Quality accommodation all en suite with TV [+ satellite & video channels], clock/radio, kettle, fridge, hairdryer. Local leisure club membership. B&B from £20 pn.
Friendly service. Pets welcome.

Phone Ian & Helen Burt 015394 33364

☆ Rothay Garth Hotel, Rothay Road, LA22 0EE. ☎ (015394) 32217 • Map 90/374043 • BB **D** • EM included in overnight price, 7-8pm • S2 D9 T2 F3 • 1-12 • Ⓥ Ⓑ Ⓓ Ⓢ Ⓡ 🍴 • 4Cr/C • Guided walks also

☙ HEART OF THE LAKE DISTRICT ❧

Distinctive & finely appointed hotel in delightful setting.
Elegant Loughrigg Restaurant
Four Crowns—Ashley Courtenay, AA & Civic Trust Awards
Brochure, exceptional value breaks.
Rothay Garth Hotel, Ambleside
LA22 0EE Tel. (015394) 32217

☆ Helen Green, Lyndhurst Hotel, Wansfell Road, LA22 0EG. ☎ (015394) 32421 • Map 90/375040 • BB **C/D** • EM book first £13.50, 6.30pm • D5 T1 • 1-12 • Ⓥ Ⓑ Ⓓ • 2Cr/C

Lyndhurst Hotel

Wansfell Road, Ambleside LA22 0EG

 Commended   **RAC** *Acclaimed*   **AA** QQQ

Attractive Lakeland stone family run hotel with private car park. Quietly situated, fully ensuite, lovely food, cosy bar and lounge. Four poster bedroom for that special occasion. Friendly service.
For colour brochure telephone:
Helen & Chris Green
(015394) 32421

Queens Hotel, Market Place, LA22 9BU. ☎ (015394) 32206 • Map 90/376044 • BB **D** • EM £13, 7-9.30pm • S4 D14 T3 F5 • 1-12 • Ⓥ Ⓑ Ⓓ Ⓢ • 3Cr/C

☆ Mrs Rosemary Russ, Croyden House, Church Street, LA22 0BU. ☎ (015394) 32209 • Map 90/376043 • BB **B/C** • S1 D5 T1 • 1-12 • Ⓑ Ⓓ Ⓢ

☆ Liz & Tim Melling, Nab Cottage, Rydal, LA22 9SD. ☎ (015394) 35311 • Map 90/355064 • BB **C** • EM £12, 7pm • S1 D2 T2 F2 • 10-6 • Ⓥ Ⓑ Ⓓ Ⓢ 🍴

☆ Smallwood House Hotel, Compston Road, LA22 9DJ. ☎ (015394) 32330 • Map 90/375044 • BB **C** • EM £10, 6-8pm • S2 D11 T7 F3 • 1-12 NX • Ⓥ Ⓑ Ⓓ 🍴 • 3Cr/C • Groups also

■ AMBLESIDE (CONTINUED)

☆ Judith Ireton, Holmeshead Farm, Skelwith Fold, LA22 0NU. ☎ 015394 33048 • Map 96,97/352982 • BB **C** • EM book first £11, 7pm • D1 T1 F1 • 1-12 • Ⓥ Ⓓ Ⓢ ♨ • List

Maureen Owens, Mill Cottage, Rydal Road, LA22 9AN. ☎ (015394) 34830 • Map 90/375046 • BB **C** • EM £6-£10, 6.30-9pm • D3 T1 F1 • 1-12 • Ⓥ Ⓑ Ⓓ Ⓢ

■ APPLEBY-IN-WESTMORLAND

E Pigney, Howgill House, CA16 6UW. ☎ (017683) 51574/51240 • Map 91/689198 • BB **B** • S1 T1 F3 • 4-9 • Ⓓ Ⓡ • 1Cr/C

☆ Anne & Malcolm Dayson, Bongate House, CA16 6UE. ☎ (017683) 51245 • Map 91/689200 • BB **C** • EM £8, 7pm • S1 D3 T2 F2 • 1-12 NX • Ⓥ Ⓑ Ⓓ Ⓡ ♨ • 3Cr/C • Groups also

Appleby Manor Ctry Hse Hotel, Roman Road, CA16 6JB. ☎ (017683) 51571 • Map 91/693205 • BB **D** • EM £20, 7-9pm • D14 T8 F8 • 1-12 NX • Ⓥ Ⓑ Ⓓ Ⓢ Ⓡ ♨ Ⓜ • 4Cr/HC • Groups also

Mrs K M Coward, Limnerslease, Bongate, CA16 6UE. ☎ (017683) 51578 • Map 91/689200 • BB **B** • D2 T1 • NX • Ⓓ Ⓢ Ⓡ ♨

Susan Hirst, Wemyss House, 48 Boroughgate, CA16 6XG. ☎ (017683) 51494 • Map 91/684201 • BB **B** • S1 D1 T1 • 4-10 NX • Ⓑ Ⓓ Ⓡ Ⓜ

■ ARNSIDE (Carnforth, Lancs)
CUMBRIA COASTAL WAY

Janet & Ian Kerr, Willowfield Hotel, The Promenade, LA5 0AD. ☎ (01524) 761354 • Map 97/456788 • BB **C/D** • EM book first £10, 7pm • S2 D3 T3 F2 • 1-12 • Ⓥ Ⓑ Ⓓ Ⓢ Ⓡ ♨ • 3Cr/C

■ BAMPTON GRANGE (Penrith)
COAST TO COAST WALK

Colin & Maureen Barber, Leyton Barn, CA10 2QR. ☎ (01931) 713314 • Map 90/522181 • BB **B** • T1 F1 • 1-12 NX • Ⓑ Ⓓ ♨

■ BASSENTHWAITE (Keswick)
CUMBRIA WAY

Mrs Vera M Fell, Chapel Farm, CA12 4QH. ☎ (017687) 76495 • Map 89,90/227316 • BB **B** • EM book first £7-£8, 6.30pm • T1 F1 • 1-12 NX • Ⓥ Ⓓ ♨

■ BLAWITH (Ulverston)
CUMBRIA WAY

Water Yeat Country Guest House, Water Yeat, LA12 8DJ. ☎ (01229) 885306 • Map 96,97/288892 • BB **C/D** • EM £16.50, 8pm • S2 D2 T2 F1 • 1-12 NX • Ⓑ Ⓓ Ⓢ

■ BOOT (Eskdale)

John & Leigh Gray, The Post Office, Dale View, CA19 1TG. ☎ (019467) 23236 • Map 89,90/176010 • BB **B** • S1 D2 T1 • 1-12 NX • Ⓓ Ⓢ Ⓡ

☆ Pat & Eddie Darlington, Brook House Hotel & Poachers Bar, CA19 1TG. ☎ (019467) 23288 • Map 89,90/176010 • BB **D** • EM up to 8.30pm • D4 T4 F4 • 1-12 NX • Ⓥ Ⓑ Ⓓ Ⓢ Ⓡ Ⓜ • 3Cr/C • Groups also

■ BORROWDALE (Keswick)
COAST TO COAST WALK & CUMBRIA WAY

Christine J Edmondson, 6 Chapel Howe, Stonethwaite, CA12 5XG. ☎ (017687) 77649 • Map 89, 90/260139 • BB **B** • S1 D1 T1 • 1-11 • Ⓓ 🐾

Mr & Mrs T Lopez, Derwent House, CA12 5UY. ☎ (017687) 77658 • Map 89, 90/257177 • BB **D** • EM book first £14, 7pm • S1 D5 T3 F1 • 2-12 NX • Ⓥ Ⓑ Ⓓ Ⓢ • 3Cr/C

Margaret Ann Cashen, 11 Middle Howe, Rosthwaite, CA12 5XD. ☎ (017687) 77644 • Map 89,90/257147 • BB **B** • T1 • 2-10 • Ⓓ 🐾

■ BOWNESS-ON-WINDERMERE
DALES WAY

Mr & Mrs Garvey, Field House Guest House, Kendal Road, LA23 3EQ. ☎ (015394) 42476 • Map 96,97/403967 • BB **C/D** • D4 T2 F2 • 2-11 • Ⓑ Ⓓ Ⓡ 🐾

☆ Eastbourne, Biskey Howe Road, LA23 2JR. ☎ (015394) 43525 • Map 96,97/407971 • BB **C/D** • S2 D4 T2 • 1-12 • Ⓑ Ⓓ Ⓢ Ⓡ • 2Cr/C

Eastbourne
Joyce & John Whitfield
Biskey Howe Road
Bowness on Windermere
Cumbria LA23 2JR

RAC
Highly Acclaimed

AA
ΩΩΩ

TOURIST BOARD 🏵🏵
COMMENDED

MasterCard VISA

Joyce and John welcome you to their quiet family-run hotel 400 yards from the end of the Dales Way.

Easy walking distance to lake and all amenities. Comfortable, spacious well-furnished bedrooms with private facilities and colour television.

TELEPHONE 015394 43525

The Albert, Queen's Square, LA23 3BY. ☎ (015394) 43241 • Map 96,97/403969 • BB **B** • EM £4.50, 5.30-9pm • D6 F2 • 1-12 • Ⓥ Ⓑ Ⓓ Ⓢ Ⓡ 🐾 • List • Bunkhouse also

☆ Mrs P M Mossop, Lingwood, Birkett Hill, LA23 3EZ. ☎ (015394) 44680 • Map 96,97/402963 • BB **B/C** • D3 T1 F2 • 1-12 • Ⓑ Ⓓ Ⓢ Ⓡ • 2Cr/C

Ever thought of taking a Ramblers Holiday?
Telephone 01707 331133 for a brochure

LINGWOOD
Birkett Hill Bowness-on-Windermere
Cumbria LA23 3EZ
You are assured of a warm welcome and comfortable accommodation in our family run house on the edge of Windermere. Ideal for walking. Drying room, showers, tea-makers, parking. Full English Breakfast.
B&B £16-£20. 3 nights £45 midweek.
☎ Windermere (015394) 44680

■ BROUGHTON-IN-FURNESS
CUMBRIA COASTAL WAY

Kathryne & David Hartley, Middlesyke, Church Street, LA20 6ER. ☎ (01229) 716549 • Map 96/208876 • BB **C** • EM book first £12, 7.30pm • D3 • 1-12 NX • Ⓥ Ⓑ Ⓓ Ⓢ Ⓡ Ⓜ • 1Cr

■ BURNESIDE (Kendal)
DALES WAY

Mrs J Ellis, Gateside Farm, LA9 5SE. ☎ (01539) 722036 • Map 97/496954 • BB **B/C** • EM book first £8, 6.30pm • D3 T1 F1 • 1-12 NX • Ⓑ Ⓓ Ⓡ • List/C

■ BUTTERMERE (Cockermouth)
COAST TO COAST WALK

☆ Bridge Hotel, Buttermere, Lake District, CA13 9UZ. ☎ (017687) 70252 • Map 89,90/175169 • BB **D** • EM from £3.50, 6-9.30pm • S2 D8 T12 • 1-12 • Ⓥ Ⓑ Ⓓ Ⓢ 🐾 • 4Cr/HC • SC also

BUTTERMERE VALLEY

English Tourist Board
HIGHLY COMMENDED
🏵🏵🏵🏵

THE BRIDGE HOTEL is situated in an unrivalled position between two lakes – Buttermere and Crummock Water – and overlooked by famous mountains such as Haystacks, High Stile and Red Pike.

Superb unrestricted walking country in an Area of Outstanding Natural Beauty.

Good food, wines and real ales served in comfortable surroundings.

Traditional Lakeland afternoon teas. Dogs welcome. Self-catering available. Special breaks all Year.

BRIDGE HOTEL, BUTTERMERE, LAKE DISTRICT, CUMBRIA CA13 9UZ
TEL 017687 70252

☆ See Display Advertisement

159

■ **BUTTERMERE (CONTINUED)**

Mrs Chris Knight, "Trevene", CA13 9XA. ☎ (017687) 70210 • Map 89/174172 • BB **B** • D1 T1 F1 • 1-12 NX • Ⓓ Ⓢ 🐾 Ⓜ

☆ Ramblers Holidays, Dalegarth, CA13 9XA. ☎ (017687) 70233 • Map 89,90/186160 • BB **B** • D4 T5 • 4-10 • Ⓑ Ⓓ Ⓜ

■ **CALDBECK (Wigton)**
CUMBRIA WAY

☆ Dorothy H Coulthard, The Briars, CA7 8DS. ☎ (016974) 78633 • Map 90/325399 • BB **C** • S1 D1 T1 • 3-10 • Ⓑ Ⓓ

☆ Mr & Mrs Savage, Swaledale Watch, Whelpo, CA7 8HQ. ☎ (016974) 78409 • Map 90/309396 • BB **B/C** • EM book first £10, 7pm • D2 T1 F1 • 1-12 NX • Ⓑ Ⓓ Ⓢ • 2Cr/HC

B&B ACCOMMODATION   ENGLAND   CUMBRIA

160

■ **CARLISLE**
CUMBRIA WAY & CUMBRIA COASTAL WAY

Mrs S E Fisher, Howard House, 27 Howard Place, CA1 1HR. ☎ (01228) 29159/512550 • Map 85/407559 • BB **B** • EM book first £8, 6.30pm • S2 D2 T2 F2 • 1-12 NX • Ⓥ Ⓑ Ⓓ Ⓢ • 3Cr/HC

Angus Hotel, 14 Scotland Road, Stanwix, CA3 9DG. ☎ (01228) 23546 • Map 85/400570 • BB **C/D** • EM £10, 7-9.30pm • S2 D2 T4 F4 • 1-12 NX • Ⓥ Ⓑ Ⓓ Ⓢ Ⓡ

☆ Michael & Angela Hayes, Avondale, 3 St Aidan's Road, CA1 1LT. ☎ (01228) 23012 • Map 85/410559 • BB **C** • EM book first £8, 6.30pm • D1 T2 • 1-12 NX • Ⓥ Ⓑ Ⓓ Ⓢ Ⓡ • 2Cr/HC

Chatsworth Guest House, 22 Chatsworth Square, CA1 1HF. ☎ (01228) 24023 • Map 85/406560 • BB **B** • EM book first £6, 6pm • S2 D1 T2 F1 • 1-12 NX • Ⓥ Ⓑ Ⓓ Ⓢ Ⓡ • 2Cr/C

☆ Ruth Casson, Liddel Lodge, Penton, CA6 5QN. ☎ (01228) 577335 • Map 86/469793 • BB **B** • EM book first £7.50, 6.30-8.30pm • S1 D1 T/F1 • 1-12 NX • Ⓥ Ⓑ Ⓓ Ⓢ 🐾 Ⓜ • List

■ **CARTMEL**
CUMBRIA COASTAL WAY

Mrs P C Lawson, Bank Court Cottage, The Square, LA11 6QB. ☎ (015395) 36593 • Map 96,97/378787 • BB **C** • EM book first £10.50 • S1 D1 • 1-12 NX • Ⓥ Ⓓ Ⓢ Ⓡ 🐾 • List/C

■ CARTMEL FELL (Grange-over-Sands)

☆ Mrs E Cervetti, Lightwood Farmhouse, LA11 6NP. ☎ (015395) 31454 • Map 96,97/408890 • BB **D** • EM book first £14, 7pm • D3 T3 F2 • 2-11 • Ⓥ Ⓑ Ⓓ Ⓢ • 3Cr/C

LIGHTWOOD COUNTRY GUEST HOUSE
CARTMEL FELL, GRANGE-OVER-SANDS, CUMBRIA LA11 6NP

☎ 015395 31454

A 17th Century farmhouse with original oak beams and staircase. 2 acres of lovely gardens with streams running through. Only 2½ miles from southern end of Lake Windermere. Comfort and hospitality are our speciality.

■ CLEATOR
COAST TO COAST WALK

Mrs Carol Ferguson, Ennerdale View, 1 Cleator Gate, CA23 3DN. ☎ (01946) 814180 • Map 89/015135 • BB **A/B** • T1 F1 • 1-12 NX • Ⓓ 🐾 • SC also

■ COCKERMOUTH

Mrs D Richardson, Pardshaw Hall, CA13 0SP. ☎ (01900) 822607 • Map 89/103254 • BB **B** • EM £7, 6-6.30pm • S2 D1 T/F1 F1 • 1-12 NX • Ⓥ Ⓓ 🐾

☆ Miss W Adams, The Castlegate Guest House, 6 Castlegate, CA13 9EU. ☎ (01900) 826749 • Map 89/122307 • BB **B/C** • D/S4 T1 F2 • 1-12 • Ⓑ Ⓓ Ⓢ 🐾

THE CASTLEGATE
6 CASTLEGATE, COCKERMOUTH
CUMBRIA CA13 9EU

Situated near the castle in historical market town. Within minutes of all unspoilt northern lakes. Listed Georgian building with period furniture. Expert advice on walks. Double rooms available as singles, no extra charge. Dogs welcome. TV, H&C, CH, tea/coffee in all rooms.

☎ **01900 826749**

Mrs V A Waters, The Rook Guest House, 9 Castlegate, CA13 9EU. ☎ (01900) 828496 • Map 89/122307 • BB **B/C** • D2 T1 • 1-12 NX • Ⓑ Ⓓ Ⓢ

■ CONISTON
CUMBRIA WAY

☆ Mrs C Hartshorn, Shepherds Villa Guest House, LA21 8EE. ☎ (015394) 41337 • Map 96,97/305976 • BB **C** • D2 T6 F2 • 1-12 • Ⓑ Ⓓ Ⓢ • 2Cr/App

SHEPHERDS VILLA GUEST HOUSE
Coniston, Cumbria LA21 8EE

Well established family run guest house offering good food, clean spacious accommodation in quiet spot on edge of village. Ideal touring & walking centre. H&C all rooms, some rooms with private shower and TV. TV lounge, tea-making facilities. Private parking. Walking & touring parties taken. A warm welcome to all.

For colour brochure please send sae

ETB
♔♔ **Tel. 015394 41337**
Approved   Proprietor C Hartshorn

Mrs M Knipe, Dixon Ground Farm, LA21 8HQ. ☎ (015394) 41443 • Map 96,97/299976 • BB **C** • EM £7, 6.30pm • S2 D2 • 1-12 • Ⓥ Ⓓ 🐾

☆ Beech Tree, Yew Dale Road, LA21 8DX. ☎ (015394) 41717 • Map 96/302976 • BB **C/D** • EM £12.50, 7pm • D3 T2 F1 • 2-11 • Ⓥ Ⓑ Ⓓ Ⓢ 🐾 Ⓜ

BEECH TREE
Yew Dale Road, Coniston LA21 8DX

Formerly the Old Vicarage, this delightful 18thC house set in its own grounds welcomes walkers in all seasons. Tea/coffee facilities, TV lounge. We serve excellent vegetarian meals. B&B from £17. Family and en suite rooms. Dinner optional £12.50. Drying facilities available. Tourist Board Commendation.

Tel. Jean and John Watts
Coniston 015394 41717

Diana Munton, Piper Croft, Haws Bank, LA21 8AR. ☎ (015394) 41778 • Map 96,97/300966 • BB **B** • D2 T1 • 1-12 NX • Ⓓ Ⓢ

Marilyn Hodson, Goldberry, 3 Collingwood Close, LA21 8DZ. ☎ (015394) 41379 • Map 96,97/307977 • BB **B/C** • EM book first £8.50, 6-7pm • S1 T1 • 1-12 NX • Ⓑ Ⓓ Ⓢ Ⓜ

☆ Lillian Grant, Cruachan, Collingwood Close, LA21 8DZ. ☎ (015394) 41628 • Map 96,97/307977 • BB **C/D** • D2 T1 • 1-12 NX • Ⓑ Ⓓ Ⓢ • 2Cr/C

CRUACHAN
Collingwood Close, Coniston

Very comfortable B&B village location, beautiful view of Coniston Old Man. Spacious en suite rooms with TV and tea and coffee-making facilities. Special diets. Packed lunches. Car parking. Non-smoking. No pets.

Telephone 015394 41628

ETB ♔♔
Commended

☆ See Display Advertisement

■ CONISTON

Patricia Cross, Waterhead Country Guest House, LA21 8AJ. ☎ (015394) 41442 • Map 96,97/310977 • BB **B/C** • S2 D7 T1 • 1-12 NX • Ⓑ Ⓓ Ⓢ Ⓜ

Lakeland House, LA21 8ED. ☎ (015394) 41303 • Map 96,97/304976 • BB **B/C** • S2 D5 T3 F2 • 1-12 NX • Ⓑ Ⓓ 🐾 • List

☆ Kirkbeck House, Lake Road, LA21 8EW. ☎ (015394) 41358 • Map 96,97/301973 • BB **B** • S1 D2 T1 F1 • 1-12 NX • Ⓓ • Groups also

KIRKBECK HOUSE
CONISTON

KIRKBECK HOUSE offers bed and breakfast accommodation in a comfortable and friendly family home.

Reduction for mid-week breaks and special arrangements for small groups, eg. packed lunches, evening meal and luggage transfer.

It is siutated in a quiet area of Coniston village, close to all amenities and within easy reach of some of the finest walks in England.

Tel. 015394 41358

■ COWGILL, DENTDALE (Sedbergh)
DALES WAY

Mrs Ferguson, Scow Cottage, LA10 5RN. ☎ (015396) 25445 • Map 98/774851 • BB **B** • EM book first £8, 6.30-7pm • D1 T1 • 1-12 NX • Ⓥ Ⓓ Ⓢ 🐾

Mr & Mrs Playfoot, River View, Lea Yeat, LA10 5RF. ☎ (015396) 25592 • Map 98/760870 • BB **B** • D1 T1 • 1-12 NX • Ⓓ Ⓢ Ⓡ Ⓜ

■ DENT (Sedbergh)
DALES WAY

Mrs A E Hunter, Rash House, Dent Foot, LA10 5SU. ☎ (015396) 20113 • Map 98/667897 • BB **B** • EM book first £8, 6.30pm • D1 F1 • 1-12 NX • Ⓥ Ⓓ 🐾 Ⓜ

Pat Barber, Stone Close Tea Shop, Main Street, LA10 5QL. ☎ (015396) 25231 • Map 98/705870 • BB **B** • S1 D1 F1 • 2-12 • Ⓓ Ⓢ 🐾 • Meals in teashop upto 5.30pm

Sun Inn, LA10 5QL. ☎ (015396) 25208 • Map 98/705870 • BB **B** • EM £5.99, 7-8.30pm • D1 T1 F1 • 1-12 NX • Ⓥ Ⓓ Ⓢ • List

Mrs Judith Newsham, Syke Fold, LA10 5RE. ☎ (015396) 25486 • Map 98/724858 • BB **B** • EM book first £9, 6.30pm • D1 F1 • 1-12 NX • Ⓥ Ⓓ Ⓢ 🐾

Mrs Eileen Neal, Old Vicarage, Flintergill, LA10 5QR. ☎ (015396) 25366 • Map 98/704869 • BB **B** • D1 T1 F1 • 3-11 • Ⓑ Ⓓ 🐾

Mrs P M Allen, The White House, Flintergill, LA10 5QR. ☎ (015396) 25041 • Map 98/704869 • BB **B** • D1 T1 • 1-12 NX • Ⓓ Ⓢ Ⓜ

■ DOCKRAY (Matterdale, Penrith)

☆ The Royal Hotel, CA11 0JY. ☎ (017684) 82356 • Map 90/393217 • BB **D** • EM £5.50-£12, 6-9pm • S1 D6 T1 F2 • 1-12 • Ⓥ Ⓑ Ⓓ Ⓢ 🐾

ROYAL HOTEL, DOCKRAY

16th Century coaching inn, nestled amidst lakeland fells, 1 mile from Ullswater.
An excellent base for a walking holiday, or an overnight stay on The Cumberland Way.
10 ensuite bedrooms with TV, tea-making facilities. Central heating, log fire in lounge bar, 60-seater restaurant, drying room.
Good selection real ales, wines and malt whisky.
Excellent home cooking.

Tel 017684 82356

■ DUFTON (Appleby)
PENNINE WAY

Mrs M Hullock, Ghyll View, CA16 6DB. ☎ (017683) 51855 • Map 91/691250 • BB **B** • EM book first £4, 7pm • S1 D1 T2 • 3-10 • Ⓥ Ⓑ Ⓓ Ⓢ

Mrs E M Howe, Dufton Hall Farm, CA16 6DD. ☎ (017683) 51573 • Map 91/690250 • BB **B** • D2 T2 F1 • 3-10 • Ⓑ Ⓓ Ⓢ • 1Cr/App

■ EAMONT BRIDGE (Penrith)

Mrs C O'Neil, 6 Lowther Glen, CA10 2BP. ☎ (01768) 864405 • Map 90/524285 • BB **B** • EM book first £6.50, 5-7.30pm • S2 D2 T2 F1 • 1-11 • Ⓥ Ⓑ Ⓓ Ⓢ Ⓡ 🐾

ELTERWATER (Ambleside)
CUMBRIA WAY

Audrey Whittle, Meadow Bank, LA22 9HW. ☎ (015394) 37278 • Map 90/327047 • BB **B** • D2 T1 • 1-12 NX • Ⓑ Ⓓ Ⓢ Ⓜ • SC also

ENNERDALE (Cleator)
COAST TO COAST WALK

Mrs Helen W Hinde, Low Moor End Farm, CA23 3AS. ☎ (01946) 861388 • Map 89/075156 • BB **B** • D1 T1 • 3-10 • Ⓓ Ⓢ

Mrs Liz Loxham, Beckfoot, CA23 3AU. ☎ (01946) 861235 • Map 89/103162 • BB **B/C** • EM book first £10.50, 6.30pm • D1 T1 F1 • 1-12 NX • Ⓓ Ⓢ

ENNERDALE BRIDGE (Cleator)
COAST TO COAST WALK

Mrs Lake, The Old Vicarage, CA23 3AG. ☎ (01946) 861107 • Map 89/065156 • BB **C** • S1 D1 T2 F1 • 1-12 NX • Ⓓ Ⓢ 🏂 Ⓜ

Sheila Sherwen, 6 Ehen Garth, CA23 3BA. ☎ (01946) 861917 • Map 89/069159 • BB **B** • D1 T1 • 1-12 NX • Ⓓ Ⓢ

The Shepherd's Arms Hotel, CA23 3AR. ☎ (01946) 861249 • Map 89/069158 • BB **C/D** • EM £5-£14.50, 7-8.30pm • S1 D3 T2 • 1-12 • Ⓥ Ⓑ Ⓓ Ⓢ 🏂 • 3Cr/App • SC also

ESKDALE

Stanley Ghyll House, Boot, CA19 1TF. ☎ (019467) 23327 • Map 89,90/175007 • BB **C/D** • EM £9.50, 7pm • S4 T8 F12 • 1-12 • Ⓥ Ⓓ Ⓢ Ⓡ Ⓜ • Groups also

☆ Neil & Christine Carter, Forest How Guest House, CA19 1TR. ☎ (019467) 23201 • Map 96/136999 • BB **C** • EM book first £11, 7pm • S1 D2 T3 F2 • 1-12 NX • Ⓥ Ⓑ Ⓓ Ⓡ • 2Cr/C • SC also

FOREST HOW, ESKDALE, CA19 1TR
🍃🍃 Commended
Secluded, warm, comfortable guest house. Excellent home cooking. Delightful gardens with spectacular views. TVs, H&C, beverage trays. Some ensuite. Parking. Friendly informal atmosphere. Brochure.
☎ 019467 23201

GARRIGILL (Alston)
PENNINE WAY

Mrs H D Dent, Ivy House Farm, CA9 3DU. ☎ (01434) 382079 • Map 86,87/744414 • BB **B** • D1 T/F1 • 1-3 & 5-12 NX • Ⓓ Ⓢ • List/C

GILSLAND (Carlisle)
PENNINE WAY

Elizabeth Woodmass, Howard House Farm, CA6 7AN. ☎ (016977) 47285 • Map 86/630677 • BB **C** • EM book first £10, 6pm • D1 T1 F1 • 1-12 NX • Ⓥ Ⓑ Ⓓ Ⓢ • 2Cr/HC

Mrs D J Cole, Alpha Mount, CA6 7EB. ☎ (016977) 47070 • Map 86/639662 • BB **B** • EM book first £6, 7pm • D1 F1 • 1-12 • Ⓥ Ⓓ Ⓢ 🏂 • 1Cr/C

GLENRIDDING (Penrith)
COAST TO COAST WALK

☆ Mr & Mrs J S Lake, Moss Crag Guest House, CA11 0PA. ☎ (017684) 82500 • Map 90/385170 • BB **B/C** • EM book first £12.50, 7.30 summer 6.30 winter • D6 • 1-11 • Ⓥ Ⓑ Ⓓ Ⓢ Ⓜ

MOSSCRAG
Overlooking Glenriddingbeck and Dodd. Step out the door to a walker's paradise, or sail on the Lake and come back for morning coffee, light lunch or afternoon tea.

Glenridding
(017684) 82500

GRANGE-IN-BORROWDALE (Keswick)
CUMBRIA WAY

☆ Terry & Gwen Boggild, Grange View, CA12 5XA. ☎ (017687) 77226 • Map 89,90/254174 • BB **B/C** • D2 T1 • 1-12 NX • Ⓓ Ⓢ

GRANGE VIEW
BORROWDALE
Overlooking picturesque Grange Village and River Derwent, 4 miles south of Keswick. Ideally situated for walks to Cat Bells, Maiden Moor, Castle Crag, Watendlath etc. Non-smoking • English breakfast • Central heating • Parking • Colour TV, washbasins, tea/coffee facilities in all bedrooms • Guest sitting room with stunning views • Packed lunches/evening meals available in Grange.
☎ 017687 77226

■ GRANGE-OVER-SANDS
CUMBRIA COASTAL WAY

Prospect House Hotel, Kents Bank Road, LA11 7DJ. ☎ (015395) 32116 • Map 96, 97/403773 • BB **C/D** • EM book first £10.50, 7pm • S1 D5 T2 • 1-12 • Ⓥ Ⓑ Ⓓ Ⓢ Ⓡ ⓘ • 3Cr

Gary & Ann Holden, Thornfield House, Kents Bank Road, LA11 7DT. ☎ (015395) 32512 • Map 96,97/401770 • BB **C** • EM book first £8, 6.30pm • S1 D1 T2 F2 • 1-12 NX • Ⓥ Ⓑ Ⓓ Ⓢ Ⓡ • List

Sandra & Derek Barton, Holme Lea Guest House, 90 Kentsford Road, Kents Bank, LA11 7BB. ☎ (015395) 32545 • Map 96,97/399760 • BB **C** • EM £8, 6.30pm • S1 D2 T1 F1 • 3-11 • Ⓑ Ⓓ Ⓡ ⓘ

■ GRASMERE (Ambleside)
COAST TO COAST WALK

Forest Side, LA22 9RN. ☎ (015394) 35250 • Map 90/343081 • BB **C/D** • EM £9.50, 7pm • S10 D6 T16 • 1-12 • Ⓥ Ⓑ Ⓓ Ⓢ Ⓜ • Groups also

Mrs Gloria Clarke, Fairy Glen, Swan Lane, LA22 9RH. ☎ (015394) 35620 • Map 90/337075 • BB **C** • D2 T2 • 1-12 • Ⓑ Ⓓ ⓘ

Mrs Alison Dixon, Oak Lodge, Easedale Road, LA22 9QJ. ☎ (015394) 35527 • Map 90/331081 • BB **C** • D1 T1 • 3-11 • Ⓓ Ⓢ • List

■ GRAYRIGG (Kendal)
DALES WAY

Mrs J Bindloss, Grayrigg Hall Farm, LA8 9BU. ☎ (01539824) 689 • Map 97/579975 • BB **B** • EM book first £6, 6.30-7pm • S1 D1 F/T1 • 3-10 • Ⓥ Ⓓ ⓘ • List

Mrs D Johnson, Punchbowl House, LA8 9BU. ☎ (01539) 824345 • Map 97/580972 • BB **B/C** • EM book first £13.50, 7.30pm • D2 T1 • 1-12 • Ⓥ Ⓑ Ⓓ Ⓢ • 2Cr/C • SC also

■ GREAT ASBY (Appleby)

Mrs D Hayton, Asby Grange Farm, CA16 6HF. ☎ (017683) 52881 • Map 91/687106 • BB **B** • EM book first £8, 6.30-7pm • D1 F1 • 5-9 NX • Ⓥ Ⓑ Ⓓ ⓘ • 1Cr

■ GREAT LANGDALE (Ambleside)
CUMBRIA WAY

Mrs J Rowand, Baysbrown Farm, LA22 9JZ. ☎ (015394) 37300 • Map 90/309057 • BB **C** • EM book first £9, 6.30pm • D1 T1 F1 • 3-11 • Ⓥ Ⓓ Ⓢ ⓘ

Jean Rowand, Stool End Farm, LA22 9JU. ☎ (015394) 37615 • Map 97/277058 • BB **B** • D/F1 • 1-12 • Ⓑ Ⓢ ⓘ

■ HAWKSHEAD (Ambleside)

The Squires Family, Greenbank House Hotel, LA22 0NS. ☎ (015394) 36497 • Map 96,97/351982 • BB **C** • EM book first £11, 6.30pm • S3 D6 T2 F1 • 1-12 • Ⓥ Ⓑ Ⓓ Ⓢ ⓘ • 2Cr

Mrs O Taylforth, Keen Ground Farm, LA22 0NW. ☎ (015394) 36228 • Map 96,97/347983 • BB **B** • D2 T1 • 1-12 NX • Ⓓ Ⓢ

Mrs Margaret Lambert, Little Ees Wyke, Near Sawrey, LA22 0JZ. ☎ (015394) 36335 • Map 96,97/366957 • BB **C** • EM book first £9, 7pm • D1 T2 • 1-12 • Ⓑ Ⓓ ⓘ

■ HESKET NEW-MARKET (Caldbeck, Wigton)
CUMBRIA WAY

☆ Mrs Margaret Monkhouse, Denton House, CA7 8JG. ☎ (016974) 78415 • Map 90/341385 • BB **C** • EM book first £8, 6.30pm • S1 D1 T2 F3 • 1-12 • Ⓥ Ⓑ Ⓓ ⓘ

HESKET NEW-MARKET, CALDBECK
A warm, friendly atmosphere welcomes everyone. Ideal stop when travelling to or from Scotland, walking the Cumbria Way and touring the lakes.
Tel. 016974 78415

■ KENDAL
DALES WAY

Newlands Guest House, 37 Milnthorpe Road, LA9 5QG. ☎ (01539) 725340 • Map 97/515916 • BB **B/C** • EM book first £7.50, 6.30-7.30pm • S1 D2 T1 F1 • 1-12 NX • Ⓥ Ⓑ Ⓓ Ⓡ ⓘ • 2Cr/App

Mr & Mrs C Wilkinson, Sonata, 19 Burneside Road, LA9 4RL. ☎ (01539) 732290 • Map 97/513933 • BB **B** • EM £7.50, 6-7.30pm • S1 D1 T1 F2 • 1-12 • Ⓥ Ⓑ Ⓓ Ⓡ ⓘ • List

Eileen & Brian Kettle, Holmfield, 41 Kendal Green, LA9 5PP. ☎ (01539) 720790 • Map 97/512939 • BB **C** • D2 T1 • 1-12 NX • Ⓓ Ⓢ Ⓡ • List/Deluxe • Food nearby

Mrs Brenda Denison, Hillside Guest House, 4 Beast Banks, LA9 4JW. ☎ (01539) 722836 • Map 97/513925 • BB **B/C** • S3 D3 T1 • 3-11 • Ⓑ Ⓓ Ⓢ Ⓡ ⓘ • 2Cr/C • Food nearby

■ KENTMERE (Kendal)

Christine Foster, Maggs Howe, LA8 9JP. ☎ (01539) 821689 • Map 90/462041 • BB **B** • EM book first £8, 7pm • D2 T/F1 • 1-12 NX • Ⓑ Ⓓ Ⓢ ⓘ

■ KESWICK
CUMBRIA WAY & CUMBRIA COASTAL WAY

Sharon & Arnold Helling, Beckside, 5 Wordsworth Street, CA12 4HU. ☎ (017687) 73093 • Map 89,90/270235 • BB **C** • EM book first £11, 6pm • D3 T1 • 1-12 NX • Ⓥ Ⓑ Ⓓ Ⓢ • 2Cr

☆ Mr & Mrs G Williams, Glendale Guest House, 7 Eskin Street, CA12 4DH. ☎ (017687) 73562 • Map 89,90/269231 • BB **B/C** • EM book first £9, 6.30pm • S2 D2 T1 F2 • 1-12 NX • B S

☆ Highfield Hotel, The Heads, CA12 5ER. ☎ (017687) 72508 • Map 89,90/264232 • BB **D** • EM £12, 6.30-8pm • S5 D8 T3 F3 • 1-12 • V B D S 🐾 • 3Cr/C

Kelvyn & Christine Sheppard, Lynwood Hotel, 12 Ambleside Road, CA12 4DL. ☎ (017687) 72081 • Map 89,90/268231 • BB **C/D** • EM £11.50, 6.30-7pm • S2 D4 T1 F1 • 2-12 NX • V B D S Ⓜ • 3Cr/C • Open New Year

☆ Richmond House, 37/39 Eskin Street, CA12 4DG. ☎ (017687) 73965 • Map 89,90/270232 • BB **B/C** • EM book first £9.50, 7pm • S2 D4 T2 F1 • 1-12 NX • V B S • 3Cr • Groups & SC also

☆ Mr K Pechartscheck, Chaucer House Hotel, Derwentwater Place, CA12 4DR. ☎ (017687) 72318/73223 • Map 89,90/268232 • BB **D** • EM £12.50, 6.30-9 (8 Sun) • S9 D13 T10 F3 • 2-12 NX • V B D S 🐾 • 3 Cr/C • SC also

☆ Mrs Jean McNichol, Glendene, 8 Southey Street, CA12 4EF. ☎ (017687) 73548 • Map 89,90/268233 • BB **B** • EM book first £8, 6pm • D2 T1 F1 • 2-11 NX • V D S

Acorn House Hotel, Ambleside Road, CA12 4DL. ☎ (017687) 72553 • Map 89,90/268231 • BB **D** • D5 T2 F3 • 2-11 • B D S • 2Cr/HC • SC also

Dave & Vicky Wright, Kylesku Guest House, 22 Skiddaw Street, CA12 4BY. ☎ (017687) 72184 • Map 89,90/271233 • BB **B** • EM book first £9, 6.30pm • S2 D1 T1 F1 • 2-10 NX • V D S

☆ See Display Advertisement   **165**

Side tab: B&B ACCOMMODATION ENGLAND CUMBRIA KESWICK

☆ Foye House, 23 Eskin Street, CA12 4DQ. ☎ (017767) 73288 • Map 89,90/270232 • BB **B** • EM £9, 6.30-8pm • S2 D3 T1 F1 • 1-12 • Ⓥ Ⓑ Ⓓ Ⓢ 🍴 Ⓜ • 3Cr

---

FOYE HOUSE

23 Eskin Street, Keswick, Cumbria CA12 4DQ

Comfortable, friendly non-smoking guesthouse close to town centre, lake and fells. CH, CTV, tea/coffee facilities in all bedrooms. Four course dinner (optional), vegetarians catered for. Table licence, packed lunches, drying facilities available.

Tel. Keswick (017687) 73288

ETB

AA listed   **CTB**

☆ Mrs R B Wharton, Braemar, 21 Eskin Street, CA12 4DQ. ☎ (017687) 73743 • Map 89,90/270232 • BB **B** • S3 D2 T1 • 1-12 NX • Ⓓ • 1Cr

---

BRAEMAR
21 Eskin Street, Keswick, Cumbria CA12 4DQ

Situated five minutes walk from Keswick Moot Hall • Single, twin and double rooms • Colour TVs in all bedrooms • Own keys • Warm welcome.

☎ 017687 73743

☆ Silverdale Hotel, Blencathra Street, CA12 4HT. ☎ (017687) 72294 • Map 89,90/270234 • BB **C** • EM £10.50, 6.45pm • S3 D6 T2 F1 • 2-11 AND XMAS • Ⓥ Ⓑ Ⓓ Ⓢ • 3Cr • SC also

---

RAC
Highly Acclaimed

FREE – Walking advice Bike Storage

SILVERDALE HOTEL
and self-catering cottage
Keswick

Bar	(017687) 72294	Parking
Packed lunches		T.V.s in rooms
Groups welcome		Tea making facilities

Mrs B Lathan, Glaramara, 9 Acorn Street, CA12 4EA. ☎ (017687) 73216 • Map 89,90/269232 • BB **B** • EM £8.50, 6.30pm • S1 D2 T1 F2 • 1-10 • Ⓥ Ⓑ Ⓓ Ⓢ 🍴 • SC also

☆ Jean Scott, Seven Oaks Guest House, Acorn Street, CA12 4EA. ☎ (017687) 72088 • Map 89,90/269232 • BB **B** • EM £8, 6.30pm • S1 D2 F3 • 3-11 NX • Ⓥ Ⓓ Ⓢ 🍴 • SC also

166

SEVEN OAKS
Acorn Street, Keswick, Cumbria

Small, family-run guesthouse, homely atmosphere, situated in quiet area, 5 mins town centre. All meals home cooked, fresh produce, all rooms have H&C, tea/coffee-making facilities and showers. Separate TV lounge. Cleanliness guaranteed. Packed lunches available. Parties welcome.

Tel. Keswick 017687 72088

☆ Tarn Hows Guest House, 5 Eskin Street, CA12 4DH. ☎ (017687) 73217 • Map 89,90/269231 • BB **B** • EM £8, 6.30pm • S1 D4 T2 F1 • 1-12 • Ⓥ Ⓑ Ⓓ Ⓢ 🍴 Ⓜ • List

---

TARN HOWS GUEST HOUSE
5 Eskin Street, Keswick, Cumbria CA12 4DH

Long established reputation for good food and warm hospitality. Pleasantly situated quiet residential area. All bedrooms heated (some with shower en suite) and tea/coffee makers. Two delightful lounges, drying room, private parking and packed lunches available.

Phone Keswick (017687) 73217 for colour brochure

☆ Mr & Mrs Chris Knox, Rivendell, 23 Helvellyn Street, CA12 4EN. ☎ (017687) 73822 • Map 89,90/269233 • BB **B/C** • EM book first £9.50, 6.30pm • S1 D4 T1 F1 • 1-12 NX • Ⓑ Ⓓ Ⓢ 🍴

RIVENDELL
23 Helvellyn Street, Keswick
Warm and comfortable family guest house for non-smokers. Hearty helpings of delicious home cooking.
B&B £15   En-suite £18
Phone 017687 73822

Annemarie & Ian Townsend, Latrigg House, St Herbert Street, CA12 4DF. ☎ (017687) 73068 • Map 89,90/270233 • BB **B** • EM £9, 7-7.30pm • S1 D2 T2 F1 • 1-12 • Ⓥ Ⓑ Ⓓ Ⓢ • 2Cr

Glaramara, Seatoller, CA12 5XQ. ☎ (017687) 77222 • Map 89,90/245133 • BB **C/D** • EM £9.50, 7pm • S19 T14 • 1-12 • Ⓥ Ⓓ Ⓢ Ⓜ • Groups also

☆ Easedale Hotel, Southey Street, CA12 4EG. ☎ (017687) 72710 • Map 89,90/268233 • BB **B/C** • S1 D4 T3 F2 • 1-12 • Ⓑ Ⓓ Ⓢ • Groups also

Easedale Hotel

**Southey Street,
Keswick-on-Derwentwater
Cumbria CA12 4EG
Tel. 017-687-72710
Fax. 017-687-71127**

With easy access to local felltops, this town centre hotel is an ideal base for walking or touring holidays. Personal attention by the owners ensures high standards of service, care and cooking. Several en-suite rooms, all have tea/coffee making sets. Two TV lounges with plenty of local and touring information. The main lounge is available for smokers, as we ask our guests for health and safety reasons to refrain from smoking elsewhere, *particularly in the bedrooms.* For similar reasons we admit guide-dogs but no pets.

☆ Mr Stephen Mason, Stonegarth, 2 Eskin Street, CA12 4DH. ☎ (017687) 72436 • Map 89,90/269231 • BB **C/D** • EM £10, 6.30pm • S2 D4 T1 F2 • 1-12 NX • Ⓑ Ⓓ 🐾 • 3Cr/C

Stonegarth

Commended

2 ESKIN STREET · KESWICK · CUMBRIA · CA12 4DH

RAC
HIGHLY
ACCLAIMED

*The Mason Family
welcomes you to Stonegarth.*
☆ *All rooms with en-suite facilities,* ☆
colour TVs, & tea/coffee makers
☆ *Generous portions of home-cooked food* ☆
☆ *Packed lunches* ☆
☆ *Large private Car Park* ☆
☆ *Group Bookings available* ☆
AA
TEL: (017687) 72436

☆ Mrs Redfern, Heatherlea, 26 Blencathra St, CA12 4HP. ☎ (017687) 72430 • Map 89,90/269233 • BB **C** • D2 T1 F1 • 1-12 NX • Ⓑ Ⓓ Ⓢ

Heatherlea

26 Blencathra Street, Keswick
Tel. 017687 72430
Friendly, welcoming house, substantial home cooking. All rooms en-suite, some with views, colour TV, central heating.
Packed lunches available.
Non-smoking.
Muddy boots welcome.

AA
QQQ

☆ Jim & Christine, Melbreak House, 29 Church Street, CA12 4DX. ☎ (017687) 73398 • Map 89,90/269232 • BB **B** • S1 D5 T4 • 1-12 NX • Ⓥ Ⓑ Ⓓ Ⓢ 🐾 Ⓜ • 2Cr/App

MELBREAK HOUSE
29 Church Street
Keswick
☎ 017687 73398

Jim and Christine welcome you to Melbreak House • Traditional home cooking • We are licensed • Relax in our comfortable lounge • Within easy walking distance of the town centre and all amenities • Attractive rates for everyone including walking groups • Evening meals available for large parties and packed lunches available upon arrangement • Pets welcome • Non-smoking • Open all year.

☆ Mr Andrew Peters, Seymour House, 36 Lake Road, CA12 5DQ. ☎ (017687) 72764 • Map 89,90/266232 • BB **B/C** • EM £8.50, 6.30pm • S1 D4 T2 F4 • 1-12 • Ⓑ Ⓓ Ⓢ 🐾 • List

SEYMOUR HOUSE

36 LAKE ROAD, KESWICK CA12 5DQ
TEL. 017687 72764 / FAX 71289
Situated in a quiet cul-de-sac midway between Keswick town centre and Derwentwater "Queen of the Lakes", a comfortable friendly base for exploring the Lake District National Park. Our breakfast will set you up for the day's activities. Comfortable bedrooms equipped with colour TVs and tea/coffee trays, a drying room for those rare wet days.

☆ Kalgurli Guest House, 33 Helvellyn Street, CA12 4EP. ☎ (017687) 72935 • Map 89,90/270233 • BB **B** • EM £9, 6.30pm • D3 F1 • 1-12 • Ⓥ Ⓑ Ⓓ Ⓢ • 2Cr/C

KALGURLI GUEST HOUSE
33 HELVELLYN STREET
KESWICK, CUMBRIA CA12 4EP

ETB 2 Crown Commended • Non-smoking • B&B (evening meal optional) • All rooms CTV, tea & coffee facilities, H&C • Some en suite • Own Key • Prices from £15-£18.

Please ring 017687 72935 for brochure

☆ W.J. & J. Hardman, Lindisfarn Guest House, 21 Church Street, CA12 4DX. ☎ (017687) 73261 • Map 89,90/269232 • BB **B/C** • EM book first £9.50, 6pm • S2 D4 T1 • 1-10 • Ⓥ Ⓑ Ⓓ Ⓢ

LINDISFARNE GUEST HOUSE
21 Church Street, Keswick
Cumbria CA12 4DX

A friendly, non-smoking guest house • Close to town centre • B&B or DB&B • HC • CH • CTV • Radio • Some en-suite rooms • Packed lunches • Drying facilities.

017687 73261

☆ Bill & Elizabeth Riding, Derwentdale Guest House, 8 Blencathra St, CA12 4HP. ☎ (017687) 74187 • Map 89,90/269234 • BB **B/C** • EM book first £9.50, 6.30pm • S2 D3 T1 • 1-12 • Ⓥ Ⓑ Ⓓ Ⓢ • List/C

DERWENTDALE GUEST HOUSE
8 Blencathra Street, Keswick CA12 4HP

ETB commended • Non-smoking • Friendly comfortable guest house 4 mins walk from town centre • Full central heating • En-suite available • Front rooms with views of Skiddaw mountain range • Colour TV in all bedrooms • Traditional Cumbrian breakfast • Evening meals available.

☎ 017687 74187

George & Joan Lancaster, Lyndhurst Guesthouse, 22 Southey Street, CA12 4EF. ☎ (017687) 72303 • Map 89,90/268233 • BB **B** • EM book first £9, 6pm • D2 T1 F2 • 1-12 NX • Ⓥ Ⓓ • 1Cr/App

Langdale Guest House, 14 Leonard Street, CA12 4EL. ☎ (017687) 73977 • Map 89,90/269233 • BB **B/C** • D2 T1 • 4-1 NX • Ⓑ Ⓓ Ⓢ

☆ Ann & Tony Atkin, Glencoe Guest House, 21 Helvellyn, CA12 4EN. ☎ (017687) 71016 • Map 89, 90/269233 • BB **B/C** • S1 D3 T2 • 1-12 NX • Ⓑ Ⓓ Ⓢ

GLENCOE GUEST HOUSE
KESWICK

Double, single and twin rooms available, both standard and en-suite, all with colour TV and tea and coffee making facilities. Full CH with individual thermostatic control. 5 min stroll to centre Keswick and amenities. Recently renovated Victorian home retains much of its original character. Warm friendly atmosphere. B&B from £15.

Tel 017687 71016

☆ Greenside, 48 Saint John's Street, Keswick-on-Derwentwater, CA12 5AG. ☎ (017687) 74491 • Map 89,90/267233 • BB **A/B** • S1 D1 T1 • 1-12 • Ⓑ Ⓓ Ⓢ

GREENSIDE
48 Saint John's Street,
Keswick on Derwentwater
Cumbria CA12 5AG

Charming little Georgian guest house. All bedrooms en-suite with colour TV and snack-making facilities. Lovely views. Private parking. Close to lake and town centre.
From £13.20 B&B
(20% discount on weekly stays)

Brochure from ☎ 017687 74491

Mrs Denise Wilmot, The Cartwheel, 5 Blencathra Street, CA12 4HW. ☎ (017687) 73182 • Map 89,90/269234 • BB **B/C** • EM book first £9, 6.30pm • S2 D2 T2 • 1-12 NX • Ⓥ Ⓑ Ⓓ Ⓢ • List

☆ Barry & Cathy Colam, Cumbria Hotel, 1 Derwentwater Place, Ambleside Road, CA12 4DR. ☎ (017687) 73171 • Map 89,90/268232 • BB **C** • EM book first £10, 6.45pm • S2 D3 T1 F1 • 1-12 NX • Ⓥ Ⓑ Ⓢ Ⓜ • 2Cr/C

Cumbria Hotel

3 min walk from the centre of Keswick - an ideal base for your Lakeland walking holiday. Lounge with library of walking books, dining room with small bar. English breakfast with home-made rolls: dinner and packed lunches on request.

COMMENDED   PRIVATE CAR PARK

1 Derwentwater Place, Ambleside Road
Keswick CA12 4DR   Tel/Fax: 017687 73171

☆ Mrs Joy Harrison, Bramblewood Cottage, Greta Street, CA12 4HS. ☎ (017687) 75918 • Map 89,90/270234 • BB **C** • S1 D4 T1 • 1-12 NX • Ⓑ Ⓓ

Bramblewood Cottage

Greta Street, Keswick CA12 4HS

Situated three minutes walk from the centre of town. Facing across river and park to Skiddaw. B&B £17.50. Four-poster £19.50. Off road parking available.

WINTER BREAKS

5 Nov 96 to 28 March 97, three nights or more, Sun-Thurs. £16 per person per night

All en suite • TV • Tea/coffee • Drying facilities

Joy & Colin Harrison

017687 75918

HOME FROM HOME

☆ Parkfield Guest House, The Heads, CA12 5ES. ☎ (017687) 72328 • Map 89,90/264232 • BB **C/D** • EM £12.75, 7.30pm • D6 T2 • 1-12 NX • Ⓥ Ⓑ Ⓓ Ⓢ Ⓜ • 2Cr/C

AS RECOMMENDED IN
"RAMBLING TODAY" VOL 19 WINTER 1995

PARKFIELD

THE HEADS, KESWICK CA12 5ES

• Delightful Lakeland residence in superb position between town and lake

• Dramatic views

• Home-cooked food — vegetarian specialities

• Excellent choice at breakfast

• CAR PARK • DRYING FACILITIES • EN-SUITE ROOMS

RAC *Acclaimed*   Tel. 017687 72328   Commended

Tom & Betty Forsyth, "Anworth House", 27 Eskin Street, CA12 4DQ. ☎ (017687) 72923 • Map 89,90/270232 • BB **C** • S1 D2 T2 F2 • 1-12 NX • Ⓑ Ⓓ Ⓢ • List • Discounts to RA members

Ian Picken, Lynwood House, 35 Helvellyn Street, CA12 4EP. ☎ (017687) 72398 • Map 89,90/270233 • BB **B** • EM book first £9.50, 6.30-7.30pm • S1 D3 T1 F1 • 1-12 • Ⓥ Ⓓ Ⓢ • 1Cr/C

■ KIRKBY LONSDALE (Carnforth, Lancs)

Simon Nutter, Nutters, 1 Market Sqare, LA6 2AN. ☎ (015242) 72130/72818 • Map 97/612787 • BB **C** • D1 T1 • 1-12 NX • Ⓑ Ⓓ • SC & groups also

■ KIRKBY STEPHEN
COAST TO COAST WALK

☆ Mrs C J Prime, Redmayne House, CA17 4RB. ☎ (017683) 71441 • Map 91/774088 • BB **B** • S1 D1 T1 F1 • 3-10 NX • Ⓓ Ⓢ Ⓡ 🐾

Redmayne House
Kirkby Stephen
Cumbria

A spacious and attractive Georgian home set in a large garden. Children and dogs welcome. Home made bread, walkers' breakfasts, private lounge, parking. £15.00.

Mrs C J Prime   Tel. 017683 71441

☆ Phil & Carol Pepper, Jolly Farmers Guest House, 63 High Street, CA17 4SH. ☎ (017683) 71063 • Map 91/774083 • BB **B/C** • EM £8, 6-9.30pm • S1 D2 T4 F1 • 1-12 • Ⓥ Ⓑ Ⓓ Ⓡ 🐾

Jolly Farmers
Guest House
Kirkby Stephen
Cumbria

Tel. **017683 71063**

Ideally situated on the Coast to Coast Walk. Excellent home cooking: 4 course evening meal £8. Homemade biscuits and tea on arrival. Warm, friendly and informal atmosphere.

Mrs Mary Graham, "Lockholme", 48 South Road, CA17 4SN. ☎ (017683) 71321 • Map 91/772078 • BB **B** • S1 D1 T2 • 1-12 NX • Ⓑ Ⓓ Ⓢ Ⓡ

Mrs C Rennison, Claremont, Nateby Road, CA17 4AJ. ☎ (017683) 71787 • Map 91/775083 • BB **B** • T1 F1 • 3-10 • Ⓑ Ⓓ Ⓢ Ⓡ 🐾

☆ The Old Rectory, Crosby Garrett, CA17 4PW. ☎ (017683) 72074 • Map 91/729094 • BB **C** • EM book first £10 • D2 T1 • 1-12 NX • Ⓑ Ⓓ Ⓢ 🐾 • List/HC • SC also. Display on next page.

☆ See Display Advertisement

B&B ACCOMMODATION ENGLAND CUMBRIA

☆ Jackie & Peter Sriven, Gordon House, 22 North Road, CA17 4RH. ☎ (017683) 71077 • Map 91/774089 • BB **B** • EM book first £8.50 • T2 • 1-12 NX • [V] [D] [S] [R] 🐕

■ LOW ROW (Brampton)

Mrs Annabel Forster, High Nook, CA8 2LU. ☎ (016977) 46273 • Map 86/589644 • BB **A/B** • EM book first £6, 6.30pm • D1 F1 • 5-10 • [V] [D] [S] 🐕 • List

■ LOWICK (Ulverston)

CUMBRIA WAY

Everard Lodge, LA12 8ER. ☎ (01229) 885245 • Map 96,97/285863 • BB **B** • D1 T1 F1 • 1-12 • [D] [S] 🐕 • List/C

Jenny Wickens, Garth Row, Lowick Green, LA12 8EB. ☎ (01229) 885633 • Map 96,97/289856 • BB **B** • D1 F1 • 1-12 NX • [D] [S] 🐕 Ⓜ • List • Transport provided

■ MALLERSTANG (Kirkby Stephen)

ALTERNATIVE PENNINE WAY

Mrs Pauline Hasted, Aisgill Crafts, CA17 4JX. ☎ (017683) 72011 • Map 98/774975 • BB **B** • EM book first £10.50, 7pm • D2 T1 • 1-12 • [V] [D] [S] [R] 🐕 • SC also

Val & John Porter, Faraday Cottage, Outhgill, CA17 4JU. ☎ (017683) 72351 • Map 91/784015 • BB **B** • EM book first £6 • D1 T1 • 1-12 NX • [V] [D] [S] 🐕

■ MILNTHORPE

CUMBRIA COASTAL WAY

Mavis & Trevor Carey, The Homestead, Ackenthwaite, LA7 7DH. ☎ (015395) 63708 • Map 97/504818 • BB **B/C** • EM book first £6, 7pm • S1 T1 F1 • 1-12 • [V] [B] [D] [S]

■ MORLAND (Penrith)

☆ Brian & May Smith, Hill Top House, CA10 3AX. ☎ (01931) 714561 • Map 91/596225 • BB **C** • EM book first £12, 7pm • S1 D1 T1 • 1-12 NX • [V] [B] [D] • 2Cr/C

■ MOTHERBY (Penrith)

☆ Jacquie Freeborn, Motherby House, CA11 0RS. ☎ (017684) 83368 • Map 90/424281 • BB **B** • EM book first £9, 7pm • F4 • 1-12 NX • [V] [B] [D] [S] • SC also

■ MUNGRISDALE (Penrith)

Mr & Mrs G Bambrough, The Old Vicarage, CA11 0XR. ☎ (017687) 79274 • Map 90/363302 • BB **C** • S1 D1 T1 F1 • 1-12 NX • [D] [S]

Mike & Penny Sutton, Bannerdale View, CA11 0XR. ☎ (017687) 79691 • Map 90/363302 • BB **C** • EM book first £12.50, 7pm • D1 T1 • 1-12 NX • [B] [D] [S] 🐕

☆ Colin & Lesley Smith, Mosedale House, Mosedale, CA11 0XQ. ☎ (017687) 79371 • Map 90/362322 • BB **C/D** • EM £12, 7pm • S1 D2 T2 F1 • 1-12 NX • [V] [B] [D] [S] 🐕 • 3Cr/C • Disabled facilities, SC also

NORTH LAKES

Stay in our traditionally built farmhouse, set in magnificent scenery in a quiet corner of the Lakes. Home-baked bread, our own free-range eggs and farm produce. En suite bedrooms B&B or DB&B, packed lunches. Vegetarians welcome. Excellent facilities for disabled people. Non-smokers. Quality cottage to let. Open all year.

SAE for brochure: Mosedale Guest House, Mosedale, Mungrisdale, Cumbria CA11 0XQ.

☎ 017687 79371

BRANDELHOW GUEST HOUSE
1 PORTLAND PLACE, PENRITH
CUMBRIA CA11 7QN
Tel: 01768 864470

Carole & Geoff Tully welcome you to
"BRANDELHOW"

We have 5 tastefully decorated spacious bedrooms all with washbasins, tea/coffee facilities, colour TV and full central heating.
Full English breakfast is served and packed lunches are available.

■ **NEW HUTTON (Kendal)**

Hayside Cottage, LA8 0AG. ☎ (01539) 725827 • Map 97/537905 • BB **B** • EM book first £7 • D1 T1 • 1-12 NX • Ⓥ Ⓓ Ⓢ Ⓡ 🌣

■ **NEWBIGGIN-ON-LUNE (Kirkby Stephen)**
COAST TO COAST WALK

Mrs B Boustead, Tranna Hill, CA17 4NY. ☎ (015396) 23227 • Map 91/705053 • BB **B** • EM book first £8, 6pm • S1 D1 T1 • 1-12 NX • Ⓥ Ⓑ Ⓓ Ⓢ • List

■ **NEWLANDS (Keswick)**
CUMBRIA WAY

Mrs M E Harryman, Keskadale Farm, Newlands Valley, CA12 5TS. ☎ (017687) 78544 • Map 89/ 211193 • BB **B/C** • D2 T1 • 3-11 • Ⓓ Ⓢ • 1Cr/C • SC also

M Beaty, Birkrigg Farm, Newlands Valley, CA12 5TS. ☎ (017687) 78278 • Map 89,90/214194 • BB **B** • S1 D2 T2 F1 • 3-11 • Ⓢ • List/App • SC also

■ **ORTON (Penrith)**
COAST TO COAST WALK

Mrs J Dunford, Berwyn House, CA10 3RQ. ☎ (015396) 24345 • Map 91/623084 • BB **B** • EM book first £7-£9 • D1 T2 • 1-12 • Ⓥ Ⓓ Ⓢ 🌣

Melissa & Colin Levey, The Vicarage, CA10 3RQ. ☎ (015396) 24873 • Map 91/622083 • BB **B** • EM book first £9 • D1 T2 • 1-12 • Ⓥ Ⓓ Ⓢ 🌣 • List/C

■ **PENRITH**

Miss D Robinson, Corner House, 36 Victoria Road, CA11 8HR. ☎ (01768) 863566 • Map 90/518297 • BB **B** • EM book first £9, from 6pm • D2 T1 • 3-10 • Ⓥ Ⓓ Ⓡ 🌣

Mrs Ann Clark, The Friargate, Friargate, CA11 7XR. ☎ (01768) 863635 • Map 90/517300 • BB **B/C** • S1 D1 T1 F1 • 4-9 • Ⓓ Ⓢ Ⓡ 🌣

☆ Mrs Carole Tully, Brandelhow Guest House, 1 Portland Place, CA11 7QN. ☎ (01768) 864470 • Map 90/514305 • BB **B** • D2 T2 F1 • 1-12 • Ⓓ Ⓢ Ⓡ 🌣 • 1Cr/C

Even if 🌣 is in the listing, check with the proprietor before bringing yours

---

■ **POOLEY BRIDGE (Penrith)**

Mrs Janet Ardley, Elm House, CA10 2NH. ☎ (017684) 86334 • Map 90/472244 • BB **B/C** • D4 T1 • 4-10 • Ⓑ Ⓓ Ⓢ 🌣

☆ Pooley Mill House, Dalemain, CA11 0HB. ☎ (017684) 86063 • Map 90/477260 • BB **B** • D2 F1 • 1-12 NX • Ⓑ Ⓓ Ⓢ

Pooley Mill House
Dalemain, Nr Pooley Bridge

Renovated mill nestling by the River Eamont in a unique peaceful setting with beautiful rural views. Ideal for walking, situated on the route of many footpaths and close to Ullswater Lake and the fells.

Tel: 017684 86063

■ **PORTINSCALE (Keswick)**
CUMBRIA WAY

☆ Bryan & Jenny Jackson, The Mount, CA12 5RD. ☎ (017687) 73070 • Map 89,90/254236 • BB **B/C** • S1 D3 T1 • 1-12 NX • Ⓑ Ⓓ Ⓢ Ⓜ • 2Cr • SC also

---

THE MOUNT
PORTINSCALE, KESWICK, CUMBRIA CA12 5RD

A comfortable Victorian guest house in quiet location overlooking Derwentwater. Non-smoking. En-suite rooms. Private car park. Drying facilities. A warm welcome and good breakfast guaranteed.

☎ 017687 73070

■ **RAVENGLASS**
CUMBRIA COASTAL WAY

☆ "Rosegarth", Main Street, CA18 1SQ. ☎ (01229) 717275 • Map 96/084964 • BB **C** • S1 D3 T1 F1 • 1-12 NX • Ⓑ Ⓓ Ⓢ Ⓡ • 2Cr. Display on next page.

■ **RAVENSTONEDALE (Kirkby Stephen)**
COAST TO COAST WALK

Mr & Mrs C Irwin, The Book House, Grey Garth, CA17 4NQ. ☎ (015396) 23634 • Map 91/723041 • BB **B** • S1 T1 F1 • 1-12 NX • Ⓓ Ⓢ 🐾

■ **ROSGILL (Penrith)**
COAST TO COAST WALK

John & Julia Gowling, Rosgill Head Farm, CA10 2QX. ☎ (01931) 716 254 • Map 90/543169 • BB **B** • EM book first £7, 7.30pm • D/S1 F/T1 • 1-12 • Ⓥ Ⓓ 🐾

■ **SEDBERGH**
DALES WAY

☆ Mike & Liz Clark, Farfield Country Guest House, Hawes Road, LA10 5LP. ☎ (015396) 20537 • Map 98/677919 • BB **C/D** • EM £11, 6.30pm • S1 D4 T1 F1 • 1-12 NX • Ⓥ Ⓑ Ⓓ Ⓢ 🐾 • SC & groups also

☆ Mrs J Snow, Randall Hill, LA10 5HJ. ☎ (015396) 20633 • Map 97/649917 • BB **B** • D1 T2 • 1-12 • Ⓓ Ⓢ 🐾

Mrs S Sharrocks, Holmecroft, Station Road, LA10 5DW. ☎ (015396) 20754 • Map 97/650919 • BB **B** • D2 T1 • 1-12 NX • Ⓓ Ⓢ 🐾

☆ Mrs Jill Jarvis, The Moss House, Garsdale Road, LA10 5JL. ☎ (015396) 20940 • Map 98/670917 • BB **B** • EM book first £9.50, 7pm • D1 T1 F1 • 3-11 • Ⓥ Ⓑ Ⓓ Ⓢ

Miss M Thurlby, Stable Antiques, 15 Back Lane, LA10 5AQ. ☎ (015396) 20251 • Map 97/659921 • BB **B** • D1 T1 • 1-12 • Ⓓ 🐾

D Liddey-Smith, Turvey House, LA10 5DJ. ☎ (015396) 20841 • Map 97/654921 • BB **B** • D1 T1 F1 • 1-12 • Ⓓ Ⓢ • C

☆ Pat & Paul Ramsden, Sun Lea, Joss Lane, LA10 5AS. ☎ (015396) 20828 • Map 97/658922 • BB **B** • D2 T1 • 1-12 NX • Ⓓ Ⓢ • List

SUN LEA
Joss Lane
Sedbergh,
Cumbria LA10 5AS
Tel. 015396 20828

Enjoy superb walking on the Howgill Fells from the door of our Victorian house. Close to the Dales Way and the Western Yorkshire Dales. Run by walkers — maps, guidebooks and local knowledge available. Eating places close by.

Pat & Paul Ramsden

Mrs M R Swainbank, 25 Bainbridge Road, LA10 5AU. ☎ (015396) 20685 • Map 97/657922 • BB **A/B** • D1 T1 F1 • 3-10 • Ⓑ Ⓓ Ⓢ Ⓜ

Mrs J C Baines, 19 Bainbridge Road, LA10 5AU. ☎ (015396) 20638/20799 • Map 97/657922 • BB **A/B** • S1 D1 T1 • 1-12 NX • Ⓓ Ⓢ

Mrs M C Hoggarth, The Myers, Joss Lane, LA10 5AS. ☎ (015396) 20257 • Map 97/658922 • BB **A/B** • S1 D1 T1 • 1-12 • Ⓓ Ⓢ

☆ Mrs Barbara Wilson, St Mark's, Cautley, LA10 5LZ. ☎ (015396) 20287 • Map 98/690944 • BB **C** • EM book first £10, 7-7.30pm • S1 T3 F1 • 1-12 NX • Ⓥ Ⓑ Ⓓ Ⓢ 🐾 • 2Cr • Groups also

ST. MARK'S
CAUTLEY, SEDBERGH LA10 5LZ

Treat yourself to the tranquility of the Howgill Fells and Western Dales. Outstanding setting, National Park, comfortable en-suite rooms, Grade II listed, open fires, home cooking. Also courses—guided walks, calligraphy, needlecrafts.

☎ Barbara Wilson 015396 20287

Mrs Anne Jones, Yew Tree Cottage, 35 Loftus Hill, LA10 5SQ. ☎ (015396) 21600 • Map 97/658917 • BB **C** • EM book first £9.50, 7pm • D1 T1 • 1-12 NX • Ⓥ Ⓓ Ⓢ 🐾

■ SHAP (Penrith)
COAST TO COAST WALK

Mrs Audrey Kirkby, New Ing Farm, CA10 3LX. ☎ (01931) 716661 • Map 90/562156 • BB **B** • S2 D7 T4 F2 • 4-10 • Ⓑ Ⓓ 🐾

Mrs Margaret Brunskill, "Brookfield", CA10 3PZ. ☎ (01931) 716397 • Map 90/565144 • BB **B** • EM book first £14, 8pm • S1 D4 T3 F2 • 3-12 NX • Ⓥ Ⓑ Ⓓ Ⓢ

Val & Peter Harrison, Fell House, CA10 3NY. ☎ (01931) 716343 • Map 90/564147 • BB **B** • S2 T4 F1 • 1-12 NX • Ⓓ 🐾

☆ Jean & Joshua Jackson, The Hermitage, CA10 3LX. ☎ (01931) 716671 • Map 90/562154 • BB **A/B/C** • EM book first £9, 6.30-8.30pm • S1 D1 T2 • 1-12 NX • Ⓥ Ⓑ Ⓓ Ⓢ

THE HERMITAGE GUEST HOUSE
Shap, Cumbria

Charming old Jacobean farmhouse in the village of Shap. **Coast to Coast Walk** goes past the door. Walkers very welcome. Ideally situated for the Fells of the Eastern Lakes and the Howgills. Very convenient for overnighting en route to **Scotland** and for **Birdwatching at Haweswater**. Discount for parties of six or more. Delicious home cooking. En suite facilities with colour TV etc.

Tel. 01931 716671

■ SKELWITH BRIDGE (Ambleside)
CUMBRIA WAY

Lilian & Phil Green, Greenbank, LA22 9NW. ☎ (015394) 33236 • Map 90/343027 • BB **C** • D2 T1 • 1-12 NX • Ⓑ Ⓓ Ⓢ • 2Cr/HC

■ ST BEES
COAST TO COAST WALK & CUMBRIA COASTAL WAY

☆ Mrs E M Smith & Ms C M Smith, Stonehouse Farm, Main Street, CA27 0DE. ☎ (01946) 822224 • Map 89/971119 • BB **B** • D1 T4 F1 • 1-12 • Ⓑ Ⓓ Ⓡ 🐾 Ⓜ • App/List

STONEHOUSE FARM
Main Street
St Bees, Cumbria
(two mins railway station)

Comfortable modernised Georgian farmhouse, all amenities. CH, CTV, B&B band B. Warm welcome. Coast to Coast route, near shops and beach, ideal walking area, golf, fishing. Car park. Centre of village.

Tel. Mrs E M Smith & Ms C M Smith
Egremont (01946) 822224

Mrs L Moffat, Outrigg House, CA27 0AN. ☎ (01946) 822348 • Map 89/972115 • BB **B** • S1 T1 F/T/D1 • 1-11 NX • Ⓓ Ⓢ Ⓡ 🐾 • List

Mrs Barbara Barwise, Bell House Farm, St Bees Road, CA28 9UE. ☎ (01946) 692584 • Map 89/978143 • BB **B** • S2 T2 F1 • 1-12 NX • Ⓑ Ⓓ Ⓡ 🐾

☆ Mr & Mrs Whitehead, 1 Tomlin House, Beach Road, CA27 0EN. ☎ (01946) 822284 • Map 89/963118 • BB **B** • EM book first £6.50, 6.30pm • D1 T2 F1 • 1-12 NX • Ⓥ Ⓑ Ⓓ Ⓢ Ⓡ 🐾. Display over page.

FOUND A GOOD B&B THAT'S NOT IN THE YEARBOOK?
Send us recommendations for future editions

CUMBRIA ENGLAND ACCOMMODATION B&B

173

■ STAVELEY (Kendal)
DALES WAY

Mrs Betty Fishwick, Stock Bridge Farm, LA8 9LP. ☎ (01539) 821580 • Map 97/475977 • BB **B** • S1 D4 F1 • 3-10 NX • Ⓓ Ⓡ ♨ • List/C

■ THORNTHWAITE (Keswick)
CUMBRIA WAY

Mr & Mrs J & M Pepper, Beckstones Farm, CA12 5SQ. ☎ (017687) 78510 • Map 89,90/221264 • BB **C** • D3 T2 • 2-11 • Ⓑ Ⓓ Ⓢ ♨ • 2Cr/C

■ ULPHA (Broughton-in-Furness)

Ray & Susan Batten, Oakbank Guest House, Ulpha, Duddon Valley, LA20 6DZ. ☎ (01229) 716393 • Map 96/201938 • BB **C** • EM book first £9, 7pm • D2 T1 • 1-11 NX • Ⓥ Ⓓ ♨ • 1Cr

■ ULVERSTON
CUMBRIA WAY & CUMBRIA COASTAL WAY

☆ Trinity House Hotel, Princes Street, LA12 7NB. ☎ (01229) 587639 • Map 96,97/285780 • BB **C/D** • EM £15.95, 7-9pm • S1 D4 T2 F1 • 1-12 • Ⓥ Ⓑ Ⓓ Ⓡ ♨ • 3Cr/C

Mike & Pat Ramsay, "Rock House", 1 Alexander Road, LA12 0DE. ☎ (01229) 586879 • Map 96,97/287779 • BB **B** • EM book first £8.50, 6pm • S1 F/D/T3 • 1-12 NX • Ⓥ Ⓓ Ⓢ Ⓡ • 1Cr/C

■ WASDALE HEAD (Gosforth)
COAST TO COAST WALK & CUMBRIA WAY

Mrs A Buchanan, Burnthwaite Farm, Seascale, CA20 1EX. ☎ (019467) 26242 • Map 89/193091 • BB **C** • EM book first £12, 7pm • S2 D3 T2 F1 • 3-10 • Ⓓ

■ WATERMILLOCK (Penrith)

Ian & Dorothy Bewley, Fair Place, CA11 0LR. ☎ (017684) 86235 • Map 90/435228 • BB **C** • S1 D1 T1 F1 • 2-11 • Ⓑ Ⓓ Ⓢ ♨ • Food nearby

Barbara Holmes, Land Ends, Watermillock, Ullswater, CA11 0NB. ☎ (017684) 86438 • Map 90/437252 • BB **D** • S3 D4 T2 • 1-12 • Ⓑ Ⓓ Ⓢ Ⓜ • 2Cr/C • SC also

■ WINDERMERE
DALES WAY

Cynthia & Tony Roberts, Kenilworth Guest House, Holly Road, LA23 2AF. ☎ (015394) 44004 • Map 96,97/413981 • BB **B** • S1 D2 T2 F1 • 1-12 • Ⓑ Ⓓ Ⓢ Ⓡ ♨ • Transport also

☆ Bob & Maureen Theobald, Oldfield House, Oldfield Road, LA23 2BY. ☎ (015394) 88445 • Map 96,97/411979 • BB **C/D** • S2 D3 T1 F2 • 2-12 • Ⓑ Ⓓ Ⓢ Ⓡ 2Cr/C

Mr & Mrs Tyson, Holly-wood Guest House, Holly Road, LA23 2AF. ☎ (015394) 42219 • Map 96,97/413981 • BB **B/C** • S1 D2 T2 F2 • 3-11 NX • Ⓑ Ⓓ Ⓢ Ⓡ

Mr & Mrs Capper, Upper Oakmere, 3 Upper Oak Street, LA23 2LB. ☎ (015394) 45649 • Map 96,97/415982 • BB **B** • EM book first £6.95, 5.30-6.30pm • S1 D2 T/D1 F2 • 1-12 • Ⓥ Ⓑ Ⓡ ♨

☆ Rod & Pauline Charnock, Thornbank Hotel, Thornbarrow Road, LA23 2EW. ☎ (015394) 43724 • Map 96,97/409975 • BB **C** • EM book first £12, 6.45pm • S1 D8 T2 F2 • 1-12 NX • Ⓥ Ⓑ Ⓢ Ⓡ • 2Cr/C

B&B ACCOMMODATION ENGLAND CUMBRIA

THORNBANK PRIVATE HOTEL

Thornbarrow Road, Windermere, Cumbria LA23 2EW

Small, family-run hotel situated in a quiet residential area close to all amenities. Comfortable rooms, some ensuite, all with Sky TV. Ample car parking. Free use of leisure club facilities. Bargain breaks. B&B or D,B&B available. Table licence. 🏆🏆 COMMENDED

Tel/Fax Windermere (015394) 43724

Mrs P Wood, The Haven, 10 Birch Street, LA23 1EG. ☎ (015394) 44017 • Map 96,97/413984 • BB **B** • S1 F3 • 1-12 • D S R 🛁

Stephanie Townsend, "Aaron Slack", 48 Ellerthwaite Road, LA23 2BS. ☎ (015394) 44649 • Map 96,97/412980 • BB **B/C** • S1 D2 T1 • 1-12 • B D S R • 1Cr/C

☆ Mr & Mrs A S Priestley, Holly Lodge, 6 College Road, LA23 1BX. ☎ (015394) 43873 • Map 96,97/411985 • BB **B/C** • EM book first £11, 6.30pm • S1 D5 T2 F3 • 1-12 NX • B D S R • 2Cr/C

HOLLY LODGE GUEST HOUSE

6 College Rd,
Windermere,
Cumbria,
LA23 1BX

Situated in the village close to shops, buses and trains. B&B. EM optional. Family run. Good home cooking. Friendly atmosphere.

Tel/Fax: 015394 43873

☆ Mrs F Holcroft, Lynwood, Broad Street, LA23 2AB. ☎ (015394) 42550 • Map 96,97/413982 • BB **B/C** • S1 D4 T1 F3 • 1-12 NX • B D S R • 2Cr/C • Groups also

LYNWOOD

Broad Street, Windermere LA23 2AB

Relax in our elegant Victorian house in the heart of Windermere. Each bedroom is individually furnished and smoke-free with en-suite shower and wc, colour TV, hairdryer & beverages. Convenient for bus and train stations and close to parking. From £26 per night for a double room with reductions for families.

Tel (015394) 42550

AA QQQ   RAC acclaimed   ETB commended 🏆🏆

☆ John & Liz Christopherson, "Villa Lodge", Cross Street, LA23 1AE. ☎ (015394) 43318 • Map 96,97/412986 • BB **C** • S1 D2 T2 F2 • 1-12 • B D S R • 2Cr/C

Villa Lodge Guest House
Windermere

Friendliness and cleanliness guaranteed. Two minutes from Station/ Restaurants. Seven lovely bedrooms mostly en suite, with beautiful views. Full central heating. All rooms with colour TV, tea/coffee facilities. Private safe parking. Open all year. Excellent base for exploring whole of Lake District.

Tel. John & Liz Christopherson
015394 43318

DERBYSHIRE

■ ALDERWASLEY (Belper)

☆ Ye Olde Bear Inn, DE4 4GD. ☎ (01629) 822585 • BB **C** • EM £5, 6.30-9.30pm • S2 D6 T1 F1 • 1-12 • V B D R 🛁

Ye Olde Bear Inn
by Alderwasley
on the Belper-Wirksworth road

Coaching Inn dating back to 16th century. Ideal for rambling and exploring the Peak District. Nine ensuite rooms. Caravan/camping facilities. Restaurant open 7 days a week.
Telephone 01629 822585

■ ALSTONEFIELD
WHITE PEAK WAY

Beverley Griffin, Greenhills Cottage, DE6 2FT. ☎ (01335) 310499 • Map 119/127566 • BB **B** • D1 F1 • 1-12 NX • D S 🛁

☆ See Display Advertisement

■ ASHBOURNE

Mrs Carole Eastwood, The Old Kennels, Birdsgrove Lane, Mayfield, DE6 2BP. ☎ (01335) 344418 • Map 128,119/156470 • BB **B** • D1 F1 • 3-10 • Ⓓ • List

☆ Blore Hall, DE6 2BS. ☎ (01335) 350525 • Map 119/138495 • BB **C/D** • EM £6.95, 5.30-9pm • D18 T8 F18 • 1-12 NX • Ⓥ Ⓑ Ⓓ • 3Cr/C

BLORE HALL

👑👑👑 Commended

Fourteenth century farmhouse overlooking Dovedale. Miles of footpaths and open access. Log fires, heated indoor pool. Freshly cooked traditional food. Licensed bar. Ensuite rooms/cottages sleeping 2-8

Brochure 01335 350525

■ BAKEWELL

WHITE PEAK WAY

☆ Mrs K Pheasey, Bourne House, The Park, Haddon Road, DE45 1AW. ☎ (01629) 813274 • Map 119/219682 • BB **B/C** • D2 T1 • 1-12 NX • Ⓑ Ⓓ Ⓢ

BOURNE HOUSE

The Park, Haddon Road, Bakewell

Friendly and comfortable accommodation in former manse alongside Bakewell's park. A short riverside stroll to town centre amenities. 2 rooms en-suite. All rooms have CH, tea-making and H&C. Residents' TV lounge. Private off-road car park.

Mrs K. H. Pheasey
☎ **Bakewell (01629) 813274**

☆ Fieldsview, Station Road, Great Longstone, DE45 1TS. ☎ (01629) 640593 • Map 119/198714 • BB **B** • EM book first £7, 7pm • D2 T/S1 • 1-12 NX • Ⓥ Ⓓ Ⓢ • List

FIELDSVIEW

Station Road, Great Longstone, Bakewell

Stone built house in peaceful, rural position in the Peak National Park. Ideally situated for walks and touring. Lots of local knowledge, books and maps available for use of guests. Central heating, open fire in lounge and delicious home cooking.

☎ **01629 640593**

☆ Mrs J M Westley, Avenue House, Haddon Road, DE45 1EP. ☎ (01629) 812467 • Map 119/221678 • BB **C** • D2 T1 • 2-11 NX • Ⓑ Ⓓ Ⓢ • 2Cr

AVENUE HOUSE

HADDON ROAD, BAKEWELL DE45 1EP

Situated in the centre of the Peak District, near to town centre. A large elegant Victorian house with central heating. Comfortable rooms, 3 en suite, with H&C, TV, tea/coffee. Lounge with TV. Car Parking.

Mrs J M Westley
01629 812467

Mr & Mrs G Lunn, Riversdale Farm, Coombs Road, DE45 1AR. ☎ (01629) 813586 • Map 119/237676 • BB **C** • EM book first £8, 6.30pm • S1 D1 T1 • 1-12 NX • Ⓥ Ⓓ Ⓢ 🐾 • 1Cr

☆ Mrs J Parker, Lathkill Cottage, Over Haddon, DE45 1JE. ☎ (01629) 814518 • Map 119/204664 • BB **C** • T1 • 1-12 NX • Ⓑ Ⓓ Ⓢ • SC also

LATHKILL COTTAGE

Over Haddon, Bakewell, Derbyshire DE45 1JE

Self-contained, en suite room overlooking Lathkill Dale. Excellent breakfasts.

Mrs Judith Parker

Tel/Fax 01629 814518

Melbourne House, Buxton Road, DE45 1DA. ☎ (01629) 815357 • Map 119/216686 • BB **C** • D2 T1 • 1-12 • Ⓑ Ⓓ Ⓢ 🐾 • 2Cr/C

■ BAMFORD (Hope Valley)

WHITE PEAK WAY

☆ Janet Treacher, Pioneer House, Station Road, S30 2BN. ☎ (01433) 650638 • Map 110/207825 • BB **B/C** • D2 T1 • 1-12 • Ⓑ Ⓓ Ⓢ Ⓡ Ⓜ • 2Cr/C

PIONEER HOUSE

Station Road, Bamford, Derbyshire

Delightfully furnished, comfortable accommodation in the heart of the Peak District provides ideal base for rambling, climbing etc. All rooms have en suite/private facilities, colour television and tea/coffee provided. Ample parking and secure cycle facilities, drying room. Transport to the start of your walk available.

Please contact Dave and Janet Treacher on:
Hope Valley (01433) 650638

Ye Derwent Hotel

Main Road, Bamford, Derbyshire S30 2AY
Tel. 01433 651395   AA QQ   ETB 👑👑

*Set amongst the
rolling hills of the
Peak National Park,
the Derwent Hotel is
a traditional 100 year
old inn with 10
bedrooms ◆ Noted for its food, ale and country
friendliness ◆ Open all year ◆ B&B from £20.
DB&B from £27.50 pp/pn ◆ Secure area for cycles.*

Sue Davies, Apple Croft, Fidler's Well, S30 2AR. ☎
(01433) 651495 • Map 110/208835 • BB **B/C** • S1 D1
T/F1 • 1-12 NX • Ⓓ Ⓢ Ⓡ

■ **BASLOW (Bakewell)**
WHITE PEAK WAY

Mrs Ruth Evans, The Fountain House, Hydro Close,
DE45 1SH. ☎ (01246) 582156 • Map 119/257726 •
BB **B** • S1 D1 T1 • 1-11 • Ⓓ Ⓢ • List/C

■ **BIGGIN (Buxton)**
WHITE PEAK WAY

☆ Biggin Hall, SK17 0DH. ☎ (01298) 84451 • Map
119/153594 • BB **C/D** • S2 D5 T6 F4 • 1-12 • Ⓑ Ⓓ
Ⓢ • Groups also

BIGGIN HALL

Biggin-by-Hartington, Buxton, Derbyshire SK17 0DH

Small 17thC Old Hall, 1,000ft up in the
Peak District National Park, close to
Dovedale, in peaceful open countryside
with beautiful uncrowded footpaths and
bridleways. Baths en suite, log fires,
warmth, comfort, quiet, and fresh home
cooked dinner. Licensed. For free brochure
telephone:

Hartington (01298) 84451

■ **BONSALL (Matlock)**

Sycamore Guest House, 76 High Street, Town Head,
DE4 2AA. ☎ (01629) 823903 • Map 119/279580 • BB
C/D • S1 D2 T2 F1 • 1-12 • Ⓑ Ⓓ Ⓢ Ⓡ

Mrs L E Cordin, Townhead Farmhouse, 70 High
Street, DE4 2AR. ☎ (01629) 823762 • Map 119/
278584 • BB **C** • D3 T1 • 1-12 • Ⓑ Ⓓ Ⓡ 🐾 • 2Cr

■ **BRADWELL (Sheffield)**
WHITE PEAK WAY

Janet Maskrey, Ashbrook, Brookside, S30 2HF. ☎
(01433) 620803 • Map 110/173811 • BB **B/C** • D2 T1
• 1-12 NX • Ⓓ Ⓢ Ⓡ

■ **BUXTON**

☆ Mrs S Pritchard, Devonshire Lodge Guest House,
2 Manchester Road, SK17 6SB. ☎ (01298) 71487 •
Map 119/055738 • BB **B** • D2 T1 • 3-11 • Ⓑ Ⓓ Ⓡ 🐾
• 2Cr

DEVONSHIRE LODGE GUEST HOUSE

2 Manchester Road, Buxton Derbyshire SK17 6SB

Family guesthouse run to highest standards. Ideally
situated for Goyt Valley, Manifold and Dovedale.
3 minutes from Buxton Opera House and Pavilion
Gardens. TV and tea-making facilities in all rooms.
Private car park. Good home cooking.
B&B from £14. 3 & 5 day breaks from £13.80
—not available bank holidays.

Tel. 01298 71487

☆ M A Roberts, Ford Side House, 125 Lightwood
Road, SK17 6RW. ☎ (01298) 72842 • Map
119/059743 • BB **C** • EM book first £11, 7pm • D3 T1
• 3-10 NX • Ⓥ Ⓑ Ⓓ Ⓢ Ⓡ 🐾 • 3Cr/C

FORD SIDE HOUSE
125 Lightwood Road
Buxton, Derbyshire SK17 6RW

*Elegant Edwardian house for non-smokers,
situated in a premier residential area yet very close
to town attractions, Peaks and Dales.
All guest rooms en-suite with full amenities,
drying facilities for walkers, private parking. Full
Fire Certificate. We are licensed to supply wines
and spirits to compliment our delicious food.
B&B £19. Short Break, Long Stay and
Low Season Discounts
Brochure Available.*
Proprietors John & Margaret Roberts

Tel 01298 72842

ETB
👑👑👑
Commended

☆ Mr & Mrs F Howlett, Buxton View, 74 Corbar Road, SK17 6RJ. ☎ (01298) 79222 • Map 119/056742 • BB **C** • EM £10, 7pm • S1 D2 T1 F1 • 1-12 NX • Ⓥ Ⓑ Ⓓ Ⓢ Ⓡ ⚓ • 3Cr/C

Mrs H R Taylor, "Hilldene", 97 Dale Road, SK17 6PD. ☎ (01298) 23015 • Map 119/061731 • BB **B** • S1 T1 F1 • 3-11 NX • Ⓑ Ⓓ Ⓡ ⚓ • 2Cr

☆ Bernard & Jill Harrison, Overglen, 4 White Knowle Road, SK17 9NH. ☎ (01298) 23004 • Map 119/061723 • BB **C** • EM book first £9.50, 7pm • S1 D1 T1 • 1-12 NX • Ⓥ Ⓑ Ⓓ Ⓢ Ⓡ • 2Cr/C

☆ Patty & Alex Hoskin, Stoneridge, 9 Park Road, SK17 6SG. ☎ (01298) 26120 • Map 119/055737 • BB **C** • D2 T1 F1 • 2-12 NX • Ⓑ Ⓓ Ⓢ Ⓡ ⚓ • 2Cr/HC

☆ The Buckingham Hotel, 1 Burlington Road, SK17 9AS. ☎ (01298) 70481 • Map 119/054734 • BB **D** • EM £14, 7.30-9.30pm • S3 D15 T9 F4 • 1-12 • Ⓥ Ⓑ Ⓓ Ⓡ ⚓ • 4Cr/HC • Groups also

☆ Mrs Hilary Parker, Grendon, Bishops Lane, SK17 6UN. ☎ (01298) 78831 • Map 119/044731 • BB **C** • EM £8, 6-9pm • S1 D2 T1 • 1-12 NX • Ⓥ Ⓑ Ⓓ Ⓢ Ⓡ ⚓ • 2Cr/C

■ **CALVER**
WHITE PEAK WAY

Dianne Payne, Pear Tree Cottage, Main Street, S30 1XR. ☎ (01433) 631243 • Map 119/238745 • BB **B** • EM book first £8, 6-7.30pm • S2 • 1-12 NX • Ⓥ Ⓑ Ⓓ Ⓢ Ⓡ

■ **CASTLETON (Sheffield)**
WHITE PEAK WAY

Mrs L Farrand, The Lodge, Back Street, S30 2WE. ☎ (01433) 620526 • Map 110/150828 • BB **C** • S1 D1 T1 • 3-11 • Ⓓ Ⓢ Ⓡ

Mrs B Johnson, Myrtle Cottage, Market Place, S30 2WQ. ☎ (01433) 620787 • Map 110/150828 • BB **C** • D3 F2 • 1-12 NX • Ⓑ Ⓓ Ⓡ

B&B ACCOMMODATION ENGLAND DERBYSHIRE

☆ Swiss House, How Lane, S30 2WJ. ☎ (01433) 621098 • Map 110/153831 • BB **D** • EM £12.50, 6.30-8pm • S1 D5 T3 F1 • 1-12 • Ⓥ Ⓑ Ⓓ Ⓢ Ⓡ • 3Cr/C

☆ Hillside House, Pindale Road, S30 2WU. ☎ (01433) 620312 • Map 110/151827 • BB **C** • D2 T1 • 1-11 • Ⓑ Ⓓ Ⓢ Ⓡ • 2Cr

Mr & Mrs T Skelton, Cryer House, S30 2WG. ☎ (01433) 620244 • Map 110/149829 • BB **B** • D2 F1 • 1-12 NX • Ⓓ Ⓢ Ⓡ 🐾

☆ Mary Gillott, Rambler's Rest, Back Street, Mill Bridge, S30 2WR. ☎ (01433) 620125 • Map 110/150831 • BB **B/C/D** • S2 D5 T2 F1 • 1-12 NX • Ⓑ Ⓓ Ⓡ 🐾 • C

■ **EDALE (Sheffield)**
PENNINE WAY & WHITE PEAK WAY

J E Chapman, Brookfield, S30 2ZL. ☎ (01433) 670227 • Map 110/113847 • BB **B** • D1 T1 • 3-10 • Ⓓ Ⓢ Ⓡ

Mrs J Beney, The Old Parsonage, Grindsbrook, S30 2ZD. ☎ (01433) 670232 • Map 110/122860 • BB **A/B** • S1 D1 T1 • 3-10 • Ⓓ Ⓢ Ⓡ

☆ Julia Reid, Stonecroft, S30 2ZA. ☎ (01433) 670262/0378 517656 • Map 110/122854 • BB **D** • EM book first £15, 7.30pm • D2 • 1-12 NX • Ⓥ Ⓑ Ⓓ Ⓢ Ⓡ • 2Cr/C

Mrs Judith Shirt, Ladybooth Hall Farm, S30 2ZH. ☎ (01433) 670282 • Map 110/142861 • BB **B** • EM book first £7, 6-7.30pm • S1 D1 T1 F1 • 2-11 • Ⓥ Ⓓ Ⓡ 🐾

Mrs Sally Gee, Cotefield Farm, S30 2ZG. ☎ (01433) 670273 • Map 110/129858 • BB **B** • D1 F1 • 1-12 NX • Ⓢ Ⓡ • SC also

☆ See Display Advertisement

B&B ACCOMMODATION ENGLAND DERBYSHIRE

179

■ ELTON (Matlock)
WHITE PEAK WAY

☆ J Hirst, Elton Guest House, Moor Lane, DE4 2DA. ☎ (01629) 650217 • Map 119/221608 • BB **B** • D2 T1 F1 • 1-12 NX • Ⓑ Ⓓ Ⓢ • SC also

■ GLOSSOP
PENNINE WAY

R & A Mills, Birds Nest Cottage, 40 Primrose Lane, SK13 8EW. ☎ (01457) 853478 • Map 110/025939 • BB **B** • S1 T3 F1 • 1-12 NX • Ⓓ Ⓢ Ⓡ

Margaret Child, Rock Farm, Monks Road, SK13 9JZ. ☎ (01457) 861086 • Map 110/027907 • BB **B** • D1 T1 • 1-12 NX • Ⓓ

Stanley Farm, Chunal, SK13 9JY. ☎ (01457) 863727 • Map 110/033905 • BB **B** • EM book first £8.50, 7.30pm • D2 T1 • 1-12 • Ⓥ Ⓑ Ⓓ Ⓢ Ⓡ

1 Manor Park Road, Old Glossop, SK13 9SQ. ☎ (01457) 852559 • Map 110/042946 • BB **B** • D1 T1 • 1-12 NX • Ⓑ Ⓓ Ⓢ Ⓡ

■ GRANGEMILL (Matlock)
WHITE PEAK WAY

Avondale Farm, Ible, DE4 4HT. ☎ (01629) 650820 • Map 119/244577 • BB **C/D** • T1 • 1-12 NX • Ⓑ Ⓓ Ⓢ • 2Cr

■ HARTINGTON (Buxton)
WHITE PEAK WAY

Mrs B Blackburn, Bank House, Market Place, SK17 0AL. ☎ (01298) 84465 • Map 119/128604 • BB **B/C** • EM book first £8.50, 6pm • D2 T2 F1 • 1-12 NX • Ⓥ Ⓑ Ⓓ Ⓢ Ⓜ

The Devonshire Arms, Market Place, SK17 0AW. ☎ (01298) 84232 • Map 119/131605 • BB **C** • EM £5, 7-9pm • D2 T2 • 1-12 NX • Ⓥ

■ HATHERSAGE (Sheffield)
WHITE PEAK WAY

Mrs M Venning, The Old Vicarage, Church Bank, S30 1AB. ☎ (01433) 651099 • Map 110/234818 • BB **C** • D2 T1 • 1-12 NX • Ⓑ Ⓓ Ⓢ Ⓡ • 2Cr

Mrs Joyce Waterhouse, Tall Trees, Ranmoor Lane, S30 1BW. ☎ (01433) 650680 • Map 110/226818 • BB **B** • S2 D1 • 1-12 NX • Ⓓ Ⓡ

Mrs J Wilcockson, Hillfoot Farm, Castleton Rd, S30 1AH. ☎ (01433) 651673 • Map 110/219818 • BB **B/C** • D3 T2 • 1-12 • Ⓑ Ⓓ Ⓢ Ⓡ • List/C

Nora Hickey, York Villa, Station Road, S30 1DD. ☎ (01433) 650339 • Map 110/230813 • BB **B** • D1 T2 • 1-12 • Ⓓ Ⓢ Ⓡ

■ HAYFIELD (High Peak)
PENNINE WAY

Sheila Collier, The Old Bank House, SK12 5EP. ☎ (01663) 747354 • Map 110/036871 • BB **C** • EM book first £12, 7.30pm • D2 T1 F1 • 1-12 • Ⓥ Ⓓ Ⓢ Ⓜ

■ HIGHAM (Alfreton)

Bettyann Banham, Holly Tree Farm, DE55 6EF. ☎ (01773) 832614 • Map 119/391593 • BB **B/C** • EM book first £6.50-£8.50, 6-8pm • S1 D1 T1 F2 • 1-12 NX • Ⓥ Ⓑ Ⓓ Ⓢ • List/App

■ HOLYMOORSIDE (Chesterfield)

P Bentley, 35 Holymoor Road, S42 7EB. ☎ (01246) 566925 • Map 119/338695 • BB **B** • EM £4.50, 6-8pm • S1 D2 F1 • 1-12 • Ⓥ Ⓓ Ⓢ Ⓜ • List/App • Transport also

■ HOPE
WHITE PEAK WAY

☆ The Woodroffe Arms Hotel, 1 Castleton Road, S30 2RD. ☎ (01433) 620351 • Map 110/172835 • BB **D** • EM bar menu • D2 T1 • 1-12 • Ⓥ Ⓑ Ⓓ Ⓢ Ⓡ • 3Cr/C

DERBYSHIRE   ENGLAND   ACCOMMODATION B&B

☆ Underleigh House, Off Edale Road, S30 2RF. ☎ (01433) 621372 • Map 110/172836 • BB **D** • EM book first £15.25, 7.30pm • S1 D4 T2 • 1-12 • Ⓥ Ⓑ Ⓓ Ⓢ Ⓡ • 3Cr/HC

Underleigh House

off Edale Road, Hope, Derbyshire S30 2RF

19thC farmhouse-style home. All double rooms en suite with glorious views and resident teddybear. Renowned for Gourmet house party dinners and hearty breakfasts. Ideally situated for walkers.

WINNER OF NATIONAL GARDEN COMPETITION FOR BEST HOTEL/GUEST HOUSE GARDEN.

Tel. 01433 621372   Highly
                                      Commended
AA QQQQQ Premier Selected   ❀❀❀

Moorgate, off Edale Road, S30 2RF. ☎ (01433) 621219 • Map 110/172836 • BB **C/D** • EM £9.50, 7pm • S8 D3 T16 • 1-12 • Ⓥ Ⓑ Ⓓ Ⓢ Ⓡ Ⓜ • Groups also

☆ Mill Farm, Edale Road, S30 2RF. ☎ (01433) 621181 • Map 110/171838 • BB **C** • D1 T2 • 1-12 • Ⓓ Ⓢ Ⓡ • List

---

PEAK DISTRICT

Traditional farmhouse home in village setting. Exposed beams, log fires, delightful gardens. Near to footpaths and local hostelries. SUPERB CENTRE FOR WALKING. Private parking • Packed lunches available • Drying facilities • Open all year round • Friendly hospitality with full English breakfast.

Mill Farm, Edale Road, Hope, Derbys S30 2RF
Tel. 01433 621181

■ **ILAM (Ashbourne)**
WHITE PEAK WAY

Mrs M A Richardson, Throwley Hall Farm, DE6 2BB. ☎ (01538) 308202/308243 • Map 119/110526 • BB **B** • D2 T1 F1 • 1-11 NX • Ⓑ Ⓓ 🎨 • 2Cr/C • SC also

Mrs Sue Prince, Beechenhill Farm, DE6 2BD. ☎ (01335) 310274 • Map 119/131512 • BB **C** • D1 F1 • 3-12 NX • Ⓑ Ⓓ Ⓢ • 2Cr/HC • SC also

■ **LITTLE HAYFIELD (High Peak)**
PENNINE WAY

☆ Michael & Diane Dean, Pool Cottage, Park Hall, SK12 5NN. ☎ (01663) 742463 • Map 110/037883 • BB **B/C** • S1 D1 F1 • 1-12 NX • Ⓑ Ⓓ Ⓢ 🎨

This Yearbook now has a special section for people offering accommodation for groups.
See pages 106-119

POOL COTTAGE

Park Hall, LITTLE HAYFIELD, High Peak

Situated in National Trust woodlands in the Peak National Park. Ideally situated for walks and touring. Direct access to open country from door step — Kinder Scout 3 miles. Full central heating, TV lounge with open fire. Drying room.
Telephone 01663 742463

■ **MAPPLETON (Ashbourne)**

Mrs E J Harrison, Little Park Farm, DE6 2BR. ☎ (01335) 350341 • Map 119/157481 • BB **B** • D2 T1 • 3-10 • Ⓓ Ⓢ • SC also

■ **MATLOCK**

Mrs S Elliott, Glendon, Knowleston Place, DE4 3BU. ☎ (01629) 584732 • Map 119/301598 • BB **B** • S1 D2 T2 F1 • 1-12 NX • Ⓓ Ⓢ Ⓡ • 1Cr

☆ Mrs K M Potter, Woodside, Stanton Lees, DE4 2LQ. ☎ (01629) 734320 • Map 119/254632 • BB **B/C** • EM book first £8.50, from 7pm • D2 T1 • 1-12 • Ⓥ Ⓑ Ⓓ Ⓢ

WOODSIDE
Stanton Lees, Matlock

When visiting the Peak District/Derbyshire Dales enjoy a friendly welcoming B&B in a rural Peakland village with panoramic views. Ideal for walking/sightseeing/bird watching. En suite or own bathroom in each bedroom, TV, tea/coffee facilities. EM available. Sorry, no smoking. Chatsworth/Bakewell/Matlock 4½ miles.

Tel Matlock (01629) 734320

Mrs L Buxton, Winstaff Guest House, Derwent Avenue, DE4 3LX. ☎ (01629) 582593 • Map 119/299599 • BB **C** • D5 T1 F1 • 1-12 • Ⓑ Ⓓ Ⓡ 🎨 • 2Cr/App

Jan Rodgers, Derwent House, Knowleston Place, DE4 3BY. ☎ (01629) 584681 • Map 119/301599 • BB **C** • S2 D1 T1 • 1-12 NX • Ⓥ Ⓑ Ⓓ Ⓢ Ⓡ • 2Cr

G N Foster, "The Orchard", 12 Greenaway Lane, Darley Dale, DE4 2QB. ☎ (01629) 734140 • Map 119/281624 • BB **B** • S1 T1 F1 • 3-11 • Ⓓ Ⓢ Ⓡ Ⓜ • List

■ **MATLOCK BATH**

Mrs B Swallow, Beech Hurst, 228 Dale Road, DE4 3RT. ☎ (01629) 56013 • Map 119/297597 • BB **B** • EM book first £7, 6-8pm • S1 D1 T/D/F1 • 1-12 NX • Ⓥ Ⓓ Ⓡ 🎨 • List

☆ See Display Advertisement

■ MAYFIELD (Ashbourne)

☆ Mrs Christine Mellor, Lichfield Guest House, Bridgeview, DE6 2HN. ☎ (01335) 344422 • Map 128,119/156456 • BB **C** • S1 D1 T1 F1 • 1-12 NX • Ⓑ Ⓓ Ⓢ • 2Cr/HC • SC also

■ MIDDLETON-BY-WIRKSWORTH

Pat & Allan Jennings, Rise End House, 10 Rise End, DE4 4LS. ☎ (01629) 825359 • Map 119/279553 • BB **B/C** • D1 F1 • 1-12 NX • Ⓓ Ⓢ

Anne R Jackson, Newlands House, 1 Duke Street, DE4 4NB. ☎ (01629) 825292 • Map 119/276561 • BB **B** • EM book first £6 • S1 D2 • 1-12 NX • Ⓥ Ⓑ Ⓓ Ⓢ Ⓡ 🐾 • List

■ MIDDLETON-BY-YOULGRAVE (Bakewell)
WHITE PEAK WAY

Mrs G F Butterworth, Castle Farm, DE45 1LS. ☎ (01629) 636746 • Map 119/192631 • BB **C** • T1 F1 • 1-12 NX • Ⓑ Ⓓ Ⓢ 🐾 • List

■ MILLER'S DALE (Buxton)
WHITE PEAK WAY

Mrs B McAuliffe, Dale Cottage, SK17 8SN. ☎ (01298) 872400 • Map 119/140734 • BB **C** • EM book first £12, 7-7.30pm • D1 T1 F1 • 1-12 NX • Ⓥ Ⓓ Ⓢ • List/C

■ MONSAL HEAD (Bakewell)

☆ Mrs S Gilbert, Castle Cliffe Private Hotel, DE45 1NL. ☎ (01629) 640258 • Map 119/185716 • BB **D** • EM book first £13, 7pm • D3 T4 F2 • 1-12 • Ⓥ Ⓑ Ⓓ Ⓢ • 2Cr/C

■ MONYASH

Mr & Mrs R H Tyler, Sheldon House, Chapel Street, DE45 1JJ. ☎ (01629) 813067 • Map 119/150666 • BB **C** • D3 • 1-12 NX • Ⓑ Ⓓ Ⓢ • 2Cr/HC • SC also

☆ Gary Mycock, Cheney Lodge, Rowson Farm, Church Street, DE45 1JH. ☎ (01629) 815336/813521 • Map 119/150665 • BB **B/C** • S3 D3 T1 • 1-12 • Ⓑ Ⓓ Ⓢ 🐾 • EM by arrangement

■ SHATTON (Bamford)

Fiona Middleton, The White House, S30 2BG. ☎ (01433) 651487 • Map 110/200818 • BB **B** • S2 D1 T1 • 1-12 • Ⓓ Ⓢ Ⓡ

■ STANSHOPE (Ashbourne)

☆ Naomi Chambers, Stanshope Hall, DE6 2AD. ☎ (01335) 310278 • Map 119/127542 • BB **C/D** • EM book first £18, 7-8pm • D2 T1 • 1-12 NX • Ⓥ Ⓑ Ⓓ Ⓢ • 2Cr/C

■ STANTON-BY-BRIDGE (Derby)

Mrs M Kidd, Ivy House Farm, DE73 1HT. ☎ (01332) 863152 • Map 128/373272 • BB **B/C** • EM book first £8, 8pm • S4 D3 T2 • 1-12 • Ⓥ Ⓑ Ⓓ Ⓢ 🐾

DERBYSHIRE   ENGLAND   B&B ACCOMMODATION

THORPE (Ashbourne)
WHITE PEAK WAY

Mrs B Challinor, The Old Orchard, Stoney Lane, DE6 2AW. ☎ (01335) 350410 • Map 119/157503 • BB **B/C** • S2 D2 • 3-10 • Ⓑ Ⓓ Ⓢ 🐾 • List

☆ Mr F Gould, St Leonard's Cottage, DE6 2AW. ☎ (01335) 350224 • Map 119/155504 • BB **C** • S2 D1 T1 • 1-12 NX • Ⓑ Ⓓ Ⓢ

ST LEONARD'S COTTAGE
THORPE, DOVEDALE
ASHBOURNE, DERBYSHIRE DE6 2AW
The Cottage is situated on Thorpe village green. Central for touring or walking in the Peak District. All rooms en suite and 1 single room. Central heating, parking, tea/coffee. Licenced, fire certificate, TV lounge. Sorry no smoking or pets in the house.
Tel. (01335) 350224

TIDESWELL (Buxton)
WHITE PEAK WAY

Mrs Pat Harris, Laurel House, The Green, Litton, SK17 8QP. ☎ (01298) 871971 • Map 119/165750 • BB **B/C** • D1 T1 • 3-11 • Ⓑ Ⓓ Ⓢ 🐾 Ⓜ • 2Cr/C

TWO DALES (Matlock)

Joan Bennett, Top O' The Hill, Sydnope Hill, DE4 2FN. ☎ (01629) 734548 • Map 119/287635 • BB **B** • EM book first £9 • D2 T1 • 3-12 NX • Ⓥ Ⓓ Ⓢ 🐾 • List/C

WARSLOW (Buxton)

The Greyhound Inn, SK17 0JN. ☎ (01298) 84249 • Map 119/087586 • BB **B** • EM £5.50, 7-9pm • S2 D2 • 1-12 NX • Ⓥ 🐾 • Live band Sat. nights

Sandra Gordon, "Holly Bank", Emmanuels Lane, SK17 0JN. ☎ (01298) 84984 • Map 119/087586 • BB **B** • D2 T1 • 1-12 • Ⓓ 🐾

WHALEY BRIDGE (High Peak)

Ann & Mike Beddows, The Old Bakery Guest House, 80 Buxton Road, SK12 7JE. ☎ (01663) 732359 • Map 110/010806 • BB **B/C** • EM book first £9.50 or snacks, 7.30pm • D2 T1 • 1-12 • Ⓥ Ⓓ Ⓡ • 2Cr/C

YOULGRAVE (Bakewell)
WHITE PEAK WAY

"Fairview", Bradford Road, DE45 1WG. ☎ (01629) 636043 • Map 119/213640 • BB **B** • D1 T1 • 1-12 NX • Ⓓ Ⓢ 🐾 • List

Anne Croasdell, The Old Bakery, DE45 1UR. ☎ (01629) 636887 • Map 119/210643 • BB **B** • T2 • 1-12 • Ⓥ Ⓓ Ⓢ 🐾 • 1Cr/C

Ann Knowles, Garden House, Fountain Square, DE45 1UR. ☎ (01629) 636362 • Map 119/210643 • BB **B** • T2 • 1-12 • Ⓑ Ⓓ Ⓢ

DEVON

APPLEDORE (Bideford)
SOUTH WEST COAST PATH & TARKA TRAIL

Mrs Margaret Cox, Riverside Guest House, 4 Marine Parade, EX39 1PJ. ☎ (01237) 478649 • Map 180/464303 • BB **B** • EM book first £9, 6.30pm • S/T1 D1 F1 • 1-12 NX • Ⓥ Ⓑ Ⓓ Ⓢ

AVETON GIFFORD (Kingsbridge)
SOUTH WEST COAST PATH

Mrs Jill Balkwill, Court Barton Farmhouse, TQ7 4LE. ☎ (01548) 550312 • Map 202/695478 • BB **C/D** • S1 D2 T2 F2 • 1-12 NX • Ⓑ Ⓓ Ⓢ • 2Cr/C

BAMPTON (Tiverton)

☆ Mrs Lindy Head, Harton Farm, Oakford, EX16 9HH. ☎ (01398) 351209 • Map 181/905225 • BB **B** • EM book first £6, 7.30pm • D1 T2 • 1-12 NX • Ⓥ Ⓓ Ⓢ 🐾 • 1Cr

---

HARTON FARM
Bampton, Oakford, Devon EX16 9HH
Country lovers and walkers welcome on our traditional, non-intensive, friendly farm near Exmoor. Home-baking and hearty meals using our own home-produced and additive-free meat and vegetables. Comfortable, secluded and tranquil stone farmhouse, bedrooms with tea trays and washbasins. Seasonal log fires.
Tel: 01398 351209

BARNSTAPLE

Bernard & Olive Capp, Crossways, Braunton Road, EX31 1JY. ☎ (01271) 79120 • Map 180/553337 • BB **B/C** • D1 T2 F1 • 1-12 • Ⓑ Ⓓ Ⓢ Ⓡ

BELSTONE (Okehampton)
TARKA TRAIL

P Cowley, The Barton, EX20 1RA. ☎ (01837) 840371 • Map 191/620935 • BB **B/C** • D2 T1 • 1-12 NX • Ⓑ Ⓓ

Moorlands House, EX20 1QZ. ☎ (01837) 840549 • Map 191/620935 • BB **B** • D1 T2 • 1-12 • Ⓓ 🐾 • Food nearby

The Tors Inn, EX20 1QZ. ☎ (01837) 840689 • Map 191/620935 • BB **C** • EM £7.50, 7-10pm • D1 T2 • 1-12 NX • Ⓥ Ⓓ Ⓢ Ⓡ 🐾

BICKINGTON (Newton Abbot)

Justin & Debbie Dashwood, Kellinch Farm, TQ12 6PB. ☎ (01626) 821252 • Map 202/790720 • BB **C** • EM £8.90, 7pm • S1 D1 T1 • 1-12 • Ⓑ Ⓓ Ⓢ 🐾

☆ See Display Advertisement

■ BIDEFORD
SOUTH WEST COAST PATH & TARKA TRAIL

☆ Mike & Janet Taylor, The Mount Hotel, Northdown Road, EX39 3LP. ☎ (01237) 473748 • Map 190, 180/447269 • BB **C/D** • EM book first £8.50, 6.30pm • S2 D3 T2 F1 • 1-12 NX • Ⓥ Ⓑ Ⓓ Ⓢ Ⓜ • 3Cr

■ BLACK DOG (Crediton)
TWO MOORS WAY

Mrs H Wedlake, Lower Brownstone Farm, EX17 4QE. ☎ (01363) 877256 • Map 191/789089 • BB **A** • EM £5, 6-8pm • D1 F1 • 3-12 • Ⓥ Ⓓ 🛁 • Camping also; lifts

■ BRANSCOMBE (Seaton)
SOUTH WEST COAST PATH

☆ Amanda Hart, Hole Mill, EX12 3BX. ☎ (01297) 680314 • Map 192/195885 • BB **B/C** • D2 T1 • 1-12 • Ⓓ Ⓢ 🛁 • Lifts also

■ BRAUNTON
SOUTH WEST COAST PATH & TARKA TRAIL

Mrs Jean Watkins, North Cottage, 14 North Street, EX33 1AJ. ☎ (01271) 812703 • Map 180/485367 • BB **A/B** • EM book first £5, 6-7pm • S2 D2 T1 • 1-12 • Ⓑ Ⓓ Ⓡ 🛁

■ BRAYFORD (Barnstaple)
TARKA TRAIL

Mrs Renee Dover, Rockley Farmhouse, EX32 7QR. ☎ (01598) 710429 • Map 180/704383 • BB **B** • EM book first £8.50, 6.30pm • D2 T1 • 1-12 NX • Ⓥ Ⓓ Ⓢ 🛁 • List/HC • SC also

■ BRIDESTOWE (Nr. Okehampton)

☆ Mrs Helen Kemp, Way Barton Barn, EX20 4QH. ☎ (01837) 861513 • Map 191/494898 • BB **B** • EM book first £6.50, 7pm • D1 T1 F1 • 2-11 • Ⓥ Ⓓ • List/C • SC also

■ BRIDFORD (Exeter)

Mr & Mrs R Joslin, Horse Engine House, Lowton Farm, EX6 7EN. ☎ (01647) 252209 • Map 191/807876 • BB **B** • EM book first £7.50 • D1 T1 • 1-12 • Ⓓ Ⓢ

■ BRIXHAM
SOUTH WEST COAST PATH

Ian & Carol Hayhurst, Richmond House, Higher Manor Road, TQ5 8HA. ☎ (01803) 882391 • Map 202/921560 • BB **B/C** • S1 D3 T1 F2 • 2-12 NX • Ⓑ Ⓓ Ⓢ 🛁 • 2Cr/C

Paul & Fay Barnett, Tor Haven Hotel, 97 King Street, TQ5 9TH. ☎ (01803) 882281 • Map 202/926561 • BB **C/D** • EM 6-9pm • S2 D5 T1 F1 • 1-12 NX • Ⓥ Ⓑ Ⓓ 🛁 Ⓜ • 2Cr/C

■ BUDLEIGH SALTERTON
SOUTH WEST COAST PATH

Mr & Mrs S Lovett, Lufflands, Yettington, EX9 7BP. ☎ (01395) 568422 • Map 192/053857 • BB **B/C** • S2 D1 F1 • 1-12 NX • Ⓑ Ⓓ Ⓢ

■ CHAGFORD (Newton Abbot)
TWO MOORS WAY

☆ Glendarah House, TQ13 8BZ. ☎ (01647) 433270 • Map 191/702879 • BB **D** • D3 T3 • 1-12 NX • Ⓑ Ⓓ Ⓢ 🛁 • 2Cr/HC

Mrs Catherine Prysor-Jones, Yellam Country House B&B, TQ13 8JH. ☎ (01647) 432211 • Map 191/716871 • BB **C** • D2 T1 • 1-12 NX • Ⓑ Ⓓ 🐾 • Food nearby

☆ Judith Pool, Ring o Bells, 44 The Square, TQ13 8AH. ☎ (01647) 432466 • Map 191/700875 • BB **C** • EM £3.50-£10, 6-9.15pm • S1 D2 T2 • 1-12 • Ⓥ Ⓑ Ⓓ Ⓢ 🐾

Ring O'Bells

The Square
Chagford
Devon

Tel. 01647 432466

Freehouse inn with central town square position for Two Moors Way and Dartmoor walking. Bar snacks and full meals seven days a week. Bed & Breakfast with TV, tea & coffee. Non smoking accommodation.

■ **CHALLACOMBE (Barnstaple)**
TARKA TRAIL

☆ Helen Asher, Twitchen Farm, EX31 4TT. ☎ (01598) 763568 • Map 180/693410 • BB **C** • EM £12.50, 7pm • S1 D3 T3 F2 • 1-12 • Ⓥ Ⓑ Ⓓ Ⓢ 🐾 • 3Cr/C • Also one room for disabled person

Twitchen Farm

Farmhouse Hotel

* High quality, en-suite bedrooms
* Tarka Trail and other excellent walking
* Panoramic views of Exmoor National Park
* ETB 🌺🌺🌺 Commended

Contact Jaye or Helen on 01598 763568

http://bigweb.castlelink.co.uk/north_devon/group/twitchen.html

■ **CLOVELLY (Bideford)**
SOUTH WEST COAST PATH

Mrs P Vanstone, The Old Smithy, Slerra Hill, EX39 5ST. ☎ (01237) 431202 • Map 190/310250 • BB **B/C** • D1 T1 F2 • 1-12 • Ⓑ Ⓓ Ⓢ 🐾

Mrs S Curtis, Fuchsia Cottage, Burscott Lane, EX39 5RR. ☎ (01237) 431398 • Map 190/314231 • BB **A/B** • EM book first £6.50, 6.30ish • S1 D1 F1 • 1-12 NX • Ⓑ Ⓓ Ⓢ 🐾 • C

■ **COLYTON**

Martin Rudd, The Tollhouse, Umborne Bridge, EX13 6EY. ☎ (01297) 553739 • Map 192,193/250943 • BB **B** • S1 D2 T1 F1 • 1-12 • Ⓓ Ⓢ

The Ramblers

■ **COMBE MARTIN (Ilfracombe)**
SOUTH WEST COAST PATH & TARKA TRAIL

Mrs A Waldon, Idle Hour, Borough Road, EX34 0AN. ☎ (01271) 883217 • Map 180/577471 • BB **A** • S1 D2 T1 • 4-9 • Ⓓ 🐾 Ⓜ

☆ Saffron House Hotel, King Street, EX34 0BX. ☎ (01271) 883521 • Map 180/581469 • BB **B/C** • EM £9, 6.30-7pm • D4 T1 F4 • 1-12 • Ⓥ Ⓑ Ⓓ Ⓢ 🐾 • 3Cr/C

Saffron House Hotel

King Street, Combe Martin, N. Devon

Charming 17thC hotel on edge of Exmoor. All rooms with CTV, tea-making, CH, most en suite. Cosy bar with log fire. Excellent Devon fayre, packed lunches. Drying facilities. Group discounts. Directions from coast path: From Little Hangman take West Challacombe Lane Footpath on left to hotel.

Tel: 01271 883521   Commended 🌺🌺🌺

Hillview Guest House, Woodlands, EX34 0AT. ☎ (01271) 882331 • Map 180/575469 • BB **B** • S1 D4 T1 • 4-10 • Ⓑ Ⓓ Ⓢ

■ **COUNTISBURY (Lynton)**
SOUTH WEST COAST PATH & TARKA TRAIL

R S & S M Pile, Coombe Farm, EX35 6NF. ☎ (01598) 741236 • Map 180/766488 • BB **B/C** • D2 T1 F2 • 3-11 • Ⓑ Ⓓ Ⓢ 🐾 • 2Cr/C

■ **CROYDE**
SOUTH WEST COAST PATH & TARKA TRAIL

Mrs Gwen Adams, Combas Farm, EX33 1PH. ☎ (01271) 890398 • Map 180/449396 • BB **C** • EM £9, 6.30pm • S1 D2 F2 • 3-12 NX • Ⓥ Ⓑ Ⓓ Ⓢ 🐾 • 2Cr/C

■ **CULLOMPTON**

Mr & Mrs Frankpitt, Knightswood Farm, Old Hill, EX15 1RW. ☎ (01884) 33272 • Map 192/027054 • BB **C** • EM book first £8, 7pm • D1 T2 • 1-12 NX • Ⓥ Ⓓ 🐾

■ **DARTMOUTH**
SOUTH WEST COAST PATH

Mrs C Haddock, Coleton Barton Farm, Brownstone Road, Kingswear, TQ6 0EQ. ☎ (01803) 752795 • Map 202/907511 • BB **B** • EM £11, 8pm • D1 T1 F1 • 1-12 • Ⓥ Ⓓ Ⓡ 🐾

■ **DAWLISH**
SOUTH WEST COAST PATH

Sheila & Bill Tindal, Woodford, 14 Westcliff, EX7 9DN. ☎ (01626) 866013 • Map 192/961765 • BB **B** • D3 F1 • 4-10 • Ⓑ Ⓓ Ⓡ 🐾

☆ See Display Advertisement

185

■ **DODDISCOMBSLEIGH (Exeter)**

Mrs Barbara Lacey, Whitemoor Farm, EX6 7PU. ☎ (01647) 252423 • Map 191/861866 • BB **B/C** • EM book first £8, 7.30pm • S2 D1 T1 • 1-12 NX • Ⓥ Ⓑ Ⓓ Ⓢ ⅍ • 1Cr/App

■ **DOWN THOMAS (Plymouth)**
SOUTH WEST COAST PATH

Margaret MacBean, Gabber Farm, PL9 0AW. ☎ (01752) 862269 • Map 201/507497 • BB **B/C** • EM book first £8, 7.30pm • D1 T2 F2 • 2-11 + XMAS • Ⓥ Ⓑ Ⓓ Ⓢ ⅍ • 2Cr/C

■ **DREWSTEIGNTON (Exeter)**
TWO MOORS WAY

Mrs Emanuel, The Old Rectory, EX6 6QT. ☎ (01647) 281269 • Map 191/737908 • BB **B/C** • EM book first £15 • D2 T1 • 1-12 NX • Ⓥ Ⓑ Ⓓ Ⓢ ⅍

■ **DUNSFORD (Exeter)**

Mark & Judy Harrison, The Royal Oak Inn, EX6 7DA. ☎ (01647) 52256 • Map 191/813892 • BB **C** • EM £4-£8, 7-9pm • D5 T2 F1 • 1-12 NX • Ⓥ Ⓑ Ⓓ Ⓢ ⅍

■ **EXETER**

☆ Park View Hotel, 8 Howell Road, EX4 4LG. ☎ (01392) 71772 • Map 192/917933 • BB **C** • S3 D7 T3 F2 • 1-12 NX • Ⓑ Ⓓ Ⓡ ⅍ • 2Cr/C

☆ C Morris, Clock Tower Hotel, 16 New North Road, EX4 4HF. ☎ (01392) 424545 • Map 192/920931 • BB **A/B** • EM book first £7.50, 7pm • S3 D7 T3 F3 • 1-12 • Ⓥ Ⓑ Ⓓ Ⓢ Ⓡ ⅍ • 2Cr

☆ Mrs Sally Glanvill, Rydon Farm, Woodbury, EX5 1LB. ☎ (01395) 232341 • Map 192/002872 • BB **C** • D1 T1 F1 • 1-12 • Ⓑ Ⓓ Ⓢ Ⓡ ⅍ • 2Cr/HC

Mo Pearmain, 12 Devonshire Place, EX4 6JA. ☎ (01392) 58147 • Map 192/925937 • BB **B** • S2 T2 • 2-12 NX • Ⓓ Ⓢ Ⓡ ⅍

Barbara & Donald Bligh, Hillcrest Corner, 1 Hillcrest Park, EX4 4SH. ☎ (01392) 277443 • Map 192/923944 • BB **B** • EM book first £6.50 • S1 D1 T1 • 1-12 NX • Ⓥ Ⓓ Ⓢ Ⓡ • SC also, veg. food only

■ **EXMOUTH**
SOUTH WEST COAST PATH

Mrs M Shobbrook, 30 Withycombe Road, EX8 1TG. ☎ (01395) 277025 • Map 192/005815 • BB **B** • EM book first £4.50, 6pm • S1 D1 F1 • 3-10 • Ⓓ Ⓡ ⅍

■ **HARTLAND (Bideford)**
SOUTH WEST COAST PATH

Mrs Y Heard, West Titchberry Farm, EX39 6AU. ☎ (01237) 441287 • Map 190/235272 • BB **B** • EM book first £7, 6.30ish • D1 T1 F1 • 1-12 NX • Ⓓ • SC also

Mrs G Johns, Hartland Quay Hotel, EX39 6DU. ☎ (01237) 441218 • Map 190/235246 • BB **C** • EM £9, 7-8pm plus bar food • S2 D4 T4 F4 • 3-10 • Ⓥ Ⓑ Ⓓ ⅍ • 2Cr

☆ Mrs Thirza Goaman, Elmscott Farm, EX39 6ES. ☎ (01237) 441276 • Map 190/231215 • BB **C** • EM book first £8.50, 6pm • D1 T1 F1 • 3-10 • Ⓥ Ⓑ Ⓓ Ⓢ • 2Cr/HC

■ HOLNE (Ashburton)
TWO MOORS WAY

Mrs Anne Torr, Middle Leat, TQ13 7SJ. ☎ (01364) 631413 • Map 202/707695 • BB **B** • D1 F1 • 1-12 NX • Ⓑ Ⓓ Ⓢ

Mr & Mrs Henderson, Dodbrooke Farm, Michelcombe, TQ13 7SP. ☎ (01364) 631461 • Map 202/697688 • BB **B** • EM book first £9, 7.30-8pm • S2 T2 • 2-11 NX • Ⓥ Ⓑ Ⓓ Ⓢ 🐾 Ⓜ • List

Anne Mortimore, Hazelwood, TQ13 7SJ. ☎ (01364) 631235 • Map 202/707695 • BB **B** • EM book first £10, 7-7.30pm • S1 D1 • 1-12 NX • Ⓥ Ⓑ Ⓓ Ⓢ 🐾 • SC also

Pamela Neal, Middle Stoke Farm, Holne, Dartmoor, TQ13 7SS. ☎ (01364) 631444 • Map 202/697705 • BB **B/C** • D/T1 • 1-12 NX • Ⓑ Ⓓ Ⓢ 🐾

■ HOLSWORTHY

Dave & Pat Regardsoe, South Worden Farm, Bradworthy, EX22 7TW. ☎ (01409) 241827 • Map 190/307147 • BB **B** • EM £8.50 • S1 D1 T1 • 1-12 • Ⓥ Ⓓ Ⓢ 🐾 • List/C

■ HONITON

Mandy Dalton, Splatthayes, Buckerell, EX14 0ER. ☎ (01404) 850464 • Map 192,193/122007 • BB **C** • EM book first £10-£15, 7.30pm • T1 F2 • 1-12 NX • Ⓥ Ⓑ Ⓓ Ⓢ 🐾 • 2Cr/C

■ HOPE COVE (Kingsbridge)
SOUTH WEST COAST PATH

☆ The Cottage Hotel, TQ7 3HJ. ☎ (01548) 561555 • Map 202/676401 • BB **D** • EM 7.30-8.30pm • S10 D/T20 F5 • 2-12 • Ⓥ Ⓓ Ⓢ 🐾 • 3Cr • B&B price includes dinner. Open New Year

Hope Cove, South Devon TQ7 3HJ
The hotel enjoys a magnificent position in this pretty and secluded fishing village. Heritage coastline • National Trust land • Ideally situated for walks • Log fire in winter • Drying facilities • Group rates • Friendly and efficient service • Good food and wine. **Brochure Tel: (01548) 561555**

Mrs J Fisher, "Surfview", 5 Sea View Gardens, TQ7 3XB. ☎ (01548) 561010 • Map 202/678402 • BB **B** • EM £6.50, 7pm • D1 T2 F1 • 9-7 • Ⓥ Ⓓ Ⓢ • SC also

■ ILFRACOMBE
SOUTH WEST COAST PATH & TARKA TRAIL

☆ Epchris Hotel, Torrs Park, EX34 8AZ. ☎ (01271) 862751 • Map 180/512475 • BB **C** • EM book first £8, 6.30pm • S1 D1 T/F7 • 2-12 • Ⓥ Ⓑ Ⓓ Ⓢ • 3Cr/App • Transport available

☆ Ilfracombe Youth Hostel, Ashmour House, 1 Hillsborough Terrace, EX34 9NR. ☎ (01271) 865337 • Map 180/524474 • BB **A** • EM £4.25, 7pm • T3 F9 • 1-12 • Ⓥ Ⓓ Ⓢ • Open for groups at Xmas. SC & bunkhouse also

☆ Bryan & Janet Cath, Combe Lodge Hotel, Chambercombe Park, EX34 9QW. ☎ (01271) 864518 • Map 180/530473 • BB **C** • EM book first £11, 6.45pm • S1 D4 F3 • 1-12 NX • Ⓥ Ⓑ Ⓓ Ⓢ 🐾 • Guided walks also

■ INSTOW (Bideford)
SOUTH WEST COAST PATH & TARKA TRAIL

Jean & John Gardner, Pilton Cottage, Victoria Terrace, Marine Parade, EX39 4JW. ☎ (01271) 860202 • Map 180/472303 • BB **B** • S1 D1 T1 F1 • 3-9 • Ⓑ Ⓓ Ⓢ

■ **IVYBRIDGE**
TWO MOORS WAY

Mr and Mrs Hancox, The Toll House, Exeter Road, PL21 0DE. ☎ (01752) 893522 • Map 202/643563 • BB **C** • D1 T2 • 1-12 • Ⓑ Ⓓ Ⓢ Ⓡ 🐾

■ **KINGSBRIDGE**
SOUTH WEST COAST PATH

☆ Carole Light, Hallsands Hotel, North Hallsands, TQ7 2EY. ☎ (01548) 511264 • Map 202/818385 • BB **C** • EM £7, 7pm • S2 D5 T4 F5 • 1-12 NX • Ⓥ Ⓑ Ⓓ 🐾

HALLSANDS HOTEL

North Hallsands, Kingsbridge, Devon

Friendly family hotel on coastal path overlooking Start Bay with wonderful views. Bed, Breakfast & Evening meal. Good food and variety of beers, wines available. Open to non-residents, children and dogs welcome. Drying facilities available.

Tel. 01548 511264

Duncan & Sheila Johnston, The Globe Inn, Frogmore, TQ7 2NR. ☎ (01548) 531351 • Map 202/775426 • BB **B/C** • EM £8, 6-10pm • D3 T1 F2 • 1-12 • Ⓥ Ⓑ Ⓓ 🐾 • 2Cr

■ **KINGSWEAR (Dartmouth)**
SOUTH WEST COAST PATH

L Congdon, Carlton House, Higher Street, TQ6 0AG. ☎ (01803) 752244 • Map 202/880510 • BB **B** • EM book first £7.50, 6-7pm • S2 D2 T1 F1 • 1-12 • Ⓓ Ⓡ 🐾

■ **KNOWSTONE (South Molton)**
TWO MOORS WAY

Mrs J Bray, West Bowden Farm, EX36 4RP. ☎ (01398) 341224 • Map 181/833224 • BB **B/C** • EM £7.50, 6.30pm • S1 D3 T2 F2 • 1-12 • Ⓥ Ⓑ Ⓓ 🐾 • 2Cr

■ **LYNMOUTH**
SOUTH WEST COAST PATH & TWO MOORS WAY

☆ Mrs J Pile, Oakleigh, 4 Tors Road, EX35 6ET. ☎ (01598) 752220 • Map 180/727494 • BB **B** • EM book first £8, 6.45pm • S2 D3 T2 F2 • 1-12 NX • Ⓓ 🐾

OAKLEIGH

Lynmouth, North Devon

Small comfortable guesthouse. Central, sunny position at entrance to famous Watersmeet Valley. Close to coastal footpath and Two Moors Way, sea and cliff railway. All rooms with tea/coffee-making facilities. Own car park adjoining. B&B with dinner optional.

Tel. (01598) 752220

☆ Mr & Mrs C & J Parker, Tregonwell Riverside Hotel, 1 Tors Road, EX35 6ET. ☎ (01598) 753369 • Map 180/727494 • BB **B/C** • EM book first £15, 6pm • S1 D3 T1 F2 • 2-12 NX • Ⓥ Ⓑ Ⓓ Ⓢ 🐾 Ⓜ • 2Cr/App

Tregonwell Riverside Guest House

1 Tors Road, Lynmouth
Exmoor National Park

Warm welcomes guaranteed at the best place to be for you Exmoor ramblers. Our elegant Victorian riverside guesthouse is snuggled alongside deep wooded valleys, waterfalls, cascades, England's highest clifftops/most enchanting harbour. Pretty en-suite bedrooms with dramatic views, log fires, tea/coffee/drying facilities. Garaged parking. 2 crown approved. Group discounts.

Telephone 01598 753369

☆ Tricia & Alan Francis, Glenville House, 2 Tors Road, EX35 6ET. ☎ (01598) 752202 • Map 180/727494 • BB **B/C** • EM book first £11, 7pm • S1 D4 T1 F1 • 2-11 NX • Ⓥ Ⓑ Ⓓ Ⓢ

GLENVILLE HOUSE

Lynmouth, Devon

☎ 01598 752202

Charming, licensed Victorian house by riverside. Ideal for touring/walking Exmoor and coastal path. Rooms with ensuite shower. Tea/coffee facilities. TV lounge. A warm welcome, good food and friendly hospitality. B&B with dinner optional.

■ **LYNTON**
SOUTH WEST COAST PATH & TWO MOORS WAY & TARKA TRAIL

☆ Hazeldene Hotel, 27 Lee Road, EX35 6BP. ☎ (01598) 752364 • Map 180/717495 • BB **C** • EM book first £12.50, 7pm • D7 T1 F1 • 1-11 NX • Ⓥ Ⓑ Ⓢ 🐾 • 3Cr/C

HAZELDENE

AA/RAC Acclaimed   〰〰〰 Commended

Lee Road, Lynton, Devon

Delightful Victorian house where you are assured every comfort, good food and hospitality. Pretty en suite bedrooms with colour televisions and tea/coffee-making facilities. Two comfortable lounges and small bar. Full central heating. Traditional English breakfast. Pets welcome. Free parking.

Tel/Fax 01598 752364 for colour brochure

Mrs V A Ashby, Rodwell, 21 Lee Road, EX35 6BP. ☎ (01598) 753324 • Map 180/717495 • BB **B** • EM book first £9, 6.30pm • S1 D3 T1 • 3-10 • Ⓑ Ⓓ Ⓢ 🐾

☆ Sandrock Hotel, Longmead, EX35 6DH. ☎ (01598) 753307 • Map 180/715495 • BB **C/D** • EM £11.50, 7pm • S2 D4 T3 • 2-11 NX • Ⓥ Ⓑ Ⓓ 🐾 • 3Cr/C

The Retreat, 1 Park Gardens, Lydiate Lane, EX35 6DF. ☎ (01598) 753526 • Map 180/717493 • BB **B** • S1 D2 T2 • 3-11 • Ⓓ 🐾 • 1Cr/C

☆ David & Judith Woodland, Rockvale Hotel, Lee Road, EX35 6HW. ☎ (01598) 752279/753343 • Map 180/720495 • BB **D** • EM book first £13, 7pm • S1 D5 F2 • 3-10 • Ⓥ Ⓑ Ⓓ Ⓢ • 3Cr/C

☆ St Vincent House, Castle Hill, EX35 6JA. ☎ (01598) 752244 • Map 180/722493 • BB **C** • EM book first £12, 7.30pm • S1 D2 T2 F1 • 2-11 • Ⓥ Ⓑ Ⓓ Ⓢ • 2Cr/C

☆ Helen & John Christian, Woodlands, Lynbridge Road, EX35 6AX. ☎ (01598) 752324 • Map 180/722491 • BB **B/C/D** • EM £12, 7.30pm • S1 D4 T2 • 3-10 • Ⓥ Ⓑ Ⓓ Ⓢ • 3Cr/C

■ **MAIDENCOMBE (Torquay)**
SOUTH WEST COAST PATH

☆ Mrs Pamela Hill, Bowden Close Hotel, TQ1 4TJ. ☎ (01803) 328029 • Map 202/923686 • BB **C/D** • EM £8, 6.30-7.30pm • S1 D5 T3 F1 • 1-12 • Ⓥ Ⓑ Ⓓ Ⓢ 🐾 • 3Cr • SC also

■ **MORCHARD BISHOP (Crediton)**
TWO MOORS WAY

Oldborough Retreat, Oldborough, EX17 6SQ. ☎ (01363) 877437 • Map 191/773064 • BB **B** • EM book first £6, 6pm • D1 T1 F1 • 1-12 NX • Ⓥ Ⓓ Ⓢ Ⓡ 🐾

■ **MORETONHAMPSTEAD (Newton Abbot)**

M Cuming, Wooston Farm, TQ13 8QA. ☎ (01647) 440367 • Map 191/764886 • BB **C** • D2 T1 • 1-12 NX • Ⓥ Ⓑ Ⓓ Ⓢ • 2Cr/HC

Mrs Trudie Merchant, Great Slon Combe Farm, TQ13 8QF. ☎ (01647) 440595 • Map 191/736862 • BB **C** • EM £11, 6.30-7pm • D2 T1 • 1-12 • Ⓑ Ⓓ Ⓢ 🐾 • 3Cr/HC

■ **MORTEHOE (Woolacombe)**
SOUTH WEST COAST PATH & TARKA TRAIL

☆ Mr & Mrs V R Bassett, Sunnycliffe Hotel, Chapel Hill, EX34 7EB. ☎ (01271) 870597 • Map 180/454446 • BB **D** • EM £15, 7pm • D6 T2 • 2-11 • Ⓥ Ⓑ Ⓓ Ⓢ • 3Cr/C. For display see next page.

Want to know how to interpret the tourist board classifications?
See page 87

B&B ACCOMMODATION ENGLAND DEVON

SUNNYCLIFFE HOTEL
CHAPEL HILL
MORTEHOE
DEVON

Small award winning quality hotel set above picturesque Devon cove on heritage coastal path. All bedrooms have seaviews, CTV, beverage trays and are en-suite. Delicious traditional English food. Proprietor chef. Someone here cares about your stay.

Phone 01271 870597   Fax 01271 870597
Mr & Mrs VR Bassett

■ NEWTON ABBOT

☆ Liz & Gray Ross, East Burne Farm, Bickington, TQ12 6PA. ☎ (01626) 821496 • Map 202/799711 • BB **C** • D1 T2 • 1-12 NX • B D S • SC also

SOUTH DEVON

Peaceful 15th Century farmhouse. Ideal centre for Dartmoor and South Coast walks. B&B with private facilities from £19.50. Self-catering in clean, warm, converted barns. AA ❶❶❶❶

East Burne Farm, Bickington, Newton Abbot TQ12 6PA   Tel. 01626 821496

Mrs Val Bates, Cleavelands, Lustleigh, TQ13 9SH. ☎ (01647) 277349 • Map 191/780809 • BB **C** • EM book first £8, from 7pm • S1 D1 T1 F1 • 1-12 NX • V B D S

■ NORTH TAWTON
TARKA TRAIL

Margaret Wills, 23 Gostwyck Close, EX20 2HR. ☎ (01837) 82495 • Map 191/661017 • BB **A** • EM book first £5-£7, 5-7pm • T2 • 1-12 • D S

■ NOSS MAYO (Plymouth)
SOUTH WEST COAST PATH

Mrs P Steer, Rookery Nook, PL8 1EJ. ☎ (01752) 872296 • Map 201/547474 • BB **B** • EM book first £7, 7pm • T1 F2 • 1-12 • V B D S • SC also

Brenda Sherrell, Brookindale, PL8 1EN. ☎ (01752) 872665 • Map 201/547475 • BB **B** • EM book first £8 • D2 T1 • 1-12 • V D S M

Mr Francis Gregory, Little Lawford Cottage, Bridgend, PL8 1DX. ☎ (01752) 872521 • Map 202/555481 • BB **B** • EM book first £7 • S2 D2 • 1-12 NX • V D S

■ OKEHAMPTON
TARKA TRAIL

Mrs I Courtney, Ifold House, 27 New Road, EX20 1JE. ☎ (01837) 52712 • Map 191/586950 • BB **A/B** • EM book first £4, 7pm • D2 T1 • 1-12 NX • V D

Jane Seigal, Heathfield House, EX20 1EW. ☎ (01837) 54211 • Map 191/589946 • BB **D** • EM £14, 7.30-8pm • S1 D3 T1 F1 • 2-11 • V B D S • 3Cr/C

■ OTTERY ST MARY

Mrs E A Forth, Fluxton Farm Hotel, EX11 1RJ. ☎ (01404) 812818 • Map 192/086934 • BB **C/D** • EM book first £7, 6.45pm • S3 D3 T4 F2 • 1-12 • B D S • 3Cr

■ PAIGNTON
SOUTH WEST COAST PATH

Mrs P Whitlam, Cheltor Hotel, 20 St Andrews Road, TQ4 6HA. ☎ (01803) 551507 • Map 202/891600 • BB **A/B** • EM book first £5.50, 6pm • S1 D2 T1 F5 • 1-12 NX • V B D R S M • 2Cr

■ PLYMOUTH
SOUTH WEST COAST PATH

Mrs L Hallam, The Staymor, 66 North Road East, PL4 6AL. ☎ (01752) 660801 • Map 201/480553 • BB **B** • EM book first £8, 6pm • S2 D2 T2 F1 • 1-12 NX • B D R

Mrs J Turner, Rusty Anchor, 30 Grand Parade, West Hoe, PL1 3DJ. ☎ (01752) 663924 • Map 201/472536 • BB **B** • EM £8, 6-7pm • S2 D1 T2 F4 • 1-12 • V D S R S M • SC also

Jean & Red Lake, 'Sea Breezes', 28 Grand Parade, West Hoe, PL1 3DJ. ☎ (01752) 667205 • Map 201/472536 • BB **B** • EM book first £10, 6-7.30pm • S1 D2 T2 F3 • 1-12 • V B D R S M

■ PONSWORTHY (Newton Abbot)
TWO MOORS WAY

Mrs E Fursdon, Old Walls Farm, TQ13 7PN. ☎ (01364) 631222 • Map 191/701747 • BB **C** • EM book first £6, 7pm • S1 D2 T1 • 1-12 NX • V B D S M

■ POSTBRIDGE (High Dartmoor)

Mr & Mrs J L Bishop, Hartyland, PL20 6SZ. ☎ (01822) 880210 • Map 191/644795 • BB **C** • EM book first £8.50 • S2 T2 F1 • 1-12 NX • V D S

■ POUNDSGATE (Ashburton, Newton Abbot)
TWO MOORS WAY

☆ Mrs Margaret Phipps, New Cott Farm, TQ13 7PD. ☎ (01364) 631421 • Map 202/703727 • BB **C** • EM book first £10, 6.30pm • D2 T1 F1 • 1-12 • V B S • 2Cr/C

See the last page of the book for the key to symbols used in this Guide

ENGLAND   DEVON   B&B ACCOMMODATION

190

■ SALCOMBE
SOUTH WEST COAST PATH

☆ Heron House Hotel, Thurlestone Sands, TQ7 3JY. ☎ (01548) 561308 • Map 202/677413 • BB **C/D** • EM 7.15-9pm • S1 D7 T9 F7 • 1-12 • Ⓥ Ⓑ Ⓓ Ⓢ 🐾 Ⓜ • 4Cr/C • Groups also

Geoff & Sheila Sharp, Lyndhurst Hotel, Bonaventure Road, TQ8 8BG. ☎ (01548) 842481 • Map 202/737390 • BB **C/D** • EM £15, 7pm • D3 T4 F1 • 2-10 • Ⓥ Ⓑ Ⓓ Ⓢ • 3Cr/C • Groups also

☆ Julie & Arthur Bouttle, Torre View Hotel, Devon Road, TQ8 8HJ. ☎ (01548) 842633 • Map 202/735385 • BB **C/D** • EM book first £11.50, 7pm • S1 D4 T2 F1 • 2-10 NX • Ⓥ Ⓑ Ⓓ Ⓢ • 3Cr/C

Roger & Anne Petty-Brown, Rocarno, Grenville Road, TQ8 8BJ. ☎ (01548) 842732 • Map 202/736389 • BB **B** • EM book first £9 • S1 D1 T1 F1 • 1-12 • Ⓥ Ⓓ Ⓢ 🐾

Mr & Mrs D Griffiths, Meadow Barn, High House, East Portlemouth, TQ8 8PN. ☎ (01548) 843085 • Map 202/759377 • BB **B** • EM book first £6-£8 • D1 T1 • 1-11 • Ⓥ Ⓓ Ⓢ

■ SAMPFORD SPINEY (Yelverton)

Linda Landick, Eggworthy Farm, PL20 6LJ. ☎ (01822) 852142 • Map 201/544719 • BB **B** • S1 D2 • 1-12 • Ⓓ 🐾 • 1Cr/C

■ SEATON
SOUTH WEST COAST PATH

Leslie Singer, Sea Swift House, Sea Hill, EX12 2QT. ☎ (01297) 21820 • Map 192/246899 • BB **B** • S1 D1 T2 • 1-12 NX • Ⓓ Ⓢ

■ SHALDON (Teignmouth)
SOUTH WEST COAST PATH

K & P Underwood, Glenside Hotel, Ringmore Road, TQ14 0EP. ☎ (01626) 872448 • Map 192/926723 • BB **C** • EM £13, 7pm • S2 D3 T2 F3 • 1-12 • Ⓥ Ⓑ Ⓢ Ⓡ 🐾 • 3Cr/C

■ SHIRWELL (Barnstaple)

Mrs Janet Pelling, The Spinney Guest House, EX31 4JR. ☎ (01271) 850282 • Map 180/590370 • BB **B/C** • EM book first £7.50, 7pm • S1 D2 T1 F1 • 1-12 • Ⓥ Ⓑ Ⓓ Ⓢ 🐾 • 2Cr/C • No meals at Xmas

■ SIDBURY (Sidmouth)

☆ Cotfordbridge Hotel & Restaurant, Cotford Road, EX10 0SQ. ☎ (01395) 597351 • Map 192,193/140920 • BB **C** • EM £12, 6.30-9pm • D2 T1 F1 • 1-12 NX • Ⓥ Ⓑ Ⓢ   For display ad see next page.

COTFORDBRIDGE
HOTEL & RESTAURANT
Cotford Road, Sidbury, Devon

Lovely small hotel set in own gardens and surrounded by beautiful countryside in the heart of the Sid Valley. Half way on East Devon Walk and many other famous walks, and only 3 miles from the beach. Large private car park.

For Details 01395 597351

■ SIDMOUTH
SOUTH WEST COAST PATH

Mrs L Lever, Canterbury House, Salcombe Road, EX10 8PR. ☎ (01395) 513373 • Map 192/127878 • BB **C** • EM book first £8, 6pm • S1 D2 T3 F2 • 2-11 NX • Ⓥ Ⓑ Ⓓ Ⓢ ⚌ • 2Cr

☆ Mrs E Tancock, Lower Pinn Farm, Peak Hill, EX10 ONN. ☎ (01395) 513733 • Map 192/102868 • BB **C** • D2 T1 • 1-12 • Ⓑ Ⓓ ⚌ • 2Cr/C

LOWER PINN FARM
Peak Hill, Sidmouth, Devon
Situated in an Area of Outstanding Natural Beauty 2 miles west of Sidmouth. Comfortable centrally heated rooms. Colour TV, hot drink-making facilities, some en-suite rooms. Keys for access at all times. Substantial breakfast served.

Tel 01395 513733   COMMENDED

Sue Pink, Ferndale, 92 Winslade Rd, EX10 9EZ. ☎ (01395) 515495 • Map 192/125886 • BB **C** • D1 T2 • 1-12 NX • Ⓥ Ⓑ Ⓓ Ⓢ • 2Cr/C

Mrs Dilys Wharton, Newland House, 35 Temple Street, EX10 9BA. ☎ (01395) 514155 • Map 192/126883 • BB **B** • S1 D2 T1 • 4-10 • Ⓑ Ⓓ Ⓢ

■ SLAPTON (Kingsbridge)
SOUTH WEST COAST PATH

V J Mercer, Old Walls, TQ7 2QN. ☎ (01548) 580516 • Map 202/824448 • BB **B** • S1 D/F2 T1 • 1-12 • Ⓥ Ⓓ Ⓢ ⚌ Ⓜ

■ SOUTH ZEAL (Okehampton)
TARKA TRAIL

Peter Wilkens, Poltimore, EX20 2PD. ☎ (01837) 840209 • Map 191/652932 • BB **D** • EM 7-9pm • S2 D3 T2 • 1-12 • Ⓥ Ⓑ Ⓓ ⚌ Ⓜ • 3Cr • SC also

■ SOUTHLEIGH (Colyton)

Mrs Jo Connor, South Bank, EX13 6JB. ☎ (01404) 871251 • Map 192/205936 • BB **A** • EM book first £7, 6-9pm • D3 • 1-12 NX • Ⓥ Ⓓ Ⓢ ⚌

■ STOKENHAM (Kingsbridge)
SOUTH WEST COAST PATH

Esme Heath, Brookfield, TQ7 2SL. ☎ (01548) 580615 • Map 202/802428 • BB **B/C** • D1 T1 • 1-12 • Ⓑ Ⓓ Ⓜ

■ TAVISTOCK

Mrs Maureen Toland, Kingfisher Cottage, Mount Tavy Road, PL19 9JB. ☎ (01822) 613801 • Map 201,191/485745 • BB **B/C** • D2 T1 • 1-12 • Ⓑ Ⓓ Ⓢ ⚌ • 2Cr/C

Graham & Joanna Moule, Mount Tavy Cottage, PL19 9JL. ☎ (01822) 614253 • Map 201,191/495747 • BB **B/C** • EM book first £15, 7pm • D/F2 T1 • 1-12 NX • Ⓥ Ⓑ Ⓓ Ⓢ ⚌ • SC also

Mrs A Küttschreutter, Broadacre, Gulworthy, PL19 8HX. ☎ (01822) 832470 • Map 201/453727 • BB **B** • D1 T1 • CLOSED OCT • Ⓓ Ⓢ

■ TIVERTON

Bridge Guest House, 23 Angel Hill, EX16 6PE. ☎ (01884) 252804 • Map 181/953125 • BB **B/C** • EM £10, 6.30-7pm • S4 D2 T1 F2 • 1-12 • Ⓥ Ⓑ Ⓓ ⚌ • 3Cr/C

Angel Guest House, 13 St Peter Street, EX16 6NU. ☎ (01884) 253392 • Map 181/954126 • BB **B** • S1 D3 T1 F2 • 1-12 • Ⓑ Ⓓ Ⓢ ⚌ • 2Cr

R S H Cochrane, Bickleigh Cottage Hotel, Bickleigh Bridge, EX16 8RS. ☎ (01884) 855230 • Map 192/923057 • BB **D** • EM book first £11.50, 7pm • S1 D4 T3 • 4-10 • Ⓥ Ⓑ Ⓓ Ⓢ

■ TORQUAY
SOUTH WEST COAST PATH

☆ Windsurfer Hotel, St Agnes Lane, TQ2 6QD. ☎ (01803) 606550 • Map 202/905635 • BB **B/C** • EM book first £10, 6.30pm • D6 T1 F2 • 3-11 • Ⓥ Ⓑ Ⓓ Ⓢ Ⓡ Ⓜ • 3Cr/C

WINDSURFER HOTEL
TORQUAY
ST AGNES LANE, CHELSTON
Comfortable ensuite accommodation in friendly family hotel. Attractive outlook close to seafront in quiet location. Specialists in rambling group holidays but enjoy helping couples/individuals walking Dartmoor or South West Way. Good home cooking.
Telephone 01803 606550 for brochure/details

■ TOTNES

Mrs Janet Hooper, "Great Court Farm", Weston Lane, TQ9 6LB. ☎ (01803) 862326 • Map 202/819601 • BB **B** • EM book first £9, 6.30pm • D2 T1 F1 • 1-12 NX • Ⓓ Ⓢ Ⓡ • 1Cr/HC

Mrs Jeannie Allnutt, The Old Forge At Totnes, TQ9 5AY. ☎ (01803) 862174 • Map 202/809602 • BB **D** • S1 D3 T2 F4 • 1-12 • Ⓑ Ⓓ Ⓢ Ⓡ • 2Cr/HC • SC also

Mrs Geraldine Nicholls, Berry Farm, Berry Pomeroy, TQ9 6LG. ☎ (01803) 863231 • Map 202/827610 • BB **B** • EM book first £9.50, 6-7pm • S1 D1 T1 F1 • 1-12 NX • Ⓥ Ⓓ Ⓢ Ⓡ 🍴 • List/C

■ TWO BRIDGES (Yelverton, Dartmoor)

☆ The Two Bridges Hotel, PL20 6SW. ☎ (01822) 890581 • Map 191/610758 • BB **D** • EM from £4.95, 6-10pm • S1 D15 T6 F2 • 1-12 • Ⓥ Ⓑ Ⓓ Ⓢ 🍴 • 3Cr • Groups also

■ WEMBURY (Plymouth)
SOUTH WEST COAST PATH

Bay Cottage, 150 Church Road, PL9 0HR. ☎ (01752) 862559 • Map 201/519487 • BB **C/D** • EM book first £13, 7-9pm • D2 T1 • 3-12 NX • Ⓥ Ⓑ Ⓓ Ⓢ 🍴

■ WEST ANSTEY (South Molton)
TWO MOORS WAY

☆ Mrs H Milton, Partridge Arms Farm, Yeo Mill, EX36 3NU. ☎ (01398) 341217 • Map 181/842263 • BB **C** • EM £9.50, 7.30pm • S1 D3 T1 F2 • 1-12 NX • Ⓥ Ⓑ Ⓓ 🍴 Ⓜ • 2Cr/C • Bunkhouse also

■ WEST BUCKLAND (Barnstaple)
TARKA TRAIL

Mrs Payne, Huxtable Farm, EX32 0SR. ☎ (01598) 760254 • Map 180/665308 • BB **D** • EM £13, 7.30pm • D3 T1 F2 • 1-12 NX • Ⓑ Ⓓ Ⓢ • 3Cr/C • Camping also

■ WESTWARD HO (Bideford)
SOUTH WEST COAST PATH & TARKA TRAIL

Mr M & Mrs P Kivell, Buckleigh Lodge, Bay View Road, EX39 1BJ. ☎ (01237) 475988 • Map 180/436288 • BB **C** • EM book first £8, 7pm • S1 D2 T2 F1 • 1-12 NX • Ⓥ Ⓑ Ⓓ • 3Cr/C

■ WHIMPLE (Exeter)

Jean Darbey, Saundercroft, EX5 2PF. ☎ (01404) 822380 • Map 192/011974 • BB **B** • EM book first £7.50, 7pm • T1 F1 • 1-12 NX • Ⓑ Ⓓ Ⓡ 🍴

■ WRANGATON (South Brent)

Mrs P E Wakeham, West Cannamore Farm, TQ10 9HA. ☎ (01364) 72250 • Map 202/689573 • BB **B** • EM book first £8, 6pm • D/F2 • 1-12 NX • Ⓓ Ⓢ

■ YELVERTON

Waverley Guest House, 5 Greenbank Terrace, PL20 6DR. ☎ (01822) 854617 • Map 201/521679 • BB **C** • S1 D1 T1 F2 • 1-12 • Ⓑ Ⓓ Ⓢ 🍴

Mrs Bridget Cole, Greenwell Farm, Meavy, PL20 6PY. ☎ (01822) 853563 • Map 201/534659 • BB **C** • EM book first £12, 6.30pm • D2 T1 • 1-12 NX • Ⓥ Ⓑ Ⓓ • 3Cr/C

DORSET

■ ABBOTSBURY (Weymouth)
SOUTH WEST COAST PATH

Swan Lodge, DT3 4JL. ☎ (01305) 871249 • Map 194/578852 • BB **C/D** • EM £5, 6-10pm • D3 T1 F1 • 1-12 • Ⓥ Ⓑ Ⓓ Ⓢ 🍴 • 2Cr/C

Mrs Pat Arnold, Chesil House, DT3 4JT. ☎ (01305) 871324 • Map 194/570853 • BB **C** • D1 T2 • 1-12 NX • Ⓑ Ⓓ Ⓢ

■ AFFPUDDLE (Dorchester)

Appletrees, DT2 7HH. ☎ (01929) 471300 • Map 194/805935 • BB **B** • EM £5, 7pm • S1 T2 • 4-10 • Ⓥ Ⓓ Ⓢ Ⓡ 🍴

■ ALTON PANCRAS (Dorchester)
WESSEX RIDGEWAY

Mrs Hilary Webb, High Barton, DT2 7RT. ☎ (01300) 348225 • Map 194/699028 • BB **B** • EM book first £6.50, 6.30-8.30pm • S1 D1 T1 • 1-12 NX • Ⓥ Ⓓ Ⓢ 🍴

■ BEAMINSTER
WESSEX RIDGEWAY

Mrs Jane Rose, The Old Vicarage, 1 Clay Lane, DT8 3BU. ☎ (01308) 863200 • Map 193/476014 • BB **B** • D1 T1 • 5-10 • Ⓑ Ⓓ Ⓢ 🍴 Ⓜ • List • Food nearby

☆ See Display Advertisement

Judy Thompson, Higher Langdon, DT8 3NN. ☎ (01308) 862537 • Map 194/506025 • BB **C** • EM £12 • D2 F1 • 1-12 NX • Ⓥ Ⓑ Ⓓ Ⓢ Ⓜ • 2Cr/C • SC also

■ BLANDFORD FORUM

Mr & Mrs J Atkins, Methven, 25 White Cliff Mill Street, DT11 7BQ. ☎ (01258) 452834 • Map 194/884065 • BB **B** • S1 D1 T1 • 1-12 NX • Ⓓ Ⓢ 🐾

■ BOURNEMOUTH
SOUTH WEST COAST PATH

Mrs E Davies, St Michaels Guest House, 42 St Michaels Road, Westcliff, BH2 5DY. ☎ (01202) 557386 • Map 195/082910 • BB **B** • EM £6, 6pm • S1 D2 T2 F1 • 1-12 • Ⓥ Ⓓ Ⓡ 🐾

Mrs E Rising, "Victoria", 120 Parkwood Road, Southbourne, BH5 2BN. ☎ (01202) 423179 • Map 195/127919 • BB **A** • D1 T1 • 5-10 • Ⓓ Ⓡ 🐾

■ BRIDPORT
SOUTH WEST COAST PATH

☆ Britmead House, West Bay Road, DT6 4EG. ☎ (01308) 422941 • Map 193/465912 • BB **C/D** • EM £13, 7pm • D4 T2 F1 • 1-12 • Ⓑ Ⓓ Ⓢ 🐾 • 3Cr/HC • SC also

---
── BRITMEAD HOUSE ──
Bridport - West Bay
ETB 💐💐💐 Highly Commended
Renowned for offering our guests comfort, a high standard of facilities, with delightful food and good service. An elegant detached house, just ¾ mile from West Bay Harbour/Dorset Coastal Path. Six full en suite bedrooms, (one on ground floor) with TVs etc. Optional Dinners. Parking. Open all year.
Tel Bridport 01308 422941
AA QQQQ Selected   RAC Acclaimed
Guestaccom Good Room Award

Mrs Val Vallard, Egdon, Third Cliff Walk, West Bay, DT6 4HX. ☎ (01308) 422542 • Map 193/458906 • BB **B/C** • D1 T1 F1 • 1-12 • Ⓓ Ⓢ 🐾 • List

Mr Keith Baylis, Seatown Cottage, Seatown, DT6 6JT. ☎ (01297) 489027 • Map 193/420917 • BB **B** • D1 T1 • 1-12 • Ⓓ Ⓢ 🐾 • Food nearby

Mikki & Robert Hansowitz, Cranston Cottages, 27 Church Street, DT6 3PS. ☎ (01308) 456240 • Map 193/467927 • BB **B** • S1 D3 T3 • 1-12 • Ⓑ Ⓓ Ⓢ 🐾 Ⓜ • 1Cr • SC also

Mrs J Ellis, Wisteria Cottage, Taylors Lane, Morcombelake,, DT6 6ED. ☎ (01297) 489019 • Map 193/400947 • BB **B/C** • EM book first £8.50, 6.30-7.30pm • D1 T1 • 1-12 NX • Ⓥ Ⓑ Ⓓ Ⓢ

Mrs S Long, The Old Dairy House, Walditch, DT6 4LB. ☎ (01308) 458021 • Map 193/482926 • BB **C** • D1 T1 • 1-12 • Ⓓ Ⓢ

■ BUCKLAND NEWTON (Dorchester)
WESSEX RIDGEWAY

Mrs K V Bunkall, Holyleas House, DT2 7DP. ☎ (01300) 345214 • Map 194/696054 • BB **B/C** • EM book first £10 • S1 D1 T1 • 1-12 NX • Ⓥ Ⓑ Ⓓ Ⓢ 🐾 • 1Cr

Mr & Mrs Phipps, The Old Farmhouse, DT2 7DJ. ☎ (01300) 345549 • Map 194/706053 • BB **C/D** • EM book first £12 • D2 T1 • 1-12 NX • Ⓥ Ⓑ Ⓓ Ⓢ • 2Cr/C

■ BURTON BRADSTOCK
SOUTH WEST COAST PATH

Iris Jennings, The Bramleys, Annings Lane, DT6 4QN. ☎ (01308) 897954 • Map 194/490897 • BB **B** • EM book first £6.50, 6.30pm • D2 T1 • 1-12 NX • Ⓥ Ⓓ Ⓢ • 1Cr/C

■ CERNE ABBAS (Dorchester)
WESSEX RIDGEWAY

Mr & Mrs R J Munn, The Singing Kettle, 7 Long Street, DT2 7JF. ☎ (01300) 341349 • Map 194/66411 • BB **C** • D1 T2 • 3-10 • Ⓑ Ⓢ • Food nearby

Ginny Williams-Ellis, Cerne River Cottage, 8 The Folly, DT2 7JR. ☎ (01300) 341355 • Map 194/6650015 • BB **C/D** • EM book first £8, 7pm • D1 T1 • 1-12 NX • Ⓥ Ⓑ Ⓓ Ⓢ • 2Cr

■ CHARMOUTH (Bridport)
SOUTH WEST COAST PATH

Newlands House, Stonebarrow Lane, DT6 6RA. ☎ (01297) 560212 • Map 193/371934 • BB **C/D** • EM book first £14, 7-7.30pm • S3 D4 T3 F2 • 3-10 • Ⓥ Ⓑ Ⓓ Ⓢ • 3Cr/C

Fernhill Hotel & Self-catering Chalets, DT6 6BX. ☎ (01297) 560492 • Map 193/350941 • BB **D** • S2 D6 T2 F4 • 2-11 • Ⓑ Ⓓ 🐾 • 3Cr • SC & groups also

■ CHIDEOCK (Bridport)
SOUTH WEST COAST PATH

☆ Sarah & Russell Balchin, Park Farmhouse, Main Street, DT6 6JD. ☎ (01297) 489157 • Map 193/426928 • BB **B/C/D** • EM book first £14, 7.30 ish • S1 D4 T1 F1 • 1-12 • Ⓥ Ⓑ Ⓓ 🐾 • 3Cr/C

Mr T and Mrs J Yerworth, Chimneys Guest House, Main Street, DT6 6JH. ☎ (01297) 489368 • Map 193/424928 • BB **C/D** • EM book first £14, 7.15pm • D3 T1 F1 • 1-12 NX • Ⓥ Ⓑ Ⓓ Ⓢ

■ CRANBORNE (Wimborne)

C Hancock, The Fleur de Lys Hotel, BH21 5PP. ☎ (01725) 517282 • Map 195/054132 • BB **D** • EM £10-£12, 7-9.30pm • S1 D4 T3 • 1-12 NX • Ⓥ Ⓑ Ⓓ 🛁 • 3Cr

■ DORCHESTER

☆ Church View Guest House, Winterbourne Abbas, DT2 9LS. ☎ (01305) 889296 • Map 194/610900 • BB **C/D** • EM £11, 7pm • S1 D4 T3 F1 • 1-12 NX • Ⓥ Ⓑ Ⓓ Ⓢ 🛁 • 3Cr/C • Groups also

Churchview Guest House
Winterbourne Abbas, Dorchester DT2 9LS

AA
♀♀♀
♨♨♨
COMMENDED

Our beautiful 17C Guest House set in picturesque countryside makes an ideal rambling base. Period dining room, two lounges, licenced bar. Delicious evening meals. Non-smoking. **Groups a speciality.**
Call Michael and Jane Deller ☎ **01305 889296**

Elizabeth Adams, 1 Vicarage Lane, Fordington, DT1 1LH. ☎ (01305) 262911 • Map 194/697906 • BB **B** • S1 D1 T1 • 1-12 NX • Ⓓ Ⓢ Ⓡ Ⓜ • List

Marian Tomblin, Lower Lewell Farmhouse, West Stafford, DT2 8AP. ☎ (01305) 267169 • Map 194/743897 • BB **B** • D1 T1 F1 • 1-12 NX • Ⓓ Ⓡ 🛁

Mrs Ann Bamlet, Yalbury Park, Frome Whitfield Farm, DT2 7SE. ☎ (01305) 250336 • Map 194/697914 • BB **C** • D1 T1 F1 • 1-12 • Ⓑ Ⓓ Ⓡ 🛁 • 1Cr/HC • Food nearby

Mrs Louise Dale, 10 Hillfort Close, DT1 2QT. ☎ (01305) 268476 • Map 194/685895 • BB **A/B** • S1 T1 • 1-12 NX • Ⓢ Ⓡ Ⓜ • List

■ EAST STOKE (Wareham)

Mrs L S Barnes, Luckford Wood Farmhouse, BH20 6AW. ☎ (01929) 463098 • Map 194/871870 • BB **C** • D1 T1 F1 • 1-12 • Ⓑ Ⓓ Ⓢ Ⓡ 🛁 • List

■ HAZELBURY BRYAN (Sturminster Newton)

Maureen & Jim Kirby, Droop Farm, DT10 2ED. ☎ (01258) 817244 • Map 194/753082 • BB **D** • EM book first £12.50 • D1 T1 • 1-12 • Ⓥ Ⓑ Ⓓ Ⓢ • Transport from station

■ HINTON ST MARY (Sturminster Newton)

Mrs S Sofield, The Old Post Office, DT10 1NG. ☎ (01258) 472366 • Map 183/784163 • BB **B/C** • EM book first £8, 7pm • D1 T1 F1 • 1-12 • Ⓥ Ⓑ Ⓓ Ⓢ 🛁 Ⓜ

■ IBBERTON (Blandford Forum)
WESSEX RIDGEWAY

Mrs C Old, Manor House Farm, DT11 0EN. ☎ (01258) 817349 • Map 194/788077 • BB **A/B** • D2 T1 • 1-12 • Ⓑ Ⓢ 🛁 • SC also

■ IWERNE MINSTER (Blandford Forum)

Mark & Mary Richardson, The Talbot Hotel, DT11 8QN. ☎ (01747) 811269 • Map 194/859128 • BB **C** • EM £6, 7-9.30pm • S1 D2 T1 F2 • 1-12 • Ⓥ Ⓑ Ⓓ 🛁

■ KIMMERIDGE (Wareham)
SOUTH WEST COAST PATH

Mrs G Hole, Bradle Farm, BH20 5NU. ☎ (01929) 480712 • Map 195/916799 • BB **C** • D2 T1 • 1-12 NX • Ⓑ Ⓓ Ⓢ • 2Cr/C • Food nearby; SC also

Mrs Annette Hole, Kimmeridge Farmhouse, BH20 5NU. ☎ (01929) 480990 • Map 195/916799 • BB **C** • EM book first £10, 7.30pm • D2 T1 • 1-12 NX • Ⓥ Ⓑ Ⓓ Ⓢ • List

■ LANGTON HERRING (Weymouth)
SOUTH WEST COAST PATH

A W Freeman, East Cottage Bed & Breakfast, DT3 4HZ. ☎ (01305) 871627 • Map 194/610820 • BB **B/C** • D2 T/D1 • 1-12 • Ⓑ Ⓓ Ⓢ 🛁 • Food nearby

■ LEIGH (Sherborne)

☆ George Taylor, The Carpenters Arms, DT9 6HJ. ☎ (01935) 872438 • Map 194/616086 • BB **C/D** • EM £5-£10, 7-10pm • D2 T1 F1 • 1-12 • Ⓥ Ⓑ Ⓢ Ⓡ • List/C

■ LULWORTH COVE (Wareham)
SOUTH WEST COAST PATH

☆ Mrs Catriona Miller, Cromwell House Hotel, BH20 5RJ. ☎ (01929) 400253/400332 • Map 194/822802 • BB **D** • EM £12, 7-8.30pm • D8 T4 F2 • 1-12 NX • Ⓥ Ⓑ Ⓓ 🛁 Ⓜ • 3Cr/C. For display ad see next page.

Do you know your rights when you're out walking in the countryside? See pages 32-39

DORSET

ENGLAND

B & B ACCOMMODATION

☆ See Display Advertisement

■ LYME REGIS
SOUTH WEST COAST PATH & WESSEX RIDGEWAY

Jenny & Ivan Harding, Coverdale Guest House, Woodmead Road, DT7 3AB. ☎ (01297) 442882 • Map 193/338924 • BB **B/C** • EM book first £9, 6.30pm • S2 D2 T3 F1 • 2-11 NX • Ⓥ Ⓑ Ⓓ Ⓢ 🐾 • 2Cr/C

☆ Mr & Mrs J Edmondson, The White House, 47 Silver Street, DT7 3HR. ☎ (01297) 443420 • Map 193/338921 • BB **C** • D5 T2 • 4-10 • Ⓑ Ⓓ Ⓢ 🐾 Ⓜ • 2Cr/C

Keith Owen Lovell, Lucerne, View Road, DT7 3AL. ☎ (01297) 443752 • Map 193/339925 • BB **B/C** • D3 T2 • 1-12 NX • Ⓑ Ⓓ Ⓢ • SC also

☆ John & Rion Culpan, Springfield, Woodmead Road, DT7 3LJ. ☎ (01297) 443409 • Map 193/338924 • BB **B/C** • S1 D3 T2 F1 • 2-11 • Ⓑ Ⓓ 🐾 • 2Cr/C

Mrs D Lake, Rashwood Lodge, Clappentail Lane, DT7 3LZ. ☎ (01297) 445700 • Map 193/333922 • BB **C** • D2 • 2-11 • Ⓑ Ⓓ Ⓢ

☆ Geoffrey & Elizabeth Griffin, Willow Cottage, Ware Lane, DT7 3EL. ☎ (01297) 443199 • Map 193/332920 • BB **C/D** • S1 D1 • 3-11 • Ⓑ Ⓓ 🐾

Mrs Rosalind Price, Coombe Street Gallery, 33 Coombe Street, DT7 3PP. ☎ (01297) 442924 • Map 193/347928 • BB **A/B** • D/T/F3 • 1-12 NX • Ⓑ Ⓓ Ⓢ 🐾 • Food nearby

Victoria Hotel, Uplyme Road, DT7 3LP. ☎ (01297) 444801 • Map 193/333924 • BB **C/D** • EM £6, 7-11pm • D5 T3 F1 • 1-12 • Ⓥ Ⓑ Ⓓ 🐾

■ MAIDEN NEWTON (Dorchester)
WESSEX RIDGEWAY

Mrs B Gorard, Threbs House, Bull Lane, DT2 0BQ. ☎ (01300) 321141 • Map 194/598977 • BB **B** • S1 D1 T1 • 1-12 NX • Ⓑ Ⓓ Ⓢ Ⓡ

■ MARTINSTOWN (Dorchester)
SOUTH WEST COAST PATH

Jane Rootham, The Old Post Office, DT2 9LF. ☎ (01305) 889254 • Map 194/641890 • BB **B** • EM book first £12.50, 7pm • D1 T2 • 1-12 • Ⓥ Ⓓ Ⓡ 🐾 • List/App

■ MELCOMBE BINGHAM (Dorchester)
WESSEX RIDGEWAY

Lesley Dowsett, Badgers Sett, Cross Lanes, DT2 7NY ☎ (01258) 880697 • Map 194/761023 • BB **B/C** • EM book first £10, 7pm • T1 F/D1 • 1-12 NX • Ⓥ Ⓑ Ⓢ 🐾 • 1Cr/C

■ NETTLECOMBE (Bridport)

Ian & Anne Barrett, The Marquis of Lorne, DT6 3SY. ☎ (01308) 485236 • Map 194/517957 • BB **D** • EM £5-£12, 7-9.30pm • D4 T2 • 1-12 NX • Ⓥ Ⓑ Ⓓ

■ PENTRIDGE (Salisbury, Wilts)

Mrs Gill Edmonds, "Roman Way", SP5 5QU. ☎ (01725) 552465 • Map 184/025184 • BB **B** • EM book first £7, 7.45pm • T2 • 1-12 • Ⓥ Ⓑ Ⓓ Ⓢ 🐾 • Host also

■ POOLE
SOUTH WEST COAST PATH

Rosemount, 167 Bournemouth Road, Lower
Parkstone, BH14 9HT. ☎ (01202) 732138 • Map
195/048917 • BB **B** • S2 D3 T2 F2 • 1-11 NX • Ⓑ Ⓓ
Ⓡ ⚥ ⑳ • List

Mrs North, The Laurels, 60 Britannia Road, BH14
8BB. ☎ (01202) 723369 • Map 195/033913 • BB **B** •
T1 F1 • 1-12 NX • Ⓑ Ⓓ Ⓢ Ⓡ

■ PORTESHAM (Weymouth)
SOUTH WEST COAST PATH

D & P Saunders, The Old Vicarage, 2 Church Lane,
DT3 4HB. ☎ (01305) 871296 • Map 194/602858 • BB
A • S/T1 D1 F1 • 2-11 NX • Ⓓ ⚥

■ PUDDLETOWN

Mrs J Stephens, Zoar House, DT2 8SR. ☎ (01305)
848498 • Map 194/762942 • BB **B** • EM book first
£10, from 6.30pm • D1 T1 F1 • 1-12 • Ⓥ Ⓑ Ⓓ Ⓢ
⚥ • SC also

■ SHAFTESBURY

Mrs K P Heasman, Vale Mount, 17A Salisbury Street,
SP7 8EL. ☎ (01747) 852991 • Map 183/864230 • BB
B • S2 D1 T1 • 1-12 NX • ⚥

■ SHILLINGSTONE (Blandford Forum)
WESSEX RIDGEWAY

White Pit Cottage, (Steve & Jennifer Burton), DT11
0SZ. ☎ (01258) 860725 • Map 194/830103 • BB **C** •
EM book first £8 • S1 D2 • 1-12 NX • Ⓑ Ⓓ Ⓢ

Mrs Rosemary Watts, Pennhills Farm, Sandy Lane,
Off Lanchards Lane, DT11 0TF. ☎ (01258) 860491 •
Map 194/821104 • BB **C** • D/F1 T/S1 • 1-11 • Ⓑ Ⓓ
Ⓢ

■ SHROTON (Blandford)
WESSEX RIDGEWAY

Mrs W Wright, Lattemere, Frog Lane, DT11 8QL. ☎
(01258) 860115 • Map 194/860129 • BB **B/C** • EM
book first £7.50-£10 • D1 T1 • 1-12 • Ⓥ Ⓑ Ⓓ ⚥

Mrs Jane Moss, "Foxhangers", 4 Old Mill Cottages,
DT11 8TW. ☎ (01258) 861049 • Map 194/858131 •
BB **C** • D1 • 1-12 NX • Ⓑ Ⓓ Ⓢ

■ SIXPENNY HANDLEY (Salisbury, Wilts)

Mrs J M Howes, The Barleycorn House, Deanland,
SP5 5PD. ☎ (01725) 552583 • Map 184/991186 • BB
B • EM book first £9 • S1 D1 T1 • 1-12 • Ⓑ Ⓓ Ⓢ ⚥ •
2Cr/C

■ SWANAGE
SOUTH WEST COAST PATH

Verulam Lodge, 26 Cluny Crescent, BH19 2BT. ☎
(01929) 422079 • Map 195/031785 • BB **B** • D1 T1
• 4-10 • Ⓓ ⚥

Mrs M Smith, Berkleigh, 35 Prospect Crescent, BH19
1BD. ☎ (01929) 423441 • Map 195/023793 • BB **B** •
D1 T1 F1 • 1-12 NX • Ⓓ ⚥

☆ White Lodge Hotel, Grosvenor Road, BH19 2DD.
☎ (01929) 422696 & 425510 • Map 195/032783 •
BB **C** • EM £9-£11, 6.30pm • S1 D4 T5 F4 • 1-12 NX •
Ⓥ Ⓑ Ⓓ Ⓢ ⚥ • 3Cr/C • Groups also

☆ Chris & Jenny Davison, Pennyfarthings, 124 Kings
Road West, BH19 1HS. ☎ (01929) 422256 • Map
195/024788 • BB **B** • EM book first £8, 6.30pm • S1
D2 T1 • 1-12 NX • Ⓥ Ⓑ Ⓓ Ⓢ Ⓡ ⚥

☆ Mr D V Joseph, Chines Hotel, 9 Burlington Road,
BH19 1LR. ☎ (01929) 422457 • Map 195/031799 •
BB **C** • EM book first £10.50, 6pm • S2 D3 T4 F3 • 3-
10 • Ⓥ Ⓑ Ⓓ Ⓢ Ⓡ

DORSET ENGLAND N ACCOMMODATION B&B

☆ See Display Advertisement

■ SWANAGE (CONTINUED)

Susan Pickering, Hermitage Guesthouse, 1 Manor Road, BH19 2BH. ☎ (01929) 423014 • Map 195/031785 • BB **B** • D2 T1 F4 • 3-11 NX • Ⓓ 🐾

Mrs J M Pike, Downshay Farm, Haycrafts Lane, BH19 3EB. ☎ (01929) 480316 • Map 195/981797 • BB **B** • D1 F1 • 3-10 • Ⓓ Ⓢ

■ SYDLING ST NICHOLAS (Dorchester)
WESSEX RIDGEWAY

Mrs J Wareham, City Cottage, DT2 9NX. ☎ (01300) 341300 • Map 194/632994 • BB **B** • S1 D1 • 1-12 NX • Ⓓ

Mrs Barraclough, Magiston Farm, DT2 9NR. ☎ (01300) 320295 • Map 194/637967 • BB **B** • EM book first £9.50, 7pm • S1/2 D1 T3 • 1-12 NX • Ⓥ Ⓑ Ⓓ Ⓢ 🐾 • List

■ TOLLER PORCORUM (Dorchester)
WESSEX RIDGEWAY

☆ Nigel Spring, The Kingcombe Centre, DT2 0EQ. ☎ (01300) 320684 • Map 194/554991 • BB **B** • EM book first £10, 7.30pm • S3 D1 T6 F1 • 1-12 • Ⓥ Ⓓ Ⓢ 🐾 • List • SC also

---

THE
KINGCOMBE CENTRE
Toller Porcorum, Dorchester
100 yards from the Wessex Ridgeway
and Jubilee Way !
A residential study centre with facilities for
B&B and self-catering in one of the least
spoilt areas of Dorset. Friendly welcome
and excellent cooking.
Tel. (01300) 320684

Mrs Rachael Geddes, Colesmoor Farm, DT2 0DU. ☎ (01300) 320812 • Map 194/556971 • BB **B/C** • EM book first £9.50, 8pm • D1 T1 • 1-2 & 4-11 • Ⓥ Ⓑ Ⓓ Ⓢ Ⓡ • 1Cr/C

■ UPWEY (Weymouth)
SOUTH WEST COAST PATH

Mr & Mrs Scott, Friars Way, 190 Church Street, DT3 5QE. ☎ (01305) 813243 • Map 194/660854 • BB **C** • D3 T1 • 1-12 NX • Ⓥ Ⓑ Ⓓ Ⓢ Ⓡ • List

■ WAREHAM

Mr & Mrs Cake, Ashcroft, 64 Furzebrook Road, Stoborough, BH20 5AX. ☎ (01929) 552392 • Map 195/929850 • BB **B** • EM book first £7, 6pm • S1 D1 T1 F1 • 1-12 NX • Ⓥ Ⓑ Ⓓ Ⓢ Ⓡ 🐾

Mrs I K Gegg, Glen Ness, 1 The Merrows, Off St Helens Road, Sandford, BH20 7AX. ☎ (01929) 552313/550274 • Map 195/931896 • BB **B** • S3 D3 • 1-12 NX • Ⓑ Ⓓ Ⓢ Ⓡ 🐾

■ WEST LULWORTH (Wareham)
SOUTH WEST COAST PATH

☆ Shirley Hotel, BH20 5RL. ☎ (01929) 400358 • Map 194/822802 • BB **D** • EM price not supplied • S3 D8 T4 F3 • 2-11 • Ⓥ Ⓑ Ⓓ Ⓢ 🐾 • 3Cr/HC

LULWORTH COVE

The Shirley Hotel is the ideal base for those wishing
to take advantage of the area's beautiful scenery on foot.
It is a family run hotel that has superb facilities offering
delicious home-cooked food, fully equipped en-suite rooms,
indoor heated swimming pool and spa, boot room and
drying facilities and on-site parking.
Our local knowledge of the footpath network
is available to help in planning walks.

FOR FULL DETAILS INCLUDING
SPECIAL BREAKS CONTACT:
✓ *SHIRLEY HOTEL*
AA★★ ETB 🕸🕸🕸 HIGHLY COMMENDED
TEL: 01929 400358

Val & Barry Burrill, Graybank Guest House, Main Road, BH20 5RL. ☎ (01929) 400256 • Map 194/822802 • BB **C** • S1 D2 T3 F1 • 2-11 • Ⓓ Ⓢ 🐾 • List

Mr & Mrs M Else, The Old Barn, BH20 5RL. ☎ (01929) 400305 • Map 194/822802 • BB **B/C** • S2 D2 T2 F2 • 1-12 • Ⓓ 🐾 • List • Food nearby

Mrs B D Hamlet, Lulworth House, Bindon Road, BH20 5RU. ☎ (01929) 400604 • Map 194/822802 • BB **B/C** • EM book first £9 • D2 • 1-12 NX • Ⓥ Ⓑ Ⓓ Ⓢ 🐾

Mrs Jan Ravensdale, Elads-Nevar, West Road, BH20 5RZ. ☎ (01929) 400467 • Map 194/825805 • BB **B** • D1 T1 F1 • 1-12 NX • Ⓓ 🐾

Diane Coade, Churchfield House, West Road, BH20 5RY. ☎ (01929) 400598 • Map 194/825805 • BB **B** • D2 T1 • 1-12 NX • Ⓑ Ⓓ Ⓢ

The Copse, School Lane, BH20 5SA. ☎ (01929) 400581 • Map 194/825805 • BB **B** • S1 T2 • 1-12 NX • Ⓓ 🐾 Ⓜ • SC also

■ WEYMOUTH
SOUTH WEST COAST PATH

Hotel Rembrandt, 12-16 Dorchester Rd, DT4 7JU. ☎ (01305) 764000 • Map 194/679805 • BB **D** • EM £11.50, 6-9.15pm • S11 D50 T40 F13 • 1-12 • Ⓥ Ⓑ Ⓓ Ⓢ Ⓡ 🐾 Ⓜ • 4Cr/C

Chris & Sylvie, 6 Goldcroft Avenue, DT4 0ET. ☎
(01305) 789953 • Map 194/675795 • BB **C** • S1 D2
T1 F2 • 1-12 • ⒟ Ⓡ

■ WIMBORNE

Suzanne Hunt, Wits End, Parkelea, Sturminster
Marshall, BH21 4DG. ☎ (01258) 857041 • Map
195/946996 • BB **B** • EM book first £7.50, 7pm • D/F1
T1 • 1-12 NX • Ⓥ Ⓑ ⒟ Ⓢ • 2Cr

■ WIMBORNE MINSTER

Turi, 21 Grove Road, BH21 1BN. ☎ (01202) 884818
• Map 195/015997 • BB **B** • T1 F1 • 1-12 • ⒟ Ⓢ Ⓜ

■ WORTH MATRAVERS (Swanage)
SOUTH WEST COAST PATH

Mrs G I Modley, Chiltern Lodge, Newfoundland
Close, BH19 3LX. ☎ (01929) 439282 • Map
195/977778 • BB **C** • EM book first £8, 7pm • D1 T1 •
1-11 • Ⓥ ⒟ Ⓢ

COUNTY DURHAM

■ BARNARD CASTLE

Mrs D Jameson, Low Startforth Hall, Boldron Lane,
Startforth, DL12 9AR. ☎ (01833) 637957 • Map
92/046158 • BB **C** • EM book first £9, 7pm • T2 F1 •
2-10 • Ⓥ Ⓑ ⒟ Ⓢ • 2Cr

■ BISHOP AUCKLAND

Miss M Gordon, Albion Cottage Guest House, Albion
Terrace, Cockton Hill, DL14 6EL. ☎ (01388) 602217
• Map 93/210290 • BB **B** • S2 D1 T1 • 1-12 • ⒟ Ⓡ

■ BOWES (Barnard Castle)
PENNINE WAY

Trish & William Milner, East Mellwaters Farm, DL12
9RH. ☎ (01833) 628269 • Map 91,92/968126 • BB **C**
• EM book first £10, 5.30-7.30pm • S1 D2 T1 F1 •
MID JAN-MID DEC • Ⓥ Ⓑ ⒟ Ⓢ • 3Cr/C

■ BOWES MOOR (Barnard Castle)
PENNINE WAY

Bowes Moor Hotel, DL12 9RH. ☎ (01833) 628331 •
Map 91,92/929121 • BB **C/D** • EM £7.25, up to 9pm •
3 D5 T2 • 1-12 • Ⓥ Ⓑ ⒟ • 3Cr

CASTLESIDE (Consett)

Liz Lawson, Bee Cottage Farm, DH8 9HW. ☎
(01207) 508224 • Map 87/070453 • BB **C/D** • EM
12, 7-9pm • S1 D3 T2 F3 • 1-12 • Ⓥ Ⓑ ⒟ •
Cr/HC • SC and groups also

■ CORNFORTH (Durham)

Ash House, 24 The Green, DL17 9JH. ☎ (01740)
654654 • Map 93/313345 • BB **C/D** • D1 T1 F1 • 1-12
NX • ⒟ Ⓢ

■ COWSHILL (Wearhead)

☆ Janet Ellis, Alston & Killhope Riding Centre, Low
Cornriggs Farm, DL13 1AQ. ☎ (01388) 537600 •
Map 86,87/845413 • BB **C** • EM £9.50-£11, 6-9.30pm
• S1 D1 T2 F1 • 1-12 • Ⓥ Ⓑ ⒟ Ⓢ • 3Cr/C

■ DURHAM

Mark Nimmins, 14 Gilesgate (Top of Claypath), DH1
1QW. ☎ 0191-384 6485 • Map 88/278427 • BB **B** •
S2 D2 T2 F3 • 1-12 NX • ⒟ Ⓢ Ⓡ • 1Cr

■ EGGLESTON (Barnard Castle)

Frank & Eileen Bell, Cloud High, DL12 0AU. ☎
(01833) 650644 • Map 92/994245 • BB **C** • EM book
first £13, 7.30pm • D1 T1 • 3-10 • Ⓥ Ⓑ ⒟ • 2Cr/HC

■ FOREST-IN-TEESDALE (Barnard Castle)
PENNINE WAY

J W & J Collin, Langdon Beck Hotel, DL12 0XP. ☎
(01833) 622267 • Map 91,92/853312 • BB **C** • EM
book first £7 or bar meals, 6.30pm • S3 D2 T1 F1 • 1-
12 NX • Ⓥ Ⓑ ⒟ • List

■ MIDDLETON-IN-TEESDALE (Barnard Castle)

Mrs June Dent, Wythes Hill Farm, Lunedale, DL12
0NX. ☎ (01833) 640349 • Map 91,92/928228 • BB **B**
• EM book first £8, 6.30pm • T1 F1 • 3-11 • Ⓥ Ⓑ ⒟
Ⓢ • 1Cr/C • SC also

■ MIDDLETON-IN-TEESDALE (CONTINUED)

Andrew & Sheila Milnes, Brunswick House, 55 Market Place, DL12 0QH. ☎ (01833) 640393 • Map 91,92/946255 • BB **C** • EM £15, 7.30pm • D2 T1 F1 • 1-12 NX • Ⓥ Ⓑ Ⓢ • 3Cr/C

The Bridge Inn, Bridge Street, DL12 0QB. ☎ (01833) 640283 • Map 92/946255 • BB **B** • EM £3.50, 7-9pm • F2 • 1-12 • Ⓥ Ⓑ Ⓓ 🐾

ESSEX

■ ALDHAM (Colchester)
ESSEX WAY

R & P Mitchell, Old House, Fordstreet, CO6 3PH. ☎ (01206) 240456 • Map 168/920270 • BB **C/D** • S1 T1 F1 • 1-12 • Ⓑ Ⓓ Ⓢ Ⓡ • 1Cr/C • Food nearby.

■ ARDLEIGH (Colchester)

Doreen & Ian Le May, Dundas Place, Colchester Road, CO7 7NP. ☎ (01206) 230625 • Map 168/053294 • BB **B/C** • D1 T2 • 1-12 NX • Ⓑ Ⓓ Ⓢ 🐾 • 2Cr/C • Food nearby

■ BRADFIELD
ESSEX WAY

☆ Penny Linton, Emsworth House, Ship Hill, CO11 2UP. ☎ (01255) 870860 • Map 168,169/142310 • BB **D** • EM book first £8 • S3 D2 T1 • 1-12 NX • Ⓥ Ⓑ Ⓓ 🐾 • C

EMSWORTH HOUSE
Ship Hill, Bradfield, Essex CO11 2UP

Stunning view of the river and countryside on the Essex Way. Comfort and hospitality my speciality!

Penny Linton 01255 870860

■ CHIPPING ONGAR

Mrs Joyce Withey, "Bumbles", Moreton Road, CM5 0EZ. ☎ (01277) 362695 • Map 167/546052 • BB **C** • T3 • 1-12 NX • Ⓓ Ⓢ Ⓡ • List

■ COGGESHALL (Colchester)
ESSEX WAY

Mr & Mrs Shaw, White Heather Guest House, 19 Colchester Rd, CO6 1RP. ☎ (01376) 563004 • Map 168/861228 • BB **C/D** • S3 D2 T1 • 1-11 • Ⓑ Ⓓ Ⓢ Ⓡ

■ COLCHESTER

S F & J Powell, Scheregate Hotel, 36 Osborne Street, CO2 7DB. ☎ (01206) 573034 • Map 168/996250 • BB **C** • S15 D4 T10 F1 • 1-12 NX • Ⓑ Ⓓ Ⓡ • 1Cr/App

Four Sevens Guest House, 28 Inglis Road, CO3 3HU. ☎ (01206) 546093 • Map 168/987246 • BB **B** • EM book first £10, 6-7.30pm • D4 T1 F1 • 1-12 • Ⓑ Ⓓ Ⓡ • 2Cr

■ DUDDENHOE END (Saffron Walden)

Mrs T Westerhuis, Rockells Farm, CB11 4UY. ☎ (01763) 838053 • Map 154/467364 • BB **C** • EM book first £8, 7pm • S1 T1 F1 • 1-12 • Ⓑ • 2Cr/C • SC also. No meals Jul-Sept.

■ EPPING
ESSEX WAY

Mrs E M Stacy, Uplands, 181a Lindsey Street, CM16 6RF. ☎ (01992) 573733 • Map 167/456033 • BB **B** • S2 F2 • 1-12 • Ⓓ Ⓢ Ⓡ • List/App

■ FORDHAM (Colchester)
ESSEX WAY

Mrs I Tweed, Kings Vineyard, Fossetts Lane, CO6 3NY. ☎ (01206) 240377 • Map 168/936279 • BB **B/C** • D1 T1 F1 • 1-12 • Ⓑ Ⓓ Ⓢ • 2Cr/C

■ GOLDHANGER

The Chequers Inn, The Square, CM9 8AS. ☎ (01621) 788203 • Map 168/905088 • BB **B/C** • EM £5-£10, up to 9.30pm • D2 T3 • 1-12 • Ⓥ Ⓑ Ⓓ Ⓢ 🐾

■ GREAT CHESTERFORD (Nr Saffron Walden)
ICKNIELD WAY

Mrs Christine King, Mill House, CB10 1NS. ☎ (01799) 530493 • Map 154/504431 • BB **C** • S1 D4 T1 • 1-12 • Ⓓ Ⓢ Ⓡ 🐾 • List/C

■ MARGARET RODING (Nr Great Dunmow)
ESSEX WAY

Mrs Joyce Matthews, "Greys", Ongar Road, CM6 1QR. ☎ (01245) 231509 • Map 167/605112 • BB **C** • D2 T1 • 1-12 NX • Ⓓ Ⓢ • List/C

■ PURLEIGH (Chelmsford)

Mr & Mrs K Ascott, Purleigh Law, Walton Hall Lane, CM3 6PR. ☎ (01621) 828682 • Map 168/827023 • BB **B** • EM book first £7.50, 7-8pm • S1 D1 T1 • 1-12 NX • Ⓥ Ⓓ Ⓢ Ⓜ

■ SIBLE HEDINGHAM

Patricia Patterson, Hedingham Antiques, 100 Swan Street, CO9 3HP. ☎ (01787) 460360 • Map 155/782340 • BB **C** • D1 T1 F1 • 1-12 NX • Ⓑ Ⓓ Ⓢ 1Cr

■ WOODHAM FERRERS

Jill Oliver, Woolfe's Cottage, The Street, CM3 8RG. ☎ (01245) 320037 • Map 167/798995 • BB **B** • D1 T2 • 1-12 NX • Ⓓ Ⓢ Ⓡ • List

GLOUCESTERSHIRE

INCLUDING THE UNITARY AUTHORITIES OF SOUTH GLOUCESTER-SHIRE AND BRISTOL, AREAS PREVIOUSLY IN THE COUNTY OF AVON

■ ADLESTROP (Moreton-in-Marsh)

Mrs M J Warrick, Honeybrook Cottage, 2 Main Street, GL56 0YN. ☎ (01608) 658884 • Map 163/242269 • BB **C** • D1 T1 • 2-11 • Ⓑ Ⓓ Ⓢ • 2Cr/C

■ ALDERLEY
COTSWOLD WAY

Mrs Julie James, Hillesley Mill, Alderley, GL12 7QT. ☎ (01453) 843258 • Map 172,162/770905 • BB **C/D** • D1 T/F1 • 1-12 NX • Ⓑ Ⓓ ⛵ • 2Cr • Food nearby

■ BIRDLIP (Gloucester)
COTSWOLD WAY

P M Carter, Beechmount, GL4 8JH. ☎ (01452) 862262 • Map 163/925143 • BB **B/C** • EM book first £8, 7pm • S1 D2 T2 F2 • 1-12 • Ⓥ Ⓑ Ⓓ Ⓢ ⛵ • 2Cr/C

■ BLAKENEY

Viney Hill Country Guesthouse, GL15 4LT. ☎ (01594) 516000 • Map 162/659067 • BB **D** • EM £14, 7pm • D4 T2 • 1-12 • Ⓥ Ⓑ Ⓓ Ⓢ • 3Cr/C

■ BLEDINGTON
OXFORDSHIRE WAY

Mrs J A Watson, The Old Stores, Foscot, OX7 6RH. ☎ (01608) 659844 • Map 163/249220 • BB **B/C** • D2 • 4-10 • Ⓓ Ⓢ Ⓡ

■ BOURTON-ON-THE-WATER (Cheltenham)
OXFORDSHIRE WAY

Mrs Joan Mustoe, 6 Moore Road, GL54 2AZ. ☎ (01451) 820767 • Map 163/169210 • BB **B** • D1 T1 • 1-11 NX • Ⓑ Ⓓ Ⓢ ⛵

Bourton Lodge Hotel, Whiteshoots Hill, GL54 2LE. ☎ (01451) 820387 • Map 163/150200 • BB **D** • EM £12, 7-9pm • D11 T4 F3 • 1-12 • Ⓥ Ⓑ Ⓓ ⛵ Ⓜ • 3Cr/App

■ BRISTOL

...rches Hotel, 132 Cotham Brow, Cotham, BS6 6AE. ☎ 0117-924 7398 • Map 172/588745 • BB **C/D** • S3 ...4 T1 F2 • 1-12 NX • Ⓑ Ⓓ Ⓢ Ⓡ ⛵ • 1Cr/C

■ BROOKTHORPE (Gloucester)
COTSWOLD WAY

Richard & Judith Cockroft, Brookthorpe Lodge, Stroud Road, GL4 0UQ. ☎ (01452) 812645 • Map 162/835128 • BB **C/D** • EM £9.50, up to 9pm • S2 D2 ...3 F2 • 1-12 • Ⓥ Ⓑ Ⓓ Ⓢ ⛵ Ⓜ • 2Cr/C

CHALFORD

Mrs J Bateman, Green Court, High Street, GL6 8DS. ☎ (01453) 883234 • Map 163/892025 • BB **B/C** • T1 • 1-12 • Ⓑ Ⓓ Ⓢ ⛵ • List

■ CHARLTON KINGS (Cheltenham)
COTSWOLD WAY

L & R Seeley, 239A London Road, GL52 6YE. ☎ (01242) 583660 • Map 163/965209 • BB **B** • D1 T1 F1 • 1-12 NX • Ⓑ Ⓓ Ⓢ Ⓡ ⛵ Ⓜ • List

☆ Charlton Kings Hotel, London Road, GL52 6UU. ☎ (01242) 231061 • Map 163/977201 • BB **D** • EM £15.95, 7-9pm • S2 D8 T2 F2 • 1-12 • Ⓥ Ⓑ Ⓓ Ⓢ ⛵ • 4Cr/HC

CHARLTON KINGS HOTEL
CHELTENHAM

English Tourist Board — HIGHLY COMMENDED

Welcomes Walkers. Ideally situated, on edge of town just half a mile from Cotswold Way. All rooms have bath/shower. For Brochure:
Tel. 01242 231061

Brookthorpe Lodge
LICENSED GUEST HOUSE AND TEA ROOMS
Stroud Road, Brookthorpe, Gloucester GL4 0UQ
Tel. (01452) 812645

ETB — COMMENDED

Three storey Georgian house on outskirts of Gloucester. Set in lovely countryside with open views at the foot of the Cotswold escarpment. High standard of comfort and friendliness. Good home cooking. Vegetarian meals. (City & Guilds trained cooks). Short break packages. Children & animals welcome. Guided walks available. RA member.

☆ See Display Advertisement

ENGLAND   GLOUCESTERSHIRE

B & B ACCOMMODATION

■ CHELTENHAM
COTSWOLD WAY

North Hall Hotel, Pittville Circus Road, GL52 2PZ. ☎ (01242) 520589 • Map 163/958227 • BB **C/D** • EM £10.50, 6.30-7.30pm • S8 D6 T6 • 1-12 NX • Ⓥ Ⓑ Ⓓ Ⓡ 🛁 • 3Cr/C

Hamilton House, 65 Bath Road, GL53 7LH. ☎ (01242) 527772 • Map 163/948217 • BB **C** • S2 D1 T2 F1 • 1-12 NX • Ⓑ Ⓓ Ⓡ 🛁 • 2Cr/C

Pauline Lyons, 374 Old Bath Road, Leckhampton, GL53 9AD. ☎ (01242) 513313 • Map 163/949193 • BB **C** • EM book first £10, 8pm • D1 • 2-11 NX • Ⓥ Ⓑ Ⓓ Ⓢ

Ruth Jennings, "St Cloud", 97 Leckhampton Road, GL53 0BZ. ☎ (01242) 575245 • Map 163/946202 • BB **C** • EM book first £8, 7-8pm • D1 T1 F1 • 1-12 NX • Ⓥ Ⓓ Ⓢ Ⓡ • 1Cr

J Cox, Langett, London Road, GL54 4HG. ☎ (01242) 820192 • Map 163/988198 • BB **C** • D1 T1 • 1-12 NX • Ⓑ Ⓓ Ⓢ Ⓡ Ⓜ

■ CHIPPING CAMPDEN
COTSWOLD WAY & HEART OF ENGLAND WAY

Mrs D Bendall, Sandalwood House, Back-Ends, GL55 6AU. ☎ (01386) 840091 • Map 151/143387 • BB **C** • T/D1 F/D1 • 1-12 NX • Ⓑ Ⓓ Ⓢ • 2Cr/C • Food nearby

Mr & Mrs Sinclair, Volunteer Inn, Lower High Street, GL55 6DY. ☎ (01386) 840688 • Map 151/150392 • BB **C/D** • EM £3.95-£7.25, 7-9pm • S1 D3 T2 F1 • 1-12 • Ⓥ Ⓑ Ⓓ 🛁 Ⓜ • SC also

Mrs M Benfield, Lower High Street, GL55 6DZ. ☎ (01386) 840163 • Map 151/150392 • BB **B/C** • D1 T1 • 3-11 • Ⓑ Ⓓ 🛁 • 1Cr/App

Mrs J Whitehouse, Weston Park Farm, Dovers Hill, GL55 6UW. ☎ (01386) 840835 • Map 151/130390 • BB **C** • F1 • 1-12 • Ⓑ Ⓓ • 2Cr • SC also

Mrs Janet Rawlings, Marnic B&B, Broad Campden, GL55 6UR. ☎ (01386) 840014 • Map 151/159378 • BB **C** • D2 T1 • 1-12 NX • Ⓑ Ⓓ Ⓢ • 2Cr/HC

Mrs Judy Wadey, "Wyldlands", Broad Campden, GL55 6UR. ☎ (01386) 840478 • Map 151/159378 • BB **C** • D2 T1 • 1-12 NX • Ⓑ Ⓓ Ⓢ Ⓜ • List/C • Food nearby

Lygon Arms Hotel, High Street, GL55 6HB. ☎ (01386) 840318 • Map 151/153394 • BB **D** • EM £6 or £15, 6-10pm • D3 T1 FT/2 • 1-12 NX • Ⓥ Ⓑ Ⓓ Ⓢ 🛁

■ CINDERFORD

☆ Littledean House Hotel, Littledean, GL14 3JT. ☎ (01594) 822106 • Map 162/668136 • BB **C** • EM book first £10, 7pm • S15 T23 F6 • 3-10 • Ⓥ Ⓑ Ⓓ 🛁

■ CLEEVE HILL (Cheltenham)
COTSWOLD WAY

Mrs L Blankenspoor, Cleyne Hage, Southam Lane, GL52 3NY. ☎ (01242) 518569/(0468) 753625 • Map 163/965257 • BB **B** • EM book first £10, 7-8.30pm • S2 D1 T1 F1 • 1-12 NX • Ⓥ Ⓑ Ⓓ Ⓢ 🛁 Ⓜ • 2Cr/App

Malvern View, GL52 3PR. ☎ (01242) 672017 • Map 163/983270 • BB **C** • S2 D1 T1 • 1-12 • Ⓑ Ⓓ Ⓢ • 2Cr/C

Edward Saunders, "Heronhaye", GL52 3PW. ☎ (01242) 672516 • Map 163/987273 • BB **C** • S1 D2 • 1-12 • Ⓓ Ⓢ 🛁 • List

Mrs Maria Wilson, The Pines, GL52 3PW. ☎ (01242) 674887 • Map 163/988273 • BB **B/C** • D1 T1 • 1-12 NX • Ⓑ Ⓓ Ⓢ 🛁 • List

■ COLD ASHTON (Chippenham, Wilts)
COTSWOLD WAY

Peter & Beryl Williamson, High Lanes, SN14 8JU. ☎ (01225) 891255 • Map 172/749726 • BB **B/C** • S1 T1 • 3-11 NX • Ⓑ Ⓓ Ⓢ

Mrs J Bishop, Toghill House Farm, Wick, BS15 5RT. ☎ (01225) 891261 • Map 172/731724 • BB **C/D** • S1 D1 T2 F2 • 1-12 • Ⓑ Ⓓ Ⓢ 🛁 • List/C • SC also, food nearby

Pat Hacker, Whittington Farmhouse, SN14 8JS. ☎ (01225) 891628 • Map 172/749726 • BB **C** • D2 • 2-10 • Ⓑ Ⓓ Ⓢ • 2Cr/HC

■ COLEFORD
OFFA'S DYKE

Mrs S Davis, Lower Tump Farm, Eastbach, English Bicknor, GL16 7EU. ☎ (01594) 860253/(0836) 536674 • Map 162/588152 • BB **B** • D1 T1 F1 • 1-12 Ⓑ Ⓓ 🛁 Ⓜ

Doug & Barbara Bond, Graygill, Staunton, GL16 8PL ☎ (01600) 712536 • Map 162/534126 • BB **B** • D1 T • 1-12 • Ⓑ Ⓓ Ⓢ

D J & J M Atherley, "Westlands House", 20 Grove Road, Berry Hill, GL16 8QY. ☎ (01594) 837143 • Map 162/573122 • BB **B** • D1 T1 • 1-12 NX • Ⓢ 🛁

GLOUCESTERSHIRE   ENGLAND

B&B ACCOMMODATION

■ **COWLEY (Cheltenham)**
COTSWOLD WAY

Linda Roff, Manor Barn, GL53 9NN. ☎ (01242)
870229 • Map 163/961144 • BB **C** • D2 T1 • 1-12 NX
• Ⓑ Ⓓ Ⓢ • 2Cr/C • Free transport

■ **CRANHAM (Gloucester)**
COTSWOLD WAY

Rest Harrow, Cranham Corner, GL4 8HB. ☎ (01452)
813302 • Map 163/882130 • BB **C** • EM book first
£12.50 • D/T/F1 • 1-12 • Ⓥ Ⓑ Ⓓ Ⓢ ⌂

■ **DURSLEY**
COTSWOLD WAY

Mrs Elizabeth Williams, Claremont House, 66
Kingshill Road, GL11 4EG. ☎ (01453) 542018 • Map
162/754984 • BB **B/C** • S1 D2 T1 • 1-12 NX • Ⓑ Ⓓ
Ⓢ • 2Cr/C

Highlands, Stinchcombe Hill Golf Course, GL11 6AQ.
☎ (01453) 542539 • Map 162/753980 • BB **C/D** • EM
book first £12.50, 6-8.30pm • S1 D2 T1 • 1-12 • Ⓥ
Ⓑ Ⓓ Ⓢ Ⓡ Ⓜ • 2Cr

Mr & Mrs P G Roberts, "Ingleside", 26 The Slade,
GL11 4JX. ☎ (01453) 542735 • Map 162/755981 •
BB **B** • EM book first £7-£8, 7-8pm • T2 • 1-5, 7-12 •
Ⓥ Ⓓ Ⓢ • Veg. EM but carnivore breakfast

☆ Stanthill House, Uley Road, GL11 4PF. ☎ (01453)
549037 • Map 162/759979 • BB **C** • D2 T1 • 1-12 • Ⓑ
Ⓓ Ⓢ

■ **EDGE (Stroud)**
COTSWOLD WAY

Mrs A Sanders, Wild Acre, Back Edge Lane, GL6 6PE.
☎ (01452) 813077 • Map 162/849099 • BB **B** • D1 T1
• 1-10 • Ⓑ Ⓓ Ⓢ ⌂ • Food nearby

■ **FALFIELD (Wotton-under-Edge)**

Mr & Mrs Burrell, Green Farm Guest House, GL12
8DL. ☎ (01454) 260319 • Map 172,162/686943 • BB
C • EM £10, 7pm • S2 D3 T2 F1 • 1-12 • Ⓥ Ⓑ Ⓢ

Want to know more about tourist
board classifications? See page 87

■ **GREET (Winchcombe)**
COTSWOLD WAY

Mrs P D Bloom, The Homestead, Smithy Lane, GL54
5BP. ☎ (01242) 603808 • Map 150/024303 • BB **B** •
D2 T1 F1 • 3-10 • Ⓑ Ⓓ ⌂

■ **HARESFIELD VILLAGE (Stonehouse)**
COTSWOLD WAY

☆ The Beacon Hotel, GL10 3DX. ☎ (01452) 728884 •
Map 162/812099 • BB **D** • EM £5-£10, 7pm • D1 T/D2
F/T/D2 • 1-12 NX • Ⓥ Ⓑ Ⓓ Ⓢ

■ **HAWKESBURY (Badminton)**
COTSWOLD WAY

Anna, Ivy Cottage, Inglestone Common, GL9 1BX. ☎
(01454) 294237 • Map 172,162/754887 • BB **B** • EM
£8-£10.50, 6.30-8pm • S1 D3 T2 F1 • 1-12 NX • Ⓥ
Ⓑ Ⓓ Ⓢ ⌂ • Transport back to Way

■ **KEMBLE (Cirencester)**
THAMES WALK

Valerie Benson, Smerrill Barns, GL7 6BW. ☎ (01285)
770907 • Map 163/003975 • BB **D** • S1 D4 T1 F1 • 1-
12 • Ⓑ Ⓓ Ⓢ Ⓡ • 2Cr/C

■ **KING'S STANLEY (Stonehouse)**
COTSWOLD WAY

Jean Hanna, Old Chapel House, Broad Street, GL10
3PN. ☎ (01453) 826289 • Map 162/813033 • BB **C** •
EM from £6, 6.30-8pm • S1 D1 T1 F1 • 1-11 • Ⓥ Ⓑ
Ⓓ Ⓡ • List

☆ See Display Advertisement

B&B ACCOMMODATION ENGLAND GLOUCESTERSHIRE

■ KING'S STANLEY (CONTINUED)

Mrs Mavis Rollins, Nurashell, Bath Road, GL10 3JG.
☎ (01453) 823642 • Map 162/811034 • BB **B** • D1 T1
• 1-12 • Ⓓ Ⓢ Ⓡ 🛁 Ⓜ

Lesley Williams, Orchardene, Castle Street, GL10
3JH. ☎ (01453) 822684 • Map 162/810032 • BB **B** •
EM £7 • T1 • 1-12 NX • Ⓥ Ⓓ Ⓡ 🛁

Mrs Louise Walker, "Stantone", Coldwell Lane,
Middleyard, GL10 3PR. ☎ (01453) 822204 • Map
162/816030 • BB **B** • T1 • 1-11 • Ⓓ Ⓢ Ⓡ • Food
nearby

■ KINGSCOTE (Tetbury)

Mrs Jane Bateman, Bumpers Island Farm, GL8 8YQ.
☎ (01453) 860498 • Map 162,173/815965 • BB **B** •
S2 D1 T1 • 4-9 • Ⓑ Ⓓ Ⓢ

■ LECHLADE
THAMES PATH

Mr John Titchener, Cambrai Lodge, Oak Street, GL7
3AY. ☎ (01367) 253173 • Map 163/214998 • BB **B/C**
• S1 D1 T1 F/D1 • 1-12 • Ⓑ Ⓓ Ⓢ 🛁 • List/C

■ LEONARD STANLEY (Stonehouse)
COTSWOLD WAY

R Reeves, The Grey Cottage, Bath Road, GL10 3LU.
☎ (01453) 822515 • Map 162/803035 • BB **D** • EM
book first £15 • S1 D1 T1 • 1-12 NX • Ⓥ Ⓑ Ⓓ Ⓢ
Ⓡ • 2Cr/HC

■ LITTLE WITCOMBE (Gloucester)
COTSWOLD WAY

Miss J Bickell, Springfields Farm, GL3 4TU. ☎
(01452) 863532 • Map 163/924160 • BB **B** • EM book
first £6, 6.30-7pm • S1 D2 F/T1 • 1-12 • Ⓥ Ⓓ Ⓢ 🛁
• List

■ MARSHFIELD (Chippenham, Wilts)
COTSWOLD WAY

Mrs Cynthia Bond, Knowle Hill Farm, Beeks Lane,
SN14 8AA. ☎ (01225) 891503 • Map 172/788717 •
BB **B** • EM book first £7, 7pm • D1 T1 F1 • 1-12 NX •
Ⓥ Ⓑ Ⓓ Ⓢ 🛁

■ MICKLETON (Chipping Campden)
HEART OF ENGLAND WAY

Mrs J Lodge, Old Barn House, Mill Lane, GL55 6RT.
☎ (01386) 438668 • Map 151/160434 • BB **C** • D1 T1
• 1-12 NX • Ⓑ Ⓓ Ⓢ 🛁 • 2Cr

■ NAILSWORTH
COTSWOLD WAY

☆ Mrs Victoria Jennings, Apple Orchard House,
Springhill, GL6 0LX. ☎ (01453) 832503 • Map
162/848997 • BB **C** • EM book first £13, 6-8.30pm •
S1 D1 T2 F1 • 1-12 • Ⓥ Ⓑ Ⓓ Ⓢ 🛁 • 2Cr/C • SC
also

Mrs L Williams-Allen, The Laurels at Inchbrook, GL5
5HA. ☎ (01453) 834021 • Map 162/842008 • BB **C/D**
• EM book first £11, 7.30pm • D2/S2 T/S1 F/S1 • 1-
12 • Ⓥ Ⓑ Ⓓ Ⓢ 🛁 • 3Cr • Transport avail.

■ NEWENT

Cherry Grove B&B, Mill Lane, Kilcot, GL18 1NY. ☎
(01989) 720126 • Map 162/689253 • BB **B** • D2 F1 •
1-12 NX • Ⓑ Ⓢ • List

■ NORTH NIBLEY (Dursley)
COTSWOLD WAY

Diana A Eley, Nibley House, GL11 6DL. ☎ (01453)
543108 • Map 162/737958 • BB **B** • D1 T2 F1 • 1-12
Ⓑ Ⓓ Ⓢ 🛁 • Camping also. Luggage transport

■ NYMPSFIELD (Stonehouse)
COTSWOLD WAY

☆ Rose & Crown Inn, GL10 3TU. ☎ (01453) 86024(
• Map 162/800007 • BB **D** • EM £9.50, 6-10pm • D1
F3 • 1-12 • Ⓥ Ⓑ Ⓓ • 3Cr/C

■ OLD SODBURY (Bristol)
COTSWOLD WAY

John & Daphne Paz, Dornden Guest House, Church Lane, BS17 6NB. ☎ (01454) 313325 • Map 172/756818 • BB **D** • EM book first £10, 6.45pm • S2 T2 F5 • 1-12 NX • Ⓑ Ⓓ 🛁 • 2Cr

David & Margaret Warren, Sodbury House Hotel, Badminton Rd, BS17 6LU. ☎ (01454) 312847 • Map 172/746817 • BB **D** • EM Mon-Thurs £12.50-£15, 7-8pm • S6 D2 T2 F3 • 1-12 NX • Ⓥ Ⓑ Ⓓ Ⓢ Ⓡ 🛁 • 2Cr/C

■ PAINSWICK
COTSWOLD WAY

Mrs B Blatchley, Thorne, Friday Street, GL6 6QJ. ☎ (01452) 812476 • Map 162/867098 • BB **C** • T2 • 3-10 • Ⓑ Ⓓ Ⓢ • 2Cr

Pat Dean, "Armamy", Golf Course Road, GL6 6TJ. ☎ (01452) 812242 • Map 162/869108 • BB **C** • T1 F1 • 1-12 NX • Ⓑ Ⓓ Ⓢ Ⓜ

Alison Bancroft-Livingston, Beaconsfield House, New Street, GL6 6UN. ☎ (01452) 813001 • Map 162 /866097 • BB **C** • D1 T1 • 1-12 NX • Ⓑ Ⓓ Ⓢ 🛁 Ⓜ

☆ Jean Hernen, Brookhouse Mill Cottage, Tibbiwell Lane, GL6 6YA. ☎ (01452) 812854 • Map 162/869096 • BB **C** • D1 F1 • 1-12 • Ⓑ Ⓓ Ⓢ • List

**Brookhouse Mill
Tibbiwell Lane,
Painswick GL6 6YA
☎ (01452) 812854**

Beautiful C17th cottage set in gardens straddling a trout stream and waterfall. En-suite bedrooms, with all facilities. Beds are covered with hand-stitched patchwork quilts. No-smoking. Use of indoor swimming pool. Near Cotswold Way.

Michele Burdett, Damsels Farm, GL6 6UD. ☎ (01452) 812148 • Map 162/875114 • BB **C** • EM book first £15.50, 7pm • D1 T2 F2 • 3-9 • Ⓥ Ⓑ Ⓓ 🛁 Ⓜ • 2Cr

■ RANDWICK (Stroud)
COTSWOLD WAY

Mr & Mrs J Taylor, Court Farm, GL6 6HH. ☎ (01453) 764210 • Map 162/830068 • BB **B** • EM book first £7-£8, 7-7.30pm • S1 D1 T1 F1 • 1-12 NX • Ⓥ Ⓑ Ⓓ Ⓡ 🛁 • Luggage transport avail.

Mrs M Parish, Laurel Cottage, GL6 6HL. ☎ (01453) 763942 • Map 162/830068 • BB **B** • EM book first £6.50, from 6pm • D2 • 1-12 NX • Ⓓ Ⓡ 🛁

VEGETARIANS
Many establishments do a veggie breakfast even if they don't do an evening meal

---

■ SHURDINGTON (Cheltenham)
COTSWOLD WAY

Allards Hotel, GL51 5XA. ☎ (01242) 862498 • Map 163/928196 • BB **D** • EM £11.95, 6-8.30pm • S1 D5 T4 F2 • 1-12 • Ⓥ Ⓑ Ⓓ • 3Cr

■ ST BRIAVELS (Lydney)
OFFA'S DYKE & WYE VALLEY WALK

Keith & Marion Allen, Woodcroft, Lower Meend, GL15 6RW. ☎ (01594) 530083 • Map 162/552043 • BB **B** • EM book first £12 • F2 • 1-12 • Ⓑ Ⓓ Ⓢ 🛁

C Parker, Blue Barn, The Hudnalls, GL15 6RT. ☎ (01594) 530252 • Map 162/532037 • BB **C** • EM £9, from 6.30pm • S2 D3 T3 • 1-12 • Ⓥ Ⓑ Ⓓ Ⓢ • 3Cr • SC also

Ann Sabin, The Florence Country Hotel, Bigsweir, GL15 6QQ. ☎ (01594) 530830 • Map 162/544063 • BB **D** • EM book first £12, 7.30pm • D2 T2 F1 • 1-12 NX • Ⓥ Ⓑ Ⓓ Ⓢ 🛁 • 3Cr/C

■ STANWAY (Nr Cheltenham)
COTSWOLD WAY

Mrs S H Garwood, The Old Bakehouse, GL54 5PH. ☎ (01386) 584204 • Map 150/061323 • BB **B** • D2 T1 • 1-12 NX • Ⓓ Ⓢ

■ STONEHOUSE
COTSWOLD WAY

Mrs D Hodge, Merton Lodge, Ebley Road, GL10 2LQ. ☎ (01453) 822018 • Map 162/815047 • BB **B** • D3 • 1-12 NX • Ⓑ Ⓓ Ⓢ Ⓡ 🛁 • 2Cr • Food nearby

■ STOW-ON-THE-WOLD
OXFORDSHIRE WAY

Helen & Graham Keyte, The Limes, Tewkesbury Road, GL54 1EN. ☎ (01451) 830034 • Map 163/181264 • BB **B/C** • S1 D3 T1 F1 • 1-12 NX • Ⓑ Ⓓ 🛁

Robert & Dawn Smith, Corsham Field Farm House, Bledington Road, GL54 1JH. ☎ (01451) 831750 • Map 163/211259 • BB **B/C** • D2 T2 F3 • 1-12 • Ⓑ Ⓓ 🛁 • 2Cr/App

Jane Beynon, Orchard Cottage, Back Lane, Upper Oddington, GL56 0XL. ☎ (01451) 830785 • Map 163/222257 • BB **C** • EM book first £12.50, 7-8pm • D1 T1 • 3-11 • Ⓥ Ⓑ Ⓓ Ⓢ 🛁 • 2Cr/HC

Valerie Keyte, Fifield Cottage, Fosse Lane, GL54 1EH. ☎ (01451) 831056 • Map 163/189258 • BB **B/C** • D1 T1 F1 • 1-12 NX • Ⓑ Ⓓ 🛁

■ STROUD
COTSWOLD WAY

Mary Humphries, "Praha", 11 Heazle Place, Off Folley Lane, GL5 1UW. ☎ (01453) 751428 • Map 162/852056 • BB **A** • D1 • 1-12 • Ⓑ Ⓓ Ⓡ

☆ See Display Advertisement

■ STROUD (CONTINUED)

☆ Downfield Hotel, Cainscross Road, GL5 4HN. ☎ (01453) 764496 • Map 162/841051 • BB **B/C** • EM £8.50, 6.30-8pm • S4 D8 T7 F2 • 1-12 NX • Ⓥ Ⓑ Ⓓ Ⓡ 🛇 • 3Cr • Groups also

☆ Bell Hotel & Restaurant, Wallbridge, GL5 3JA. ☎ (01453) 763556 • Map 162/848050 • BB **C/D** • EM £7.50, 7-9pm • S1 D6 T4 F1 • 1-12 • Ⓥ Ⓑ Ⓓ Ⓢ Ⓡ 🛇 • 3Cr

■ TEWKESBURY
SEVERN WAY

Mr & Mrs C J Dickenson, Carrant Brook House, Rope Walk, GL20 5DS. ☎ (01684) 290355 • Map 150/896329 • BB **C** • S1 D1 T1 • 1-12 • Ⓑ Ⓓ Ⓢ Ⓜ

■ TODDINGTON (Cheltenham)
COTSWOLD WAY

Mrs Heather Butler, Stanway Grounds, GL54 5DR. ☎ (01242) 620079 • Map 150/054333 • BB **C** • EM book first £12.50 • D2 T1 • 1-12 • Ⓥ Ⓑ Ⓓ 🛇 • 2Cr/App

■ TORMARTON (Badminton)
COTSWOLD WAY

The Compass Inn, GL9 1JB. ☎ (01454) 218242/218577 • BB **D** • EM £5-£16.95, up to 10.30pm • S1 D11 T16 F3 • 1-12 NX • Ⓥ Ⓑ Ⓓ Ⓢ 🛇 Ⓜ • Charge for dogs

Heather Cadei, Chestnut Farm, GL9 1HS. ☎ (01454) 218563 • Map 172/769791 • BB **C** • EM £9.50, 8.30pm • D3 T2 • 1-12 • Ⓥ Ⓑ Ⓓ 🛇 Ⓜ

■ ULEY (Dursley)
COTSWOLD WAY

G & N Kent, Hill House, Crawley Hill, GL11 5BH. ☎ (01453) 860267 • Map 162/788996 • BB **B** • EM book first £9, 6.30pm • S1 D1 T1 F1 • 1-12 NX • Ⓥ Ⓑ Ⓓ Ⓢ

Mrs Susan Strain, Cotswold House, 57 The Street, GL11 5SL. ☎ (01453) 860305 • Map 162/790985 • BB **C** • D2 T1 • 1-11 • Ⓑ Ⓓ Ⓢ

■ WHITTINGTON (Cheltenham)
COTSWOLD WAY

Mrs A E Hughes, Ham Hill Farm, GL54 4EZ. ☎ (01242) 584415 • Map 163/985213 • BB **C** • S2 D2 T2 F1 • 1-12 NX • Ⓑ Ⓓ Ⓢ 🛇 • 2Cr/C

■ WINCHCOMBE (Cheltenham)
COTSWOLD WAY

Mrs J G Saunders, Great House, Castle Street, GL54 5JA. ☎ (01242) 602490 • Map 150,163/026282 • BB **B/C** • D1 F1 • 1-12 NX • Ⓓ Ⓢ

Mrs S Simmonds, Gower House, 16 North Street, GL54 5LH. ☎ (01242) 602616 • Map 150,163/025284 • BB **B** • D1 T2 • 1-12 NX • Ⓑ Ⓓ • 2Cr/C

☆ Mrs C M Rand, Clevely Cottage, Loadfield Farm, Corndean Lane, GL54 5AL. ☎ (01242) 602059 • Map 163/025263 • BB **B** • EM book first £7.50, 6.30pm • D1 T1 F1 • 1-12 NX • Ⓥ Ⓑ Ⓓ • List/C

☆ David Gould, The Plaisterers Arms, Abbey Terrace, GL54 5LL. ☎ (01242) 602358 • Map 150,163/024282 • BB **B/C** • EM £7, 6.30-9.30pm • D2 T2 F1 • 1-12 • Ⓥ Ⓑ Ⓓ 🛇 • 2Cr/App

Courtyard House, 18 High Street, GL54 5LJ. ☎ (01242) 602441 • Map 150,163/025282 • BB **C** • S1 D2 T2 • 1-12 • Ⓑ Ⓓ 🍴 • 2Cr/C

Mrs J E Upton, Mercia, Hailes Street, GL54 5HU. ☎ (01242) 602251 • Map 150,163/026285 • BB **C** • D2 T1 • 1-12 NX • Ⓑ Ⓓ Ⓢ 🍴 • 2Cr/C

Mrs Janet Cooper, Pilgrim House, Hailes, GL54 5PB. ☎ (01242) 603011 • Map 150/047304 • BB **B/C** • EM book first £10-£12, 7.30pm • D1 T2 • 1-12 NX • Ⓥ Ⓑ Ⓓ Ⓢ 🍴 Ⓜ

Mrs M Robins, 1 Stancombe View, GL54 5LE. ☎ (01242) 603654 • Map 150,163/023285 • BB **B** • S1 D1 • 4-10 • Ⓑ Ⓓ Ⓢ • List

Mrs S Chisholm, Blair House, 41 Gretton Road, GL54 5EG. ☎ (01242) 603626 • Map 150,163/023287 • BB **B** • S2 T2 • 1-12 • Ⓑ Ⓢ

Ms Adeline Rucklidge, Rutland Court, Cowl Lane, GL54 5RA. ☎ (01242) 603101 • Map 150,163/024284 • BB **C** • S1 D2 • 1-12 NX • Ⓢ • List

☆ Annie Hitch, Almsbury Farm, Vineyard Street, GL54 5LP. ☎ (01242) 602403 • Map 150, 163/024280 • BB **C/D** • D1 T1 • 2-11 • Ⓑ Ⓓ Ⓢ • 2Cr/HC

Almsbury Farm
Vineyard Street
Winchcombe
☎ **01242 602403**

Ideally located on the Cotswold Way only 150 yards from village, 17th C Almsbury Farm is set in peaceful country-side. We offer a high standard of accommodation including a "scrummy" breakfast, tea making facilities, TVs in rooms, all ensuite. 🏵🏵 Highly Commended

Mrs R Wilson, Parks Farm, Sudeley, GL54 5BX. ☎ (01242) 603874 • Map 150/046266 • BB **C** • EM book first £9.50, 7pm • T2 • 1-12 NX • Ⓑ Ⓓ Ⓢ 🍴 • C

■ WOTTON-ÜNDER-EDGE
COTSWOLD WAY

Mrs K P Forster, Under-the-Hill House, Adey's Lane, GL12 7LY. ☎ (01453) 842557 • Map 172,162/758937 • BB **B/C** • D1 T1 • 4-10 • Ⓓ Ⓢ

Mrs Sandra Nixon, The Coffee Shop, 31a Long Street, GL12 7BX. ☎ (01453) 843158 • Map 172,162/757933 • BB **C** • S1 D4 T4 • 1-12 • Ⓑ Ⓓ Ⓢ 🍴

Sylvia McIlroy, The Old Repository, Church Street B&B, 3 Church Street, Old Town, GL12 7HB. ☎ (01453) 843272/521650 • Map 172,162/758934 • BB **C** • D1 T2 • 3-10 • Ⓑ Ⓓ Ⓢ

Mrs S Mayo, Coombe Lodge, GL12 7NB. ☎ (01453) 845057 • Map 172,162/769940 • BB **C** • EM book first £12 • D2/F1 T1/F1 • 1-12 NX • Ⓥ Ⓓ Ⓢ 🍴 • 1Cr/HC

Mrs April Haddrell, Falcon Cottage, 15 Station Road, Charfield, GL12 8SY. ☎ (01453) 843528 • Map 172,162/724922 • BB **B** • T2 • 1-12 • Ⓓ Ⓢ • List

Mrs C Rollo, The Fleece Inn, Hillesley, GL12 7RD. ☎ (01453) 843189 • Map 172,162/769895 • BB **C** • EM £10, 7-9pm • D2 T1 • 1-12 NX • Ⓥ Ⓓ 🍴

HAMPSHIRE

■ ALTON

Mrs Wendy Bradford, The Vicarage, East Worldham, GU34 3AS. ☎ (01420) 82392 • Map 186/751381 • BB **B** • EM book first £6 Monday only, 6-7pm • S/T2 D/F1 • 1-12 NX • Ⓥ Ⓓ Ⓡ 🍴 • Food nearby (not Monday)

■ ANDOVER

Mr & Mrs Norton, Staggs, Windmill Hill, Ibthorpe, Hurstbourne Tarrant, SP11 0BP. ☎ (01264) 736235 • Map 185/374536 • BB **B** • EM £6, 6-9pm • S1 D1 T1 • 1-12 NX • Ⓥ Ⓓ

■ BASHLEY

Mrs H Bursey, Wayward Cottage, New Lane, BH25 5TD. ☎ (01425) 611500 • Map 195/236967 • BB **C** • D1 T1 • 2-10 • Ⓑ Ⓓ Ⓢ Ⓡ • 2Cr/HC

■ BURITON (Petersfield)
SOUTH DOWNS WAY

Mrs M Bray, Nursted Farm, GU31 5RW. ☎ (01730) 264278 • Map 197/754214 • BB **B** • T3 F1 • 5-2 • Ⓑ Ⓓ Ⓢ Ⓡ

Sarah Moss, Pillmead House, North Lane Burian, GU31 5RS. ☎ (01730) 266795 • Map 197/740200 • BB **C** • EM book first £12.50, 7-7.30pm • T2 • 1-12 NX • Ⓥ Ⓑ Ⓓ Ⓢ 🍴

■ BURLEY (Ringwood)

Mrs G Russell, Charlwood, Longmead Road, BH24 4BY. ☎ (01425) 403242 • Map 195/205037 • BB **C** • D1 T1 • 1-11 • Ⓓ Ⓢ 🍴

Robin & Mary Ford, Holmans, Bisterne Close, BH24 4AZ. ☎ (01425) 402307 • Map 195/229025 • BB **C** • D2 T2 • 1-12 NX • Ⓑ Ⓓ Ⓢ 🍴 • 2Cr/HC

Jenny Hardman, "Miracle Trees", Cott Lane, BH24 4BB. ☎ (01425) 403380 • Map 195/218030 • BB **C** • S1 D1 T1 • 1-12 NX • Ⓑ Ⓓ Ⓢ 🍴 • Food nearby

■ CHERITON (Alresford)

Margaret Hoskings, Brandy Lea, SO24 0QQ. ☎ (01962) 771534 • Map 185/581283 • BB **B** • S1 T1 • 1-12 • Ⓑ Ⓓ 🍴

☆ See Display Advertisement

■ DUMMER (Basingstoke)

☆ Mrs E Hutton, Oakdown Farm, RG23 7LR. ☎ (01256) 397218 • Map 185/587472 • BB **B** • D1 T2 • 1-12 • Ⓑ Ⓓ 🐾 Ⓜ • 1Cr/C

■ EAST MEON (Petersfield)
SOUTH DOWNS WAY

Mrs J Rockett, Drayton Cottage, Drayton, GU32 1PW. ☎ (01730) 823472 • Map 185/669232 • BB **C** • EM book first £12 • D1 T1 • 1-12 NX • Ⓥ Ⓑ Ⓓ Ⓢ • List/HC

■ EMSWORTH

☆ Merry Hall Hotel, 73 Horndean Road, PO10 7PU. ☎ (01243) 431377 • Map 197/743072 • BB **D** • EM book first £8, 7pm • S3 D4 T2 F3 • 1-12 • Ⓥ Ⓑ Ⓓ Ⓢ Ⓡ 🐾 • 2Cr • Groups also

■ FORDINGBRIDGE

Mr & Mrs R Harte, Alderholt Mill, Sandleheath Road, SP6 1PU. ☎ (01425) 653130 • Map 195/119143 • BB **C** • EM book first £12.50, 7-8.30pm • S1 D3 T1 • 1-12 NX • Ⓥ Ⓑ Ⓓ Ⓢ 🐾

■ GODSHILL (Fordingbridge)

J & B Grigg, The Old Post Office, SP6 2LW. ☎ (01425) 653719 • Map 184/166158 • BB **B** • EM £7, 8pm • D1 T2 • 1-12 • Ⓥ Ⓓ

■ HALE (Fordingbridge)

Forest Cottage, Hatchet Green, SP6 2NE. ☎ (01725) 510529 • Map 184/194193 • BB **C** • S1 D2 • 1-12 NX • Ⓑ Ⓢ

■ HAMBLEDON (Waterlooville)
WAYFARER'S WALK

Mr & Mrs Lutyens, Mornington House, PO7 4RW. ☎ (01705) 632704 • Map 196/644149 • BB **B/C** • T2 • 1-12 NX • Ⓓ Ⓢ 🐾 • List

■ HIGHCLERE (Newbury, Berks)

Westridge Open Centre, Andover Road, RG20 9PJ. ☎ (01635) 253322 • Map 174/436604 • BB **A** • EM book first £5, 6.30pm • S3 T2 • 1-12 NX • Ⓥ Ⓓ Ⓢ • Extra for cooked breakfast. Closed public holidays

■ HOUGHTON (Stockbridge)

Mrs M Shea, Rowans, SO20 6LT. ☎ (01794) 388551 • Map 185/340318 • BB **D** • S1 D1 F1 • 1-12 NX • Ⓑ Ⓓ Ⓢ 🐾

■ HYTHE (Southampton)
SOLENT WAY

Mrs C Archdeacon, Dale Farm House, Manor Road, Applemore Hill, Dibden, SO45 5TJ. ☎ (01703) 849632 • Map 196/395078 • BB **C** • EM book first £11.50, 6-7pm • S1 D2 T1 F2 • 1-12 NX • Ⓥ Ⓑ Ⓓ • 2Cr

Mr & Mrs G A Swain, "Changri-La", 12 Ashleigh Close, SO45 3QP. ☎ (01703) 846664 • Map 196/423058 • BB **B** • D1 T1 • 1-12 NX • Ⓓ Ⓢ • 1Cr/HC

■ KINGSCLERE (Newbury, Berks)

Mrs S A Salm, Cleremede, Fox's Lane, RG20 5SL. ☎ (01635) 297298 • Map 174/521587 • BB **C** • EM book first £10, 7.30-8pm • S1 T2 • 1-12 • Ⓑ Ⓓ Ⓢ 🐾 • 2Cr/HC

■ LYMINGTON
SOLENT WAY

P & R Davies, Altworth 12, North Close, SO41 9BT. ☎ (01590) 674082 • Map 196/325958 • BB **B** • S1 D1 F/T1 • 3-10 • Ⓓ Ⓢ Ⓡ • List/App

■ LYNDHURST (New Forest)

Lyndhurst House, 35 Romsey Road, SO43 7AR. ☎ (01703) 282230 • Map 196/298084 • BB **B** • D1 T4 F2 • 2-12 NX • Ⓑ Ⓓ Ⓡ 🐾 • SC also

William & Mary Dibben, Stable End, Emery Down, SO43 7FJ. ☎ (01703) 282504 • Map 196/290089 • BB **B/C** • D1 T1 • 1-12 • Ⓑ Ⓓ Ⓢ

Grove House, Minstead, SO43 7GG. ☎ (01703) 813211 • Map 195/272107 • BB **B/C** • T/F1 • 1-12 • Ⓑ Ⓓ Ⓢ 🐾 • List

■ MEONSTOKE
SOUTH DOWNS WAY

Mrs Claire Allan, Harvestgate Farm, Stocks Lane, SO32 3NQ. ☎ (01489) 877675 • Map 185/628200 • BB **C** • EM book first £10, 7.30pm • D1 T1 F1 • 1-12 NX • Ⓥ Ⓑ Ⓓ Ⓢ 🐾 Ⓜ

■ NEW MILTON

Mr & Mrs M Pearce, St Ursula, 30 Hobart Road, BH25 6EG. ☎ (01425) 613515 • Map 195/239947 • BB **C** • EM book first £7, 6.30-7pm • S2 D1 T2 F1 • 1-12 • Ⓥ Ⓑ Ⓓ Ⓢ Ⓡ 🐾

■ PETERSFIELD
SOUTH DOWNS WAY

Mrs B West, Ridgefield, Station Road, GU32 3DE. ☎ (01730) 261402 • Map 197/743237 • BB **C** • D1 T2 • 1-12 NX • Ⓓ Ⓢ Ⓡ

Mrs P Scurfield, Heath Farmhouse, GU31 4HU. ☎ (01730) 264709 • Map 197/757224 • BB **B** • D1 T1 F1 • 1-12 NX • Ⓑ Ⓓ Ⓡ • 2Cr/C

Jennifer Tarver, 1 The Spain, GU31 4AD. ☎ (01730) 261678 • Map 197/748232 • BB **B/C** • S1 D1 T2 • 1-12 • Ⓑ Ⓓ Ⓢ Ⓡ

■ PORTCHESTER (Fareham)

Mrs R L Jones, 144 Castle Street, PO16 9QH. ☎ (01705) 370376 • Map 196/622047 • BB **B** • S1 T1 • 1-12 • Ⓥ Ⓢ ·Ⓡ 🐾 • Food nearby

■ RINGWOOD

Mrs M Burt, Fraser House, Salisbury Road, Blashford, BH24 3PB. ☎ (01425) 473958 • Map 195/149068 • BB **C** • S1 D2 T2 • 1-12 • Ⓑ Ⓓ Ⓢ 🐾

■ ROMSEY (New Forest)

Mrs Christina Pybus, Pyesmead Farm, Plaitford, SO51 6EE. ☎ (01794) 323386 • Map 184/280193 • BB **B** • EM book first £9, 7pm • D2 T1 • 1-12 NX • Ⓥ Ⓑ Ⓓ Ⓢ 🐾 • List/C

■ SHIPTON BELLINGER (Tidworth)

Col & Mrs J Peecock, Parsonage Farm, SP9 7UF. ☎ (01980) 842404 • Map 184/232453 • BB **C** • T2 F1 • 1-12 NX • Ⓑ Ⓓ Ⓢ • 1Cr/C • Food nearby

■ SOBERTON (Droxford, Southampton)

Rosemary Taylor, Moortown Farm, Station Road, SO32 3QU. ☎ (01489) 877256 • Map 185/612179 • BB **C** • T1 F1 • 1-12 NX • Ⓑ Ⓓ Ⓢ 🐾 • List/C

■ SOUTHSEA

Glenroy Guest House, 28 Waverley Road, PO5 2PW. ☎ (01705) 814922 • Map 196/650985 • BB **B** • S2 D2 T2 F2 • 1-12 • Ⓑ Ⓓ Ⓡ

■ STOCKBRIDGE

Carbery Guest House, Salisbury Hill, SO20 6EZ. ☎ (01264) 810771 • Map 185/350351 • BB **D** • EM £12, 7pm • S4 D3 T2 F2 • 1-11 NX • Ⓥ Ⓑ Ⓓ

■ WARNFORD (Southampton)

Mrs Sarah Broadbent, Hayden Barn Cottage, SO32 3LF. ☎ (01730) 829454 • Map 185/627230 • BB **C** • S1 T2 • 1-12 NX • Ⓑ Ⓓ Ⓢ 🐾

■ WINCHESTER
THREE CASTLES WALK & SOUTH DOWNS WAY

Mrs A Farrell, 5 Ranelagh Road, SO23 9TA. ☎ (01962) 869555 • Map 185/476286 • BB **C** • S1 D1 T1 F1 • 1-12 NX • Ⓑ Ⓓ Ⓢ Ⓡ Ⓜ • 2Cr/C

Mrs S Pell, The Lilacs, 1 Harestock Close, off Andover Road North, SO22 6NP. ☎ (01962) 884122 • Map 185/468321 • BB **B** • EM book first £8, 7-9pm • D/F1 T1 • 1-12 NX • Ⓥ Ⓑ Ⓓ Ⓢ Ⓡ 🐾

Mrs S Tisdall, 32 Hyde Street, SO23 7DX. ☎ (01962) 851621 • Map 185/480300 • BB **B** • D1 F1 • 1-12 NX • Ⓢ Ⓡ • 1Cr

Mrs R Ashby, Mays Farm, Longwood Dean, SO21 1JR. ☎ (01962) 777486 • Map 185/547243 • BB **C** • EM book first £7.50-£12, 7.30pm • D1 T1 F1 • 1-12 NX • Ⓥ Ⓑ Ⓓ Ⓢ 🐾 • SC also

HEREFORD & WORCESTER

■ BALLINGHAM (Hereford)
WYE VALLEY WALK

Mrs J Williams, "Wailea", HR2 6NH. ☎ (01432) 840255 • Map 149/577317 • BB **B/C** • EM book first £6 upwards, up to 9pm • T1 • 1-12 NX • Ⓥ Ⓑ Ⓓ Ⓢ 🐾 Ⓜ • 2Cr

■ BEWDLEY

Mrs P A Grainger, Lightmarsh Farm, Crundalls Lane, DY12 1NE. ☎ (01299) 404027 • Map 138/788768 • BB **C** • D1 T1 • 1-12 NX • Ⓑ Ⓓ Ⓢ Ⓡ 🐾 • 2Cr/HC • Steam railway - seasonal

☆ See Display Advertisement

■ BREDWARDINE
WYE VALLEY WALK

Mrs Sue Whittall, Old Court Farm, HR3 6BT. ☎ (01981) 500375 • Map 161,148,149/335445 • BB **C** • EM book first £13-£17, 7-7.30pm • D3 F1 • 1-12 NX • Ⓥ Ⓑ Ⓓ • 1Cr • SC also

■ BROADWAY
COTSWOLD WAY

Olive Branch Guest House, 78 High Street, WR12 7AJ. ☎ (01386) 853464 • Map 161,148,149/098375 • BB **D** • S2 D2 T2 F2 • 1-12 • Ⓑ Ⓓ • 3Cr/C • SC also

Southwave House, Station Road, WR12 7DE. ☎ (01386) 853681 • Map 150/091378 • BB **C** • S1 D4 T2 • 1-12 NX • Ⓑ Ⓓ 🛁 • 2Cr/C

Mrs P Renfrew, West Bank, Station Road, WR12 7DE. ☎ (01386) 852372 • Map 150/090380 • BB **B** • T1 F1 • 3-10 • Ⓓ Ⓢ • List

Helen Richardson, Whiteacres Guest House, Station Road, WR12 7DE. ☎ (01386) 852320 • Map 150/090380 • BB **C** • D5 T1 • 3-11 • Ⓑ Ⓓ Ⓢ • 2Cr/HC

Mrs B Gwilliams, The Orchard B&B, Leamington Road, WR12 7EB. ☎ (01386) 852534 • Map 150/099388 • BB **B** • D1 T1 • 1-12 NX • Ⓓ Ⓢ 🛁 • List

Anne C Evans, Eastbank, Station Drive, WR12 7DF. ☎ (01386) 852659 • Map 150/090380 • BB **B/C/D** • EM book first £13.50-16.50, 7pm • D2 T2 F2 • 1-12 NX • Ⓥ Ⓑ Ⓓ Ⓢ 🛁 • 3Cr

D J & I Porter, Pathlow House, 82 High Street, WR12 7AJ. ☎ (01386) 853444 • Map 150/101376 • BB **C/D** • D4 T2 • 1-12 NX • Ⓑ Ⓓ • List

☆ Mr Andrew Scott, Crown & Trumpet Inn, Church Street, WR12 7AE. ☎ (01386) 853202 • Map 150/095374 • BB **C/D** • EM £5-£6, 6.15pm • D3 T1 • 1-12 • Ⓥ Ⓑ 🛁 • 3Cr/App

■ BROMYARD

Mrs E Whiteley, Park House, 28 Sherford Street, HR7 4DL. ☎ (01885) 482294 • Map 149/656545 • BB **B** • S1 D1 T1 F2 • 1-12 • Ⓑ Ⓓ Ⓢ • 2Cr • SC also

■ BYFORD (Hereford)
WYE VALLEY WALK

Mrs Audrey Mayson, Old Rectory, HR4 7LD. ☎ (01981) 590218 • Map 161,148,149/396429 • BB **C** • EM book first £12, 7pm • D2 T1 • 3-11 • Ⓥ Ⓑ Ⓓ Ⓢ • Dogs OK outside

■ CLIFFORD (Hereford)
OFFA'S DYKE & WYE VALLEY WALK

☆ Mrs Julie Jones, Cottage Farm, Middlewood, HR3 5SX. ☎ (01497) 831496 • Map 161,148/288447 • BB **B** • T1 F1 • 1-12 NX • Ⓓ Ⓢ • Part of Golden Valley & Black Mountains B&B group. See Display opposite.

■ CROPTHORNE (Pershore)

Joan & Doug Faulkner, The Cedars Guest House, Evesham Road (A44), WR10 3JU. ☎ (01386) 860219 • Map 150/997443 • BB **B/C** • EM £8, 6.30pm • S1 D1 T2 F2 • 1-12 NX • Ⓥ Ⓑ Ⓓ 🛁 • 2Cr

■ EVESHAM

Mrs D Salter, Dayleen Guest House, 16 Broadway Road, WR11 6BQ. ☎ (01386) 446676 • Map 150/047433 • BB **C** • D2 T1 • 3-10 NX • Ⓑ Ⓓ Ⓢ Ⓡ

Park View Hotel, Waterside, WR11 6BS. ☎ (01386) 442639 • Map 150/038433 • BB **C** • EM for groups £9 • S10 D3 T11 F2 • 1-12 NX • Ⓥ Ⓓ Ⓡ 🛁 • 1Cr •

Mrs M W Addy, "Whitening Close", Arrow Lane, North Littleton, WR11 5QR. ☎ (01386) 832095 • Map 150/080473 • BB **B** • D1 T1 • 1-12 • Ⓑ Ⓓ Ⓢ Ⓜ

■ FOWNHOPE (Hereford)
WYE VALLEY WALK

The Squirrels, HR1 4PB. ☎ (01432) 860413 • Map 149/579347 • BB **B/C** • D1 T1 • 1-12 NX • Ⓑ Ⓓ • Food nearby

■ HEREFORD

R & D A Burrough, Cedar Guest House, 123 Whitecross Road, Whitecross, HR4 0LS. ☎ (01432) 267235 • Map 149/500403 • BB **B** • T1 F3 • 1-12 NX • Ⓓ Ⓡ • 1Cr

Castle Pool Hotel, Castle Street, HR1 2NR. ☎ (01432) 356321 • Map 149/513397 • BB **D** • EM £14.50, from 7.30pm • S9 D8 T8 F2 • 1-12 • Ⓥ Ⓑ Ⓓ Ⓡ 🛁 • 4Cr/C

■ HERGEST (Kington)
OFFA'S DYKE

Mrs E Protheroe, Bucks Head House, School Farm, HR5 3EW. ☎ (01544) 231063 • Map 148/262550 • BB **B** • EM £8, 6.30pm • S2 D2 T1 F1 • 1-12 • Ⓥ Ⓓ 🛁 • SC also

■ HIMBLETON (Droitwich)

Mrs P Havard, Phepson Farm, WR9 7JZ. ☎ (01905) 391205 • Map 150/940598 • BB **C** • D2 T1 F1 • 1-12 NX • Ⓑ Ⓓ Ⓢ 🛁 • 2Cr/C • SC also

■ HOARWITHY (Hereford)
WYE VALLEY WALK

☆ Carol Probert, The Old Mill, HR2 6QH. ☎ (01432) 840602 • Map 149/545292 • BB **B** • EM book first £10, 7pm • S1 D6 • 1-12 • Ⓥ Ⓑ Ⓓ Ⓢ • 2Cr/C • SC also

The Old Mill, Hoarwithy, situated in small unspoilt village, 18th century farmhouse, an ideal base for exploring a county of truly outstanding natural beauty. Home cooking a speciality.
Friendly atmosphere.
Write or telephone

Carol Probert, The Old Mill, Hoarwithy,
Hereford HR2 6QH. 01432 840602

■ KIMBOLTON (Leominster)
Mrs Jean Franks, The Fieldhouse Farm,, HR6 0EP. ☎ (01568) 614789 • Map 137,149,138/524606 • BB **B** • EM £11, 7pm • D1 T1 F1 • 3-11 NX • Ⓥ Ⓑ Ⓓ Ⓢ Ⓡ 🐾 • List

■ KINGTON
OFFA'S DYKE

☆ Burton Hotel, Mill Street, HR5 3BQ. ☎ (01544) 230323 • Map 148/296565 • BB **D** • EM £7.70-£14, from 7.30pm • S1 D6 T5 F3 • 1-12 • Ⓥ Ⓑ Ⓓ 🐾 • 4Cr/App

Mr & Mrs Darwin, Church House, Church Road, HR5 3AG. ☎ (01544) 230534 • Map 148/291567 • BB **C** • D1 T1 • 1-12 NX • Ⓓ Ⓢ 🐾

■ LEDBURY
☆ The Royal Oak Hotel, The Southend, HR8 2EY. ☎ (01531) 632110 • Map 149/711373 • BB **C** • EM £5, 6.30-10pm • S8 D2 T4 F2 • 1-12 • Ⓥ Ⓑ Ⓓ Ⓡ Ⓜ • 3Cr/C • Groups also. See display over page.

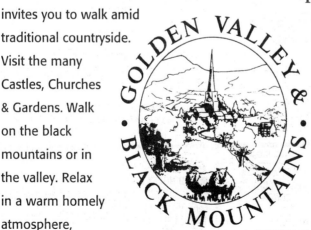
HEREFORD & WORCESTER

B&B ACCOMMODATION ENGLAND

ENGLAND HEREFORD & WORCESTER

B&B ACCOMMODATION

■ LEOMINSTER
GLYNDWR'S WAY & OFFA'S DYKE

Mrs J Ruell, Ladymeadow Farm, Luston, HR6 0AS.
☎ (01568) 780262 • Map 148,137,149,138/485640 •
BB **B/C** • S1 D1 T1 F1 • 3-10 NX • Ⓑ Ⓓ Ⓢ • 1Cr

Mrs M Longworth, Bramlea, Barons Cross Road,
HR6 8RW. ☎ (01568) 613406 • Map
148,149/492591 • BB **C** • S1 T1 F1 • 1-12 NX • Ⓑ Ⓓ
Ⓢ Ⓡ ♨ • 1Cr/C

■ LONGTOWN (Hereford)
OFFA'S DYKE

Mrs I Pritchard, Olchon Cottage, HR2 0NS. ☎
(01873) 860233 • Map 161/306287 • BB **C** • EM book
first £10, 6.30pm • F/T/D2 • 1-12 NX • Ⓥ Ⓑ Ⓓ ♨ •
2Cr/C

■ MALVERN

☆ Rock House, 144 West Malvern Road, WR14 4NJ.
☎ (01684) 574536 • Map 150/764470 • BB **C** • EM
book first £11, 6.30pm • D5 T3 F2 • 2-11 + XMAS •
Ⓥ Ⓑ Ⓓ Ⓢ Ⓡ ♨ • 1Cr/C • SC & groups also

☆ Sidney House, 40 Worcester Road, WR14 4AA. ☎
(01684) 574994 • Map 150/775463 • BB **C/D** • S1 D4
T2 F1 • 1-12 NX • Ⓑ Ⓓ Ⓢ Ⓡ ♨ • 2Cr/C • Guided
walks also

Barbara & Richard Rowan, The Red Gate, 32 Avenue
Road, WR14 3BJ. ☎ (01684) 565013 • Map
150/785457 • BB **D** • S1 D4 T2 • 1-12 NX • Ⓑ Ⓓ Ⓢ
Ⓡ • 3Cr/HC

Mrs Ann Porter, Croft Guest House, Bransford, WR6
5JD. ☎ (01886) 832227 • Map 150/795524 • BB **C** •
EM book first £9-£11, 7-7.30 • D4 T/F1 • 1-12 • Ⓥ
Ⓑ Ⓓ Ⓢ ♨ • 2Cr

☆ Thornbury House Hotel, Avenue Road, WR14 3AR.
☎ (01684) 572278 • Map 150/781457 • BB **D** • EM
£15, 6.30-9pm • S5 D6 T3 F1 • 1-12 NX • Ⓥ Ⓑ Ⓓ
Ⓡ ♨ • 3Cr/C • Groups also

"Strathmore", West Malvern Road, Upper Wyche,
WR14 4EL. ☎ (01684) 562245 • Map 150/768440 •
BB **C** • D1 T1 • 1-12 NX • Ⓓ Ⓢ Ⓡ

■ MUCH MARCLE
WYE VALLEY WALK

Mrs Ann Jordan, New House Farm, HR8 2PH. ☎
(01531) 660604 • Map 149/640321 • BB **B** • EM £10
• D1 T1 • 1-12 NX • Ⓥ Ⓓ • 1Cr/C • Transport avail.

■ ODDINGLEY (Droitwich)

Mrs Gwen Jackson, Wessex House Farm, Trench
Lane, WR9 7NB. ☎ (01905) 772826 • Map
150/914604 • BB **B** • D1 F1 • 3-10 • Ⓓ Ⓢ

■ ROSS-ON-WYE
WYE VALLEY WALK

Mrs M Ryder, Broadlands, Ledbury Road, HR9 7AU.
☎ (01989) 563663 • Map 162/602246 • BB **B** • S2
D3 • 1-12 NX • Ⓑ Ⓓ Ⓜ

☆ P & G Williams, Sunnymount Hotel, Ryefield Road, HR9 5LU. ☎ (01989) 563880 • Map 162/606242 • BB **C/D** • EM £14.50, 7pm • S3 D3 T3 • 1-12 NX • Ⓑ Ⓓ Ⓢ • 3Cr/C

☆ Vaga House, Wye Street, HR9 7BS. ☎ (01989) 563024 • Map 162/596241 • BB **C** • EM book first £9.50, 7pm • S1 D3 T2 F1 • 1-12 NX • Ⓓ Ⓢ 🐾 Ⓜ • 1Cr/C

☆ Mrs Jean Jones, The Arches Country House, Walford Road, HR9 5PT. ☎ (01989) 563348 • Map 162/597230 • BB **C** • EM book first £7, 7.30pm • S1 D3 T2 F2 • 1-12 • Ⓑ Ⓓ Ⓢ 🐾

☆ The Skakes, Glewstone, HR9 6AZ. ☎ (01989) 770456 • Map 162/547225 • BB **B/C** • EM book first £8, 7pm • S1 D4 T2 • 1-12 NX • Ⓑ Ⓓ Ⓢ 🐾 Ⓜ • 2Cr

☆ Patrick & Clare O'Reilly, Linden House, 14 Church Street, HR9 5HN. ☎ (01989) 565373 • Map 162/598241 • BB **C** • S3 D3 T1 • 1-12 • Ⓑ Ⓓ Ⓢ 🐾 • List/C

■ **STOKE PRIOR (Bromsgrove)**

Mrs P Dexter, Astwood Court Farm, Astwood Lane, B60 4BB. ☎ (01527) 821362 • Map 150/940657 • BB **C/D** • D/S1 T/S1 F/S1 • 1-12 NX • Ⓑ Ⓓ Ⓢ • List

■ **UPTON-UPON-SEVERN (Worcester)**

E Denley, 1 Elm Villas, Holly Green, WR8 0PD. ☎ (01684) 592182 • Map 150/860410 • BB **A** • S1 D1 T1 F1 • 1-12 • Ⓥ Ⓑ Ⓢ 🐾 Ⓜ

■ **VOWCHURCH (Hereford)**

Mrs J Powell, Little Green Farm, Newton St Margarets, HR2 0QJ. ☎ (01981) 510205 • Map 161, 149/332340 • BB **B** • D2 F1 • 4-10 • Ⓥ Ⓓ Ⓢ 🐾

☆ See Display Advertisement

HERTFORDSHIRE

■ CROXLEY GREEN (Rickmansworth)
GRAND UNION CANAL WALK

Beryl Millward, Moorside, 30 Hazelwood Road, WD3 3EB. ☎ (01923) 226666/233751 • Map 176,166/080953 • BB **B/C** • S1 T3 • 1-12 • D S R ॐ • List

■ HEMEL HEMPSTEAD
GRAND UNION CANAL WALK

Southville Private Hotel, 9 Charles Street, HP1 1JH. ☎ (01442) 251387 • Map 166/053066 • BB **C** • S10 D2 T6 F1 • 1-12 • R ॐ M • List

■ ST ALBANS

Alison Burroughes, Amaryllis, 25 Ridgmont Road, AL1 3AG. ☎ (01727) 862755/(0589) 542126 • Map 166/154069 • BB **B** • S1 T1 F1 • 1-12 • D S R • List

■ TRING
RIDGEWAY & GRAND UNION CANAL WALK

Royal Hotel, Station Road, HP23 5QR. ☎ (01442) 827616 • Map 165/950122 • BB **C** • EM £8, 6-11pm • S2 D6 T8 F4 • 1-12 • V B D S R ॐ

■ WATFORD
GRAND UNION CANAL WALK

Mr & Mrs Troughton, 33 Courtlands Drive, WD1 3HU. ☎ (01923) 220531 • Map 176,166/093988 • BB **C** • T2 • 1-12 • D S R

HUMBERSIDE

COUNTY NO LONGER EXISTS. SEE EAST RIDING OF YORKSHIRE AND LINCOLNSHIRE FOR ENTRIES PREVIOUSLY LISTED HERE.

ISLE OF WIGHT

■ ALVERSTONE
ISLE OF WIGHT COAST PATH

Mrs G Watling, The Grange Country House Hotel, PO36 0EZ. ☎ (01983) 403729 • Map 196/577856 • BB **C/D** • EM book first £13.50, 6.30-7.30pm • S1 D3 T2 F1 • 2-11 NX • V B D S R • 3Cr/C

■ BONCHURCH (Ventnor)

☆ The Lake Hotel, Shore Road, PO38 1RF. ☎ (01983) 852613 • Map 196/572778 • BB **C/D** • EM £8, 6.30-7pm • S2 D8 T6 F4 • 3-10 • V B D S ॐ • 3Cr/C

■ BRIGHSTONE (Newport)
ISLE OF WIGHT COAST PATH

Buddlebrook Guest House, Moortown Lane, PO30 4AN. ☎ (01983) 740381 • Map 196/426832 • BB **C** • D2 T1 • 1-12 NX • B D S ॐ • 1Cr/C

■ CARISBROOKE (Newport)

Mrs V Skeats, The Mount, 1 Calbourne Road, PO30 5AP. ☎ (01983) 522173/524359 • Map 196/479881 • BB **B** • EM book first £5, 7pm • S1 D1 T1 • 3-10 NX • V D S

■ CHALE (Ventnor)
ISLE OF WIGHT COAST PATH

Wendy Hardy, Yew Tree Cottage, PO38 2HL. ☎ (01983) 730660 • Map 196/482772 • BB **B** • S1 D2 • 3-10 • D

Mrs E L Whittington, Cortina, Gotten Lane, PO38 2HQ. ☎ (01983) 551292 • Map 196/487791 • BB **B** • EM book first £6.50, 6.30pm • D1 T1 • 1-11 NX • V B D S M

■ COWES
ISLE OF WIGHT COAST PATH

Mrs J Finch, Caledon Guest House, 59 Mill Hill Road, PO31 7EG. ☎ (01983) 293599 • Map 196/495956 • BB **B** • S2 D1 T1 F2 • 1-12 NX • D S ॐ

Jane Gibbons, 14 Milton Road, PO31 7PX. ☎ (01983) 295723 • Map 196/496949 • BB **B** • EM book first £6.50, 7pm • S1 D1 T1 F1 • 3-12 NX • V B D S ॐ M • C • SC also

■ FRESHWATER
ISLE OF WIGHT COAST PATH

Royal Standard Hotel, School Green Road, PO40 9AJ. ☎ (01983) 753227 • Map 196/336871 • BB **C** • EM £5, 6-9pm • S4 D3 T1 F3 • 1-12 • V B D S ॐ • 3Cr

Brookside Forge Hotel, Brookside Road, PO40 9ER. ☎ (01983) 754644 • Map 196/336870 • BB **C** • EM £7.95, 7pm • S1 D5 T2 F2 • 1-12 • V B D S R ॐ • 3Cr/C

■ NEWPORT

Mrs C Simms, Fairways, 99 St Johns Road, PO30 1LS. ☎ (01983) 522254 • Map 196/498884 • BB **B** • D2 • 3-11 NX • D S

ISLE OF WIGHT · HERTFORDSHIRE · ENGLAND · B&B ACCOMMODATION

Mrs Carol Corke, Salween House, 7 Watergate Road, PO30 1XN. ☎ (01983) 523456 • Map 196/499882 • BB **B** • T3 • 1-12 NX • Ⓑ Ⓓ Ⓢ Ⓜ • 1Cr/HC

Mrs Elgar, Newport Quay Hotel, Quay Street, PO30 5BA. ☎ (01983) 528544 • Map 196/500892 • BB **B/C/D** • EM book first £9.95, 6.30pm • S3 D4 T3 F2 • 1-12 • Ⓥ Ⓑ Ⓓ Ⓢ • 2Cr/App

■ NITON
ISLE OF WIGHT COAST PATH

Brook Lodge, Rectory Lane, PO38 2AY. ☎ (01983) 730927 • Map 196/508766 • BB **B** • S1 D1 T1 F1 • 1-12 NX • Ⓑ Ⓓ

■ RYDE
ISLE OF WIGHT COAST PATH

Rowantrees, 63 Spencer Road, PO33 3AF. ☎ (01983) 568081 • Map 196/585926 • BB **B** • S2 D2 • 1-12 NX • Ⓓ Ⓡ 🐾 • List • SC also

David Wood, Seaward Guest House, 14/16 George Street, PO33 2EW. ☎ (01983) 563168 • Map 196/593928 • BB **B/C** • EM book first £7, 6.30pm • D3 T1 F3 • 1-12 • Ⓥ Ⓑ Ⓓ Ⓢ Ⓡ • List/C

■ SANDOWN
ISLE OF WIGHT COAST PATH

Mrs G Watson, Sunnyside, 6 Pier Street, PO36 8JR. ☎ (01983) 406022 • Map 196/598841 • BB **B** • EM book first £3.50, 6pm • D2 T1 • 4-11 • Ⓥ Ⓓ Ⓡ 🐾 Ⓜ

■ SHALFLEET
ISLE OF WIGHT COASTAL PATH

M Young, The Old Malthouse, 1 Mill Road, PO30 4NE. ☎ (01983) 531329 • Map 196/414892 • BB **B/C** • D1 F1 • 1-12 NX • Ⓑ Ⓓ Ⓢ • 2Cr/C • Food nearby

■ SHANKLIN
ISLE OF WIGHT COAST PATH

☆ Mrs P Metcalf, Culham Lodge, 31 Landguard Manor Road, PO37 7HZ. ☎ (01983) 862880 • Map 196/580820 • BB **C** • EM £7, 6pm • S1 D4 T5 • 1-12 NX • Ⓥ Ⓑ Ⓓ Ⓢ Ⓡ Ⓜ • 3Cr/C

☆ Hambledon Hotel, Queens Road, PO37 6AW. ☎ (01983) 862403 • Map 196/584814 • BB **C** • EM £8, 6.30pm • S1 D5 T2 F3 • 1-12 • Ⓥ Ⓑ Ⓓ Ⓢ Ⓡ 🐾 • 3Cr/C • Groups also

Chris & Molly Bland, Atholl Court, 1 Atherley Road, PO37 7AT. ☎ (01983) 862414 • Map 196/582818 • BB **B** • EM book first £5, 6pm • S4 D3 T3 • 3-10 • Ⓥ Ⓑ Ⓓ Ⓢ Ⓡ • List/C

☆ Brian Norton, Bondi Hotel, Clarence Road, PO37 7BH. ☎ (01983) 862507 • Map 196/583820 • BB **C/D** • EM book first £7-£10, 6.30pm • S10 D15 T20 F5 • 1-12 • Ⓥ Ⓑ Ⓓ Ⓡ 🐾 • 3Cr • Groups also

Mrs J James, The Glen, 4 Avenue Road, PO37 7BG. ☎ (01983) 862154 • Map 196/582819 • BB **B** • D4 T2 • 3-10 • Ⓑ Ⓓ Ⓢ Ⓡ

■ TOTLAND
ISLE OF WIGHT COAST PATH

Ontario Hotel, Colwell Common Road, PO39 0DD. ☎ (01983) 753237 • Map 196/328875 • BB **C** • EM book first £8, 6.30pm • S1 D2 T1 F3 • 2-11 NX • Ⓥ Ⓑ Ⓓ 🐾 • 3Cr

☆ See Display Advertisement

■ TOTLAND (CONTINUED)

Sandford Lodge, 61 The Avenue, PO39 0DN. ☎ (01983) 753478 • Map 196/329872 • BB **C** • EM book first £11.50, 6.30-7pm • S2 D5 T2 F2 • 2-11 • Ⓥ Ⓑ Ⓓ Ⓢ • 3Cr/C • Near ferry

Maureen Wright, Littledene Lodge Hotel, Granville Road, PO39 0AX. ☎ (01983) 752411 • Map 196/326870 • BB **C** • EM £9.50, 6.30pm • D2 T2 F2 • 3-10 • Ⓥ Ⓑ Ⓓ 🛁 • 3Cr/C • SC also

■ TOTLAND BAY
ISLE OF WIGHT COAST PATH

☆ The Nodes Country Hotel, Alum Bay Old Road, PO39 0HZ. ☎ (01983) 752859 • Map 196/316856 • BB **C** • EM £9.50, 6.30-8pm • D3 T3 F5 • 1-12 NX • Ⓥ Ⓑ Ⓓ Ⓢ 🛁 • 3Cr

The Nodes Country Hotel
Alum Bay Old Road, Totland Bay, IOW

A lovely old country house hotel in extensive grounds with glorious views of Tennyson Downs and the coast. Marvellous walking country. Fine food, CH, courtyard, bar, real ale, rooms en suite. Children welcome at reduced rates. Beaches nearby. AA, RAC approved. Open all year.

Tel. 01983 752859

Vera McMullan, Strang Hall, Uplands Road, PO39 0DZ. ☎ (01983) 753189 • Map 196/327867 • BB **C** • EM book first £10, 7.30pm • S1 D1 T1 F1 • 1-12 NX • Ⓥ Ⓓ Ⓢ Ⓜ • SC also

■ UPPER VENTNOR
ISLE OF WIGHT COAST PATH

Greenfields, Down Lane, PO38 1AH. ☎ (01983) 852702 • Map 196/557778 • BB **A** • D1 T1 • 2-11 • Ⓓ 🛁

■ VENTNOR
ISLE OF WIGHT COAST PATH

☆ Hillside Hotel, 151 Mitchell Avenue, PO38 1DR. ☎ (01983) 852271 • Map 196/565779 • BB **C** • EM £8.50, from 7pm • S1 D7 T2 F1 • 1-12 • Ⓥ Ⓑ Ⓓ Ⓢ 🛁 Ⓜ • 3Cr/C

HILLSIDE HOTEL
Mitchell Avenue, Ventnor

Thatched 'Hillside' offers superb sea views, gardens and relaxed atmosphere. Minutes from town, beach, esplanade. All bedrooms have en suite/private facilities, TV, and tea/coffee facilities. Licensed bar. Extensive breakfast, 5-course evening meal. Open all year. Dogs welcome.

For brochure Tel 01983 852271

AA QQQQ   RAC acclaimed   ETB ♨♨♨ Commended

Channel View Hotel, Hambrough Road, PO38 1SQ. ☎ (01983) 852230 • Map 196/562774 • BB **B** • EM £7.50, 6-7pm • S3 D4 T3 F4 • 3-10 NX • Ⓥ Ⓑ Ⓓ 🛁

☆ Anne & Peter Everett, Seagulls, Belle Vue Road, PO38 1DB. ☎ (01983) 852085 • Map 196/560776 • BB **B** • EM book first £7, 6.30pm • S1 D2 T3 F1 • 2-10 • Ⓥ Ⓑ Ⓓ Ⓢ 🛁 • 3Cr/C

"Seagulls"
♨♨♨ Commended

Charming Victorian hotel in quiet location, with excellent home cooking, superb coastal and country scenery. Close to downland and coastal footpaths, botanical gardens, park and town.

Ensuite rooms with TV and tea/coffee. Central heating, licensed, non-smoking, car parking, drying facilities.
Anne & Peter Everett   **Tel. (01983) 852085**

■ WOOTTON CREEK
ISLE OF WIGHT COAST PATH

Carol Pearce, Ashlake Farmhouse, Ashlake Farm Lane, PO33 4LF. ☎ (01983) 882124 • Map 196/550924 • BB **B** • EM book first £8.50, 7-8.30pm • D1 T1 F1 • 1-12 NX • Ⓥ Ⓑ Ⓓ Ⓢ 🛁 • Seasonal steam train. SC also

■ WROXALL (Ventnor)

Mrs F J Corry, Little Span Farm, Rew Lane, PO38 3AU. ☎ (01983) 852419 • Map 196/546790 • BB **B/C** • EM book first £7, 7-8pm • D2 T1 • 1-12 • Ⓥ Ⓑ Ⓓ Ⓢ Ⓡ 🛁

■ YARMOUTH
ISLE OF WIGHT COAST PATH

Mrs J Manfield, St Hilda, Victoria Road, PO41 0QW. ☎ (01983) 760814 • Map 196/356895 • BB **B** • D1 T1 • 3-10 • Ⓥ Ⓓ 🛁

Quinces, Cranmore Avenue, PO41 0XS. ☎ (01983) 760080 • Map 196/390903 • BB **C** • D1 T1 • 1-12 NX • Ⓑ Ⓓ Ⓢ 🛁 • Transport to pubs

ISLES OF SCILLY

■ ST MARY'S

☆ R & J Graham, Carnwethers Country House, Pelistry Bay, TR21 0NX. ☎ (01720) 422415 • Map /924117 • BB **D** • EM £15, 6.30pm • S1 D4 T3 F2 • 5-9 • Ⓥ Ⓑ Ⓓ Ⓢ 🛁 • 3Cr/C

IF YOU CAN'T FIND THE PLACE YOU'RE AFTER TRY THE INDEX

KENT

■ **ASHURST (Tunbridge Wells)**
WEALDWAY & LONDON COUNTRYWAY

Mrs Soyke & Miss Berwick, Manor Court Farm, Stonecross, TN3 9TB. ☎ (01892) 740279 • Map 188/520390 • BB **C** • D1 T2 • 1-12 NX • Ⓑ Ⓓ Ⓢ Ⓡ 🐾 • 2Cr • Camping also

■ **BARHAM (Canterbury)**
NORTH DOWNS WAY

C Stewart, The Duke of Cumberland, The Street, CT4 6NY. ☎ (01227) 831396 • Map 189,179/207501 • BB **C/D** • EM £6-£9, 6.30-9.30pm • D2 T1 • 1-12 NX • Ⓥ Ⓑ Ⓓ Ⓡ 🐾 • 3Cr

■ **BILSINGTON (Ashford)**
SAXON SHORE WAY & GREENSAND WAY

Mrs Hopper, Willow Farm, Stone Cross, TN25 7JJ. ☎ (01233) 720484 • Map 189/028366 • BB **C** • EM book first £5 • S2 D1 F1 • 1-12 NX • Ⓥ Ⓓ Ⓢ

■ **BIRLING (West Malling)**
NORTH DOWNS WAY & WEALDWAY & LONDON COUNTRYWAY

Mrs Caroline Moorhead, The Stable Block, 25 Ryarsh Road, ME19 5JW. ☎ (01732) 873437 • Map 177,188,178/679605 • BB **B** • EM book first £10, 7-7.30pm • T2 • 3-11 • Ⓥ Ⓓ Ⓢ Ⓡ

■ **BOROUGH GREEN (Sevenoaks)**
NORTH DOWNS WAY & WEALDWAY

Stone Ridge, 168 Maidstone Road, St Marys Platt, TN15 8JD. ☎ (01732) 882053 • Map 188/616572 • BB **B/C** • EM book first £5.50, 7-8pm • S2 D2 T2 F2 • 1-12 NX • Ⓥ Ⓑ Ⓓ Ⓢ Ⓡ • 2Cr

■ **CANTERBURY**
NORTH DOWNS WAY

London Guest House, 14 London Road, CT2 8LR. ☎ (01227) 765860 • Map 179/142584 • BB **C** • S2 D1 T2 F1 • 1-12 • Ⓓ Ⓡ Ⓜ • List/C

Castle Court Guest House, 8 Castle Street, CT1 2QF. ☎ (01227) 463441 • Map 179/148576 • BB **B/C** • S3 D5 T3 F1 • 1-12 • Ⓑ Ⓓ Ⓢ Ⓡ 🐾 • List

Mrs J Wright, Milton House, 9 South Canterbury Road, CT1 3LH. ☎ (01227) 765531 • Map 179/150567 • BB **B** • D1 T1 • 1-12 NX • Ⓓ Ⓢ Ⓡ 🐾 • List

■ **CAPEL-LE-FERNE (Folkstone)**
NORTH DOWNS WAY

Mrs D Strutt, Xaipe, 18 Alexandra Road, CT18 7LD. ☎ (01303) 257956 • Map 179/252385 • BB **B** • D1 T1 • 3-10 • Ⓓ Ⓢ Ⓜ

■ **CHARING (Ashford)**
NORTH DOWNS WAY

E & R Bigwood, Timberlodge, Charing Hill, TN27 0NG. ☎ (01233) 712822 • Map 189/959499 • BB **C** • EM book first £5-£10 • D1 F1 • 1-12 NX • Ⓥ Ⓑ Ⓓ Ⓢ Ⓡ Ⓜ • List

Mrs Margaret Micklewright, 23 The Moat, TN27 0JH. ☎ (01233) 713141 • Map 189/955492 • BB **C** • T1 • 4-10 • Ⓑ Ⓓ Ⓢ Ⓡ Ⓜ

■ **CHILHAM (Canterbury)**
NORTH DOWNS WAY

Mrs J Wood, Bagham Cross, CT4 8DU. ☎ (01227) 730264 • Map 189,179/070536 • BB **B** • D1 T1 • 4-10 • Ⓓ Ⓢ Ⓡ

Mr & Mrs L Easthope, Bagham Farm House, Canterbury Road, CT4 8DX. ☎ (01227) 730306 • Map 189,179/078538 • BB **C/D** • EM book first £7.50 • D1 T2 • 1-12 NX • Ⓥ Ⓑ Ⓓ Ⓡ

■ **CRANBROOK**

Mrs D M Waddoup, The Hollies, Old Angley Road, TN17 2PN. ☎ (01580) 713106 • Map 188/775367 • BB **C** • EM book first £10 • S1 T1 F1 • 1-12 NX • Ⓑ Ⓓ Ⓢ 🐾

■ **DEAL**
SAXON SHORE WAY

Mr & Mrs H A Wiggins, Beaconhill Cottage, Beaconhill, Gt Mongeham, CT14 0HW. ☎ (01304) 372809 • Map 179/339511 • BB **B** • EM £9, 7pm • T4 • 1-12 • Ⓥ Ⓓ Ⓢ Ⓡ • Walking holidays also

■ **DOVER**
NORTH DOWNS WAY & SAXON SHORE WAY

Amanda Guest House, 4 Harold Street, CT16 1SF. ☎ (01304) 201711 • Map 179/320418 • BB **B** • D1 T2 F2 • 1-12 NX • Ⓓ Ⓢ Ⓡ • List

Mr & Mrs Oakley, Walletts Court Ctry Hse Hotel, West Cliffe, St Margarets, CT15 6EW. ☎ (01304) 852424 • Map 179/349447 • BB **D** • EM £23, 7-9pm • D5 T2 F1 • 1-12 NX • Ⓥ Ⓑ Ⓓ Ⓢ • 4Cr/HC

Rodney & Elizabeth Dimech, Castle House, 10 Castle Hill Road, CT16 1QW. ☎ (01304) 201656 • Map 179/323416 • BB **B/C** • EM £8, 6-8pm • S1 D3 T1 F1 • 1-12 • Ⓥ Ⓑ Ⓓ Ⓢ Ⓡ 🐾 • 3Cr

☆ See Display Advertisement

☆ Mrs M Sames, Coldred Court Farm, Church Road, Coldred, CT15 5AQ. ☎ (01304) 830816 • Map 179/273475 • BB **C/D** • EM book first £12.50, 6-8pm • D2 T1 • 1-12 NX • Ⓥ Ⓑ Ⓓ Ⓢ Ⓡ • 2Cr/HC

☆ Alistair & Betty Dimech, Cleveland Guest House, 2 Laureston Place, CT16 1QX. ☎ (01304) 204622 • Map 179/322416 • BB **C** • EM book first £12.50, 7-8.30pm • D2 T1 F2 • 1-12 NX • Ⓥ Ⓑ Ⓓ Ⓡ 🛁 • 2Cr/C

■ **DYMCHURCH**

Waterside Guest House, 15 Hythe Road, TN29 0LN. ☎ (01303) 872253 • Map 189/105298 • BB **B/C** • EM £3.50, 5.30-8pm • S1 D3 T2 F1 • 1-12 • Ⓥ Ⓑ Ⓓ • 2Cr/C

■ **EDENBRIDGE**
NORTH DOWNS WAY & LONDON COUNTRYWAY

Marjorie & Peter McEwan, Four Oaks, Swan Lane, TN8 6BA. ☎ (01732) 863556 • Map 187/441478 • BB **C** • S2 D1 • 1-11 + XMAS • Ⓑ Ⓓ Ⓢ Ⓡ

■ **EGERTON (Ashford)**
GREENSAND WAY

Ragged Barn, Munday Bois Road, TN27 9ER. ☎ (01233) 756358 • Map 189/904461 • BB **C** • D2 T2 F1 • 1-12 NX • Ⓑ Ⓓ Ⓢ Ⓡ 🛁 • Food nearby

■ **FAIRSEAT (Wrotham)**
NORTH DOWNS WAY

Mrs E Gray, The Old Post House, TN15 7LU. ☎ (01732) 822444 • Map 177,188/622614 • BB **C** • EM book first £12 • S1 D1 T1 • 1-12 NX • Ⓥ Ⓓ Ⓢ • Station 2.5 miles

■ **FAVERSHAM**
NORTH DOWNS WAY

Mr & Mrs A Brightman, The Granary, Plumford Lane, Off Brogdale Road, ME13 0DS. ☎ (01795) 538416 • Map 178/002583 • BB **C** • D1 T1 F1 • 1-12 • Ⓑ Ⓓ Ⓢ Ⓡ • 2Cr/HC

■ **FOLKESTONE**
NORTH DOWNS WAY

Mrs Young, Sunny Lodge Guest House, 85 Cheriton Road, CT20 2QL. ☎ (01303) 251498 • Map 189,179/222361 • BB **B** • S2 D2 T2 F2 • 1-12 NX • Ⓓ Ⓢ Ⓡ 🛁 • 1Cr/App

Normandie Guest House, 39 Cheriton Road, CT20 1DD. ☎ (01303) 256233 • Map 189,179/225360 • BB **B** • S1 D1 T2 F2 • 1-12 NX • Ⓢ Ⓡ • List

Abbey House Hotel, 5-6 Westbourne Gardens, (off Sandgate Road), CT20 2JA. ☎ (01303) 255514 • Map 189,179/217355 • BB **B/C** • EM book first £6, 6-7pm • S3 D3 T4 F4 • 1-12 • Ⓥ Ⓑ Ⓓ Ⓢ Ⓡ 🛁 • 2Cr • Groups also

Wycliffe Hotel, Mr & Mrs Shorland, 63 Bouverie Road West, CT20 2RN. ☎ (01303) 252186 • Map 189,179/219357 • BB **B** • EM book first £8, 6.30pm • S2 D5 T4 F2 • 1-12 • Ⓥ Ⓑ Ⓓ Ⓢ Ⓡ 🛁

■ **GREAT CHART (Ashford)**
GREENSAND WAY

Mr & Mrs P Wynn-Green, Goldwell Manor, TN23 3BY. ☎ (01233) 631495 • Map 189/968425 • BB **D** • EM book first £10 • S1 D1 T/F1 • 1-12 NX • Ⓥ Ⓑ Ⓓ 🛁

■ **HADLOW (Tonbridge)**
WEALDWAY

Mrs Lesley Tubbs, Dunsmore, Hadlow Park, TN11 0HX. ☎ (01732) 850611 • Map 188/634504 • BB **C** • T1 • 1-12 • Ⓑ Ⓓ

■ **HARRIETSHAM (Maidstone)**
NORTH DOWNS WAY

Mrs H Atkins, Mannamead, Pilgrims Way, ME17 1BT. ☎ (01622) 859336 • Map 189/883533 • BB **B** • S1 D1 T1 • 1-12 NX • Ⓑ Ⓓ Ⓢ Ⓡ Ⓜ • 2Cr

ENGLAND KENT

B&B ACCOMMODATION

■ HERNE BAY

Foxden, 5 Landon Road, off Beltinge Road, CT6 6HP.
☎ (01227) 363514/369820 • Map 179/190680 • BB
B • S2 D2 • 1-12 • Ⓓ Ⓢ Ⓡ • List

■ HOLLINGBOURNE (Maidstone)
NORTH DOWNS WAY

Frances Leer, Manorfield, Pilgrims Way, ME17 1RD.
☎ (01622) 880373 • Map 188,178/843554 • BB **C** •
EM book first £10 • D1 T1 F1 • 1-12 NX • Ⓥ Ⓑ Ⓓ
Ⓢ Ⓡ

■ KINGSDOWN (Deal)
SAXON SHORE WAY

☆ Mr J A Thompson, Kingsdown Country Hotel,
Cliffe Road, CT14 8AJ. ☎ (01304) 373755 • Map
179/378487 • BB **D** • EM book first £12, 7-8pm • S1
D2 T1 • 1-12 • Ⓥ Ⓑ Ⓓ Ⓢ Ⓡ • 3Cr

KINGSDOWN COUNTRY HOTEL

Cliffe Road, Kingsdown, Near Deal, Kent CT14 8AJ
Take a Special Three Day Half Board Break
@ £199 per Couple and

WALK THE SAXON SHORE WAY

5 Miles Sandwich ← ← KINGSDOWN → → Dover 5 miles

AA
ۤۤۤ
Recommended

ۤۤۤ
Commended

Conveniently situated on the Saxon Shore Way,
nestling in a quaint, quiet, historic fishing village
and surrounded by cliff and country walks.
Large, safe, secluded rear car park and gardens with
a gate to the beach. All rooms are fully ensuite and
Three Day Half Board Breaks are offered at £199
per couple with packed lunches provided free.
Julian and Yvonne THOMPSON

Tel/Fax 01304 373755

■ LINTON (Maidstone)
GREENSAND WAY

Mrs Elizabeth Johnston, Hill Place, ME17 4AL. ☎
(01622) 743834 • Map 188/754505 • BB **C/D** • D2 T1
• 1-12 NX • Ⓑ Ⓓ Ⓢ • Food nearby. Dogs not in
bedrooms.

■ LYMINGE (Fokestone)
NORTH DOWNS WAY

Southfields, Farthing Common, CT18 8DH. ☎
(01303) 862391 • Map 189,179/138404 • BB **C** • EM
book first £7.50, from 7pm • T1 F/T1 • 4-10 • Ⓥ Ⓓ
Ⓢ Ⓡ

■ MAIDSTONE

Lesley King, Wits End Guest House, 78 Bower Mount
Road, ME16 8AT. ☎ (01622) 752684 • Map
188,178/748557 • BB **C** • EM book first £7, 6-9pm •
S2 D1 T2 F2 • 1-12 • Ⓥ Ⓑ Ⓢ Ⓡ • 3Cr

■ MARDEN

Mrs L R Mannington, Tanner House, Tanner Farm,
Goudhurst Road, TN12 9ND. ☎ (01622) 831214 •
Map 188/733415 • BB **C** • EM book first £12.50, 7pm
• D1 T2 • 1-12 NX • Ⓥ Ⓑ Ⓓ Ⓢ • 3Cr/C

■ OTFORD (Sevenoaks)
NORTH DOWNS WAY

Mr G A Levien, Moat Bungalow, Station Road, TN14
5QU. ☎ (01959) 524165 • Map 188/530590 • BB **C** •
S1 T1 • 1-12 NX • Ⓓ Ⓢ Ⓡ Ⓜ • Food nearby

Mrs C M Hord, 24a Pilgrims Way East, TN14 5QN. ☎
(01959) 523743 • Map 188/536593 • BB **C** • S2 T1 •
1-11 • Ⓑ Ⓓ Ⓢ Ⓡ • List

■ PRESTON (Canterbury)

Mrs E M Scott, Forstal House, The Forstal, CT3 1DT.
☎ (01227) 722282 • Map 179/246607 • BB **B/C** • EM
book first £12.50, 6-8pm • D1 T1 • 1-12 NX • Ⓥ Ⓑ
Ⓓ Ⓢ • Transport avail.

■ ROCHESTER
NORTH DOWNS WAY

Mrs S Beggs, 98 Borstal Road, ME1 3BD. ☎ (01634)
843528 • Map 178/736673 • BB **B** • S1 D1 T1 • 1-12
NX • Ⓓ Ⓢ Ⓡ 🦮

■ RYARSH (West Malling)
WEALDWAY & NORTH DOWNS WAY

Mrs J Edwards, Heavers Farm, Chapel Lane, ME19
5JU. ☎ (01732) 842074 • Map 177/665603 • BB **B** •
EM 7.30pm • D1 T2 • 1-12 NX • Ⓥ Ⓓ Ⓢ 🦮

■ SHEPHERDSWELL (Dover)
NORTH DOWNS WAY

B & L Popple, Sunshine Cottage, The Green, Mill
Lane, CT15 7LQ. ☎ (01304) 831359/831218/(0589)
572676 • Map 179/261478 • BB **C** • EM £6.50 or £14,
6-8.30pm • D4 T1 F1 • 1-12 • Ⓥ Ⓑ Ⓓ Ⓢ Ⓡ 🦮 Ⓜ •
2Cr/C

■ SOUTHBOROUGH (Tunbridge Wells)
WEALDWAY

Anneke Leemhuis, 10 Modest Corner, TN4 0LS. ☎
(01892) 522450 • Map 188/571423 • BB **C** • EM book
first £8.50, 7-8pm • D2 F1 • 1-12 • Ⓥ Ⓓ Ⓢ Ⓡ 🦮

■ STELLING MINNIS (Canterbury)

Mrs L Castle, Greatfield Farm, Misling Lane, CT4
6DE. ☎ (01227) 709223 • Map 189,179/134452 • BB
C • D2 T1 • 1-12 • Ⓑ Ⓓ Ⓢ 🦮 • List/HC • SC also

☆ See Display Advertisement

■ **STOWTING (Ashford)**
NORTH DOWNS WAY

Mrs Carole Cole, Water Farm, TN25 6BA. ☎ (01303) 862401 • Map 189,179/121412 • BB **C** • S1 T1 F1 • 1-12 NX • Ⓑ Ⓓ Ⓢ • SC also, food nearby

■ **SUTTON VALENCE (Maidstone)**
GREENSAND WAY

June & Tony King, West Belringham, Chart Road, ME17 3AW. ☎ (01622) 843995 • Map 188/809491 • BB **C** • T2 • 1-11 • Ⓑ Ⓓ Ⓢ • 1Cr/C • Food nearby

■ **TENTERDEN**

Margaret & Dave Wilkinson, The Hollies, Appledore Road, TN30 7BE. ☎ (01580) 763069 • Map 189/894334 • BB **C** • S2 T1 • 1-12 NX • Ⓢ

■ **TROTTISCLIFFE (West Malling)**
NORTH DOWNS WAY & WEALDWAY

Bramble Park, Church Lane, ME19 5EB. ☎ (01732) 822397 • Map 177/644604 • BB **C** • S1 T1 F1 • 1-12 • Ⓓ • Food nearby

■ **WEST PECKHAM (Tonbridge)**
WEALDWAY & GREENSAND WAY

M Wright, Crooked Chimneys House, Gover Hill, Roughway, TN11 9SP. ☎ (01732) 810726 • Map 188/634531 • BB **C** • D1 T1 • 1-12 NX • Ⓑ Ⓓ Ⓢ

■ **WHITSTABLE**
NORTH DOWNS WAY & SAXON SHORE WAY

Elisabeth Dyke, Windy Ridge, Wraik Hill, CT5 3BY. ☎ (01227) 263506 • Map 179/102642 • BB **C** • EM book first £12, 7pm • S3 D2 T1 F2 • 1-12 • Ⓥ Ⓑ Ⓓ Ⓡ ⚒ • 3Cr/HC

■ **WINGHAM (Canterbury)**

☆ Mrs Nicola Ellen, Crockshard Farm House, CT3 1NY. ☎ (01227) 720464 • Map 179/248559 • BB **C** • T1 F3 • 1-12 • Ⓑ Ⓓ Ⓢ ⚒ • Camping barn also

CANTERBURY

Once you've been here, you'll be back! Rural and beautiful (own transport advisable). Ideally located for exploring whole of Kent. B&B £17.50 (quad room £59).

**Nicola Ellen
Crockshard Farm House
Wingham
☎ 01227 720464**

■ **WOULDHAM (Nr Rochester)**
NORTH DOWNS WAY

Mrs A Parnell, Wouldham Court Farmhouse, 246 High Street, ME1 3TY. ☎ (01634) 683271 • Map 188,178/714643 • BB **B/C** • EM £4, 7-9pm • S1 D1 F1 • 1-12 • Ⓥ Ⓓ Ⓢ ⚒

■ **WROTHAM (Borough Green, Sevenoaks)**
NORTH DOWNS WAY

The Bull Hotel, TN15 7RF. ☎ (01732) 885522 • Map 188/612591 • BB **D** • EM £10, 7-10pm • S2 D2 T4 F1 • 1-12 • Ⓥ Ⓑ Ⓓ Ⓡ ⚒ • 3Cr

■ **WYE (Ashford)**
NORTH DOWNS WAY

Joan & John Morris, Akermans, 38 High Street, TN25 5AL. ☎ (01233) 812133 • Map 189,179/055468 • BB **C** • D1 T2 • 1-12 NX • Ⓑ Ⓓ Ⓢ Ⓡ

LANCASHIRE

■ **ANGLEZARKE (Chorley)**

Mr & Mrs Hilton, Jepsons Farm, Moor Road, PR6 9DQ. ☎ (01257) 481691 • Map 109/622167 • BB **C** • EM book first £6-£10, 7pm • S1 D/F1 T1 • 1-12 NX • Ⓓ

■ **BLACKPOOL**

Mr & Mrs R Gray, Southern House Private Hotel, 1A King Edward Avenue, FY2 9TD. ☎ (01253) 352712 • Map 102/322385 • BB **A/B** • EM £4.50, 5.30pm • S2 D6 T1 F1 • 1-12 • Ⓥ Ⓑ Ⓓ Ⓢ Ⓡ ⚒ Ⓜ

■ **BURNLEY**

Julie Whitehead, 121/123 Ormerod Road, BB11 3QW. ☎ (01282) 423255 • Map 103/846331 • BB **B/C** • S4 D2 T3 F1 • 1-12 • Ⓑ Ⓓ Ⓡ ⚒ • 2Cr/HC

■ **CAPERNWRAY (Carnforth)**

☆ Mrs Melanie Smith, Capernwray House, LA6 1AE. ☎ (01524) 732363 • Map 97/534718 • BB **B/C** • EM book first £8, 6-9pm • S1 D2 T1 • 1-12 NX • Ⓥ Ⓑ Ⓓ Ⓢ • 2Cr/C

Capernwray House
Capernwray Nr. Carnforth Lancashire

Beautifully kept Country House in 5½ acres. Panoramic Views, T.V. lounge. Close to Lakes, Dales, Lancaster, Canal 5 mins walk. No smoking. From £16 p.p. En-suite available. Warm welcome. Phone for brochure.

Tel/Fax Roy & Melanie Smith 01524 732363

■ **CARNFORTH**

Dorothy Dickinson, 26 Victoria Street, LA5 9ED. ☎ (01524) 732520 • Map 97/497702 • BB **B** • D1 T1 F1 • 1-12 • Ⓓ Ⓡ

■ CHIPPING

Mrs Pat Gifford, Rakefoot Farm, Chaigley, BB7 3LY. ☎ (01995) 61332/0589 279063 • Map 103/663416 • BB **A/B/C** • EM book first £8-£10, 5-7pm • S2 D2 T2 F2 • 1-12 • Ⓥ Ⓑ Ⓓ ⅋ • List/C • SC also

■ CLAYTON-LE-DALE (Ribble Valley)

Marj Adderley, 2 Rose Cottage, Longsight Road, BB1 9EX. ☎ (01254) 813223 • Map 103/663330 • BB **C** • D1 T2 F1 • 1-12 • Ⓑ Ⓓ Ⓢ Ⓡ ⅋ • Food nearby

■ CLITHEROE
RIBBLE WAY

Mrs A Haslewood, 8 Lingfield Avenue, off Littlemoor Rd, BB7 1HA. ☎ (01200) 422360 • Map 103/745408 • BB **A** • S1 T1 F1 • 1-12 • Ⓡ ⅋

Mr & Mrs R E Berry, Lower Standen Farm, Whalley Road, BB7 1PP. ☎ (01200) 424176 • Map 103/739400 • BB **B** • D2 T1 • 1-12 • Ⓑ Ⓓ Ⓡ ⅋ • 2Cr • SC also

Jean & Ken Lord, Brooklands, 9 Pendle Road, BB7 1JQ. ☎ (01200) 422797 • Map 103/750414 • BB **B** • EM book first £10, 6.30-7.30pm • D1 T2 • 1-12 • Ⓑ Ⓓ Ⓡ ⅋ • List/C • Transport avail.

■ COLNE

Mrs Etherington, 148 Keighley Road, BB8 0PJ. ☎ (01282) 862002 • Map 103/897402 • BB **B/C** • S1 D1 T1 • 3-12 NX • Ⓑ Ⓓ Ⓢ Ⓡ • 2Cr/HC

Mrs Carole Mitson, Higher Wanless Farm, Red Lane, BB8 7JP. ☎ (01282) 865301 • Map 103/871413 • BB **C** • EM book first £10.50, 7pm • S1 T1 F1 • 2-11 • Ⓥ Ⓑ Ⓓ Ⓡ • 2Cr/HC • Transport available

■ DUTTON (Longridge, Preston)

Mrs M Jackson, Smithy Farm, Huntingdon Hall Lane, PR3 2ZT. ☎ (01254) 878250 • Map 103/660380 • BB **A** • EM book first £5, 7.30-9.30pm • D1 T1 F1 • 3-12 NX • Ⓥ Ⓓ ⅋ • List

■ ECCLESTON (Chorley)

Mrs K Motley, Parr Hall Farm, Parr Lane, PR7 5SL. ☎ (01257) 451917 • Map 108/518174 • BB **C** • D4 • 1-12 NX • Ⓑ Ⓓ Ⓢ Ⓜ

■ GARSTANG (Preston)

Esther Heaton, Castleview, Bonds Lane, PR3 1ZB. ☎ (01995) 602022 • Map 102/493448 • BB **B** • S1 T4 • 1-12 NX • Ⓑ Ⓓ ⅋ Ⓜ • 2Cr

Tom M. Wilkinson, Sandbriggs, Lancaster Road, PR3 1JA. ☎ (01995) 603080 • Map 102/492459 • BB **B** • S1 D2 T1 F1 • 1-12 • Ⓑ Ⓓ ⅋ • SC also

■ LANCASTER

Shakespeare Hotel, 96 St Leonardgate, LA1 1NN. ☎ (01524) 841041 • Map 97/479619 • BB **B** • S3 D2 T2 F2 • 1-11 • Ⓑ Ⓓ Ⓢ Ⓡ • 2Cr

■ MORECAMBE

Eric & Alma Amos, 25 Chatsworth Road, LA4 4JQ. ☎ (01524) 424527 • Map 96,97/426635 • BB **A** • S1 D2 T1 F1 • 1-12 NX • Ⓥ Ⓓ Ⓡ ⅋ • Food nearby

■ PRESTON

Mrs E J Ibison, Jenkinsons Farmhouse, Longridge, PR3 3BD. ☎ (01772) 782624 • Map 102,103/602360 • BB **C** • EM book first £12.50, 7pm • S1 D2 T3 • 1-12 NX • Ⓥ Ⓑ Ⓓ Ⓢ ⅋

■ RIBCHESTER (Preston)
RIBBLE WAY

Roy & June Bamber, New House Farm, Preston Road, PR3 3XL. ☎ (01254) 878954 • Map 102,103/648354 • BB **C/D** • D1 T1 F1 • 1-12 • Ⓑ Ⓓ Ⓢ • Food nearby

■ ROCHDALE
PENNINE WAY

Jane Neave, Leaches Farm Bed & Breakfast, Ashworth Valley, OL11 5UN. ☎ (01706) 41116/7 or 228520 • Map 109/851127 • BB **C** • S1 D1 T1 F1 • 1-12 NX • Ⓓ Ⓢ ⅋ • List

■ SABDEN (Clitheroe)

Beech Cottage, 12 Wesley Street, BB7 9EH. ☎ (01282) 772348 • Map 103/781377 • BB **A** • EM book first £5 • S2 D1 • 1-12 NX • Ⓓ Ⓢ

■ SILVERDALE (Carnforth)

Noel & Andree Livesey, The Limes, 23 Stankelt Road, LA5 0TF. ☎ (01524) 701454 • Map 97/463749 • BB **C** • EM book first £5.50/£12.50, 6pm/7.30pm • D1 T1 F1 • 1-12 • Ⓥ Ⓑ Ⓓ Ⓢ Ⓡ

■ SLAIDBURN (Clitheroe)

Mary & Peter Cowking, Pages Farm, Woodhouse Lane, BB7 3AH. ☎ (01200) 446205 • Map 103/696538 • BB **B** • EM book first £10, 6-8.30pm • D2 T1 • 1-12 NX • Ⓥ Ⓑ Ⓓ Ⓢ • 2Cr/C

■ WYCOLLER (Nr Colne)

Pat Hodgson, Parson Lee Farm, BB8 8SU. ☎ (01282) 864747 • Map 103/937385 • BB **B** • EM book first £6-£7, 6.30-8pm • D1 T1 F1 • 1-12 NX • Ⓥ Ⓑ Ⓓ ⅋ • 1Cr

LEICESTERSHIRE & RUTLAND

■ BELTON IN RUTLAND (Oakham)

☆ The Old Rectory, LE15 9LE. ☎ (01572) 717279 • Map 141/814010 • BB **B/C/D** • S2 D2 T2 F2 • 1-12 • Ⓑ Ⓓ Ⓢ ⅋ • 2Cr/C • Food nearby. SC and groups also

☆ See Display Advertisement

The Old Rectory
Belton in Rutland, Oakham LE15 9LE
(01572) 717279

Macmillan Way,
Leicestershire Round
and lots more.
Comfortable guest
house accommodation
in attractive conserva-
tion village with
shop/pub and nice people. Children & pets welcome.
❤❤❤ Commended

■ **GREAT DALBY (Melton Mowbray)**

Mrs Lynn Parker, Dairy Farm, LE14 2EW. ☎ (01664) 62783 • Map 129/743143 • BB **B** • D1 T1 F1 • 1-12 • B D 🐾

■ **LOUGHBOROUGH**

Valerie Wood, Peachnook Guest House, 154 Ashby Road, LE11 3AG. ☎ (01509) 264390 • Map 129/529196 • BB **A/C/D** • S1 D1 T1 F1 • 1-12 • B R ⓜ • List

■ **MARKET BOSWORTH (Nuneaton)**

Bosworth Firs, Bosworth Road, CV13 0DW. ☎ (01455) 290727 • Map 140/417037 • BB **C** • EM £6, 6-9pm • S2 D1 T1 F1 • 1-12 • V B D S • 2Cr/C

■ **MARKET HARBOROUGH**

Mrs J Neal, Westgate Cottage, 27 Westgate Lane, Lubenham, LE16 9TS. ☎ (01858) 462182 • Map 141/703871 • BB **B/C** • D1 T1 F1 • 1-12 NX • D S R ⓜ

■ **NORTH LUFFENHAM**

Mrs Joan Cook, Pinfold House, 6 Pinfold Lane, LE15 8LE. ☎ (01780) 720175 • Map 141/934034 • BB **B** • D2 T1 F1 • 2-11 • D S 🐾

■ **OAKS IN CHARNWOOD (Coalville)**

Mr & Mrs J Havers, St Josephs, Abbey Road, LE67 4UA. ☎ (01509) 503943 • Map 129/459155 • BB **C** • S2 D1 T2 • 4-10 • D S

■ **OLD DALBY (Melton Mowbray)**

Mr & Mrs Anderson, Home Farm, Church Lane, LE14 3LB. ☎ (01664) 822622 • Map 129/674236 • BB **C/D** • S2 T3 • 1-12 NX • B D S • Food nearby. Groups also

■ **REDMILE (Nottingham)**

P & M Need, Peacock Farm Guesthouse & Country Restaurant, NG13 0GQ. ☎ (01949) 842475 • Map 129/790359 • BB **B/C** • EM £13.50 • S1 D2 T2 F4 • 1-12 • V B D S R 🐾 • 2Cr • Bunkhouse and SC also

■ **TILTON**

Knebworth House, Loddington Road, Launde, LE7 9DF. ☎ 0116-259 7257 • Map 141/767055 • BB **B** • S1 D1 T1 • 2-11 •

LINCOLNSHIRE

INCLUDING THE UNITARY AUTHORITES OF NORTH AND NORTH EAST LINCOLNSHIRE, PREVIOUSLY HUMBERSIDE

■ **BARNETBY**
VIKING WAY

☆ Mrs Angela Vora, Holcombe House, Victoria Road, DN38 6JR. ☎ (0850) 764002 • Map 112/059097 • BB **C** • EM £9, 6-8pm • S4 D1 T2 F2 • 1-12 • V B D S R 🐾 • 3Cr/C

Holcombe Guest House
34 Victoria Road
Barnetby, Lincolnshire
(VIKING WAY)

ETB ❤❤❤ Commended

Comfortable homely accommodation to rest your feet. Centrally heated, TV, beverage-making facilities, residents lounge with video. £17.50/person. Evening meals (inc. vegetarian) by arrangement.
Call Angela on 0850 764002

■ **BARTON-UPON-HUMBER**

Mrs R Havercroft, Southgarth, 2 Caistor Road, DN18 5AH. ☎ (01652) 632833 • Map 106,112,107/023223 • BB **B** • T3 • 1-12 • R 🐾

■ **CARLTON SCROOP (Grantham)**
VIKING WAY

Mrs M Hutchins, Stonehouse Farm, Hough Lane, NG32 3BB. ☎ (01400) 250147 • Map 130/941453 • BB **B** • EM book first £7, 6.30-7.30pm • D1 T1 • 1-12 NX • V D S 🐾

■ **CRANWELL (Sleaford)**
VIKING WAY

Mrs A Wood, Byards Leap Cottage, NG34 8EY. ☎ (01400) 261537 • Map 130/011498 • BB **B** • EM book first £6.50, 6.30pm • T1 F1 • 1-12 NX • V D S

■ **FULLETBY (Horncastle)**
VIKING WAY

☆ The Old Rectory, LN9 6JX. ☎ (01507) 533533 • Map 122/289731 • BB **C/D** • EM book first £12, 7.30pm • D3 T1 • 1-12 NX • V B D S 🐾

Want to know more about the tourist board classifications?
See page 87

THE OLD RECTORY

Fulletby, Nr Horncastle, Lincs LN9 6JX
(Viking Way)

Experience our lovely country house, nestling in the Wolds, an area of outstanding natural beauty.

Enjoy unspoilt rural tranquillity
superb undiscovered walks
—transport, maps, information provided.

We offer aga-cooking, books, log fires, gardens, wonderful views, — peace, comfort, relaxation!

Superior B&B ensuite from £20 pp
Optional 4-course dinner £12.
Short Breaks 10% discount (min. 3 nights)
Dogs welcome (kennels)

Tel: 01-507-533-533

■ GRANTHAM

Mrs J Standish, The Lanchester Guest House, 84 Harrowby Road, NG31 9DS. ☎ (01476) 574169 • Map 130/920353 • BB **B/C** • D1 T2 • 1-12 • Ⓑ Ⓓ Ⓢ Ⓡ • 2Cr

■ LINCOLN
VIKING WAY

Mr & Mrs T Cain, ABC Guest House, 126 Yarborough Road, LN1 1HP. ☎ (01522) 543560 • Map 121/969723 • BB **C** • S2 D6 T2 F1 • 1-12 NX • Ⓑ Ⓓ Ⓢ Ⓡ

Mayfield Guest House, 213 Yarborough Road, LN1 3NQ. ☎ (01522) 533732 • Map 121/969720 • BB **C** • S1 D2 T1 F2 • 1-12 NX • Ⓑ Ⓓ Ⓢ Ⓡ • 2Cr/C

Tony Downes, Old Rectory Guest House, 19 Newport, LN1 3DQ. ☎ (01522) 514774 • Map 121/975722 • BB **C** • S1 D3 T1 F1 • 1-12 NX • Ⓑ Ⓓ Ⓢ Ⓡ

■ MABLETHORPE

Mrs J Harvey, White Heather, 114 Victoria Road, LN12 2AJ. ☎ (01507) 472626 • Map 122/510844 • BB **B** • EM book first £3.50, 5.30pm • S3 D2 T2 F2 • 1-12 NX • Ⓥ Ⓑ

■ MALTBY-LE-MARSH (Alford)

Mrs Ann Graves, Grange Farm, LN13 0JP. ☎ (01507) 450267 • Map 122/471825 • BB **B** • EM book first £8, 6-7pm • D1 T3 F3 • 1-12 NX • Ⓓ 🦮 • SC also

---

Vegetarian meals are sometimes available by arrangement even if we don't give the Ⓥ sign in the listing

---

■ MARKET RASEN
VIKING WAY

☆ Mrs M E Dawson-Margrave, The Waveney Guest House, Willingham Road, LN8 3DN. ☎ (01673) 843236 • Map 121,113/111890 • BB **B/C** • EM book first £7, 6-7.30pm • T2 F1 • 1-12 • Ⓥ Ⓑ Ⓓ Ⓢ Ⓡ 🦮 • 2Cr/C

■ SKEGNESS

Amanda Lucie Collingwood, South Lodge Hotel, 147 Drummond Road, PE25 3BT. ☎ (01754) 765057 • Map 122/565620 • BB **C** • EM £6.50, 5.30-7.30pm • S1 D2 T/D3 F1 • 1-12 NX • Ⓥ Ⓓ Ⓢ Ⓡ

■ SKILLINGTON (Grantham)
VIKING WAY

Mrs E M Whatton, Sproxton Lodge Farm, NG33 5HJ. ☎ (01476) 860307 • Map 130/881252 • BB **B** • EM book first £6, 6-6.30pm • S1 D1 F1 • 1-12 NX • Ⓥ Ⓓ Ⓢ • List

■ STAMFORD

Mrs J Headland, Birch House, 4 Lonsdale Road, PE9 2RW. ☎ (01780) 754876/(0850) 185759 • Map 141/015067 • BB **B** • S2 D1 T1 • 1-12 NX • Ⓓ Ⓢ Ⓡ • List/C

Mrs H Nichols, Barash, 10 Stirling Road, PE9 2XG. ☎ (01780) 63065 • Map 141/016075 • BB **B** • S1 T1 F/D1 • 1-12 • Ⓓ Ⓢ Ⓡ 🦮 • List

■ WOODHALL SPA
VIKING WAY

Claire Brennan, Claremont Guest House, 9/11 Witham Road, LN10 6RW. ☎ (01526) 352000 • Map 122/191630 • BB **B/C** • EM book first £5, 6.30pm • S2 D3 T2 F2 • 1-12 • Ⓥ Ⓑ Ⓓ Ⓢ 🦮 • 2Cr

GREATER LONDON

■ CENTRAL LONDON
THAMES PATH

St Athan's Hotel, 20 Tavistock Place, WC1H 9RE. ☎ 0171-837 9140 • Map 176,177/300823 • BB **D** • EM book first £12.50, 7pm • S16 D20 T10 F8 • 1-12 • Ⓥ Ⓑ Ⓓ Ⓡ 🦮 • List

■ **HIGHGATE/HORNSEY**
THAMES PATH

☆ Penny & Laurence Solomons, Parkland Walk Guesthouse, 12 Hornsey Rise Gardens, N19 3PR. ☎ 0171-263 3228/(0973) 382982 • Map 176/299877 • BB **C/D** • S2 D1 T1 F1 • 1-12 • Ⓑ Ⓓ Ⓢ Ⓡ • List/C

PARKLAND WALK GUEST HOUSE
12 Hornsey Rise Gardens, London N19 3PR

North London, Highgate/Crouch End, on The Parkland Walk. Small, friendly B&B in beautiful Victorian house. Easy access to central London, Kings Cross, Euston, Alexandra Palace and Hampstead Heath. No Smoking. Tea/coffee facilities, TV and radio in rooms. Most rooms en-suite.

Tel. 0171-263 3228   ETB COMMENDED
Fax. 0171-831 9489   Listed

■ **PUTNEY**
THAMES PATH

Pip & Robert Neil Taylor, One Fanthorpe Street, SW15 1DZ. ☎ 0181-785 7609 • Map 176/233758 • BB **C** • EM book first £10, 8pm • D2 • 1-12 NX • Ⓥ Ⓑ Ⓓ Ⓢ Ⓡ

■ **WANSTEAD**
THAMES PATH

Mrs A Foster, 71 Grosvenor Road, Wanstead, E11 2ES. ☎ (0181) 530 6970 • Map 177/407888 • BB **B** • S1 D1 T1 F1 • 1-12 NX • Ⓑ Ⓢ Ⓡ

GREATER MANCHESTER

■ **DENSHAW (Oldham)**
PENNINE WAY

Mrs Norma Hall, Boothstead Farm, Rochdale Road, OL3 5UE. ☎ (01457) 878622 • Map 109/967110 • BB **C** • EM book first £6, 6.30-7pm • S1 D1 T1 • 1-12 NX • Ⓥ Ⓓ Ⓢ 🛁 • List/C

■ **SALFORD**
CHESHIRE RING CANAL

White Lodge Hotel, 89 Great Cheetham Street West, M7 2JA. ☎ 0161-792 3047 • Map 109/823004 • BB **C** • S3 D3 T3 F1 • 1-12 NX • Ⓓ Ⓢ Ⓡ 🛁 • 1Cr

---

MERSEYSIDE

■ **NEW BRIGHTON (Wallasey, Wirral)**

Mrs S Brereton, Sherwood Guest House, 55 Wellington Road, L45 2ND. ☎ 0151-639 5198 • Map 108/307941 • BB **B** • EM book first £5, 6.30pm • S2 D2 T2 F2 • 1-12 NX • Ⓥ Ⓑ Ⓓ Ⓡ 🛁

■ **WEST KIRBY**

Mrs Joyce Fishel, 120 Frankby Road, L48 9UX. ☎ 0151-625 6215 • Map 108/230871 • BB **A** • S1 D1 T1 F1 • 1-12 • Ⓓ Ⓡ 🛁 Ⓜ

NORFOLK

■ **AYLSHAM (Norwich)**
WEAVERS WAY

"Birchdale", Blickling Road, NR11 6ND. ☎ (01263) 734827 • Map 133, 134/191270 • BB **B** • S1 D1 T1 • 1-12 NX • Ⓑ Ⓓ Ⓢ Ⓡ Ⓜ

☆ Enid Parry, The Old Bank House, 3 Norwich Road, NR11 6BN. ☎ (01263) 733843 • Map 133,134/194267 • BB **C** • EM book first £9.50, 7pm • D1 T1 F1 • 1-12 NX • Ⓥ Ⓑ Ⓓ Ⓢ 🛁 • 2Cr/HC

THE OLD BANK HOUSE, 3 NORWICH RD, AYLSHAM, NORFOLK NR11 6BN

AA ♦♦♦ Recommended   ETB Highly Commended

A warm & friendly welcome with hearty breakfasts & spacious rooms with CH/HC/TV/Radio/Tea, Coffee, retaining many original features. Homely atmosphere. Lovely walks, beautiful woodland & National Trust properties all nearby. £17pp. Packed lunches and home-cooked evening meals by arrangement.
Tel: 01263 733843

☆ The Old Pump House, Holman Road, NR11 6BY. ☎ (01263) 733789 • Map 133,134/190269 • BB **C/D** • EM book first £9.50, 6.30-7pm • S1 D2 T2 • 1-12 NX • Ⓑ Ⓓ Ⓢ 🛁 • 2Cr/HC

THE OLD PUMP HOUSE
Holman Road, Aylsham, Norfolk NR11 6BY

1750s family home by thatched pump near marketplace, convenient for Weavers Way. Centrally heated rooms (three en-suite). Two bathrooms with constant hot water. Hearty breakfasts in Red Sitting Room overlooking garden. Evening meals by arrangement. Non smoking. ETB ★★ Highly Commended.
Telephone 01263-733789

■ **BARTON TURF (Norwich)**

The White House, Pennygate, NR12 8BG. ☎ (01692) 536057 • Map 133/354225 • BB **C** • EM book first £12, 6.30-8.30pm • D1 T1 F1 • 4-12 • Ⓥ Ⓑ Ⓓ 🛁 • SC also

■ **BRECKLES (Attleborough)**
PEDDARS WAY & NORFOLK COAST PATH

☆ Peter & Margaret Morfoot, Church Cottage, NR17 1EW. ☎ (01953) 498286 • Map 144/961944 • BB **C** • D2 T1 • 1-12 NX • Ⓓ Ⓢ 🛁 • 1Cr/C

■ BURNHAM OVERY STAITHE (King's Lynn)

Domville Guest House, Glebe Lane, PE31 8JQ. ☎ (01328) 738298 • Map 132/846440 • BB **C** • EM book first £8, 7pm • S4 D2 T2 • 1-12 NX • Ⓥ Ⓑ Ⓓ Ⓢ • 1Cr/C

■ CAISTER-ON-SEA

Mrs M Driver, 7 Villarome, NR30 5TQ. ☎ (01493) 720711 • Map 134/513120 • BB **B** • EM book first £7 • D1 • 1-12 NX • Ⓥ Ⓑ Ⓓ Ⓢ

■ CASTLE ACRE (King's Lynn)
PEDDARS WAY & NORFOLK COAST PATH

Miss G Bannister, Home Farm, PE32 2BW. ☎ (01760) 755342 • Map 132/793184 • BB **C** • EM book first £10, 7pm • S1 D1 T1 • 4-10 NX • Ⓥ Ⓓ Ⓢ

Alison M Loughlin, The Old Red Lion, Bailey Street, PE32 2AG. ☎ (01760) 755557 • Map 132/818149 • BB **A/D** • EM book first £5 - veg. wholefood only • D2 T2 F1 • 1-12 • Ⓥ Ⓑ Ⓓ Ⓢ 🐾 • Groups also - dorms/bunkhouse

Willow Cottage, Stocks Green, PE32 2AE. ☎ (01760) 755551 • Map 132/816151 • BB **B/C** • D2 T2 • 3-12 NX • Ⓓ Ⓢ 🐾 • Food nearby

■ CLEY NEXT THE SEA (Holt)
PEDDARS WAY & NORFOLK COAST PATH

☆ Mr & Mrs S Bragg, Whalebone House, High Street, NR25 7RN. ☎ (01263) 740336 • Map 133/045438 • BB **C** • D2 T1 • 1-12 NX • Ⓑ Ⓓ Ⓢ

■ COLTISHALL

Mrs P Dack, Broad Gates, NR12 7DU. ☎ (01603) 737598 • Map 133,134/274197 • BB **C** • S1 T2 • 1-12 NX • Ⓑ Ⓓ • List

■ CROMER
PEDDARS WAY & NORFOLK COAST PATH & WEAVERS WAY

Mrs R Votier, Morden House, 20 Cliff Avenue, NR27 0AN. ☎ (01263) 513396 • Map 133/221417 • BB **C** • EM £12, 7pm • S1 D3 T2 • 1-12 • Ⓥ Ⓑ Ⓓ Ⓢ Ⓡ 🐾 • 2Cr/HC

■ DISS
ANGLES WAY

Strenneth, Airfield Road, Fersfield, IP22 2BP. ☎ (01379) 688182 • Map 144/070842 • BB **C** • S1 D4 T2 • 1-12 • Ⓑ Ⓓ Ⓢ 🐾 • 2Cr/C

■ EAST WINCH (King's Lynn)

Miss I E Bass, Field Cottage, Station Road, PE32 1NR. ☎ (01553) 841231 • Map 132/698162 • BB **A** • EM £3-£4, 6pm • S1 D2 • 1-12 NX • Ⓥ Ⓓ 🐾

■ GARBOLDISHAM (Diss)
ANGLES WAY

Beverley & Alan Boreham, Ingleneuk Lodge, Hopton Road, IP22 2RQ. ☎ (01953) 681541 • Map 144/002802 • BB **C/D** • EM book first £14.50, 7pm • S2 D3 T2 F1 • 1-12 NX • Ⓥ Ⓑ Ⓢ 🐾 • 3Cr/C

■ GREAT YARMOUTH
WEAVERS WAY & ANGLES WAY

Mrs R Albone, Beaumont House, 52 Wellesley Road, NR30 1EX. ☎ (01493) 843957 • Map 134/529080 • BB **B** • EM book first £6, 5.15pm • S1 D4 T1 F2 • 5-10 NX • Ⓓ Ⓡ

■ HAPPISBURGH

Cliff House Teashop/Guesthouse, Beach Road, NR12 0PP. ☎ (01692) 650775 • Map 133/384309 • BB **B** • EM £6, up to 8pm • S2 D1 T1 • 1-12 NX • Ⓥ Ⓓ Ⓢ • SC also

■ HEMPTON (Fakenham)

T Beales, Yew Tree House, 2 East View, NR21 7LW. ☎ (01328) 851450 • Map 132/909287 • BB **B** • EM book first £7.50, 6-8pm • S1 D1 T2 F1 • 1-12 NX • Ⓥ Ⓓ Ⓢ 🐾

■ HUNSTANTON
PEDDARS WAY & NORFOLK COAST PATH

G B Wellard, Gate Lodge, 2 Westgate, PE36 5AL. ☎ (01485) 533549 • Map 132/672406 • BB **C** • EM £10, 6.45pm • D3 T3 • 2-11 • Ⓥ Ⓑ Ⓓ Ⓢ 🐾 • 2Cr/C

Vanessa Bamfield, Northgate House, 46 Northgate, PE36 6DR. ☎ (01485) 533269 • Map 132/674413 • BB **B** • EM book first £7.50, 6.30pm • S1 D2 T2 F1 • 1-12 NX • Ⓥ Ⓑ Ⓓ Ⓢ 🐾 Ⓜ • 1Cr

☆ See Display Advertisement

NORFOLK

ENGLAND

B&B ACCOMMODATION

■ KING'S LYNN

Mrs J Bastone, Maranatha Guest House, 115 Gaywood Road, PE30 2PU. ☎ (01553) 774596 • Map 132/627204 • BB **B** • EM £5, 6pm • S3 D1 T3 F2 • 1-12 • [V] [B] [D] [R] • 2Cr/App

Havana Guest House, 117 Gaywood Road, PE30 2PU. ☎ (01553) 772331 • Map 132/627204 • BB **B/C** • S1 D3 T2 F1 • 1-12 NX • [B] [D] [S] [R] • 2Cr/C

■ LESSINGHAM (Norwich)

☆ John & Jean Murden, The Seafarers, North Gap Eccles Beach, NR12 0SW. ☎ (01692) 598218 • Map 134/412292 • BB **C** • S1 D1 T2 • 1-12 NX • [B] [D] [S]

BED & BREAKFAST

Telephone 01692 598218

For coastal and countryside walks, stay with Jean & John Murden at **The Seafarers (Former 18th Century Manor Farm house), North Gap, Eccles Beach, Near Lessingham, Norwich NR12 0SW** (O/S Map 134. Grid ref. 412292)

Our accommodation offers a high standard of comfort and friendliness. We are near the Broads National Park and have unspoilt beaches and wildlife sanctuaries close to hand.

■ MUNDFORD (Thetford)

Mrs Marion Ford, Old Bottle House, Cranwich, IP26 5JL. ☎ (01842) 878012 • Map 144/782948 • BB **B/C** • EM book first £10, 7.30pm • D1 T2 F1 • 1-12 NX • [V] [B] [D] [S]

■ NEATISHEAD (Norwich)

Sue Wrigley, Regency Guest House, The Street, NR12 8AD. ☎ (01692) 630233 • Map 133,134/340210 • BB **C** • EM Light suppers • D2 T2 F1 • 1-12 • [V] [B] [D] [S] • 2Cr/C • SC also

■ NORTH PICKENHAM

PEDDARS WAY & NORFOLK COAST PATH

Mrs B J Norris, Riverside House, Meadow Lane, PE37 8LE. ☎ (01760) 440219 • Map 144/865065 • BB **B** • T2 • 1-12 NX • [D] • Food nearby

■ NORWICH

Mrs D Solomon, The Old Rectory, Crostwick, NR12 7BG. ☎ (01603) 738513 • Map 133,134/256159 • BB **D** • EM £8.50, 7pm • S1 D3 T10 F2 • 1-12 • [V] [B] [D] [S] • 3Cr

☆ Arrow Hotel, 2 Britannia Road, NR1 4HP. ☎ (01603) 628051 • Map 134/244092 • BB **B/C** • EM book first £8, 6.30pm • S5 D3 T2 F2 • 1-12 NX • [V] [B] [D] [S] [R] • 2Cr

ARROW HOTEL

On the edge of Mousehold Heath

Within easy walking distance of city centre. Colour TV and tea-making facilities in each room. Covered outdoor heated swimming pool May-Oct. Ample parking.

2 BRITANNIA ROAD
NORWICH NR1 4HP

Peter & Ann Redgrave Tel 01603 628051

☆ Sally Clarke, Kingsley Lodge, 3 Kingsley Road, NR1 3RB. ☎ (01603) 615819 • Map 134/227078 • BB **D** • S1 D1 T1 • 2-12 NX • [B] [D] [S] [R] • 2Cr/C • SC also

NORWICH CITY CENTRE

KINGSLEY LODGE

3 KINGSLEY ROAD, NORWICH NR1 3RB

Quiet cul-de-sac 5 minutes walk from bus station and shops • B&B • All rooms with en-suite bathroom, TV, tea/coffee facilities • No smoking.

☎/Fax 01603 615819

COMMENDED

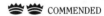

■ REEDHAM (Norwich)

Fred Monk, "Briars", Riverside, NR13 3TF. ☎ (01493) 700054 • Map 134/422017 • BB **C** • EM book first £8, until 8pm • D3 • 1-12 • [V] [B] [D] [S] [R] • 2Cr

■ ROUGHTON (Norwich)

WEAVERS WAY

Mrs D I Varden, Chalden Cottage, Felbrigg Road, NR11 8PA. ☎ (01263) 513353 • Map 133/215384 • BB **B** • D2 • 1-12 NX • [B] [D] [S] [R] Ⓜ

■ SEDGEFORD (Hunstanton)

Mrs J Frost, Park View, PE36 5LT. ☎ (01485) 571352 • Map 132/720357 • BB **B** • EM book first £8 • S2 D2 T1 • 3-11 • [V] [B] [D] [S] • 1Cr

■ SHERINGHAM

Mrs E Meakin, Wykeham Guest House, Morley Road North, NR26 8JB. ☎ (01263) 823818 • Map 133/158427 • BB **B** • S1 D1 T1 F1 • 4-10 • Ⓑ Ⓓ Ⓢ Ⓡ Ⓜ

Achimota, 31 North Street, NR26 8LW. ☎ (01263) 822379 • Map 133/154432 • BB **B/C** • EM book first £9, 6.30pm • D2 T1 • 1-12, Xmas B&B only • Ⓥ Ⓑ Ⓓ Ⓢ Ⓡ 🦮 Ⓜ • 2Cr/C

Christine Perkins, Holly Cottage, 14a The Rise, NR26 8QB. ☎ (01263) 822807 • Map 133/161426 • BB **B** • D1 F2 • 1-12 NX • Ⓑ Ⓓ Ⓢ Ⓡ

Mr P Pigott, Bayleaf Guest House, 10 Saint Peters Road, NR26 8QY. ☎ (01263) 823779 • Map 133/156431 • BB **C** • EM book first £10, 6-7pm • D6 T3 F3 • 1-12 NX • Ⓥ Ⓑ Ⓢ Ⓡ 🦮 • 1Cr/C

■ STALHAM
WEAVERS WAY

Mrs S Durrell-Walsh, The Old Surgery, High Street, NR12 9BB. ☎ (01692) 581248 • Map 133,134/372252 • BB **C** • EM book first £9 • S1 D1 T1 • 1-12 NX • Ⓥ Ⓓ

■ SWAFFHAM
PEDDARS WAY & NORFOLK COAST PATH

Mrs C Webster, Purbeck House, Whitsands Road, PE37 7BJ. ☎ (01760) 721805/725345 • Map 144/815090 • BB **B** • S2 T2 F2 • 1-12 NX • Ⓑ Ⓓ 🦮

■ TAVERHAM (Norwich)

Foxwood Guest House, Fakenham Road, NR8 6HR. ☎ (01603) 868474 • Map 133/154152 • BB **C** • EM book first £7.50, 6.30pm • D1 T2 • 1-12 NX • Ⓥ Ⓑ Ⓓ Ⓢ

■ THOMPSON (Thetford)
PEDDARS WAY & NORFOLK COAST PATH

Lavender Garnier, College Farm, IP24 1QG. ☎ (01953) 483318 • Map 144/933966 • BB **C** • D1 T2 • 1-12 • Ⓑ Ⓓ • List

Brenda Mills, Thatched House, Pockthorpe Corner, IP24 1PJ. ☎ (01953) 483577 • Map 144/917967 • BB **B** • EM £5, 7pm • D1 T2 • 1-12 • Ⓥ Ⓑ Ⓓ Ⓢ 🦮 Ⓜ

■ WELLS-NEXT-THE-SEA
PEDDARS WAY & NORFOLK COAST PATH

Mrs J Court, Eastdene, Northfield Lane, NR23 1LH. ☎ (01328) 710381 • Map 132/919435 • BB **B** • S1 D2 T1 • 1-12 NX • Ⓑ Ⓓ Ⓢ 🦮 Ⓜ

& S Cox, West End House, Dogger Lane, NR23 BE. ☎ (01328) 711190 • Map 132/913437 • BB **B** • 1 D1 T1 F1 • 1-12 NX • Ⓓ 🦮

& L Shayes, Meadowside, Two Furlong Hill, NR23 HQ. ☎ (01328) 710470 • Map 132/913433 • BB **C** • 1 T1 • 1-12 • Ⓑ Ⓓ Ⓢ

Mr & Mrs D Bramley, Brambledene, Warham Road, NR23 1NE. ☎ (01328) 711143 • Map 132/922429 • BB **B** • D2 • 11-9 • Ⓓ Ⓢ

☆ Carolyn Stocker, Wingate, Two Furlong Hill, NR23 1HQ. ☎ (01328) 711814 • Map 132/913433 • BB **C** • D2 T1 • 1-12 NX • Ⓑ Ⓓ Ⓢ 🦮 • 2Cr/HC

WINGATE

TWO FURLONG HILL, WELLS-NEXT-THE-SEA

A FINE EDWARDIAN HOUSE offering a high standard of Bed and Breakfast accommodation, set in ¾ acre garden. Well situated for the Norfolk Coastal Path, Wingate, with its warm and relaxing atmosphere, is an ideal place to rest and explore local footpaths.

TELEPHONE 01328 711814
〰〰 Highly Commended

■ WORSTEAD
WEAVERS WAY

Mrs Dirkie Lowe, Hall Farm, NR28 9RS. ☎ (01692) 536124 • Map 133,134/301252 • BB **B** • EM book first £10 • S2 D1 F1 • 1-12 • Ⓥ Ⓑ Ⓓ Ⓢ Ⓡ

NORTHAMPTONSHIRE

■ ABTHORPE (Towcester)

Mrs S Brodie, Stone Cottage, Main Street, NN12 8QN. ☎ (01327) 857544 • Map 152/650465 • BB **C** • S1 D1 T1 F1 • 1-12 • Ⓑ Ⓓ 🦮 Ⓜ • List/C

■ BRAUNSTON (Daventry)
GRAND UNION CANAL WALK

The Old Castle, London Road, NN11 7HB. ☎ (01788) 890887 • Map 152/533660 • BB **C** • S/T/D1 D2 T1 F1 • 1-12 NX • Ⓓ 🦮

■ CHACOMBE (Banbury, Oxfordshire)

Mrs Noelene Cummins, "Berry Furze", 12 Silver Street, OX17 2JR. ☎ (01295) 710145 • Map 151/491439 • BB **C** • EM book first £8 • D2 • 1-12 • Ⓥ Ⓑ Ⓓ Ⓢ Ⓡ 🦮 • 1Cr/C

☆ See Display Advertisement

CRANFORD (Kettering)

Audrey E Clarke, Dairy Farm, NN14 4AQ. ☎ (01536) 330273 • Map 141/923773 • BB **D** • EM book first £10-£12, 7pm • D2 T1 F1 • 1-12 NX • Ⓥ Ⓑ Ⓓ Ⓡ • 3Cr/C

DAVENTRY
GRAND UNION CANAL WALK

Ann Spicer, Drayton Lodge, NN11 4NL. ☎ (01327) 702449 • Map 152/577620 • BB **D** • S1 D1 T3 • 1-12 NX • Ⓑ Ⓓ ⅏ • 3Cr

KETTERING

Pennels Guest House, 175 Beatrice Road, NN16 9QR. ☎ (01536) 81940 • Map 141/868801 • BB **B** • EM £9.50, 6-7pm • S3 D1 T1 F2 • 1-12 • Ⓥ Ⓑ Ⓓ Ⓡ ⅏ Ⓜ • C

LITTLE BRAUNSTON (Daventry)
GRAND UNION CANAL WALK

Sue Goodchild, Nelson Cottage, Dark Lane, NN11 7HJ. ☎ (01788) 891806 • Map 152/545661 • BB **B/D** • D1 T1 • 3-1 NX • Ⓑ Ⓓ Ⓢ ⅏ • Plus double room on boat

MORETON PINKNEY (Daventry)

Mrs M Lainchbury, Barewell Fields, NN11 3NJ. ☎ (01295) 760754 • Map 152/573491 • BB **B** • S1 D1 T1 • 1-11 NX • Ⓓ Ⓢ • List/HC

MOULTON (Northampton)

Poplars Hotel, Cross Street, NN3 7RZ. ☎ (01604) 643983 • Map 152/782661 • BB **C** • EM £12, 6.30-7.45pm • S12 D4 T1 F4 • 1-12 NX • Ⓥ Ⓑ Ⓓ Ⓢ ⅏

NETHER HEYFORD
GRAND UNION CANAL WALK

Pam Clements, 27 Church Street, NN7 3LH. ☎ (01327) 340872 • Map 152/659586 • BB **B/C** • EM book first £6, 5-8pm • T3 • 1-12 • Ⓥ Ⓑ Ⓓ ⅏ • List

OUNDLE (Peterborough, Cambridgeshire)

Paul & Jayne Kirkby, Shuckburgh Arms, Stoke Doyle, PE8 5TG. ☎ (01832) 272339 • Map 141/025860 • BB **D** • EM £6.50, 7-9.30pm • S2 D1 T2 • 1-12 • Ⓥ Ⓑ Ⓓ ⅏ • 3Cr/C

QUINTON (Northampton)

Mrs M Turney, Quinton Green Farm, NN7 2EG. ☎ (01604) 863685 • Map 152/782531 • BB **C** • S1 D1 T1 • 1-12 NX • Ⓑ Ⓓ ⅏ • 2Cr

SIBBERTOFT (Market Harborough, Leics)

☆ Mrs M J Hart, The Wrongs, LE16 9UJ. ☎ (01858) 880886 • Map 141/666829 • BB **B** • S2 D1 • 1-12 • Ⓓ Ⓢ ⅏ • List • SC also

STOKE BRUERNE (Towcester)
GRAND UNION CANAL WALK

Pam Hart, Beam End, Stoke Park, NN12 7RZ. ☎ (01604) 864802/864638 • Map 152/740489 • BB **C** • EM book first £6-£10 • D1 T1 • 1-12 NX • Ⓥ Ⓓ Ⓢ ⅏ • List/C • SC also

WAKERLEY (Oakham, Rutland)

The Exeter Arms, Main Street, LE15 8PA. ☎ (01572) 747817 • Map 141/957955 • BB **C** • EM £5, 6-9.30pm • D3 T2 • 1-12 • Ⓥ Ⓑ Ⓓ ⅏ • List/C

WELLINGBOROUGH

Mr & Mrs D Lam, High View Hotel, 156 Midland Road, NN8 1NG. ☎ (01933) 278733 • Map 152/901678 • BB **C/D** • EM £8, 6.30-8.30pm • S5 D5 T4 F2 • 1-12 NX • Ⓥ Ⓑ Ⓓ Ⓢ Ⓡ • 3Cr

WILBARSTON (Market Harborough, Leics)

Mr McHarg, The Fox Inn, LE16 8QG. ☎ (01536) 771270 • Map 141/814882 • BB **B/C** • EM £5-£10, 6.30-9.45pm • D2 T1 F1 • 1-12 NX • Ⓥ Ⓑ • 2Cr/C

WOODEND (Towcester)

Mrs A Davey-Turner, Rose Cottage, Top Green, NN12 8RZ. ☎ (01327) 860968 • Map 152/615495 • BB **C** • EM book first £12, 7pm • D1 T1 • 1-12 NX • Ⓑ Ⓓ ⅏

NORTHUMBERLAND

■ ALNMOUTH (Alnwick)

☆ The Famous Schooner Hotel, Northumberland Street, NE66 2RS. ☎ (01665) 830216 • Map 81/246108 • BB **D** • EM £10, 7-9.30pm • S3 D4 T5 F14 • 1-12 • Ⓥ Ⓑ Ⓓ Ⓢ Ⓡ 🖳 ⓜ • 4Cr/App

17th Century coaching inn, only 100yds from beach, river & golf course, with many rooms overlooking the beautiful hotel gardens & the Aln estuary. Renowned for its superb cuisine and extensive real ale selection.
The Famous Schooner Hotel, Alnmouth Northumberland NE66 2RS

01665 830216

■ ALNWICK

Mrs Ann Bowden, Roseworth, Alnmouth Road, NE66 2PR. ☎ (01665) 603911 • Map 81/195128 • BB **C** • D2 T1 • 3-11 • Ⓑ Ⓓ Ⓢ • 2Cr/HC

■ ALWINTON (Morpeth)

Mr & Mrs Pulman, Clennell Hall, Clennell, NE65 7BG. ☎ (01669) 650341 • Map 80/929071 • BB **B** • EM £8, 7-9pm • S3 D3 T5 F2 • 1-12 • Ⓥ Ⓑ Ⓓ Ⓢ 🖳 ⓜ • SC and bunkhouse also

■ BARDON MILL (Hexham)
PENNINE WAY

Mrs J Davidson, Crindledykes Farm, House Steads, NE47 7AF. ☎ (01434) 344316 • Map 86/782672 • BB **B** • EM book first £11-£12, 6.30-7pm • D1 T1 • 3-11 • Ⓓ Ⓢ Ⓡ ⓜ • HC

■ BELLINGHAM (Hexham)
PENNINE WAY

Mrs J Gaskin, Lyndale Guest House, Off Main Square, NE48 2AW. ☎ (01434) 220361 • Map 80/839833 • BB **C/D** • EM £12.50, 7pm • S1 D2 T1 • 1-12 NX • Ⓥ Ⓑ Ⓓ Ⓢ ⓜ • 3Cr/HC • SC also

Mrs H Young, Victoria House, NE48 2JR. ☎ (01434) 220229 • Map 80/839833 • BB **A/B** • S1 D1 F1 • 5-9 • Ⓓ ⓜ

Mr & Mrs Minchin, Westfield House, NE48 2DP. ☎ (01434) 220340 • Map 80/835835 • BB **C/D** • EM book first £14, 7.30pm • D2 T2 F1 • 1-12 • Ⓥ Ⓑ Ⓓ Ⓢ 🖳 • 2Cr/HC

Mrs M J Forster, Crofters End, The Croft, NE48 2JY. ☎ (01434) 220034 • Map 80/834835 • BB **B** • S1 F2 • 3-10 • Ⓓ Ⓢ

■ BERWICK-UPON-TWEED

☆ Mr & Mrs John Hoggan, Wallace Guest House, 1 Wallace Green, TD15 1EB. ☎ (01289) 306539 • Map 75/999531 • BB **B/C** • EM £8.50, 6.30-7.30pm • S1 D1 T1 F3 • 2-12 NX • Ⓥ Ⓑ Ⓓ Ⓢ Ⓡ • List/C

WALLACE HOUSE
Wallace Green
Berwick-upon-Tweed
The forgotten jewel of the North
Quiet central position inside Elizabethan Walls. Many picturesque walks. All meals home cooked. Private parking. NON-SMOKING.

**John & Joanne Hoggan
Tel. 01289 306539**

Cherry Trees, Fenwick Village, TD15 2PJ. ☎ (01289) 381437 • Map 75/066400 • BB **B** • EM book first £9, 7pm • S1 D1 T1 F1 • 3-10 • Ⓥ Ⓓ 🖳

■ CATTON (Allendale, Hexham)
ALTERNATIVE PENNINE WAY

Nick & Heather Coulson, The Old Hostel, 1 Allen View, NE47 9QQ. ☎ (01434) 683780 • Map 86, 87/831575 • BB **B** • S1 D2 T1 F1 • 1-12 • Ⓓ Ⓢ 🖳

■ CORBRIDGE

☆ Mr F J Matthews, The Hayes, Newcastle Road, NE45 5LP. ☎ (01434) 632010 • Map 87/996643 • BB **B** • S3 D2 T3 F2 • 1-11 NX • Ⓓ Ⓢ Ⓡ 🖳 • 1Cr • SC also

HAYES GUEST HOUSE
Newcastle Road, Corbridge
Northumberland NE45 5LP
RAMBLERS WELCOMED
Highly recommended accommodation in 7½ acres of gardens, lawns and woodland. BB £16. H&C all rooms, some with showers. Also 3 self-catering cottages, flat & caravan available. Stair lift for disabled. Private parking. Full fire certificate. Packed lunches.
Tel 01434 632010

■ CORNHILL-ON-TWEED (Coldstream)

Lynne Anderson, The Coach House at Crookham, TD12 4TD. ☎ (01890) 820293 • Map 74/913380 • BB **D** • EM £15.50, 7.30pm • S2 D2 T5 • 4-10 • Ⓥ Ⓑ Ⓓ Ⓢ 🖳 • 3Cr/HC

■ EMBLETON (Alnwick)

Audrey & Douglas Turnbull, Doxford Farmhouse, Chathill, NE67 5DY. ☎ (01665) 579235 • Map 75/183233 • BB **B** • EM book first £10, 6.45pm • D2 T1 F1 • 1-12 NX • Ⓥ Ⓑ Ⓓ Ⓢ 🖳 • 2Cr/C • SC and bunkhouse also

■ **EMBLETON (CONTINUED)**

K & B Robson, Brunton House, Brunton, NE66 3HQ.
☎ (01665) 589238 • Map 75/209247 • BB **C** • EM
book first £12, 7pm • S2 D2 T3 • 1-12 NX • Ⓥ Ⓑ Ⓓ
Ⓢ • 2Cr/C

■ **FALSTONE (Nr Kielder Water)**
ALTERNATIVE PENNINE WAY

Mrs M Grimwood, Woodside, Yarrow, NE48 1BG. ☎
(01434) 240443 • Map 80/714874 • BB **B** • EM book
first £8.50-£9, 6.30pm • D1 T2 • 4-10 NX • Ⓥ Ⓓ Ⓢ
• List

■ **GREENHEAD-IN-NORTHUMBERLAND (Carlisle,
Cumbria)**
PENNINE WAY

☆ Mrs P Staff, Holmhead Farm, Hadrians Wall/PW,
CA6 7HY. ☎ (016977) 47402 • Map 86/661659 • BB
D • EM £17, 7.30pm • D1 T2 F1 • 1-12 NX • Ⓥ Ⓑ Ⓓ
Ⓢ • 3Cr/C • Bunkhouse and SC also

holmhead
A Licensed Guest House and Holiday Cottage

🏵🏵🏵 COMMENDED 🍴🍴🍴🍴 COMMENDED
for non-smokers

**Pauline and Brian Staff, Holmhead Farm,
Hadrian's Wall, Greenhead, Carlisle CA6 7HY
Tel/Fax: (016977) 47402 or 0586 661659
OS 86/661659**
COME AND ENJOY PEACE, TRANQUILITY, BREATHTAKING
VIEWS AND A LOVELY WARM WELCOME AT
OUR HOME IN THE SOUTH WEST CORNER OF
NORTHUMBERLAND'S NATIONAL PARK.

★ Completely non-smoking
★ All rooms shower/toilet
★ Home cooking using fresh produce
★ Licensed mini bar
★ Longest breakfast menu! Award winning
★ Drying room
★ ON Pennine Way and Hadrian's Wall Path
★ Loan of footpath maps and advice from
 your host, a former tour guide and expert
 on Hadrian's Wall
★ Walking holidays (with or without guide)
 planned for you

Mrs B Smith, Prospect House, Longbyre, CA6 7HN.
☎ (016977) 47471 • Map 86/654660 • BB **B/C** • D1
T1 • 3-10 • Ⓑ Ⓢ • 2Cr • SC also

Wallend Farm, CA6 7HN. ☎ (016977) 47339 • Map
86/654660 • BB **B** • D3 • 1-12 NX • Ⓓ Ⓢ

■ **HALTWHISTLE**
PENNINE WAY

Mrs J Brown, Broomshaw Hill Farm, Willia Road,
NE49 9NP. ☎ (01434) 320866 • Map 86,87/723670 •
BB **B/C** • D1 T1 F1 • 3-10 NX • Ⓑ Ⓓ Ⓢ Ⓡ • 2Cr/HC

Mrs Heather Humes, Hall Meadows, Main Street,
NE49 0AZ. ☎ (01434) 321021 • Map 86,87/708641 •
BB **B** • S1 D1 T1 • 1-12 NX • Ⓓ Ⓡ • 1Cr/C

■ **HAYDON BRIDGE (Hexham)**

Mrs Lyn Murray, Sewing Shields Farm, Hadrian's
Wall, NE47 6NW. ☎ (01434) 684418 • Map
86/809701 • BB **B** • EM book first £8, 7pm • D1 T1 F1
• 1-12 • Ⓥ Ⓓ Ⓢ 🐾 • List/C

■ **HEXHAM**

Carmen Robinson, Amber House, 2 Woodlands,
Corbridge Road, NE46 1HT. ☎ (01434) 602148 •
Map 87/946638 • BB **B** • EM book first £9, 7pm • S2
D1 • 1-12 NX • Ⓥ Ⓓ Ⓢ Ⓡ

Mavis McCormick, Topsy Turvy, 9 Leazes Lane, NE46
3BA. ☎ (01434) 603152 • Map 87/921642 • BB **B** •
EM book first £7.50, 6-6.30pm • D2 • 1-12 NX • Ⓥ
Ⓑ Ⓓ Ⓢ Ⓡ 🐾 • List/C

Mrs E Elliott, Middlemarch, Hencotes, NE46 2EB. ☎
(01434) 605003 • Map 87/936638 • BB **C/D** • D1 T1
F1 • 1-12 • Ⓑ Ⓓ Ⓢ Ⓡ 🐾 • Food nearby

Mrs Joan Liddle, Peth Head Cottage, Juniper, Steel,
NE47 0LA. ☎ (01434) 673286 • Map 87/938587 • BB
C • S1 D1 T1 • 1-12 NX • Ⓑ Ⓓ Ⓢ • 2Cr/HC

Mrs D A Theobald, "Dukeslea", 32 Shaws Park, NE46
3BJ. ☎ (01434) 602947 • Map 87/925645 • BB **C** •
D2 • 1-12 NX • Ⓑ Ⓓ Ⓢ Ⓡ • 2Cr/HC

Pat & Jim Mattinson, Ingarth, Leazes Lane, NE46
3AE. ☎ (01434) 603625 • Map 87/925642 • BB **B/C** •
T1 • 1-12 NX • Ⓢ Ⓡ 🐾

■ **ONCE BREWED/TWICE BREWED (Bardon Mill,
Hexham)**
PENNINE WAY

Mr & Mrs J Wright, Vallum Lodge Hotel, Military
Road, Twice Brewed, NE47 7AN. ☎ (01434) 344248
• Map 86/748669 • BB **C** • EM £14, 7.30pm • S1 D3
T3 • 2-11 • Ⓥ Ⓑ Ⓓ Ⓢ 🐾 • 2Cr/C

■ **OTTERBURN**

Barbara Hill, The Butterchurn Guest House, NE19
1NP. ☎ (01830) 520585 • Map 80/888930 • BB **C** •
EM £9, 7pm • D2 T2 F3 • 1-12 NX • Ⓥ Ⓑ Ⓓ 🐾 •
3Cr/C

Miss Debbie Cranston, Low Byrness, NE19 1TF. ☎ (01830) 520648 • Map 80/779012 • BB **B/C** • EM book first £7, 7pm • D3 F1 • 1-12 NX • [V] [B] [D] [S] 🐾

■ ROTHBURY (Morpeth)

M & S Jefferson, Orchard Guest House, High Street, NE65 7TL. ☎ (01669) 620684 • Map 81/056017 • BB **C** • EM £13.50, 7pm • D2 T3 F1 • 3-11 • [V] [B] [D] [S] • 3Cr/HC

Tim & Alison Giles, Thropton Demesne, Thropton, NE65 7LT. ☎ (01669) 620196 • Map 81/026023 • BB **C** • D1 T1 F1 • 1-12 NX • [B] [D] [S] • 2Cr/HC

Helen & David Edes, Well Strand, NE65 7UD. ☎ (01669) 620794 • Map 81/056016 • BB **B** • S1 D1 T1 • 1-12 NX • [D] [S] 🐾

Mrs Ann Foggin, "Tosson Tower Farm", Great Tosson, NE65 7NW. ☎ (01669) 620228 • Map 81/028006 • BB **C** • D1 T1 F1 • 1-11 • [B] [D] 🐾 • 2Cr/HC • SC also

Mrs June Taylor, Wagtail Farm, NE65 7PL. ☎ (01669) 620367 • Map 81/073008 • BB **B** • D2 T1 • 5-10 • [D] [S] • List

Mrs J Hewison, "Silverton Lodge", Silverton Lane, NE65 7RJ. ☎ (01669) 620144 • Map 81/064013 • BB **C** • EM £11, 7pm • D1 T1 • 1-12 NX • [V] [B] [D] [S] • 3Cr/HC • SC also

■ SEAHOUSES

"Slate Hall", 174 Main Street, NE68 7UA. ☎ (01665) 720320 • Map 75/212315 • BB **C** • D1 T1 F1 • 1-12 NX • [B] [D] [S] 🐾 • 2Cr/HC

■ SLAGGYFORD (Carlisle)
PENNINE WAY

Margaret Graham, Stonehall Farm, CA6 7PB. ☎ (01434) 381349 • Map 86,87/678542 • BB **B** • EM book first £6, 7pm • D1 T1 F1 • 3-10 • [V] [B] [D] 🐾 Ⓜ

■ STANNERSBURN (Falstone, Kielder Water)

☆ The Pheasant Inn, NE48 1DD. ☎ (01434) 240382 • Map 80/721866 • BB **D** • EM £5.95-£15, 7-9pm • D4 T3 F1 • 1-12 NX • [V] [B] [S] 🐾 • 3Cr/C

■ WARK (Hexham)
PENNINE WAY

Mrs Ann Bell, Woodpark Farm, NE48 3PZ. ☎ (01434) 230259 • Map 86/847798 • BB **B** • D1 F1 • 4-10 • [D] [S]

Mrs A Nichol, Hetherington, NE48 3DR. ☎ (01434) 230260 • Map 86,87/824782 • BB **B/C** • S1 D2 T1 • 3-11 • [D] [S] 🐾 • Food nearby. SC also

■ WARKWORTH (Morpeth)

Mrs D Graham, Bide a While, 4 Beal Croft, NE65 0XL. ☎ (01665) 711753 • Map 81/249053 • BB **B/C** • D1 F1 • 1-12 • [B] [D] 🐾 • List/C

■ WHITLEY BAY

Parkholme Guest House, 8 Ocean View, NE26 1AL. ☎ Tyneside 0191-253 0370 • Map 88/356724 • BB **B/C** • S1 D1 T1 F2 • 1-12 NX • [B] [S] [R]

Mrs L Smith, 12 Ocean View, NE26 1AL. ☎ 0191-252 5591 • Map 88/356724 • BB **B** • D2 • 1-12 NX • [D] [S] [R]

■ WOOLER

Joan Kelly, "Southgate", 20 High Street, NE71 6BY. ☎ (01668) 282004 • Map 75/990280 • BB **B** • D1 T2 • 4-9 • [D] [S] 🐾 • 1Cr/C

Mrs M Hugall, 6 Church Street, NE71 6DA. ☎ (01668) 281340 • Map 75/990280 • BB **B** • S1 D1 T2 F1 • 1-12 • [D] [S] 🐾 • C

Mr T F Gilbert, Winton House, 39 Glendale Road, NE71 6DL. ☎ (01668) 281362 • Map 75/991283 • BB **B/C** • D2 T1 • 3-10 • [B] [D] [S] • 2Cr/C • Transport avail.

NOTTINGHAMSHIRE

■ BURTON JOYCE (Nottingham)

Phyllis Sturgeon, Owston, 32 Main Street, NG14 5DZ. ☎ 0115-9313398 • Map 129/648438 • BB **C** • S1 T1 F1 • 1-12 • [B] [D] [S] [R] 🐾

■ CARBURTON (Nr Worksop)
ROBIN HOOD'S WAY

Beverley & Martin Beevers, Duncan Wood-Lodge Guest House, S80 3BP. ☎ (01909) 483614 • Map 120/612716 • BB **C/D** • EM £8, 6.30-8pm • D2 T3 F1 • 1-12 • [V] [B] [D] [S] 🐾 • 2Cr/C

■ EDWINSTOWE (Mansfield)
ROBIN HOOD'S WAY

Mrs H Bott, Friars Lodge Guest House, Mill Lane, NG21 9QY. ☎ (01623) 823405 • Map 120/625662 • BB **C** • S1 D1 T2 F1 • 1-12 • [B] [D] 🐾 • 2Cr • SC also

☆ See Display Advertisement

■ **NOTTINGHAM**
ROBIN HOOD'S WAY

Mrs I G Grenville, Forest Hills Hotel, 100 Musters Road, West Bridgford, NG2 7PS. ☎ 0115-981 1133 • Map 129/583374 • BB **C/D** • EM £8, 6-10pm • S9 D4 T3 F3 • 1-12 NX • Ⓥ Ⓑ Ⓓ Ⓡ 🐾

■ **OXTON**

Pilgrim Cottage, Water Lane, NG25 0SH. ☎ 0115-965 2913 • Map 120/629510 • BB **D** • EM book first £10, up to 8pm • F1 • 1-12 NX • Ⓥ Ⓑ Ⓓ Ⓢ

■ **UPPER BROUGHTON (Melton Mowbray, Leics)**

Mrs H Dowson, Sulney Fields, Colonelis Lane, LE14 3BD. ☎ (01664) 822204 • Map 129/683263 • BB **B/C** • S1 D2 T3 • 1-12 NX • Ⓑ Ⓓ Ⓢ 🐾

Ian Jalland, Swan Lodge, LE14 3BH. ☎ (01664) 823686 • Map 129/677260 • BB **C** • EM £7, 6-7pm • S1 T2 F1 • 1-12 • Ⓥ Ⓑ Ⓓ 🐾 • SC & bunkhouse also

OXFORDSHIRE

■ **ASCOTT-UNDER-WYCHWOOD (Chipping Norton)**
OXFORDSHIRE WAY

Anne & Nigel Braithwaite, The Mill, OX7 6AP. ☎ (01993) 831282 • Map 164/292181 • BB **C** • EM book first £5 • S1 D/T2 • 1-12 • Ⓥ Ⓓ Ⓢ Ⓡ

■ **BANBURY**

Belmont Guest House, Crouch Street, OX16 9PR. ☎ (01295) 262308 • Map 151/452402 • BB **C** • S1 D3 T3 F1 • 1-12 NX • Ⓑ Ⓓ Ⓡ

■ **BLETCHINGDON**
OXFORDSHIRE WAY

Mrs Pat Hedges, Stonehouse Farm, Weston Road, OX5 3EA. ☎ (01869) 350585 • Map 164/521191 • BB **C** • S1 D1 T1 F1 • 1-12 NX • Ⓓ Ⓢ Ⓡ • List

■ **BUSCOT (Faringdon)**
THAMES PATH

Mrs E Reay, Apple Tree House, SN7 8DA. ☎ (01367) 252592 • Map 163/228981 • BB **B/C** • D2 T1 • 1-12 • Ⓑ Ⓓ Ⓢ • 2Cr

■ **CHALGROVE**
OXFORDSHIRE WAY

Mrs Margaret Duxbury, Cornerstones, 1 Cromwell Close, OX44 7SE. ☎ (01865) 890298 • Map 164/641966 • BB **C** • T2 • 1-12 NX • Ⓓ Ⓢ 🐾 • List

■ **CHARLBURY (Oxford)**
OXFORDSHIRE WAY

Angela Widdows, Banbury Hill Farm, Enstone Road, OX7 3JH. ☎ (01608) 810314 • Map 164/363209 • BB **C** • S1 D2 T1 F1 • 1-12 NX • Ⓑ Ⓓ Ⓢ Ⓡ • 2Cr/C • SC also

■ **CHIPPING NORTON**

Mrs Barnard, Kingsmoor Cottage, Chapel Lane, Salford, OX7 5YN. ☎ (01608) 643276 • Map 163/288280 • BB **B** • T1 • 1-12 • Ⓓ Ⓢ 🐾 • List

■ **COMBE (Oxford)**
OXFORDSHIRE WAY

Mrs Rosemary Fox, Mayfield Cottage, West End, OX8 8NP. ☎ (01993) 898298 • Map 164/410159 • BB **B/C** • S1 D1 T1 • 3-10 • Ⓓ Ⓢ Ⓡ • List/HC • Food nearby

■ **DEDDINGTON (Oxford)**

Joan White, Hill Barn, Milton Gated Road, OX15 0TS. ☎ (01869) 338631 • Map 151/466328 • BB **B/C** • D1 T2 F1 • 1-12 NX • Ⓢ 🐾

■ **EAST HENDRED**

Mrs Iris Newman, Ridgeway Lodge Hotel, Skeats Bush, OX12 8LH. ☎ (01235) 833360 • Map 174/457884 • BB **D** • EM £8, 6-8.30pm • S4 D2 T4 F1 • 1-12 • Ⓥ Ⓑ Ⓓ 🐾

■ **FOREST HILL (Oxford)**

Audrey Dunkley, Mead Close, OX33 1DY. ☎ (01865) 872248 • Map 164/584077 • BB **B/C** • EM book first £7-£10, 6-7pm • S1 D1 T1 • 1-12 NX • Ⓥ Ⓓ Ⓢ • C

■ **GORING-ON-THAMES (Reading, Berks)**
RIDGEWAY & THAMES PATH

Mrs B Wiltshire, "Leyland", 3 Wallingford Road, RG8 0AX. ☎ (01491) 872119 • Map 175/602809 • BB **B/C** • D1 T1 F1 • 3-10 • Ⓓ Ⓡ 🐾 Ⓜ

Mrs Ewen, 14 Mountfield, Wallingford Road, RG8 0BE. ☎ (01491) 872029 • Map 175/602813 • BB **C** • S1 D1 T1 F1 • 1-12 • Ⓓ Ⓡ • Taxi service also

■ **HENLEY-ON-THAMES**
OXFORDSHIRE WAY & THAMES PATH

Mrs J Williams, Lenwade, 3 Western Road, RG9 1JL. ☎ (01491) 573468/(0374) 941629 • Map 175/760817 • BB **C** • D2 T1 • 1-12 • Ⓑ Ⓓ Ⓡ 🐾 • 1Cr/HC

Mr & Mrs E G Willis, Avalon, 36 Queen Street, RG9 1AP. ☎ (01491) 577829 • Map 175/762824 • BB **C/D** • S1 D1 T1 • 1-12 • Ⓑ Ⓓ Ⓢ Ⓡ • List

Mr & Mrs Brooks, Jacksons Farm, Fawley Bottom, RG9 6JJ. ☎ (01491) 575330 • Map 175/747879 • BB **C** • EM book first £from £7.50, from 7pm • D/F1 T1 • 1-12 NX • Ⓥ Ⓓ

■ **HOOK NORTON**

Valerie & Donald Cornelius, Symnel, High Street, OX15 5NH. ☎ (01608) 737547 • Map 151/352331 • BB **B** • EM book first £7, 7pm • D1 T2 • 1-12 NX • Ⓥ Ⓓ Ⓢ Ⓜ

■ KIDLINGTON (Oxford)
OXFORDSHIRE WAY

Mrs A C Holmes, Cherwell Croft, 72 Church Street, OX5 2BB. ☎ (01865) 373371 • Map 164/498146 • BB **B** • S1 D1 T1 • B D S 🏠 Ⓜ • 2Cr/C

■ LONG HANBOROUGH (WOODSTOCK) (Witney)

Tom & Carol Ellis, Wynford House, 79 Main Road, OX8 8JX. ☎ (01993) 881402 • Map 164/425143 • BB **C** • EM book first £10, 7pm • D1 T1 F1 • 1-12 • Ⓥ B D S R 🏠 • List

☆ Mrs Barbara Jones, Gorselands Farmhouse Auberge, Boddington Lane, OX8 6PU. ☎ (01993) 881895 • Map 164/399135 • BB **C** • EM £12.95, 7-9pm • S1 D2 T1 F1 • 1-12 • Ⓥ B D S R 🏠 • 2Cr • SC also

Gorselands Farmhouse Auberge
Long Hanborough

Old Cotswold stone house with flagstone floors and oak beams, situated in idyllic countryside. Lovely walks by the river Windrush and Cotswolds hills. Billiards Room, Grass Tennis Court, B&B from £17.00pp, All rooms en-suite. Evening meals from £10.95. Licensed.
🌊🌊 **Tel. (01993) 881895** RAC HOTEL ★★

Mrs Ann Warwick, The Close Guest House, Witney Road, OX8 8HF. ☎ (01993) 882485 • Map 164/409140 • BB **C** • S1 F3 • 1-12 NX • B D S R 🏠 • 2Cr/C

■ LONG WITTENHAM (Abingdon)
THAMES PATH

Mrs Jill Mellor, Witta's Ham Cottage, High Street, OX14 4QH. ☎ (01865) 407686 • Map 174,164/546937 • BB **C** • D1 T1 • 1-12 NX • D S R 🏠 • Food nearby

■ MILTON-UNDER-WYCHWOOD (Chipping Norton)
OXFORDSHIRE WAY

N J Perry, Little Spinney, 30 Church Meadow, OX7 6JG. ☎ (01993) 831239 • Map 163/266185 • BB **C** • EM book first £10, 7pm • S1 T1 • 2-12 • Ⓥ D S R 🏠

■ MINSTER LOVELL (Oxford)

☆ Katharine Brown, Hill Grove Farm, Crawley Dry Lane, OX8 5NA. ☎ (01993) 703120 • Map 164/323115 • BB **C** • S1 D1 T1 • 1-12 NX • B D S • 2Cr/HC • SC also

> **Do you know your rights when you're out walking in the countryside? See pages 32-39**

■ NORTH STOKE
RIDGEWAY

Mrs H Lucey, The Old Farm House, OX10 6BL. ☎ (01491) 837079 • Map 175/609863 • BB **C** • EM book first £10 • T2 • 3-10 • Ⓥ D S Ⓜ

Mrs Tanner, Footpath Cottage, The Street, OX10 6BJ. ☎ (01491) 839763 • Map 175/610863 • BB **C** • EM book first £9 • S1 D1 • 3-11 NX • Ⓥ B D 🏠 • List

■ OXFORD
THAMES PATH

Mr & Mrs P I Welding, Combermere House, 11 Polstead Road, OX2 6TW. ☎ (01865) 56971 • Map 164/506079 • BB **D** • S4 D1 T2 F2 • 1-12 • B D S R 🏠 • List

Mr & Mrs Price, Arden Lodge, 34 Sunderland Avenue, North Oxford, OX2 8DX. ☎ (01865) 552076/(0402) 068697 • Map 164/502102 • BB **C/D** • S1 D1 T1 • 1-12 NX • B D S • List

Ascot House, 283 Iffley Road, OX4 4AQ. ☎ (01865) 240259 • Map 164/528048 • BB **D** • S1 D2 T2 F2 • 1-12 • B D S R Ⓜ

Nest Lewis, Acorn Guest House, 260 Iffley Road, OX4 1SE. ☎ (01865) 247998 • Map 164/527049 • BB **B/C/D** • S2 T1 F3 • 1-12 NX • B D S R • List

■ PISHILL (Henley-on-Thames)
OXFORDSHIRE WAY

Mrs E Lakey, Bank Farm, RG9 6HJ. ☎ (01491) 638601 • Map 175/723898 • BB **B** • S1 F1 • 1-12 • B D 🏠

■ STEEPLE ASTON (Bicester)

Westfield Motel, Fenway, OX6 3SS. ☎ (01869) 340591 • Map 164/465255 • BB **D** • EM £14.50, 7-8.30pm • S2 D2 T2 F1 • 1-12 • Ⓥ B D R 🏠 • 3Cr/C

■ TETSWORTH
OXFORDSHIRE WAY

Julia Tanner, Little Acre, Tetsworth, Nr Thame, OX9 7AT. ☎ (01844) 281423 • Map 164,165/682022 • BB **B** • S1 D1 T2 F1 • 1-12 • B D 🏠

☆ See Display Advertisement

233

■ UFFINGTON (Faringdon)
RIDGEWAY

☆ C Wadsworth, The Craven, Fernham Road, SN7 7RD. ☎ (01367) 820449 • Map 174/303895 • BB **B/C/D** • EM £12.50, 7-8pm • S3 D3 T1 F1 • 1-12 • Ⓥ Ⓑ Ⓓ Ⓢ

THE CRAVEN
Uffington, Oxon

Quietly situated on the outskirts of this pretty village, and close to the Ridgeway path, the Craven, a thatched and beamed farmhouse, offers relaxed and comfortable accommodation. Log fires in winter, gardens in summer. Evening meal, packed lunches, cycle shelter.
Tel. Mrs C.A. Wadsworth 01367 820449

Mrs F Oberman, Norton House, Broad Street, SN7 7RA. ☎ (01367) 820230 • Map 174/304894 • BB **B** • D1 T1 F1 • 1-12 NX • Ⓑ Ⓓ Ⓢ 🐾

■ WALLINGFORD
THAMES PATH

Mrs Hilary Warburton, North Farm, Shillingford Hill, OX10 8NB. ☎ (01865) 858406 • Map 174,164/586924 • BB **C/D** • EM book first £10, 7.30pm • D1 T1 • 1-12 NX • Ⓥ Ⓑ Ⓓ Ⓢ Ⓜ • 2Cr/HC

Mrs J Standbridge, Dormer Cottage, High Street, Ewelme, OX10 6HQ. ☎ (01491) 833987 • Map 164,175/643916 • BB **B/C** • S1 D1 • 1-12 NX • Ⓓ

■ WANTAGE
RIDGEWAY

Viv & John Haigh, Orpwood House, Ardington, OX12 8PN. ☎ (01235) 833300 • Map 174/430883 • BB **C/D** • EM book first £8 • S1 T1 F1 • 1-12 NX • Ⓥ Ⓑ Ⓓ Ⓢ

■ WESTCOT (Wantage)
RIDGEWAY

Mrs P Upton, Westcot Lodge, OX12 9QA. ☎ (01235) 751251 • Map 174/338874 • BB **C** • EM book first £12 from 7pm • S1 D1 T1 • 1-12 NX • Ⓥ Ⓑ Ⓓ Ⓢ 🐾 Ⓜ

■ WITNEY (Oxford)

Mrs Elizabeth Simpson, Field View, Wood Green, OX8 6DE. ☎ (01993) 705485/0468 614347 • Map 164/362105 • BB **C** • D1 T2 • 1-12 NX • Ⓑ Ⓓ Ⓢ • 2Cr/HC

Mrs S Strainge, Ducklington Farm, Coursehill Lane, Ducklington, OX8 7YG. ☎ (01993) 772175 • Map 164/344073 • BB **C** • S1 T1 F1 • 1-12 NX • Ⓑ Ⓓ Ⓢ • 2Cr/C

■ WOOTTON (Woodstock)
OXFORDSHIRE WAY

Mrs Nancy Fletcher, 8 Manor Court, OX20 1EU. ☎ (01993) 811186 • Map 164/438199 • BB **B** • S2 T1 • 1-11 • Ⓑ Ⓓ Ⓢ • App • Food nearby

234

SHROPSHIRE

■ ACTON SCOTT (Church Stretton)
SHROPSHIRE WAY

Mrs M Jones, Acton Scott Farm, SY6 6QN. ☎ (01694) 781260 • Map 137,138/456898 • BB **B/C** • D2 T1 • 2-11 NX • Ⓑ Ⓢ • 2Cr/C

■ ASTON MUNSLOW

Robert & Muriel White, Chadstone, SY7 9ER. ☎ (01584) 841675 • Map 137,138/513866 • BB **C** • EM £12, 6.30pm • S1 D2 T1 • 1-12 • Ⓥ Ⓑ Ⓓ Ⓢ • 3Cr/HC

■ BISHOPS CASTLE
OFFA'S DYKE & SHROPSHIRE WAY

Peter & Phyllis Hutton, The Old Brick Guesthouse, 7 Church Street, SY9 5AA. ☎ (01588) 638471 • Map 137/323885 • BB **C** • EM book first £10, 7-7.30pm • S1 D2 T2 F1 • 1-12 NX • Ⓥ Ⓑ Ⓓ 🐾 • 2Cr

■ BRIDGNORTH

Mr & Mrs R N Lloyd, Bearwood Lodge Hotel, Kidderminster Road, WV15 6BW. ☎ (01746) 762159 • Map 138/721923 • BB **C/D** • D3 T3 F1 • 1-12 • Ⓑ Ⓓ Ⓢ 🐾 • 3Cr

■ BRONYGARTH, WESTON RHYN (Oswestry)
OFFA'S DYKE

John & Sheila Bampfield, The Old School, SY10 7NB. ☎ (01691) 772546 • Map 126/267370 • BB **B** • S1 T2 • 1-12 NX • Ⓑ Ⓓ Ⓢ Ⓡ 🐾 Ⓜ • Transport to eatery

■ BROSELEY

Diane Kaiser, Orchard House, 40 King Street, TF12 5NA. ☎ (01952) 882684 • Map 127/671022 • BB **B** • EM book first £8, 6.30pm • D1 T1 F1 • 1-12 NX • Ⓥ Ⓑ Ⓓ 🐾 • 2Cr

■ BUCKNELL

Mrs C Price, The Hall, SY7 0AA. ☎ (01547) 530249 • Map 148,137/354738 • BB **C** • EM book first £9, 6-8pm • D2 T1 • 3-11 NX • Ⓑ Ⓢ Ⓡ • 2Cr/C

■ CARDINGTON (Church Stretton)

Mrs O Pennington, Grove Farm, SY6 7JZ. ☎ (01694) 771451 • Map 137,138/505952 • BB **B** • EM book first £5 • T1 F1 • 1-12 • Ⓥ Ⓓ 🐾 Ⓜ • List/App

■ CHURCH STRETTON

Mrs C Wharton, Dalesford, Carding Mill Valley, SY6 6JF. ☎ (01694) 723228 • Map 137/448943 • BB **C** • EM book first £8.50, 7pm • D2 T1 • 1-12 NX • Ⓥ Ⓑ Ⓓ Ⓡ 🐾 Ⓜ

☆ Belvedere Guest House, Burway Road, SY6 6DP. ☎ (01694) 722232 • Map 137/451941 • BB **C/D** • EM £9.50, 7pm • S3 D4 T3 F2 • 1-12 NX • Ⓥ Ⓑ Ⓓ Ⓢ Ⓡ 🐾 • 3Cr/C • Groups also

Belvedere Guest House
BURWAY ROAD
CHURCH STRETTON
ETB 🏅🏅🏅 Commended

In superb walking country, a comfortable house on slopes of Long Mynd, minutes from Church Stretton. Bedroom tea-making facilities. Two lounges (one with TV). Packed lunches, evening meals. 10% reduction for weekly or party bookings. Well-behaved pets and children welcome.

 AA   **Tel. 01694 722232**   **RAC**
            Fax. 01694 722232   *Acclaimed*

☆ Joanna Brereton, Woolston Farm, Woolston, SY6 6QD. ☎ (01694) 781201 • Map 137/424871 • BB **B/C** • EM book first £8.50, 6.30pm • D2 T1 • 2-11 • Ⓥ Ⓑ Ⓓ Ⓢ 🐾

Woolston Farm
Church Stretton

Victorian farmhouse situated above Wistanstow. Long Mynd and Stiperstones nearby. Friendly atmosphere and good home cooking. ETB 🏅

Contact Joanna Brereton
Marshbrook (01694) 781201

Mrs Christine Hughes, "Bycroft", 59 Shrewsbury Road, SY6 6EX. ☎ (01694) 722582 • Map 137, 138/454942 • BB **B** • D2 T1 • 3-11 • Ⓑ Ⓓ Ⓢ Ⓡ 🐾

Mrs Margaret Knight, Rheingold, 9 The Bridleways, SY6 7AN. ☎ (01694) 723969 • Map 137,138/462934 • BB **B** • EM book first £9, 7.15pm • D1 T1 • 1-12 NX • Ⓑ Ⓢ Ⓡ • 2Cr

Stewart Blower, Brookfields Guest House, Watling Street North, SY6 7AR. ☎ (01694) 722314 • Map 137,138/459937 • BB **D** • EM £15.50, 7-9.30pm • D2 T1 F1 • 1-12 • Ⓥ Ⓑ Ⓓ Ⓢ Ⓡ 🐾 • 3Cr/C

■ CLEE HILL (Ludlow)
SHROPSHIRE WAY

☆ Studley Cottage, SY8 3NP. ☎ (01584) 890990 • Map 138/599747 • BB **B/C** • EM £10, 7-8pm • S1 D1 T1 • 4-10 • Ⓥ Ⓑ Ⓓ Ⓢ • 3Cr/C

This Yearbook now has 4 accommodation sections:

☆ **Hostels & Bunkhouses**
☆ **Centres for Groups**
☆ **Self-catering**
☆ **Bed & Breakfast**

STUDLEY COTTAGE
Clee Hill, near Ludlow,
South Shropshire SY8 3NP

Explore beautiful, unspoiled S. Shropshire from our secluded, comfortable home, surrounded by wonderful views and walks from the gate. Enjoy hearty meals and home-grown produce. CTV, coffee/tea in all rooms. Relax in a friendly, peaceful atmosphere. ☎

(01584) 890990 for brochure

■ CLEOBURY MORTIMER (Kidderminster, Hereford & Worcs)

The Redfern Hotel, DY14 8AA. ☎ (01299) 270395 • Map 138/675759 • BB **D** • EM £15, 7.30-9.30pm • D6 T3 F2 • 1-12 • Ⓥ Ⓑ Ⓓ Ⓢ 🐾 • 4Cr/C

Dinah M Thompson, Cox's Barn, Bagginswood, DY14 8LS. ☎ (01746) 718415/(0860) 135011 • Map 138/682805 • BB **B** • EM £7-£10, 6.30-8.30pm • D2 T/F1 • 1-12 • Ⓥ Ⓑ Ⓢ 🐾 • 1Cr

■ CLUN (Craven Arms)

☆ M Ellison, New House Farm, SY7 8NJ. ☎ (01588) 638314 • Map 137/275863 • BB **C** • EM book first £10.50, 7.30pm • D1 T1 F1 • 2-10 • Ⓥ Ⓑ Ⓓ Ⓢ 🐾 • 2Cr/HC

New House Farm
High in Clun Hills

Walks from the doorstep surround this peaceful and isolated 18th century farmhouse—Offa's Dyke, Shropshire Way and Kerry Ridgeway. "New House Farm is an example of superb farmhouse Bed & Breakfast," *Yorkshire Evening Post.* **Tel. 01588 638314**

ETB 🏅🏅   **AA**
Highly Commended   ००००
               Selected

Chris & Mal Lewis, Clun Farm, High Street, SY7 8JB. ☎ (01588) 640432 • Map 137/302808 • BB **B/C** • S2 T1 F1 • 1-12 NX • Ⓑ Ⓓ Ⓢ 🐾 • List

Reg Maund & Judy Bailey, Crown House, Church Street, SY7 8JN. ☎ (01588) 640780 • Map 137/300805 • BB **B/C** • D1 T1 • 1-12 • Ⓑ Ⓓ Ⓢ 🐾 Ⓜ • 2Cr

Mrs J Williams, Hurst Mill Farm, Clunton, SY7 0JA. ☎ (01588) 640224 • Map 137/323811 • BB **B** • EM £7, 6-8pm • D1 T1 F1 • 1-12 NX • Ⓥ Ⓑ Ⓓ Ⓢ 🐾 Ⓜ • 2Cr/C • SC also

Gill Dellacasa, Birches Mill, SY7 8NL. ☎ (01588) 640409 • Map 137/280820 • BB **C** • EM book first £14, 8pm • D2 T1 • 4-10 • Ⓓ Ⓢ 🐾 • 1Cr/HC • SC also

☆ See Display Advertisement

Mrs V Lewis, Lawn Farm, Newcastle, SY7 8PN. ☎ (01588) 640303 • Map 137/218826 • BB **B** • EM book first £6, 6-6.30pm • D2 F1 • EASTER-OCT • Ⓥ Ⓓ ⅋ Ⓜ • Lifts to Offa's Dyke

■ COALBROOKDALE (Telford)
SHROPSHIRE WAY

Rosemary Clegg, 2 School Road, TF8 7DY. ☎ (01952) 432210 • Map 127/668048 • BB **B/C** • EM book first £9.50, 6.30pm • D1 T1 F1 • 1-12 NX • Ⓥ Ⓑ Ⓓ Ⓢ • 2Cr

■ CRAVEN ARMS
SHROPSHIRE WAY

☆ Roger & Sheila Davies, Hesterworth Holidays, Hopesay, SY7 8EX. ☎ (01588) 660487 • Map 137/391817 • BB **C** • EM book first £, 6-7.30pm • S3 D6 T10 F2 • 1-12 • Ⓥ Ⓑ Ⓓ Ⓡ ⅋ • SC and groups also

HESTERWORTH HOLIDAYS
HOPESAY, CRAVEN ARMS, SHROPSHIRE SY7 8EX

On Shropshire Way
• ETB up to Commended •
Comfortable homely accommodation in countryside apartments and cottages surrounded by 12 acres of beautiful gardens and grounds. Large communal/dining room, good home-cooked meals, ideal for families or groups. Ludlow 10 miles. Private bathroom, CTV, pay phone, tea/coffee, licenced. B&B £16.25. Evening meals from £6. Packed lunch by arrangement.
Tel. Roger & Sheila Davies 01588 660487

■ ELLESMERE

The Watergate Guest House, Watergate Street, SY12 0EU. ☎ (01691) 622747 • Map 126/401348 • BB **B** • S2 D2 T1 F1 • 1-12 • Ⓓ Ⓢ

Mrs H Rodenhurst, Hordley Hall, Hordley, SY12 9BB. ☎ (01691) 622772 • Map 126/381308 • BB **B/C** • EM book first £10, 7-8pm • S1 D1 T1 F1 • 1-12 • Ⓥ Ⓓ Ⓢ ⅋ • List/App

■ GOBOWEN (Oswestry)

Miss O Powell, Clevelands, Station Road, SY11 3JS. ☎ (01691) 661359 • Map 126/302334 • BB **B** • S2 D1 • 1-12 • Ⓓ Ⓢ Ⓡ ⅋ • Food nearby

■ IRONBRIDGE

Mrs M Gilbride, Paradise House, Coalbrookdale, TF8 7NR. ☎ (01952) 433379 • Map 127/668039 • BB **C** • D1 T1 F1 • 3-11 NX • Ⓑ Ⓓ • 1Cr/App • SC also

■ LITTLE STRETTON (Church Stretton)
SHROPSHIRE WAY

☆ Jane Blake, The Elms, SY6 6RD. ☎ (01694) 723084 • Map 137/443917 • BB **B/C** • D2 T1 • 1-12 NX • Ⓓ Ⓢ Ⓡ ⅋ • List

THE ELMS
Little Stretton,
Church Stretton, Shropshire

Attractive Victorian residence close to quaint village with cheerful pubs. Five minutes walk to Ashes Valley, Long Mynd and other easy rambles. Pleasant cycling on traffic-free roads. Tea-making facilities in rooms. Towels supplied. Lounge with TV. Parking. B&B.

Tel. 01694 723084

■ LLANFAIR WATERDINE (Knighton, Powys)
OFFA'S DYKE & GLYNDWR'S WAY

☆ Chris & Judy Stevenson, Red Lion Inn, LD7 1TU. ☎ (01547) 528214 • Map 148,137/240762 • BB **C** • EM £8-£10, 7-9pm • D1 T2 • 1-12 • Ⓥ Ⓑ Ⓢ

RED LION INN
LANFAIR WATERDINE
SHROPSHIRE LD7 1TU

16th Century Drovers Inn just 1½ miles from the best section of Offa's Dyke. Peaceful riverside location. An excellent cellar of Cask Conditioned Ales, great home cooked food and a warm welcome await you at
THE RED LION INN.
☎ **01547 528214**
Grid ref 324067 276260

SHROPSHIRE ENGLAND B&B ACCOMMODATION

■ LLANYMYNECH (Powys)
OFFA'S DYKE

Roy & Joan Beeston, Lion Hotel, SY22 6EJ. ☎ (01691) 830234 • Map 126/267208 • BB **C** • EM book first £6.50, 6pm • S3 D2 T4 F1 • 12-10 NX • Ⓥ Ⓑ Ⓓ 🐾 • App

Mrs Carol Fahey, "Hospitality", Vyrnwy Bank, Llanymynech, Nr Oswestry, SY22 6LG. ☎ (01691) 830427 • Map 126/274209 • BB **B** • EM book first £8.50, 7pm • S1 D1 T1 • 3-1 NX • Ⓥ Ⓓ Ⓢ 🐾 • List/C • Camping also

■ LONGVILLE-IN-THE-DALE

Patrick & Madeline Egan, The Longville Arms, TF13 6DT. ☎ (01694) 771206 • Map 137,138/538937 • BB **B/C** • EM from £4.50, 7-9pm • D4 T2 F1 • 1-12 • Ⓥ Ⓑ Ⓓ Ⓢ 🐾 Ⓜ • SC also. No meals Tuesdays

■ LUDLOW
SHROPSHIRE WAY

☆ Cecil Guest House, Sheet Road, SY8 1LR. ☎ (01584) 872442 • Map 137,138/525742 • BB **C/D** • EM book first £11.50, 7pm • S2 D1 T5 F1 • 1-12 NX • Ⓥ Ⓑ Ⓓ Ⓢ Ⓡ 🐾 • 2Cr/C • Groups also

Mrs J Bowen, Arran House, 42 Gravel Hill, SY8 1QR. ☎ (01584) 873764 • Map 148,137/313749 • BB **B** • EM £7.50, 6pm • S2 D1 T1 • 1-12 • Ⓓ Ⓢ Ⓡ 🐾 • 1Cr

■ MINSTERLEY (Shrewsbury)

☆ Debbie & Paul Costello, Cricklewood Cottage, Plox Green, SY5 0HT. ☎ (01743) 791229 • Map 126/366039 • BB **C** • EM Oct-Mar, book first £11.50, 6.30pm • D2 T1 • 1-12 NX • Ⓥ Ⓑ Ⓓ Ⓢ • 2Cr/HC

■ OSWESTRY
OFFA'S DYKE

☆ The Bear Hotel & Restaurant, Salop Road, SY11 2NR. ☎ (01691) 652093 • Map 126/292295 • BB **C/D** • EM £7, 7-9.30pm • S3 D4 T2 F1 • 1-11 NX • Ⓥ Ⓑ Ⓓ 🐾 • 3Cr/C • Groups also

■ RATLINGHOPE (Shrewsbury)
SHROPSHIRE WAY

Stuart & Carol Buxton, Marehay Farm, Ratlinghope, Pontesbury, SY5 0SJ. ☎ (01588) 650289 • Map 137/381983 • BB **B/C** • T2 • 1-12 NX • Ⓑ Ⓓ Ⓢ • 2Cr/HC

■ SELATTYN (Oswestry)
OFFA'S DYKE

Mrs Kay Brown, Carreg-y-Big, SY10 7HX. ☎ (01691) 654754 • Map 126/252322 • BB **B** • EM book first £7.50, 6-8pm • T3 • 9-6 NX • Ⓥ Ⓑ Ⓓ 🐾

■ SHREWSBURY
SHROPSHIRE WAY

Abbey Court House, 134 Abbey Foregate, SY2 6AU. ☎ (01743) 364416 • Map 126/506122 • BB **B/C** • S2 D3 T3 F2 • 1-12 NX • Ⓑ Ⓓ Ⓢ Ⓡ 🐾 • 2Cr

Lucroft Hotel, Castlegates, SY1 2AD. ☎ (01743) 362421 • Map 126/492128 • BB **B/C** • S4 D3 T3 F2 • 1-12 NX • Ⓓ Ⓡ 🐾 • 1Cr

☆ Restawhile Guest House, 36 Coton Crescent, SY1 2NZ. ☎ (01743) 240969 • Map 126/491134 • BB **B/C** • EM book first £12.50, 6.30pm • S1 D1 T1 • 1-12 • Ⓑ Ⓓ Ⓡ

SHROPSHIRE
ENGLAND
B&B ACCOMMODATION

Gill Oldham-Malcolm, The Bancroft, Coton Crescent, SY1 2NY. ☎ (01743) 231746 • Map 126/490135 • BB B/C • EM book first £10, 6.30-8pm • S2 T1 F1 • 1-12 NX • Ⓥ Ⓑ Ⓓ Ⓡ ⚄ • List/C

■ SMETHCOTT (Church Stretton)

Mr & Mrs J Scarratt, Lawley House, SY6 6NX. ☎ (01694) 751236 • Map 137,138/452998 • BB B • EM £10 • S1 D1 T2 • 1-12 NX • Ⓥ Ⓑ Ⓓ ⚄ • Transport to Shropshire Way

■ STIPERSTONES (Minsterley, Shrewsbury)
SHROPSHIRE WAY

Roy & Sylvia Anderson, Tankerville Lodge, SY5 0NB. ☎ (01743) 791401 • Map 137/355995 • BB B/C • EM book first £9.50, 7pm • D1 T3 • 1-12 • Ⓥ Ⓓ Ⓢ ⚄ • 1Cr/C • SC also

The Stiperstones Inn, SY5 0LZ. ☎ (01743) 791327 • Map 126/365003 • BB A • EM £4 • S1 D2 T1 F1 • 1-12 • Ⓥ Ⓓ ⚄ • SC also

Mrs R Lawton, Hill Cottage, The Bog, SY5 0NL. ☎ (01743) 791918 • Map 126, 137/359981 • BB B/C • EM book first £13.50, 7pm • S1 D1 T1 • 4-10 • Ⓥ Ⓑ Ⓓ Ⓢ • List/HC

■ STOKESAY (Craven Arms)
SHROPSHIRE WAY

Mrs Ruth Grizzell, Castle View Bed & Breakfast, SY7 9AL. ☎ (01588) 673712 • Map 137/435816 • BB B • S1 D1 T1 • 1-12 NX • Ⓑ Ⓓ Ⓡ ⚄ • List/HC

■ WEM
SHROPSHIRE WAY

Mrs Anne James, Forncet, Soulton Road, SY4 5HR. ☎ (01939) 232996 • Map 126/521292 • BB B • EM book first £10, 6.30-8pm • S1 D1 T1 • 1-12 NX • Ⓥ Ⓓ Ⓢ Ⓡ • List/C

■ WENTNOR (Bishops Castle)
SHROPSHIRE WAY

R Middleton, Brook House, Prollymoor, SY9 5EQ. ☎ (01588) 650666 • Map 137/391941 • BB B • S1 D1 T1 • 4-10 • Ⓓ ⚄

SOMERSET

INCLUDING THE UNITARY AUTHORITIES OF BATH AND NORTH EAST SOMERSET AND NORTH WEST SOMERSET, AREAS PREVIOUSLY IN THE COUNTY OF AVON

■ ALLERFORD
SOUTH WEST COAST PATH

Sheila Wright, Pack Horse, TA24 8HW. ☎ (01643) 862475 • Map 181/904469 • BB C • D1 • 1-12 • Ⓑ Ⓓ ⚄ • SC also

☆ Jean & Ian Hamilton, Fern Cottage, TA24 8HN. ☎ (01643) 862215 • Map 181/904470 • BB D • EM £11.25, 7pm • S1 D2 T2 • 1-12 NX • Ⓥ Ⓑ Ⓓ Ⓢ ⚄ • 3Cr/C

Fern Cottage, Allerford, Nr Porlock,
West Somerset TA24 8HN
Telephone: Porlock (01643) 862215
Exhilarating Exmoor! Walk the coombes, moors, hills and forests. Stay in our tiny village set in 20sq miles of National Trust estate within the National Park. Walks from doorstep. Cosy large old cottage. Noted for classic cooking and wine list. CH, logfires, non-smoking. Credit cards.

■ BATH
COTSWOLD WAY

Mrs P J Rowe, Abode, 7 Widcombe Crescent, Widcombe Hill, BA2 6AH. ☎ (01225) 422726 • Map 172/757641 • BB C • S2 D/S2 T1 F1 • 1-11 NX • Ⓑ Ⓓ Ⓢ • 2Cr

Mrs M Gould, 3 Pulteney Terrace, BA2 4HJ. ☎ (01225) 316578 • Map 172/756645 • BB B • D1 T1 F1 • 1-12 NX • Ⓓ Ⓡ • SC also

☆ Cranleigh, 159 Newbridge Hill, BA1 3PX. ☎ (01225) 310197 • Map 172/724656 • BB D • D2 T2 F2 • 1-12 • Ⓑ Ⓓ Ⓢ Ⓡ • 2Cr

CRANLEIGH
BATH

The Cotswold Way goes past our door—this is the perfect spot to begin or end your walk! Lovely Victorian house with beautiful veiws, spacious en suite bedrooms and generous breakfasts. Non-smoking, private parking.

Tel (01225) 310197

Jane & John Shepherd, 21 Newbridge Road, BA1 3HE. ☎ (01225) 314694 • Map 172/731651 • BB C • S1 D1 T1 • 1-12 NX • Ⓓ Ⓢ Ⓡ • 1Cr

Jenny Bennett, Kinlet Guest House, 99 Wellsway, BA2 4RX. ☎ (01225) 420268 • Map 172/746635 • BB C • S1 D1 F1 • 1-12 • Ⓓ Ⓢ Ⓡ • 1Cr

Marion Dodd, Brocks, 32 Brock Street, BA1 2LN. ☎ (01225) 338374 • Map 172/746652 • BB D • D2 T2 F2 • 1-12 NX • Ⓑ Ⓓ Ⓢ Ⓡ • 2Cr/C

M A Cooper, Flaxley Villa, 9 Newbridge Hill, BA1 3LE. ☎ (01225) 313237 • Map 172/724653 • BB C • S1 D1 T2 F1 • 1-12 • Ⓑ Ⓡ • 1Cr

Sarah Danny, The Manor House, Wellow, BA2 8QQ. ☎ (01225) 832027 • Map 172/740583 • BB C • S1 D1 T1 • 1-12 NX • Ⓑ Ⓓ Ⓢ • List • Food nearby

☆ Mrs A Kitching, Wentworth House Hotel, 106 Bloomfield Road, BA2 2AP. ☎ (01225) 339193 • Map 172/745635 • BB D • EM book first £15, 7pm • D10 T6 F2 • 1-12 NX • Ⓥ Ⓑ Ⓢ Ⓡ ⚄ • 3Cr

Mr & Mrs Delaney, Homely Guest House, 9 Pulteney Terrace, Pulteney Road, BA2 4HJ. ☎ (01225) 316159 • Map 172/756645 • BB **C** • S1 D1 T1 F1 • 1-11 • Ⓑ Ⓓ Ⓡ • 1Cr

☆ Nicole & Anthony O'Flaherty, Oldfields, 102 Wells Road, BA2 3AL. ☎ (01225) 317984 • Map 172/742641 • BB **C/D** • D8 T6 F2 • 1-12 • Ⓑ Ⓡ ⛱

Janet Cross, Clearbrook Farm, Midford, BA2 7DE. ☎ (01225) 723227 • Map 172/765615 • BB **B/C** • S1 D2 T1 F1 • 1-12 • Ⓓ Ⓢ ⛱ • Food nearby

Judith Goddard, Cherry Tree Villa, 7 Newbridge Hill, BA1 3PW. ☎ (01225) 331671 • Map 172/731651 • BB **B/C** • S1 D/T1 F1 • 1-12 NX • Ⓓ Ⓡ ⛱ • 1Cr

■ BATHFORD (Bath)

Beverley Smart, Garston Cottage, Ashley Road, BA1 7TT. ☎ (01225) 852510 • Map 172/792668 • BB **B/C** • EM book first £8, 6-8pm • S2 D2 T2 F1 • 1-12 NX • Ⓥ Ⓑ Ⓓ Ⓢ ⛱ • 2Cr • Groups also

■ BICKNOLLER (Taunton)

Quantock Moor Farm Cottage, TA4 4ER. ☎ (01984) 656626 • Map 181/118392 • BB **B** • EM £9, 7-7.30pm • S1 D1 T1 • 1-12 NX • Ⓥ Ⓓ Ⓢ ⛱ • Steam railway nearby

■ BISHOPS LYDEARD

☆ Jane & David Hinton, The Mount, Mount Street, TA4 3AN. ☎ (01823) 432208 • Map 181,193/168296 • BB **B** • EM book first £10.50, from 6.30pm • S1 T3 • 1-12 • Ⓓ Ⓢ • SC also, Steam railway

■ BISHOPSWOOD (Nr Chard)

Roger & Sarah Newman-Coburn, Hawthorne House, TA20 3RS. ☎ (01460) 234482 • Map 193/259127 • BB **C** • EM book first £10, 6.30-7.30pm • D2 T1 • 1-12 • Ⓥ Ⓑ Ⓓ Ⓢ ⛱ • 2Cr/C

■ BRIDGWATER

Mrs D Chappell, Cokerhurst Farm, 87 Wembdon Hill, TA6 7QA. ☎ (01278) 422330/(0850) 692065 • Map 182/280378 • BB **B/C** • D1 T1 F1 • 1-12 NX • Ⓑ Ⓓ Ⓢ Ⓡ • 2Cr/HC

■ BRUTON

Chris Dunn, "The Old Forge", 89 High Street, BA10 0AL. ☎ (01749) 812585 • Map 183/682348 • BB **B/C** • D2 T1 F1 • 1-11 NX • Ⓑ Ⓓ Ⓢ Ⓡ

■ BURRINGTON (Bristol)

Mrs P Hicks, Holly Wood, Ham Link, BS18 7AW. ☎ (01761) 462221 • Map 182,172/483592 • BB **B/C** • D1 T1 • 4-10 • Ⓑ Ⓓ Ⓢ ⛱ Ⓜ

■ CHEDDAR
WEST MENDIP WAY

P A Phillips, The Forge, Cliff Street, BS27 3PL. ☎ (01934) 742345 • Map 182/460534 • BB **B** • D1 F1 • 1-12 NX • Ⓓ Ⓢ

Mrs C Ladd, Tor Farm, Nyland, BS27 3UD. ☎ (01934) 743710 • Map 182/455503 • BB **C/D** • EM book first £11, 6pm • S2 D4 T1 F1 • 1-12 NX • Ⓥ Ⓑ Ⓢ ⛱

■ CHEW MAGNA (Bristol)

Mrs Judi Hasell, Woodbarn Farm, Denny Lane, BS18 8SZ. ☎ (01275) 332599 • Map 182,172/574620 • BB **C** • D1 F1 • 3-12 NX • Ⓑ Ⓓ Ⓢ • 2Cr/C

☆ See Display Advertisement

SOMERSET   ENGLAND   B&B ACCOMMODATION

■ CHEW STOKE (Bristol)

Mrs Ann Hollomon, Orchard House, Bristol Road, BS18 8UB. ☎ (01275) 333143 • Map 182, 172/561618 • BB **C** • EM book first £10, 6.45pm • S1 D2 T3 F1 • 1-12 • Ⓥ Ⓑ Ⓓ • 2Cr/C

■ CHURCHINFORD (Taunton)

☆ The York Inn, TA3 7RF. ☎ (01823) 601333 • Map 193/213124 • BB **D** • EM from £6.50, 7-10pm • S1 D1 T2 F1 • 1-12 • Ⓥ Ⓑ ⚬

■ CLEVEDON

Mrs E Potter, 'Bibury', 5 Sunnyside Road, BS21 7TE. ☎ (01275) 873315 • Map 171,172/405713 • BB **B** • D1 F1 • 1-12 NX • Ⓓ Ⓢ

■ CREWKERNE

Heather McQue, Merefield Vegetarian Guest House, East Street, TA18 7AB. ☎ (01460) 73112 • Map 193/443097 • BB **C** • EM book first £8, veg. only, 7pm • D1 T2 • 1-12 NX • Ⓥ Ⓑ Ⓓ Ⓢ Ⓡ • SC also

Frank & Lina Joyce, George Hotel and Restaurant, Market Square, TA18 7LP. ☎ (01460) 73650 • Map 193/441098 • BB **C/D** • EM £5-£15, 6.30-9.30pm • S3 D5 T2 F3 • 1-12 • Ⓥ Ⓑ Ⓓ Ⓡ ⚬ • 3Cr/App

Mr & Mrs Rouse, Beverley, Hewish Lane, TA18 8RE. ☎ (01460) 77742 • Map 193/436096 • BB **C** • EM book first £8, 6-8pm • D2 • 2-11 • Ⓥ Ⓑ Ⓓ Ⓢ Ⓡ

■ CROWCOMBE (Taunton)

Mrs J Lamacraft, Town End Farm, TA4 4AA. ☎ (01984) 618655 • Map 181/140365 • BB **B/C** • D2 T2 • 1-12 NX • Ⓑ Ⓓ Ⓡ • 2Cr

■ DULVERTON (Exmoor)

Mrs Jane Buckingham, Town Mills, TA22 9HB. ☎ (01398) 323124 • Map 181/914279 • BB **C** • D4 T1 • 1-12 NX • Ⓑ Ⓓ • 2Cr/HC

Exton House Hotel, Exton, TA22 9JT. ☎ (01643) 851365 • Map 181/926336 • BB **C/D** • EM £14, 7.30pm • S1 D3 T2 F3 • 1-12 • Ⓑ Ⓓ Ⓢ Ⓜ ⚬ • 3Cr/HC

Mrs P Vellacott, Springfield Farm, Ashwick Lane, TA22 9QD. ☎ (01398) 323722 • Map 181/868314 • BB **B/C** • EM book first £11.75, 6.30pm • D2 T1 • 2-11 • Ⓑ Ⓓ Ⓢ ⚬ • 2Cr/C

Mrs C Nurcombe, Marsh Bridge Cottage, TA22 9QG. ☎ (01398) 323197 • Map 181/904288 • BB **B/C** • EM book first £11, 7pm • D1 T1 F1 • 1-12 • Ⓥ Ⓑ Ⓓ ⚬

Gillian Aldridge, Scatterbrook Farm, Hinam Cross, TA22 9QQ. ☎ (01398) 323857 • Map 181/917279 • BB **A/B** • EM book first £8, 7pm • D2 T1 • 1-12 • Ⓥ Ⓑ Ⓓ ⚬ • List/App

■ DUNSTER (Minehead)
SOUTH WEST COAST PATH

☆ The Yarn Market Hotel, 25/27 High St, Dunster, Minehead TA24 6SF. ☎ (01643) 821425 • Map 181/992437 • BB **D** • EM £10 • S1 D1 T1 F1 • 1-12 • Ⓥ Ⓑ Ⓓ Ⓢ Ⓡ ⚬ • 3Cr/App

☆ The Luttrell Arms, 32-36 High Street, TA24 6SG. ☎ (01643) 821555 • Map 181/992438 • BB **D** • EM £10, 7-9pm • T27 • 1-12 • Ⓥ Ⓑ Ⓓ Ⓢ Ⓡ ⚬

■ EXFORD (Minehead)
TWO MOORS WAY

☆ Gillian Lamble, Edgcott House, TA24 7QG. ☎ (01643) 831495 • Map 181/847387 • BB **C** • EM book first £11, 7.30pm • S2 D1 T1 • 1-12 • Ⓥ Ⓑ Ⓓ ⚬ • 2Cr/C

EDGCOTT HOUSE
Exford, Minehead, Somerset
Charming old country house, peacefully situated in the heart of Exmoor National Park. Quarter mile from village. H&C in all rooms, private bathrooms available. Excellent home cooking with full English breakfast, optional dinner, packed lunches. Boot & drying room, dogs welcome.
Tel 01643 831495

☆ Nigel Winter, Exmoor Lodge, Chapel Street, TA24 7PY. ☎ (01643) 831694 • Map 181/853384 • BB **B/C** • EM book first £11, 7-9pm • S1 D3 T1 • 1-12 • Ⓥ Ⓑ Ⓓ Ⓢ 🐾 • Veg. food only

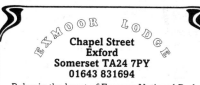

EXMOOR LODGE
Chapel Street
Exford
Somerset TA24 7PY
01643 831694
Relax in the heart of Exmoor National Park and enjoy the beautiful surroundings. No smoking. Exclusively vegetarian and vegan food. Most rooms en-suite, all with tea/coffee facilities. Contact Nigel for details
Telephone 01643 831694

■ **FROME**

Mrs O Allen, Gioia, 2 Vallis Farm Cottages, Egford, BA11 3JQ. ☎ (01373) 463545 • Map 183/758488 • BB **A/B** • EM book first £6, 6.30-7pm • T1 • 1-12 NX • Ⓥ Ⓓ Ⓢ Ⓡ

■ **HINTON ST GEORGE**

Mrs B Hudspith, "Rookwood", West Street, TA17 8SA. ☎ (01460) 73450 • Map 193/417126 • BB **B** • S1 T1 • 1-12 NX • Ⓑ Ⓓ Ⓢ

■ **HOLFORD (Bridgwater)**

☆ Mrs P Laidler, Quantock House, TA5 1RY. ☎ (01278) 741439 • Map 181/158413 • BB **C** • EM book first £12, 6.30pm • D1 T1 F1 • 1-12 NX • Ⓥ Ⓑ Ⓓ 🐾 Ⓜ

Quantock House
Holford
Bridgwater

Relax in our 300yr old thatched house, we're in a small village at the foot of the Quantock Hills. Evening meals available or use the excellent local pubs. Accommodation includes 3 large rooms with full en-suite facilities. Guest sitting-room with inglenook fireplace.

Tel. Pam Laidler on Holford (01278) 741439

Mrs Susan Ayshford, Forge Cottage, TA5 1RY. ☎ (01278741) 215 • Map 181/158413 • BB **A** • EM book first £7, 6-7pm • D2 T1 • 1-12 NX • Ⓥ Ⓓ 🐾 Ⓜ • List

☆ Richard Bjergfelt, Combe House Hotel, TA5 1RZ. ☎ (01278) 741382 • Map 181/151416 • BB **D** • EM £16.50 • S4 D7 T8 F1 • 1-12 NX • Ⓥ Ⓑ Ⓓ Ⓢ 🐾 • 3Cr/HC

COMBE HOUSE HOTEL
Holford, Bridgwater, Somerset
TA5 1RZ
The Quantock hills are an Area of Outstanding Natural Beauty. The ideal area to explore for the relaxed rambler. Spoil yourself and take a short break or holiday in the 17th Century Combe House Hotel.

❖ Relax in total peace and quiet away from all traffic noise.

❖ Enjoy the period and antique furniture in the bedrooms and public rooms.

❖ You will enjoy the well-equipped bedrooms.

❖ Leave your car at the hotel and start your ramble from the front door.

❖ Ideal base for groups (special group rates).

❖ Run by the same family for over 20 years.

Phone now 01278 741382 for colour brochure
AA 2 Star with Rosette
RAC 2 Star with Merits

HIGHLY COMMENDED

■ **ILMINSTER**

Ruth Hayter, Shipley House Holidays, Hylands, 22 New Road, TA19 9AF. ☎ (01460) 52560 • Map 193/357148 • BB **A** • S/T1 D/T/F1 T/S1 • 1-12 NX • Ⓓ Ⓢ 🐾

■ **MIDSOMER NORTON (Bath)**

Mrs M Gentle, Ellsworth, Fosseway, BA3 4AU. ☎ (01761) 412305 • Map 183/671534 • BB **B** • S/T1 D/T/F/S1 • 1-12 NX • Ⓓ Ⓢ 🐾

☆ See Display Advertisement

■ MINEHEAD
SOUTH WEST COAST PATH

Colin & Maureen Smith, Fernside, The Holloway, TA24 5PB. ☎ (01643) 707594 • Map 181/966464 • BB **B** • EM £7.50, 6-6.30pm • D2 F1 • 1-12 NX • Ⓥ Ⓑ Ⓓ Ⓢ Ⓡ • 2Cr/C

☆ Mayfair Hotel, The Avenue, TA24 5AY. ☎ (01643) 702719 • Map 181/971463 • BB **D** • EM £9, 7pm • S4 D7 T9 F6 • 3-10 NX • Ⓥ Ⓑ Ⓓ Ⓢ Ⓡ 🐾 • 3Cr

■ MUDFORD (Yeovil)

Mrs E Tavener, The Old Kiln, Higher Brickyard, Main Street, BA21 5TG. ☎ (01935) 850958 • Map 183/572195 • BB **B** • EM book first £8 • S2 D1 T1 F1 • 1-12 • Ⓑ Ⓓ • List/C

■ NETHER STOWEY (Bridgwater)

☆ Susan Lilienthal, Parsonage Farm, TA5 1HA. ☎ (01278) 733237 • Map 181/185387 • BB **B/C** • EM book first £11, 7.30pm • D1 T1 F1 • 1-12 • Ⓥ Ⓑ Ⓓ Ⓢ 🐾 Ⓜ

■ PORLOCK (Minehead)
SOUTH WEST COAST PATH

Mr & Mrs D Urry, Overstream Hotel, TA24 8QJ. ☎ (01643) 862421 • Map 181/886466 • BB **C/D** • EM £10.50, 7pm • S2 D2 T3 F2 • 3-10 NX • Ⓥ Ⓑ Ⓓ Ⓢ • Guided walks also

☆ Mrs J Stiles-Cox, Leys - The Ridge, Off Bossington Lane, TA24 8HA. ☎ (01643) 862477 • Map 181/892469 • BB **B** • EM book first £9, 7pm • S2 D/T1 • 1-12 NX • Ⓥ Ⓑ Ⓓ Ⓢ 🐾

R G Thornton, The Lorna Doone Hotel, High Street, TA24 8PS. ☎ (01643) 862404 • Map 181/887469 • BB **C** • EM £12, 6.15-8.30pm • S3 D6 T4 F2 • 1-12 NX • Ⓥ Ⓑ Ⓓ Ⓢ 🐾 • 3Cr • Group rates

Doverhay Place, TA24 8EX. ☎ (01643) 862398 • Map 181/888468 • BB **C/D** • EM £9.50, 7pm • S9 D6 T12 • 1-12 • Ⓥ Ⓑ Ⓓ Ⓢ Ⓜ • Groups also

■ RADSTOCK (Bath)

Mr & Mrs R Sims, The Rookery, Wells Road, BA3 3RS. ☎ (01761) 432626 • Map 183/684547 • BB **D** • EM from £7 (not Sun.), 7-9pm • D2 T2 F2 • 1-12 • Ⓥ Ⓑ Ⓢ 🐾 • 3Cr/App

■ SHIPHAM (Winscombe)
WEST MENDIP WAY

Mrs Helen Stickland, Herongates, Horseleaze Lane, BS25 1UQ. ☎ (01934) 843280 • Map 182/437579 • BB **B/C** • EM book first £10, 7-7.30pm • D1 T1 F1 • 1-12 NX • Ⓥ Ⓑ Ⓓ Ⓢ • 2Cr

☆ Penscot Farmhouse Hotel, BS25 1TW. ☎ (01934) 842659 • Map 182,172/444575 • BB **D** • EM £12, 7-8pm • S4 D6 T7 F1 • 2-11 NX • Ⓥ Ⓑ Ⓓ 🐾

SOMERSET   ENGLAND   B & B ACCOMMODATION

■ SIMONSBATH
TWO MOORS WAY

Mrs L Roberts, Winstitchen, TA24 7JT. ☎ (01643) 831505 • Map 180/782394 • BB **C** • EM book first £12, 7-8pm • D1 T1 • 7-5 • Ⓥ Ⓓ 🐾

■ SOMERTON

Mr & Mrs Cooper, Etsome Dairy Farm, TA11 6JD. ☎ (01458) 274500 • Map 193/482306 • BB **A/B** • EM book first £8, 6-8pm • D1 T1 • 1-12 • Ⓑ Ⓓ 🐾

■ TIMSBURY (Bath)

Old Malt House Hotel & Restaurant, Radford, BA3 1QF. ☎ (01761) 470106 • Map 172/672578 • BB **D** • EM £9-£16, 7-8.30pm • S2 D3 T3 F2 • 1-12 NX • Ⓥ Ⓑ Ⓓ Ⓢ 🐾 • 3Cr/C

■ UPPER LANGFORD (Bristol)

Mrs C Wade, Holly Cottage, Langford Green, BS18 7DG. ☎ (01934) 852557 • Map 182,172/471597 • BB **B** • EM book first £10, 6.30pm • S1 D1 T1 • 4-10 • Ⓥ Ⓑ Ⓓ Ⓢ

■ WATCHET

Mr & Mrs R M Brown, "Green Bay", Washford, TA23 0NN. ☎ (01984) 640303 • Map 181/048411 • BB **B** • EM book first £9.50, 7pm • D1 T2 • 3-10 • Ⓥ Ⓑ Ⓡ Ⓜ • 2Cr/C

■ WEDMORE

Charles Hicks, Upper Farm, Sand, BS28 4XF. ☎ (01934) 712595 • Map 182/432465 • BB **C** • D2 T2 • 1-12 • Ⓑ Ⓢ 🐾

■ WELLS
WEST MENDIP WAY

Mrs J Gould, Milton Manor Farm, Old Bristol Road, Upper Milton, BA5 3AH. ☎ (01749) 673394 • Map 182,183/546474 • BB **B** • D1 T1 F1 • 1-12 NX • Ⓓ Ⓢ • 1Cr

☆ Tor House, 20 Tor Street, BA5 2US. ☎ (01749) 672322 • Map 182,183/553458 • BB **C** • S1 D4 T2 F1 • 1-12 NX • Ⓑ Ⓓ Ⓢ • HC

Robert & Margaret Pletts, Cadgwith, Hawkers Lane, BA5 3JH. ☎ (01749) 677799 • Map 182/559462 • BB **B** • S2 D2 T1 F1 • 1-12 NX • Ⓑ Ⓓ 🐾

Linda Parker, Carmen B&B, Bath Road, BA5 3LQ. ☎ (01749) 677331 • Map 182,183/563461 • BB **B** • D1 • 1-12 NX • Ⓑ Ⓓ Ⓢ

☆ Lyn & John Howard, Furlong House, Lorne Place, St Thomas Street, BA5 2XF. ☎ (01749) 674064 • Map 182,183/554460 • BB **C** • S2 D1 T1 • 1-12 NX • Ⓑ Ⓓ Ⓢ

SOMERSET

ENGLAND

B&B ACCOMMODATION

■ WEST QUANTOXHEAD (Taunton)

Miss A Kennard, Blakes House, Lower Weacombe, TA4 4ED. ☎ (01984) 632588 • Map 181/111408 • BB **B** • S1 D1 T1 • 4-9 • Ⓓ Ⓢ 🌡 • Food nearby

■ WESTON-SUPER-MARE

☆ Braeside Hotel, 2 Victoria Park, BS23 2HZ. ☎ (01934) 626642 • Map 182/317620 • BB **C** • EM book first £11.50, 6.30pm • S2 D5 T1 F1 • 1-12 NX • Ⓥ Ⓑ Ⓓ Ⓢ Ⓡ 🌡 Ⓜ • 3Cr/C

■ WHEDDON CROSS (Minehead)

Mr Bob Cody-Boutcher, Little Quarme Farm, Wheddon Cross, Exmoor, TA24 7EA. ☎ (01643) 841249 • Map 181/917390 • BB **C** • EM £10, 7pm • D2 T1 • 4-10 • Ⓥ Ⓑ Ⓓ Ⓢ • List/HC • SC also

Gunns Farm, Luckwell Bridge, TA24 7EL. ☎ (01643) 841156 • Map 181/905385 • BB **B** • D1 • 1-12 • Ⓑ Ⓓ Ⓢ

■ WINSFORD (Exmoor)

☆ Maureen & Nigel Messett, Karslake House Hotel, TA24 7JE. ☎ (01643) 851242 • Map 181/907352 • BB **C/D** • EM £15.50, 7.30-8pm • D4 T3 • 3-11 • Ⓥ Ⓑ Ⓓ Ⓢ 🌡 • 3Cr/C

■ YEOVIL

Mrs C Smith, Wyndham Guest House, 142 Sherborne Road, BA21 4HQ. ☎ (01935) 421468 • Map 183/564162 • BB **C** • S1 D2 T2 F1 • 1-12 NX • Ⓓ Ⓢ Ⓡ 🌡 • List

■ YEOVILTON (Yeovil)

Mrs Susie Crang, Cary Fitzpaine Farmhouse, Cary Fitzpaine, BA22 8JB. ☎ (01458) 223250 • Map 183/548270 • BB **C** • EM book first £10, 7pm • S1 D1 T1 F1 • 1-12 NX • Ⓥ Ⓑ Ⓓ Ⓢ 🌡 • 2Cr/App

STAFFORDSHIRE

■ ARMITAGE (Rugeley)
HEART OF ENGLAND WAY

Mrs M Lewis, Park Farm, Hawkesyard, Armitage Lane, WS15 1ED. ☎ (01889) 583477 • Map 128/059162 • BB **B** • S1 T1 F1 • 1-12 • Ⓑ Ⓓ Ⓡ 🌡 • 1Cr/C

■ CHEDDLETON (Leek)
STAFFORDSHIRE WAY

Nancy Sherratt, Little Brookhouse Farm, ST13 7DF. ☎ (01538) 360350 • Map 118/964508 • BB **C** • EM book first £9, 6.30pm • D2 T1 • 1-12 NX • Ⓑ Ⓓ Ⓢ • 3Cr/HC

■ CHORLEY (Farewell, Lichfield)

Mrs E Clewley, Little Pipe Farm, WS13 8BS. ☎ (01543) 683066 • Map 128/078105 • BB **B** • EM book first £8, 6.30-7pm • S1 D1 T1 F1 • 1-12 • Ⓥ Ⓓ

■ FROGHALL
STAFFORDSHIRE WAY

Heath House Farm, Ross Road, Whiston, ST10 2JF. ☎ (01538) 266497 • Map 128, 119/033468 • BB **A** • D2 T1 • 1-12 NX • Ⓓ Ⓢ

■ GRINDON (Leek)
WHITE PEAK WAY

☆ Mrs P Simpson, Summerhill Farm, ST13 7TT. ☎ (01538) 304264 • Map 119/083534 • BB **B/C** • EM book first £10, 6.30-7pm • D2 T1 • 1-12 • Ⓥ Ⓑ Ⓓ Ⓢ 🌡 • 2Cr/C • SC also

■ HORTON (Leek)
STAFFORDSHIRE WAY

Mrs Irene Harrison, Croft Meadows Farm, ST13 8QE. ☎ (01782) 513039 • Map 118/921577 • BB **B** • S3 D1 T1 • 1-12 • Ⓑ Ⓓ Ⓢ • 1Cr/C

■ KINVER
STAFFORDSHIRE WAY

Mrs A Harris, Old Vicarage, Vicarage Drive, DY7 6HJ. ☎ (01384) 872784 • Map 138/843834 • BB **C** • T2 • 1-12 NX • Ⓓ ⁂

■ LONGSDON (Stoke-on-Trent)
STAFFORDSHIRE WAY

Mrs B White, Micklea Farm, Micklea Lane, ST9 9QA. ☎ (01538) 385006 • Map 118/959540 • BB **B** • EM £11, 6-8pm • S2 T/D2 • 1-12 NX • Ⓥ Ⓓ Ⓢ • List/C

■ NORBURY (Stafford)

Judy Palmer, Oulton House Farm, ST20 0PG. ☎ (01785) 284264 • Map 127/780220 • BB **C** • D2 T1 • 1-12 • Ⓑ Ⓓ

■ OAKAMOOR (Stoke-on-Trent)
STAFFORDSHIRE WAY

The Old Furnace, Greendale, ST10 3AP. ☎ (01538) 703331 • Map 128,119/041435 • BB **B** • S1 D1 • 1-12 • Ⓓ Ⓢ ⁂ • Walking holidays also

■ RUGELEY
STAFFORDSHIRE WAY

☆ Mrs C Miller, 13 Moss Green, WS15 2NU. ☎ (01889) 582653 • Map 128/034187 • BB **A** • T1 • 1-12 NX • Ⓢ

RUGELEY STAFFORDSHIRE

For a warm welcome, good food, comfortable beds, stay B&B at a small house near beautiful Cannock Chase, The Staffordshire Moorlands, and the Staffordshire Way.

Telephone 01889 582653

■ RUSHTON SPENCER (Macclesfield, Cheshire)
STAFFORDSHIRE WAY

Mrs J Brown, Barnswood Farm, SK11 0RA. ☎ (01260) 226261 • Map 118/945608 • BB **B** • D1 T1 F1 • 1-12 NX • Ⓓ

■ STOKE-ON-TRENT

Peacock Hay Guest House, Peacock Hay Road, Talke, ST7 1UN. ☎ (01782) 773511 • Map 118/835518 • BB **B** • S3 D3 T3 F1 • 1-12 NX • Ⓑ Ⓓ Ⓡ ⁂ • 2Cr

■ THREAPWOOD (Nr Cheadle, Stoke-on-Trent)
STAFFORDSHIRE WAY

Bradley Elms Farm, ST10 4RA. ☎ (01538) 753135 • Map 128,119/010430 • BB **C** • EM £10, 6.30-7.45pm • D4 T3 F2 • 1-12 NX • Ⓥ Ⓑ • 3Cr/C

■ WINKHILL (Leek)

Mrs Joyce Saul, Lower Broomyshaw Farm, ST13 7QZ. ☎ (01538) 308298 • Map 119/075503 • BB **B** • D1 F1 • 1-12 • Ⓑ Ⓓ ⁂ • SC also

SUFFOLK

■ BECCLES
ANGLES WAY

Mr & Mrs W T Renilson, Catherine House, 2 Ringsfield Road, NR34 9PQ. ☎ (01502) 716428 • Map 156/418897 • BB **B** • EM book first £10 • S1 D1 F1 • 1-12 • Ⓥ Ⓑ Ⓓ Ⓢ Ⓡ Ⓜ • 2Cr/C

■ BEYTON (Bury St Edmunds)

Mrs Kay Dewsbury, Manorhouse, The Green, IP30 9AF. ☎ (01359) 270960 • Map 155/935634 • BB **C** • EM book first £11, 6.30-7.30pm • S1 D1 T1 • 1-12 NX • Ⓑ Ⓓ Ⓢ Ⓡ • SC also

■ BLYTHBURGH

Mrs S E Harris, Little Thorbyns, The Street, IP19 9LS. ☎ (01502) 478664 • Map 156/452752 • BB **C** • EM £7.50, 6.30pm • S1 D1 T1 F1 • 1-12 NX • Ⓥ Ⓑ Ⓓ Ⓢ • 2Cr/C • SC also

■ BRAMFIELD (Halesworth)

Mrs Patricia Kemsley, Broad Oak Farm, IP19 9AB. ☎ (01986) 784232 • Map 156/385736 • BB **B** • EM £9, 7-8pm • D1 T2 • 1-12 • Ⓥ Ⓑ Ⓓ Ⓢ ⁂ • 2Cr/C

■ BURY ST EDMUNDS

M E Hanson, Hilltop, 22 Bronyon Close, off Flemyng Road, IP33 3XB. ☎ (01284) 767066 • Map 155/832640 • BB **B** • EM £6 • S1 T1 F1 • 1-12 • Ⓑ Ⓓ Ⓢ Ⓡ ⁂ • List

■ CHILLESFORD (Woodbridge)

Alistair & Joy Shaw, The Froize Inn, IP12 3PU. ☎ (01394) 450282 • Map 156/387522 • BB **C** • EM £12, 7-9pm • D1 T1 F1 • 1-12 NX • Ⓥ Ⓑ Ⓓ ⁂

■ CLARE (Sudbury)
STOUR VALLEY PATH

Jean & Alistair Tuffill, Cobwebs, 26 Nethergate Street, CO10 8NP. ☎ (01787) 277539 • Map 155/768451 • BB **C/D** • S1 T2 • 1-12 • Ⓑ Ⓓ Ⓢ ⁂ • List

■ DARSHAM (Saxmondham)

Priory Farm, IP17 3QD. ☎ (01728) 668459 • Map 156/416700 • BB **C** • D1 T1 • 4-9 • Ⓑ Ⓓ Ⓢ Ⓡ • 2Cr/C • SC also

■ EAST BERGHOLT (Colchester, Essex)
ESSEX WAY

Mrs Natalie Finch, Rosemary, Rectory Hill, CO7 6TH. ☎ (01206) 298241 • Map 155,169/073344 • BB **C** • S1 T2 • 1-12 • Ⓓ Ⓢ Ⓡ ⁂ • List • Food nearby

■ EYKE (Woodbridge)

☆ Mrs J Warnock, The Old House, IP12 2QW. ☎ (01394) 460213 • Map 156/315516 • BB **C** • EM book first £12-£14, 6-8pm • D/T/S3 • 1-12 NX • Ⓥ Ⓑ Ⓓ Ⓢ 🛁 • 2Cr/HC

THE OLD HOUSE

Eyke, Woodbridge, Suffolk IP12 2QW

Lovely listed house, C1600, beams, open fires and home cooking, large, attractive garden. Ideal centre for a feast of music, birdwatching and walking. T.V., C.H., tea/coffee facilities, all rooms en suite. B&B from £19. EM and packed lunches on request. Diets catered for.

ETB 〰️〰️
Tel. Eyke (01394) 460213   COMMENDED

■ FLEMPTON (Bury St Edmunds)

Lindsay School House, IP28 6EG. ☎ (01284) 728792 • Map 155/813698 • BB **A/B** • T1 F1 • 1-12 • Ⓓ Ⓢ 🛁 • List • Food nearby

■ FRAMLINGHAM (Woodbridge)

Brian & Phyllis Collett, Shimmens Pightle, Dennington Road, IP13 9JT. ☎ (01728) 724036 • Map 156/277643 • BB **B/C** • S1 D1 T1 F1 • 1-12 NX • Ⓓ Ⓢ • List/C

■ HACHESTON (Woodbridge)

G E Hall, Cherry Tree House, IP13 0DR. ☎ (01728) 746371 • Map 156/309589 • BB **B** • EM book first £7.50, 7pm • S1 D1 T1 • 1-12 • Ⓥ Ⓑ Ⓓ Ⓢ

■ HENGRAVE (Bury St Edmunds)

Mrs M Ferguson, Minstrels, Bury Road, IP28 6LS. ☎ (01284) 703677 • Map 155/826686 • BB **C** • D1 T1 • 1-12 NX • Ⓑ Ⓓ Ⓢ 🛁

■ HIGHAM (Colchester, Essex)
STOUR VALLEY PATH & ESSEX WAY

Mr & Mrs Watkins, The Bauble, CO7 6LA. ☎ (01206) 337254 • Map 155/031355 • BB **C/D** • S1 D/T2 • 1-12 • Ⓑ Ⓓ Ⓢ • 2Cr/HC

■ HORAM (Eye)

Mrs N Cudmore, Thick Thorn Farm, IP21 5ER. ☎ (01379) 384005 • Map 156/218714 • BB **B** • EM book first £8.50, 7pm • S1 D1 T1 • 1-12 NX • Ⓥ Ⓑ Ⓓ Ⓢ

■ HORRINGER-CUM-ICKWORTH

☆ Rose Cottages & Laurels Stables, IP29 5SN. ☎ (01284) 735281 • Map 155/825613 • BB **B** • EM book first £7 • D1 T1 F1 • 1-12 NX • Ⓥ Ⓑ Ⓓ Ⓢ Ⓡ 🛁 Ⓜ

SUFFOLK
ENGLAND
B&B ACCOMMODATION

Rose Cottages & Laurels Stables, Horringer
Within charming village, adjacent N.T. Parkland. Two good pub/restaurants nearby. Wet walkers welcome. Small working farm with animals. T.B. Regd. Any pet by arrangement.
(01284) 735281 Mrs. Ann James

■ IXWORTH (Bury St Edmunds)

Robert Peel House, IP31 2HH. ☎ (01359) 230555 • Map 155,144/931703 • BB **B/C** • T6 F1 • 1-11 • Ⓑ Ⓓ

■ LAVENHAM (Sudbury)

Mrs Hazel Rhodes, Weaners Farm, Bears Lane, CO10 9RX. ☎ (01787) 247310 • Map 155/917481 • BB **C** • D1 T2 • 1-12 NX • Ⓓ Ⓢ

■ MIDDLETON (Saxmundham)

Mrs D Crowden, Rose Villa, The Street, IP17 3NJ. ☎ (01728) 648489 • Map 156/429678 • BB **B** • S1 D1 T1 • 1-12 • Ⓡ

■ NAYLAND (Colchester)
ESSEX WAY & STOUR VALLEY PATH

Mrs P Heigham, Hill House, Gravel Hill, CO6 4JB. ☎ (01206) 262782 • Map 155/976345 • BB **B/C** • S1 T1 F1 • 1-12 NX • Ⓑ Ⓓ Ⓢ • C • Food nearby

■ SNAPE (Saxmundham)

Mrs I A Edwards, Flemings Lodge, Gromford Lane, IP17 1RG. ☎ (01728) 688502 • Map 156/393582 • BB **C** • D1 T1 • 1-12 NX • Ⓓ Ⓢ • List/C

■ SOUTHWOLD

Acton Lodge, 18 South Green, IP18 6HB. ☎ (01502) 723217 • Map 156/508759 • BB **C/D** • S1 D1 T1 • 1-12 • Ⓑ Ⓓ Ⓢ

Linda & Christopher Whiting, Saxon House, 86 Pier Avenue, IP18 6BL. ☎ (01502) 723651 • Map 156/510767 • BB **D** • D4 T2 F1 • 1-12 • Ⓑ Ⓓ Ⓢ 🛁 • 2Cr/HC

"Mardale", 54 Halesworth Road, Reydon, IP18 6NR. ☎ (01502) 724850 • Map 156/496770 • BB **B** • S1 D1 • 3-10 • Ⓓ Ⓢ

Joan Ratcliff, Shanklin House, 6 Chester Road, IP18 6LN. ☎ (01502) 724748 • Map 156/509763 • BB **C/D** • D1 T1 F1 • 1-12 NX • Ⓑ Ⓓ Ⓢ 🛁

■ SPEXHALL (Halesworth)

☆ Mary Ball, Mahn House, IP19 0RJ. ☎ (01986) 874396 • Map 156/388806 • BB **C** • S1 D1 F1 • 1-12 NX • Ⓑ Ⓓ Ⓢ Ⓡ

MAHN HOUSE, Spexhall
Halesworth, Suffolk IP19 0RJ
Grade II Listed 16thC Farmhouse • Ideal for exploring
North Suffolk • Situated between Halesworth and Bungay
on A144 • Fully heated • TV • Tea/coffee facilities.
Telephone 01986 874396

■ **STEEPLE BUMPSTEAD (Haverhill)**

Mrs S J Stirling, Yew Tree House, 15 Chapel Street,
CB9 7DQ. ☎ (01440) 730364 • Map 154/680411 •
BB **B/C** • EM book first £8.50, 6-8pm • S1 D1 T1 • 3-
12 NX • Ⓥ Ⓑ Ⓓ Ⓢ • 1Cr/C

■ **STOKE-BY-NAYLAND (Colchester, Essex)**
ESSEX WAY & STOUR VALLEY PATH

Mrs Deirdre Wollaston, Thorington Hall, CO6 4SS. ☎
(01206) 337329 • Map 155/004357 • BB **B/C** • S1 D2
T1 F1 • 4-9 • Ⓑ Ⓓ Ⓢ 🐾 • List/App

■ **SUDBOURNE (Woodbridge)**

Mrs A Wood, Long Meadows, Gorse Lane, IP12 2BD.
☎ (01394) 450269 • Map 156/412532 • BB **B** • EM
book first £6 • S1 D1 T1 • 1-12 NX • Ⓑ Ⓓ Ⓢ 🐾 •
List/C

■ **TUNSTALL (Woodbridge)**

Mrs J Pegrum, The Old Rectory, IP12 2JP. ☎
(01728) 688534 • Map 156/363551 • BB **C** • EM book
first £8 veg. only, 6.30pm • S2 D1 T1 F1 • 4-10 • Ⓥ
Ⓓ Ⓢ

■ **WESTLETON (Saxmundham)**

Ron & Jose Allen, Barn Cottage, Mill Street, IP17
3BD. ☎ (01728) 648437 • Map 156/441688 • BB **B** •
D1 T2 • 1-12 NX • Ⓓ Ⓢ

■ **WOODBRIDGE**

☆ Sylvia Hall, Meadow View, Bromeswell, IP12 2PY.
☎ (01394) 460635 • Map 156/302506 • BB **B** • S1
D1 T1 F1 • 1-12 NX • Ⓑ Ⓓ Ⓡ 🐾 • List

MEADOW VIEW
BROMESWELL, WOODBRIDGE,
SUFFOLK

A warm welcome and a good English
breakfast awaits you in our 400 year old
cottage set in a quiet village 2 miles from
Woodbridge. Indoor heated swimming
pool. Prices from £16 per person.

☎ **(01394) 460635**

Mrs Susan Ferguson, Spion Kop, Spring Lane,
Ufford, IP13 6EF. ☎ (01394) 460277 • Map
156/298527 • BB **C/D** • D1 T2 • 1-12 • Ⓑ Ⓓ Ⓡ

SURREY

■ **BRAMLEY (Guildford)**
NORTH DOWNS WAY

Mr & Mrs J Cook, Beevers Farm, Chinthurst Lane,
GU5 0DR. ☎ (01483) 898764 • Map 186/008459 •
BB **B/C** • T2 F1 • 3-10 • Ⓑ Ⓓ Ⓢ Ⓡ • List

■ **DORKING**
NORTH DOWNS WAY

Mrs Treays, Steyning Cottage, Horsham Road, South
Holmwood, RH5 4NE. ☎ (01306) 888481 • Map
187/172449 • BB **B** • EM book first £8, 8pm • S1 T1 •
1-12 • Ⓥ Ⓓ Ⓢ Ⓡ 🐾 • List

The Waltons, 5 Rose Hill, RH4 2EG. ☎ (01306)
883127 • Map 187/166491 • BB **B/C** • EM book first
£10.50, 7-8.30pm • S3 D2 T1 F2 • 1-12 • Ⓥ Ⓓ Ⓢ
Ⓡ 🐾 • List

Fairdene Guest House, Moores Road, RH4 2BG. ☎
(01306) 888337 • Map 187/169496 • BB **C** • D2 T2
F1 • 1-12 • Ⓓ Ⓢ Ⓡ 🐾 • 1Cr

Mrs Beryl Davis, Ashcombe Cottage, Ranmore
Common, RH5 6SP. ☎ (01306) 881599 • Map
187/155511 • BB **C** • EM book first £8, 6-7pm • S1
T1 • 1-12 NX • Ⓥ Ⓓ Ⓢ

■ **EWHURST (Cranleigh)**
GREENSAND WAY

Mrs Carol Franklin-Adams, High Edser, Shere Road,
GU6 7PQ. ☎ (01483) 278214 • Map 187/089409 •
BB **C** • D2 T1 • 1-12 NX • Ⓓ Ⓢ 🐾 • List/C • Food
nearby

A M Nutting, Yard Farm, GU6 7SN. ☎ (01483)
276649 • Map 187/106406 • BB **C** • EM book first
£15, 7-8.30pm • S1 D1 T2 F1 • 1-12 NX • Ⓑ Ⓓ 🐾

■ **GATWICK**
SEE HORLEY, SURREY; AND COPTHORNE, WEST SUSSEX

■ **GRAYSHOTT (Hindhead)**
GREENSAND WAY

Mrs Burgess, The Valleys, School Road, GU26 6LR.
☎ (01428) 606987 • Map 186/869355 • BB **B/C** • S1
D1 • 1-12 • Ⓓ Ⓢ 🐾 Ⓜ • Food nearby

■ **GUILDFORD**
NORTH DOWNS WAY

Mr & Mrs Bourne, Weybrook House, 113 Stoke
Road, GU1 1ET. ☎ (01483) 302394 • Map 186/
997503 • BB **B/C** • S1 D1 F1 • 1-12 NX • Ⓓ Ⓢ Ⓡ 🐾

☆ See Display Advertisement

■ HASLEMERE

Mrs S G Lipscomb, Pound Close, Three Gates Lane, GU27 2LE. ☎ (01428) 643661 • Map 186/907332 • BB **D** • S1 D1 • 1-12 NX • Ⓓ Ⓢ Ⓡ 🛁

■ HOLMBURY ST MARY (Dorking)
GREENSAND WAY

Gill Hill, Bulmer Farm, RH5 6LG. ☎ (01306) 730210 • Map 187/114441 • BB **C** • D3 T5 • 1-12 • Ⓑ Ⓓ Ⓢ • 2Cr • SC also, food nearby

■ HORLEY (Nr Gatwick)

Prinsted Guest House, Oldfield Road, RH6 7EP. ☎ (01293) 785233 • Map 187/277424 • BB **C/D** • S2 D2 T2 F1 • 1-12 NX • Ⓑ Ⓓ Ⓢ Ⓡ • List

☆ Woodlands Guest House, 42 Massetts Road, RH6 7DS. ☎ (01293) 782994 • Map 187/286426 • BB **C/D** • S1 D3 T3 F1 • 1-12 NX • Ⓑ Ⓓ Ⓢ Ⓡ Ⓜ • 2Cr

---

Near Gatwick
WOODLANDS GUEST HOUSE
42 Massetts Road, Horley RH6 7DS

Flying from Gatwick? We are one and a quarter miles from the airport. Ideal for early departures & late return flights. All bedrooms of high standard, with colour TV, tea/coffee, CH & double glazing. All en suite. Courtesy car, car parking on premises. No smoking. Full English breakfast.

(01293) 782994 (Res)
(01293) 776358 (Fax)

Oakdene Guest House, 32 Massetts Road, RH6 7DS. ☎ (01293) 772047 • Map 187/286426 • BB **C/D** • S3 D2 T2 F1 • 1-12 NX • Ⓓ Ⓡ • List

■ MYTCHETT (Camberley)

☆ HEHNB, Basingstoke Canal Centre, Mytchett Place Road, GU16 6DD. ☎ (0831) 566373 • Map 175,186/893550 • BB **D** • EM includes dinner, 7pm • S6 D1 T1 • 3-9 • Ⓑ Ⓓ Ⓢ • Location varies - boats! See next column for display ad.

■ OXTED
NORTH DOWNS WAY & VANGUARD WAY

Mr D I Nunn, The New Bungalow, Old Hall Farm, Tandridge Lane, RH8 9NS. ☎ (01342) 892508 • Map 187/376483 • BB **B/C** • D1 T1 F1 • 1-12 NX • Ⓓ Ⓢ Ⓡ 🛁 • List • Transport also

Rosehaven, 12 Hoskins Road, RH8 9HT. ☎ (01883) 712700 • Map 187/392527 • BB **C** • S1 T2 • 3-12 NX • Ⓓ Ⓢ Ⓡ

■ REDHILL
NORTH DOWNS WAY

Lynwood Guest House, 50 London Road, RH1 1LN. ☎ (01737) 766894 • Map 187/280511 • BB **D** • S2 D2 T2 F3 • 1-12 • Ⓑ Ⓓ Ⓡ

■ REIGATE
NORTH DOWNS WAY

Cranleigh Hotel, 41 West Street, RH2 9BL. ☎ (01737) 240600/223417 • Map 187/250502 • BB **D** • EM 7-9pm • S2 D3 T3 F1 • 1-12 NX • Ⓥ Ⓑ Ⓓ Ⓡ • 3Cr

Norfolk Lodge Hotel, 23/25 London Road, RH2 9PY. ☎ (01737) 248702 • Map 187/252505 • BB **C** • S6 D3 T4 F3 • 1-12 • Ⓓ Ⓡ 🛁

■ SHERE (Guildford)
NORTH DOWNS WAY

Mrs M James, Manor Cottage, GU5 9JE. ☎ (01483) 202979 • Map 187/072479 • BB **B** • S1 D1 • 4-10 NX • Ⓓ Ⓢ Ⓡ Ⓜ

■ THURSLEY (Godalming)

Mrs P Roe, Hindhead Hill Farm, Portsmouth Road, GU8 6DD. ☎ (01428) 684727 • Map 186/906387 • BB **B/C** • EM book first £8.50 • T1 F1 • 1-12 NX • Ⓑ Ⓢ • Dogs OK in kennel

■ WEST CLANDON
NORTH DOWNS WAY

Mrs D Hughes, Ways Cottage, Lime Grove, GU4 7UT. ☎ (01483) 222454 • Map 186/044531 • BB **C** • EM book first £10, 7-9pm • T2 • 1-12 NX • Ⓑ Ⓓ Ⓢ Ⓡ • List/C

■ WESTCOTT (Dorking)
NORTH DOWNS WAY

Mr & Mrs Nyman, Corner House, Guildford Road, RH4 3QE. ☎ (01306) 888798 • Map 187/143486 • BB **B** • S1 D1 T1 F1 • 1-12 • Ⓓ Ⓢ Ⓡ 🛁

SURREY

ENGLAND

B & B ACCOMMODATION

EAST SUSSEX

■ ALFRISTON (Polegate)
SOUTH DOWNS WAY

Mrs D Savage, Pleasant Rise Farm, BN26 5TN. ☎ (01323) 870545 • Map 199/515027 • BB **B/C** • S1 D1 T1 F1 • 1-12 NX • Ⓑ Ⓓ Ⓢ Ⓡ

Elizabeth & David Brown, Riverdale House, Seaford Road, BN26 5TR. ☎ (01323) 871038 • Map 199/516024 • BB **C/D** • D3 T2 F1 • 1-12 NX • Ⓑ Ⓓ Ⓡ

Mrs Lesley Goodchild, Winton Street Farmhouse, BN26 5UH. ☎ (01323) 870293 • Map 199/522038 • BB **C** • S1 D1 T1 • 1-12 NX • Ⓑ Ⓓ 🐾

Mrs Irene Fitch, Winton Street Farm Cottage, BN26 5UH. ☎ (01323) 870118 • Map 199/522038 • BB **B/C** • S1 D1 T2 F1 • 1-12 • Ⓓ Ⓢ Ⓡ 🐾 • Groups also

■ BISHOPSTONE (Newhaven)
SOUTH DOWNS WAY

Karen Fay, The Old Farmhouse, Foxhole Farm, BN9 0EE. ☎ (01273) 515966 • Map 198/461011 • BB **B** • EM book first £7.50, 7pm • S1 D2 T1 F1 • 1-12 • Ⓥ Ⓑ Ⓓ Ⓢ Ⓡ 🐾 Ⓜ • SC also

■ BLACKBOYS (Uckfield)
WEALDWAY & VANGUARD WAY

Cider Cottage, TN22 5JD. ☎ (01825) 890294 • Map 199/519195 • BB **B/C** • D1 T2 • 1-12 • Ⓑ Ⓓ Ⓢ

■ BRIGHTON
SOUTH DOWNS WAY

☆ Brighton Marina House Hotel, 8 Charlotte Street, BN2 1AG. ☎ (01273) 605349/679484 • Map 198/319038 • BB **B/C/D** • EM book first £10 upwards • S3 D7 T4 F3 • 1-12 • Ⓥ Ⓑ Ⓡ • 3Cr • Groups also. See next column for display ad.

■ BUXTED (Uckfield)
WEALDWAY

Mr & Mrs Bailey, Buxted Inn, High Street, TN22 4LA. ☎ (01825) 733510 • Map 199/498234 • BB **C** • EM bistro & restaurant, 6pm till late • S2 D2 T1 F1 • 1-12 • Ⓥ Ⓓ Ⓢ Ⓡ 🐾

■ CHELWOOD GATE (Ashdown Forest)
VANGUARD WAY

Mrs D A Birchell, Holly House, Beaconsfield Road, RH17 7LF. ☎ (01825) 740484 • Map 187/419297 • BB **C** • EM book first £12 • S1 D2 T2 • 1-12 • Ⓥ Ⓑ Ⓓ 🐾 • 2Cr/C

■ CHIDDINGLY (Lewes)
WEALDWAY & VANGUARD WAY

Sheilah-Ann Farrier, 'Holmes Hill', Holmes Hill, BN8 6JA. ☎ (01825) 872746 • Map 199/533127 • BB **C** • S1 D1 T1 • 1-12 NX • Ⓑ Ⓓ Ⓢ

Mr & Mrs Alsop, The Orchard, The Street, BN8 6HE. ☎ (01825) 872679 • Map 199/543144 • BB **B** • S1 T1 • 1-12 NX • Ⓓ Ⓢ • Food nearby

■ COLEMANS HATCH (Hartfield)
VANGUARD WAY & WEALDWAY

Mrs L Hawker, Gospel Oak, TN7 4ER. ☎ (01342) 823840 • Map 187/447327 • BB **C** • EM book first £9.50, 8pm • D1 T1 • 1-12 • Ⓥ Ⓑ Ⓓ Ⓢ Ⓜ

■ CROWBOROUGH
VANGUARD WAY & WEALDWAY

June & Alan Peck, Chillies Granary, Chillies Lane, Nr High Hurstwood, TN6 3TB. ☎ (01892) 655560 • Map 188/497283 • BB **C** • D1 T1 F1 • 3-12 • Ⓓ Ⓢ

■ DANEHILL (Haywards Heath, West Sussex)

Mrs J M Jennings, Greenacres, Horsted Lane, RH17 7HP. ☎ (01825) 790863 • Map 187,198/397278 • BB **A** • EM book first £6, 6-8.30pm • S2 T1 • 1-11 NX • Ⓥ Ⓑ Ⓓ Ⓢ Ⓜ

■ EASTBOURNE
SOUTH DOWNS WAY & WEALDWAY

J Pattenden, Ambleside Hotel, 24 Elms Avenue, BN21 3DN. ☎ (01323) 724991 • Map 199/616989 • BB **C** • EM book first £6.50, 6pm • S2 D6 T6 • 1-12 • Ⓥ Ⓓ Ⓢ Ⓡ 🐾 Ⓜ

Mr R F Cooke, Beachy Rise Guest House, Beachy Head Road, BN20 7QN. ☎ (01323) 639171 • Map 199/600972 • BB **D** • EM book first £10, 6.30pm • D4 T2 F1 • 1-12 NX • Ⓑ Ⓓ Ⓢ Ⓡ 🐾 • 3Cr

EAST SUSSEX

ENGLAND

B&B ACCOMMODATION

249

EASTBOURNE (CONTINUED)

Brian Jones, Arden Hotel, 17 Burlington Place, BN21 4AR. ☎ (01323) 639639 • Map 199/613985 • BB **C/D** • EM book first £9, 6pm • S2 D3 T4 F1 • 2-11 • Ⓥ Ⓑ Ⓓ Ⓢ Ⓡ • 3Cr

Mrs Doreen Sisley, 29 Manvers Road, BN20 8HH. ☎ (01323) 726645 • Map 199/588992 • BB **B** • EM £5 • S1 T1 • 2-12 NX • Ⓥ Ⓓ Ⓡ

■ GLYNDE (Lewes)
SOUTH DOWNS WAY

Mr & Mrs B Tolton, Ranscombe House, Ranscombe Lane, BN8 6AA. ☎ (01273) 858538 • Map 198/439086 • BB **B/C** • S1 D2 T1 F1 • 1-12 NX • Ⓑ Ⓓ Ⓡ Ⓑ

■ HAILSHAM
WEALDWAY

David & Jill Hook, Longleys Farm Cottage, Harebeating Lane, BN27 1ER. ☎ (01323) 841227 • Map 199/598105 • BB **B** • EM book first £7 • S1 D1 F1 • 1-12 NX • Ⓥ Ⓑ Ⓓ Ⓢ Ⓑ

■ HARTFIELD
WEALDWAY

Mrs G Pring, Stairs Farmhouse, High Street, TN7 4AB. ☎ (01892) 770793 • Map 188/477355 • BB **C** • EM £10 • D1 T1 F1 • 1-12 • Ⓥ Ⓑ Ⓓ Ⓢ • List/C • Bunkhouse also

■ HERSTMONCEUX (Hailsham)

☆ Cleavers Lyng Country Hotel, Church Road, BN27 1QJ. ☎ (01323) 833131 • Map 199/639108 • BB **D** • EM £12.75, 7pm • D3 T3 F1 • 1-12 NX • Ⓥ Ⓑ Ⓓ Ⓢ Ⓑ

■ HORAM (Heathfield)
VANGUARD WAY & WEALDWAY

The Gun Inn (Freehouse), Gun Hill, TN21 0JU. ☎ (01825) 872361 • Map 199/565145 • BB **B/C** • EM £6-£10, 6-10pm • D1 T1 F1 • 1-12 NX • Ⓥ Ⓑ Ⓓ Ⓑ

■ JEVINGTON (Polegate)
SOUTH DOWNS WAY & WEALDWAY

Mr J Ryder-Smith, The Homestead, BN26 5QL. ☎ (01323) 482505 • Map 199/563013 • BB **B** • D1 T1 • 1-12 NX • Ⓑ Ⓓ Ⓢ Ⓡ Ⓑ

■ KINGSTON (Lewes)
SOUTH DOWNS WAY

Geoff & Jean Hudson, "Nightingales", The Avenue, BN7 3LL. ☎ (01273) 475673 • Map 198/389083 • BB **C/D** • D1 T1 • 1-12 NX • Ⓑ Ⓓ Ⓢ Ⓡ Ⓑ • HC • SC also

■ LEWES
SOUTH DOWNS WAY

Mrs M Whitehead, Felix Gallery, 2 Sun Street, BN7 2QB. ☎ (01273) 472668 • Map 198/415104 • BB **C** • S1 T1 • 1-12 • Ⓓ Ⓡ

Vic & Veronica Newman, The Black Horse Inn, Western Road, BN7 1RS. ☎ (01273) 473653 • Map 198/409100 • BB **C/D** • D/S3 T/S1 • MID JAN-MID DEC • Ⓓ Ⓢ Ⓡ Ⓑ

Mrs Kathy Hole, Dairy Farmhouse, Firle, BN8 6NB. ☎ (01273) 858280/(0589) 155493 • Map 198/469079 • BB **C** • S1 D1 F1 • 1-12 NX • Ⓓ Ⓡ Ⓑ

■ MAYFIELD

B Powner, April Cottage Guest House and Tearoom, West Street, TN20 6BA. ☎ (01435) 872160 • Map 188,199/585269 • BB **C** • S1 D1 T1 • 1-12 • Ⓑ Ⓓ Ⓢ Ⓑ

■ PEVENSEY BAY

Rosalie & Brian Scales, Montana, The Promenade, BN24 6HD. ☎ (01323) 764651 • Map 199/658039 • BB **B** • S1 T2 • 1-12 NX • Ⓓ Ⓢ Ⓡ

■ PLUMPTON GREEN
SOUTH DOWNS WAY

Mrs M Baker, Farthings, Station Road, BN7 3BY. ☎ (01273) 890415 • Map 198/360162 • BB **C** • D2 T1 F1 • 1-12 • Ⓑ Ⓓ Ⓢ Ⓡ • Bunkhouse also

■ RODMELL (Lewes)
SOUTH DOWNS WAY

Mr & Mrs Fraser, Barn House, BN7 3HE. ☎ (01273) 477865 • Map 198/419060 • BB **C** • EM book first £10-£15, 6-7pm • S1 D3 T3 • 3-1 NX • Ⓥ Ⓑ Ⓓ Ⓢ • Groups also

■ RYE
SAXON SHORE WAY

☆ F & J Hadfield, Jeake's House, Mermaid Street, TN31 7ET. ☎ (01797) 222828 • Map 189/919203 • BB **C/D** • S1 D7 T1 F2 • 1-12 • Ⓑ Ⓓ Ⓢ Ⓡ Ⓑ Ⓜ • 2Cr/HC

EAST SUSSEX

ENGLAND

B&B ACCOMMODATION

Tel. Rye (01797) 222828 Fax (01797)222623

Beautiful listed building built in 1689. Set in medieval cobblestoned street, renowned for its smuggling associations. Breakfast—served in eighteenth century galleried former chapel—is traditional or vegetarian. Oak beamed and panelled bedrooms overlook the marsh and roof-tops to the sea. Brass or mahogany bedsteads, linen sheets and lace, En-suite bathrooms, hot drink trays, direct dial telephones and televisions. Four poster honeymoon suite and family room available. Residential license. Wonderful walking country. Bike hire nearby.

■ SEAFORD
SOUTH DOWNS WAY

Abbots Lodge, Marine Parade, BN25 2RB. ☎ (01323) 891055 • Map 198/469000 • BB **C** • EM £7.50, 7-9.30pm • D40 T30 • 1-12 • Ⓥ Ⓑ Ⓓ Ⓡ ⬮ • 3Cr • Groups also

Mrs B M Friend, Bentley Guest House, 23 Pelham Road, BN25 1ES. ☎ (01323) 893171 • Map 198/481988 • BB **B** • S3 D4 T2 • 1-12 NX • Ⓑ Ⓓ Ⓡ ⬮

■ STREAT
SOUTH DOWNS WAY

Valerie & John Eastwood, North Acres, BN6 8RX. ☎ (01273) 890278 • Map 198/353154 • BB **B** • EM book first £5 • S1 T2 F3 • 1-12 NX • Ⓥ Ⓓ Ⓢ Ⓡ • Groups also. Transport avail.

■ VINES CROSS (Horam)

Sue Newbold, Woodgate Cottage, Laundry Lane, TN21 9ED. ☎ (01435) 812834 • Map 199/592173 • BB **B** • S1 D1 T1 • 1-12 NX • Ⓓ Ⓢ ⬮ • Cot available

■ WILMINGTON (Polegate)
SOUTH DOWNS WAY & WEALDWAY & VANGUARD WAY

Miss P Forrest, Fairview, BN26 5SQ. ☎ (01323) 870210 • Map 199/547048 • BB **B** • T2 • 4-10 NX • Ⓓ Ⓢ Ⓡ ⬮

Clive Jones, The Giant's Rest, The Street, BN26 5SQ. ☎ (01323) 870207 • Map 199/546045 • BB **C** • EM 7-9pm • F/D/S2 • 1-12 NX • Ⓥ Ⓢ Ⓡ ⬮

David Stott, Crossways Hotel, BN26 5SG. ☎ (01323) 482455 • Map 199/547048 • BB **D** • EM £23.95, 7.30-8.45pm • S2 D3 T2 • 2-12 NX • Ⓑ Ⓓ Ⓢ Ⓡ

■ AMBERLEY (Arundel)
SOUTH DOWNS WAY

Mrs Bridget Jollands, Bacons, BN18 9NJ. ☎ (01798) 831234 • Map 197/031131 • BB **C** • T2 • 1-12 NX • Ⓓ ⬮

Mr & Mrs G Hardy, "Woodybanks", Crossgates, BN18 9NR. ☎ (01798) 831295 • Map 197/041136 • BB **B/C** • D1 T1 • 1-12 NX • Ⓓ Ⓢ Ⓡ • Some facilities for disabled

■ ARUNDEL
SOUTH DOWNS WAY

Arden Guest House, 4 Queen's Lane, BN18 9JN. ☎ (01903) 882544 • Map 197/019068 • BB **B/C** • D5 T3 • 1-12 • Ⓑ Ⓓ Ⓢ Ⓡ

Jack Hutchinson, Bridge House, 18 Queen Street, BN18 9JG. ☎ (01903) 882142 • Map 197/020069 • BB **B/C** • EM £8, 6-7.30pm • S2 D9 T2 F6 • 1-12 NX • Ⓥ Ⓑ Ⓓ Ⓡ ⬮ • 3Cr/C • Groups also

Mrs J Carter, 9 Dalloway Road, BN18 9HJ. ☎ (01903) 882253/730068 • Map 197/006064 • BB **B** • S1 T1 • 1-12 NX • Ⓓ Ⓢ Ⓡ

Peter & Sarah Fuente, Mill Lane House, Slindon, BN18 0RP. ☎ (01243) 814440 • Map 197/964084 • BB **C/D** • EM book first £9.85, 7pm • S1 D3 T2 F1 • 1-12 • Ⓥ Ⓑ Ⓓ ⬮ • 2Cr/C • SC also

■ BURY (Pulborough)
SOUTH DOWNS WAY

Mrs Carol Clarke, Harkaway, 8 Houghton Lane, RH20 1PD. ☎ (01798) 831843 • Map 197/012130 • BB **B** • D1 T2 • 1-12 • Ⓑ Ⓓ Ⓢ Ⓡ

■ CHICHESTER

Ethel & Tony Hosking, "Hedgehogs", 45 Whyke Lane, PO19 2JT. ☎ (01243) 780022 • Map 197/867044 • BB **B/C** • D1 T1 • 1-12 • Ⓓ Ⓢ Ⓡ ⬮ • List/C

■ CHIDHAM (Chichester)

Mr & Mrs Blencowe, The Old Rectory, PO18 8TA. ☎ (01243) 572088 • Map 197/787040 • BB **C/D** • D2 T1 • 1-12 NX • Ⓑ Ⓓ Ⓢ Ⓡ • Food nearby

■ CLAYTON (Hassocks)
SOUTH DOWNS WAY

Mrs C Bailey, Dower Cottage, Underhill Lane, BN6 9PL. ☎ (01273) 843363 • Map 198/309136 • BB **C/D** • EM book first £8.50 • S2 D3 T1 F1 • 1-12 • Ⓥ Ⓑ Ⓓ Ⓢ Ⓡ • SC also

Mrs S Calver, Halfway, BN6 9PH. ☎ (01273) 843540 • Map 198/305145 • BB **C** • EM book first £10 • S1 D1 T1 • 1-12 NX • Ⓥ Ⓓ Ⓢ Ⓡ ⬮

☆ See Display Advertisement

■ COCKING (Midhurst)
SOUTH DOWNS WAY

Village Tea Rooms, Chichester Road, GU29 0HN. ☎ (01730) 813336 • Map 197/877176 • BB **C** • D2 T1 • 1-12 NX • D ⛺

S C Wooldridge, Alpen Rose, GU29 0HN. ☎ (01730) 813298 • Map 197/878177 • BB **B** • T1 • 1-12 NX • D S

Blue Bell Inn, Bell Lane, GU29 0HN. ☎ (01730) 813449 • Map 197/877176 • BB **C** • EM £5, 6-10pm • D1 T2 F1 • 1-12 • V D S

■ COPTHORNE
☆ The Smyth Family, Linchens, New Domewood, RH10 3HF. ☎ (01342) 713085 • Map 187/342401 • BB **B/C/D** • D2 T2 F4 • 1-12 NX • B D S ⛺ Ⓜ

■ DITCHLING
SOUTH DOWNS WAY

☆ Bob & Annie Norfolk, The Old Rectory, Westmeston, BN6 8RL. ☎ (01273) 843711 • Map 198/342135 • BB **B/C/D** • S1 D1 T1 F1 • 1-12 • B D S

■ EAST ASHLING (Chichester)
Sylvia Jones, Englewood, PO18 9AS. ☎ (01243) 575407 • Map 197/820075 • BB **B** • EM book first £7, 6pm • D1 T1 • 1-12 NX • B D R

■ FINDON (Worthing)
SOUTH DOWNS WAY

Thurza & Tony Smith, Findon Tower, Cross Lane, Findon Village, BN14 0UG. ☎ (01903) 873870 • Map 198/123083 • BB **C** • D2 T1 • 1-12 NX • B D S ⛺ • 2Cr/C

■ FULKING (Henfield)
SOUTH DOWNS WAY

Mr & Mrs Downer, Downers Vineyard, Clappers Lane, BN5 9NH. ☎ (01273) 857484 • Map 198/245129 • BB **C** • F2 • 1-12 NX • D S ⛺ • List/App

■ HENFIELD
Mrs M Wilkin, Great Wapses Farm, BN5 9BJ. ☎ (01273) 492544 • Map 198/238182 • BB **C** • EM book first £8, 7.30pm • D3 T1 F1 • 1-12 NX • B ⛺

■ HEYSHOTT (Midhurst)
SOUTH DOWNS WAY

Robert & Judith Ralph, Little Hoyle, Hoyle Lane, GU29 0DX. ☎ (01798) 867359 • Map 197/906187 • BB **C** • D1 • 1-12 NX • B D S

■ HORSHAM
P & A Churcher, Copsale Farm, Copsale, RH13 6QU. ☎ (01403) 731114 • Map 187,198/172248 • BB **C** • D2 T1 • 1-12 • D S ⛺

■ LOWER BEEDING (Horsham)
G S & M Murby, The Old Posthouse, RH13 6NU. ☎ (01403) 891776 • Map 187,198/223274 • BB **C** • EM book first £8, 7pm • S2 D2 T1 F1 • 1-12 • V B D ⛺

■ LYMINSTER
Sandfield House, BN17 7PG. ☎ (01903) 724129 • Map 197/027039 • BB **C** • D1 • 1-12 NX • D R • 1Cr/C

■ OREHAM COMMON (Henfield)
SOUTH DOWNS WAY

Mrs J Forbes, Little Oreham Farm, BN5 9SB. ☎ (01273) 492931 • Map 198/224137 • BB **C** • EM £12, 6.30pm • D2 T1 • 1-12 NX • V B D S • SC also

■ POYNINGS (Brighton, East Sussex)
SOUTH DOWNS WAY

Mrs Carol Revell, Manor Farm, BN45 7AG. ☎ (01273) 857371 • Map 198/262122 • BB **C** • EM book first £10, 7pm • D1 T2 • 3-12 NX • V B D S • 1Cr/C

■ PULBOROUGH
Chequers Hotel, Church Place, RH20 1AD. ☎ (01798) 872486 • Map 197/047187 • BB **D** • EM £16.95, 7.30-8.30pm • D4 T4 F3 • 1-12 NX • V B D S R ⛺ • 4Cr/HC

■ STEYNING
SOUTH DOWNS WAY

Mrs J Morrow, 5 Coxham Lane, BN44 3LG. ☎ (01903) 812286 • Map 198/176116 • BB **B** • S1 T2 • 1-12 NX • 🅱 🅳 🏊 ⓜ

Mrs E M Dawson, The Old Museum House, 93 High Street, BN44 3RE. ☎ (01903) 812317 • Map 198/176112 • BB **B** • S1 D1 T1 • 1-12 NX • 🅳 🆂

Mrs Marilyn McKenna, 47 Hills Road, BN44 3QG. ☎ (01903) 814506 • Map 198/173109 • BB **B** • EM book first £6, 7pm • S1 T1 • 1-12 NX • 🆅 🅳 🆂 🏊 ⓜ

■ STORRINGTON (Pulborough)
SOUTH DOWNS WAY

☆ Mrs M Smith, Willow Tree Cottage, Washington Road, RH20 4AF. ☎ (01903) 740835 • Map 198/101138 • BB **C/D** • D2 T2 F1 • 1-12 NX • 🅱 🅳 🆂 🏊

WILLOW TREE COTTAGE
Storrington, West Sussex

Situated between 2 exits of the South Downs, one down Barns Farm Lane, the other past Sullington Parish Church. Family-run B&B, set in beautiful gardens, swimming pool available. All rooms en suite. Colour TV, H&C, tea making, good food. Good service.

Tel. 01903 740835

Mrs Fiona Warton, No. 1 Lime Chase, RH20 4LX. ☎ (01903) 740437 • Map 197/089147 • BB **C/D** • D1 T1 F1 • 1-12 NX • 🅱 🅳 🆂

■ WASHINGTON (Pulborough)
SOUTH DOWNS WAY

Barry & Mary Sturgess, Long Island, School Lane, RH20 4AP. ☎ (01903) 892237 • Map 198/120129 • BB **C** • D1 T1 F1 • 1-12 • 🅳 🆂 🏊

Judy Ward, Brook House, London Road, RH20 4AL. ☎ (01903) 892142 • Map 198/122130 • BB **B** • S1 T2 • 1-12 • 🅱 🅳 🆂 🏊 • SC also

■ WEST BURTON (Pulborough)
SOUTH DOWNS WAY

Mrs Angela Azis, Cokes Barn, RH20 1HD. ☎ (01798) 831636 • Map /000139 • BB **C** • S1 T2 • 1-12 NX • 🅳 🆂 🆁 🏊

■ WEST HARTING (Petersfield)
SOUTH DOWNS WAY

Mrs Patricia Stevens, 3 Quebec, GU31 5PG. ☎ (01730) 825386 • Map 197/780214 • BB **C** • EM book first £6.50, 6-8pm • S1 F1 • 1-12 • 🆅 🅱 🅳 🆂 🏊 • List/C

■ WISBOROUGH GREEN

Jacky Miller, Meadowbank House, Petworth Road, RH14 0BJ. ☎ (01403) 700482 • Map 186,197/045258 • BB **B** • D1 T1 • 1-12 NX • 🅳 🆂

■ WORTHING

Alan Trudgett, Tregalan, 3 Alexandra Road, BN11 2DX. ☎ (01903) 206613 • Map 198/158028 • BB **B** • EM 5.30-6.30pm • D2 T2 • 1-12 • 🆅 🅳 🆁 🏊 ⓜ • 1Cr

WARWICKSHIRE

■ ALCESTER
COTSWOLD WAY

John & Margaret Canning, Glebe Farm, Exhall, B49 6EA. ☎ (01789) 772202 • Map 150/102550 • BB **C** • S2 D1 T1 • 1-12 NX • 🅳 🆂 🏊 • 1Cr/C • SC also

■ BROADWELL (Rugby)
GRAND UNION CANAL WALK

Mr & Mrs John Pickering, High House, The Green, CV23 8HD. ☎ (01926) 812687 • Map 151/453658 • BB **B** • F1 • 1-12 NX • 🅱 🅳 🏊 ⓜ

■ HASELEY KNOB (Warwick)
GRAND UNION CANAL WALK

Mrs Pat Clapp, The Croft, CV35 7NL. ☎ (01926) 484447 • Map 139/233711 • BB **C** • S1 D1 T1 F2 • 1-12 NX • 🅱 🅳 🆂 🏊 • 2Cr/C

■ ILMINGTON (Shipston-on-Stour)

Meadow Hill, Mickleton Road, CV36 4JQ. ☎ (01608) 682456 • Map 151/214464 • BB **B/C** • D2 • 1-12 • 🅱 🅳

■ KENILWORTH

Trevor & Angela Jefferies, The Abbey Guest House, 41 Station Road, CV8 1JD. ☎ (01926) 512707 • Map 140/290717 • BB **C** • EM book first £7, 7pm • S1 D2 T3 F1 • 1-12 • 🆅 🅱 🆂 ⓜ • 2Cr/C

Mrs Patricia Snelson, Banner Hill Farmhouse Accom., Rouncil Lane, CV8 1NN. ☎ (01926) 52850 • Map 140/268708 • BB **B** • EM £7.50 • S2 D2 T4 F2 • 1-12 NX • 🆅 🅱 🅳 🆂 🏊 • 1Cr • Groups also

■ KINETON (Warwick)

Carolyn Howard, Willowbrook Farmhouse, Lighthorne Road, CV35 0JL. ☎ (01926) 640475 • Map 151/330510 • BB **B/C** • D2 T1 • 1-12 NX • 🅱 🅳 🆂 🏊 • 2Cr

■ LONG COMPTON (Shipston-on-Stour)

Jim & Doreen Cunnington, Archways, Crockwell Street, CV36 5JN. ☎ (01608) 684358 • Map 151/286333 • BB **B** • D1 T1 • 1-12 NX • 🅳 🆂 • 1Cr/C

☆ See Display Advertisement

■ **LONG MARSTON (Stratford-upon-Avon)**
HEART OF ENGLAND WAY

Mrs Taylor, Church Farm, CV37 8RH. ☎ (01789) 720275 • Map 151/153484 • BB **C** • T1 F/D1 • 1-12 NX • Ⓑ Ⓓ Ⓢ ⬧ • 2Cr/C

■ **MERIDEN (Coventry)**
HEART OF ENGLAND WAY

☆ Cooperage Farm B&B, Old Road, CV7 7JP. ☎ (01676) 523493 • Map 140/251820 • BB **D** • EM £8, 6-9pm • D2 T2 F2 • 2-12 NX • Ⓥ Ⓑ Ⓡ ⬧ • 1Cr

---

Cooperage Farm
Meriden
Warwickshire

B&B in the attractive village of Meriden on the Heart of England Way.
Tea/coffee facilities and a good English breakfast. Ample car parking.
Cooperage Farm is a 300-year-old Listed farmhouse.

Tel. 01676 523493

■ **SHIPSTON-ON-STOUR**

Lower Farm Barn, Great Wolford, CV36 5NQ. ☎ (01608) 674435 • Map 151/247345 • BB **B** • D1 T1 F1 • 1-12 • Ⓑ Ⓓ Ⓢ Ⓡ ⬧ • 2Cr • SC also

■ **SOUTHAM (Leamington Spa)**
GRAND UNION CANAL WALK

Mrs E Bishop, "Briarwood", 34 Warwick Road, CV33 0HN. ☎ (01926) 814756 • Map 151/414615 • BB **C/D** • D1 • 1-12 NX • Ⓑ Ⓓ Ⓢ

■ **STRATFORD-UPON-AVON**
HEART OF ENGLAND WAY

☆ Jo & Roger Pettitt, Parkfield Guest House, 3 Broad Walk, CV37 6HS. ☎ (01789) 293313 • Map 151/197546 • BB **C** • S1 D3 T2 F1 • 1-12 • Ⓑ Ⓓ Ⓢ Ⓡ ⬧ • 2Cr

---

STRATFORD-UPON-AVON
Parkfield Guest House, 3 Broad Walk CV37 6HS

An attractive Victorian house in a quiet location, 5 minutes' walk to town centre & Royal Shakespeare Theatre and one minute from start of Greenway leading to Heart of England Way. Rooms have colour TV and tea/coffee-making facilities. Most rooms en suite. Full English or vegetarian breakfast. Brochure on request. Large private car park. A no-smoking house.

AA
RAC   ☎ 01789 293313   ETB 🏵

The Hunter's Moon Guest Hse, 150 Alcester Road, CV37 9DR. ☎ (01789) 292888 • Map 151/186552 • BB **C** • EM book first £10, 6pm • S2 D4 T3 F3 • 1-12 • Ⓥ Ⓑ Ⓓ Ⓢ Ⓡ ⬧ • 2Cr

Nando's, 18/19 Evesham Place, CV37 6HT. ☎ (01789) 204907 • Map 151/197547 • BB **B/C** • EM book first £7-£8, 6pm • S5 D5 T6 F5 • 1-12 • Ⓑ Ⓢ Ⓡ ⬧ • 2Cr

☆ Travellers Rest Guest House, Joan & Clive Horton, 146 Alcester Road, CV37 9DR. ☎ (01789) 266589 • Map 151/186553 • BB **B/C** • S/D1 T1 F/D/T1 • 1-12 NX • Ⓑ Ⓓ Ⓢ Ⓡ • List/C

Travellers Rest Guest House
146 Alcester Road, Stratford-upon-Avon

Explore Shakespeare's historic countryside and enjoy a stay at Travellers Rest Guest House situated betweeen the town centre and Ann Hathaway's Cottage. All rooms are en-suite, comfortable with tea/coffee tray, hairdryer and colour TV. A friendly welcome and good home cooking awaits you.

☎ **01789 266589**

H of E Tourist Board
LISTED COMMENDED

R & V Lilley, Braeside Guest House, 129 Shipston Road, CV37 7LW. ☎ (01789) 261648 • Map 151/206540 • BB **C** • S1 D1 T1 F1 • 1-12 NX • Ⓑ Ⓓ Ⓢ Ⓡ ⬧ • 2Cr • Food nearby

■ **STRETTON ON FOSSE (Moreton-in-Marsh, Gloucs)**

Mrs A Campbell Smith, Jasmine Cottage, GL56 9SA. ☎ (01608) 661972 • Map 151/223384 • BB **B** • EM book first £7 • D1 T1 • 3-11 • Ⓥ Ⓑ Ⓓ Ⓢ ⬧ • 1Cr

■ **WARWICK**
GRAND UNION CANAL WALK

Avon Guest House, 7 Emscote Road, CV34 4PH. ☎ (01926) 491367 • Map 151/292653 • BB **B** • EM boo first £7, 6.30pm • S3 D2 T2 F2 • 1-12 • Ⓥ Ⓑ Ⓓ Ⓢ Ⓡ Ⓜ • 2Cr/App

The Seven Stars, Friars Street, CV34 6HD. ☎ (01926 492658 • Map 151/278646 • BB **C** • EM book first £5 7-8pm • D2 T1 • 1-12 • Ⓥ Ⓑ Ⓓ Ⓡ ⬧ • 1Cr/C

■ **WILMCOTE (Stratford-upon-Avon)**

Dosthill Cottage, 2 The Green, CV37 9XJ. ☎ (01789) 266480 • Map 151/160580 • BB **C** • D2 T1 • 1-12 NX • Ⓑ Ⓓ Ⓢ Ⓡ • 2Cr/C

■ **WIMPSTONE (Stratford-Upon-Avon)**

Joan James, Whitchurch Farm, CV37 8NS. ☎ (01789) 450275 • Map 151/215488 • BB **C** • EM £10 6.30pm • D2 T1 • 1-12 NX • Ⓥ Ⓑ Ⓓ • 2Cr/App

■ **WIXFORD (Alcester)**
HEART OF ENGLAND WAY

Mrs Margaret Kember, Orchard Lawns, B49 6DA. ☎ (01789) 772668 • Map 150/087547 • BB **C** • S1 D1 T1 • 1-12 NX • Ⓑ Ⓓ Ⓢ ⬧ • 2Cr/s/HC • Food nearby

■ **WOOTTON WAWEN (Stratford-upon-Avon)**
HEART OF ENGLAND WAY

Mrs J S McCall, Wootton Park Farm, B95 6HJ. ☎
(01564) 792673 • Map 151/ 141627 • BB **C** • D1 T1
F2 • 1-12 NX • Ⓑ Ⓓ Ⓡ 🛁 • 2Cr

WEST MIDLANDS

■ **COVENTRY**

June Beecham, Northanger Guest House, 35
Westminster Road, CV1 3GB. ☎ (01203) 226780 •
Map 140/327785 • BB **B/C** • EM £4, 7pm • S4 T3 F2
• 1-12 NX • Ⓥ Ⓓ Ⓡ • 2Cr/App

■ **DUDLEY**

Mrs J Green, "Merdeka", 16 Dawlish Road,
Woodsetton, DY1 4LU. ☎ (01902) 884775 • Map
139/927930 • BB **B** • EM book first £6, 6-8pm • S1
T1 • 1-12 NX • Ⓥ Ⓓ Ⓢ Ⓡ 🛁

■ **KNOWLE (Solihull)**
HEART OF ENGLAND WAY & GRAND UNION CANAL WALK

Jennifer Watson, Dowland Cottage, 24 Kenilworth
Road, B93 0JA. ☎ (01564) 779889 • Map
139/184766 • BB **D** • EM book first £8.50, 7-8pm •
S2 D1 T2 F1 • 1-12 • Ⓥ Ⓑ Ⓓ Ⓡ

■ **SELLY PARK (Birmingham)**

The Awentsbury Hotel, 21 Serpentine Road, B29
7HU. ☎ (0121) 472 1258 • Map 139/050830 • BB
C/D • EM book first £7.50, 8pm • S6 D2 T6 F2 • 1-12
• Ⓥ Ⓑ Ⓓ Ⓡ 🛁

■ **SOLIHULL**
GRAND UNION CANAL WALK

Mr & Mrs J Townsend, Ivy House, Warwick Road,
Heronfield Knowle, B93 0EB. ☎ (01564) 770247 •
Map 139/194750 • BB **C/D** • S3 D2 T2 F1 • 1-12 • Ⓑ
Ⓢ Ⓡ 🛁 • 2Cr/C

WILTSHIRE

■ **ALVEDISTON (Salisbury)**

Samways Farm, SP5 5LQ. ☎ (01722) 780286 • Map
184/974233 • BB **C** • T3 • 1-12 NX • Ⓑ Ⓓ 🛁 • SC
also, food nearby

■ **BRADFORD-ON-AVON**

Mr & Mrs J Benjamin, The Locks, 265 Trowbridge
Road, BA15 1UA. ☎ (01225) 863358 • Map
173/833597 • BB **B/C** • S1 D1 T1 F1 • 1-12 • Ⓑ Ⓓ
Ⓢ Ⓡ

VEGETARIANS
Many establishments do a veggie breakfast
even if they don't do an evening meal

■ **BREMHILL (Calne)**

Elizabeth Sinden, Lowbridge Farm, SN11 9HE. ☎
(01249) 815889 • Map 173/987737 • BB **B** • EM
book first £7.50, 7-9pm • T1 F1 • 1-12 • Ⓥ Ⓓ Ⓢ

■ **CALNE**

G Brandani, White Hart Hotel, 2 London Road, SN11
0AB. ☎ (01249) 812413 • Map 173/999706 • BB **C** •
EM £9, 6-10pm • S3 D4 T4 F3 • 1-12 • Ⓥ Ⓑ Ⓓ 🛁 •
1Cr • Groups also

■ **CHICKLADE (Hindon, Salisbury)**
WESSEX RIDGEWAY

Mrs W A Jerram, Chicklade Lodge, SP3 5SU. ☎
(01747) 820389 • Map 184/910345 • BB **B** • EM
book first £8.50, 7.30pm • T2 • 1-12 NX • Ⓥ Ⓓ Ⓢ
🛁

■ **CHIPPENHAM**
RIDGEWAY

Ian & Audrey Smith, Home Farm, Harts Lane,
Biddestone, SN14 7DQ. ☎ (01249) 714475 • Map
173/866735 • BB **B/C** • D1 F1 • 1-12 • Ⓑ Ⓓ Ⓢ •
List/C • Food nearby

■ **CORSHAM**

Anne Venus, Owl House, Lower Kingsdown Road,
Box, SN13 8BB. ☎ (01225) 743883 • Map
173/812675 • BB **C** • S1 T2 • 1-10 • Ⓓ Ⓢ Ⓜ • C

■ **CRICKLADE**
THAMES PATH

Mrs J Rumming, Waterhay Farm, Leigh, SN6 6QY.
☎ (01285) 861253 • Map 173, 163/061931 • BB **C** •
S1 D1 T1 • 1-12 • Ⓑ Ⓓ Ⓢ • 2Cr/C

■ **CROCKERTON (Nr Warminster)**

Rachel & Colin Singer, Springfield, BA12 8AU. ☎
(01985) 213696 • Map 183/866427 • BB **C/D** • EM
book first £15, 7-8pm • D2 T1 • 1-12 NX • Ⓥ Ⓑ Ⓓ
Ⓢ Ⓡ

■ **DEVIZES**
WESSEX RIDGEWAY

May & Philip Linton, Pinecroft, Potterne Road
(A360), SN10 5DA. ☎ (01380) 721433 • Map 173/
006607 • BB **B/C** • D2 T2 F1 • 1-12 • Ⓑ Ⓓ Ⓢ • 2Cr

■ **EASTON ROYAL (Pewsey)**

Mrs Margaret Landless, Follets, SN9 5LZ. ☎
(01672) 810619/0468 560302 • Map 174/208606 •
BB **C** • EM book first £12, 7pm • D1 T1 F1 • 1-12 NX
• Ⓥ Ⓑ Ⓓ Ⓢ

■ **ENFORD (Nr Pewsey)**
WESSEX RIDGEWAY

Enford House, SN9 6DJ. ☎ (01980) 670414 • Map
184/140500 • BB **B** • EM book first £15 • D1 T2 • 1-
12 NX • Ⓑ Ⓓ Ⓢ 🛁 • 1Cr

■ ERLESTOKE (Devizes)

Pam Hampton, Longwater, SN10 5UE. ☎ (01380) 830095 • Map 184/964544 • BB **C** • EM £11.50, 7pm • D2 T2 F1 • 1-12 NX • Ⓥ Ⓑ Ⓓ Ⓢ 🐾 • 3Cr/C

■ LACOCK (Chippenham)

Mrs S McDowell, Lacock Pottery, The Tanyard, SN15 2LB. ☎ (01249) 730266 • Map 173/916686 • BB **C/D** • D1 T3 • 1-12 NX • Ⓑ Ⓓ Ⓢ 🐾 • 2Cr/C

Mrs Margaret Addison, The Old Rectory, Cantax Hill, SN15 2JZ. ☎ (01249) 730335 • Map 173/914687 • BB **D** • D2 T1 • 1-12 NX • Ⓑ Ⓓ Ⓢ • 2Cr/C

■ LUDWELL (Shaftesbury, Dorset)
WESSEX RIDGEWAY

Mrs Ann Rossiter, Birdbush Farm, SP7 9NH. ☎ (01747) 828252 • Map 184/914227 • BB **B** • S1 D1 • 3-10 NX • Ⓓ Ⓢ

■ MARKET LAVINGTON (Devizes)
WESSEX RIDGEWAY

☆ R & J Mattingly, The Old Coach House, 21 Church Street, SN10 4DU. ☎ (01380) 812879 • Map 184/014541 • BB **C** • EM book first £11.50 • S1 D1 T2 • 1-12 NX • Ⓑ Ⓓ Ⓢ • 2Cr/C

■ MARLBOROUGH
WESSEX RIDGEWAY

Mrs S Harrison, Cartref, 63 George Lane, SN8 4BY. ☎ (01672) 512771 • Map 173/190688 • BB **B** • D2 T1 • 1-12 NX • Ⓓ 🐾 • Lift to Ridgeway

Mrs M Young, Kennet Beeches, 54 George Lane, SN8 4BY. ☎ (01672) 512579 • Map 173/190688 • BB **B** • S2 T2 • 1-12 NX • Ⓓ Ⓢ • Rail Link service

Mrs P A Waite, 5 Reeds Ground, London Road, SN8 2AW. ☎ (01672) 513926 • Map 173/190680 • BB **C** • S1 D1 • 1-12 NX • Ⓑ Ⓓ Ⓢ

■ MERE

Midwinter House, Castle Street, BA12 6JF. ☎ (01747) 861226 • Map 183/810324 • BB **B** • EM book first £8, 6-8pm • D1 T1 • 1-11 • Ⓥ Ⓑ Ⓓ Ⓢ

■ OGBOURNE ST GEORGE (Marlborough)
RIDGEWAY

Mr G H Edwins, Foxlynch, Bytham Road, SN8 1TD. ☎ (01672) 841307 • Map 173/190740 • BB **B** • 1-12 • Ⓑ Ⓓ • Bunk room only

☆ Parklands Hotel & Restaurant, High Street, SN8 1SL. ☎ (01672) 841555 • Map 174/200744 • BB **D** • EM £14.50, 7-9.30pm • S2 D2 T6 • 1-12 • Ⓥ Ⓑ Ⓢ 🐾 • 3Cr/C

Mr & Mrs Shaw, The Old Crown, Marlborough Road, SN8 1SQ. ☎ (01672) 841445 • Map 173/195746 • BB **B** • EM £5.50, 6-10pm, 7-9pm Sun. • T1 • 1-12 NX • Ⓥ Ⓑ Ⓓ Ⓢ 🐾 • 2Cr

■ PEWSEY

Mrs Margot Andrews, Huntleys Farm, Manningford Abbotts, SN9 6HZ. ☎ (01672) 563663 • Map 173/145593 • BB **B/C** • EM book first £10 • S1 D1 T1 • 1-12 • Ⓥ Ⓑ Ⓓ Ⓢ Ⓡ 🐾

■ REDLYNCH (Salisbbury)

Angela Churchill, Yew Tree Cottage, Grove Lane, SP5 2NR. ☎ (01725) 511730 • Map 184/202212 • BB **B/C** • S1 D1 T1 • 1-12 NX • Ⓓ Ⓢ Ⓜ

■ SALISBURY

Holmhurst Guest House, Downton Road, SP2 8AR. ☎ (01722) 410407 • Map 184/145286 • BB **B/C** • S1 D2 T2 F1 • 1-12 • Ⓑ Ⓓ Ⓢ Ⓡ 🐾 • List

Mrs Gill Rodwell, Farthings, 9 Swaynes Close, SP1 3AE. ☎ (01722) 330749 • Map 184/145306 • BB **C** • S2 D1 T1 • 1-12 NX • Ⓑ Ⓓ Ⓢ Ⓡ Ⓜ • 2Cr

Mrs Kay Bugden, Avon View House, 287 Castle Road, SP1 3SB. ☎ (01722) 333723 • Map 184/141319 • BB **B** • D2 T1 • 1-12 NX • Ⓑ Ⓓ Ⓢ Ⓡ Ⓜ

Mrs S A Combes, Manor Farm, Burcombe, SP2 0EJ. ☎ (01722) 742177 • Map 184/071308 • BB **B/C** • S1 D1 T1 • 3-11 • Ⓓ Ⓢ • List/C

■ SEMINGTON (Trowbridge)

Mrs M Bruges, Brook House, BA14 6JR. ☎ (01380) 870232 • Map 173/898607 • BB **C** • D1 T1 F1 • 2-11 • Ⓑ Ⓓ Ⓢ 🐾

■ STAPLEFORD (Salisbury)

Mrs Christine Sykes, Elm Tree Cottage, SP3 4LH. ☎ (01722) 790507 • Map 184/072370 • BB **D** • D2 F1 • 4-9 • B D S 🐾 • 2Cr/HC

■ WANBOROUGH (Swindon)
RIDGEWAY

G & M Sadler, Ducksbridge, Bury Croft, SN4 0AP. ☎ (01793) 790338 • Map 174/206837 • BB **C** • S1 D1 T1 • 1-12 • B D S 🐾 • Food nearby

■ WARMINSTER

Farmers' Hotel, 1 Silver Street, BA12 8PS. ☎ (01985) 213815 • Map 183/871451 • BB **C** • EM £8.50, 6-10pm • S8 D4 T5 F3 • 1-12 • V B D R 🐾 • 1Cr • Groups also

■ WEST LAVINGTON (Devizes)

Mrs Judy Noble, "Long Thatch", 34 High Street, SN10 4JB. ☎ (01380) 812117 • Map 184/007530 • BB **C** • D1 T1 • 1-12 NX • B D S

■ WEST WINTERSLOW (Salisbury)

Mrs Jackie Martin, Dunstable Cottage, Pitton Road, SP5 1SA. ☎ (01980) 862485 • Map 184/221330 • BB **B** • EM book first £10 • D1 T1 • 1-12 NX • V D Ⓜ

■ WESTBURY
WESSEX RIDGEWAY

Mrs C Knight, Birchanger Farm, Bratton Road, BA13 4TA. ☎ (01373) 822673 • Map 184/900520 • BB **B/C** • EM book first £9, 7.30pm • S3 D1 T1 • 1-12 NX • B D R • List • SC also

Sue Tricker, Rock Villa, 81 Westbury Leigh, BA13 3SF. ☎ (01373) 864238 • Map 183/862500 • BB **B** • S1 D1 T2 F1 • 1-12 • B D S R 🐾

■ ZEALS (Longcross)

Irene & John Snook, Corner Ways Cottage, BA12 6LL. ☎ (01747) 840477 • Map 183/787320 • BB **B/C** • EM book first £9 • D2 T1 • 1-12 NX • V B D S Ⓜ • 2Cr/C

EAST RIDING OF YORKSHIRE

■ BEVERLEY

Mr & Mrs C Anderson, Eastgate Guest House, 7 Eastgate, HU17 0DR. ☎ (01482) 868464 • Map 107/036394 • BB **B/C** • S5 D5 T4 F4 • 1-12 • B D S R 🐾 • 2Cr/C

1 Woodlands, HU17 8BT. ☎ (01482) 862752 • Map 106,107/029395 • BB **C** • EM £12, 7pm • S1 D1 T1 F1 • 1-12 NX • V B D S R 🐾

■ LONDESBOROUGH (York)
WOLDS WAY

Mrs P Rowlands, Towthorpe Grange, YO4 3LB. ☎ (01430) 873814 • Map 106/876438 • BB **B** • EM book first £5 • D2 T1 F1 • 1-12 NX • V D S 🐾 • SC also

■ MILLINGTON (York)
WOLDS WAY

Mrs M Dykes, Laburnum Cottage, YO4 2TX. ☎ (01759) 303055 • Map 106/830517 • BB **B** • EM book first £6, 7pm • S1 F1 • 2-10 • V D S 🐾

■ POCKLINGTON (York)
WOLDS WAY

Kay & David West, Ashfield Farm, Canal Head, YO4 2NW. ☎ (01759) 305238 • Map 106/800474 • BB **B** • D1 T2 F1 • 1-12 • D S 🐾

■ WELWICK (Holderness)

Wheatsheaf House, Main Street, HU12 0RY. ☎ (01964) 630390 • Map 107,113/342210 • BB **B** • D2 T1 • 1-12 • D S

NORTH YORKSHIRE

■ APPLETREEWICK (Skipton)
DALES WAY

Alyson Coney, Blundellstead, BD23 6DB. ☎ (01756) 720632 • Map 98/053601 • BB **C** • S2 D1 • 1-12 NX • D S 🐾 • List • Food nearby

■ ARKENGARTHDALE (Reeth)
COAST TO COAST WALK

☆ Charles Bathurst Inn, DL11 6EN. ☎ (01748) 884567 • Map 92/000031 • BB **C/D** • EM £12, from 7pm • S2 D7 • 1-12 • V B D S 🐾

■ ARRATHORNE (Bedale)

☆ Jim & Edith Lillie, Elmfield House, DL8 1NE. ☎ (01677) 450558 • Map 99/201933 • BB **C/D** • EM book first £11.50, 6.30pm • D4 T3 F2 • 1-12 NX • V B D S • 3Cr/C

☆ See Display Advertisement

ASKRIGG (Leyburn)

☆ Mr & Mrs J Drew, Helm, DL8 3JF. ☎ (01969) 650443 • Map 98/939916 • BB **D** • EM book first £15.50, 7pm • D2 T1 • 1-10 • V B D S • 3Cr/HC

Mr & Mrs B Bowe, Syke's House, DL8 3HT. ☎ (01969) 650535 • Map 98/947910 • BB **C** • EM book first £10, 7pm • D2 T1 F1 • 1-12 NX • V D ⚓ • SC also

Mrs Kate Empsall, Whitfield Helm, DL8 3JF. ☎ (01969) 650565 • Map 98/934916 • BB **B/C** • D1 T1 • 1-12 • B D S ⚓ • 2Cr/C • SC also

Stoney End, Worton, DL8 3ET. ☎ (01969) 650652 • Map 98/955900 • BB **C** • D/T1 F1 • 1-12 NX • D S ⚓ • 1Cr/HC

Mollie Gilyeat, Thornsgill Guest House, Moor Road, DL8 3HH. ☎ (01969) 650617 • Map 98/948910 • BB **C** • EM book first £13, 6.30pm • D2 T1 • 1-12 NX • V B D S ⚓ • 2Cr/HC

☆ Mrs B Percival, Milton House, DL8 3HJ. ☎ (01969) 650217 • Map 98/948910 • BB **C** • EM book first £10.50, 7pm • D3 • 1-12 • B D ⚓ • 2Cr/C

AYSGARTH (Nr Leyburn)

☆ Stow House Hotel, Aysgarth Falls, DL8 3SR. ☎ (01969) 663635 • Map 98/014883 • BB **D** • EM book first £12, 7.30pm • D5 T4 • 1-12 • V B D

BAINBRIDGE (Leyburn)

Riverdale House Country Hotel, DL8 3EW. ☎ (01969) 650311, Nov-Mar 663381 • Map 98/933952 • BB **C/D** • EM £16, 7.30pm • D6 T4 F2 • 3-11 NX • V B D S ⚓ • 3Cr/C

BEDALE

Mrs Jacky Rudd, Tentrees, Exelby, DL8 2HF. ☎ (01677) 426541 • Map 99/295871 • BB **B/C** • S1 D/F1 • 3-11 • B D S M

BLAKEY (Kirkbymoorside)
COAST TO COAST WALK

The Lion Inn, YO6 6LQ. ☎ (01751) 417320 • Map 100,94/678997 • BB **B/C/D** • EM £5.75 • D6 T1 F3 • 1-12 • V B D ⚓ M

High Blakey House, YO6 6LQ. ☎ (01751) 417641/417296 • Map 100,94/678997 • BB **C** • T2 F1 • 1-12 NX • B D S

B&B ACCOMMODATION ENGLAND NORTH YORKSHIRE

■ BUCKDEN (Skipton)
DALES WAY

Mrs A Oxford, Mullions, BD23 5JA. ☎ (01756) 760252 • Map 98/942772 • BB **B** • S1 D1 T1 • 1-12 NX • Ⓓ Ⓢ

Jack & Shirley Leach, Beck Cottage, BD23 5JA. ☎ (01756) 760340 • Map 98/942772 • BB **B** • D1 T1 • 1-12 NX • Ⓓ Ⓢ

Mrs Joy Tupling, Romany Cottage, BD23 5JA. ☎ (01756) 760365 • Map 98/942772 • BB **B** • S1 D1 T1 • 2-12 NX • Ⓓ Ⓢ 🐕 Ⓜ

■ BURNSALL (Skipton)
DALES WAY

☆ W T Haighton, Manor House, BD23 6BW. ☎ (01756) 720231 • Map 98/032614 • BB **C** • EM book first £9.50, 7pm • D4 T3 • 1-11 NX • Ⓥ Ⓑ Ⓓ Ⓢ 🐕 2Cr • Groups also

☆ Mrs Carol Fitton, Valley View Guest House, BD23 6BN. ☎ (01756) 720314 • Map 98/032614 • BB **C/D** • D1 T1 F1 • 1-12 NX • Ⓑ Ⓓ Ⓜ

■ CASTLETON (Whitby)

☆ Mr A Abrahams, The Moorlands Hotel/Inn, YO21 2DB. ☎ (01287) 660206 • Map 94/687080 • BB **D** • EM £10, 6-9.30pm • S3 D2 T2 F1 • 1-12 • Ⓥ Ⓑ Ⓓ Ⓢ Ⓡ 🐕 • 3Cr • Groups also

You'll find more accommodation in the Hostels & Bunkhouses, Self-catering and Groups sections of this YEARBOOK

■ CHOPGATE (Stokesley)
CLEVELAND WAY & COAST TO COAST WALK

Jean Bowes, Raisdale Mill House, TS9 7JG. ☎ (01642) 778254 • Map 93/538006 • BB **B** • EM £6, from 6pm • D1 T1 • 1-12 NX • Ⓥ Ⓓ Ⓢ • SC also

■ CLAY BANK TOP (Bilsdale)
COAST TO COAST WALK

Wendy & Gerry Broad, Maltkiln House, Urra, Chop Gate, TS9 7HZ. ☎ (01642) 778216 • Map 93/571019 • BB **B** • EM £8.50, 7pm • S1 D1 T1 • 1-12 NX • Ⓥ Ⓑ Ⓓ Ⓢ 🐕

■ CLOUGHTON (Scarborough)
CLEVELAND WAY

Cober Hill, YO13 0AR. ☎ (01723) 870310 • Map 101/010948 • BB **C** • EM £8.50, 7pm • S21 D11 T28 F10 • 1-12 • Ⓥ Ⓑ Ⓓ Ⓢ 🐕 • Groups also

Mrs M A Martin, Gowland Farm, Gowland Lane, YO13 0DU. ☎ (01723) 870924 • Map 94,101/991961 • BB **B** • EM book first £7.50, 6pm • S1 D1 T1 • 4-10 • Ⓓ Ⓜ • SC also

■ DANBY (Whitby)
COAST TO COAST WALK

Mrs B Tindall, Rowantree Farm, YO21 2LE. ☎ (01287) 660396 • Map 94/704073 • BB **B** • EM book first £7, 6.30pm • S1 T1 F1 • 1-12 NX • Ⓥ Ⓓ Ⓢ Ⓡ 🐕

J & M Lowson, Sycamore House, YO21 2NW. ☎ (01287) 660125 • Map 94/688058 • BB **B** • EM book first £9, 6-8pm • S1 D2 T1 F2 • 3-11 • Ⓥ Ⓓ Ⓢ 🐕

■ DANBY WISKE (Northallerton)
COAST TO COAST WALK

Mrs Merlyn Watson, The White Swan Inn, DL7 0NQ. ☎ (01609) 770122 • Map 99/337987 • BB **B** • EM £6.50, 7-9.30pm • S1 T3 • 1-12 • Ⓥ Ⓓ 🐕 • Camping also

■ DARLEY (Harrogate)
NIDDERDALE WAY

Mrs Judy Barker, Brimham Guest House, Silverdale Close, HG3 2PQ. ☎ (01423) 780948 • Map 104/206593 • BB **B** • D2 T1 • 1-12 NX • Ⓥ Ⓑ Ⓓ Ⓢ

NORTH YORKSHIRE • ENGLAND • B&B ACCOMMODATION

☆ See Display Advertisement

259

■ EASINGWOLD (York)

Rachel Ritchie, The Old Rectory, Thormanby, YO6 3NN. ☎ (01845) 501417 • Map 100/527698 • BB **B/C** • D1 T1 F1 • 1-12 NX • B D S 🛁 • SC also. Food nearby

■ EAST HESLERTON (Malton)
WOLDS WAY

Elizabeth Lumley, Manor Farm, YO17 8RN. ☎ (01944) 728268 • Map 101/926767 • BB **B** • F2 • 4-10 • B D S 🛁 • 2Cr/C • Food nearby

■ EGTON BRIDGE

Mr & Mrs D White, Broom House, Broom House Lane, YO21 1XD. ☎ (01947) 895279 • Map 94/796054 • BB **B/C** • D1 T1 F1 • 1-12 • B D S R 🛁 • SC also

■ FARNDALE (York)

Mrs M Featherstone, Keysbeck Farm, YO6 6UZ. ☎ (01751) 433221 • Map 100/665950 • BB **A** • EM book first £6, 6-7pm • D2 T1 • 1-12 • V S 🛁

■ FILEY
WOLDS WAY

Seafield Hotel, 9/11 Rutland Street, YO14 9JA. ☎ (01723) 513715 • Map 101/117804 • BB **C** • EM £5.50, 6pm • S2 D4 T1 F7 • 1-12 NX • V B D S R • 3Cr/C • Small groups also

Windmill House, Malton Road, Hunmanby, YO14 0PG. ☎ (01723) 891459 • Map 101/091770 • BB **B** • EM book first £6.50 upwards, from 6.30pm • T1 F1 • 1-12 NX • V D S R 🛁

■ GLAISDALE (Whitby)
COAST TO COAST WALK

Jean & Andy Hogben, Sycamore Dell, Dale Road, YO21 2PZ. ☎ (01947) 897345 • Map 94/769048 • BB **B** • S2 D2 T1 • 1-12 • D S R

☆ T J & S K Spashett, Red House Farm, YO21 2PZ. ☎ (01947) 897242 • Map 94/772049 • BB **C** • S1 D1 T1 F1 • 1-12 NX • B D S R • SC also

Mrs Jean Lister, Browside Farm, YO21 2PZ. ☎ (01947) 897228 • Map 94/750041 • BB **B** • EM book first £7, 6.30pm • S1 D1 F1 • 4-10 • V D S

Mrs A Mortimer, Hollins Farm, YO21 2PZ. ☎ (01947) 897516 • Map 94/753042 • BB **B** • D1 T1 F1 • 1-12 NX • D S R 🛁 • SC and camping also

Mr Mike Westwood, Arncliffe Arms, YO21 2QL. ☎ (01947) 897209 • Map 94/782054 • BB **B** • EM £3.50, 7-9pm • S1 D2 T2 F1 • 1-12 • V D S R 🛁 • Lift to Walk

Ann Richardson, Egton Banks Farm, YO21 2QP. ☎ (01947) 897289 • Map 94/785065 • BB **B** • EM £7, 6.30pm • S1 T1 F1 • 3-10 • D S R • 1Cr/C • SC caravan also

■ GOATHLAND (Whitby)

☆ Mrs C Chippindale, Barnet House Guest House, YO22 5NG. ☎ (01947) 896201 • Map 94/837011 • BB **C** • EM book first £8, 6.30pm • D3 T3 F1 • 3-11 NX • V D S R

Mrs V MacCaig, Prudon House, YO22 5AN. ☎ (01947) 896368 • Map 94/830099 • BB **C** • EM book first £9, 7pm • D4 T2 F3 • 1-12 NX • V B D S R 🛁

Mr & Mrs K Laflin, Fairhaven Hotel, The Common, YO22 5AN. ☎ (01947) 896361 • Map 94/830099 • BB **C** • EM £10, 7pm • S1 D3 T2 F3 • 1-12 NX • V B D S R 🛁 • 2Cr

■ GRASSINGTON (Skipton)
DALES WAY

☆ R M Richardson, Foresters Arms, Main Street, BD23 5AA. ☎ (01756) 752349 • Map 98/003642 • BB **C** • EM £6, 6-8.30pm • S1 D4 F2 • 1-12 NX • V B 🛁 • List/App

Mr G Berry, Springroyd House, 8a Station Road, BD23 5NQ. ☎ (01756) 752473 • Map 98/001639 • BB **B** • D1 T1 • 1-12 • Ⓓ Ⓢ 🐾

Mrs Trewartha, Mayfield, Low Mill Lane, BD23 5BX. ☎ (01756) 753052 • Map 98/007633 • BB **B/C** • D2 T1 F1 • 1-12 • Ⓑ Ⓓ Ⓢ 🐾 Ⓜ

Mrs I Wallace, Craiglands, 1 Brooklyn, Threshfield, BD23 5ER. ☎ (01756) 752093 • Map 98/998639 • BB **C/D** • EM book first £10.50, 6.30pm • S1 D2 T1 • 1-12 NX • Ⓥ Ⓑ Ⓓ Ⓢ • 2Cr/C

■ **GREAT AYTON (Middlesbrough)**
CLEVELAND WAY

Hazel Petch, 1 Park Rise, TS9 6ND. ☎ (01642) 722436 • Map 93/562106 • BB **B/C** • D1 T1 • 1-12 NX • Ⓑ Ⓓ Ⓢ Ⓡ • 2Cr/C

Mr & Mrs Houghton, Eskdale Cottage, 31 Newton Road, TS9 6DT. ☎ (01642) 724306 • Map 93/563112 • BB **B** • EM book first £9, 6.30pm • T2 • 1-12 NX • Ⓥ Ⓑ Ⓓ Ⓢ Ⓡ

■ **GREAT BROUGHTON (Middlesbrough)**
CLEVELAND WAY & COAST TO COAST WALK

☆ Mrs M Sutcliffe, Ingle Hill, Great Broughton, Stokesley, TS9 7ER. ☎ (01642) 712449 • Map 93/548063 • BB **B** • D1 T1 F1 • 1-12 NX • Ⓑ Ⓓ Ⓢ 🐾

Ingle Hill, Gt Broughton
Stokesley, Middlesbrough

Friendly welcome and very comfortable accommodation. Spectacular views of Cleveland Hills. Sun Lounge. Home cooking, Tea on arrival. CH & open fire, TVs. Drying facilities. Near village inns. Transport can be arranged back to C to C. Cleveland Way Walks. "Home from Home".

Margaret Sutcliffe
Telephone: 01642 712449

☆ Mrs S Mead, Hilton House, 52 High Street, TS9 7EG. ☎ (01642) 712526 • Map 93/547062 • BB **B** • D1 T2 • 1-12 NX • Ⓑ Ⓓ Ⓢ

HILTON HOUSE

Great Broughton, Stokesley

15 years caring for walkers. We offer tea and home-baking on arrival, drying, comfortable sitting room with many books, good beds, excellent breakfast, transport to path. Friendly atmosphere in lovely sandstone house near shop, pub, packhorse drop. No smoking.

Shirley Mead   **01642 712526**

Don Robinson, Holme Farm, 12 The Holme, TS9 7HF. ☎ (01642) 712345 • Map 93/546062 • BB **B** • D2 T2 • 1-12 • Ⓓ Ⓢ

Mrs Jean Noble, 4 Manor Grove, TS9 7AJ. ☎ (01642) 712291 • Map 93/537060 • BB **B** • S2 D1 T1 • 3-10 NX • Ⓑ Ⓢ Ⓡ

■ **GRINTON (Richmond)**
COAST TO COAST WALK

Mrs K Brown, Scarr House, DL11 6JA. ☎ (01748) 884479 • Map 98/047985 • BB **B** • D1 T1 • 5-3 • Ⓓ 🐾

■ **GROSMONT (Whitby)**
COAST TO COAST WALK

Mr B Atha, Hazelwood, Front Street, YO22 5QE. ☎ (01947) 895292 • Map 94/829052 • BB **B** • S1 D2 T2 • 3-12 NX • Ⓑ Ⓓ Ⓢ 🐾

3 New Houses, Eskdaleside, YO22 5PP. ☎ (01947) 095495 • Map 94/835054 • BB **B** • T1 • 1-12 • Ⓑ Ⓓ Ⓢ Ⓡ

■ **HARROGATE**

Mrs E Barker, Barker's Guest House, 202/204 Kings Road, HG1 5JG. ☎ (01423) 568494 • Map 104/304563 • BB **C** • S1 D1 F/T/D1 • 1-12 NX • Ⓑ Ⓓ Ⓢ Ⓡ 🐾 • 3Cr • Food nearby

Sylvia Barnes, Amadeus Vegetarian Hotel, 115 Franklin Road, HG1 5EN. ☎ (01423) 505151 • Map 104/303560 • BB **C/D** • EM book first £13, 7.30pm • S1 D1 T2 F1 • 1-12 NX • Ⓥ Ⓑ Ⓓ Ⓢ Ⓡ 🐾

■ **HAWES**
PENNINE WAY

Mrs L Ward, East House, Gayle Lane, DL8 3RZ. ☎ (01969) 667405 • Map 98/871892 • BB **B** • S1 D1 T1 • 3-11 • Ⓑ Ⓓ Ⓢ • 2Cr/C

Mrs S McGregor, Gayle Laithe, DL8 3RR. ☎ (01969) 667397 • Map 98/869896 • BB **B** • S1 D1 T1 • 3-11 • Ⓓ Ⓜ

☆ Gordon Sleightholm, White Hart Inn, Main Street, DL8 3QL. ☎ (01969) 667259 • Map 98/875897 • BB **B/C** • EM £6, 7-8.30pm • S1 D4 T2 • 2-11 • Ⓥ Ⓓ Ⓢ 🐾 • 1Cr/App

---

WHITE HART INN

SITUATED ON THE PENNINE WAY

Main Street, Hawes DL8 3QL
Tel. Wensleydale (01969) 667259

Small country inn with a friendly welcome, offering home-cooked meals using local produce. An ideal centre for exploring the Yorkshire Dales. Bed & breakfast from £17.50. Parking.   Ⓔ Approved

---

☆ See Display Advertisement

HAWES (CONTINUED)

Steppe Haugh Guest House, Town Head, DL8 3RH. ☎ (01969) 667645 • Map 98/869898 • BB B/D • EM book first £13, 7.30pm • S1 D4 T1 • 1-12 • Ⓥ Ⓑ Ⓓ Ⓢ ⬛ • 2Cr/C

Old Station House, Hardraw Road, DL8 3NL. ☎ (01969) 667785 • Map 98/875898 • BB C • D1 T2 • 1-12 NX • Ⓑ Ⓓ Ⓢ Ⓜ • 2Cr/HC

Mrs F Garnett, The Bungalow, Spring Bank, DL8 3NW. ☎ (01969) 667209 • Map 98/875897 • BB C • D2 F1 • 4-10 • Ⓑ Ⓓ Ⓢ ⬛ Ⓜ

Mrs Gwen Clark, Ebor Guest House, Burtersett Road, DL8 3NT. ☎ (01969) 667337 • Map 98/876897 • BB B/C • S1 D2 T1 • 1-12 NX • Ⓑ Ⓓ Ⓢ ⬛ • 2Cr

Mrs M C Guy, Halfway House, DL8 3LL. ☎ (01969) 667442 • Map 98/865902 • BB B • D1 T1 • 2-11 • Ⓓ Ⓢ ⬛

Chris Taplin, Stonehouse Hotel, Sedbusk, DL8 3PT. ☎ (01969) 667571 • Map 98/879909 • BB D • EM £16.50, 7-8pm • S1 D8 T7 F2 • 2-12 • Ⓥ Ⓑ Ⓓ Ⓢ ⬛ • 3Cr/C

Mrs Gladys Ramsden, Beech House, DL8 3NP. ☎ (01969) 667486 • Map 98/876897 • BB B • D1 T1 • 4-11 • Ⓓ Ⓢ Ⓜ • List

☆ F Bedford, Cocketts Hotel, Market Place, DL8 3RD. ☎ (01969) 667312 • Map 98/871898 • BB D • EM from £12, 7pm • D6 T2 • 2-12 NX • Ⓥ Ⓑ Ⓓ Ⓢ • 3Cr/HC

HAWES, WENSLEYDALE

COCKETT'S HOTEL

NORTH YORKSHIRE

COCKETT'S HOTEL is a 17th Century stone-built hotel in the heart of North Yorkshire National Park. Pennine Way passes through Hawes with many walks to suit everyone.

• 8 ensuite rooms
• Excellent food
Telephone 01969 667312

HIGHLY COMMENDED

■ HAWNBY (Helmsley)

Sarah Wood, Easterside Farm, Hawnby, York, YO6 5QT. ☎ (01439) 798277 • Map 100/552895 • BB C • EM book first £12, 6.30pm • D1 T1 F1 • 1-12 NX • Ⓑ Ⓓ Ⓢ • 2Cr/C

■ HEBDEN (Grassington, Skipton)
DALES WAY

Mrs P J Kitching, Court Croft, Church Lane, BD23 5DX. ☎ (01756) 753406 • Map 98/026630 • BB B • T2 • 1-12 • Ⓓ ⬛

■ HELMSLEY (York)
CLEVELAND WAY

Mrs M L Houlston, 20 Ashdale Road, YO6 5DB. ☎ (01439) 770324 • Map 100/616837 • BB B • S1 F1 • 1-11 NX • Ⓓ Ⓢ ⬛

Mrs H O'Neil, Ashberry, 41 Ashdale Road, YO6 5DE. ☎ (01439) 770488 • Map 100/616838 • BB B • S1 D1 T1 • 1-12 NX • Ⓓ Ⓢ ⬛

Carlton Lodge, Bondgate, YO6 5EY. ☎ (01439) 770557 • Map 100/614839 • BB D • EM £12, 7-8.30pm • D8 T3 F1 • 1-12 • Ⓥ Ⓑ Ⓓ Ⓢ ⬛ • 3Cr/C • Groups also

■ HORTON-IN-RIBBLESDALE (Settle)
PENNINE WAY

J Wagstaff, Wagi's, Townend Cottage, BD24 0EX. ☎ (01729) 860320 • Map 98/812724 • BB C • D1 T2 • 1-12 • Ⓑ Ⓓ Ⓢ Ⓡ ⬛

Mrs M Pilkington, Middle Studfold Farm, BD24 0ER. ☎ (01729) 860236 • Map 98/813704 • BB B • EM book first £7.50, 7-7.30pm • S1 D1 T1 F1 • 1-12 • Ⓥ Ⓓ Ⓢ Ⓡ ⬛

Frank & Margaret Lane, The Rowe House, BD24 0HT. ☎ (01729) 860212 • Map 98/804729 • BB C • D2 T2 • 3-11 • Ⓑ Ⓓ Ⓢ Ⓡ

☆ Margaret Kenyon, South House Farm, BD24 0HU. ☎ (01729) 860271 • Map 98/786741 • BB B • EM book first £9, 6.30pm • D2 T1 F1 • 1-12 NX • Ⓥ Ⓓ Ⓢ Ⓡ ⬛

SOUTH HOUSE FARM
Horton-in-Ribblesdale, Settle, North Yorks BD24 0HU

Farmhouse Bed and Breakfast, evening meal optional. Centre of Three Peaks area with lovely moorland views. Lounge and colour TV. Open fire. Central heating. Open all year.

Telephone Margaret Kenyon
Horton-in-Ribblesdale (01729) 860271

Colin & Joan Horsfall, Studfold House, BD24 0ER. ☎ (01729) 860200 • Map 98/812701 • BB B • EM book first £7.50, 6.30pm • D2 T1 F1 • 1-12 NX • Ⓥ Ⓓ Ⓡ ⬛ • SC also

Michael & Tricia Johnson, The Golden Lion Hotel, BD24 0HB. ☎ (01729) 860206 • Map 98/807721 • BB **B/C** • EM £8, 7-9.30pm • S1 D2 T2 • 1-12 NX • Ⓥ Ⓑ Ⓓ Ⓡ

■ **HUBBERHOLME (Skipton)**
DALES WAY

Mrs Gill Huck, Church Farm, BD23 5JE. ☎ (01756) 760240 • Map 98/935773 • BB **B** • T1 F1 • 1-12 • Ⓓ

☆ The George Inn, BD23 5JE. ☎ (01756) 760223 • Map 98/935773 • BB **B/C/D** • EM £5.25-£12, 6.30-9pm • D2 T2 F2 • 1-12 • Ⓥ Ⓑ Ⓓ 👢 • SC also and bunkbarn nearby

---

The George Inn

STONE FLAGGED FLOORS AND 16TH CENTURY CHARM
IN THE HEART OF YORKSHIRE'S WALKING COUNTRY
AND RIGHT ON THE DALES WAY.

HOME COOKED FOOD • TRADITIONAL ALES •
ACCOMMODATION • DRYING FACILITIES

Hubberholme, Skipton, North Yorks BD23 5JE
Telephone & Fax 01756 760223

■ **HUGGATE (York)**

Peter & Patricia Elliott, The Wolds Inn, Driffield Road, YO4 2YH. ☎ (01377) 288217 • Map 106/882550 • BB **C** • EM £9, 7-9.30pm • D2 T1 • 1-12 • Ⓥ Ⓑ 👢 Ⓜ

■ **HUTTON-LE-HOLE**

The Barn Hotel, YO6 6UA. ☎ (01751) 417311 • Map 100,94/705900 • BB **C/D** • EM £11, 7.30pm • S2 D4 T1 F1 • 1-12 NX • Ⓥ Ⓑ Ⓓ Ⓢ 👢 • 2Cr/C

■ **INGLEBY ARNCLIFFE (Northallerton)**
COAST TO COAST WALK & CLEVELAND WAY

Mrs E Backhouse, Monks House, DL6 3ND. ☎ (01609) 882294 • Map 93/449007 • BB **B** • S1 D1 • 3-10 • Ⓑ Ⓓ Ⓢ

■ **INGLEBY CROSS (Northallerton)**
COAST TO COAST WALK

North York Moors Adventure Centre, Park House, DL6 3PE. ☎ (01609) 882571 • Map 99/453995 • BB **B** • EM book first £6, 6pm • S3 D3 T3 F2 • 1-12 NX • Ⓥ Ⓓ 👢 • Groups also

■ **INGLETON (Carnforth, Lancs)**

Springfield Private Hotel, Main Street, LA6 3HJ. ☎ (015242) 41280 • Map 98/695732 • BB **C** • EM £10, 6.30pm • D3 T1 F1 • 1-12 NX • Ⓥ Ⓑ Ⓓ Ⓢ 👢 • 3Cr/App

Mrs Anne Brown, Ingleborough View Guest House, Main Street, LA6 3HH. ☎ (015242) 41523 • Map 98/695732 • BB **B** • D2 T1 F1 • 1-12 NX • Ⓑ Ⓓ • 2Cr/C

Mrs P A Garner, Bridge End Guest House, Mill Lane, LA6 3EP. ☎ (015242) 41413 • Map 98/695733 • BB **B/C** • EM £4 • S1 D2 T1 F1 • 1-12 • Ⓥ Ⓑ Ⓓ • 2Cr

Mrs Mollie Bell, Langber Country Guest House, Tatterthorne Road, LA6 3DT. ☎ (015242) 41587 • Map 98/689709 • BB **B** • EM £7, 6.30pm • S1 D2 T2 F2 • 1-12 NX • Ⓥ Ⓑ Ⓓ Ⓢ Ⓡ 👢 • 2Cr

☆ Ferncliffe Country Guest House, LA6 3HJ. ☎ (015242) 42405 • Map 98/695732 • BB **C/D** • EM £12.5, 6.30-8.30pm • D1 T4 • 2-11 • Ⓥ Ⓑ Ⓓ 👢 • 3Cr/C

Ferncliffe
Country
Guest House
ETB Commended

A lovely detached stone built house dated 1897. All rooms en-suite with T.V. Excellent food by owner/chef. Ideally situated for the Dales & the Lakes.
Main St. Ingleton Via Carnforth LA6 3HJ
Tel. 015242 42405

Mr R B Sanbrook, The Craven Heifer Inn, LA6 3HG. ☎ (015242) 41427 • Map 98/692729 • BB **B** • EM from £5, 7-9.30pm • D2 F1 • 1-12 • Ⓥ Ⓑ Ⓓ 👢

■ **KELD (Richmond)**
PENNINE WAY & COAST TO COAST WALK

☆ Doreen Whitehead, East Stonesdale Farm, DL11 6LJ. ☎ (01748) 886374 • Map 91/895012 • BB **B** • EM book first £9, 7.30pm • S1 D1 T2 • 3-8 NX • Ⓥ Ⓑ Ⓓ Ⓢ 👢

EAST STONESDALE FARM
KELD, RICHMOND, N YORKS, DL11 6LJ

Farmhouse Bed & Breakfast on Coast to Coast Walk, Pennine Way & Herriot Way.
ALSO AVAILABLE: the original Coast to Coast Accommodation Guide (1997 edition due out 14th January price £2 + sae 5" x 7")

DOREEN WHITEHEAD
TEL 01748 886374

■ **KETTLEWELL (Skipton)**
DALES WAY

Mrs Lorna Thornbrow, Lynburn, BD23 5RF. ☎ (01756) 760803 • Map 98/970720 • BB **C** • D1 T1 • 3-10 • Ⓓ

Mr & Mrs R Elliott, Langcliffe Country Guest House, BD23 5RJ. ☎ (01756) 760243/760896 • Map 98/969723 • BB **D** • EM £16, 7pm • D3 T2 F1 • 1-12 • Ⓥ Ⓑ Ⓢ 👢 • 4Cr/C

☆ See Display Advertisement

■ KILBURN (York)
CLEVELAND WAY

Mrs C Thompson, Church Farm, YO6 4AH. ☎ (01347) 868318 • Map 100/516796 • BB **B** • EM book first £7 • T1 F1 • 1-12 NX • Ⓥ Ⓓ ⚲

■ KILDALE (Whitby)
CLEVELAND WAY

A Addison, Bankside Cottage, YO21 2RT. ☎ (01642) 723259 • Map 94/604101 • BB **B** • EM £10, 7pm • D1 T1 F1 • 1-12 NX • Ⓥ Ⓓ Ⓢ Ⓡ

☆ M Gutteridge, Glebe Cottage, Station Road, YO21 2RH. ☎ (01642) 724470/712793 • Map 94/606095 • BB **C** • EM £8, 5.30-7pm • S1 T2 • 1-12 • Ⓥ Ⓓ Ⓢ Ⓡ ⚲ • SC also

Glebe Cottage (Cleveland Way)
Kildale, North York Moors YO21 2RH

Lovely restored stone built longhouse in idyllic setting. Directly on the Cleveland Way.
This delightful cottage is a perfect centre for endless excellent walking and off-road cycling, with the added facility of superb home cooking with vegetarian dishes a speciality.

☎ **01642 724470/712793**

■ LEYBURN

Anne Suttill, Coverlea, Carlton-Coverdale, DL8 4AY. ☎ (01969) 640248 • Map 99/064847 • BB **B** • D1 F1 • 2-11 • Ⓓ ⚲ Ⓜ

Mrs E Allinson, Middleham House, Carlton, DL8 4BB. ☎ (01969) 640645 • Map 99/060840 • BB **B** • EM book first £10, 6pm • D2 T1 • 3-10 • Ⓓ Ⓢ ⚲

☆ Golden Lion Hotel, Market Square, DL8 5AS. ☎ (01969) 622161 • Map 99/115905 • BB **D** • EM £10.50, 7-9pm • S3 D5 T3 F4 • 1-12 NX • Ⓥ Ⓑ Ⓓ ⚲ • 3Cr/C • Disabled facilities

GOLDEN LION HOTEL

A traditional market square inn specialising in comfortable en suite accommodation, good food served in friendly surroundings. Disabled facilities, lift to all floors. A great centre for Dales walkers.
References supplied. **Tel. 01969 622161**

■ LITTON (Skipton)
DALES WAY

Lyn & Bryan Morgan, Park Bottom, BD23 5QJ. ☎ (01756) 770235 • Map 98/904740 • BB **C/D** • D1 T2 F1 • 1-12 NX • Ⓑ Ⓓ ⚲

■ LOW ROW (Richmond)
COAST TO COAST WALK

☆ Ann Chamberlain, Rowleth End, DL11 6PY. ☎ (01748) 886327 • Map 98/972974 • BB **C** • EM book first £8, 6.30pm • D2 F2 • 1-12 • Ⓥ Ⓓ Ⓢ ⚲ • SC caravan also

ROWLETH END GUEST HOUSE
Low Row, Richmond, N Yorks

Our family-run guesthouse offers you comfortable, quiet accommodation. Guests' lounge and dining-room have open fires. All bedrooms CH with washbasin and shaving socket. Home cooking, friendly service and the beauty of Swaledale can be yours. Why not ring Ann Chamberlain and reserve a room.

Tel. (01748) 886327

■ MALHAM (Skipton)
PENNINE WAY

Sparth House Hotel, BD23 4DA. ☎ (01729) 830315 • Map 98/901628 • BB **C/D** • EM £13.50, 7.30pm • S1 D6 T3 • 1-12 • Ⓥ Ⓑ Ⓓ Ⓢ • Groups also

R Boatwright, Beck Hall Guest House, BD23 4DJ. ☎ (01729) 830332 • Map 98/898631 • BB **B/C** • S1 D7 T4 F2 • 1-12 NX • Ⓑ

Mrs Sharp, The Miresfield Farm, BD23 4DA. ☎ (01729) 830414 • Map 98/901628 • BB **D** • EM £10, 6.30pm • S1 D6 T6 F2 • 1-12 • Ⓑ Ⓓ Ⓢ ⚲ • 3Cr • Groups also

G & H J Boocock, The Buck Inn, BD23 4DA. ☎ (01729) 830317 • Map 98/901628 • BB **D** • EM £10, 7-9pm • D6 T2 F2 • 1-12 • Ⓥ Ⓑ Ⓓ • 3Cr/C • SC also

■ MALTON

☆ Mrs Janet Hawes, Leonard House, 45 Old Maltongate, YO17 0EH. ☎ (01653) 695711/692033/(0378) 740645 • Map 100/788717 • BB **B/C** • D1 T2 F1 • 1-12 NX • Ⓑ Ⓓ Ⓢ Ⓡ

Leonard House
45 Old Maltongate, Malton YO17 0EH

Highly Recommended Spacious Georgian House, the ideal base for N.Yorks Moors/Wolds/Ryedale, York and East Coast, 5 mins bus/rail. Large bedrooms, TV, CH, tea/coffee, washbasins, parking & gardens.
Private bathroom available. Non-smoking
Tel: Janet Hawes 01653 695711/692033
Mobile (0378) 740645

■ MARKET WEIGHTON (York)
WOLDS WAY

Mrs D M Stephenson, Arras Farmhouse, Arras, YO4 3RN. ☎ (01430) 872404 • Map 106/924417 • BB **B/C** • EM book first £7, 6.15pm • D2 T1 • 1-12 NX • Ⓥ Ⓑ Ⓓ • List

■ MASHAM (Ripon)

Bank Villa Guest House, HG4 4DB. ☎ (01765) 689605 • Map 99/224810 • BB **C** • EM book first £15, 7.30pm • D4 T3 • 4-10 • Ⓥ Ⓑ Ⓓ Ⓢ 🐾

■ MIDDLEHAM (Leyburn)

☆ Mrs Pauline Robinson, The Priory Guest House, DL8 4QC. ☎ (01969) 623279 • Map 99/127877 • BB **B/C** • EM £9, 6.30pm • S2 D3 T2 F1 • 3-11 • Ⓥ Ⓑ Ⓓ Ⓢ 🐾 • 3Cr/App

■ NEWBIGGIN-IN-BISHOPDALE (Leyburn)

Mrs D M Proctor, Newbiggin House, DL8 3TD. ☎ (01969) 663583 • Map 98/000857 • BB **B** • S1 D1 T1 • 2-11 • Ⓓ Ⓢ 🐾 • 1Cr/C • SC also

■ NORTHALLERTON
COAST TO COAST WALK

Mrs M M Pearson, Lovesome Hill Farm, Lovesome Hill, DL6 2PB. ☎ (01609) 772311 • Map 99/360997 • BB **C** • EM book first £9.95, 7-7.30pm • S1 D1 T1 F1 • 3-10 NX • Ⓥ Ⓑ Ⓓ Ⓢ • 2Cr/C • Camping Barn also

---
VEGETARIANS
Many establishments do a veggie breakfast even if they don't do an evening meal

---

■ OSMOTHERLEY (Northallerton)
CLEVELAND WAY & COAST TO COAST WALK

Mr Allan Abbott, Vane House, 11A North End, DL6 3BA. ☎ (01609) 883448 • Map 99/456974 • BB **B** • T3 • 1-12 • Ⓓ Ⓢ 🐾 Ⓜ

☆ Dr R I Bainbridge, Quintana House, Back Lane, DL6 3BJ. ☎ (01609) 883258 • Map 99/457974 • BB **B** • EM book first £8, 7pm • D1 T1 • 1-12 NX • Ⓥ Ⓓ Ⓢ • List/C

Marion Wood, Oak Garth Farm, North End, DL6 3BH. ☎ (01609) 883314 • Map 99/456976 • BB **B** • D1 T1 • 1-11 • Ⓑ Ⓓ Ⓢ 🐾 Ⓜ

■ PATELEY BRIDGE

Mrs J Lubeck, Windy Nook, Wath-in-Nidderdale, HG3 5PL. ☎ (01423) 711088 • Map 99/148675 • BB **A/B** • S1 D1 • 5-9 • Ⓓ Ⓢ

☆ Peter & Rita Briggs, Roslyn Hotel, 9 King St, HG3 5AT. ☎ (01423) 711374 • Map 99/157656 • BB **B/C** • EM £9, 7pm • D3 T1 F2 • 1-12 • Ⓥ Ⓑ Ⓓ • 3Cr/App

Mrs Pauline Shaw, Woodlands Bewerley, HG3 5HS. ☎ (01423) 711175 • Map 99/157648 • BB **B** • D1 T1 • 1-12 NX • Ⓑ Ⓓ Ⓢ

■ PICKERING

Mrs R Metcalf, 103 Westgate, YO18 8BB. ☎ (01751) 472500 • Map 100/793840 • BB **B** • D2 T1 • 1-12 NX • Ⓡ

Mrs M Rayner, Kirkham Garth, Whitby Road, YO18 7AT. ☎ (01751) 474931 • Map 100/800840 • BB **B** • S1 D1 T1 F1 • 1-12 • Ⓓ Ⓢ Ⓡ

☆ Ms E Bleasdale, The Old Manse Guest House, Middleton Road, YO18 8AL. ☎ (01751) 476484 • Map 100/792841 • BB **C** • EM book first £10, 6.30-7pm • D5 T2 F1 • 3-11 • Ⓥ Ⓑ Ⓓ Ⓢ

The
Old Manse
GUEST HOUSE
Middleton Road, Pickering,
North Yorkshire YO18 8AL
Tel. (01751) 476484
Fax (01751) 477124

Warm comfortable Guest House set in own grounds with private car park. All rooms en-suite with colour TV and tea-making facilities. Just 4 minutes walk to North York Moors Steam Railway.
Ideal base for walking and touring.

☆ Keith & Judy Russell, Heathcote House, 100 Eastgate, YO18 7DW. ☎ (01751) 476991 • Map 100/802836 • BB **C** • EM book first £12, 7pm • D3 T2 • 1-12 NX • Ⓥ Ⓑ Ⓓ Ⓢ Ⓡ Ⓜ • 2Cr/C

AN INVITATION TO STAY AT

Heathcote House

• L I C E N C E D •

100 Eastgate, Pickering YO18 7DW

Enjoy a relaxing, care-free stay in the friendly atmosphere of R.A.member's delightful home. For your comfort, each bedroom has en-suite facilities, colour TV and hostess tray. Delicious dinners and packed lunches available. Totally non-smoking. Secluded parking.

For colour brochure
Tel: 01751 476991

COMMENDED

VISA

MasterCard

EUROCARD

Jackie Heaton, Swan Cottage, Newton upon Rawcliffe, YO18 8QA. ☎ (01751) 472502 • Map 100,94/812907 • BB **B** • EM book first £8.50, 7-8pm • S1 D1 T/F1 • 1-12 • Ⓥ Ⓓ Ⓢ Ⓡ ♨ Ⓜ

■ **RAISGILL (Yockenthwaite)**
DALES WAY

☆ Mrs S M Middleton, Low Raisgill Cottage, BD23 5JQ. ☎ (01756) 760351 • Map 98/906786 • BB **C** • EM book first £12, 6.30-7.30pm • S1 D1 T1 F1 • 1-12 • Ⓥ Ⓑ Ⓓ Ⓢ ♨

■ **RAMSGILL (Pateley Bridge)**

Mrs M Crosse, Longside House, HG3 5RH. ☎ (01423) 755207 • Map 99/119718 • BB **C/D** • D1 T1 F1 • 2-11 • Ⓑ Ⓓ • List

■ **RAVENSCAR (Scarborough)**
CLEVELAND WAY & COAST TO COAST WALK

☆ Mrs J Greenfield, Smugglers Rock, Country Guest House, YO13 0ER. ☎ (01723) 870044 • Map 94/975006 • BB **C** • EM book first £9, 6.30pm • S2 D3 T2 F1 • 3-11 • Ⓥ Ⓑ Ⓓ Ⓢ ♨ • 2Cr • SC also

☆ Mrs B Leach, Bide-a-While, 3 Lorings Road, YO13 0LY. ☎ (01723) 870643 • Map 94/984011 • BB **B** • EM £6, 5-6.30pm • D3 F2 • 1-12 • Ⓥ Ⓓ • List/App

☆ Geoff & Rita Kirkham, Crag Hill, Ravenhall Road, YO13 0NA. ☎ (01723) 870925 • Map 94/979012 • BB **B/C** • EM £9, 6.30pm • D3 T2 F2 • 1-12 NX • Ⓥ Ⓑ Ⓓ Ⓢ ♨ • 3Cr/App

■ **RIBBLEHEAD (Ingleton, Carnforth, Lancashire)**
DALES WAY & PENNINE WAY

☆ Neil & June Warwick, Station Inn, LA6 3AS. ☎ (015242) 41274 • Map 98/783801 • BB **B/C** • EM £5.50, 6.30-8.30pm • D3 T1 F1 • 1-12 • Ⓥ Ⓑ Ⓓ Ⓡ • App • SC also

■ **RICHMOND**
COAST TO COAST WALK

Mrs S M Lee, 27 Hurgill Road, DL10 4AR. ☎ (01748) 824092 • Map 92/169011 • BB **C** • S1 D1 T2 • 1-12 NX • Ⓓ Ⓢ • List

Mrs D M Irwin, Hillcrest Sleegill, DL10 4RH. ☎ (01748) 823280 • Map 92/170003 • BB **B** • S1 D2 T1 • 4-10 • Ⓓ Ⓢ

■ **ROBIN HOOD'S BAY (Whitby)**
CLEVELAND WAY & COAST TO COAST WALK

Clarence Dene, Station Road, YO22 4RL. ☎ (01947) 880272 • Map 94/951053 • BB **B/C** • EM book first £8, 6.30-7.30pm • D2 T1 • 1-12 • Ⓥ Ⓑ Ⓓ Ⓢ

Mrs G Luker, Meadowfield, Mount Pleasant North, YO22 4RE. ☎ (01947) 880564 • Map 94/951054 • BB **B** • S1 D3 T2 • 1-12 NX • Ⓑ Ⓓ Ⓢ • Vegan & veg. breakfasts avail.

Victoria Hotel, Station Road, YO22 4RL. ☎ (01947) 880205 • Map 94/951053 • BB **D** • S1 D6 T2 F2 • 1-12 NX • Ⓥ Ⓑ Ⓓ

Richard & Julia Price, Glen-Lyn, Station Road, YO22 4RA. ☎ (01947) 880391 • Map 94/950054 • BB **B** • EM book first £8, 6.30-7.30pm • S1 D2 • 1-12 NX • Ⓥ Ⓓ Ⓢ

■ **ROSEDALE ABBEY (Pickering)**

Mrs S Smith, Low Bell End Farm, YO18 8RE. ☎ (01751) 417127 • Map 100,94/717970 • BB **B** • EM book first £7, 7pm • D1 T1 F1 • 1-12 NX • Ⓓ Ⓢ 🐾

☆ Mrs Linda Sugars, Sevenford House, Thorgill, YO18 8SE. ☎ (01751) 417283 • Map 100,94/724949 • BB **C** • S1 D1 T1 • 1-12 • Ⓑ Ⓓ Ⓢ • 2Cr/HC • SC also. Food nearby

■ **RUNSWICK BAY (Saltburn)**
CLEVELAND WAY

Mrs S Smith, 10 Hinderwell Lane, TS13 5HR. ☎ (01947) 840758 • Map 94/791168 • BB **A** • D1 T2 • 3-10 • Ⓓ 🐾 • Food nearby

☆ Jennifer Smith, Cockpit House, The Old Village, TS13 5HU. ☎ (01947) 840504/603047 • Map 94/810161 • BB **B** • T2 • 3-10 • Ⓓ 🐾

NORTH YORKSHIRE   B&B ACCOMMODATION

☆ See Display Advertisement

■ SALTBURN-BY-THE-SEA
CLEVELAND WAY

☆ Albany Guest House, 15 Pearl Street, TS12 1DU.
☎ (01287) 622221 • Map 94/664215 • BB **B** • S1 D1
T1 • 1-12 NX • Ⓓ Ⓢ Ⓡ • 1Cr

ALBANY
GUEST HOUSE
**15 Pearl Street, Saltburn by the Sea,
Cleveland TS12 1DU**

Central position, close to shops, sea and moors.
All rooms have colour TVs and coffee/
tea-making facilities. Member of the English
Tourist Board (1 crown).

Tel. Guisborough (01287) 622221

■ SANDSEND (Whitby)
CLEVELAND WAY

Bungalow Hotel, YO21 3TG. ☎ (01947) 893272 •
Map 94/859128 • BB **D** • EM £12 • S6 D5 T3 F10 • 3-
11 • Ⓥ Ⓑ Ⓓ Ⓡ 🐾 • Groups also

■ SCARBOROUGH
CLEVELAND WAY

Mrs P Cooper, Capria Guest House, 16 The Dene
Peasholm, YO12 7NJ. ☎ (01723) 370234 • Map
101/036891 • BB **B** • EM book first £5.50, 5.30pm •
S1 D1 T1 F1 • 2-11 • Ⓥ Ⓑ Ⓓ Ⓢ Ⓡ • No single
nights July/August

Brincliffe Edge Private Hotel, 105 Queens Parade,
YO12 7HY. ☎ (01723) 364834 • Map 101/039895 •
BB **C** • EM book first £7, 5.30pm • S1 D6 T2 F2 • 3-
10 • Ⓥ Ⓑ Ⓓ Ⓢ Ⓡ

Ted & Margaret Marsh, Highbank Hotel, 5 Givendale
Road, YO12 6LE. ☎ (01723) 365265 • Map
101/031898 • BB **C** • EM £6.50, 5.30pm • S2 D3 T1
F1 • 1-12 NX • Ⓥ Ⓑ Ⓓ Ⓢ Ⓡ 🐾 Ⓜ • 2Cr/C

■ SELBY

Mr & Mrs J Leake, Hazeldene, 34 Brook Street,
Doncaster Road, YO8 0AR. ☎ (01757) 704809 • Map
105/610321 • BB **B** • S2 D2 T3 F1 • 1-12 NX • Ⓑ Ⓓ
Ⓢ Ⓡ • List/App

■ SETTLE
PENNINE WAY & RIBBLE WAY

Mrs P Houlton, Whitebeam Croft, Duke Street, BD24
9AN. ☎ (01729) 822824 • Map 98/817634 • BB **B** •
T1 F/D1 • 1-12 NX • Ⓓ Ⓢ Ⓡ 🐾 • Food nearby

Mrs S Beecroft, Penmar Court, Duke Street, BD24
9AS. ☎ (01729) 823258 • Map 98/816631 • BB **B** •
S2 D3 T1 • 1-12 NX • Ⓑ Ⓓ Ⓡ 🐾 Ⓜ

☆ The Oast Guest House, 5 Pen-y-Ghent View,
Church Street, BD24 9JJ. ☎ (01729) 822989 • Map
98/817639 • BB **B/C** • EM book first £10, 6.30-7pm •
S1 D2 T3 F1 • 1-12 • Ⓥ Ⓑ Ⓓ Ⓢ Ⓡ • 2Cr

NORTH YORKSHIRE

B&B ACCOMMODATION

---

5 Pen-y-Ghent View
Church Street
Settle
ETB

Margaret and Tony King

AA
Recommended

The Oast Guest House
Ideal for Yorkshire Dales, Lake District, Settle-Carlisle
railway. A warm welcome awaits you. English
traditional cooking. Caters for diets. Rooms have
own showers, basins, some en suite. CH, TV lounge,
licensed, packed lunches. Special Christmas breaks.
Reduced rates for out of season.
Tel. 01729 822989

☆ Whitefriars Country Guest House, Church Street,
BD24 9JD. ☎ (01729) 823753 • Map 98/819637 • BB
C • EM book first £10.50, 7-8pm • S1 D3 T2 F3 • 1-12
NX • Ⓥ Ⓑ Ⓓ Ⓢ Ⓡ • 2Cr/App

Whitefriars
Country Guesthouse
Church Street, Settle
North Yorks BD24 9JD
Delightful 17th Century, family-run,
no-smoking, guesthouse, in spacious
gardens in heart of Settle. Ideal for walking,
touring & cycling, Yorkshire Dales National
Park, and Settle/Carlisle railway.

Tel. Settle (01729) 823753

Greta & Robert Duerden, Liverpool House Guest
House & Tearoom, Chapel Square, BD24 9HR. ☎
(01729) 822247 • Map 98/822635 • BB **C** • S4 D2 T2
• 1-12 • Ⓓ Ⓢ Ⓡ

☆ Golden Lion Hotel, Duke Street, BD24 9DU. ☎
(01729) 822203 • Map 98/819635 • BB **C/D** • EM
£8.50, 6-10pm • S1 D5 T5 • 1-12 • Ⓥ Ⓑ Ⓓ Ⓡ 🐾 •
1Cr/App

Golden Lion Hotel
Duke Street, Settle, North Yorkshire

17th century Coaching
Inn with log fires, in
Settle's bustling market
place. Prime centre for
exploring Yorkshire
Dales, Three Peaks and
5 minutes walk from
Settle-Carlisle Railway.
Groups welcome.

Tel 01729 822203   Fax: 01729 824103

■ SKELTON (Saltburn-by-the-Sea)
CLEVELAND WAY

B Bull, Westerland's Guest House, 27 East Parade,
TS12 2BJ. ☎ (01287) 650690 • Map 94/655185 • BB
B • EM £6, 6.30-7pm • S2 D3 F1 • 3-10 • Ⓥ Ⓑ Ⓓ
Ⓢ Ⓡ 🐾

■ SKIPTON

Highfield Hotel, 58 Keighley Road, BD23 2NB. ☎ (01756) 793182 • Map 103/988512 • BB **C** • EM £7, 6-8pm • S1 D6 T1 F2 • 2-12 NX • Ⓥ Ⓑ Ⓡ 🏷 • 3Cr

Phillis Sapsford, Alton House, 5 Salisbury St, BD23 1NQ. ☎ (01756) 794780 • Map 103/984519 • BB **B** • S1 D2 T2 F2 • 1-12 NX • Ⓑ Ⓓ Ⓢ Ⓡ Ⓜ

■ SLEIGHTS (Whitby)
COAST TO COAST WALK

☆ Pat Beale, Ryedale House, 154 Coach Road, YO22 6EQ. ☎ (01947) 810534 • BB **B/C** • D2 T1 • 3-11 • Ⓑ Ⓓ Ⓢ Ⓡ • 2Cr • SC also

North York Moors National Park
Near Whitby

"Heartbeat" country 3½ miles Whiby, magnificent walking. Relaxing, non-smoking house with high standards. Comfortable beds, private facilities, landscaped gardens. Extensive breakfast menu; snacks, picnics. Regret no pets or young children. Tourist Board member.

Pat Beale, Rydale House, Sleights.
Tel: (01947) 810534

■ STAITHES (Saltburn-by-the-Sea, Cleveland)
CLEVELAND WAY

☆ Betty & Trevor Readman, Captain Cook Inn, 60 Staithes Lane, TS13 5AD. ☎ (01947) 840200 • Map 94/781184 • BB **B/C** • EM £3.50-£9.50, till 9pm • D2 T1 F1 • 1-12 • Ⓥ Ⓑ Ⓓ 🏷

THE CAPTAIN COOK INN
Staithes, North York Moors National Park
Tel. 01947 840200

Friendly family inn in scenic fishing village. H&C, colour TV, tea & coffee making facilities in all rooms.

Five day break with two guided walks from £70 per person (minimum party of 4).

Guided Sunday morning walk and 4-course lunch £8 per person or dawn walk and full English breakfast £6 per person (minimum parties of 4).

■ STARBOTTON (Skipton)
DALES WAY

Mrs A Close, Gill Croft, BD23 5HY. ☎ (01756) 760866 • Map 98/952749 • BB **B** • D2 • 1-12 NX • Ⓓ

■ STOCKTON-ON-FOREST (York)

Mr Mike Cundall, Orillia House, 89 The Village, YO3 9UP. ☎ (01904) 400600/738595 • Map 105,106/656560 • BB **B/C** • EM book first £7.50, 6.30-7pm • D2 T2 F2 • 1-12 • Ⓑ Ⓓ Ⓢ 🏷 • SC also

■ SUMMERBRIDGE (Harrogate)

Mrs J E Smith, Dalriada, Cabin Lane, Dacre Banks, HG3 4EE. ☎ (01423) 780512 • Map 99/196621 • BB **B** • EM book first £6, 6-7pm • D1 T1 • 1-12 NX • Ⓑ Ⓓ Ⓢ 🏷

Alan & Sheila Melville, The Laurels, HG3 4HP. ☎ (01423) 780530 • Map 99/202623 • BB **B** • S1 T2 F1 • 1-12 • Ⓑ Ⓓ Ⓢ 🏷

■ SUTTON BANK (Thirsk)
CLEVELAND WAY

Mrs K M Hope, Hambleton High House, YO7 2HA. ☎ (01845) 597557 • Map 100/523830 • BB **C** • EM £9, from 6pm • D1 T1 F1 • 4-11 • Ⓥ Ⓓ • 1Cr

Mrs J Jeffray, Cote Faw, YO7 2EZ. ☎ (01845) 597363 • Map 100/522829 • BB **B** • S1 D1 F1 • 1-12 NX • Ⓓ Ⓢ • SC also

■ THIRSK

Mrs T Williamson, Thornborough House Farm, South Kilvington, YO7 2NP. ☎ (01845) 522103 • Map 99/426846 • BB **B** • EM book first £9, 6.30pm • S1 D1 T1 F1 • 1-12 • Ⓥ Ⓑ Ⓓ Ⓢ 🏷 • 2Cr/C • SC also

■ THIXENDALE (Malton)
WOLDS WAY

Mrs S Anstey, "Round-The-Bend", YO17 9TG. ☎ (01377) 288237 • Map 100/843610 • BB **C** • S1 D1 F1 • 3-10 • Ⓓ Ⓢ

■ THORNTON DALE (Pickering)

Mrs S Wardell, Tangalwood, Roxby Road, YO18 7SX. ☎ (01751) 74688 • Map 100/832829 • BB **B** • D2 T1 • 3-10 • Ⓑ Ⓓ

■ THWAITE (Richmond)
PENNINE WAY

I & J Danton, Kearton Guest House, DL11 6DR. ☎ (01748) 886277 • Map 98/892982 • BB **C** • EM book first £5, 6.30pm • S1 D3 T7 F2 • 2-12 • Ⓥ Ⓑ Ⓓ 🏷 • List

■ WHITBY
CLEVELAND WAY & COAST TO COAST WALK

Leeway Guest House, 1 Havelock Place, YO21 3ER. ☎ (01947) 602604 • Map 94/896112 • BB **B/C** • EM £8, 6-7pm • S1 D2 T1 F5 • 1-12 NX • Ⓥ Ⓑ Ⓓ Ⓢ Ⓡ • 3Cr/C

☆ Wentworth House, 27 Hudson Street, YO21 3EP. ☎ (01947) 602433 • Map 94/895112 • BB **B/C** • S1 D4 T3 • 1-12 NX • Ⓑ Ⓓ Ⓢ Ⓡ • 2Cr

Wentworth House

27 Hudson Street, Whitby
North Yorkshire YO21 3EP

Enjoy comfortable smoke-free accommodation in our spacious Victorian house. Some rooms en-suite. Traditional and vegetarian food using wholefoods and free range eggs. Full CH. Lounge with CTV. B&B. H&C.

Joy and John Dixon
Tel. Whitby (01947) 602433

☆ Flora & Harry Collett, Ashford, 8 Royal Crescent, YO21 3EJ. ☎ (01947) 602138 • Map 94/894113 • BB **B/C** • S1 D4 T1 F3 • 1-12 NX • Ⓑ Ⓓ Ⓡ 🛇

ASHFORD

8 Royal Crescent, Whitby

A warm and friendly welcome. All bedrooms CH, H&C, tea/coffee, en suite, TV. Situated on the West Cliff with outstanding sea views. An ideal centre for moorland, forest or coastal walks.

Flora & Harry Collett
Tel. Whitby (01947) 602138

Falcon Guest House, 29 Falcon Terrace, YO21 1EH. ☎ (01947) 603507 • Map 94/896106 • BB **B** • D1 T1 F1 • 1-12 • Ⓓ Ⓢ Ⓡ

☆ J & C Gledhill, Prospect Villa, 13 Prospect Hill, YO21 1QE. ☎ (01947) 603118 • Map 94/894105 • BB **B** • EM book first £8.75, 6.30pm • S3 D2 T1 F2 • 1-12 • Ⓑ Ⓓ Ⓢ Ⓡ • Caravan also

Prospect Villa

Janice & Chris Gledhill
13 PROSPECT HILL
WHITBY YO21 1QE
Tel: 01947 603118

A large Victorian house, easy walking distance centre of Whitby.
◆ *Licensed bar* ◆ *TV lounge* ◆ *Dining Room*
◆ *Large bedrooms* ◆ *Breakfasts & Evening meals*
◆ *Open all year including Christmas and New Year*
◆ *Car park*

Abbey House, East Cliff, YO22 4JT. ☎ (01947) 600557 • Map 94/902111 • BB **C/D** • EM £8.50, 7pm • S6 T19 F6 • 1-12 • Ⓥ Ⓓ Ⓢ Ⓡ • Groups also

Mrs R C Woodall, Rosewood, 3 Ocean Road, YO21 3HY. ☎ (01947) 820534 • Map 94/890113 • BB **B** • S1 D2 T1 F1 • 3-11 • Ⓓ Ⓢ Ⓡ • 1Cr/C

☆ Anne & Tom Wheeler, Lansbury Guest House, 29 Hudson Street, YO21 3EP. ☎ (01947) 604821 • Map 94/895112 • BB **C** • EM book first £9, 6pm • S2 D5 T1 • 2-12 NX • Ⓥ Ⓑ Ⓓ Ⓢ Ⓡ • 2Cr/C

LANSBURY GUEST HOUSE
Whitby, N Yorks

Be comfy in our large Victorian Guest House. Bedrooms have CTVs, tea/coffee, H&C — all doubles en suites — a homely lounge complete with real open fire. Just the job for wintery nights. Enjoy good food and a warm welcome — a step from the Cleveland Way. BB/EM, Packed lunches.

Tel 01947 604821   Commended ETB ♨♨

■ YORK

Mrs J Cundall, Wellgarth House, Wetherby Road, Rufforth, YO2 3QB. ☎ (01904) 738592/738595 • Map 105/526514 • BB **B/C** • S1 D3 T2 F1 • 1-12 NX • Ⓑ Ⓓ Ⓢ 🛇 • 2Cr/C

☆ Dairy Wholefood Guest House, 3 Scarcroft Road, YO2 1ND. ☎ (01904) 639367 • Map 105/601509 • BB **B/C** • S1 D2 T1 F2 • 2-11 • Ⓑ Ⓢ Ⓡ 🛇 • List/C

DAIRY
GUESTHOUSE
Traditional and Wholefood

Beautifully appointed Victorian town-house, once the local Dairy! Well equipped cottage-style rooms have colour TV, CD players, hairdryers and hot drink facilities. Some en suite. One four-poster. Informal, non-smoking environment. Traditional or vegetarian B&B from £17pp.

For colour brochure contact Keith Jackman
3 Scarcroft Road, **YORK** YO2 1ND
Telephone (01904) 639367

☆ Priory Hotel, 126/128 Fulford Road, YO1 4BE. ☎ (01904) 625280 • Map 105/607508 • BB **D** • EM £10.50, 6.30-9.30pm • S1 D10 T5 F4 • 1-12 NX • Ⓥ Ⓑ Ⓓ Ⓡ 🛇 • 3Cr

PRIORY HOTEL
126-128 FULFORD ROAD
YORK YO1 4BE
TEL. & FAX (01904) 625280

All rooms with private facilities. Restaurant and bar available. AA and RAC listed. Private car park. Ten minutes riverside walk to city centre.

☆ Mr Tracey, Holmlea Guest House, 6/7 Southlands Road, YO2 1NP. ☎ (01904) 621010 • Map 105/600507 • BB **B** • D4 T2 F3 • 2-11 NX • Ⓑ Ⓓ Ⓢ Ⓡ • 3Cr/C

Holmlea Guest House
6/7 Southlands Road, York
🏵🏵🏵 Commended
★ Lowest price for Ramblers! From £15.

★ Close city and centre and rambling country.

★ Twin/ensuite/double rooms

★ All Satellite TV

★ Top Hotel quality at Ramblers prices

01904 621010

☆ R & C Whitbourn-Hammond, Nunmill House, 85 Bishopthorpe Road, YO2 1NX. ☎ (01904) 634047 • Map 105/601507 • BB **C** • D6 T1 F1 • 2-11 • Ⓑ Ⓓ Ⓢ Ⓡ • 2Cr/HC

NUNMILL HOUSE
85 Bishopthorpe Road, York
An elegant Victorian residence lovingly restored to enhance the original architectural features, now offers Bed & Breakfast and the benefit of an easy walk to all of York's historic attractions.
Each ensuite bedroom, individually furnished and smoke free, is for those who are looking for comfortable yet affordable accommodation.
Send S.A.E. for colour brochure.
Tel 01904 634047   Fax 01904 655879

☆ D & E Mowbray, Arrow Lodge, 8 Queen Annes Road, Bootham, YO3 7AA. ☎ (01904) 642344 • Map 105/596524 • BB **B** • S1 T1 F1 • 2-12 NX • Ⓓ Ⓢ Ⓡ

ARROW LODGE
8 Queen Annes Road
Bootham, York
We are a small B&B within a mile from York railway station. We have 3 rooms—family, single and twin. Colour TV and tea/coffee in each room. Central heating and drying facilities.
Tel 01904 642344

Mrs Margaret Stothard, Bank House, 9 Southlands Road, YO2 1NP. ☎ (01904) 627803 • Map 105/600507 • BB **B/C** • D2 T1 F1 • 1-12 NX • Ⓑ Ⓓ Ⓢ Ⓡ • 2Cr

☆ Bill Pitts & Rosie Blanksby, Holmwood House, 114 Holgate Road, YO2 4BB. ☎ (01904) 626183 • Map 105/590512 • BB **D** • EM book first £20, 6.30-9.30pm • D9 T3 F1 • 1-12 • Ⓥ Ⓑ Ⓓ Ⓢ Ⓡ Ⓜ • 2Cr/HC

HOLMWOOD HOUSE

YORK
We offer luxury en-suite rooms (13) with excellent breakfasts, close to the city centre and railway station
(2 hours from Edinburgh/London).
Dales and moors are close and we can organise guided walks with transport as far as the borders. Try our mid-week DB&B break.

Tel: 01904 626183
Fax: 01904 670899
Bill Pitts & Rosie Blanksby

SOUTH YORKSHIRE

■ SHEFFIELD
Zillertal, 15 Thornsett Road, S7 1NB. ☎ 0114-258 7431 • Map 110,111/344855 • BB **B** • S1 D1 T1 • 1-12 NX • Ⓢ Ⓡ Ⓜ

WEST YORKSHIRE

■ ADDINGHAM (Ilkley)
DALES WAY

Mrs B Goodwin, 27 Wharfe Park, LS29 0QZ. ☎ (01943) 831370 • Map 104/083497 • BB **B** • EM book first £8, 6.30-7pm • S1 D1 T1 • 4-12 • Ⓥ Ⓓ 🐾

■ BINGLEY
Mrs L Jean Warin, March Cote Farm, Cottingley, BD16 1UB. ☎ (01274) 487433 • Map 104/104375 • BB **C** • EM book first £8, 6-8pm • D1 T1 F1 • 1-12 NX • Ⓑ Ⓓ Ⓢ Ⓡ • List/C • SC also

■ BLACKSHAWHEAD (Hebden Bridge)
PENNINE WAY

Mrs Miriam Whitaker, Badger Fields Farm, Badger Lane, HX7 7JX. ☎ (01422) 845161 • Map 103/957274 • BB **B** • D1 F1 • 3-11 • Ⓓ Ⓢ Ⓡ

■ BRADFORD
Ivy Guest House, 3 Melbourne Place, BD5 0HZ. ☎ (01274) 727060 • Map 104/159324 • BB **B** • EM book first £6, 7pm • S3 D2 T4 F1 • 1-12 • Ⓥ Ⓓ Ⓡ • List

■ EMLEY (Nr Huddersfield)

Marie Gill, White Cross Farm, HD8 9QU. ☎ (01924) 848339 • Map 110/256128 • BB **B/C** • S1 D1 F1 • 1-12 NX • ⑧ ⑩ 🛁 • List/App

■ GREETLAND (Halifax)
CALDERDALE WAY

Mrs Sylvia Shackleton, Crawstone Knowl Farm, Rochdale Road, Upper Greetland, Calderdale, HX4 8PX. ☎ (01422) 370470 • Map 104/081213 • BB **C** • EM book first £7, 7pm • S1 D1 T1 F1 • 1-12 • ⑰ ⑧ ⑩ ⑤ ⑱ 🛁 • 2Cr/C

■ HAWORTH (Keighley)

Mr & Mrs D Bell, Ebor House, Lees Lane, BD22 8RA. ☎ (01535) 645869 • Map 104/039376 • BB **A/B** • S1 T1 F1 • 1-12 NX • ⑩ ⑱ 🛁 • 1Cr/App

■ HEBDEN BRIDGE
PENNINE WAY & CALDERDALE WAY

Ann Anthon, Prospect End, 8 Prospect Terrace, Savile Road, HX7 6NA. ☎ (01422) 843586 • Map 103/982272 • BB **B/C** • EM book first £7.50, 7pm • D1 T1 • 1-12 • ⑰ ⑧ ⑩ ⑤ ⑱ • 1Cr/C

☆ Mrs M J Audsley, Myrtle Grove, Old Lees Road, HX7 8HL. ☎ (01422) 846078 • Map 103/994278 • BB **B/C** • D1 F1 • 1-12 • ⑰ ⑧ ⑩ ⑤ ⑱ • 2Cr/HC

■ HOLME VILLAGE (Holmfirth)
PENNINE WAY

Ms J Hayfield & J Sandford, Holme Castle Country Hotel, HD7 1QG. ☎ (01484) 686764 • Map 110/107058 • BB **C/D** • EM book first £10 & £19, 7.30pm • S1 D3 T2 F2 • 1-12 • ⑧ ⑩ ⑤

■ ILKLEY
DALES WAY

Summerhill Guest House, 24 Crossbeck Road, LS29 9JN. ☎ (01943) 607067 • Map 104/119471 • BB **B** • EM book first £7.50, 6.30pm • S1 D1 T3 • 1-12 NX • ⑰ ⑧ ⑩ ⑤ ⑱

Mrs P Bradbury, Osborne House, 1 Tivoli Place, LS29 8SU. ☎ (01943) 609483 • Map 104/120474 • BB **B** • D1 T2 F1 • 1-12 NX • ⑩ ⑤ ⑱ 🛁

Mrs S M Read, 126 Skipton Road, LS29 9BQ. ☎ (01943) 600635 • Map 104/108480 • BB **B** • T1 • 1-12 NX • ⑧ ⑩ ⑤ ⑱

Mrs Y O'Neill, Poplar View Guest House, 8 Bolton Bridge Road, LS29 9AA. ☎ (01943) 608436 • Map 104/113477 • BB **B** • D1 T1 F1 • 1-12 NX • ⑩ ⑤ ⑱ 🛁 ⑩

Alfred & Pat Below, Archway Cottage, 24 Skipton Road, LS29 9EP. ☎ (01943) 603399 • Map 104/113478 • BB **B/C** • D2 T2 • 1-12 NX • ⑩ ⑱ 🛁 ⑩

Petra Roberts, 63 Skipton Road, LS29 9HF. ☎ (01943) 817542 • Map 104/110479 • BB **C/D** • EM book first £5 • D2 T1 • 1-12 • ⑰ ⑧ ⑩ ⑤ ⑱ 🛁 • List

■ LEEDS

☆ Aragon Hotel, 250 Stainbeck Lane, LS7 2PS. ☎ (0113) 275 9306 • Map 104/293373 • BB **C/D** • EM £8.50, 7-9pm • S4 D5 T3 F1 • 1-12 NX • ⑰ ⑧ ⑩ ⑱ 🛁 ⑩ • 3Cr

■ MARSDEN (Huddersfield)
PENNINE WAY

Mr & Mrs T Fussey, Forest Farm Guest House, Mount Road, HD7 6NN. ☎ (01484) 842687 • Map 110/042105 • BB **B** • EM book first £6, 7pm • D1 T1 F1 • 1-12 NX • ⑰ ⑧ ⑩ ⑱ 🛁 • Bunkhouse also

■ NORLAND (Sowerby Bridge, Halifax)
CALDERDALE WAY

☆ The Hobbit Country Hotel, Hob Lane, HX6 3QL. ☎ (01422) 832202 • Map 104/058226 • BB **C/D** • EM £8, up to 10pm • S3 D10 T7 F2 • 1-12 • ⑰ ⑧ ⑤ ⑱ • 4Cr/C • Groups also

■ OAKWORTH (Keighley)

☆ Railway Cottage, 59 Station Road, BD22 0DZ. ☎ (01535) 642693 • Map 104/038383 • BB **B/C** • S2 D3 • 1-12 NX • ⒷⒹⒾ ⓈⓇ • List/App

■ OTLEY

Mrs P M Davison, 11 Newall Mount, LS21 2DY. ☎ (01943) 462898 • Map 104/200460 • BB **B** • S1 D1 T1 F1 • 1-12 • ⒷⒹⒾ ⓈⓇ

■ OXENHOPE (Keighley)

☆ Mrs Julie Hargreaves, Springfield Guest House, Shaw Lane, BD22 9QL. ☎ (01535) 643951 • Map 104/030348 • BB **B** • EM £8.50, 6pm • S1 D1 T1 F1 • 1-12 • ⓋⒷⒹⒾ ⓈⓇ

■ STANBURY (NR HAWORTH) (Keighley)
PENNINE WAY

☆ Mrs Taylor, Ponden Hall, BD22 0HR. ☎ (01535) 644154 • Map 103/987370 • BB **C** • EM £9.50, 7pm • D1 F1 • 1-12 NX • ⓋⒷⒹⒾ Ⓢ Ⓜ

■ STANDEDGE (Delph, Oldham, Lancs)
PENNINE WAY

Mrs J Mayall, Globe Farm Guest & Bunk House, Huddersfield Road (nr Saddleworth), OL3 5LU. ☎ (01457) 873040 • Map 110/012097 • BB **C** • EM £6.50, 6.30pm • S3 D2 T2 F6 • 1-12 NX • ⓋⒷⒹ • 2Cr/C • Bunkhouse & camping also

Isle of Man

■ DOUGLAS
ISLE OF MAN COASTAL PATH

☆ Mrs Betty Quirk, Rangemore, 12 Derby Square, IM1 3LS. ☎ (01624) 674892 • BB **B** • EM book first £8.50, 6pm • S1 D4 T2 F3 • 3-11 NX • ⓋⒷⒹⒾ Ⓢ ⓇⓀ • 3Cr/C • Ferry nearby

■ RAMSEY
ISLE OF MAN COASTAL PATH

Mrs J G Bass, Thorncliffe, Ballure Road. ☎ (01624) 813885 • BB **C** • EM £6, 7-8pm • S2 D2 T2 F1 • 1-12 • ⓋⒹⒾ ⓈⓇⓀ • 1Cr/C

Mr & Mrs E Grantham, "Solway", Windsor Mount, IM8 3EA. ☎ (01624) 816471 • Map 95/816471 • BB **B** • D1 T1 • 1-12 NX closed part Sept. • ⒹⒾ ⓈⓇⓀ • List/C

Scotland

ARGYLL & BUTE

■ BRIDGE OF ORCHY
WEST HIGHLAND WAY

Mrs F Aitken, Achallader, PA36 4AG. ☎ (01838) 400253 • Map 50/323444 • BB **B** • EM £7, 5-9pm • S2 D1 T1 F1 • 2-11 • ⓋⒹ Ⓜ

■ CARRADALE (Campbeltown)

Mrs D MacCormick, Mains Farm, PA28 6QG. ☎ (015833) 216 • Map 68,69/798380 • BB **B** • EM book first £6, 6.30pm • S1 D1 F1 • 4-10 NX • ⓋⒹ Ⓚ • List/C

■ DALMALLY (Argyll)

A W Cressey, Craig Villa Guest House, PA33 1AX. ☎ (01838) 200255 • Map 50/176271 • BB **C** • EM book first £12, 7pm • D2 T2 F2 • 3-10 • Ⓥ Ⓑ Ⓓ Ⓢ Ⓡ • 3Cr/C

■ HELENSBURGH (Dunbartonshire)

Anne & John Urquhart, Thorndean, 64 Colquhoun St, G84 9JP. ☎ (01436) 674922 • Map 56/ 297830 • BB **D** • D1 T1 F1 • 1-12 • Ⓑ Ⓓ Ⓢ Ⓡ • 2Cr/C

■ OBAN

Mrs M Wardhaugh, Kathmore, Soroba Road, PA34 4JF. ☎ (01631) 562104 • Map 49/860292 • BB **B/C/D** • EM book first £8, 6.30pm • D3 T1 F1 • 1-12 NX • Ⓥ Ⓑ Ⓓ Ⓢ 🛁 • C

Mrs J Clark, Blair Villa, Rockfield Road, PA34 5DQ. ☎ (01631) 564813 • Map 49/860299 • BB **B** • D1 T1 F1 • 3-10 • Ⓡ

Ruth Rodaway, Pinmacher, Polvinister Road, PA34 5TN. ☎ (01631) 563553 • Map 49/866300 • BB **C** • EM book first £8, 7pm • D2 T1 • 3-10 • Ⓥ Ⓑ Ⓓ Ⓡ 🛁 Ⓜ • 3Cr/C

CENTRAL BELT

THE AUTHORITIES OF AYRSHIRE (EAST, NORTH & SOUTH), CLACK-MANNANSHIRE, DUNBARTONSHIRE (WEST & EAST), DUNDEE CITY, EDINBURGH CITY, FALKIRK, FIFE, GLASGOW CITY, INVERCLYDE, LANARKSHIRE (NORTH & SOUTH), LOTHIAN (EAST & WEST), MID-LOTHIAN, RENFREWSHIRE & EAST RENFREWSHIRE,

■ ARROCHAR (Argyll & Bute)

Mr & Mrs Chandler, Lochside Guest House, G83 7AA. ☎ (01301) 702467 • Map 56/299045 • BB **C** • EM £10, 6.30pm • S2 D3 T1 F1 • 1-12 • Ⓥ Ⓑ Ⓓ Ⓢ Ⓡ 🛁 • 2Cr/App • Situated in Dunbartonshire

■ CUMBERNAULD (Glasgow)

S & M Abercrombie, 68 Lammermoor Drive, Greenfaulds, G67 4BE. ☎ (01236) 721307 • Map 64/751735 • BB **B** • T3 • 1-12 • Ⓓ Ⓢ Ⓡ • List/C

■ DAILLY (Girvan, South Ayrshire)

Mrs Marion Whiteford, Maxwelston Farm, KA26 9RH. ☎ (01465) 811210 • Map 76/262003 • BB **B** • EM book first £12, 6pm • D1 T1 • 4-10 • Ⓥ Ⓓ Ⓢ 🛁 • HC

■ DOLLAR (Clackmannanshire)

Rosemary Cranfield, "Tigh Ur", 4 Hillfoots Road, FK14 7BB. ☎ (0374) 182799 • Map 58/964985 • BB **B** • T2 • 1-12 NX • Ⓓ 🛁 • SC also

■ DRYMEN (Loch Lomond, Glasgow)
WEST HIGHLAND WAY

Mrs Julia Cross, Easter Drumquhassle Farm, Gartness Road, G63 0DN. ☎ (01360) 660893 • Map 57/486871 • BB **B/C** • EM £8, 6.30-7.30pm • D/T1 F1 • 1-12 • Ⓥ Ⓑ Ⓓ Ⓢ 🛁 • List/C • SC and bunkhouse also

■ DUNURE (South Ayrshire)

Mrs Lesley Wilcox, Fisherton Farm (below Carrick Hills), KA7 4LF. ☎ (01292) 500223 • Map 70/273173 • BB **B** • T2 • 3-11 • Ⓓ Ⓢ 🛁 • 1Cr/C • SC also

■ EDINBURGH

Mrs Y Pretty, Barrosa Guest House, 21 Pilrig Street, EH6 5AN. ☎ (0131) 554 3700 • Map 66/264753 • BB **C/D** • D3 T3 F2 • 1-12 NX • Ⓑ Ⓢ Ⓡ 🛁 • C

Mrs H Donaldson, Invermark, 60 Polwarth Terrace, EH11 1NJ. ☎ 0131-337 1066 • Map 66/235717 • BB **C** • S1 T1 F1 • 1-12 NX • Ⓓ Ⓢ Ⓡ 🛁 • 1Cr/C • SC also

Mrs C A Darlington, Borodale, 7 Argyle Place, (off Melville Drive), EH9 1JU. ☎ 0131-667 5578 • Map 66/256724 • BB **C** • S1 D1 T1 F1 • Ⓑ Ⓓ Ⓢ Ⓡ 🛁 • List/C

Anne McTavish, 9B Scotland Street, EH3 6PP. ☎ 0131-556 5080 • Map 66/255746 • BB **D** • S2 D1 T2 • 5-10 • Ⓑ Ⓓ Ⓡ 🛁 • C

■ HADDINGTON (Lothian)

Barbara Williams, Eaglescairnie Mains, EH41 4HN. ☎ (01620) 810491 • Map 66/516689 • BB **B/C** • S2 D1 T1 • 1-12 NX • Ⓑ Ⓓ Ⓢ 🛁 • 2Cr/C

■ LARGS (Ayrshire)

Mrs M Watson, South Whittlieburn Farm, Brisbane Glen, KA30 8SN. ☎ (01475) 675881 • Map 63/218632 • BB **B/C** • D1 T1 F1 • 1-12 NX • Ⓑ Ⓓ Ⓢ Ⓡ • 2Cr/C

■ MILNGAVIE (Glasgow)
WEST HIGHLAND WAY

Mrs Heather Ogilvie, 13 Craigdhu Avenue, G62 6DX. ☎ (0141) 956 3439 • Map 64/547742 • BB **B** • T1 F1 • 4-9 • Ⓓ Ⓢ Ⓡ 🛁

DUMFRIES & GALLOWAY

■ GATEHOUSE OF FLEET (Castle Douglas, Kirks)

Murray Arms Hotel, DG7 2HY. ☎ (01557) 814207 • Map 83/602563 • BB **D** • EM £15, 5-9.30pm • S1 D6 T4 F2 • 1-12 • Ⓥ Ⓑ Ⓓ Ⓢ 🛁 • 4Cr/C

■ GLENLUCE (Newton Stewart, Wigtownshire)

Mr John Thomas, Rowan Tree Guest House, DG8 0PS. ☎ (01581) 300244 • Map 82/198575 • BB **A/B** • S1 D2 T1 F1 • 1-12 • Ⓑ Ⓓ Ⓢ 🛁 • 2Cr/C

■ LANGHOLM

☆ Paul Hayhoe, The Reivers Rest, 81 High Street, DG13 0DJ. ☎ (013873) 81343 • Map 79/365845 • BB **C/D** • EM £5-£12, 6-9pm • S1 D3 T2 F1 • 1-12 NX • Ⓥ Ⓑ Ⓓ Ⓢ 🛁 • List/C

■ MOFFAT
SOUTHERN UPLAND WAY

Mrs M Struthers, Wykeham Lodge, Old Well Road, DG10 9AW. ☎ (01683) 220188 • Map 78/086054 • BB **B** • S1 D1 T1 • 3-10 NX • 🛁

Mr D Cheetham, Ramlodge Guest House, High Street, DG10 9RU. ☎ (01683) 220594 • Map 78/080063 • BB **B** • D2 T2 F1 • 1-12 • Ⓑ 🛁 • Bunk room also

Linda Harvie, Berriedale House, Beechgrove, DG10 9RU. ☎ (01683) 220427 • Map 78/080063 • BB **B** • EM £7.50 • D2 T1 • 1-12 • Ⓥ Ⓓ 🛁 Ⓜ

Joan & John Marchington, Seamore House, Academy Road, DG10 9HW. ☎ (01683) 220404 • Map 78/083055 • BB **B/C** • EM book first £7, 6.45pm • S1 D2 T2 F2 • 1-12 NX • Ⓥ Ⓑ Ⓓ Ⓢ 🛁 • 2Cr/C

Mr & Mrs D Armstrong, "Boleskine", 4 Well Road, DG10 9AS. ☎ (01683) 220601 • Map 78/085054 • BB **B** • S1 D2 T1 • 1-12 • Ⓑ Ⓓ Ⓢ 🛁 • 2Cr/HC

Mrs L Taylor, Morag, 19 Old Carlisle Road, DG10 9QJ. ☎ (01683) 220690 • Map 78/093046 • BB **B** • EM £7, 5.30-7pm • S1 D1 T1 • 1-12 NX • Ⓥ Ⓓ Ⓢ 🛁

■ NEW GALLOWAY (Kirkcudbrightshire)

James McPhee, Smithy Restaurant & Shop, High St, DG7 3RN. ☎ (01644) 420269 • Map 77/ 633773 • BB **B** • EM £8.50, all day • D1 T1 • 3-10 • Ⓥ Ⓓ 🛁

■ NEWTON STEWART (Wigtownshire)

☆ Geoff & Linda Inker, Flowerbank Guest House, Millcroft Road, Minnigaff, DG8 6PJ. ☎ (01671) 402629 • Map 83/410660 • BB **B/C** • EM £8, 6.30pm • D2 T1 F3 • 2-11 • Ⓥ Ⓑ Ⓓ Ⓢ 🛁 • 2Cr/C

Corsbie Villa, Corsbie Road, DG8 6JB. ☎ (01671) 402124 • Map 83/404665 • BB **B** • EM £6.50, 6.30-7pm • S1 D3 T4 F2 • 1-12 • Ⓥ Ⓓ Ⓢ 🛁 • Groups also

■ NEWTON WAMPHRAY (Moffat)

Mrs Val Wilson, The Red House Hotel, DG10 9NF. ☎ (01576)470470 • Map 78/107948 • BB **B/C** • S1 D1 T1 • 1-12 NX • Ⓑ Ⓓ Ⓢ • Transport avail.

■ PORTPATRICK
SOUTHERN UPLAND WAY

Michael & Eileen Pinder, Melvin Lodge, South Crescent, DG9 8LE. ☎ (01776) 810238 • Map 82/000538 • BB **C** • S2 D3 T1 F/T4 • 1-12 • Ⓑ Ⓓ Ⓢ 🛁 • 2Cr/C

■ SANQUHAR (Dumfries-shire)
SOUTHERN UPLAND WAY

Mrs Mary McDowall, "Penhurst", Townhead Street, DG4 6DA. ☎ (01659) 50751 • Map 71,78/779101 • BB **A** • EM £4 • D1 T1 F1 • 1-12 • Ⓥ Ⓓ Ⓢ Ⓡ 🛁 • List/C

Mrs N Turnbull, 28 High Street, DG4 6BL. ☎ (01659) 58143 • Map 71,78/781098 • BB **A** • EM book first £5, 6.30-9.30pm • D1 T1 • 1-12 • Ⓥ Ⓓ Ⓡ 🛁 • List/App

■ WATERBECK (Lockerbie)

Mrs Cecilia Hislop, Carik Cottage, DG11 3EU. ☎ (01461) 600652 • Map 85/242778 • BB **B/C** • EM book first £7, 7pm • D2 T1 • 1-11 • Ⓑ Ⓓ Ⓢ • List/HC

HIGHLAND

■ ACHARACLE (Ardnamurchan, Argyll)

Yuzan Lodges, Mingarry, PH36 4JX. ☎ (01967) 431384 • Map 40/702697 • BB **B** • EM £10, 6-7.30pm • T1 F1 • 3-1 • Ⓥ Ⓓ Ⓢ Ⓜ • SC also

■ AULTBEA (Achnasheen, Ross-shire)

Mrs H MacLeod, The Croft, IV22 2JA. ☎ (01445) 731352 • Map 19/876892 • BB **B** • D2 T1 • 3-10 • Ⓓ 🛁 • 1Cr/C

■ AVIEMORE (Inverness-shire)

Mrs Margaret Hall, Kinapol Guest House, Dalfaber Road, PH22 1PY. ☎ (01479) 810513 • Map 35,36/896124 • BB **B** • D3 T/D2 • 1-12 • Ⓓ Ⓡ 🛁 • 1Cr/C

☆ Shona Anderson, Glenmore Lodge, PH22 1QU. ☎ (01479) 861276 • Map 36/987095 • BB **B** • EM book first £6.75, 6.45pm • S1 T23 F3 • 2-11 • Ⓥ Ⓑ Ⓓ Ⓢ

GLENMORE LODGE
Northern Cairngorms

Recently refurbished throughout.
Comfortable twin rooms.
Unique location, ideally situated in the heart of Glenmore Forest with the Cairngorms right on the doorstep.
Tel: 01479 861256

■ BALLACHULISH (Argyll)

☆ Mr W & Mrs J Watson, Craiglinnhe Guest House, PA39 4JX. ☎ (01855) 811270 • Map 41/059591 • BB **C** • EM book first £11, 7pm • D3 T3 • 3-10 • Ⓥ Ⓑ Ⓓ Ⓢ • 3Cr/C

CRAIGLINNHE GUEST HOUSE
Ballachulish

Nineteenth century villa of charm and character in magnificent lochside setting beneath Beinn a'Bheithir. Small, personally managed establishment offering traditional Scottish hospitality in well-appointed accommodation. Excellent centre for exploring the Western Highlands. Superb hill and forest walks. Brochure on request.

☎ **(01855) 811270**

STB 🦢🦢🦢 COMMENDED

Mrs Jeanette Watt, Riverside House, PA39 4JE. ☎ (01855) 811473 • Map 41/081580 • BB **B** • D2 T1 • 3-10 NX • Ⓑ Ⓓ Ⓢ 🛁 • 2Cr/C

Mrs Diana Macaskill, Park View, 18 Park Road, PA39 4JS. ☎ (01855) 811560 • Map 41/080582 • BB **A/B** • D3 T2 • 1-12 NX • Ⓓ Ⓢ 🛁 • 1Cr/C

■ BALMACARA (Wester Ross)

Mrs Anne Porter, "Feorlig", Kirkton, IV40 8EG. ☎ (01599) 566281 • Map 33/832273 • BB **B** • EM £7, 7pm • S1 D2 T1 • 2-11 • Ⓥ Ⓓ Ⓢ 🛁

■ BANAVIE (Fort William)
WEST HIGHLAND WAY

☆ Glen Loy Lodge, PH33 7PD. ☎ (01397) 712700 • Map 41,34/120828 • BB **C/D** • EM £11, 7pm • S2 D4 T3 • 4-10 NX • Ⓥ Ⓑ Ⓓ Ⓢ 🛁 Ⓜ • 3Cr/C

Glen Loy Lodge
Banavie, Fort William PH33 7PD

Convenient base for the Western Highlands. Licensed. Centrally heated throughout. H&C in all bedrooms all with private facilities. Packed lunches. Drying facilities. Children welcome. Pets accepted. Enjoy good food and wine in a friendly atmosphere. STB 3 Crown classification and commended grade.

Tel. 01397 712 700

■ BERRIEDALE (Caithness)

Mrs S Steven, Mulberry Croft, 2 East Newport, KW7 6HA. ☎ (01593) 751245 • Map 17/131246 • BB **B** • EM book first £7.50, 6-8pm • D/F1 T1 • 1-12 NX • Ⓥ Ⓓ 🛁

■ CARRBRIDGE (Inverness-shire)

Craigellachie Guest House, Main Street, PH23 3AS. ☎ (01479) 841641 • Map 36/907228 • BB **B/C/D** • EM book first £10, 7-8pm • S1 D2 T2 F2 • 1-12 NX • Ⓥ Ⓑ Ⓓ Ⓢ Ⓡ • 2Cr/C

■ CAWDOR (Nairn)

Mrs J Macleod, Dallaschyle, IV12 5XS. ☎ (01667) 493422 • Map 27/820490 • BB **B** • EM book first £10, 7pm • D1 F1 • 4-11 • Ⓓ Ⓢ • List/C

■ DIABAIG (Torridon, Achnasheen, Ross-s)

Mrs I Ross, Ben Bhraggie, IV22 2HE. ☎ (01445) 790268 • Map 24,19/802605 • BB **A** • EM £8, 7.30pm • D1 T1 • 3-10 • Ⓥ Ⓑ Ⓓ 🛁 • SC also

Ms Anne Ross, Croft No 3, IV22 2HE. ☎ (01445) 790240 • Map 24, 19/802605 • BB **B** • EM £11, 7.30pm • S1 D1 T1 • 1-12 NX • Ⓥ Ⓑ Ⓓ Ⓢ • List/C • SC also. Postbus from station

■ DRUMNADROCHIT (Inverness-shire)

Sandra & Bill Silke, Westwood, Lower Balmacaan, IV3 6UL. ☎ (01456) 450826 • Map 26, 35/503285 • BB **B/C** • EM book first £9, 6-8pm • D1 T2 • 1-12 • Ⓥ Ⓑ Ⓓ 🛁 Ⓜ • C/List

■ FORT AUGUSTUS (Inverness-shire)

Bob & Judy Burnett, Kettle House, Golf Course Road, PH32 4BY. ☎ (01320) 366408 • Map 34/377064 • BB **B** • S2 D1 T1 • 1-12 NX • Ⓑ Ⓓ Ⓢ 🛁

■ FORT WILLIAM (Inverness-shire)
WEST HIGHLAND WAY

Rhu Mhor Guest House, Alma Road, PH33 6BP. ☎ (01397) 702213 • Map 41/107740 • BB **C** • EM book first £10.50, 7pm • D3 T3 F1 • 4-10 • Ⓓ Ⓢ Ⓡ 🛁 • List/C

Craig Nevis Guest House, Belford Road, PH33 6BU. ☎ (01397) 702023 • Map 41/108741 • BB **B** • S1 D1 T2 F2 • 1-12 NX • Ⓑ Ⓓ Ⓡ • 1Cr/C

☆ Mrs D Macbeth, Glenlochy Guest House, Nevis Bridge, PH33 6PF. ☎ (01397) 702909 • Map 41/114742 • BB **B/C** • D5 T4 F2 • 1-12 • Ⓑ Ⓓ Ⓢ Ⓡ • 2Cr/C • SC also

Abrach House, Caithness Place, PH33 6JP. ☎ (01397) 702535 • Map 41/097729 • BB **B/C** • S1 D2 T1 • 1-12 NX • Ⓑ Ⓓ Ⓢ Ⓡ 🛁 • 2Cr/C • SC also

"Taransay", Seafield Gardens, PH33 6RJ. ☎ (01397) 703303 • Map 41/093729 • BB **B** • S1 T1 F1 • 1-12 NX • Ⓑ Ⓓ Ⓢ Ⓡ

Mrs J Macleod, 25 Alma Road, PH33 6HD. ☎ (01397) 703735 • Map 41/107739 • BB **B** • D1 T1 • 1-12 • Ⓓ Ⓡ

Mrs Diane Young, Achintee Farm Guest House, Glen Nevis, PH33 6TE. ☎ (01397) 702240 • Map 41/124731 • BB **C** • S1 D2 T1 F1 • 1-12 • Ⓑ Ⓓ Ⓢ Ⓡ 🛁 • 2Cr/C • Bunkhouse & SC also

Shona MacGillivray, Alexandra Hotel, The Parade, PH33 6AZ. ☎ (01397) 701177 • Map 41/104740 • BB D • EM £9, up to 11pm • S22 D10 T51 F14 • 1-12 • Ⓥ Ⓑ Ⓓ Ⓡ 🛁 • 4Cr/C • Groups also

Patricia Archibald, Milton Hotel, North Road, PH33 6TG. ☎ (01397) 701177 • Map 41/124754 • BB **D** • EM £9, up to 9pm • S19 D19 T74 F7 • 1-12 • Ⓥ Ⓑ Ⓓ Ⓡ 🛁 • 4Cr/C • Groups also

▌ GAIRLOCH (Ross-shire)

Horisdale House, Strath, IV21 2DA. ☎ (01445) 712151 • Map 19/791774 • BB **C** • EM book first £11.50, 7pm • S2 D2 T1 F1 • 5-9 NX • Ⓥ Ⓑ Ⓓ Ⓢ • 2Cr/HC

GARVE (Ross-shire)

& P Hollingdale, The Old Manse, IV23 2PX. ☎ (01997) 414201 • Map 20/388625 • BB **B** • D2 T1 • 1-1 NX • Ⓑ Ⓓ Ⓢ Ⓡ

☆ Mr & Mrs R Miller, Tigh-Na-Drochit, Little Garve, IV23 2PU. ☎ (01997) 414256 • Map 20/395629 • BB • S1 D1 T1 • 1-12 NX • Ⓑ Ⓓ Ⓡ 🛁 Ⓜ • SC also

▌ GLENCOE (Ballachulish, Argyll)

Sally Mortimer, Scorrybreac Guest House, Hospital Drive, PA39 4HT. ☎ (01855) 811354 • Map 41/104589 • BB **B** • EM book first £12.50, 6.30-7pm • D3 T3 • 1-10 & 12 • Ⓥ Ⓑ Ⓓ Ⓢ 🛁 • 2Cr/C

▌ GLENFINNAN (Fort William)

Sue & Gilbert Scott, Craigag Lodge, PH37 4LT. ☎ (01397) 722240 • Map 40/901806 • BB **C** • EM £10, 7.30pm • D1 T1 F1 • 3-10 + DEC • Ⓥ Ⓓ Ⓢ Ⓡ 🛁 • List/App

▌ INVERGARRY (Inverness-shire)

Mrs M Waugh, North Laggan Farmhouse, by Spean Bridge, PH34 4EB. ☎ (01809) 501335 • Map 34/271961 • BB **B** • EM book first £9.50, 7pm • T1 F1 • 5-9 NX • Ⓓ Ⓢ Ⓡ 🛁 • List/C • SC also

Lilac Cottage, South Laggan, by Spean Bridge, PH34 4EA. ☎ (01809) 501410 • Map 34/335995 • BB **B** • EM £10, 7pm • D1 T1 F1 • 1-12 • Ⓓ Ⓢ 🛁 • List/C

▌ INVERINATE (Kyle, Ross-shire)

Mrs J MacIntosh, Forester's Bungalow, IV40 8HE. ☎ (01599) 511329 • Map 33,25/939210 • BB **B/C** • D1 T/D1 • 3-10 • Ⓑ Ⓓ 🛁

▌ INVERNESS

Mrs I Geddes, Tanera, 8 Fairfield Road, IV3 5QA. ☎ (01463) 230037 • Map 26/661452 • BB **B** • D2 T1 • 1-12 NX • Ⓑ Ⓓ Ⓡ 🛁

Christine Mackenzie, Malvern, 54 Kenneth Street, IV3 5PZ. ☎ (01463) 242251 • Map 26/661453 • BB **B/C** • D1 T1 F2 • 1-12 NX • Ⓑ Ⓓ Ⓢ Ⓡ 🛁 • 2Cr/C

B&B ACCOMMODATION   SCOTLAND   HIGHLAND

277

■ KINCRAIG (Kingussie, Inverness-shire)

Nick & Patsy Thompson, Insh House Guest House, PH21 1NU. ☎ (01540) 651377 • Map 35/837037 • BB **B** • EM book first £10, 7pm • S2 D1 T1 F1 • 1-12 NX • Ⓥ Ⓑ Ⓓ 🐾 • 2Cr/C • SC also

■ KINGUSSIE (Inverness-shire)

The Osprey Hotel, Ruthven Road, PH21 1EN. ☎ (01540) 661510 • Map 35/756005 • BB **C/D** • EM £19.95, 7.30-8pm • S2 D4 T3 • 1-12 • Ⓥ Ⓑ Ⓓ Ⓢ Ⓡ 🐾 • 3Cr/C

Bhuna Monadh, 85 High Street, PH21 1HX. ☎ (01540) 661186/(0385) 931345 • Map 35/759007 • BB **B** • EM £10.50, 7pm • D1 T1 F2 • 1-12 • Ⓥ Ⓑ Ⓓ Ⓢ Ⓡ 🐾 • 2Cr/C

■ KINLOCHEWE (Achnasheen, Ross-shire)

Clive & Fiona Hunt, "Alltan Domhain", 2 Cromasaig, IV22 2PE. ☎ (01445) 760297 • Map 19/026607 • BB **B** • EM £8, 7-7.30pm • S1 D1 T1 • 1-12 • Ⓥ Ⓓ Ⓢ Ⓜ

■ KINLOCHLEVEN (Argyll, Lochaber)
WEST HIGHLAND WAY

Miss MacAngus, "Hermon", PA40 4RA. ☎ (01855) 831383 • Map 41/189622 • BB **B** • D2 T1 • 3-10 • Ⓑ Ⓓ Ⓢ 🐾

Elsie Robertson, Edencoille, PA40 4SE. ☎ (01855 831) 358 • Map 41/180617 • BB **B** • EM £8, 6-9.30pm • T3 • 1-12 • Ⓥ Ⓓ Ⓢ • 1Cr/C

Tailrace Inn, Riverside Road, PA40 4QH. ☎ (01855) 831777 • Map 41/185620 • BB **B/C** • EM £5, 5-9pm • D2 T3 F1 • 1-12 • Ⓥ Ⓑ Ⓓ

■ KISHORN (Strathcarron)

P Van Hinsbergh, Craigellachie, Achintraid, IV54 8XB. ☎ (01520) 733253 • Map 24/840387 • BB **B** • EM £10, 6-8pm • D1 T1 • 4-9 • Ⓥ Ⓑ Ⓓ Ⓢ 🐾 • 1Cr/C • SC also

■ KYLE (Glenshiel, Wester Ross)

Mrs Camilli, Wild Firs, Ratagan, IV40 8HP. ☎ (01599) 511266 • Map 33/919198 • BB **A** • EM book first £3-£8, 7pm • D2 • 1-12 • Ⓥ Ⓓ Ⓢ • SC also

Mary Grant, Craigellachie, IV40 8HP. ☎ (01599) 511331 • Map 33/919198 • BB **B** • D1 T1 • 3-9 • Ⓓ Ⓢ

■ KYLESKU (Sutherland)

☆ Newton Lodge, IV27 4HN. ☎ (01971) 502070 • Map 15/251216 • BB **D** • EM £13, 7-7.30pm • D4 T3 • 4-mid Oct • Ⓑ Ⓓ Ⓢ 🐾 • 3Cr/HC

■ LAIRG (Sutherland)

Mrs J B MacIntosh, 77 Dalcharn, Tongue, IV27 4XU. ☎ (01847) 611251 • Map 10/622587 • BB **B** • EM book first £7, 6.30-7pm • S1 D1 T1 F1 • 1-12 NX • Ⓥ Ⓑ Ⓓ Ⓢ

■ LATHERON (Caithness)

Mrs Cath Falconer, Tacher Farm, KW5 6DX. ☎ (01593) 741313 • Map 11,12/179428 • BB **B** • EM book first £8, 6pm • D1 T1 F1 • 5-9 • Ⓥ Ⓑ Ⓓ 🐾 • 2Cr/C

■ LOCHINVER (Sutherland)

Mrs Sue Munro, Ardglas Guest House, IV27 4LJ. ☎ (01571) 844257 • Map 15/093231 • BB **B** • S1 D4 T1 F2 • 1-12 NX • Ⓓ Ⓢ 🐾 • 1Cr/C

■ LYBSTER (Caithness)

Mr & Mrs Gunn, Bolton House, Main Street, KW3 6AE. ☎ (01593) 721282 • Map 11/248355 • BB **B** • EM £7, 6-8pm • S11 D1 T1 • 1-12 • Ⓥ Ⓑ Ⓓ Ⓢ 🐾

■ MALLAIG

J & T Smith, Springbank Guest House, East Bay, PH41 4QF. ☎ (01687) 462459 • Map 40/678967 • BB **B** • EM book first £7.50, 7pm • S2 D2 T3 F1 • 1-12 NX • Ⓥ Ⓓ Ⓢ Ⓡ 🐾 • 1Cr/App

Mrs C King, Seaview, PH41 4QS. ☎ (01687) 462059 • Map 40/676969 • BB **B** • D2 T1 F1 • 1-12 NX • Ⓓ Ⓡ Ⓜ • App

■ MORAR BY MALLAIG (Inverness-shire)

Mrs U Clulow, Sunset Guest House, PH40 4PA. ☎ (01687) 462259 • Map 40/677933 • BB **A/B** • EM book first £7, 6.30-9pm • S1 D1 T1 F2 • 1-12 • Ⓥ Ⓓ Ⓢ Ⓡ • 1Cr/App

■ NEWTONMORE (Inverness-shire)

Maureen & George Johnston, "Ardnabruach", Glen Road, PH20 1DZ. ☎ (01540) 673339 • Map 35/714993 • BB **B** • EM book first £7, 7-9pm • S1 D1 T1 F1 • 1-12 • Ⓥ Ⓓ Ⓢ Ⓡ 🐾 Ⓜ • List/C

Don & Dorothy Muir, Greenways, Golf Course Road, PH20 1AT. ☎ (01540) 673325 • Map 35/716991 • BE **B** • S1 D1 T1 • 1-12 NX • Ⓓ Ⓢ Ⓡ Ⓜ • 1Cr/C • Food nearby

---

You'll find more accommodation in the Hostels & Bunkhouses, Self-catering and Groups sections of this YEARBOOK

278

■ **ONICH (Fort William,Inverness-shire)**

☆ Ronald & Helen Young, Camus House Lochside Lodge, PH33 6RY. ☎ (01855) 821200 • Map 41/038613 • BB **C/D** • EM book first £14.50, 7.15pm • D3 T2 F2 • 1-10 • Ⓥ Ⓑ Ⓓ Ⓢ ♿ • 3Cr/C

Camus House

**LOCHSIDE GUEST HOUSE
ONICH
INVERNESS-SHIRE
PH33 6RY**

This is an ideal Highland base for hill walkers, climbers and Munro-baggers central to the Etive Hills, Mamores, Glencoe, Glen Nevis, Appin and Knoydart. Relax after a strenuous day by our log fire and enjoy our excellent home cooking. En suite accommodation, central heating, drying facilities, licensed. Hotel standard of comfort at affordable prices!

Please write for brochure or phone Mr Young. Tel (01855) 821200

Mrs J Maclean, Foresters Bungalow, Inchree, PH33 6SE. ☎ (01855) 821285 • Map 41/028634 • BB **B** • EM £7, 6pm • D1 T2 • 3-10 • Ⓥ Ⓓ ♿ • 1Cr/C

■ **OPINAN (Laide, Achnasheen)**

☆ Roger & Mairi Beeson, Obinan Croft, IV22 2NU. ☎ (01445) 731548 • Map 19/883973 • BB **D** • EM £15, 8pm • D2 T2 • 3-10 • Ⓥ Ⓓ Ⓢ ♿.See next column for display ad.

■ **POOLEWE (Wester Ross)**

Madge Macleod, Bruach Ard, Inverasdale, IV22 2LN. ☎ (01445) 781214 • Map 19/818849 • BB **C** • EM book first £10, 7.30pm • D2 T1 • 3-10 • Ⓥ Ⓑ Ⓓ Ⓢ • 2Cr/C

■ **SHIELDAIG (Strathcarron, Ross-shire)**

Chris & Erica Sermon, Innis Mhor, Ardheslaig, IV54 8XH. ☎ (01520) 755339 • Map 24/779562 • BB **B** • EM £10, 7pm • S2 D2 T1 • 1-12 NX • Ⓥ Ⓓ Ⓢ ♿ • 1Cr/C

■ **STRATHPEFFER (Ross-shire)**

Mrs Janet Greathead, Hideaway, Craigdarroch Drive, Contin, IV14 9EL. ☎ (01997) 421127 • Map 26/447573 • BB **B** • EM £7, 6.30-8pm • D2 T/S1 • 1-12 NX • Ⓑ Ⓓ Ⓢ

■ **THURSO (Caithness)**

Barbara MacIvor, "Ivordene", Janetstown, KW14 7XF. ☎ (01847) 894760 • Map 11,12/089656 • BB **A** • EM book first £6, 6-7.30pm • S1 D1 T1 F1 • 1-12 • Ⓥ Ⓓ Ⓢ Ⓡ ♿

■ **TORRIDON (Achnasheen, Ross-shire)**

Mrs P Rose, Heather Cliff, Inveralligin, IV22 2HB. ☎ (01445) 791256 • Map 24/849577 • BB **B** • EM book first £8.50, 7pm • S1 D1 F1 • 2-11 NX • Ⓥ Ⓓ Ⓢ

Mrs M MacKay, Shalimar, Inver Alligin, IV22 2HB. ☎ (01445) 791315 • Map 24/845577 • BB **B** • EM book first £9, 7.30pm • D1 • 4-9 • Ⓓ Ⓢ ♿

Mrs Mary Mackay, "Benview", Alligin, Loch Torridon, IV22 2HB. ☎ (01445) 791333 • Map 24/845577 • BB **B** • D2 T1 • 1-12 NX • Ⓓ • SC also

■ **ULLAPOOL (Ross-shire)**

Tony Weston, Taigh Na Mara Veg. Guest House, The Shore, Ardindrean, Lochbroom, IV23 2SE. ☎ (01854) 655282 • Map 20/158880 • BB **C** • EM £13.50, 8pm • D2 T1 • 1-12. SC available • Ⓥ Ⓑ Ⓓ Ⓢ ♿ • SC also

The Ceilidh Place Clubhouse, West Argyle Street, IV26 2TY. ☎ (01854) 612103 • Map 19/126939 • BB **C** • EM £12, 7-9.30pm • S4 T3 F4 • 1-12 • Ⓥ Ⓓ ♿ • Bunkhouse accommodation, groups also

Gruinard Bay - Wester Ross - Scotland

Obinan Croft is hospitality, welcome, laughter and being at peace with yourself. It is a kitchen bursting with good local food; a cellar of find wines and memorable malts; and everywhere windows filled with sea, shore, mountain and sky. Great walks, visit "The Last Great Wilderness" see An Teallach from your window.

OBINAN CROFT
—— The last house by the shore ——

Roger & Mairi Beeson Tel: 01445 731548

For key to symbols used see the last page of the book

☆ See Display Advertisement

B&B ACCOMMODATION SCOTLAND HIGHLAND

ISLAY, JURA, GIGHA & COLONSAY

ISLAY (Argyll & Bute)

Mick Stuart, The Bothy, 91 Lennox Street, Port Ellen, PA42 7BW. ☎ (01496) 302391 • Map 60/368452 • BB **B** • EM £7, 6-10pm • D2 T1 • 1-12 • Ⓥ Ⓓ Ⓢ 🛁

Mr & Mrs Kent, Tighcargaman, Port Ellen, PA42 7BX. ☎ (01496) 302345 • Map 60/362458 • BB **C** • EM book first £10, 7pm • D1 T2 • 1-12 NX • Ⓑ Ⓢ Ⓜ • SC also

JURA (Argyll)

Mr & Mrs Walton, Jura Hotel, Craighouse, PA60 7XU. ☎ (01496) 820243 • Map 60,61/485636 • BB **D** • EM £16.25, 7.30pm • S7 D2 T6 F2 • 1-12 NX • Ⓥ Ⓑ Ⓓ Ⓢ 🛁 • 3Cr/C

ISLE OF ARRAN

BRODICK

☆ Invermay Hotel, Whiting Bay, KA27 8PZ. ☎ (01770) 700431 • Map 69/046270 • BB **D** • EM £11, 6pm • S3 D6 T2 • 3-10 • Ⓥ Ⓑ Ⓓ Ⓢ Ⓜ • 3Cr/C

☆ Glencloy Farm Guesthouse, Glencloy, KA27 8DA. ☎ (01770) 302351 • Map 69/008361 • BB **C/D** • EM £12.50, 7pm • S1 D2 T2 • 3-11 • Ⓥ Ⓑ Ⓓ Ⓢ 🛁 • 2Cr/C

CORRIE (Brodick)

☆ D & M Wilkinson, Blackrock Guest House, KA27 8JP. ☎ (01770) 810 282 • Map 69,63/023439 • BB **C** • EM 6.30pm • S2 D2 T2 F2 • 1-11 NX • Ⓥ Ⓓ Ⓢ 🛁 • 1Cr/C

LAGG

Mrs B Caldwell, Kilmory House, KA27 8PQ. ☎ (01770) 870342 • Map 68,69/956214 • BB **B** • EM book first £10, 7.30pm • S1 D1 T1 • 1-12 NX • Ⓥ Ⓓ Ⓢ

LOCHRANZA (Brodick)

Mr & Mrs G Bannatyne, Fairhaven, Catacol, KA27 8HN. ☎ (01770) 830237 • Map 62,69/912494 • BB **B** • S2 D3 T3 F1 • 1-12 NX • Ⓑ Ⓓ • SC also

ISLE OF LUING

ISLE OF LUING (Argyll & Bute)

Birgit & Andrew Whitmore, Bardrishaig Farm, PA34 4TZ. ☎ (01852) 314364 • Map 55/735089 • BB **B** • EM £7, 6-10pm • S1 D2 T1 • 1-12 NX • Ⓥ Ⓓ

ISLE OF MULL

DERVAIG (Tobermory)

Mr N A Shilling, Ardbeg House Hotel, PA75 6QJ. ☎ (01688400) 254 • Map 47/427520 • BB **C** • EM £10, 7-8.30pm • S2 D2 T1 F1 • 1-12 • Ⓥ Ⓑ Ⓓ 🛁 • List

FIONNPHORT

J & E Wagstaff, Red Bay Cottage, Deargphort, PA66 6BP. ☎ (01681) 700396 • Map 48/312242 • BB **B** • EM £10, 7.30-10pm • D1 T2 • 1-12 • Ⓥ Ⓓ 🛁

PENNYGHAEL

Fiona Brown & Norman Salkeld, Tigh Na H-Abhann, PA70 6HB. ☎ (01681) 704229 • Map 48/534282 • BB **B** • S1 D1 T1 • 1-12 NX • Ⓓ Ⓢ

■ **TOBERMORY**

T V & B M Bettley, The Cedars, Dervaig Road, PA75 6PY. ☎ (01688) 302096 • Map 47/501553 • BB **B** • D1 T1 • 1-12 NX • Ⓓ

ISLE OF SKYE

■ **BROADFORD**

Mrs D Robertson, Westside, IV49 9AB. ☎ (01471) 822320 • Map 32/634235 • BB **C** • S1 D1 T1 • 2-12 NX • Ⓑ Ⓓ Ⓢ ⚍ Ⓜ • 2Cr/HC

Mrs J Donaldson, Fairwinds, Elgol Road, IV49 9AB. ☎ (01471) 822270 • Map 32/634235 • BB **C** • D2 T1 • 3-10 • Ⓑ Ⓓ Ⓢ ⚍ Ⓜ • 2Cr/C • Bicycles for hire

P D & V Tordoff, Millbrae House, IV49 9AE. ☎ (01471) 822310 • Map 32/648231 • BB **B/C** • S1 D1 T1 • 1-12 NX • Ⓑ Ⓓ Ⓢ

■ **CARBOST, GLEN EYNORT**

Mr Robert Van Der Vliet, "The Blue Lobster", IV47 8SG. ☎ (01478) 640320 • Map 32/376264 • BB **B** • EM £6-£15, 6-9pm • T6 • 1-12 • Ⓥ Ⓓ ⚍ • SC also

■ **ELGOL**

John & Jenny Kubale, Strathaird House, Strathaird, IV49 9AX. ☎ (01471) 866269 • Map 32/515187 • BB **D** • EM £12.50, 7.30pm • S2 D1 F4 • 4-9 • Ⓥ Ⓑ Ⓓ Ⓢ ⚍ • List/App • SC also

■ **GLENBRITTLE (Carbost)**

Mrs Bernadette Roberts, Forest View, IV47 8TA. ☎ (01478) 640391 • Map 32/409214 • BB **B** • EM £7-£8, 6-7pm • D1 T1 • 1-12 NX • Ⓥ Ⓓ Ⓢ

■ **PORTREE**

Joan MacDonald, Creag An Fhithich, 10 Achachork, IV51 9HT. ☎ (01478) 612213 • Map 23/471466 • BB **B** • S1 D1 T1 F1 • 3-11 • Ⓓ ⚍

■ **SCONSER**

Morag Nicolson, "Sgoirebreac", IV48 8TD. ☎ (01478) 650322 • Map 32,24/536304 • BB **B** • D2 T1 • 3-10 • Ⓓ • SC also

■ **SLEAT**

Mr & Mrs Fraser, Half of 10 Calgary, IV45 8RU. ☎ (01471) 844312 • Map 32/627030 • BB **B** • EM £6, 6.30-8.30pm • D2 T1 • 1-12 • Ⓥ Ⓓ ⚍ • Caravan also

■ **STRUAN**

Mrs M Mackinnon, "Seaforth", Coillore, IV56 8FX. ☎ (01470) 572230 • Map 23,32/354376 • BB **B** • EM book first £10, 7pm • D1 T1 F1 • 4-10 • Ⓓ

NORTH EAST SCOTLAND

THE UNITARY AUTHORITIES OF CITY OF ABERDEEN, ABERDEEN-SHIRE, ANGUS AND MORAY

■ **ABERDEEN**

☆ Colin & Frances Moore, Roselea Hotel, 12 Springbank Terrace, AB11 6LS. ☎ (01224) 583060 • BB **B/C** • D2 T2 F3 • 1-12 • Ⓑ Ⓓ Ⓡ ⚍ • List/C

ROSELEA HOTEL
12 Springbank Terrace,
ABERDEEN
Tel/Fax: 01224 583060

Family-run city centre hotel, convenient for bus/railway stations and P & O ferry terminal • Commended by STB • Vegetarian breakfasts available • TV and tea/coffee making facilities in all rooms • Ideal base for coastal and country walks in North East Scotland • Drying facilities • B&B £15-£22.

■ **ABERLEMNO (Brechin, Angus)**

Jean Stewart, Wood of Auldbar, DD9 6SZ. ☎ (01307) 830218 • Map 54/553556 • BB **B** • EM £8.50-£9.50, 6-8pm • S1 T1 F1 • 1-12 NX • Ⓥ Ⓓ Ⓢ ⚍ • List/C

■ **BALLATER (Aberdeenshire)**

Gairnshiel Lodge, Glengairn, AB35 5UQ. ☎ (013397) 55582 • Map 37/277014 • BB **C** • EM £13, 7.30pm • D2 F8 • 1-12 • Ⓥ Ⓑ Ⓓ Ⓢ ⚍

■ **BRAEMAR (Aberdeenshire)**

Mrs I C McKellar, Morningside, Kindrochit Drive, AB35 5YQ. ☎ (013397) 41370 • Map 43/153914 • BB **B/C** • EM book first £6-£10 • D/S1 T/S1 • 1-10 • Ⓥ Ⓓ ⚍

■ **DUFFTOWN (Moray)**

SPEYSIDE WAY

Mrs J Smart, Errolbank, 134 Fife Street, AB55 4DP. ☎ (01340) 820229 • Map 28/330399 • BB **A** • EM book first £8, 6-8pm • S1 D1 F3 • 1-12 • Ⓥ Ⓓ ⚍

■ **ELGIN (Moray)**

Torr House Hotel, 8 Moss Street, IV30 1LU. ☎ (01343) 542661 • Map 28/217626 • BB **D** • EM from £5.95, 5.30-8.30pm • S2 D2 T3 F1 • 1-12 • Ⓥ Ⓑ Ⓓ Ⓡ ⚍ • 3Cr/C

■ **FORFAR (Angus)**

Mrs R Kirby, Glencoul House, Justinhaugh, DD8 3SF. ☎ (01307) 860248 • Map 54/464578 • BB **B** • EM £7.50, 6.30-8pm • D/F1 T1 • 1-11 • Ⓓ Ⓢ ⚍ • List/C

☆ See Display Advertisement

281

■ LINTRATHEN (By Kirriemuir, Angus)

Mrs Moira Clark, Purgavie Farm, DD8 5HZ. ☎ (01575) 560213/(0860) 392794 • Map 53/296552 • BB **C** • EM £10, 7pm • D1 T1 F1 • 1-12 • Ⓥ Ⓑ Ⓓ Ⓢ 🐾 • 3Cr/HC • SC also.

■ STRATHDON (Aberdeenshire)

Mrs Elizabeth Ogg, Buchaam Farm, AB36 8TN. ☎ (019756) 51238 • Map 37/393134 • BB **B** • EM book first £8, 7pm • D1 T1 F1 • 5-10 • Ⓓ Ⓢ • List/C • SC also

ORKNEY ISLANDS

■ ORPHIR

Kathy Tait, Westrow Lodge Bed & Breakfast, KW17 2RD. ☎ (01856) 811360 • Map 7,6/334045 • BB **C** • D2 T1 • 1-12 NX • Ⓑ Ⓓ Ⓢ • 2Cr/HC

PERTH & KINROSS

■ BLAIR ATHOLL (Perthshire)

Gill Sherrington, Dalgreine, Off St Andrew's Cres, PH18 5SX. ☎ (01796) 481276/481627 • Map 43/878653 • BB **B/C** • EM book first £9.50, 6.30-7.30pm • S1 D2 T2 F1 • 1-12 • Ⓥ Ⓑ Ⓓ Ⓢ Ⓡ 🐾 • 2Cr/C

■ GLENISLA (Blairgowrie, Perthshire)

Mr Simon Evans, Glenmarkie Farmhouse, PH11 8QB. ☎ (01575) 582341 • Map 44/239641 • BB **C** • EM £12.50, 7pm • D2 T1 • 1-10 & 12 NX • Ⓥ Ⓑ Ⓓ Ⓢ 🐾 • 2Cr/C

■ MEIGLE (Perthshire)

Mrs Jean Ruffhead, Arnbog Farmhouse, PH12 8QT. ☎ (01307) 840535 • Map 53/320462 • BB **B** • EM £7 • T1 F1 • 1-12 NX • Ⓥ Ⓓ 🐾

■ PERTH

Pat & Brian Smith, Beeches Bed & Breakfast, 2 Comelybank, PH2 7HU. ☎ (01738) 624486 • Map 58,53/124245 • BB **B** • EM book first £8, 6pm • S2 D1 T1 • 1-12 • Ⓥ Ⓑ Ⓓ Ⓢ Ⓡ • 3Cr/C

■ PITLOCHRY

Yvonne Chadwick, Whinrigg, Aldour, Perth Road, PH16 5LY. ☎ (01796) 472330 • Map 43, 52, 53/948575 • BB **B/C/D** • S1 D2 T1 • 1-12 • Ⓥ Ⓑ Ⓓ Ⓡ • SC also

■ TROCHRY (Dunkeld, Perthshire)

Joan Brookes, Borelick, PH8 0BX. ☎ (01350) 723222 • Map 52,53/947397 • BB **B** • EM book first £7, 7pm • T1 F1 • 3-10 NX • Ⓥ Ⓓ Ⓢ

SCOTTISH BORDERS

■ EARLSTON (Berwickshire)
SOUTHERN UPLAND WAY

☆ Gwen & John Todd, Melvaig, Lauder Road, TD4 6EE. ☎ (01896) 849303 • Map 73,74/570388 • BB **B** • EM book first £8 • D1 T2 F1 • 2-12 NX • Ⓥ Ⓑ Ⓓ Ⓢ 🐾 • 2Cr/C

■ ETTRICK VALLEY (Selkirk)

☆ Mr & Mrs S Osbourne, Tushielaw Inn, TD7 5HT. ☎ (01750) 62205 • Map 79/303185 • BB **C** • EM £5.25, 6-9pm • D2 T1 • 1-12 NX • Ⓥ Ⓑ Ⓓ Ⓢ 🐾 • 3Cr/C

■ EYEMOUTH (Berwickshire)

Mrs J McGovern, Ebba House, Upper Houndlaw, TD14 5BU. ☎ (018907) 50350 • Map 67/943642 • BB **B** • EM book first £9, 6pm • S1 D1 T/F1 • 1-12 • Ⓥ Ⓓ 🐾 • List/C

Mrs J Mackay, Hillcrest, Coldingham Road, TD14 5AN. ☎ (018907) 50463 • Map 67/939641 • BB **B** • D1 T1 • 3-10 NX • Ⓓ 🐾 Ⓜ • List/C

■ GALASHIELS
SOUTHERN UPLAND WAY

Mrs S Field, Ettrickvale, 33 Abbotsford Road, TD1 3HW. ☎ (01896) 755224 • Map 73/499352 • BB **B** • EM book first £6, 6-8pm • D1 T2 • 1-12 • Ⓥ Ⓓ Ⓢ 🐾 • 1Cr/C

Bill & Sheila Salkeld, Williamhope, Old Peel, Clovenfords, TD1 3LL. ☎ (01896) 850243 • Map 73/410335 • BB B/C • EM book first £9, 6.30-7.30pm • S1 D1 T1 • 1-12 • Ⓥ Ⓑ Ⓓ Ⓢ 🐾 • 2Cr/C • Transport available.

■ HAWICK (Roxburghshire)

Mrs J Shell, Wiltonburn Farm, TD9 7LL. ☎ (01450) 372414/(0374) 192551 • Map 79/480146 • BB B • S1 D2 F1 • 1-12 NX • Ⓑ Ⓓ Ⓢ • List/C • SC also

Mrs A Bell, Kirkton Farmhouse, TD9 8QJ. ☎ (01450) 372421 • Map 79/538138 • BB B • EM £7.50, 6-8pm • D2 T1 • 3-11 NX • Ⓥ Ⓓ Ⓢ 🐾 • C

■ INNERLEITHEN (Peebles-shire)
SOUTHERN UPLAND WAY

Mr & Mrs Djellil, Caddon View Guest House, 14 Pirn Road, EH44 6HH. ☎ (01896) 830208 • Map 73/333368 • BB B/C • EM £12, 7pm • S1 D1 T2 F1 • 1-12 NX • Ⓥ Ⓑ Ⓓ Ⓢ 🐾 • 2Cr/C

■ JEDBURGH (Roxburghshire)

☆ Alan & Christine Swanston, Ferniehirst Mill Lodge, TD8 6PQ. ☎ (01835) 863279 • Map 80/654171 • BB D • EM £13, 7.30pm • S1 D3 T4 F1 • 1-12 • Ⓥ Ⓑ Ⓓ 🐾 • 2Cr/App

---

FERNIEHIRST MILL LODGE
BY JEDBURGH, ROXBURGHSHIRE TD8 6PQ
A chalet-style guesthouse set in own grounds of 25 acres beside the River Jed. Large lounge with TV and log fire. All rooms ensuite with tea/coffee facilities. Home cooking including vegetarian.
Dogs welcome by arrangement.
Country lover's paradise.
Alan & Christine Swanston
Tel 01835 863279

■ KELSO (Roxburghshire)

E Galbraith, Border Hotel, Woodmarket, TD5 7AX. ☎ (01573) 224791 • Map 74/728340 • BB B • EM book first £7, 5-6pm • S3 D2 T1 F3 • 1-12 NX • Ⓥ Ⓓ 🐾

■ KIRK YETHOLM (Roxburghshire)
PENNINE WAY

Gail Brooker, Blunty's Mill, TD5 8PG. ☎ (01573) 420288 • Map 74/825284 • BB B • EM £10-£14, 6-8pm • D1 T1 • 1-12 • Ⓥ Ⓑ Ⓓ 🐾 • 1Cr/C

Mrs Margaret Campbell, Valleydene, High Street, TD5 8PH. ☎ (01573) 420286 • Map 74/828281 • BB B/C • EM £10, 6.30-7.30pm • D1 T1 F1 • 1-12 • Ⓥ Ⓑ Ⓓ Ⓢ 🐾 • C/List

■ LAUDER (Berwickshire)
SOUTHERN UPLAND WAY

Mr P Gilardi, The Grange, 6 Edinburgh Road, TD2 6TW. ☎ (01578) 722649 • Map 73/526479 • BB B • D1 T2 • 1-12 NX • Ⓓ Ⓢ • 1Cr/C

■ MELROSE (Roxburghshire)
SOUTHERN UPLAND WAY

Mrs Susan Graham, Dunfermline House, Buccleuch Street, TD6 9LB. ☎ (01896) 822148 • Map 73/546340 • BB C • S1 D2 T2 • 1-12 • Ⓑ Ⓓ Ⓢ 🐾 • 2Cr/HC

Mrs Margaret Aitken, The Gables, Darnick, TD6 9AL. ☎ (01896) 822479 • Map 73/531342 • BB B • EM book first £9, 6-7pm • S1 D1 T1 • 1-12 NX • Ⓥ Ⓓ Ⓢ 🐾 • 1Cr/C

Mrs Trudy Davison, "Treetops", Gattonside, TD6 9NH. ☎ (01896) 823153 • Map 73/543354 • BB B • S1 T1 • 4-10 • Ⓑ Ⓓ Ⓢ 🐾 • List/C

■ PEEBLES (Tweeddale)

Carl & Catherine Lane, Lindores, 60 Old Town, EH45 8JE. ☎ (01721) 720441 • Map 73/248404 • BB B • EM £7, 6-8pm • S1 D1 T1 F3 • 1-12 • Ⓥ Ⓑ Ⓓ Ⓢ 🐾 Ⓜ • 3Cr/C

■ SELKIRK

Mrs Janet MacKenzie, Ivy Bank, Hillside Terrace, TD7 4LT. ☎ (01750) 21270 • Map 73/473286 • BB B • S1 D1 T1 • 2-12 NX • Ⓓ Ⓢ 🐾 Ⓜ

■ TEVIOTHEAD (Hawick)

Mrs Mary Jackson, Colterscleuch, TD9 0LF. ☎ (01450) 850247 • Map 79/419067 • BB B • EM £6, 7pm • S1 D/T1 T1 F1 • 1-12 • Ⓥ Ⓑ Ⓓ 🐾 Ⓜ • 1Cr/C

■ TOWN YETHOLM (Kelso, Roxburghshire)
PENNINE WAY

Mrs L S Hurst, Lochside, TD5 8PD. ☎ (01573) 420349 • Map 74/804282 • BB C • EM book first £10, 6-7pm • D1 T1 • 5-10 NX • Ⓑ Ⓓ Ⓢ 🐾 • 2Cr/C

■ TRAQUAIR (Innerleithen, Peebles-shire)
SOUTHERN UPLAND WAY

Mrs J A Caird, Traquair Bank, EH44 6PH. ☎ (01896) 830425 • Map 73/332346 • BB B • EM book first £8, 7pm • D1 T1 F1 • 4-2 NX • Ⓥ Ⓓ Ⓢ 🐾 • C

■ WALKERBURN (Peeblesshire)
SOUTHERN UPLAND WAY

Keith Miller, Tweed Valley Hotel, EH43 6AA. ☎ (01896) 870636 • Map 73/336374 • BB D • EM from £7.50, 6.30-8.30pm • S4 D4 T5 F1 • 1-12 NX • Ⓥ Ⓑ Ⓓ Ⓢ 🐾 • 4Cr/C

STIRLING

■ CALLANDER (Perthshire)

Almardon, Leny Road, FK17 8AJ. ☎ (01877) 331597 • Map 57/621080 • BB C • D2 T1 • 2-12 NX • Ⓑ Ⓓ Ⓢ

☆ See Display Advertisement

"Annfield", North Church Street, FK17 8EG. ☎ (01877) 330204 • Map 57/630079 • BB **B** • S1 D4 T2 F1 • 2-11 NX • Ⓑ Ⓓ Ⓢ 🛁 • 2Cr/C

■ CRIANLARICH (Perthshire)
WEST HIGHLAND WAY

Glenardran Guest House, FK20 8QS. ☎ (01838) 300236 • Map 52/388253 • BB **B** • EM £10, 7pm • S1 D2 T2 F1 • 1-12 NX • Ⓥ Ⓑ Ⓓ Ⓢ Ⓡ 🛁 • List/C

☆ Suie Lodge Hotel, Glen Dochart, FK20 8QT. ☎ (01567) 820417 • Map 51/488278 • BB **B** • EM £5.50, until 9pm • S1 D4 T4 F2 • 1-12 NX • Ⓥ Ⓑ Ⓓ Ⓢ 🛁 • 2Cr • SC also in winter

☆ Ben More Lodge Hotel, FK20 8QS. ☎ (01838) 300210 • Map 51/445278 • BB **D** • EM £8, 6-8.45pm • D8 T1 F2 • 1-12 NX • Ⓥ Ⓑ Ⓓ Ⓡ 🛁 • 3Cr/C

■ DRYMEN (Loch Lomond, Glasgow)
WEST HIGHLAND WAY

Mrs D Reid, Croft Burn Cottage Bed & Breakfast, Croftamie, G63 0HA. ☎ (01360) 660796 • Map 57/484857 • BB **B** • EM book first £11, 6.30-7.30pm • D1 T1 F1 • 1-11 NX • Ⓥ Ⓑ Ⓓ Ⓢ 🛁 Ⓜ • SC caravan also

Peter Nichols, Mar Achlais, Milton of Buchanan, G63 0JE. ☎ (01360870) 300 • Map 57/443902 • BB **C** • D1 F1 • 1-12 NX • Ⓑ Ⓓ Ⓢ 🛁 • 2Cr/C

☆ Buchanan Arms Hotel, Main Street, G63 0BQ. ☎ (01360) 660588 • Map 57/474883 • BB **D** • EM £19.95, 7-9.30pm • S9 D8 T31 F4 • 1-12 • Ⓥ Ⓑ Ⓓ Ⓢ 🛁 • 4Cr/C

■ KILLIN (Perthshire)
WEST HIGHLAND WAY

Fairview House, Main Street, FK21 8UT. ☎ (01567) 820667 • Map 51/572328 • BB **B** • EM book first £10, 7.30pm • S1 D4 T2 • 1-12 NX • Ⓥ Ⓑ Ⓓ 🛁 • 2Cr/C

John & Joyce Holms, `Fernbank', FK21 8UW. ☎ (01567) 820511 • Map 51/572329 • BB **B** • D1 T1 F1 • 3-10 • Ⓑ Ⓓ Ⓢ Ⓜ

■ ROWARDENNAN (Glasgow)
WEST HIGHLAND WAY

Mrs Caroline Fraser, "Coorie Doon", 5 Forest Cottages, G63 0AW. ☎ (01360) 870320 • Map 56/385955 • BB **B/C** • EM book first £6 • D1 T1 F1 • 1-12 • Ⓥ Ⓑ Ⓓ 🛁 • Family room is caravan for 8

■ STRATHYRE (By Callander)

Mr & Mrs W Reid, Coire Buidhe, FK18 8NA. ☎ (01877) 384288 • Map 57/561170 • BB **B/C** • EM £10, 7pm • S2 D2 T2 F2 • 1-12 NX • Ⓥ Ⓑ Ⓓ • App/List

■ THORNHILL

Mrs Agnew, Braes of Boquhapple Farm, FK8 3QH. ☎ (01786) 850484 • Map 57/656019 • BB **B** • EM book first £5-£7, 7.30-8.30pm • S2 D1 F1 • 1-12 • Ⓥ Ⓓ 🛁 • SC caravan also

■ TYNDRUM (By Crianlarich, Perthshire)
WEST HIGHLAND WAY

☆ Invervey Hotel, FK20 8RY. ☎ (01838) 400219 • Map 50/329302 • BB **C/D** • EM £10, 5-9pm • S5 D5 T7 F4 • 1-12 NX • Ⓥ Ⓑ Ⓓ Ⓢ Ⓡ 🛁 • 2Cr/App • Groups also

B&B ACCOMMODATION SCOTLAND STIRLING

THE INVERVEY is a modern, comfortable, fully licensed family hotel, with a friendly and relaxed atmosphere where everyone is welcome. We are conveniently situated at Tyndrum in the Central Highlands, near the fork of the A82 and A85 for the famous Glencoe and the Pass of Brander. The West Highland Way runs close by us, and we are within easy reach of no less than 50 Munros! Of our 21 bedrooms, 18 have en-suite facilities and all rooms have telephones, tea/coffee making facilities and fully adjustable heating. With a choice of bars and lounges that

are licensed all day, the weary traveller can always find well prepared food in our restaurant. For your day out we will prepare packed lunches, and the drying room is always available when you return. We can also arrange special activity breaks such as package holidays on the West Highland Way, including pack carrying, taxi service and insurance, or ski breaks including ski hire and tuition. We also cater for functions such as weddings, club dinners and dances. Our prices are very competitive and the larger the group, the better the price!

Your hosts John and Barbara Riley will be delighted to see you

Tyndrum, by Crianlarich, Perthshire, Scotland FK20 8RY.
Telephone 01838 400219   Fax 01838 400280

STB ♛♛
Approved

WESTERN ISLES

■ HARRIS

Paula Williams, 2 Glen An T-ob, Leverburgh, HS5 3TY. ☎ (01859) 520319 • Map 18/997877 • BB **B** • EM book first £10, 7-8pm • T2 F1 • 1-12 NX • Ⓥ Ⓑ Ⓓ ♿ • SC also

Wales

CAMBRIAN WAY
CARDIFF - 274 miles - CONWY
The Association's members offer a chain of co-ordinated comfortable accommodation with daily transport to and from each stage. Guides and maps, available covering the whole length of Wales's longest long distance footpath.
Information pack and free logbook from Cambrian Way Walkers Association, Llandovery, SA20 0NB
Tel (01550) 750274 / Fax (01550) 750300

ANGLESEY

■ AMLWCH

☆ Bryn Arfor Guest House, Pen-y-Bonc, LL68 9DU. ☎ (01407) 831493 • Map 114/441933 • BB **B/C** • EM £9.95, 6-8pm • S2 D4 T2 F2 • 1-12 NX • Ⓥ Ⓑ Ⓓ Ⓢ Ⓜ • 2Cr/HC • Walking holidays also

ANGLESEY
Situated in a fabulous AONB, steeped in history. Self guided walks with maps and routes provided free of charge. Packed lunches, most rooms en-suite, hospitality guaranteed.

PEN-Y-BONC
AMLWCH. ANGLESEY LL68 9DU
TEL: (01407) 831493

HIGHLY COMMENDED BY WALES TOURIST BOARD

■ HOLYHEAD

Mrs B Simms, 4 Walthew Avenue, LL65 1AF. ☎ (01407) 762941 • Map 114/244830 • BB **B** • EM book first £6, 6-6.30pm • S1 D1 T1 • 1-12 • Ⓓ Ⓡ ♿

■ MENAI BRIDGE

☆ Ms Rosemary A Abas, Bwthyn, Brynafon, LL59 5HA. ☎ (01248) 713119 • Map 114, 115/557717 • BB **B** • EM book first £9.95, 6.30-7pm • D2 • 1-12 NX • Ⓥ Ⓑ Ⓢ Ⓡ • 2Cr/HC

CARMARTHENSHIRE

■ BRECHFA (Carmarthen)

☆ Glasfryn Guest House and Restaurant, SA32 7QY. ☎ (01267) 202306 • Map 146/526303 • BB **C** • EM £10-£12, 7-9pm • D2 T1 • 1-12 • Ⓥ Ⓑ Ⓓ Ⓢ • 3Cr/HC. See next column for display ad.

■ CARMARTHEN

Mrs Rosemary Jones, Trebersed Farm, St Peters, Travellers Rest, SA31 3RR. ☎ (01267) 238182 • Map 145,159/381200 • BB **C** • D1 T1 F1 • 1-12 NX • Ⓑ Ⓓ Ⓢ Ⓡ • 2Cr/HC

■ LLANDISSILIO (Clynderwen)
LANDSKER BORDERLANDS TRAIL

Mrs Janet Pogson, Plas y Brodyr, Rhydwilym, SA66 7QH. ☎ (01437) 563771 • Map 158/115246 • BB **B/C** • EM book first £12.50 • D2 T1 • 1-12 NX • Ⓥ Ⓑ Ⓓ Ⓢ • 2Cr/De-luxe • Collections from Clynderwen station

■ LLANDOVERY

Llwyncelyn Guest House, SA20 0EP. ☎ (01550) 720566 • Map 146/160/761347 • BB **C/D** • EM book first £12, 7pm • S1 D1 T3 F1 • 1-12 NX • Ⓥ Ⓓ Ⓢ Ⓡ • 1Cr/C

☆ Nick & Irena Bointon, LLanerchindda Farm, Cynghordy, SA20 0NB. ☎ (01550) 750274 • Map 160/807427 • BB **C** • EM £10, 7.30pm • S1 D4 T4 F1 • 1-12 NX • Ⓥ Ⓑ Ⓓ Ⓢ Ⓡ 🐾 Ⓜ • 2Cr/HC • Minibus available

■ LLANGYNOG

Margaret Thomas, Plas Farm, SA33 5DB. ☎ (01267) 211492 • Map 159/331173 • BB **B** • D1 T1 F1 • 1-12 NX • Ⓑ Ⓓ Ⓢ 🐾 • 2Cr/C

■ MYDDFAI (Llandovery)
CAMBRIAN WAY

Gill Swan, Beiliglas, SA20 0QB. ☎ (01550) 720494 • Map 146,160/782310 • BB **B** • EM book first £7, from 7pm • D1 T1 F1 • 1-12 • Ⓥ Ⓑ Ⓓ Ⓢ 🐾 • SC also

■ **RHANDIRMWYN (Llandovery)**

☆ Bryan & Pat Williams, Bwlch-y-Ffin, SA20 0PG. ☎ (01550) 760311, ring for exact location • Map 146,147/795481 • BB **B** • EM book first £10, 6.30-7.30pm • D1 T2 • 1-12 NX • Ⅴ Ⅾ Ⓢ 🐾

BWLCH-Y-FFIN
Rhandirmwyn

Close to Llyn Brianne in the southern Cambrian Mountains. Magnificent scenery, abundant wildlife – a centre for hillwalkers, naturalists & birdwatchers. H&C in all bedrooms, comfortable lounge, hearty breakfasts. Packed lunches, evening meals by arrangement. Dogs welcome.

Tel. Rhandirmwyn (01550) 760311

The Royal Oak Inn, SA20 0NY. ☎ (01550) 760201 • Map 146/785437 • BB **C/D** • EM £6.50, 6-10pm • S2 D1 T1 F1 • 1-12 • Ⅴ Ⓑ Ⅾ Ⓢ 🐾 • 1Cr

■ **ROSEBUSH (Clynderwen)**

Dot & Dave Thomas, The Old Post Office, SA66 7QU. ☎ (01437) 532205 • Map 158,145/076292 • BB **C** • EM from £6, from 7pm • D2 T1 • 1-12 • Ⅴ Ⅾ Ⓢ 🐾 • 1Cr/C

CEREDIGION

■ **ABERAERON**

Lisa Raw-Rees, Moldavia, 7 & 8 Bellevue Terr, SA46 0BB. ☎ (01545) 570107 • Map 146/457628 • BB **C/D** • S/T2 D2 F1 • 1-12 • Ⓑ Ⅾ Ⓢ 🐾 Ⓜ • 2Cr/HC

■ **ABERYSTWYTH**

Lester & Sarah Ward, Sinclair Guest House, 43 Portland Street, SY23 2DX. ☎ (01970) 615158 • Map 135/585819 • BB **D** • EM book first £10, 7pm • D1 T2 • 1-12 NX • Ⅴ Ⓑ Ⅾ Ⓢ Ⓡ • 3Cr/HC

■ **BOW STREET (Aberystwyth)**

Mrs A Edwards, Garreg Lwyd, Penygarn, SY24 5BE. ☎ (01970) 828830 • Map 135/625852 • BB **B/C** • S1 D1 T1 F1 • 1-12 NX • Ⅾ Ⓡ 🐾 • 1Cr/C

■ **CARDIGAN**

P Williams, Norbury, Napier Street, SA43 1ED. ☎ (01239) 613160 • Map 145/179463 • BB **A** • EM book first £5-£7, 6-7pm • S1 D2 T2 • 1-12 • Ⅴ Ⓑ

LAMPETER

Mrs Christine Longthorne, Tal-y-Fan, Cellan, SA48 8JA. ☎ (01570) 423158 • Map 146/603478 • BB **B** • EM book first £7.50, 7-8pm • D1 T1 • 1-11 • Ⅴ Ⅾ Ⓢ 🐾

■ **NEW QUAY**

Mrs V Kelly, Ty Hen Farm Hotel, Llwyndafydd, SA44 6BZ. ☎ (01545) 560346 • Map 145/360558 • BB **C/D** • EM book first £12.50, 7pm • D2 T2 • 3-10 • Ⅴ Ⓑ Ⅾ Ⓢ 🐾 • 3Cr/C • SC also

■ **PONTERWYD (Aberystwyth)**
CAMBRIAN WAY

☆ Islwyn & Angharad Jones, Dyffryn Castell Hotel, SY23 3LB. ☎ (01970) 890237 • Map 135/774817 • BB **C** • EM £12.50, 6.30-9pm • S2 D2 T1 F6 • 1-12 • Ⅴ Ⓑ Ⅾ Ⓢ 🐾 • 3Cr/C

DYFFRYN CASTELL HOTEL
Ponterwyd

400-year-old coaching inn on A44 London-Aberystwyth road. Well stocked bar, friendly atmosphere, wide range bar food. CH, TV lounge, games room, beer garden, children's play area. Tea/coffee facilities. Ideal rambling (5 Rivers Walk, Cambrian Way), bird watcing, trekking, fishing and magnificent scenery. Drying facilities.

Organiser—Central section of Cambrian Way

AA   **Tel. Ponterwyd (01970) 890237**   WTB

☆ John & Jill Wall, The George Borrow Hotel, SY23 3AD. ☎ (01970) 890230 • Map 135/746805 • BB **C** • EM £5.25, 6.30-9.30pm • D4 T4 F2 • 1-12 • Ⅴ Ⓑ Ⅾ 🐾 • 2Cr/C

The George Borrow Hotel
Ponterwyd, Dyfed

Aberystwyth 12 miles, famous Hotel in Cambrian Mountains WTB 2 Crown commended). Ideal for Cambrian Way or following in Borrow's footsteps. Marked walks locally. Good homemade food, packed lunches, log fires and stunning views over gorge. Central heating, TVs and tea facilities in all 9 letting rooms. En-suites available (01970) 890230

■ **TALYBONT**
DYFI VALLEY WAY

Glenys Evans, Llwyn Farm, SY24 5EQ. ☎ (01970) 832386 • Map 135/637892 • BB **B** • EM book first £7, from 6.30pm • S1 D2 T1 F1 • 1-12 NX • Ⅴ Ⓑ Ⅾ Ⓡ 🐾

■ **TREGARON**

Mrs Jacqueline Davies, Neuaddlas Country Guest House, SY25 6LG. ☎ (01974) 298905 • Map 146/669614 • BB **B** • EM book first £9.50, 7-7.30pm • D1 T2 F2 • 1-12 NX • Ⅴ Ⓑ Ⅾ Ⓢ 🐾 • 3Cr/C

☆ See Display Advertisement

CONWY

■ **BETWS-Y-COED**

☆ Fairy Glen Hotel, LL24 0SH. ☎ (01690) 710269 • Map 115/798546 • BB **C/D** • EM £12, 7-7.30pm • S1 D4 T3 F2 • 2-11 NX • Ⓥ Ⓑ Ⓓ Ⓢ Ⓡ ⬚ • 3Cr/HC

Fairy Glen Hotel, Snowdonia
BETWS-Y-COED, GWYNEDD LL24 0SH

A quiet comfortable hotel, ideally situated for exploring Snowdonia. Widely known for its comfort and excellent food. Full CH, many private bathrooms, licensed, packed lunches, drying facilities. Families, parties and individuals welcomed. Special out of season and group rates. Details from Graham Ball.

AA ★   WTB ✿ ✿ ✿ Highly Commended   RAC ★

Tel/Fax 01690 710269

Mrs N Parker, Bryn Llewelyn, LL24 0BN. ☎ (01690) 710601 • Map 115/784565 • BB **B/C** • S1 D3 T1 F2 • 1-12 • Ⓑ Ⓓ Ⓢ Ⓡ ⬚ • 2Cr/C

☆ Mrs M E Panting, Tan-y-Cyrau, LL24 0BL. ☎ (01690) 710653 • Map 115/787569 • BB **B** • EM £9.50 • S1 D3 T1 F1 • 1-12 • Ⓑ Ⓓ Ⓢ Ⓡ • 1Cr/HC

TAN-Y-CYRAU
Betwys-y-Coed

Tan-y-Cyrau is a unique Alpine-style house, situated in an elevated position on a private forestry road with superb views and lovely peaceful garden. All rooms have colour TV, washbasins, drink-making facilities. Two have own WCs. Non-smoking. WTB highly commended.

Tel 01690 710653

Mrs K Houghton, Royal Oak Farm Cottage, LL24 0AH. ☎ (01690) 710760 • Map 115/795564 • BB **B** • D2 T1 • 1-12 NX • Ⓑ Ⓓ Ⓢ Ⓡ • 2Cr

Betty & Roy Lampard, Glan Llugwy, LL24 0BN. ☎ (01690) 710592 • Map 115/784565 • BB **B** • S1 D2 T1 F1 • 1-12 NX • Ⓓ Ⓢ Ⓡ

Mr Roobottom, The Ferns, LL24 0AN. ☎ (01690) 710587 • Map 115/795562 • BB **B/C** • EM book first £10-£12, 7pm • S1 D6 T2 F2 • 1-12 • Ⓥ Ⓑ Ⓓ Ⓢ Ⓡ • 3Cr/HC

☆ Marion Betteney, Bryn Afon, LL24 0BB. ☎ (01690) 710403 • Map 115/792566 • BB **B** • S1 D4 T2 • 1-12 NX • Ⓑ Ⓓ Ⓢ Ⓡ

VEGETARIANS
Many establishments do a veggie breakfast even if they don't do an evening meal

---

Bryn Afon
Betws-y-Coed, Gwynedd

A comfortable, centrally situated guest house, with car park, by the river Llugwy. Drying facilities. TV. Coffee/tea maker in all rooms, some ensuite. Forest, mountain & lake walks at our doorstep.

Tel. 01690 710403

☆ Ray & Barbara Valadini, Henllys Hotel, The Old Courthouse, Old Church Road, LL24 0AL. ☎ (01690) 710534 • Map 115/795568 • BB **C/D** • EM £14.95, 7-7.30pm • S2 D3 T3 F2 • 2-11 & XMAS • Ⓥ Ⓑ Ⓓ Ⓢ Ⓡ Ⓜ • 3Cr/HC • Groups also

---

SNOWDONIA
Henllys – The Old Courthouse
Unique • Elegant • Antique • Peaceful riverside garden setting • Superb food • Spotless en suite rooms • Converted Victorian magistrates court. Warm welcome • No smoking • No pets.

Tel. 01690 710534

☆ Aberconwy House, Llanrwst Road, LL24 0HD. ☎ (01690) 710202 • Map 116/800565 • BB **C** • D3 T3 F2 • 3-12 • Ⓑ Ⓓ Ⓢ Ⓡ ⬚ • 3Cr/HC

ABERCONWY HOUSE
IS NESTLING IN A QUIET POSITION overlooking the picturesque village of Betws-y-Coed, Snowdonia National Park. Superbly furnished for comfort and relaxation. There are beautiful views of the valley, surrounding mountains and rivers. Central for walking, touring and other activities.

Llanrwst Road, Betws-y-Coed
Snowdonia National Park, North Wales
Tel 01690 710202

Mrs G Morris, Ty-Coch Farm, LL25 0NJ. ☎ (01690) 760248 • Map 115/773525 • BB **C** • EM book first £8, 7pm • D2 F2 • 1-12 NX • Ⓥ Ⓑ Ⓓ Ⓢ ⬚ • 3Cr • SC also

Mrs Joyce Melling, Mount Pleasant, LL24 0BN. ☎ (01690) 710502 • Map 115/789567 • BB **B/C** • D4 • 1-12 • Ⓑ Ⓓ Ⓢ Ⓡ

☆ Jim & Lillian Boughton, Bron Celyn Guest House, Llanrwst Road, LL24 0HD. ☎ (01690) 710333 • Map 116/800565 • BB **B/C** • EM £9.50, 7pm • S1 D2 T1 F1 • 1-12 • Ⓥ Ⓑ Ⓓ Ⓢ Ⓡ • 3Cr/HC • SC also

BRON CELYN

Beautiful situation in Snowdonia National Park overlooking the village of Betws-y-Coed and Conwy/Llugwy Valleys. Most rooms en-suite, all with colour TV and beverage trays. Car parking, hearty breakfasts, packed lunches, evening meals. Christmas/New Year & out of season breaks.

Jim & Lilian Boughton
Bron Celyn Guest House
Llanrwst Road
Betws-y-Coed LL24 0HD
Tel. 01690 710333
Fax 01690 710111

WTB ● ● ● HIGHLY COMMENDED

Mrs S Walsh, "Maelgwyn", LL24 0AN. ☎ (01690) 710252 • Map 115/795562 • BB **B/C** • D2 T2 • 1-12 NX • Ⓑ Ⓓ Ⓢ Ⓡ • 2Cr

☆ Margaret Martin, Mairlys Guest House, Holyhead Road, LL24 0AN. ☎ (01690) 710190 • Map 115/795562 • BB **C** • S1 D3 T1 • 3-11 + XMAS • Ⓑ Ⓓ Ⓢ Ⓡ • 2Cr/HC

Sue McGregor, Swn-y-Dwr, Pentrefelin, LL24 0BB. ☎ (01690) 710648 • Map 115/792566 • BB **B** • D2 F1 • 1-12 • Ⓑ Ⓓ Ⓢ Ⓡ

■ **CAPEL CURIG (Betws-y-Coed)**

☆ N & D Riley, Bron Eryri, LL24 0EE. ☎ (01690) 720240 • Map 115/734573 • BB **C** • D3 T1 F1 • 1-12 NX • Ⓑ Ⓓ Ⓢ • 2Cr/HC

☆ Alison Cousins, Bryn Glo Cafe, LL24 0DT. ☎ (01690) 720215/720312 • Map 115/736570 • BB **B** • EM book first £8.50, 6-7pm • D1 T1 F1 • 1-12 • Ⓥ Ⓑ Ⓓ Ⓢ • 1 Cr

Mr J Davies, Llugwy Guest House, LL24 0ES. ☎ (01690) 720218 • Map 115/719581 • BB **B** • EM book first £10, 6.30pm • S2 D2 T1 F2 • 1-12 NX • Ⓓ Ⓢ • 1Cr/C

■ **LLANDUDNO**

Mr & Mrs L P Lesiter, Carmel, 17 Craig y Don Parade, Promenade, LL30 1BG. ☎ (01492) 877643 • Map 115/795820 • BB **B** • EM book first £6.50-£7, 6.30pm • D6 T1 F2 • 3-10 • Ⓥ Ⓑ Ⓓ Ⓢ Ⓡ Ⓜ • C

Brannock Hotel, 36 St. David's Road, LL30 2UH. ☎ (01492) 877483 • Map 115/780819 • BB **B** • EM £6, 6pm (not Sun.) • S2 D3 T2 F1 • 2-12 NX • Ⓑ Ⓓ Ⓢ Ⓡ • 3Cr/HC

■ **LLANFAIRFECHAN**

Mr & Mrs Colin Goodey, The Towers, Promenade, LL33 0DA. ☎ (01248) 680012 • Map 115/679753 • BB **B/C** • S3 D4 T2 F2 • 1-12 • Ⓑ Ⓓ Ⓢ Ⓡ • SC and bunkhouse also

Plas Heulog, Mount Road, LL33 0HA. ☎ (01248) 680019 • Map 115/697747 • BB **B/C** • EM book first £8, 7pm • D2 T7 • 2-11 • Ⓥ Ⓑ Ⓓ Ⓢ Ⓡ • 2Cr/C

■ **LLANRWST**

Mr & Mrs M Richardson, Llys Cerdd, Watling Street, LL26 0LS. ☎ (01492) 640636 • Map 115/798616 • BB **A** • D2 F1 • 1-12 • Ⓓ Ⓡ Ⓜ

Mrs Eleanore Roberts, "Awelon", Plas Isa, LL26 0EE. ☎ (01492) 640047 • Map 115/805615 • BB **B** • EM book first £6, 6.30pm • D2 F1 • 3-10 • Ⓥ Ⓑ Ⓓ Ⓢ Ⓡ • 1Cr

■ **PENMACHNO (Betws-y-Coed)**

Mrs G Morris, Ty Coch Farm, LL25 0HJ. ☎ (01690) 760248 • Map 115/770525 • BB **C** • EM book first £8, 7pm • D2 F2 • 1-12 NX • Ⓥ Ⓑ Ⓓ Ⓢ • 3Cr

■ **TREFRIW**

☆ Philip Booth, Argoed Guest House, LL27 0TX. ☎ (01492) 640091 • Map 115/780631 • BB **B** • EM £10, 7pm • S2 D2 T1 F1 • 3-10 + New Year • Ⓥ Ⓑ Ⓓ Ⓢ Ⓡ Ⓜ • 2Cr/C. See over for display ad.

GWYNEDD

■ ABERDARON (Pwllheli)

Vivien Bate, Bryn Mor, LL53 8BS. ☎ (01758) 760344
• Map 123/168265 • BB **B** • EM £6.50, 6pm • S1 D1
T1 F2 • 1-11 • Ⓥ Ⓓ Ⓢ

■ ABERSOCH

Mrs Chris Stanworth, Angorfa Guest House, Lon-
Sarn-Bach, LL53 7EB. ☎ (01758) 712967 • Map
123/313279 • BB **B/C** • EM book first £9, from
6.30pm • D3 T2 F1 • 1-11 • Ⓥ Ⓑ Ⓓ Ⓢ • SC also

Mrs Janet Clark, Crowrach Isaf Guest House,
Bwlchtocyn, LL53 7BY. ☎ (01758) 712860 • Map
123/311252 • BB **C** • EM £12.50, 7pm • S1 D2 T1 • 3-
10 • Ⓑ Ⓓ Ⓢ • 3Cr/Deluxe • SC also

■ BALA

Mr T G Jones, Frondderw, Stryd-y-fron, LL23 7YD.
☎ (01678) 520301 • Map 125/915363 • BB **B/C** • EM
book first £9, 7pm • S2 D2 T2 F3 • 3-11 NX • Ⓥ Ⓑ
Ⓓ Ⓢ • 3Cr/C • Groups also

☆ Mrs J M Cunningham, Abercelyn, Llanycil, LL23
7YF. ☎ (01678) 521109 • Map 125/913352 • BB **C** •
D2 T1 F1 • 1-10+12 NX • Ⓑ Ⓓ Ⓢ ⚘ • 3Cr/HC • SC
also

BALA LAKE
Southern Snowdonia
Former Rectory in own grounds, spacious bedrooms, log fires,
home-produce cooking. Quiet walking in uncrowded
mountain scenery away from popular routes. Guided walking.
Visitors can be met by car. S/C cottage (sleeps 6) nearby.
Brochure Mrs Judy Cunningham,
Abercelyn. Tel: 01678 521109

Mrs L Andrews, Bronwylfa Guest House & Coach
House, Llandderfel, LL23 7HG. ☎ (01678)
530207/530395 • Map 125/982374 • BB **C** • EM book
first £9, 6.30-7pm • D2 T1 F1 • 1-12 • Ⓑ Ⓓ Ⓢ ⚘ •
2Cr/De Luxe

Dee & Peter Smith, Tyn-y-Fron, Crogen, Llanderfel,
LL23 7RG. ☎ (01490) 440346 • Map 125/022366 •
BB **B** • EM book first £8.50, 6.30-7.30pm • T/F2 • 1-
11 • Ⓥ Ⓓ • SC also

■ BARMOUTH
CAMBRIAN WAY

Mrs D Lewis, The Gables, Mynach Rd, LL42 1RL. ☎
(01341) 280553 • Map 124/609166 • BB **B** • EM book
first £10, 6.30-7.30pm • S1 D2 F1 • 2-11 • Ⓥ Ⓑ Ⓓ
Ⓢ Ⓡ ⚘ • 2Cr/C • Guided walks also

■ BEDDGELERT (Caernarfon)
CAMBRIAN WAY

☆ Lynda Osmond, Plas Colwyn Guest House, LL55
4UY. ☎ (01766) 890458 • Map 115/589482 • BB **B/C**
• EM restaurant • S1 D2 T1 F2 • 1-12 • Ⓥ Ⓑ Ⓓ Ⓢ •
3Cr

☆ Mr & Mrs Brian Maddison, Mizpah, Plas Tan-y-
Graig, LL55 4LT. ☎ (01766) 890329 • Map
115/591482 • BB **B** • EM book first £8.50, 7-7.30pm •
D3 T1 F3 • 1-12 NX • Ⓥ Ⓓ ⚘ • Bunkhouse also

☆ Ael Y Bryn, Caernarfon Road, LL55 4UY. ☎
(01766) 890310 • Map 115/587483 • BB **B/C** • EM
£10, 7-8pm • D2 T1 • 1-12 NX • Ⓥ Ⓑ Ⓓ Ⓢ • 1Cr

(side margin) GWYNEDD · CONWY · WALES · B&B ACCOMMODATION

Ael Y Bryn
Caernarfon Road
Beddgelert
Gwynedd
LL55 4UY

Beautiful views and warm welcome await visitors to Ael Y Bryn. Comfortable, newly refurbished accommodation now including en suite. Good home cooking, vegetarians welcome.

Tel. 01766 890310 for brochure
Fax 01766 890629

☆ Joan Williams, "Colwyn", LL55 4UY. ☎ (01766) 890276 • Map 115/587483 • BB **C** • D/T3 F1 • 1-12 NX • Ⓑ Ⓓ ⚄ Ⓜ • Food nearby

Colwyn
Beddgelert
Snowdonia

Beddgelert Village Centre
Small Cottage Guesthouse overlooking River, Most Rooms En-Suite
Muddy Boots and Pets Welcome
B&B £21   3 nts £19.50   5 nts £18.50
(booking advisable)
Joan Williams 01766 890 276
[Also Cottage Sleeps Two £165 wk]

■ CAERNARFON

Mr & Mrs Hamilton, "Parkia", Bangor Road, LL55 1TP. ☎ (01286) 676496 • Map 114,115/495645 • BB **C** • D2 • 1-12 NX • Ⓑ Ⓓ Ⓢ ⚄ • 2Cr • Bunkhouse and SC also

Plas Menai National Watersports Centre, Llanfairisgaer, LL55 1UE. ☎ (01248) 670964 • Map 114,115/502661 • BB **B/D** • EM book first £4.45, 6pm • T34 • 1-12 NX • Ⓥ Ⓑ Ⓓ Ⓢ • Groups also

■ CRICCIETH

Moelwyn Restaurant & Rooms, 27/29 Mona Terrace, LL52 0HG. ☎ (01766) 522500 • Map 124/500380 • BB **B/C** • EM £14, 6.30-8.30pm • D4 T2 • 3-12 NX • Ⓥ Ⓑ Ⓓ Ⓢ Ⓡ ⚄ • 3Cr/HC

■ DOLGELLAU
CAMBRIAN WAY

Mr & Mrs E P Rowlands, Tanyfron, Arran Road, LL40 2AA. ☎ (01341) 422638 • Map 124/735176 • BB **C** • D1 T1 F1 • 2-11 • Ⓑ Ⓓ Ⓢ • 2Cr/HC • SC also

Mrs S Harris, Bryn Ffynnon, Love Lane, LL40 1RR. ☎ (01341) 422738 • Map 124/726176 • BB **B** • EM £7.50 • D1 T1 F2 • 1-12 • Ⓥ Ⓑ Ⓓ Ⓢ ⚄ Ⓜ • SC also

☆ Baron & Margaret Westwood, Esgair Wen Newydd, Garreg Feurig, Llanfachreth Road, LL40 2YA. ☎ (01341) 423952 • Map 124/736185 • BB **B** • EM book first £7.50, 7pm • D2 T1 • 1-12 NX • Ⓥ Ⓓ Ⓢ • 1Cr/HC

Baron & Margaret Westwood
Esgair Wen Newydd
Garreg Feurig, Llanfachreth Road
Dolgellau, Gwynedd LL40 2YA

New bungalow, fantastic mountain views. Very quiet, private parking. H&C, tea/coffee all bedrooms. High standard of home cooking, comfort, cleanliness. Personal attention assured, highly recommended by past guests. Food Hygiene and Welcome Host certificates. No smoking/pets. WTB ☗ Highly Commended.

Tel. 01341 423952

☆ Mrs N Jones, Dwy Olwyn, Coed-y-Fronallt, LL40 2YG. ☎ (01341) 422822 • Map 124/734183 • BB **B** • EM £7.50, 7pm • D1 T2 F1 • 2-11 • Ⓥ Ⓓ Ⓢ • 2Cr/HC

Mrs N. Jones
DWY OLWYN
DOLGELLAU, GWYNEDD
LL40 2YG
TEL. 01341 422822

A comfortable guesthouse in an acre of landscaped gardens, magnificent views of Cader Idris. Peaceful position yet only 10 minutes walk from town. Ideal base for touring, within Snowdonia National Park. Convenient for sandy beaches, narrow gauge railways, gold mines, alternative technology centre, RSPB sanctuary, picturesque walks including famous Precipice Walk high above Mawddach estuary. Spacious bedrooms with colour TVs, hot and cold water, good home cooking; lounge with colour TV. Ample parking. Packed lunches if required. Cleanliness and personal attention assured. Tea/coffee facilities all bedrooms. WTB Approved 2 crowns and Commended. Brochure available.

☆ J S & M Bamford, Ivy House, Finsbury Square, LL40 1RF. ☎ (01341) 422535 • Map 124/727177 • BB **C/D** • EM Restaurant, 5-9.30pm • D3 T2 F1 • 1-12 • Ⓥ Ⓑ Ⓓ ⚄ • 3Cr/C

IVY HOUSE
DOLGELLAU

A country town guesthouse and restaurant, close to Cader Idris and magnificent Mawddach estuary, perfect walking area. Full central heating, lounge, cellar bar. All bedrooms TV and tea/coffee facilities, some en suite. Packed lunches.   WTB ☖☖☖
Tel. 01341 422535   Commended

■ HARLECH

Mrs J Jones, Tyddyn Gwynt, LL46 2TH. ☎ (01766) 780298 • Map 124/593298 • BB **B** • EM book first £8 • S1 D1 T1 F1 • 1-12 • Ⓓ Ⓡ 🦶 • 1Cr

Gweneth Evans, Glanygors, Llandanwg, LL46 2SD. ☎ (01341) 241410 • Map 124/570285 • BB **A/B** • EM book first £8, 6pm • D1 T1 F1 • 1-12 • Ⓥ Ⓓ Ⓢ Ⓡ 🦶 • 1Cr/HC

☆ Deborah Williams, Gwrach Ynys Country Guest Hse, Ynys, Talsarnau, LL47 6TS. ☎ (01766) 780742 • Map 124/591359 • BB **C** • EM £12, 6.30pm • S1 D2 T1 F3 • 2-11 • Ⓥ Ⓑ Ⓓ Ⓢ Ⓡ 🦶 • 3Cr/De Luxe

☆ Ann Jones, Fron Deg, Llanfair, LL46 2RE. ☎ (01766) 780448 • Map 124/575295 • BB **B** • EM book first £8, 6.30-7pm • S1 D1 T1 • 3-10 • Ⓑ Ⓓ Ⓡ 🦶 • 1Cr

■ LLANBERIS (Caernarfon)

Mount Pleasant Hotel, High Street, LL55 4HA. ☎ (01286) 870395 • Map 114,115/577602 • BB **B/C** • EM £9, 6-9pm • S2 D2 T1 F2 • 1-12 • Ⓥ Ⓑ Ⓓ 🦶 • 2Cr • Groups also

Mrs J I Watson, Beech Bank, High Street, LL55 4EN. ☎ (01286) 870414 • Map 114,115/576605 • BB **B** • S1 D4 T2 F1 • 1-12 NX • Ⓓ • 1Cr

Dolafon Hotel, High St, LL55 4SU. ☎ (01286) 870993 • Map 114,115/578600 • BB **B/C** • EM £10-£15, 7-8.30pm • S1 D2 T3 F3 • 1-11 • Ⓥ Ⓑ Ⓓ Ⓢ • 2Cr

Snowdon Cottage, Pentre Castell, LL55 4UB. ☎ (01286) 872015 • Map 115/585596 • BB **B** • EM book first £12, 7pm • S1 D1 T1 • 1-12 • Ⓥ Ⓓ Ⓢ Ⓜ • SC also

■ LLANUWCHLLYN (Bala)
DYFI VALLEY WAY

Mrs Fran Burn, Brynllech Isaf, LL23 7SU. ☎ (01678) 540374 • Map 124,125/855317 • BB **B** • S1 T1 • 2-12 NX • Ⓑ Ⓓ Ⓢ

■ MAENTWROG (Blaenau Ffestiniog)

Mrs E Jackson, Bron-y-Wern, LL41 4HN. ☎ (01766) 590210 • Map 124/665405 • BB **B** • S1 D1 T1 • 1-12 NX • Ⓓ Ⓢ

■ MALLWYD (Machynlleth, Powys)
CAMBRIAN WAY & DYFI VALLEY WAY

Brigands Inn, SY20 9HJ. ☎ (01650) 531208 • Map 124/863125 • BB **C/D** • EM £4.95-£15.50, 6.30-9.15pm • S2 D3 T4 F2 • 1-12 • Ⓥ Ⓑ Ⓓ 🦶 • 2Cr

■ NANTGWYNANT (Caernarfon)

Pen-y-Gwryd Hotel, Pen-y-Gwryd, LL55 4NT. ☎ (01286) 870211 + 870768 • Map 115/660558 • BB **C/D** • EM £15, 7.30-8pm • S1 D8 T6 F1 • 1-11 • Ⓥ Ⓑ Ⓓ Ⓢ 🦶

■ PANT GLAS

☆ Terry Gibbins, Hen Ysgol (Old School), Bwlch Derwin, LL51 9EQ. ☎ (01286) 660701 • Map 115/456474 • BB **B/C** • EM book first £8 • S1 D1 T1 F1 • 1-12 • Ⓥ Ⓑ Ⓓ Ⓢ 🦶 • Bunkhouse also

■ PENRHYNDEUDRAETH (Porthmadog)

☆ Hilary & Paul Davies, Talgarth, LL48 6DR. ☎ (01766) 770353 • Map 124/615398 • BB **B** • EM book first £6, 7pm • S3 D1 • 1-12 NX • Ⓥ Ⓑ Ⓓ Ⓢ Ⓡ

■ TRAWSFYNYDD (Blaenau Ffestiniog)

Daphne Percival, Bodyfuddau, LL41 4UW. ☎ (01766) 540553 • Map 124/730353 • BB **B** • EM book first £6.50 • S1 D1 T1 • 1-12 • Ⓥ Ⓓ Ⓢ 🗲

MONMOUTHSHIRE

■ ABERGAVENNY

Mr & Mrs B Cook, The Guest House & Mansel Restaurant, 2 Oxford Street, NP7 5RP. ☎ (01873) 854823 • Map 161/303147 • BB **B/C** • EM £9.99, 5.30-8pm • S2 D5 T5 F3 • 1-12 • Ⓥ Ⓓ Ⓢ Ⓡ • 1Cr

Julia Herring, Park Guest House, 36 Hereford Road, NP7 5RA. ☎ (01873) 853715 • Map 161/303146 • BB **B/C** • EM book first £11, 6.30pm • S1 D3 T2 F1 • 1-12 NX • Ⓥ Ⓓ Ⓡ • 1Cr/C

Chris & Sandra Belcham, Tyn y Bryn, Deriside, NP7 7HT. ☎ (01873) 856682 • Map 161/278204 • BB **C** • EM book first £8.50, 7.30-8.30pm • D1 T1 F1 • 1-12 NX • Ⓥ Ⓑ Ⓓ Ⓢ 🗲 • 3Cr • SC also

■ CHEPSTOW
OFFA'S DYKE & WYE VALLEY WALK

Eileen Grassby, Lower Hardwick House, Hardwick Hill, NP6 5PT. ☎ (01291) 622162 • Map 172, 162/531935 • BB **B/C** • S2 D2 T2 F2 • 1-12 • Ⓑ Ⓓ Ⓡ 🗲 • Camping also

Beaufort Hotel, Beaufort Square, NP6 5EP. ☎ (01291) 622497 • Map 172,162/534939 • BB **D** • EM £8, 6-9.30pm • S6 D7 T4 F2 • 1-12 • Ⓥ Ⓑ Ⓓ Ⓡ 🗲 • 3Cr/HC • Groups also

■ GILWERN (Abergavenny)
CAMBRIAN WAY

☆ B L Harris, The Wenallt, NP7 0HP. ☎ (01873) 830694 • Map 161/244136 • BB **C** • EM book first £10, 7.30pm • S6 D5 T2 F1 • 1-12 • Ⓥ Ⓑ Ⓓ Ⓡ 🗲 • 3Cr/C

The Wenallt

GILWERN, NR ABERGAVENNY, GWENT
16thC Longhouse nestling in Brecon Beacons National Park. Ideal for walking in Beacons, Black Mountains, Offa's Dyke, Brecon-Monmouth canal. Optional evening meal and packed lunch. Central heating, drying room. En suite rooms. **01873 830694**

■ LLANFIHANGEL CRUCORNEY (Abergavenny)
OFFA'S DYKE

Ann Davies, Penyclawdd Farm, NP7 7LB. ☎ (01873) 890591 • Map 161/312200 • BB **B** • EM book first £7 • S/D/F2 • 1-12 • Ⓥ Ⓓ Ⓢ Ⓡ 🗲 • List/C

■ LLANTHONY (Abergavenny)
OFFA'S DYKE

Christine Smith, The Half Moon, NP7 7NN. ☎ (01873) 890611 • Map 161/286279 • BB **B/C** • EM £5, 7-8.30pm • D4 T2 F1 • 1-12 NX • Ⓥ Ⓓ 🗲

■ LLANTILIO CROSSENNY (Abergavenny)
OFFA'S DYKE

Mrs Beryl Ford, Little Treadam, NP7 8TA. ☎ (01600) 780326 • Map 161/383149 • BB **C** • EM book first £10, 7.30pm • S1 D2 T2 • 3-12 NX • Ⓥ Ⓑ Ⓓ Ⓢ 🗲 Ⓜ • 3CrHC

■ MONMOUTH
OFFA'S DYKE & WYE VALLEY WALK

Mrs Cantrell, Wye Avon, Dixton Road, NP5 3PR. ☎ (01600) 713322 • Map 162/512134 • BB **B** • S1 D1 T1 F1 • 1-12 NX • Ⓓ Ⓢ

☆ Church Farm Guest House, Mitchel Troy, NP5 4HZ. ☎ (01600) 712176 • Map 162/493104 • BB **C** • EM book first £11, 7-7.30pm • S1 D3 T2 F2 • 1-12 NX • Ⓥ Ⓑ Ⓓ Ⓢ 🗲 Ⓜ • 2Cr/C • SC also. See also Walking Holidays section: Wysk Walks

Mrs M Evans, Tresco, Redbrook, NP5 4LY. ☎ (01600) 712325 • Map 162/536101 • BB **B** • EM £7.50, 6-6.30pm • S2 D1 T/D/F1 • 1-12 • Ⓥ Ⓓ Ⓢ 🗲 Ⓜ • SC also

The Riverside Hotel, Cinderhill Street, NP5 3EY. ☎ (01600) 715577/713236 • Map 162/504123 • BB **D** • EM £6-£12, 6-9.30pm • D6 T9 F2 • 1-12 • Ⓑ Ⓓ 🗲 • 4Cr/HC • No smoking restaurant

Yvone Beale, Cherry Orchard Farm, Lone Lane, Penallt, NP5 4AJ. ☎ (01600) 714010 • Map 162/535105 • BB **B** • EM book first £9.50, 7.30-8.30pm • D1 T1 • 1-12 NX • Ⓥ Ⓓ Ⓢ 🗲 • List/App

■ TINTERN (Chepstow)
OFFA'S DYKE & WYE VALLEY WALK

Wendy Taylor, The Old Rectory, NP6 6SG. ☎ (01291) 689519 • Map 162/530007 • BB **B** • EM book first £9, 7.30pm • S1 D2 T2 F1 • 1-12 NX • Ⓑ Ⓓ Ⓢ 🗲 • 1Cr

☆ See Display Advertisement

MONMOUTHSHIRE

GWYNEDD

WALES

B&B ACCOMMODATION

293

■ TINTERN (CONTINUED)

Judith Russill, Wye Barn, The Quay, NP6 6SZ. ☎ (01291) 689456 • Map 162/531002 • BB **C** • EM book first £12.50, 7pm • S1 T2 • 1-12 NX • Ⓑ Ⓓ Ⓢ • List

Dereck & Vickie Stubbs, Parva Farmhouse Hotel, NP6 6SQ. ☎ (01291) 689411 • Map 162/526009 • BB **D** • EM £16.50, 7-8.30pm • D3 T3 F3 • 1-12 • Ⓥ Ⓑ Ⓓ 🐾 • 4Cr/HC

G T & M M Mark, Holmleigh, Monmouth Road, NP6 6SG. ☎ (01291) 689521 • Map 162/529008 • BB **B** • S1 D1 T1 • 1-12 • Ⓓ 🐾

NORTH EAST WALES

THE AUTHORITIES OF DENBIGHSHIRE, FLINTSHIRE & WREXHAM

■ BODFARI (Denbigh)
OFFA'S DYKE

Mrs Edna Ellis, Lleweni Hall, LL16 4BW. ☎ (01745) 812908 • Map 116/081685 • BB **B** • S/T1 D2 F1 • 7-5 • Ⓓ Ⓢ 🐾

■ CHIRK (Wrexham)
OFFA'S DYKE

Len & Barbara Berry, Pedlar Corner, Colliery Rd, LL14 5PB. ☎ (01691) 772903 • Map 126/292379 • BB **B** • T2 • 1-12 NX • Ⓓ Ⓢ Ⓡ

■ CORWEN (Denbighshire)

Corwen Court Private Hotel, London Road, LL21 0DP. ☎ (01490) 412854 • Map 125/080434 • BB **B** • EM book first £7, 7pm • S6 D4 • 3-11 • Ⓥ Ⓑ Ⓓ 🐾 • 2Cr/C

☆ Central Hotel, The Square, LL21 0DE. ☎ (01490) 412462 • Map 125/079434 • BB **C/D** • EM £8.50, 7-10.30pm • S1 D4 T3 F2 • 1-12 NX • Ⓥ Ⓑ Ⓓ 🐾 Ⓜ • 2Cr

---

CENTRAL HOTEL, CORWEN
With the River Dee on its doorstep and the Berwyn Mountains rising up behind, Corwen is a haven for travellers – a gateway to the "Wilds of North Wales". The Central Hotel continues this tradition with its warm welcome and excellent cuisine. Situated in the Market Square, it is ideal for the rambler both locally and as a centre for more distant excursions. Help and assistance with your itinerary is always available. Reduced rates out of season. Licensed.
Telephone 01490 412462

■ DENBIGH

Cayo Guest House, 74 Vale Street, LL16 3BW. ☎ (01745) 812686 • Map 116/055663 • BB **B** • EM book first £9, 6.30-7pm • S1 D2 T3 • 1-12 NX • Ⓥ Ⓑ Ⓢ 🐾 • 3Cr

■ HANMER (Whitchurch, Salop)

Hanmer Arms Village Hotel, SY13 3DE. ☎ (01948) 830640/532 • Map 117/457406 • BB **B/C/D** • EM £8-£15, 6-10pm • S1 D15 T4 F4 • 1-12 • Ⓥ Ⓑ Ⓓ 🐾 Ⓜ • 4Cr/HC • Maelor Way

■ LLANARMON DYFFRYN CEIRIOG (Llangollen)

Mrs J Jones, Ty Gwyn, LL20 7LD. ☎ (01691) 600229 • Map 125/157328 • BB **A** • EM book first £8, 7-7.30pm • S1 D1 T1 • 2-11 • Ⓜ

`Hillwalk Wales'`, "Gwynfa" Guest House, LL20 7LF. ☎ (01691) 600287 • Map 125/155326 • BB **B** • EM book first £9.75, 7pm • T2 F1 • 2-11 • Ⓥ Ⓑ Ⓓ Ⓢ Ⓜ • 2Cr/HC • Guided walks also

■ LLANDEGLA (Wrexham)
OFFA'S DYKE

The Hand, LL11 3AW. ☎ (01978) 790337/790417 • Map 116/194524 • BB **B** • EM £7.50, 7-8pm • D2 T1 F1 • 1-12 NX • Ⓥ Ⓑ Ⓓ Ⓢ

■ LLANDRILLO (Corwen, Denbighshire)

Mrs S E Stille, Fron Goch Farmhouse, LL21 0NA. ☎ (01490) 440418 • Map 125/046391 • BB **C/D** • EM £10, until 7.30pm • S2 D2 T2 F1 • 1-12 • Ⓥ Ⓑ Ⓓ Ⓢ 🐾 • 3Cr

■ LLANGOLLEN (Denbighshire)
OFFA'S DYKE

Jean Lewis, Dinbren House, Dinbren Road, LL20 8TF. ☎ (01978) 860593 • Map 117/213424 • BB **B** • D2 F1 • 1-12 NX • Ⓑ Ⓓ Ⓢ 🐾 Ⓜ • 2Cr

Mrs B W Evans, The Grange, Grange Road, LL20 8AP. ☎ (01978) 860366 • Map 117/218413 • BB **C** • D2 T1 F2 • 1-12 NX • Ⓑ Ⓓ Ⓢ • 2Cr/HC

☆ Mrs Eira Jeffreys, Hendy Isa, Horseshoe Pass Road, LL20 8DE. ☎ (01978) 861232 • Map 117/201444 • BB **B** • F4 • 1-12 • Ⓑ Ⓓ Ⓢ Ⓜ • 2Cr/HC • Food nearby

---

Hendy Isa
Horseshoe Pass Road, Llangollen LL20 8DE
Quiet country house set amongst beautiful scenery in little known part of Wales. Many varied walks and other local attractions. Tastefully furnished spacious bedrooms with minibar. Private parking. Wholesome Welsh breakfasts. Hosts keen walkers.

WTB Highly Commended

☎ (01978) 861232

Mrs Joan Lloyd, Hillcrest Guest House, Hill Street, LL20 8EU. ☎ (01978) 860208 • Map 117/217418 • BB **C** • EM from £4.50, 5.30-7.30pm • D3 T2 F2 • 1-12 NX • Ⓥ Ⓑ Ⓢ • 3Cr/HC

Dee Farm, Rhewl, LL20 7YT. ☎ (01978) 861598 •
Map 125/180448 • BB **B/C** • EM book first £8, 6-7pm
• S1 T2 • 3-10 • Ⓥ Ⓑ Ⓓ Ⓢ 🍴 • 2Cr/C

☆ Jeremy & Lindsay Knibbs, Oakmere, Regent
Street, LL20 8HS. ☎ (01978) 861126 • Map
117/218418 • BB **C** • D2 T2 F2 • 1-12 • Ⓑ Ⓓ Ⓢ •
2Cr/HC

Robert Jaques, Bryn Derwen Hotel, Abbey Road,
LL20 8EF. ☎ (01978) 860583 • Map 117/209431 •
BB **D** • EM £10, 7-9pm • S4 D4 T6 F2 • 1-12 NX • Ⓥ
Ⓑ Ⓓ 🍴 • 3Cr/C • Groups also

■ LLANGYNHAFAL (Ruthin, Denbighshire)
OFFA'S DYKE

Mrs I Henderson, Esgairlygain, LL15 1RT. ☎ (01824)
704047 • Map 116/135625 • BB **B** • EM book first £9,
7pm • D1 T1 F1 • 1-12 NX • Ⓥ Ⓑ Ⓓ Ⓢ 🍴 • 3Cr

■ NANNERCH (Mold, Flintshire)
OFFA'S DYKE

☆ The Old Mill Private Hotel, Melin-y-Wern, Denbigh
Road, CH7 5RH. ☎ (01352) 741542 • Map
116/163703 • BB **D** • EM £15.95, 6-8pm • S6 D5 T3
F2 • 1-12 NX • Ⓥ Ⓑ Ⓓ Ⓢ 🍴 • 3Cr/HC

■ PRESTATYN (Denbighshire)
OFFA'S DYKE

Y Kubler, Roughsedge Guest House, 26-28 Marine
Rd, LL19 7HD. ☎ (01745) 887359 • Map
116/066833 • BB **B/C** • EM book first £9, 7pm • S2
D4 T2 F2 • 1-12 NX • Ⓥ Ⓑ Ⓓ Ⓢ Ⓡ • 2Cr/C

■ RUTHIN (Denbighshire)

Mrs M Ranson, "Rhianfa", Ffordd Llanrhydd,, LL15
1PP. ☎ (01824) 702971 • Map 116/127581 • BB **B** •
EM book first £7.50 • D2 T1 • 1-12 NX • Ⓥ Ⓑ Ⓓ Ⓢ
• List

Jen & Bert Spencer, Eyarth Station, Llanfair DC, LL15
2EE. ☎ (01824) 703643 • Map 116/130557 • BB **C** •
EM £6.50-£13, 7pm • D2 T2 F2 • 1-12 • Ⓥ Ⓑ Ⓓ 🍴 •
3Cr/HC

PEMBROKESHIRE

■ ABEREIDDY (Croesgoch)
PEMBROKESHIRE COAST PATH

Mrs P V Lloyd, Bank House Farm, SA62 6XZ. ☎
(01348) 831305 • Map 157/817303 • BB **A/B** • EM
book first £8, 6-7pm • D1 T1 • 2-11 • Ⓥ Ⓓ 🍴 • List

■ AMROTH (Narberth)
PEMBROKESHIRE COAST PATH & LANDSKER BORDERLANDS
TRAIL

Roy & Edith Williamson, Ashdale Guest House, SA67
8NA. ☎ (01834) 813853 • Map 158/160071 • BB **A/B**
• EM £6.95, 6pm • S1 T1 F4 • 3-11 • Ⓥ Ⓓ Ⓢ Ⓡ 🍴
• 2Cr

■ ANGLE (Pembroke)
PEMBROKESHIRE COAST PATH

Mrs S Reece, Timothy Lodge, 39 Angle, SA71 5AT.
☎ (01646) 641342 • Map 157/865028 • BB **B** • T1 •
3-10 • Ⓑ Ⓓ Ⓢ 🍴

■ BEREA (St David's)
PEMBROKESHIRE COAST PATH

Cwmwdig Water Guest House, SA62 6DW. ☎
(01348) 831434 • Map 157/806304 • BB **C** • EM £12,
7pm • S2 D5 T5 F1 • 1-12 NX • Ⓥ Ⓑ Ⓓ Ⓢ 🍴 •
2Cr/HC

■ BROAD HAVEN (Haverfordwest)
PEMBROKESHIRE COAST PATH

Mrs F Morgan, Ringstone Guesthouse, Haroldston
Hill, SA62 3JP. ☎ (01437) 781051 • Map
157/862148 • BB **B** • S1 D1 T1 F1 • 1-11 NX • Ⓑ Ⓓ •
2Cr/HC

Mr & Mrs Main, Lion Rock, SA62 3JP. ☎ (01437)
781645 • Map 157/860143 • BB **B/C/D** • EM book
first £8.50, 7-9pm • S2 D2 T1 • 1-12 NX • Ⓥ Ⓑ Ⓓ
Ⓢ 🍴 • 1Cr/C

■ DALE (Haverfordwest)
PEMBROKESHIRE COAST PATH

Elizabeth Webber, Point Farm , SA62 3RD. ☎
(01646) 636254 • Map 157/814053 • BB **C** • EM book
first £15 inc. wine, 7.30pm • S1 D1 T1 F1 • 1-11
+Xmas • Ⓑ Ⓓ • 2Cr/HC • SC also

■ DINAS CROSS (Newport)
PEMBROKESHIRE COAST PATH

Len & Claire Urwin, Fron Isaf Farmhouse, SA42 0SW.
☎ (01348) 811339 • Map 157/018384 • BB **C** • EM
book first £11 • S1 D1 T1 • 1-12 NX • Ⓥ Ⓓ ♨ •
Transport also

■ FISHGUARD
PEMBROKESHIRE COAST PATH

Gillian Wheat, 55 West Street, SA65 9NG. ☎ (01348)
873592 • Map 157/955371 • BB **A** • EM book first £6,
7-8pm • S1 D1 F1 • 1-12 • Ⓥ Ⓓ Ⓡ

Beatrix & Ralph Davies, Manor House Hotel, Main
Street, SA65 9HG. ☎ (01348) 873260 • Map
157/958370 • BB **D** • EM £15, 7-8.30pm • S2 D3 T2
F1 • 1-12 NX • Ⓥ Ⓑ Ⓓ Ⓡ ♨ • 3Cr/HC

■ GOODWICK (Fishguard)
PEMBROKESHIRE COAST PATH

☆ Hope & Anchor Inn, SA64 0BP. ☎ (01348)
872314 • Map 157/945382 • BB **C** • EM £5, 7-9pm •
S1 D1 T2 • 1-12 NX • Ⓥ Ⓑ Ⓓ Ⓡ ♨ • 2Cr

HOPE & ANCHOR INN

GOODWICK, PEMBROKESHIRE SA64 0BP
Small friendly inn on Coastal Path overlooking
Fishguard harbour. H&C, shaver points, tea-
making facilities. Restaurant for snacks or
evening dinner. Packed lunches. "Real ale". All
rooms en-suite & TV's. Les Routiers, WTB.
B/B £18.00 p.p.

Tel. Terry or Mary McDonald
01348 872314

Bryntirion Guest House, Glanymor Road, SA64 0ER.
☎ (01348) 872189 • Map 157/940379 • BB **B** • S1
D1 T1 F1 • 1-12 NX • Ⓓ Ⓡ ♨ • 2Cr

Monica Hendrie, Stanley House, Quay Road, SA64
0BS. ☎ (01348) 873024 • Map 157/945383 • BB **B** •
S1 D2 T1 F1 • 1-12 • Ⓑ Ⓓ Ⓡ ♨ • 1Cr/C

☆ Mayrid Rees, Berry Hill, SA64 0HG. ☎ (01348)
872260 • Map 157/942382 • BB **C** • D2 • 1-12 • Ⓑ Ⓓ
Ⓢ Ⓡ • 2Cr/HC

BERRY HILL
Goodwick, Nr Fishguard,
Pembrokeshire SA64 0HG

Smallholding with most breathtaking views looking down
on Fishguard Bay and rolling countryside. 3 mins walk
from coastal walks. Ensuite facilities. Farmhouse award.
Tel. 01348 872260 ♨♨ Highly Commended

Maureen Miller, 2 Siriole, Quay Road, SA64 0BS. ☎
(01348) 872375 • Map 157/945383 • BB **C** • D1 F1 •
1-12 • Ⓑ Ⓡ ♨

■ HAVERFORDWEST
PEMBROKESHIRE COAST PATH

☆ Margaret Davies, Cuckoo Mill, Pelcomb Bridge,
SA62 6EA. ☎ (01437) 762139 • Map
157,158/933172 • BB **B** • EM £8-£9, 6-8.30pm • S1
D2 T1 F1 • 1-12 • Ⓥ Ⓑ Ⓓ Ⓡ ♨

Cuckoo Mill Farm
Pelcomb Bridge
Haverfordwest

Mixed farm in central Pembrokeshire.
Country walks on farm. Trout stream. Six
miles from coastal path. Meal times to
suit guests. Home produce all home
cooked. H&C. Tea-making facilities.
Telephone 01437 762139

■ LAWRENNY (Narberth)
LANDSKER BORDERLANDS TRAIL

Virginia Lort-Phillips, Knowles Farm, SA68 0PX. ☎
(01834) 891221 • Map 157,158/023084 • BB **B/C** •
EM book first £11.50, 6.30-8pm • D1 T2 • 3-10 • Ⓥ
Ⓑ Ⓓ Ⓢ ♨ • 2Cr/HC

■ LITTLE HAVEN (Haverfordwest)
PEMBROKESHIRE COAST PATH

Whitegates, SA62 3LA. ☎ (01437) 781552 • Map
157/857129 • BB **C** • EM book first £14.50, 7pm • S1
D3 T1 F1 • 3-10 NX • Ⓥ Ⓑ Ⓓ ♨ Ⓜ • 3Cr/C • SC
also

John Birt-Llewellin, The Bower Farm, SA62 3TY. ☎
(01437) 781554 • Map 157/869135 • BB **C** • EM book
first £15, 7.30pm • S1 D1 T1 F1 • 1-12 NX • Ⓥ Ⓑ Ⓓ
♨ Ⓜ • 3Cr/HC

■ MANORBIER (Tenby)
PEMBROKESHIRE COAST PATH

Mrs Jill McHugh, The Old Vicarage, SA70 7TN. ☎
(01834) 871452/(0421) 595858 • Map 158/069979 •
BB **C** • D1 T1 • 1-12 • Ⓑ Ⓓ Ⓢ • List • SC also

■ MARLOES (Haverfordwest)
PEMBROKESHIRE COAST PATH

Mrs F Morgan, The Foxes Inn, SA62 3AY. ☎ (01646)
636527 • Map 157/795084 • BB **B** • S4 D4 T1 F2 • 1-
12 • Ⓓ • List

☆ Eileen Roddam-King, Foxdale, Glebe Lane, SA62
3AX. ☎ (01646) 636243 • Map 157/796083 • BB **B/C**
• D1 T2 F1 • 1-12 NX • Ⓑ Ⓓ ♨ • 2Cr/HC • Camping
also

Please mention the Rambler's Yearbook
when booking your accommodation

■ **NEWPORT**
PEMBROKESHIRE COAST PATH

Chris & Rosemary Joseph, Hafan Deg, Off Long St, SA42 0TN. ☎ (01239) 820301 • Map 145/ 057392 • BB **B/C** • S1 D1 T2 • 1-12 NX • Ⓑ Ⓓ Ⓢ ♨ • 2Cr

Mr & Mrs David Inman, 2 Spring Hill, Parrog Road, SA42 0RH. ☎ (01239) 820626 • Map 145/055393 • BB **B** • EM book first £10, 7pm • D1 T1 F1 • 1-12 • Ⓥ Ⓓ ♨ • 1Cr/HC • SC also

☆ Llysmeddyg Guest House, East Street, SA42 0SY. ☎ (01239) 820008 • Map 145/059392 • BB **C** • EM book first £13.50, 7.45pm • S1 D2 T2 • 1-12 NX • Ⓥ Ⓑ Ⓓ Ⓢ • 2Cr/HC • SC also

Ann King & Malcolm Powell, Grove Park Guest House, Pen-y-Bont, SA42 0LT. ☎ (01239) 820122 • Map 145/060393 • BB **C** • EM £12.50, 7-8pm • D3 T1 • 1-12 NX • Ⓥ Ⓑ Ⓓ Ⓢ ♨ • 3Cr/HC

Mr & Mrs N A Paul, Llys Dewi, Fishguard Road, SA42 0UF. ☎ (01239) 820177 • Map 157,145/ 039392 • BB **B/C** • S1 D1 T1 F1 • 1-12 NX • Ⓑ Ⓓ Ⓢ ♨ • 2Cr • Transport to path

Mrs A J Collenette, Kenvor, Dinas, SA42 0UY. ☎ (01348) 811242 • Map 157,145/012389 • BB **B** • F1 • 1-12 NX • Ⓓ ♨

■ **PEMBROKE**
PEMBROKESHIRE COAST PATH

☆ The Barnikel Family, High Noon Guest House, Lower Lamphey Road, SA71 4AB. ☎ (01646) 683736 + 681232 • Map 157,158/990011 • BB **C** • EM book first £8.95, 7-7.30pm • S3 D3 T1 F2 • 1-12 NX • Ⓥ Ⓑ Ⓓ Ⓢ Ⓡ ♨ • 3Cr/C • Groups also

Mrs Nannette Pearce, Merton Place House, 3 East Back, SA71 4HL. ☎ (01646) 684796 • Map 157,158/986014 • BB **B** • S1 D2 T2 • 1-12 NX • Ⓓ Ⓢ Ⓡ • List/App

■ **SOLVA (Haverfordwest)**
PEMBROKESHIRE COAST PATH

☆ Lochmeyler Farm, Pen-y-cwm, Landeloy, SA62 6LL. ☎ (01348) 837724 • Map 157/855275 • BB **B/C/D** • EM £10, 7pm • S1 D4 T4 F3 • 1-12 • Ⓥ Ⓑ Ⓓ Ⓢ • 4Cr/Deluxe • Groups also

B&B ACCOMMODATION   WALES   PEMBROKESHIRE

■ SOLVA (CONTINUED)

Patricia Cross, Whitehouse, Penycwm, SA62 6LA. ☎ (01437) 720959 • Map 157/857250 • BB **B** • EM book first £8.50, 7.30pm • S1 D1 T1 F1 • 1-12 • Ⓥ Ⓑ Ⓓ Ⓢ Ⓜ • 3Cr/HC • SC and hostel also

■ ST DAVID'S (Haverfordwest)
PEMBROKESHIRE COAST PATH

☆ Mac & Sandra Thompson, Ramsey House, Lower Moor, SA62 6RP. ☎ (01437) 720321 • Map 157/747250 • BB **D** • EM £12-£14, 7pm • D4 T3 • 1-12 • Ⓥ Ⓑ Ⓓ Ⓢ 🐾 • 3Cr/HC

ST. DAVID'S

Half mile from Pembrokeshire Coast Path

Superior non-smoking licensed guest house catering exclusively for adults. Ideally situated for daily walks on Pembrokeshire Coast Path

All rooms en-suite

Award-winning Welsh speciality menus

Dogs welcome   Private parking

Dinner, bed & breakfast from £35.00 - £40.00 p.p.p.n.

For Brochure call 01437 - 720321

Mrs Shân Williams, Gwryd Bach, Rhodiad-y-Brenin, SA62 6PJ. ☎ (01437) 720240 • Map 157/765273 • BB **B** • EM book first £ • S1 D1 T1 • 1-12 • Ⓓ 🐾

■ ST ISHMAELS (Haverfordwest)
PEMBROKESHIRE COAST PATH

Mrs M Williams, Skerryback Farmhouse, Sandy Haven, SA62 3DN. ☎ (01646) 636598 • Map 157/852074 • BB **B** • EM book first £ • S1 D1 T1 • NX • Ⓥ Ⓓ Ⓢ • 1Cr/HC

Georgina Llewellin, Bicton Farm, SA62 3DR. ☎ (01646) 636215 • Map 157/842078 • BB **B** • EM book first £8, 7pm • D2 T1 • 1-12 NX • Ⓥ Ⓑ Ⓓ 🐾 • List

■ TENBY
PEMBROKESHIRE COAST PATH

Sandra Milward, West Wales Walking, Glenholme Guest House, Picton Terrace, SA70 7DR. ☎ (01834) 843909 • Map 158/133001 • BB **A/B** • EM book first £5, 6pm • S1 D3 T1 F3 • 1-12 NX • Ⓥ Ⓑ Ⓓ Ⓢ Ⓡ 🐾 Ⓜ • 2Cr

Bryn & Shirley Draper, Hammonds Park Hotel, Narberth Road, SA70 8HT. ☎ (01834) 842696 • Map 158/126011 • BB **C** • EM £9, 6pm • S1 D4 T2 F4 • 1-12 • Ⓥ Ⓑ Ⓓ Ⓢ Ⓡ 🐾 • 3Cr/C

■ TREVINE (St Davids)
PEMBROKESHIRE COAST PATH

Jill & Robin Moore, Awel-Mor Guest House, Pen Parc, SA62 5AG. ☎ (01348) 837865 • Map 157/845312 • BB **C** • EM book first £13, 7pm • D2 T1 • 1-10 • Ⓥ Ⓑ Ⓓ Ⓢ Ⓜ • SC also

POWYS

■ BONT DOLGADFAN (Llanbrynmair)
CAMBRIAN WAY & GLYNDWR'S WAY

Liz & Andrew Fox, Cyfeiliog Guest House, SY19 7BB. ☎ (01650) 521231 • Map 137/886003 • BB **B** • EM £7.50, 7.30pm • D1 T1 F1 • 1-12 • Ⓥ Ⓑ Ⓓ Ⓢ • 2Cr/C

■ BOUGHROOD (Brecon)
WYE VALLEY WALK

Mrs K Kelleher, Upper Middle Road, LD3 0BX. ☎ (01874) 754407 • Map 161/140392 • BB **A** • EM £7 • S1 D1 T1 • 1-12 NX • Ⓥ Ⓑ Ⓓ Ⓢ • List

■ BRECON
TAFF TRAIL

☆ Mrs M Meredith, Lodge Farm, Talgarth, LD3 0DP. ☎ (01874) 711244 • Map 161/173344 • BB **C** • EM book first £11, 7pm • S1 D1 T1 F1 • 1-12 • Ⓥ Ⓑ Ⓢ 🐾 • 3Cr/HC

LODGE FARM
Talgarth, Brecon

Welcome to our 17th century farm house situated in the Brecon Beacons National Park, well placed for walking the Black Mountains and Brecon Beacons. En suite bedrooms, tea-making facilities. Good, freshly prepared food including vegetarian. Non-smoking. FHB Members.

WTB ♨♨♨ Highly Commended

Tel 01874 711244

Flag & Castle Guest House, 11 Orchard Street, LD3 8AN. ☎ (01874) 625860 • Map 160/040285 • BB **B** • S2 D2 T1 F1 • 1-12 • Ⓑ Ⓓ 🐾

Peter & Jean Abbott, Trewalter House, Llangorse, LD3 0PS. ☎ (01874) 658442 • Map 161/135299 • BB **C** • EM book first £9.50, 7.30pm • D1 T1 F1 • 2-11 NX • Ⓥ Ⓑ Ⓓ Ⓢ • 3Cr/HC • SC also

The Coach Guest House, Orchard Street, LD3 8AN. ☎ (01874) 623803 • Map 160/040285 • BB **C** • D4 T2 • 1-12 NX • Ⓑ Ⓓ Ⓢ • 4Cr/HC

☆ Mr & Mrs Smith, The Grange , The Watton, LD3 8ED. ☎ (01874) 624038 • Map 160/035282 • BB **B/C** • D3 T1 F4 • 1-12 NX • Ⓑ Ⓓ Ⓢ 🐾 Ⓜ

THE GRANGE GUEST HOUSE
Brecon

Detached Georgian guest house, standing in its own grounds. We offer a totally non-smoking establishment. All attractively decorated bedrooms have colour TV and tea-making facilities. En suite bedrooms available. Vegetarians catered for.

Private car park and gardens.

Safe garaging for cycles.

Margaret & Bob Smith

Telephone 01874 624038

☆ Beacons Guest House, 16 Bridge Street, LD3 8AH. ☎ (01874) 623339 • Map 160/042285 • BB **B/C** • EM £10, 7pm • S1 D3 T4 F2 • 1-12 NX • Ⓥ Ⓑ Ⓓ Ⓢ ⚘ • 3Cr/C • Groups also

Beacons Guest House
Brecon

Georgian guesthouse close to town centre. Comfortable en suite rooms with colour TV and beverage tray. Cosy bar, residents' lounge and private parking. Excellent home cooking - 'Taste of Wales' recommended. WTB 3 crown, AA listed. Bargain Break from £49. Brochure.

 RAC Acclaimed

Tel. 01874 623339

☆ Mrs E Moore, Maes-y-Gwernen, School Rd, Abercraf, SA9 1XD. ☎ (01639) 730218 • Map 160/816127 • BB **D** • EM £10.50, 6-8.30pm • S3 D5 T3 F2 • 1-12 • Ⓥ Ⓑ Ⓓ Ⓢ ⚘ Ⓜ • 4Cr/HC

Maes-Y-Gwernen
HOTEL
ABERCRAF, SWANSEA VALLEY SA9 1XD

Well furnished, colour TV, hairdryer, tea/coffee facilities all rooms. Ample parking in private gounds. Lounges, bar & gardens, sauna, spa and solarium exclusive to guests. Ideal walking centre for Brecon Beacons & Fforest Fawr.

LES ROUTIERS BEST GUEST HOUSE
IN BRITIAN AWARD 1995 RAC Acclaimed

Tel. 01639 730218 Fax. 01639 730765

AA QQQQ   WTB ♛♛♛♛ Highly Commended

Bill Lomas, Cambridge House, St David's Street, LD3 8BB. ☎ (01874) 624699 • Map 160/040284 • BB **B** • EM book first £8, 7-7.30pm • S1 D2 T1 • 1-12 • Ⓥ Ⓑ Ⓓ Ⓢ ⚘ • 1Cr/HC

Forge Cottage, Hay Road, LD3 7SS. ☎ (01874) 611776 • Map 160/051299 • BB **B/C** • EM book first £10, 7-8pm • D2 T1 • 3-10 • Ⓥ Ⓑ Ⓓ Ⓢ

☆ Mrs K E M Evans, Upper Cantref Farm, Cantref, LD3 8LR. ☎ (01874) 665223 • Map 160/057258 • BB **B/C** • D1 F1 • 4-10 • Ⓑ Ⓓ • 2Cr • SC and bunkhouse also

BRECON BEACONS

Family run farmhouse accommodation with excellent views and within walking distance of the main peaks of the Brecon Beacons. Comfortable spacious bedrooms in a large traditional farmhouse. Wholesome food. Set in a quiet rural location on a working sheep and pony farm with on site riding. Ideal centre for walking, biking etc.

Upper Cantref Farm, Cantref, Brecon LD3 8LR

Tel 01874 665223

☆ Canal Bridge B&B, 1 Gas Lane, LD3 7HA. ☎ (01874) 611088 • Map 160/048282 • BB **C** • S1 D1 T1 F/T/D2 • 1-12 NX • Ⓓ Ⓢ • List/C

Brecon

Whether strolling, walking or hill climbing you'll find Canal Bridge ideally situated. The Monmouthshire Canal, Marina and River Usk are only a step away. Enjoy a stay in our spacious and comfortable B&B and take in the breathtaking views of the Brecon Beacons. Be assured of a very warm welcome.

No. 1 Gas Lane, Brecon ☆ Tel. 01874 611088

■ BUILTH WELLS

R & M Wiltshire, Bron-Wye, Church Street, LD2 3BS. ☎ (01982) 553587 • Map 147/041510 • BB **B** • EM book first £7, 6.30pm • S1 D2 T1 F1 • 1-12 • Ⓑ Ⓓ Ⓢ Ⓡ ⚘ • 3Cr/C

☆ Biddy Williams, Dol-Llyn-Wydd Farm, LD2 3RZ. ☎ (01982) 553660 • Map 147/042488 • BB **B/C** • EM book first £8.50, 7.30-8.30pm • S2 D1 T2 • 2-12 NX • Ⓥ Ⓑ Ⓓ Ⓢ Ⓡ • 2Cr/C

DOL-LLYN WYDD FARM
BUILTH WELLS   WTB ♛♛

17th C farmhouse lying beneath the Eppynt Hills
• Superb area for walking-touring-birdwatching.
• Easy distance of Elan Valley, Brecon Beacons, Black Mountains • Good home cooking, comfortable rooms • One mile from Builth Wells on B4520 signed Upper Chapel, first left down quiet farm lane — 200 yards, house on left.

Tel. Mrs Williams 01982 553660

Mrs C M Hammond, Querida, 43 Garth Road, LD2 3NS. ☎ (01982) 553642 • Map 147/037511 • BB **A** • D1 F1 • 1-12 • Ⓓ Ⓡ ⚘

Zena E Hope, Caepandy Farm, Garth Road, LD2 3AR. ☎ (01982) 553793 • Map 147/037511 • BB **B** • D1 T1 F1 • 1-12 • Ⓓ Ⓡ ⚘ Ⓜ • List

POWYS

WALES

B&B ACCOMMODATION

299

■ BUTTINGTON (Welshpool)
GLYNDWR'S WAY & OFFA'S DYKE

M Broxton, 1 Plas Cefn Holding, Heldre Lane, SY21 8SX. ☎ (01938) 570225 • Map 126/266092 • BB **A/B** • D2 F1 • 1-12 NX • Ⓓ Ⓢ Ⓡ

■ CAPEL-Y-FFIN (Abergavenny, Monmouthshire)
CAMBRIAN WAY & OFFA'S DYKE

Griffiths Family, The Grange, NP7 7NP. ☎ (01873) 890215 • Map 161/251315 • BB **C** • EM £12, 7.45pm • S1 D1 T2 F2 • 3-11 • Ⓥ Ⓓ 🛁 Ⓜ • 1Cr • Camping also

■ CRICKHOWELL
CAMBRIAN WAY

☆ Dragon Hotel, High Street, NP8 1BE. ☎ (01873) 810362 • Map 161/217183 • BB **D** • EM £9.95, 6.30-8.30pm • S2 D5 T6 F2 • 1-12 • Ⓥ Ⓑ Ⓓ Ⓢ • 3Cr/HC

THE DRAGON HOTEL

Crickhowell,
Brecon Beacons
National Park
NP8 1BE
Tel: 01873 810362
Fax: 01873 811868

Very popular with guests who enjoy a traditional, character hotel and a relaxed atmosphere.
Good position in centre of Crickhowell.
On the river Usk nestling between the Beacons and Black Mountains.
Excellent base for country activities and attractions, wonderful food, outstanding walking.
Good value short breaks.

Organiser of Southern Section of The Cambrian Way

Please call for our brochure and walk programme.

WTB ♛♛♛ RAC, AA, 'Taste of Wales' Member

■ DYLIFE (Nr Staylittle, Llanbrynmair)
GLYNDWR'S WAY & CAMBRIAN WAY

The Star Inn
Set in breathtaking countryside, superb food, Real Ales, residents lounge, colour TV, H&C, showers/bath. Full central heating, excellent ambience, own tea and coffee making facilities, a warm and friendly welcome guaranteed.

WTB ❀❀ AA recommended.
Tel: 01650 521345

☆ Star Inn , SY19 7BW. ☎ (01650) 521345 • Map 135/863940 • BB **B** • EM £5.95, 7pm • S2 D2 T2 F1 • 1-12 • Ⓥ Ⓑ Ⓓ 🛁 Ⓜ

■ ERWOOD (Builth Wells)
WYE VALLEY WALK

Alistair Legge, Trericket Mill, LD2 3TQ. ☎ (01982) 560312 • Map 148, 161/112414 • BB **A/B/C** • EM £6.50-£9 veg. only, 7-8pm • S1 D2 T1 F2 • 1-12 NX • Ⓥ Ⓑ Ⓓ Ⓢ 🛁 Ⓜ • Bunkhouse and camping also.

■ FAN (Llanidloes)
GLYNDWR'S WAY

Llinos Rees, Esgairmaen, SY18 6NT. ☎ (01686) 430272 • Map 136/927893 • BB **B** • EM book first £7, 5-9pm • D1 F1 • 3-10 • Ⓥ Ⓑ Ⓓ 🛁 • 3Cr

■ FORDEN (Welshpool)
OFFA'S DYKE

Mrs M Payne, Heath Cottage, Kingswood, SY21 8LX. ☎ (01938) 580453 • Map 126/237025 • BB **C** • EM book first £10 • S1 D2 F1 • 4-10 • Ⓥ Ⓑ Ⓓ Ⓢ • 3Cr

■ GLADESTRY (Kington, Herefordshire)
OFFA'S DYKE

☆ Mrs M Hughes, Stonehouse Farm, HR5 3NU. ☎ (01544) 370651 • Map 148/231549 • BB **B** • EM book first £6, 7pm • D1 T1 • 1-12 NX • Ⓥ Ⓓ Ⓢ 🛁 Ⓜ

STONEHOUSE FARM
GLADESTRY, KINGTON, HEREFORDSHIRE
Listed building situated on
Offa's Dyke Footpath
Ideal for touring mid-Wales. Perfect for ramblers. B&B, dinner by arrangement, vegetarian cooking on request. Packed lunches. Home produced food. Friendly atmosphere. H&C in bedrooms. Razor points. Sitting room and TV. Children welcome.

Tel Gladestry (01544) 370651

■ GLANGRWYNEY (Crickhowell)

Priscilla Llewelyn, White Hall, NP8 1EW. ☎ (01873) 811155 or 840267 • Map 161/238164 • BB **B/C** • EM book first £10, 7.30pm • S1 D2 T1 F1 • 1-12 NX • Ⓥ Ⓑ Ⓓ Ⓢ 🛁 • 2Cr

■ HAY-ON-WYE (Hereford & Worcester)
OFFA'S DYKE & WYE VALLEY WALK

Linda Webb, The Old Post Office, Llanigon, HR3 5QA. ☎ (01497) 820008 • Map 161,148/213401 • BB **B/C** • D2 T1 • 2-12 • Ⓥ Ⓑ Ⓓ Ⓢ 🛁 • 2Cr/C • Veg. breakfast only

Jenny Morris, The Willows, St Marys Road, HR3 5EB ☎ (01497) 820387 day, 820174 night • Map 161,148/226420 • BB **B** • S2 D1 T1 • 2-11 • Ⓑ Ⓓ Ⓢ

☆ La Fosse Guest House, Oxford Road, HR3 5AJ. ☎ (01497) 820613 • Map 161,148/227422 • BB **C** • D4 F1 • 1-11 • B D

■ HEOL SENNI (Nr Brecon)

Mrs M J Mayo, Maeswalter Farm, LD3 8SU. ☎ (01874) 636629 • Map 160/931236 • BB **B** • EM book first £9, 6.30-7pm • D2 T1 F1 • 1-12 • V B D S ⚿ • 1Cr

■ KNIGHTON
GLYNDWR'S WAY & OFFA'S DYKE

☆ Mrs Dana Simmons, The Fleece House, Market Street, LD7 1BB. ☎ (01547) 520168 • Map 148,137/284723 • BB **C/D** • T6 • 1-12 • B D S R • 2Cr/C

Plough Hotel, 40 Market Street, LD7 1EY. ☎ (01547) 528041 • Map 148,137/284723 • BB **B** • EM £6.50, 7-9pm • S7 D2 T3 • 1-12 • V B R ⚿ Ⓜ • Camping too

■ LLANANNO (Llandrindod Wells)
GLYNDWR'S WAY

R & D Taylor, Bwlch Farm, Glyndwrs Way, LD1 6TT. ☎ (01597) 840366 • Map 147,136/085747 • BB **C** • D2 T1 • 3-10 • B D S ⚿ • 2Cr/HC • SC also

■ LLANBADARN FYNYDD
GLYNDWR'S WAY

Mr & Mrs Bainsworth, Hillside Lodge Guest House, LD1 6TU. ☎ (01597) 840364 • Map 136/085764 • BB **C** • EM book first £7 • T1 F2 • 1-12 • V B D S ⚿ • 3Cr/HC • SC also

■ LLANDDEWI'R CWM (Builth Wells)

☆ Mrs I James, New Hall, LD2 3RX. ☎ (01982) 552483 • Map 147/034487 • BB **B/C** • EM £8, 7-8pm • D3 T1 F1 • 1-12 NX • V B D S R • 3Cr/HC

■ LLANDRINDOD WELLS

☆ Llanerch 16th Century Inn, LD1 6BG. ☎ (01597) 822086 • Map 147/058613 • BB **C** • EM £5-£10, 6-9pm • S2 D4 T2 F4 • 1-12 NX • V B D R ⚿ • 3Cr/C • Groups also

Rod & Beryl Prince, Corven Hall, Howey, LD1 5RE. ☎ (01597) 823368 • Map 147/050583 • BB **B/C** • EM book first £9.50, 7-7.30pm • D2 T2 F6 • 2-10 • V B D S R ⚿ • 3Cr/HC

☆ Mrs C Nixon, Brynhir Farm, Chapel Road, Howey, LD1 5PB. ☎ (01597) 822425 • Map 147/067586 • BB **C** • EM £8, 7pm • S2 D2 T4 F1 • 3-11 + XMAS • V B D S R ⚿ • 3Cr/HC

☆ Ron, Margaret & Sarah Bufton, Three Wells Farm, Chapel Road, Howey, LD1 5PB. ☎ (01597) 824427 • Map 147/067586 • BB **C** • EM £8.50-£9.50, 7pm • S2 D6 T6 F1 • 1-12 NX • Ⓥ Ⓑ Ⓓ Ⓢ Ⓡ 🌣 • 4Cr/HC

THREE WELLS FARM

☆ Peter & Jackie Longley, Neuadd Farm Country Guest House, Penybont, LD1 5SW. ☎ (01597) 822571 • Map 147/091618 • BB **C** • EM book first £10, 7.30pm • D1 T2 • 1-12 NX • Ⓥ Ⓑ Ⓓ Ⓢ Ⓡ • 3Cr/HC

Mrs B J Jones, Rhydithon, Dyffryn Road, LD1 6AN. ☎ (01597) 822624 • Map 147/058613 • BB **B** • EM book first £7.50, 6-8pm • S1 D1 T1 • 1-12 NX • Ⓥ Ⓑ Ⓓ Ⓢ Ⓡ 🌣 • 2Cr/C

Angela & Iain Macdonald, Greylands Guest House, High Street, LD1 6AG. ☎ (01597) 822253 • Map 147/057612 • BB **B/C** • EM book first £8.50, 5.30-7.30pm • S3 D2 T2 F1 • 1-12 • Ⓥ Ⓑ Ⓓ Ⓢ Ⓡ 🌣 • 2Cr

■ **LLANFAIR CAEREINION (Welshpool)**

Ivernia Watkin, Bryn Penarth, SY21 0BZ. ☎ (01938) 810535 • Map 136/101046 • BB **B** • EM book first £7, 7-8pm • S2 D2 T1 • 4-10 • Ⓥ Ⓑ Ⓓ 🌣 • 2Cr/HC

■ **LLANFIHANGEL NANT MELAN (New Radnor, Presteigne)**

Mrs F Griffiths, Summergill, LD8 2TN. ☎ (01544) 350247 • Map 148/180582 • BB **A** • EM £7, 7pm • D2 T1 • 1-12 NX • Ⓥ Ⓑ Ⓓ Ⓢ 🌣

■ **LLANFRYNACH (Brecon)**
TAFF TRAIL

Mrs A Phillips, Tyfry Farm, LD3 7AX. ☎ (01874) 665232 • Map 160/068258 • BB **A/B** • D1 F2 • 1-12 • Ⓓ • C

Mrs A Harpur, Llanbrynean Farm, LD3 7BQ. ☎ (01874) 665222 • Map 160/076254 • BB **B** • D1 T1 F1 • 1-12 NX • Ⓑ Ⓓ Ⓢ 🌣 • 1Cr • Food nearby

■ **LLANGADFAN (FOEL) (Welshpool)**
GLYNDWR'S WAY

Lluest Fach, SY21 0PB. ☎ (01938) 820351 • Map 125/980108 • BB **B** • EM book first £8, 7.30ish • D1 T1 F2 • 1-12 NX • Ⓥ Ⓓ Ⓢ 🌣 Ⓜ • SC, groups and bunkhouse also

■ **LLANIDLOES**
GLYNDWR'S WAY

Tom Lines, Lloyds Hotel & Restaurant, Cambrian Place, SY18 6BX. ☎ (01686) 412284 • Map 136/955844 • BB **B/C** • EM book first £9 • S4 D2 T3 • 1-12 • Ⓥ Ⓑ Ⓓ • 2Cr/C • Groups also

■ **LLANRHAEADR-YM-MOCHNANT (Oswestry, Shropshire)**

Lesley Groom, Ty-Draw, SY10 0DB. ☎ (01691) 780036 • Map 125/119275 • BB **B** • EM book first £6 • D1 • 1-12 • Ⓥ Ⓑ Ⓓ 🌣 • Transport also

☆ Mrs J Morgan, Llys Morgan, SY10 0JZ. ☎ (01691) 780345 • Map 125/123261 • BB **B** • EM book first £7.50, from 6.30pm • D1 T1 F1 • 1-12 NX • Ⓥ Ⓑ Ⓓ 🌣 • 3Cr

LLYS MORGAN
Llanrhaeadr YM, Nr Oswestry SY10 0JZ

An historic house with character and charm, in ¾ acre of mature gardens. Village centre one min walk. Ideal for outdoor pursuits, close to local beauty spots, friendly homely atmosphere, peaceful & quiet. All rooms en-suite. Evening meals on request. Commended.

Tel. (01691) 780345

■ **LLANSTEPHAN (Brecon)**
WYE VALLEY WALK

Mrs M R Bowen, Neuadd-Glan-Gwy, LD3 0YT. ☎ (01982) 560645 • Map 161,148/121411 • BB **B** • D1 T1 • 4-8 • ⅅ Ⓢ Ⓜ

■ **LLANWRTYD WELLS**

☆ Gordon & Diana Green, Neuadd Arms Hotel, The Square, LD5 4RR. ☎ (01591) 610236 • Map 147/878466 • BB **C** • EM £11.50, 7.30-8.30pm • S8 D5 T6 F1 • 1-12 NX • Ⓥ Ⓑ ⅅ Ⓢ Ⓡ ⅏ Ⓜ

WELSH WAYFARING HOLIDAYS
Neuadd Arms Hotel
Llanwrtyd Wells, Powys LD5 4RR

Family run hotel in the unspoilt and relatively unknown "Welsh Lake District." Friendly, relaxing atmosphere with log fires, good food, real ales. Owner (Gordon Green) organises and often leads guided walks and rents mountain cycles. Ideal for groups of up to 32 people. Some budget accommodation with discounts. RSPB Red Kite Centre nearby. Live video shots of Goshawks and Red Kites. 2 Day Break £66. Week from £240 (All FB and includes guide). On British Rail.

Tel. 01591 610236

☆ Eileen & Bernie Dodd, Belle Vue Hotel, LD5 4RE. ☎ (01591) 610237 • Map 147/879467 • BB **A/B/C** • EM £4-£12, 6.30-9.30pm • S3 D2 T8 F2 • 1-12 • Ⓥ Ⓑ ⅅ Ⓡ ⅏ • 2Cr/App • Bunkhouse also

---

Please mention the Rambler's Yearbook when booking your accommodation

---

BELLE VUE HOTEL
LLANWRTYD WELLS, POWYS.
TEL: (01591) 610237

Built in 1843, the oldest family owned hotel in Llanwrtyd Wells offers exceptionally good value for walkers. Great traditional old pub atmosphere. Real ales. Open fires. Good home cooking. Extensive bar menu. Comfortable restaurant. Cosy residents' lounge. Minibus available for collect or take out (no charge).
2 DAY GROUP SPECIAL
2 nights bed & breakfast. 2 days packed lunch.
2 three course evening meals
2 days professional guide
£57 inclusive
10% ramblers discount off normal rates

■ **MACHYNLLETH**
GLYNDWR'S WAY & DYFI VALLEY WAY & WYE VALLEY WALK

☆ Mrs M Vince, Maenllwyd, Newtown Road, SY20 8EY. ☎ (01654) 702928 • Map 135/752008 • BB **C** • EM book first £9, 6.30pm • D4 T2 F2 • 1-12 NX • Ⓑ ⅅ Ⓢ Ⓡ ⅏ • 3Cr/HC

Maenllwyd
Newtown Road,
Machynlleth

W.T.B. Award

WTB Highly Commended

Situated in historic market town, close to all amenities, approx 10 mins walk from station. Comfortable, well equipped rooms with central heating. Packed lunches available on request. **Telephone 01654 702928**

Mrs Lona Williams, Awelon, Heol Powys, SY20 8AY. ☎ (01654) 702047 • Map 135/747008 • BB **B** • S1 D1 T1 F1 • 1-12 NX • ⅅ Ⓢ Ⓡ ⅏ Ⓜ • C

Elaine Petrie, Pendre, Maengwyn Street, SY20 8EF. ☎ (01654) 702088 • Map 135/749008 • BB **B/C** • D2 T1 F2 • 1-11 • Ⓑ ⅅ Ⓡ ⅏ • 2Cr/C

■ **MEIFOD**
GLYNDWR'S WAY

Mrs Angela Clifford, Central House, SY22 6BZ. ☎ (01938) 500482 • Map 125/154133 • BB **B** • S1 D1 T1 • 1-12 • Ⓑ ⅅ Ⓢ

■ MONTGOMERY
OFFA'S DYKE

Gaynor Bright, Little Brompton Farm, SY15 6HY. ☎ (01686) 668371 • Map 137/244941 • BB **B** • EM book first £8, 6.30pm • S1 D1 T1 F1 • 1-12 • Ⓥ Ⓑ Ⓓ Ⓢ 🐾 • 3Cr/HC

Mrs Ceinwen Richards, The Drewin Farm, Church Stoke, SY15 6TW. ☎ (01588) 620325 • Map 137/261905 • BB **B** • EM book first £8, 6.30-7pm • F/D2 • 3-11 • Ⓥ Ⓑ Ⓓ Ⓢ 🐾 • 3Cr/HC

Mark & Sue Michaels, Dragon Hotel, SY15 6PA. ☎ (01686) 668359 • Map 137/222964 • BB **D** • EM £6-£20, 7-9pm • S2 D6 T4 F3 • 1-12 • Ⓥ Ⓑ Ⓓ 🐾 Ⓜ • 4Cr/C

Mrs Kay Nicholson, The Dingle, Cwminkin, SY15 6HH. ☎ (01686) 668838 • Map 137/204959 • BB **B** • S1 D1 F1 • 1-12 • Ⓓ Ⓢ

■ NEW RADNOR (Presteigne)

Angela Hoy, Eagle Hotel, Broad Street, LD8 2SN. ☎ (01544) 350208 • Map 148,137/212609 • BB **A/B/C** • EM £8.50, till 10pm • D2 T1 F3 • 1-12 • Ⓥ Ⓑ Ⓓ 🐾 • 1Cr • Groups also

■ NEWTOWN

David & Jean Burd, Plas Canol, New Road, SY16 1AS. ☎ (01686) 625598 • Map 136/108913 • BB **B** • EM book first £8, 6pm • S1 T1 F1 • 1-12 • Ⓥ Ⓑ Ⓓ Ⓢ Ⓡ Ⓜ • HC

■ PEN-Y-CAE (Swansea Valley)
CAMBRIAN WAY

Mrs J Williams, Dderi Farm, Glyntawe, SA9 1GT. ☎ (01639) 730458 • Map 160/852174 • BB **B** • D1 F1 • 1-12 NX • Ⓑ Ⓓ Ⓢ • List

■ PENGENFFORDD (Talgarth)
CAMBRIAN WAY

☆ Paul Mountjoy, Castle Inn, LD3 0EP. ☎ (01874) 711353 • Map 161/174296 • BB **C** • EM £5.50, 7-9pm • S1 D2 T1 F1 • 1-12 NX • Ⓥ Ⓑ Ⓢ • 2Cr • Bunkhouse also

■ PRESTEIGNE
OFFA'S DYKE

Mr & Mrs Rowlatt, 14 Hereford Street, LD8 2AR. ☎ (01544) 260466 • Map 148/316643 • BB **B/C** • EM book first £8, 7pm • D1 T2 • 1-12 NX • Ⓑ Ⓓ Ⓢ

■ RHAYADER

Mrs B Lawrence, Brynteg, East St, LD6 5EA. ☎ (01597) 810052 • Map 147,136/972681 • BB **B** • EM book first £7.50 • S1 D2 T1 • 1-12 NX • Ⓑ Ⓓ 🐾 Ⓜ • 2Cr

Mr & Mrs R Price, Downfield Farm, LD6 5PA. ☎ (01597) 810394 • Map 147,136/988684 • BB **B** • D2 T1 • 3-10 • Ⓓ Ⓢ 🐾 • 1Cr

Mrs Ann Griffiths, Liverpool House, East Street, LD6 5EA. ☎ (01597) 810706 • Map 147,136/972681 • BB **B** • EM book first £8, 6.30pm • S1 D3 T1 F3 • 1-12 NX • Ⓑ Ⓓ Ⓢ 🐾 • 3Cr • Groups also

☆ Elan Valley Hotel, Elan Valley, LD6 5HN. ☎ (01597) 810448 • Map 147,136/945665 • BB **D** • EM £10.50-£12.50, 7-9pm • S4 D7 T5 F3 • 1-12 • Ⓥ Ⓑ Ⓓ Ⓢ 🐾 • 3Cr • Groups also

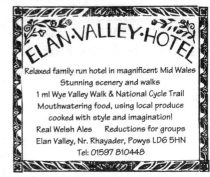

■ STAYLITTLE (Llanbrynmair)
GLYNDWR'S WAY & CAMBRIAN WAY

Mrs Paula Anwyl, Maesmedrisiol Farm, SY19 7BN. ☎ (01650) 521494 • Map 135/884945 • BB **A** • EM book first £8 • S1 D2 T1 F1 • 2-11 • Ⓥ Ⓓ Ⓢ 🐾

■ TALYBONT-ON-USK (Brecon)
TAFF TRAIL

Marjorie Taylor, Shop House, The Aber, LD3 7YS. ☎ (01874) 676276 • Map 161/105214 • BB **A** • EM book first £5, before 8pm • S1 T2 • 1-12 • Ⓥ Ⓓ Ⓢ 🐾

Mrs Jill Carr, Abercynafon Lodge, Abercynafon, LD3 7YT. ☎ (01874) 676342 • Map 161/100203 • BB **B/C** • S1 D1 T1 • 1-12 • Ⓑ Ⓓ Ⓢ 🐾 • 2Cr • Wheelchair access

■ WELSHPOOL
GLYNDWR'S WAY & OFFA'S DYKE

Mrs Freda Emberton, Tynllwyn Farm, SY21 9BW. ☎ (01938) 553175 + 553054 • Map 126/215086 • BB **B** • EM book first £8.50, 6-6.30pm • D/S2 T/S2 F/S2 • 1-12 NX • Ⓥ Ⓑ Ⓓ Ⓡ 🐾

T & J Jones, Severn Farm, SY21 7BB. ☎ (01938) 553098 • Map 126/231070 • BB **B** • EM book first £8.50, 6.30pm • S2 D1 T1 F2 • 1-12 NX • Ⓥ Ⓓ Ⓡ ⅍ Ⓜ • 1Cr

Mrs K Cleland, Bank Farmhouse, Felindre, Berriew, SY21 8QX. Map 136/147021 • BB **A** • T1 • 5-9 • Ⓓ Ⓢ • Vegetarian

SOUTH WALES

THE AUTHORITIES OF BLAENAU GWENT, BRIDGEND, CARDIFF, CAERPHILY, MERTHYR TYDFIL, NEWPORT, NEATH PORT TALBOT, RHONDDA CYNON TAFF, SWANSEA & TORFAEN.

■ CARDIFF
CAMBRIAN WAY & TAFF TRAIL

Mrs Maureen George, 39 Plasturton Gardens, Pontcanna Court, CF1 9HG. ☎ (01222) 383660 • Map 171/170769 • BB **C** • D2 T2 F1 • 1-12 NX • Ⓑ Ⓓ Ⓢ Ⓡ ⅍ • 2Cr

Mrs Wendy Oxley, Rambler Court Hotel, 188 Cathedral Road, CF1 9JE. ☎ (01222) 221187 • Map 171/ 167773 • BB **B** • S3 D4 T4 F4 • 1-12 NX • Ⓑ Ⓓ Ⓡ • 2Cr

■ CWMBRAN (Torfaen)

Mrs J Graham, Springfield Guest House, 371 Llantarnam Road, NP44 3BN. ☎ (01633) 482509 • Map 171/305934 • BB **B** • S2 D3 T2 F3 • 1-12 • Ⓑ Ⓓ Ⓢ Ⓡ ⅍ • 2Cr/C

■ CWMTAF (Merthyr Tydfil)
TAFF TRAIL

Mrs M Evans, Llwyn Onn Guest House, CF48 2HT. ☎ (01685) 384384 • Map 160/012115 • BB **C** • S1 D2 T1 • 1-12 • Ⓑ Ⓓ • 3Cr

■ LITTLE MILL (Pontypool, Torfaen)
CAMBRIAN WAY

Ann Bradley, Pentwyn Farm, NP4 0HQ. ☎ (01495) 785249 • Map 171/325035 • BB **B/C** • EM book first £12, 7.30pm • D2 T2 • 2-11 • Ⓑ Ⓓ Ⓢ • 3Cr/HC • SC also

■ LLANMADOC (Gower)

Tallizmand, SA3 1HA. ☎ (01792) 386373 • Map 159/493921 • BB **C** • EM book first £10, 6.30-8pm • S1 D1 T1 F1 • 1-12 NX • Ⓥ Ⓑ Ⓓ ⅍ • 3Cr/HC

■ MARGAM (Neath Port Talbot)

Mrs Rhiannon Gaen, Ty'n-Y-Caeau, SA13 2NF. ☎ (01639) 883897 • Map 170/790868 • BB **C** • EM book first £9, 6-6.30pm • D1 T4 F2 • 2-11 • Ⓥ Ⓑ Ⓓ Ⓢ Ⓡ ⅍ • 2Cr • SC also

Want to know more about the tourist board classifications? See page 87

■ MERTHYR TYDFIL
TAFF TRAIL

☆ Tregenna Hotel, Park Terrace, CF47 8RF. ☎ (01685) 723627 or 382055 • Map 160/049066 • BB **C/D** • EM £7, 6-10pm • S5 D6 T7 F5 • 1-12 • Ⓥ Ⓑ Ⓓ Ⓢ Ⓡ ⅍ Ⓜ • 4Cr/HC • SC also

■ NELSON (Caerphilly)
TAFF TRAIL

Mrs C Kedward, Fairmead House, 24 Gelligaer Road, CF46 6DN. ☎ (01443) 411174 • Map 171/109965 • BB **C** • EM book first £9.50, 6-7pm • S1 D1 T1 • 1-12 • Ⓥ Ⓑ Ⓓ Ⓢ Ⓡ ⅍ • 2Cr/HC

■ NEWPORT (Gwent)

Frank & Danielle Sheahan, The West Usk Lighthouse, St Brides Wentlooge, NP1 9SF. ☎ (01633) 810126/815860 • Map 171/291821 • BB **C/D** • S2 D3 T1 • 1-12 • Ⓑ Ⓢ • 2Cr

Chapel Guest House, Church Road, St Brides Wentlooge, NP1 9SN. ☎ (01633) 681018 • Map 171/294822 • BB **C** • EM £8-£10, 7-10pm • S1 D1 T1 F1 • 1-12 • Ⓥ Ⓑ Ⓓ Ⓢ Ⓡ ⅍ • 2Cr/C

■ PORT EYNON (Swansea)

Mrs Jenny Thomas, Highfield, SA3 1NL. ☎ (01792) 390357 • Map 159/465855 • BB **B** • EM book first £8, 6.30pm • D2 T1 • 4-10 • Ⓥ Ⓓ Ⓢ ⅍ • List/HC

☆ Mrs Anne Still, Culver House Hotel, SA3 1NN. ☎ (01792) 390755 • Map 159/468853 • BB **C/D** • EM £12, 6.30-8.30pm • S4 D4 T2 F3 • 1-12 • Ⓥ Ⓑ Ⓓ Ⓢ ⅍ • 3Cr/HC

SOUTH WALES POWYS WALES ACCOMMODATION B&B

305

■ **PORT TALBOT**

Mrs Jennie Williams, Bryn Teg House, 9 Craig-y-Fan, Cymmer, SA13 3LN. ☎ (01639) 851820 • Map 170/861963 • BB **B** • EM book first £6, 6.30pm • D1 T2 • 1-12 • Ⓥ Ⓓ Ⓢ 🐾

■ **PORTHCAWL (Bridgend)**

Rockybank Guest House, 15 De Breos Drive, CF36 3JP. ☎ (01656) 785823 • Map 170/819779 • BB **C** • D1 T1 F1 • 1-12 NX • Ⓑ Ⓓ • 2Cr/HC • Food nearby

■ **RHOSSILI (Gower)**

☆ David Legg, Worms Head Hotel, SA3 1PP. ☎ (01792) 390512 • Map 159/414881 • BB **D** • EM book first £12.50, 7-8.30pm • D5 T9 F5 • 1-12 • Ⓥ Ⓓ Ⓢ 🐾 • 3Cr/C

The Worms Head Hotel
Rhossili, Gower, Swansea

Outstanding natural beauty and spectacular scenery
Something for everyone! Clean beaches, ideal for sporting enthusiasts, bird lovers, walkers and those who just want to get away from it all.
20 beautiful en-suite rooms with full facilities.
Fabulous restaurant specialising in fresh, locally caught fish and local produce.
☎ **01792 390512**

Ireland

COUNTY CLARE

■ **LISDOONVARNA**

☆ Mrs Breide Casey, Benrue Farmhouse. ☎ 065 74059 • Map R/18 99 • BB **B** • EM book first £12, 7pm • D2 T1 F3 • 3-11 • Ⓥ Ⓑ Ⓓ Ⓢ 🐾 • App

DUBLIN

■ **DUBLIN**
WICKLOW WAY

Mrs Mary Clinton, Woodview Farmhouse, Margaretstown, Skerries. ☎ (01) 849 1528 • BB **B** • EM £8-£12, 6-7.30pm • D2 T2 F2 • 1-12 • Ⓥ Ⓑ Ⓓ Ⓢ Ⓡ 🐾 Ⓜ

☆ C Cassells, 24 Charleville Road, Phibsborough, Dublin 7. ☎ (01) 838 9812 • BB **B** • S1 D1 T1 • 1-12 NX • Ⓓ Ⓢ Ⓡ Ⓜ

FOUND A GOOD B&B THAT'S NOT IN THE YEARBOOK?
Send us recommendations for future editions

COUNTY KERRY

■ ANNASCAUL (Dingle Peninsula)

Mrs Kathleen O'Connor, "Four Winds". ☎ 066 57168 • Map 70/ • BB **B** • D2 T2 F1 • 1-12 • Ⓑ Ⓓ • ITB/App • SC also

■ BALLYDAVID (Dingle)

Sile & Vincent O'Gormain, Caife na Mara, Glaise Beag. ☎ (066) 55162 • Map 70/3909/ • BB **B** • EM £11, 6-9pm • S1 D1 T1 F1 • 1-12 • Ⓥ Ⓑ Ⓓ Ⓢ Ⓜ • Map ref is OS of Ireland. On Dingle Way

■ CAHIRCIVEEN

Christina O'Neill, Iveragh Heights. ☎ Killarney 066 72545 • BB **B** • EM book first £10, 6-7pm • D2 T1 F1 • 1-12 • Ⓑ Ⓓ ⛰ Ⓜ • ITB/App • SC also

■ CLOGHANE

Mrs Kitty Brosnan, "Agrainn Mhor". ☎ Tralee 066-38211 • Map 70/5011 • BB **B** • EM book first £12, 7pm • S1 D1 T1 F1 • 4-9 • Ⓥ Ⓑ Ⓓ ⛰ Ⓜ

■ FOILMORE, CAHERCIVEEN
KERRY WAY

Mary Landers, Fransal House. ☎ 066-72997 • BB **B** • EM £8-£13, 7pm • D2 T/F1 F1 • 1-12 • Ⓥ Ⓑ Ⓓ Ⓢ • ITB/App • SC also

■ GLENCAR
KERRY WAY

☆ Mrs Mary O'Connor, "Rocklands", Cappantanvalley. ☎ 066-60177 • Map 78/V720875 • BB **A/B** • EM £10 • S1 D2 T1 F1 • 1-12 NX • Ⓥ Ⓑ Ⓓ Ⓢ ⛰ • Map no is Discovery series

Johnny Walsh, Climbers Inn. ☎ 066-60101 • Map 78 /841724 • BB **B/C** • EM £12, 6.30-9.30pm • T7 F2 • 1-12 NX • Ⓥ Ⓑ Ⓓ Ⓢ ⛰ • ITB/App • Walking hols also

■ KENMARE
KERRY WAY

Mike & Anne Murphy, Laburnum House. ☎ Killarney 064-41034 • Map V/902712 • BB **B** • EM book first £13, 6.30-8pm • D2 T2 F1 • 3-10 • Ⓑ Ⓓ Ⓢ ⛰ • ITB/App • SC also

■ KILLARNEY
KERRY WAY

☆ Eileen Fitzgerald, Tuscar House, Golf Course Road. ☎ 064-31978 • BB **A** • EM book first £10, 6-9pm • S1 D2 T10 F2 • 3-10 NX • Ⓥ Ⓑ Ⓓ Ⓡ ⛰ Ⓜ

Mrs Helen Foley, Hillside, Haven Doon, Tahilla, Sneem. ☎ (064) 82065 • BB **B** • EM £13, 7-8.30pm • D2 F2 • 4-10 + XMAS • Ⓥ Ⓑ Ⓓ Ⓢ ⛰ Ⓜ

Mary R Tangney, Hillcrest Farmhouse, Gearahmeen, Black Valley. ☎ (064) 34702 • Map /878823 • BB **B** • EM £13, 7-9.30pm • D1 T4 • 3-10 • Ⓥ Ⓑ Ⓓ Ⓢ Ⓜ

■ TRALEE

Kathleen Daly, Finglas House, Camp Village, Camp. ☎ (066) 30125 • BB **B** • D2 T2 F1 • 4-10 • Ⓑ Ⓓ Ⓢ ⛰ Ⓜ

■ WATERVILLE (Ring of Kerry)
KERRY WAY

Abbie Clifford, Clifford's B & B. ☎ (066) 74283 • BB **B** • S1 D2 T2 F1 • 2-10 • Ⓑ Ⓓ ⛰

COUNTY WATERFORD

■ BALLYMACARBRY (via Clonmel)

Clonanav Farm Guest House, Nire Valley. ☎ 052-36141 • BB **D** • EM £15, 7pm • S3 D2 T4 F1 • 4-11 • Ⓥ Ⓑ Ⓓ • 3 star • SC and bunkhouse also

■ KILCLOONEY (Kilmacthomas)

☆ Pauline Humphreys, Coumshingaun Lodge. ☎ 00 353 51 646238 • Map 75/344105 • BB **B** • EM book first £13.50, 7.30pm • D2 F3 • 2-11 NX • Ⓥ Ⓑ Ⓓ Ⓢ • Wheelchair facilities. Map ref. is Discovery Series. See over for display ad.

COUMSHINGAUN LODGE
Kilclooney, Kilmacthomas
Co. Waterford

Magnificent setting near Lough Coumshingaun in the Comeragh Mountains. Enjoy excellent food, good wines, a relaxed atmosphere and occasional live traditional music. Rosslare 1½ hours. B&B, evening meals, packed lunches, all rooms en suite. Visitors with disabilities welcome.

Telephone 00 353 51 646238

■ **NIRE VALLEY (Comeragh Mountains)**

☆ Martin & Una Moore, Bennetts Church, Old School House, Ballymacarbry. ☎ 052 36217 • BB **C** • EM £13 • S1 D2 T1 F2 • 1-12 NX • Ⓥ Ⓑ Ⓓ Ⓢ ⚑

The Nire Valley Comeragh Mountains Co. Waterford, Ireland

THE NIRE VALLEY is situated in the Comeragh Mountains in Co. Waterford, Ireland. The Comeragh mountains are a glaciated mountain range containing some of the finest corrie lakes in Europe, 13 in all.

We in the Nire Valley can offer you the walker everything from high level walks to gentle low level walks. We have Guides and maps waiting for your pleasure. We are convenient to Waterford and Cork airport and Rosslare and Cork ferryports.

A Warm welcome awaits you in the Nire Valley. Contact Una at

Tel: + 353-52-36217
Fax: + 353-52-36540
E-Mail hiking@indigo.ie

☆ Seamus & Mary Wall, Hanora's Cottage Guesthouse, Nire Valley, Via Clonmel. ☎ 052-36134 • BB **D** • EM book first £20, 7-8pm • D2 T6 • Closed Dec 12-27 • Ⓥ Ⓑ Ⓓ Ⓢ • 3 star

Hanora's Cottage Guesthouse

NIRE VALLEY, COMERAGH MOUNTAINS
Ballymacarbry, Co. Waterford

We are right on the Comeragh Mountains so you walk from the door step. All our rooms are en-suite including one with jacuzzi bath! Bliss after a day on the hills. Cooking is by our son Eoin, a Ballymaloe school chef. We provide packed lunch, maps and walking sticks. All rooms have TV, telephone, hair dryer and tea/ coffee maker.
You will be very welcome at HANORA'S COTTAGE.
Contact Mary Wall
Tel: + 353-52-36134   Fax: + 353-52-36540

Richard & Nora Harte, Cnoc-Na-Ri, Knocknaree, Ballymacarbry, via Clonmel. ☎ 052-36239 • BB **C** • EM book first £14, 7pm • D2 F2 • 1-12 NX • Ⓥ Ⓑ Ⓓ ⚑

Patrick & Olive O'Gorman, "Glasha", Ballymacarbry, Via Clonmel. ☎ 052-36108 • BB **C** • EM £15 • D1 T1 F3 • 1-12 NX • Ⓥ Ⓑ Ⓓ Ⓢ ⚑ • ITB/App

COUNTY WICKLOW

■ **GLENDALOUGH**

Carmel Hawkins, Carmels, Annamoe. ☎ 0404-45297 • BB **B** • D2 T2 • 3-10 • Ⓥ Ⓑ Ⓓ Ⓢ • Bord Failte

■ **GLENEALY (Co Wicklow)**

☆ Mrs Mary Byrne, Ballyknocken House. ☎ (0404) 44614 Fax 44627 • BB **B** • EM £12, 7pm • S1 D3 T3 F1 • 3-12 NX • Ⓥ Ⓑ Ⓓ Ⓢ • SC also

Walk the Wicklow Way
Ballyknocken House
Glenealy, Ashford
Co. Wicklow

An ideal base for ramblers.
Varied routes arranged. Own exclusive walking guidebook. Packaged holidays available, incl. transport. 200-acre farm 30 miles from Dublin. Good food, wine licence, en suite rooms, log fires. Brochure

Mrs Mary Byrne
☎ (00 353) 404 44614
Fax (00 353) 404 44627

Index to the Accommodation Guide

Any town which is only listed as a "postal" town and not in its own right is not included in this index. For example, for Highclere, Newbury, only Highclere is listed. If Newbury had entries of its own, it too would be listed, but as it appears only as a postal town in this Guide, it is not. Many small villages in this index are "hidden" in the entries and it will therefore be necessary to search for them once you get to the page.

ACCOMMODATION INDEX

ACCOMMODATION INDEX

Path Problem Report Form

WHERE WAS THE PROBLEM? Please give as much information as you can.

County_____District_____

Parish/Community_____

From (place) _____

_____ Gridref._____

To (place)_____

_____ Grid ref._____

Path number if known_____

Date problem encountered_____

WHAT WAS THE PROBLEM? Be precise and quote a grid reference for any specific point. Draw a sketch map if you think it will help. If anyone spoke to you, please give details, including their name and address if known.

WHAT TO DO NEXT? Give us your details

Name_____

Address_____

_____

Telephone_____ **Tick box for more Report Forms** ❏

Send this form to
Your local Ramblers representative (see Area & Group Contacts section in this Yearbook) or Ramblers' Association, 1/5 Wandsworth Road, London SW8 2XX. Telephone 0171-582 6878.

Special Membership Offer

If you are not yet an RA member, use this coupon to get 20% off your first year's subscription. And if you are already a member of the RA why not introduce a friend to this special offer and give them this form?

Either way you will be helping the RA in its vital work of conservation and protection of the countryside and public rights of way.

It is a condition of this offer that you pay by direct debit.

I/We wish to join the RA and have completed the direct debit instructions below

Mr/Mrs/Miss/Ms (Initials)_____**Surname**_____

Address_____

_____

_____**Postcode**_____

Date(s) of Birth_____**RA Group (if you have a preference)**_____

Tick the box that suits you best

		Special Rate	Full Rate
☐	Individual	£13.60	£17.00
☐	Joint/family *	£16.80	£21.00
☐	Reduced ordinary *	£6.80	£8.50
☐	Reduced joint/family *	£8.40	£10.50

*Joint membership for 2 adults at the same address (please give both names); reduced rates for members under 18; students; disabled; unwaged and retired people.
The offer stays open until 1 October 1997 and is not open to existing members.

Instruction to your bank or building society to pay Direct Debits

Originator's identification number 922670. Membership number (office use only)

DIRECT Debit

To: The Manager (give the name of your bank or building society) _____

_____

Full address_____

_____

Name(s) of account holder(s) _____

Account No._____**Sort code** (top RH corner of cheque) _____

Please pay the Ramblers' Association Direct Debits from the account detailed on this Instruction subject to the safeguards assured by the Direct Debit Guarantee.

Signature(s)_____**Date**_____

Banks and Building Societies may not accept Direct Debit Instructions for some types of account.
Send this form to The Ramblers' Association, 1/5 Wandsworth Road, London SW8 2XX.

B

323

Where have you been staying?

IF YOU LIKED IT AND IT ISN'T IN THIS BOOK, PLEASE GIVE
DETAILS HERE
Remove this page and send it to the Yearbook Editor,
The Ramblers' Association, 1/5 Wandsworth Road, London SW8 2XX

Abbreviations and symbols used in the Accommodation Guide

☆	A display ad is either below or nearby
BB	Bed & Breakfast accommodation
SC	Self-catering accommodation
A	Price per person per night under £13
B	Price per person per night £13—£16.99
C	Price per person per night £17—£21.99
D	Price per person per night £22 or over – the price could be considerably over £22
EM	Evening meal normally available (unless 'book first' is stated) followed by average price and time it is served
S, D, T, F	Number of single, double, twin or family rooms available
1-12	Months open (1 = January)
NX	Closed Christmas
Ⓓ	Drying facilities available
Ⓥ	Vegetarian evening meals available routinely. NB Many places not showing this symbol do provide a vegetarian cooked breakfast and often provide vegetarian evening meals by arrangement
Ⓢ	Some smoking restrictions. Vary from no smoking in certain rooms to no smoking at all—make enquiries
Ⓑ	At least one room has private bath/shower and/or toilet,
Ⓡ	A railway station is within 2 miles
Ⓟ	A packed lunch can be obtained (Groups section)
🐕	You may be able to take your dog having first consulted with the proprietor
Ⓜ	The advertiser is a member of the Ramblers' Association

The following are abbreviations of tourist board awards.
See page 87 for explanation.

Cr	Crown(s)
k	Key(s)
App	Approved
C	Commended
HC	Highly Commended

Abbreviations and symbols used in the Accommodation Guide

☆	A display ad is either below or nearby
BB	Bed & Breakfast accommodation
SC	Self-catering accommodation
A	Price per person per night under £13
B	Price per person per night £13—£16.99
C	Price per person per night £17—£21.99
D	Price per person per night £22 or over – the price could be considerably over £22
EM	Evening meal normally available (unless 'book first' is stated) followed by average price and time it is served
S, D, T, F	Number of single, double, twin or family rooms available
1-12	Months open (1 = January)
NX	Closed Christmas
ⅅ	Drying facilities available
Ⅴ	Vegetarian evening meals available routinely. NB Many places not showing this symbol do provide a vegetarian cooked breakfast and often provide vegetarian evening meals by arrangement
Ⓢ	Some smoking restrictions. Vary from no smoking in certain rooms to no smoking at all—make enquiries
Ⓑ	At least one room has private bath/shower and/or toilet,
Ⓡ	A railway station is within 2 miles
Ⓟ	A packed lunch can be obtained (Groups section)
🐕	You may be able to take your dog having first consulted with the proprietor
Ⓜ	The advertiser is a member of the Ramblers' Association

The following are abbreviations of tourist board awards.
See page 87 for explanation.

Cr	Crown(s)
k	Key(s)
App	Approved
C	Commended
HC	Highly Commended